# The Katherine Mansfield Notebooks

# The
# Katherine Mansfield
## Notebooks

Complete Edition

*Katherine Mansfield*

Edited by Margaret Scott

University of Minnesota Press
Minneapolis

Published by the University of Minnesota Press
111 Third Avenue South, Suite 290
Minneapolis, MN  55401-2520
http://www.upress.umn.edu

Library of Congress Cataloging-in-Publication Data

Mansfield, Katherine, 1888-1923
The Katherine Mansfield notebooks / Katherine Mansfield ; edited by Margaret Scott.—
Complete ed.
p. cm.
Includes indexes.
ISBN 978-0-8166-4235-9 (hc : alk. paper) — ISBN 978-0-8166-4236-6 (pbk. : alk paper)
1. Mansfield, Katherine, 1888-1923—Notebooks, sketchbooks, etc. I. Scott, Margaret, 1928- II. Title.

PR9639.3.M258 A6 2002a
823'.912—dc21                                                    2002072648

Printed in the United States of America on acid-free paper

The University of Minnesota is an equal-opportunity educator and employer.


12  11  10          10  9  8  7  6  5  4  3  2

# Contents

The Katherine Mansfield Notebooks

Volume One

*Katherine Mansfield, 1917.*
*From the journals of John Middleton Murry.*

*The*
# Katherine Mansfield
*Notebooks*

Volume One

*edited by*
MARGARET SCOTT

*Manuscript page from Notebook 1, 1906, reproduced actual size.*
*For the transcription see page 60, lines 12–20, of this volume.*

ALEXANDER TURNBULL LIBRARY, NLNZ

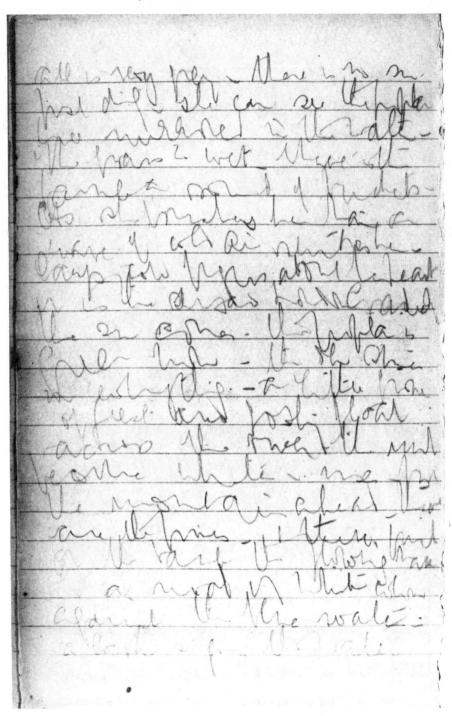

*Manuscript page from Notebook 2, 1907, written in pencil, reproduced actual size. For the transcription see page 145, second paragraph, lines 4–11, of this volume.*

ALEXANDER TURNBULL LIBRARY, NLNZ

# Contents

# *Introduction*

THESE VOLUMES consist of transcriptions of the Katherine Mansfield notebooks and unbound pages of manuscript material in the Alexander Turnbull Library in Wellington and the Newberry Library in Chicago. They do not include the manuscripts of her published stories or letters but otherwise are non-selective.

These are the papers KM left behind when she died. Where they were before that is a matter for conjecture. It is hard to imagine that, in all her flittings from one address to another in search of health during the last years of her life, she carried with her half a hundred notebooks and several hundred loose pages of scribble. It is likely that she lodged them with the London branch of the Bank of New Zealand whose manager, Alexander Kay, was obliging and helpful whenever possible to all of Sir Harold Beauchamp's daughters.

What is certain is that this huge, amorphous, nearly illegible mass of material was inherited by John Middleton Murry when KM died in 1923. The first book he produced from it was *Poems by Katherine Mansfield* in that same year. He then extracted from the notebooks pieces he thought would appeal to the general reader, put them together, and published them in a volume called *Journal of Katherine Mansfield* (1927). This book did very well and ran to many reprints so that Murry regretted having been so selective. He combed the manuscripts again and put together another volume of pieces, which he called *The Scrapbook of Katherine Mansfield* (1939), thus creating the impression that KM had kept two books to write in—one a journal and the other a scrapbook.

However, most of the contents of her 53 notebooks remained unpublished. Murry perceived that the market could stand yet more of this material and so in 1954 he published *Journal of Katherine Mansfield: Definitive Edition*, a volume incorporating the 1927 *Journal* with some of the *Scrapbook* entries as well as a good deal of hitherto unseen material. All of these, as well as two volumes of *The Letters of Katherine Mansfield* (1928), *Novels and Novelists* (1930) which was a collection of her book reviews, *Katherine Mansfield's Letters to John Middleton Murry* (1951), and two posthumous collections of her stories, *The Doves' Nest* (1923) and *Something Childish* (1924), were edited by Murry and published by Constable & Co Ltd, London.

After such labours Murry felt he had done enough with the notebook material and, although he kept the main body of it intact, he began selling off small manuscripts as his financial exigencies dictated. (A letter from him in the Alexander Turnbull Library offers one of KM's notebooks in exchange for the price of a new tractor for his farm.) The manuscripts he sold seemed invariably to be bought by the Chicago dealers Hamill and Barker, who sold them on to Mrs Edison Dick of Chicago.

Murry died in 1957 having made a will stipulating that KM's letters were to be offered to the British Museum for £1,000 and, if not bought by the British Museum, to the Turnbull Library for the same amount. The British Museum, responding to a nudge from the Turnbull Library, turned the offer down, and the letters came to Wellington. It happened that all the other Mansfield manuscripts—the 'notebooks'—were to be auctioned at Sotheby's in London at about the same time. A public appeal for funds was launched by the Friends of the Turnbull Library and, together with a special government grant, raised enough to make it possible to bid for the manuscripts at auction as well as to buy the letters. Although a couple of lots escaped (to fetch up later in the Newberry Library), most of the material came to New Zealand.

Some years later, when I was a librarian in the Manuscripts section of the Turnbull Library, I was struck by how much of the material Murry had left unused, and also by how much of what he did use he had misread, trimmed, punctuated, and generally tidied up. I found that I could read words and sentences that had baffled him and, with the blessing of A G Bagnall, the Turnbull Library's Chief Librarian at the time, I was able to spend a few minutes each day transcribing some of the barely-legible unpublished pieces from Notebook 1. We published these in successive issues of *The Turnbull Library Record* between 1970 and 1979. During this period I was aware that critics, commentators, students and others were attempting to read these manuscripts and relying too much on guess-work, while at the same time Murry's misreadings were being quoted and perpetuated in other people's books. I developed a wish to do the whole thing again from the beginning, leaving out nothing. However, I was fully engaged all that time on *The Collected Letters of Katherine Mansfield* (Clarendon Press), and knew that I could do nothing about the notebooks until I could have a whole year to devote to them alone.

The opportunity came when I applied successfully for the 1989 New Zealand National Library Research Fellowship, which gave me a room in the Turnbull Library (which occupies part of the National Library building), the use of a computer, staff privileges, and a stipend. During that good year I transcribed all the material on to the computer. Subsequently, however, there was much work to be done to get it into a publishable state, and this was made possible for me by the 1991 Non-fiction Bursary of the Queen Elizabeth II Arts Council of New Zealand.

By the time I began this work Mrs Edison Dick's collection of Katherine Mansfield manuscripts in Chicago had been discovered, although it was not well understood how closely related the two collections were. The Turnbull Library approached Mrs Dick with offers to buy her collection, and although she thought carefully about this—indeed she and her husband visited New Zealand and were shown the Turnbull Library—she decided eventually that the Newberry Library in Chicago, with which she had a long association, was where she wanted the manuscripts to go. And so they sit now, something of an anomaly, among the American Mid-West manuscripts in the Newberry—a little post-mortem irony that would have amused KM who always felt drawn to America.

The Turnbull, however, could not have asked for a more cooperative sister-repository than the Newberry which, without ado, sent to Wellington all of its Mansfield material on microfilm. Thus it was possible to see that the two collections are extraordinarily inter-related. Sometimes there is one page of a piece here, and its second page there; the first draft of a poem here and its fair copy there; pieces of almost the same date in each place. Naturally, a treatment of the Turnbull's manuscripts had to include the Newberry's, not least because when they were together in Murry's possession he drew on them all for the construction of the *Journal* and *The Scrapbook*. Having copies of the Newberry material in Wellington was an enormous help and, although it was necessary for me to go to Chicago to examine the originals, most of the work could be done at home.

This material—the whole raft of it—is so rich in reflections of, connections with, roots of, hints at, variations of her best work that to explicate it all would take more lifetimes than I have at my disposal. I have therefore confined myself to a presentation of the text of these manuscripts, together with such descriptive and explanatory notes as will help to convey their essential nature. This is the raw material for an infinite number of investigations.

## ARRANGEMENT

The principal finding aid in this edition is the table of contents in the front of each volume. The index of personal and fictional names at the back is an auxiliary aid.

Since it is impossible for an editor to know exactly what will interest any particular reader, and since people will continue to puzzle over any scraps left undeciphered, this edition includes everything; even isolated words and sentences have been included as potentially suggestive of stories in embryo.

The arrangement is, as far as possible, chronological. It has seemed important not to break up individual notebooks in order to make their contents more precisely chronological. (An exception to this rule had to be made in respect of Notebook 29, as is explained in the relevant footnote.) Because KM used some of her notebooks over long periods of time there is inevitably some overlapping, but a rough chronology has nevertheless been possible. The unbound manuscripts have been fitted in between the notebooks at the appropriate points.

Passages used by Murry, in part or in full, in either *The Scrapbook* or the Definitive Edition of the *Journal*, are followed by the relevant S or J page number. This, and all other editorial information, is contained within square brackets.

## THE TEXT

The intention of this edition is to reproduce what KM wrote. Some liberties had to be taken however. The handwriting is often so impenetrable that one cannot always be sure of the spelling of a word. But KM was a good and reliable speller (apart from her failure to double the 'l' in 'woollen' and 'appalling') and so, where it is impossible to see exactly how she has spelt a word, it has seemed safe to assume she is right.

Punctuation is a more difficult matter. While, unlike Murry, I have been strict about not supplying exclamation marks, question marks, colons and semi-colons, and have left the text, on the whole, under-punctuated, I have nevertheless had to make some minor changes in the interests of readability. In her early notebooks she was scribbling so fast that the only form of punctuation she used was a dash. A dash was quicker and easier to make than a backward-turning comma or a stationary full stop. As she wrote, at top speed, and 'heard' the need for a pause she employed a dash. Since many of these dashes function as commas or full stops I have rendered them so, but where they function as dashes I have of course kept them.[1] The ampersand has been retained for no very good reason other than that it helps to convey the breathlessly shorthand nature of the early jottings without obstructing their readability. KM tended to ignore both apostrophes and hyphens. In respect of these my transcriptions are faithful except where, occasionally, the lack of either an apostrophe or a hyphen results in momentary obscurity. In these cases I have supplied the requisite aid to clarity. Paragraphing generally follows KM's own, but there are some manuscripts in which she simply scribbled non-stop without any breaks or pauses. Such large, dense blocks of prose have required some editorial paragraphing because the transcription of these manuscripts needs to be readable as well as true.

Alas, there are some words whose illegibility all the diligence in the world cannot penetrate. These are replaced by three dots within square brackets [. . .] with an additional dot for each extra illegible word. Words for which I have had to rely to some extent on guess-work are followed by a question mark within square brackets. In order to preserve the strictly editorial function of square brackets in this edition, KM's occasional non-significant square brackets have been rendered as round brackets. Crossed-out words or passages that remain legible and may be of some interest are given within angle brackets.

Each Turnbull Library item is preceded by its catalogue identification, while Newberry Library items are preceded by [NL]. Typescripts are preceded by [ts], indicating that in those cases there was no transcribing to be done—just copying. Occasional small obvious words missed out by KM have been supplied within square brackets. I have not, in general, noted the instances of

---

[1] In order to reflect the handwriting these short dashes have been reproduced as hyphens (rather than em or en dashes).

difference between my readings and Murry's because there are simply too many of them. However, I must not leave this discussion of editorial methods without a few more words about John Middleton Murry.

One can barely imagine what it must have been like for him to find himself suddenly in possession of this vast mass of material. Not only was it scarcely legible, it was also full of judgements on him and complaints about him—sudden stinging bites, some of them poisonous. It must have been agonising for him to keep coming across KM's bitter accusations and misunderstandings. No matter how much he told himself her warped view of him was due to her illness, the pain of all these discoveries must have been intense. Yet his courage never failed him. He struggled on with the deciphering and whatever he did manage to read he published, without defensive explanations. Almost his only deliberate suppressions were names of people still alive at the time of publication. This courage and honesty (the self-revelatory honesty for which he was famously reviled) served only to harden the public perception of KM as the suffering and dying genius, and Murry as the cold, careless, inadequate husband. This was cruelly unfair to him.

During the years in which he worked on these manuscripts Murry's own life was in disarray. He did not have what this particular job demands—an initial year of undisturbed time. He was also, in working on the early manuscripts, hampered by his unfamiliarity with New Zealand. In the light of these difficulties his achievement is astonishing. Only another transcriber, coming after him, can perceive the quiet dogged hard labour he put into these volumes. He commands a respect and an admiration that no amount of disapproval of his editorial methods can diminish.

He was—inevitably, because of the job description—unable to be a perfect husband for KM, but he was a man whose aesthetic acuity and intellectual breadth and integrity were of great importance to her. That they could share so much—more, it seems, than either of them ever shared with anyone else—was why they both hung on to the relationship to the end. His indisputable stature as a literary critic and thinker is outside the scope of this comment but is fundamental to the respect and affection in which KM always held him.

Physically, the notebooks are of all shapes, sizes, thicknesses and colours. Some of them are full, most not, a few barely started. One or two were principally Murry's notebooks but were usurped, or briefly borrowed, by KM. In a couple of her early and more difficult ones he pencilled his transcription between her lines before copying it out for publication in the *Journal*. The physical characteristics of the large mass of manuscripts on unbound pages are equally varied. KM's handwriting varies enormously and is almost a new hand for every day. Sometimes it is tightly microscopic—what she called 'my neat little stitches'—and sometimes it is an elongated scrawl with spaces in the middle of words more often than in between them. Between these two extremes is every shape and variation and tension of script. And yet there is a unifying Mansfield character to it all if one spends long enough becoming sensitised to it. There is no question but that most of it is abominably difficult to read, but its ultimate elucidation affords similar satisfactions to those of solving an apparently impossibly cryptic crossword puzzle.

There are about 50 short passages in the published *Journal* for which no manuscripts exist in these two collections. More than half of these are quotations from other people's books, sometimes with a comment by KM. One assumes that these were passages which she marked in the respective books, with or without a marginal note. The 20 or so brief pieces by KM—clearly 'notebook' material—must have been taken from manuscripts which either no longer exist or ended up somewhere other than the Turnbull or Newberry Libraries.

'The New Baby', although it was written early rather than late in the last year, I have chosen to place at the end because its final words seem somehow evocative of Katherine Mansfield herself.

## BIOGRAPHICAL NOTE

The first two-thirds, more or less, of Volume One, covering the New Zealand years, consists of the notebooks and small manuscripts with which KM busied herself during her adolescence and up to the time she left New Zealand finally in 1908.

Murry used only a fraction—less than a sixth—of this material in the *Journal* and *The Scrapbook*, presumably because he thought it immature, which it is, and uninteresting, which it is not. It is a goldmine of biographical and psychological information, and clearly shows the emergence of themes and situations that were to preoccupy her for the rest of her life. It also, inevitably, changes to some extent our perception of her life at that time.

Although the main outlines of KM's life are well known, the biographical backdrop to these volumes can bear a brief retelling. Born Kathleen Mansfield Beauchamp on 14 October 1888 in Wellington, New Zealand, she was the third daughter of Harold (later Sir Harold) Beauchamp and Annie Dyer Beauchamp. The first two daughters were Vera Margaret (1885) and Charlotte Mary ('Chaddie' or 'Marie') (1887). Then came Kathleen. Gwendoline Burnell (1890) lived for only three months, and was followed by Jeanne Worthington (1892) and Leslie Heron (1894).

At the time of KM's birth the family lived in the city, in Tinakori Road, and then in 1893 moved to Karori, now a suburb of Wellington but in those days a village out in the country. The removal to Karori—to a house called 'Chesney Wold'—is described in KM's famous story 'Prelude'. Because Annie, the mother, spent so much time pregnant (not all of her pregnancies came to term) much of the care of the children devolved upon *her* mother, KM's Granny Dyer, and two of Granny's other daughters, Kitty and Belle, who also formed part of the Beauchamp household.

At the age of six KM started school in Karori village, recollected later in her story 'The Doll's House'. Three years later she began to attend Wellington

Girls' High School, commuting by coach from Karori, and when her parents returned from England later that year the family moved back into the city to a rather grand house at 75 Tinakori Road, the scene of the story 'The Garden Party'.

After only a year at Wellington Girls' High School, KM, with her two older sisters, was sent to Miss Swainson's private school in Fitzherbert Terrace.

The suburb of Thorndon, through which Tinakori Road runs, is to this day full of reminders of KM—particularly the house where she was born which is now run by the Katherine Mansfield Birthplace Society Inc as a memorial. The property at 47 Fitzherbert Terrace, also in Thorndon, where, in 1908, stood the last house in which KM lived with her family, is now the site of the Embassy of the United States of America. Visible through the fence is a plaque informing the passer-by that the Beauchamps' house was on that site when Katherine Mansfield lived with them before her final departure from New Zealand. The other side of Fitzherbert Terrace is now the Katherine Mansfield Memorial Park, an undulating grassy area of flower beds, trees, garden seats, gravel walks, and a pool shaded by large elms.

In 1903, when she was 14, KM and her two older sisters were taken to England for three years of schooling at Queen's College in London. Their aunt, Belle Dyer, went with them and remained in England *in loco parentis* during their schooling. The three years at Queen's College were crucial for KM: she was stimulated intellectually as never before and she developed an urgent longing for a kind of life quite different from the conventional one into which she was expected to fit on her return to New Zealand. When the time came for the girls to go home in October 1906 (their parents had travelled to England to collect them), KM begged to be allowed to stay in London, but to no avail.

The seven-week sea voyage to New Zealand involved a number of frustrations: a too-close confinement with her parents, anger at having her stated ambition to become a professional 'cellist condemned, and a lack (in spite of handsome cricketers and shipboard flirtations) of enough to occupy all those hours. So she spent a good deal of time scribbling in notebooks, and those scribbles may be seen here.

Back in New Zealand she spent 18 difficult months pining for the atmosphere of London and arguing with herself about how to get back to it. She was by no means single-minded about this. One part of her knew that to spurn everything home had to offer was a wild and risky thing to do. But there was another part of her which was very susceptible to such exhortations of Oscar Wilde as 'risk everything' and 'push everything as far as it will go'. Also influencing her at this time were the movements of her friends the Trowell family. Thomas Trowell was a music teacher in Wellington who taught her to play the 'cello. He and his wife had twin sons, Tom and Garnet, and a younger daughter, Dolly. Tom (whom KM called Caesar and whose professional name was Arnold) was a 'cellist and the object of KM's romantic fantasies throughout her teenage years until she returned to England in 1908.

During her stormy last months in Wellington the Trowells moved to London, making Wellington seem lonelier and greyer than ever. The struggle between the cautious and the reckless sides of herself, strongly hinted at in these notebooks, was severe and, in a sense, fatal. From the moment she knew she had won the battle with her father and was to be allowed to go, she also knew there could be no turning back to her family—ever. Even when, not much later, she found herself up to her neck in disaster, and during all her sub-sequent anguished longings for a home, she felt that she had forfeited her right to go home.

During those 18 months, though, she did have at least one enriching, happy, and stimulating experience—the month-long Urewera camping trip on which she took a thick black notebook, now the Turnbull's Notebook 2. She continued to practise writing, and during 1908 had several pieces published in the *Native Companion* in Melbourne. In July 1908, with a settlement of £100 a year from her father, she returned to London and was reunited with the Trowell family. Tom Trowell seems never to have been very interested in her and she now found Garnet much more responsive and attractive. A passionate but doomed love affair ensued.

The last entries in Notebooks 1, 2, and 39 were written on board ship and after her arrival in England. However, the notebooks are here presented complete, so there is no hard and fast line between the New Zealand years and the next phase of her life. It will be seen that the manuscripts of the first phase are mainly apprentice work. Later material has a greater preponderance of 'cogitabilia', to use Coleridge's word about his own notebooks.

During the early period KM wrote a number of 'baby stories', eight of which survive. Three of them were published in the *Queen's College Magazine* during her time at the school but this is the first time they have all been published. In a letter to her cousin Sylvia Payne on 26 December 1904 she writes, 'Some people seem to like those "baby" stories, and I love writing them.' (CLKM 1, p 15) These stories and some of KM's 'child verse' were to have constituted a book to be illustrated by her friend E K Bendall. It was probably this to which she referred in a letter to Sylvia Payne on 4 March 1908 when she wrote, 'I have finished My First Book'. The book did not find a publisher, nor does any list of its contents survive, but to give publication now to its probable contents—albeit nearly a century late—is pleasing.

Back in London, struggling to survive, KM made a series of disastrous misjudgements. In love with Garnet Trowell, she became pregnant by him, hastily married George Bowden and left him immediately, was taken by her mother to Bad Worishofen in Bavaria to await the birth of the child, suffered a miscarriage, arranged for a deprived child from London convalescing from pleurisy to be sent over to her, looked after him for a few weeks, became to some extent involved with Floryan Sobienowski, a Polish writer who later blackmailed her over the letters she had written him, returned to London, tried for a short time to live with George Bowden her legal husband, and became at some stage infected with gonorrhoea, one symptom of which was the pain she always thought of as 'my rheumatiz'.

KM's attachment, which began in 1911, and subsequent marriage to John Middleton Murry dominated the rest of her short life, as her thoughts about him and their relationship dominate her notebooks increasingly. They were much apart because of her worsening health and although she wrote to him daily she also needed the notebooks in which to make plainer, more unvarnished observations about him and herself. And all the time consumption (as pulmonary tuberculosis was usually called) was inexorably consuming her.

After Murry (Jack) the other major figure in KM's life was Ida Constance Baker whose middle name was well chosen, and who makes her presence felt in the pages of these notebooks. She was at school, Queen's College, with KM, a large, emotionally immature girl with a strong dependence on her mother who had just died. Very vulnerable, she was unconsciously looking for an emotional attachment as a prop, and fate threw her up against KM, who was partial to enslaving people.

The broad facts of their relationship are well-known—how she became KM's house-keeper/companion/nurse, how she remained faithful and constant in spite of provocation and harsh treatment to the end of KM's life. And after KM's death, she told me, she suffered what would now be recognised, but wasn't then, as a severe nervous breakdown. When they were young KM invented a pseudonym for Ida—Lesley Moore—and henceforth they usually referred to each other by the initials KM and LM. Addressing her directly KM called her Ida or Jones. Referring to her in letters to Murry she usually called her LM, and in letters to some others LM or the Faithful One (or the FO) or the Rhodesian Mountain (or the Mountain) or the Albatross. Although an editorial footnote in Miss Baker's book asserts that 'Jones' was a name by which the two women addressed each other, there is no record, anywhere, of LM calling KM 'Jones'. By the time she was old Miss Baker was known to her friends as Lesley exclusively. In these notebooks she is a shadowy, anxious recurring presence—a kind of insubstantial punch-ball whose devoted ministrations were largely taken for granted.

The first real tragedy of KM's life occurred in 1915 with the accidental death of her beloved brother, Leslie. There are evidences here—unpublished until now—that Leslie was always important to KM. Without these evidences one had been left with a suspicion that in KM's extreme reaction to his death she may have been over-dramatising him and herself and the significance of his death for her. It can now be seen that this was not so. All the pain and grief she described were truly felt.

Leslie, born in 1894, was just short of his 21st birthday when he arrived in England in 1915 to join the army. Later that same year he was (in KM's words) 'blown to bits' in France while attempting to demonstrate the use of a hand grenade. His death was devastating for the whole family. Beauchamp had lost the only person to carry on his name. (Years later he attempted to persuade at least one of his grandsons to change his name by deedpoll to Beauchamp.) For KM the death seemed to act as a focus for all the lesser losses and disappointments of her recent life, and her grief was extreme.

To judge from the letters (now in the Turnbull Library) Leslie wrote home to his parents during that year, he was indeed an attractive, bright young man. Still teetering on the edge of adolescence (inclined to get the giggles) he had been educated at Waitaki Boys' High School, a New Zealand approximation to an English Public School, and had emerged with the gloss of boyish charm and self-assurance that such a school can facilitate. On the ship coming over he saw his life stretching before him, full of interest and achievement, and getting better all the time. The war would be just a brief adventure on the way. His death, like countless thousands of others in that war, was a tragedy, but for his parents and his middle sister it was also a mini-death of their own.

The war affected KM profoundly in other ways, too. It killed not only her brother but also her friends Frederick Goodyear, Rupert Brooke, and Henri Gaudier-Brzeska. In early 1918, having been medically advised to go abroad because of the spot on her lung, KM spent two-and-a-half months in Bandol in the South of France. Very ill and trying to get back to England to get married (her divorce from Bowden having come through), she, with LM, was trapped in Paris for three weeks while it was under bombardment. Two weeks after getting home KM and Murry were married and two weeks after *that* she had to leave him and take herself and her illness south to Looe in Cornwall.

From then on (ie during her last five years) her life was dominated and circumscribed by illness. The gonorrhoea, undiagnosed for about eight years, was now advanced; the tuberculosis was pitilessly killing her.

Speeding 'like a comet' towards death (to quote Murry on Keats), aware of it but hoping to outwit it, KM wrote faster and faster. The last year (she died on 9 January 1923) was a prolific letter-writing year, and in the last two years she wrote almost all of her best stories. Physically she was grounded: to sit at a table for a few minutes at a time pushing a pen was all her body could manage. Her mind, however, was as free and active as ever, and it demanded expression. The shadow of death (those dark wings she had written of years earlier), the desperate sense of time running out, drove her to put everything down on paper lest it should be lost with her.

As well as all that, for nearly two years from April 1919 she wrote a weekly book review for the *Athenaeum*, and a good many of the isolated phrases in these notebooks are ones she noted down for use in reviews. Sometimes the reviews themselves illuminate her thoughts and her work. Thus, in a review on 11 December 1920 (her last), at least six months before starting to write 'At the Bay', and even longer before 'The Garden Party', she wrote:

And therefore the childhood that we look back upon and attempt to recreate must be—if it is to satisfy our longing as well as our memory— a great deal more than a catalogue of infant pleasures and pangs. It must have, as it were, a haunting light upon it.

During the nine months she spent in Switzerland (May 1921 to February 1922) KM enjoyed the proximity of her father's cousin 'Elizabeth', who was famous herself and had always been spoken of with admiration by the Beauchamps during KM's childhood. Elizabeth was born Mary Annette Beauchamp in Australia in 1866 and, superficially at least, had done well in life. She had left Australia (a mark of distinction in the Antipodes in those days), had married Count Henning von Arnim and lived with him and their five children on his estate in Pomerania, and had written a best-selling book (*Elizabeth and her German Garden*, 1898) at the age of 31. She continued her successful career as a writer and made enough money to build a châteàu in Randogne, Switzerland, after her husband's death in 1910. For a time she was one of H G Wells' string of interesting mistresses and then in 1916 she married, disastrously, Francis, the second Earl Russell, older brother of Bertrand Russell. By the time she and KM were able to spend some time together in Switzerland Elizabeth (as she was always called) had left her second husband and written a novel (*Vera*, 1921) about their unhappy marriage.

The two women, a generation apart in age, admired each other but were to some extent rivals. KM envied Elizabeth's literary popularity and money and luxurious mode of life, but knew that she herself was the better artist. It was a comfort to have Elizabeth living only half an hour away from the Chalet des Sapins where KM lived with Murry for that period, yet the two women never fully accepted each other. They were both constantly wary—KM's side of which is reflected here.

The late notebooks, because of their urgency, constitute an even richer and more complex omnium gatherum than the earlier ones. Inevitably, the significance of some of their bits and pieces is no longer discernible, perhaps never was to anyone other than their creator. But some of them echo in the imagination and provide their own mysterious justification. One of the most important functions of the notebooks was explained by KM herself (albeit *to* herself) in Newberry Notebook 7 in 1921:

> Queer this habit of mine of being garrulous. And I don't mean that any eye but mine should read this. This is—*really private*. But I must say nothing affords me the same relief. What happens as a rule is, if I go on long enough I *break through*. It's rather like tossing very large flat stones into the stream. The question is, though, how long this will prove efficacious. Up till now, I own, it never has failed me ...

Anything that affords relief can become an ingrained habit, and for KM this habit was ingrained. True, she did sometimes struggle against it: she referred to 'those huge complaining diaries' as if they no longer existed, suggesting she had destroyed them; she mentioned having tidied all her papers ('Tore up and ruthlessly destroyed much'); and, elsewhere, she vowed to keep silence as her mother had kept silence, and not to write down everything that had happened. But she needed the notebooks to help her to 'break through', though they also had many other functions—as memoranda, as a nursery in which to plant seedlings of ideas, as a record of events and thoughts and feelings. She certainly regarded it all as '*really private*' but the moral decision about whether to publish it was made, and for all time, by Murry. It seems to me he could hardly have decided otherwise. My job has been to complete what he began.

The last part of her life was not much more than work, and the search for health. But it was done with the high courage, honesty, wit and intelligence that were the hall-marks of her personality.

## ACKNOWLEDGEMENTS

To the two libraries concerned I owe most of all. The Manuscripts staffs in both of them gave every possible assistance, and the Turnbull Library's published guide to their Katherine Mansfield manuscripts was invaluable. The three Chief Librarians of the Turnbull Library during the period of my association with it—A G Bagnall, J E Traue, and Margaret Calder—have all supported and encouraged me. Graham Bagnall, indeed, could be said to have been the *sine qua non* of the whole enterprise. His death before I had finished the work was the hardest among a number of such blows. At the Newberry Library Diana Haskell, Curator of the Mid-West Manuscripts, was wonderfully kind and accommodating to a rather lost New Zealander.

And, of course, to the three people who generously supported my application for the National Library Research Fellowship—Dr J R Tye, Professor C K Stead (who also cast a critical and helpful eye over my introduction), and the late Dr Frank McKay—and to the National Library itself, I am warmly grateful.

Professor I A Gordon, who played a crucial part in New Zealand's successful acquisition of these manuscripts in 1957, read these volumes in draft form and was exceedingly generous in the time he gave to discussing and solving some of the problems. He alone saw my work before it was finished and his encouragement was of vital importance to me.

My thanks are due, too, to those who advised me in matters pertaining to their own specialist subjects: Wharehuia Hemara (Māori language), Nelson Wattie (German), Stephen Reid (meteorology), Gerald M Bennett (agriculture), John M Thomson (music), Kitty Wood (Karori history), Barbara Angus (Maata Mahupuku), Arnold Solomons (pharmaceuticals), Ann Rosenberg and Catherine Kelly (their father, Siegfried Eichelbaum), and Professor William Burgan of Indiana University (Charles Dickens).

The late Dan and Winnie Davin helped in ways both tangible and intangible, as did the late David Hall and his wife, Wanda. Gillian Boddy gave a lot of time during the first year of the work and helped me to organise and keep track of the material. The judicious advice and practical help of Lauris Edmond, Ian and Diana Wards, Rosemary Mercer, Ray Copland, Heather Murray, and

Margaretha Gee did much to stiffen my sinews. And Nicky Page and Paula Wagemaker of Daphne Brasell Associates Ltd, and the team of students in the Whitireia Publishing Course were indefatigable in their pursuit of excellence in copy editing and overall preparation of the typescripts. Margaret Cochran, the designer, is responsible for the elegant visual quality of the publication.

My children, Rachel, Jonathan and Kate, with their individual skills and resources, have all helped and supported me through the long years of my attention to Katherine Mansfield's manuscripts. Lastly, I should record that it all began when my long-time friend and mentor, the late Dr E H McCormick, opened a first crucial door for me many years ago.

Margaret Scott

Wellington, 1997

## ABBREVIATIONS

| | |
|---|---|
| S | *The Scrapbook of Katherine Mansfield*, ed J M Murry, Constable & Co Ltd, London, 1939 |
| J | *Journal of Katherine Mansfield: Definitive Edition*, ed J M Murry, Constable & Co Ltd, London, 1954 |
| CLKM | *The Collected Letters of Katherine Mansfield*, ed Vincent O'Sullivan and Margaret Scott, Clarendon Press, Oxford. Vol 1, 1984; Vol 2, 1987; Vol 3, 1993; Vol 4, 1996; Vol 5, forthcoming |
| ts | typescript |
| ATL | Alexander Turnbull Library |
| NL | Newberry Library |

# *Unbound Papers*

[MS-Papers-3981-105]

## ENNA BLAKE[2]
By Kathleen Beauchamp
Aged 9 years.

"Oh, mother, it is still raining, and you say I can't go out." It was a girl who spoke; she looked about ten. She was standing in a well-furnished room, and was looking out of a large bay window. "No, Enna, dear" said her mother, "you have a little cold, and I don't want it made worse." Just then the gong rang for luncheon, and they went into the dining-room. In the midst of this meal the maid came in with the letters; there was one for Enna and one for Mrs Blake. As it had stopped raining after lunch, they all went outside, where Enna seated herself in a shady nook and began to read her letter. It was a note from Lucy Brown, to ask her and her mother to spend a few weeks holiday with her at her home in Torquay. Enna was delighted, and ran to ask her mother.

And so it happened that next morning they got into the train that bore them to Torquay. When Enna was tired of looking out of the window she lay back in her seat and knew nothing more until she heard the porter shout "Torquay".

Lucy was on the platform to welcome them. "I am so glad you have come" she said, "mother thought your music might prevent you." They had a pleasant drive to Sunny Glen; it was nine o'clock at night when they reached it, and so they were told to go to bed at once, which Enna willingly did.

The next day was very fine. Mrs Brown proposed that they should go ferning. So soon after breakfast they started. "It seems just the day for enjoying

---

[2]This piece appeared in *The High School Reporter* (Wellington Girls' High School), second term 1898, Vol 23, No 20, with the following comment: 'This story, written by one of the girls who have lately entered the school, shows promise of great merit. We shall always be pleased to receive contributions from members of the lower forms. Ed.'

one's self" said Lucy, as they climbed the hill. "Yes" Enna answered, "today here is much nicer than in London." At about twelve o'clock the two girls sat on a log and ate their dinners. "I should think it would be very nice to get some moss" Enna said; so off they trudged. The girls spent a very happy day, and got a great many nice ferns and some beautiful moss. And that night Enna said she thought it was the nicest day she had ever spent in the country. The next day was very wet, so they had to stay indoors, but they made cakes, scones, ginger-nuts, and other dainties for a party she meant to have the day after next. At about eight o'clock that night a box came directed to Lucy in her uncle's hand. On opening it she found a darling little kitten; it was pure white except for a black spot on its neck. Lucy was delighted, and played with it all the rest of the evening.

The third day of Enna's stay was very pleasant. The girls went for a ride in the morning, and visited some girl friends of Lucy's in the afternoon. When they had had tea a gentleman came to see Mrs Brown and amused them for the rest of the evening. And, indeed, the weeks flew by too quickly, but when the holidays did come to an end, Enna thought it was the happiest holiday she had ever had.

- - - - - - - - - - - - - - - -

### A HAPPY CHRISTMAS EVE.[3]
### By Kathleen Beauchamp
### Aged 10½

The town clock was striking half-past twelve, and a sigh of relief came from the children in the little schoolroom at the Courteney's house. "I am glad lessons are over" said Grace the eldest one:"I could not learn today." "Well" said Fanny, "let's be quick and gather the books together and tidy the room, for mamma said she wanted to see us after the morning's lessons." The room was soon tidied, and the children ran into the study to see their mother.

"Good morning, my darlings" said Mrs Courteney, laying down the book that she was reading. "As you break up today, I am going to take you with me to town, to get the presents for our tree." For the Courteneys were going to have a tree for the poor children that year.

"How lovely!" the children answered, dancing about the room in their glee. "Will we go directly after dinner, mamma?" "Yes, I think so, darlings. And now run to nurse and get ready for dinner."

What a busy afternoon they had, buying small things and large things of every sort and description. They were thoroughly tired when they reached home, and very glad to get to bed. It was to be Christmas Eve in a week, and as the tree was to be shown that night they had to be rather quick.

The next morning when they awoke the first thought was of the presents they had bought. "I wonder if they have come" said Harold to his favourite,

---

[3]*The High School Reporter*, second term 1899, Vol 24, No 23.

Beth, "do you think they will have." "I think so" Beth said, "mamma will be very quick."

I will pass over the next few days and will resume my story on the morning of the day before Christmas. The day dawned clear and bright, and the children were up at a very early hour. "I never felt more happy before" said Harry, giving Fanny's arm a squeeze; "But there is the breakfast bell; we must hurry." It was impossible to keep silence at breakfast time, they chatted all the while about the tree.

"What are we going to do this morning mamma" said Grace. "Going for a walk, darling, to work off your spirits." They had a long and pleasant walk, and when they came back the noises that were coming out of the study were wonderful. "Oh dear! I do want to look so; but then it would spoil all the fun" said Beth.

Such a funny crowd it was that came that night, ragged and dirty, but having a look of curiosity on their faces. When they had all come, the study door was thrown open, and the Christmas tree was seen in all its splendour. I wish I could have let you see the delight on the faces of the children. Really it was a sight to behold. The tree was loaded with sweets, fruits, and presents, and there was a present for everyone besides a bag of sweets. Then there were games, supper at which the children ate very heartily, more games, and then they went home. When the guests had gone the children sat alone in the study talking over the events of the evening. Soon their mother came in, looking very tired. "Well, children" she said, "how have you enjoyed yourselves?" "Mamma" they answered, "it is the happiest Christmas Eve we have ever had."

[MS-Papers-4006-01]

Three 20th Century Girls[4]

June 4th 1901
by K. Beauchamp

Chapter 1
The great examination.

They were walking in a leisurely fashion up the stairs. They had been sent to bed as it was past nine o'clock, but that was a mere detail in their minds. There are three girls in the family, the eldest, Phoebe, is just sixteen. Phoebe is not what could be called a truly pretty girl, but she had a wealth of beautiful nut brown hair that fell in one thick plait down her back. Next in age is Kitty, or Edith, if you wish to be exact. She is what girls call, a 'real good sort', and here the writer agrees, she is one girl in twenty. And last comes Bessie, who is the one beauty in the family, though is herself entirely unconscious of the fact. Lately, she has developed a tendency to appear masculine, to the great

---

[4]This, the earliest manuscript, is comparatively easy to read. It contains a couple of spelling mistakes which have been retained.

amusement of the rest of the family. The ages of these two are fourteen and thirteen. Bessie is speaking. "Phoebe", she says, "I wish that when you wake me in the morning, that you'd roll me right out of bed. How can a fellow be expected to jump from the comfortable regions of the Equator, to the icy coldness of the North pole." "I simply couldn't", Kitty says, "really I dont see any advantage in you doing your lessons twice." "Of course you don't" the two others exclaimed both together, "but you are not trying nearly so hard for the prize as we are." "I'm like a skeleton, already", Bessie continued "if we did not break up in a week, something would go wrong with my brain. I was just trying to find the square root of the fifth Euclid prop." The three then said goodnight and departed to their respective bedrooms.

These girls have no father, their Mother is middleaged. She is passionately loved by the family and deserves it all. There are two boys, one aged twenty, whose name is Arthur, the other seventeen, named Albert.

Next morning the girls went off to school on their bicycles (the whole family had cycles, which were the presents of their Grandfather) with much fear and trepidation. It was the day of the great exam. Girls from twelve upwards were trying and it was thought to be a hard battle. Soon all the candidates assembled in a large schoolroom, where the papers were given out. Every girl described it as being very stiff, and Kitty bit the handles of two pens down to nothing in the time given them. After school all girls who had done the exam had the rest of the day free to do what they pleased. Our three went home in low spirits. "How did you get on?" queried the Mother, directly they entered the door. But a chorus of groans was the only answer she received. "Awful", said Phoebe, "dreadful", said Kitty, "terrific", said Bessie. "Really", went on Kitty, "you will have to seriously think of increasing my allowance, Mater, in the time of exams. The numbers of handles of pens that I nibble away is absolutely appaling". The Mother smiled, and told them to run away and get ready for dinner.

"What can we do with ourselves this afternoon?" said Phoebe. "For my part, I shall enjoy myself with 'Paul Dombey', in the hammock", said Bessie. "And the apples", Kitty said. "Mother, only think, the other day I found Bessie sitting under the apple tree, crying over the death of Paul". Bessie stoutly denied such "feminine weakness", as she expressed it, and turned the conversation into a different channel. A week after, the girls assembled to hear the results of the great exam and to break up. The headmistress made a short speech and then said that the prize was awarded to one of the younger girls and I have much pleasure in presenting [it] to Kitty Mahony. There was a burst of applause and Kitty went up with flaming cheeks to receive the 'Waverly Novels', bound in red morocca.

- - - - - - - - - - - - - - -

### A pleasant surprise

"Do suggest something that we can do these holidays Arthur" said Phoebe, "of course [we] want to be home for Christmas and here we are waiting till it comes." Arthur thought for a moment, and then a bright idea struck him. "Why not go on a bicycling tour, you three?" he said. "Bravo" they all shouted, "we'll go to the same place as you and Bert went last holidays." "And I'll chaperone you girls", continued Bert, "we'll have a ripping time."

[MS-Papers-3981-105 ts]

## THE PINE-TREE, THE SPARROWS, AND YOU AND I.[5]

He was a tall, stately pine-tree. So tall, so very tall, that when you stood underneath and looked right up through the branches you could not see the top. How very fond you were of that pine-tree. We used to go and see it every day. He sang the most beautiful songs and told the most lovely stories; but he always seemed a little sad, somehow. You could not understand why for days and days, until one morning I discovered quite by accident - poor, dear old pine-tree. No little bird had ever built a nest in his branches. All the other trees had two and three, but no bird ever seemed to come near this one. We decided it must be a very unfashionable quarter for birds, yet there was no reason why it should be. A dear little rippling stream ran quite near it and laughed all day long. But yet no birds came near him.

One day when we were sitting under an old apple-tree in the garden, you pointed with your finger to a little husband and wife sparrow who had evidently gone out house-hunting. They looked tidy and very respectable; so we thought what a good idea it would be for them to build in the pine-tree. We went back to the house very quickly, and while you got a nice crumby piece of bread I wrote a little letter. Then I tied it on to the bread with one of your little blue hair ribbons, and hand-in-hand we walked back to where the sparrows were sitting. Yes, they were still in just the same place, so we put the bread down quite near them, and then walked away with our heads in the air as though we knew nothing about it.

The next morning, very early, you and I went to the old pine-tree. Your little legs were going along so fast that it made me quite dizzy to look at them. Long before we came to the place I had to carry you - you had such a terrible stitch! At last we caught sight of him. His branches were all waving and his head was high in the air. When he saw us he bowed most graciously, but very proudly. I stole along ever so quietly with you in my arms, and, sure enough, there were the sparrows sitting in the branches. They did not seem at all shy, and how glad we both were. The old pine-tree looked just like you do when you have had a cold bath and Mummy has put you in a clean starched frock, and a petticoat that sticks out all round. You look as though you never made mud pies in your life and would rather die than tread in the puddles.

After that visit we came regularly every day with hay and feathers and little bits for their nest, and at last it was finished. The old pine-tree simply sang the whole day now. He never was sad. You said he always seemed to be singing "hymns of gladness", and I think you were right.

---

[5] *Queen's College Magazine*, December 1903.

One night when you were in bed and asleep, Mummy and I went for a walk all by our own selves, and suddenly we found we were standing under the old pine-tree. He was not looking half so proud that night, but very, very tender and loving. The moon shone down through the branches and we could see the little nest and suddenly we heard a little "cheep, cheep". Just a weeny-teeny sound. Then Mummy and I knew that there must be some little baby sparrows, so we came home just as fast as we could, wishing that morning would come, so that we could tell you. How excited you were, and how quickly Mummy dressed you. When we did come to the pine-tree, you kept one little hand over my mouth (I had you on my shoulder) so that I would not say a word. We listened for a long long time, and heard them saying "cheep, cheep". We would have stayed all day, I think, if I had not managed to whisper a little breath whisper that I was going to sneeze. Then you made me run, because you knew how loud my sneezing was. When we reached home your cheeks were like roses, and your eyes were shining like stars, and you tried to tell Mummy so much in one breath that I thought you would burst. We did not go and see them again all day, but when the dew had begun to fall, and the little shadow boys were coming out of school, and the air smelt full of roses, Mummy and you and I went. Mummy had hold of one of your hands and I had hold of the other, and we jumped you over all the big stones, till you shouted with laughter. All the way home I played horses with you on my back, and poor Mummy's hair nearly came down, we ran so fast. You told me it had got soft with washing, just as though she sent it to the laundry.

Late that night, when I was locking the windows, and Mummy was lighting the bedroom lamp, a huge big grandfather storm came. He shook the house 'mensely, and woke you right up. I found you underneath the bed-clothes, crying and looking so red and hot. I got you a clean "hanky" and a drink, and asked you if you were crying because you were frightened, and you said No-o-o, and the tooth glass shook so in your hand that I thought the water would spill. "Have you got a pain, darling" I said. "No-o-o-o" you said, crying much harder. "Its about zem poor 'icle spawows." I sat right down on the bed and felt like Mummy feels when the cook says she's going to leave, "dinner-party or no dinner-party."

We went to see them the first thing next morning. Alas! as soon as I saw our old friend, I knew something must be the matter. He was crying and moaning - and then - and - then, you found three little dead sparrows. Poor, poor little darlings. You held them in your pinafore, and I quite forgot Mummy would be cross.

That afternoon we had a little sad funeral. We buried them under the old pine-tree, and you planted a geranium flower on their grave.

# Notebook 40

[Notebook 40, qMS-1239]

Contents

-/8/03

"In Sobriety and Otherwise"

By Kass.

1.                    His Ideal.[6]

He was but a child when he first saw Her. Such a wee child, and, ah, so ill, so very ill. It was night. The room was dark. From his little bed he could see the tall dark trees out of the window. They were waving and bending to and fro, to and fro. He wondered vaguely if they were talking to one another, and what they were saying. He had been in pain all day, but towards evening it had left him. "If he can but sleep", said the Doctor, "sleep is his only chance." He was lying there, hot and fevered, when She came to him. He saw Her, he saw Her!: She was tall, and wore a long white robe, that shimmered like the moonbeams. Her white throat was bare. On her forehead shone a star, golden and beautiful, and there was another on her bosom. She leant over him with a face full of tenderness and pity. And he, not knowing, ah! the poor little child, not knowing, stretched out his arms for her to take him up, and soothe him, and hold him to her breast. He was so tired, so very very tired!! But she shrank back, and she looked at him with such compassion, that the tears came to his eyes, and he hid his face. When he looked again, she was gone. And he slept.

- - - - - - - - - - - - - - - - -

He did not see Her again, for many years; but Her memory haunted him always. He grew unlike other children. He did not play or laugh, but sat apart,

---

[6]Another version of this story ('She') is in the so called Notebook 29 and can be found on p 30. It is important as an illustration of KM's interest in Death, even at the age of 12.

and in silence, always thinking of Her, always longing for Her. If she would only come again. Ah, if she would only come.

One day when many years had passed, and he had grown to be a young man, he was thrown from his horse, and was found lying on the roadway, unconscious. They took him home, and laid him on his bed. He moaned and tossed about for many days, but one day he raised himself, and cried out in a strong voice:- "I have seen Her, I have seen Her!!" - - -

They thought that the fall had injured his brain for ever after. He grew more silent, more reserved, living quite by himself. He had indeed seen her, but she had not taken him, although he had longed to go. She had shaken her head, and vanished as before.

- - - - - - - - - - - - - - - -

More years passed. He grew old and feeble, and wrinkled. And one day he walked by the river. The sky was green and lowering. The wind moaned and cried through the trees. The water rushed along with an angry roar. Winter was at hand, cold, cold winter. And winter was in his heart. Pity him, the old lonely man!! And as he stood by the bank, a terrible fear rose in his heart. He felt he was going to die. Here alone, all in his terrible loneliness. He could not bear it. He must struggle, he must live. But he felt his strength leave him, and sank to the ground. He gave one hoarse cry.

And then! Ah! he saw her again. She stretched out her arms, with her lips parted, with her eyes luminous, and clasped him to her breast. And as her arms enfolded him, he felt all his sorrows, his loneliness, fade into, and become part of, the past; they were buried with the past. Then he looked up at her. "Take me with you, now", he moaned, "do not leave me". She looked at him and smiled, & clasping him more tightly to him [ie her], she took him.

And her name was - Ah! how well we know her you and I. She, who came with her forefathers, and will stay while this little Universe remains.
Her name was Death.

2.                          Concerning Cornet players.
                            (of the average type.)

The man that I really have a great admiration for in a Brass Band, is a cornet player. There is such a stern and sober air of reality about himself and his instrument, and I really think that the way in which he has his feelings under control is marvellous!! For instance, I have watched, (and heard, alas) a cornet player emit wails and sobs of anguish from his cornet, which have well nigh torn my heart out, while <u>he</u> sits in stolid silence never moving a hair.

The patience that the man has, is another matter of great wonder to me. Often "when on my couch I lie in vacant or in pensive mood", I have heard a man next door, play "Way down upon the Swannee River", with various other tunes, I believe, <u>called</u> variations, twenty times without stopping. <u>Then</u> he has only ceased because I have threatened to have him evicted if he does not change his tune. Frequently, after a dose of this kind, I have had nothing but the "Swannee River" on the brain, for weeks. I wake up with the "Swannee River", eat it with every meal I take, and go to bed eventually with "all de world am sad and weary" as a lullaby.

Now, if I played that tune myself, as my neighbour does, I am confident that after a time I should become insensible to anything else. Players of the cornet should never attempt anything approaching what is commonly termed "light" music. They should steadily stick to "Funeral Marches", "Lamentations" and a few of the average "Coronation Odes". In the course of ages they may become quite proficient in these, and give a certain degree of <u>almost</u> pleasure to the public. But when they attempt "Silvery Waves", "The Maiden's Prayer", or the "Honeysuckle and the Bee", then O public, put your respectable fingers to your ears, and depart in haste.

Dear cornet players, long may I hear your thrilling strains. You keep us in touch with the old world melodies. Good luck to the Swannee River, & to you!!!⁷

### A True Tale

Many, many miles from here, my little Saxons, many many years ago, there was a beautiful island. All round it lay the lovely laughing sea, and there were tall, green, "smelly"⁸ woods, the like of which you have never seen, down to the water's edge.

There were no white people living there, but tall, stately, copper coloured men and women, who sailed all round their country in great, carved canoes, and hunted in the woods for game, and very often, I am afraid, human people, whom they killed with aké-akés.⁹ They were always having wars among themselves, and it is about one of these wars that I am going to tell you. Let us come closer to the fire, dear children, and be glad that you did not live in the time that Motorua¹⁰ did.

Kathleen.

K.

Kathleen M.Beauchamp.

K.M.Beauchamp.

Der Tod, das ist die kühle Nacht
Das Leben ist der schwüle Tag
Es dunkelt schon, mich schläfert
Der Tag hat mich müd gemacht.

---

⁷Across the bottom of two pages of this piece KM has drawn a series of treble clefs.
⁸'Smelly': fragrant.
⁹Ake ake: literally 'forever', here it probably means 'triumphant shouts of ake ake'.
¹⁰Motorua is not a name which occurs in Māori mythology.

Über mein Bett erhebt sich ein Baum
Drin singt die junge Nachtigall
Sie singt von lauter Liebe
Ich hör es sogar im Traum.[11]

KKK
Isobel M. Dyer.[12]
   Isobel M. Dyer.
Annie
   Annie B. Beauchamp.

Twilight
Twilight is gathering round us, dearest,
It is the end of this short day
And our lives have come to the twilight, dearest,
You and I have not long to stay.

Come, stand by me at the window, dearest
Look out at the calm, quiet sky.

Annie B.Beauchamp
Your loving Mother
Annie.
Harold
Annie Harold
Harold[13]

Ober kind
too kind

12 people who would receive - - - if - - -

   Gladys
   Father & Mother
   Diddy
   Gran
   Aunt Li
   Myself
   Tommy
   Maude

---

[11]The translation of this poem by Heinrich Heine is:
Death, it is the cool night
and life is the sultry day
It grows dark, I am sleepy;
the day has made me weary.

Above my bed a tree spreads out
The young nightingale sings in it.
It sings of love alone.
I hear it even in my dream.
[12]Isobel Marion Dyer was the full name of KM's Aunt Belle.
[13]At this point one must turn the notebook over and start at the other end.

Marion
Sylvia
Uncle Val
Uncle Syd

My dear Mr Mason,

I am writing to beg a

Deutsch sentences for Conversation[14]

| | |
|---|---|
| I | Wo sind wir stehen geblieben? = when did we leave off? |
| II | Ein junges Blut = a young thing. |
| III | Auf dem Boden schlafen = to sleep on the floor. |
| IV | Der Flug macht einen Bogen = the river makes a bend. |
| V | Er war sehr böse auf mich = he was very angry with me. |
| VI | Er meinte es nicht böse = he meant no harm. |
| VII | Man brauchte es nicht = it was not needed. |
| VIII | Thränen brachen auf ihren augen = tears flowed from her eyes. |
| IX | Es brennt in der Stadt! = there is a fire in the town! |
| X | Er ist hoch ambretto! = he is at the top of the tree! |
| | ich unterschweide nicht = I do not know. |
| | nicht von Bedeutung = nothing to speak of. |
| | ich sah ihn, konnte ihn aber nicht sprechten = I saw him but could not speak to him. |
| | Es thut mir leid = I am sorry. |
| | das Violoncell = the 'cello. |

It was a big bare house surrounded with pine trees. A wilderness of a garden stretched away on all sides - no settled beds of flowers, but the whole overrun with weeds, and tall, long grass. At the back of the house were high thickly wooded hills. Beautiful hills where the tui[15] sang all day in summer and the morepork[16] cried aloud in the evenings. But the house looked desolate. There were no dainty window curtains, no creepers to soften its outlines. It was painted white. There was a broad verandah at the back, that was the only "nice" thing about it. It was a desperately hot afternoon in the middle of November. The sun streamed down, and there was not a breath of wind. Suddenly the front door opened. "Ettie" cried out a girl's voice. "Ettie, where are you." No answer. She stepped outside and looked about. "She can't have gone off with the boys" she said, "I'll go down to the gate and see if they are coming."

She was a tall thin girl. Her hair still hung down her back in masses of thick golden brown curls, which were tied back by a ribbon. Her face was beautiful, very beautiful, but she was too thin, and she looked almost old and certainly care worn. Yet she was only fifteen. She was the eldest of a family of

---

[14]These sentences contain some mistakes but are what KM wrote.
[15]Tui: *Prosthemadera novaeseelandiae*, the parson bird.
[16]Morepork: *Ninox novaeseelandiae*, the small owl.

## The old Inkstand

O, the old inkstand on the table stays
It is too shabby to sell
In truth it has seen much better days
It has many a story to tell.

There was a time when its drawers were full
Of red wax and old quill pens

## Friendship

He sat by his attic window
The moonlight was streaming
Over his furrowed face
He had sat thus for hours with his head bent
Never moving his place.

He thought of the long past sweetness
When life had started
Like a blossoming rose
Of how soon it had spent all its beauty & fragrance
And gone - no man knows

He thought of his future before him
The figure of poverty
Looked in his eyes
He saw his old friends watch him begging & praying
With silent surprise.

## Friendship

He sat at his attic window
The night was bitter cold
But he did not seem to feel it
He was so old - so old -

The moonlight silvered his grey hair
And caressed his furrowed face
The clock at the old church tower struck 12
But he did not change his place.

He thought of his happy boyhood
How life had seemed to him
Like an ever dancing river
And his eyes grew misty & dim

Then he thought of his dismal Future
Alone, and loved by none
Dark clouds lay in every direction
And hid the glorious sun.

He moaned as he sat at the window
And moved as though in pain
"O dream of my happy boyhood
Come back to me again." - - -

Suddenly all his attic
Was lit with wondrous light
And there stood up before him
Figures from out the night.

Lo, they were 5 young maidens
And they stood before him all
As though 'twere the richest castle
And his room a banqueting hall

And he said in low strained accents
What would ye have with me
For I am poor and aged
And have not heard of thee.

And the maidens sang together
"Hear us you poor old man
We have come to blight your troubles
And help you if we can.

Know then our names are beauty,
Youth, friendship, riches & peace
And we would make you happy
And cause your pain to cease.

Choose one of us, choose wisely
That whom thou lovest best
She will remain with you always
Until your eternal rest."

This is an exam

My dear uncle

Then the maidens stopped their singing
"If my sorrow would find release
I must choose that which is most perfect
And her beautiful name is <u>Peace</u>"

Then before his weary vision
The spirits faded fast
But Peace stayed still beside him          My dear Uncle Syd
And held him to her, fast.

My dear Uncle Syd

They found him the next morning
Quite dead upon the floor
The old man had ah, truly
Found Peace for evermore.

Misunderstood.

If only human nature
would be more forbearing
not
‒ ‒ ‒ ‒ ‒ ‒ ‒ ‒ ‒ ‒ ‒ ‒ ‒ ‒ ‒

It was visiting afternoon in a London hospital. Mothers, Fathers, sisters, brothers, aunts and uncles, streamed up to the door. The hospital was in one of the poorest parts of the City & was for children, whose parents could not afford to pay a doctor, and who could not, or would not, follow his instructions if they did have one. In the front ward there was only one cot which did not have a visitor. This was occupied by a child of about 8 years of age. A little curly haired dark skinned child with great luminous black eyes. She was one of the most beautiful and also one of the most eccentric children who had ever entered the Hospital. She had been run over in the streets and her ankle broken. When brought to the Hospital she was asked where she lived. "Nowhere" was the response. Had she a Mother and Father. "No". Any relations. "No". Who did she live with. "No one". And that was all they ever learnt of her circumstances. She never wished for toys, but would sit hour by hour moving her right hand up and down, as though wielding a bow, and singing a weird indescribable accompaniment. Once, when the other children wished to sleep the "little musician" as she was called persisted in singing. One of the nurses came up, and taking hold of her hands, told her she must stop instantly. The child looked up at her and then bursting into a torrent of sobs, declared it was "all gone". In vain she was asked what was gone, she only shook her head & sobbed more piteously.

It was half past three. The little musician, despite all the noise of talking in the room, had begun playing again, & singing softly. As she sat there, one of the nurses happened to be taking round an old gentleman, a patron of the Hospital, a bachelor, & intensely musical. As they came to her cot, he stopped amazed and wondering. The child did not see them. She went on swaying her body slightly from side to side and singing a plaintive minor cadence. The tears rolled down her cheeks as she sang, but the sweet voice never quavered right on to the end. When the last note had died away, Lord Hunter, strangely excited, spoke to the nurse. Who was she? Her name? Her age? the nurse told him all she knew, & then the old man leant over the child. "It was very sad" he said, "where did you learn that." The little one looked up, and seeing his kindly old face, and sympathetic eyes, she said "I didn't learn it. I just ‒ thought it." He went on talking. "Would you like to hear beautiful music, and to play beautiful music?" The child looked up at him. Her eyes were flashing. "O ‒ ‒ ‒ h" was all she said. Then "but I heard some once. It was in one of the houses of the gentry folk. It was O like just nothing else." "Do you remember the tune?" he said gently. "Why yes" she answered, "I'll tell you." She sang with her queer little bowing movement that little masterpiece which touches our hearts and brings the tears to our eyes. Ave Maria. He listened, and the same sense of awe and wonder filled him, as it had before ‒[17]

---

[17]Here there is a page of drawings of dolls, one labelled 'Leslie's petite enfant', and another labelled 'Jeanne's petite enfant'.

The Song of my Lady.

My lady sits and sings
The sunlight flings
Its beams, and brings
Ripe gold into her hair—
O my lady, knowing nothing
Fearing nothing, she sits there.

My lady sits and sighs
The autumn wind
Not overkind
Tries to unbind
Her golden hair—
O my lady, knowing all things
Fearing many, has learnt Care.

My lady sits & sews
The broidery grows
Like a summer rose
She little knows
She's aught to fear—
O my lady, be more watchful
Do not sit so blindly there![18]

---

[18]At the bottom of this page KM has written, upside down, 'Franz Liszt. Franz.'

# Notebook 37

[Notebook 37, qMS-1240]

Wedding Day 30th Jan.
Birthday 13th

"Little Fern Fronds"[19]

by Kass.

Dedicated to a fellow-songster in loving memory of a June afternoon.

## Contents

---

[19]This notebook is, to some extent, a fair copy of poems in MS Papers 4006/14, the others of which can be found on pp 22–26.

Evening.

Evening is come, the glory of the sunset
Floods the sky
The little birds lift up their hymns of praise
To God on High.

But one by one, the colours now have faded
The sky grows gray
No star is seen in all the heavens to guide us
If we should stray.

At last one wee star peeps from out its covert
Of the dull sky
To cheer the rough and stony way before us
And to be nigh.

It is a narrow path that lies before us
Hard is the way,
Almighty Guide, watch over us and shield us
Lest we should stray.

The Sea.

O the beauty, O the grandeur of the sea
What stories does its changeful visage tell
To you and me.

When fiercely rage the tempests o'er the deep
And all the slumb'ring world is waked from sleep
When the sea sobs, as if in sad distress
And none are there to cheer my lonliness
I feel for thee O Sea.

In calm and tempest and in storm and strife
In all the bitter changeful scenes of life
In death's dark hour before Eternity
I feel for thee, O Sea.

The Three Monarchs.

Day took off her azure mantle
She laid down her golden crown
And she sank to her rest on the cloudlets
On pillows of rosy down.

Twilight, clad in a sombre mantle
Ascended the vacant throne
His face was haggard and weary
And his courtiers left him alone.

When the reign of Twilight was over
Night, clad in a robe of black
Saw the far away form of the monarch
And beckoned to him to come back.

But twilight, his course pursuing
Ne'er turned, ne'er lifted his head
And the face of Night grew despairing
In low hollow tones he said

Alas! Alas! where are my brethren?
Am I left here alone to die?
Does no one care for my welfare
When I on my deathbed lie?

And he wrapt his robe around him
And down in the darkness he lay
The reign of the night was over
And back to her throne came Day.

### Music.

The world began with music,
Wist ye not the "Music of the Spheres"
And the angels will be playing harps of gold
When Judgement Day appears.

When Christ our Heavenly Lord came down to earth
And solemn stillness reignèd all around
A burst of angels song proclaimed his birth
That made the whole world tremble at the sound - - -

We pray that when our Lord may come again[20]
And when we hear that angels music ring
That we may shout with one accord "Amen"
And with the angels joyfully may sing.

All the world is music
Wist ye not the music of the sea
The music of the birds, the winds, the flowers
'Tis all in all to me.

### A Fragment.

What thing, more beautiful, more fair
To eyes of God and man is
Than a garden.

---

[20]Above 'again' KM has written '(en)' to indicate that it should be pronounced to rhyme with 'Amen'.

It is the spot where
Man first prayed to God
Craving his pardon.

### Love's Entreaty.

Lovest thou me, or lovest me not
Whisper and do not fear
Let me not wait thine answer, love
The time to part draws near.

Why standest thou, so proud, so cold
Would I thy heart might see
The moon shall wane, and the stars grow old
Ere I lose my love for thee.

If thou wouldst take my heart, my life
If I thy slave might be
I'd reck not for the world's hard strife
O my love, I would live for thee.

### Night.

When the shadows of evening are falling

27/XII/03.

I am afraid I must be very old-fashioned.[21] I used to pride myself upon being quite a Modern woman, but, within the last week I have had a rude awakening. Last Saturday afternoon when my Beloved had come home and we had drawn the curtains and poked the fire, and settled down for a lovely quiet time just by ourselves, there came a loud ring at the doorbell. A moment after the maid appeared with a suspicious looking envelope bearing the words "With Mr Johnson's Compliments". "Bother Mr Johnson", I said quickly. "Beloved I am sure they are tickets for a Horse Show or a Flower Show or something else equally objectionable." But no, I was wrong. The tickets blazed with pomp and show, and it was not without a great deal of perseverance that we managed to discover between floral wreaths, and angels blowing trumpets this notice:- Lecture on Physical Culture by Miss Mickle, at the Assembly Rooms 3 p.m.

To my infinite distress my beloved was seized with a wish to go, so we left our dear little cosy sitting room, and very soon found ourselves in a most draughty room, on the most hard chairs, surrounded by the most Physical Cultured men and women. I shuddered at the women. Great tall gaunt looking figures, and all angles. They seemed to be seized with a mania to appear masculine. Men's boots, men's gloves, men's hats, men's coats. They walked with long strides and spoke in low tones. Poor benighted dears, I am

---

[21]This piece, and the following diary entry, were written at school in London.

sure in their heart of hearts they were very sorry for themselves. They had a hungry look in their eyes. I longed to take them home and show them my babies and make their hair soft and fluffy and put them in tea gowns, and then cuddle them. I think they would never have gone back to their Physical Culture or their Society for the Promotion of Women's Rights.

At precisely 3 o'clock Miss Mickle appeared amid a burst of applause. Never shall I forget that woman. It seemed to be her great desire to squeeze out all the tenderness, all the loving, all the affectionate ways that should belong by rights to every woman, and to put in their places divided skirts and <no corsets> no figures. On the subject of children she became most eloquent. Why teach an infant the entirely foolish and senseless rhyme of Jack Horner for instance. How much better it would be for him to learn the position of his heart and the Circulation of the Blood. A great clapping followed this, and many cries of hear, hear, that's so. Now my Mother had taught me Little Jack Horner when I was about three, and I had taught it to my babies. I never considered it senseless. It always seemed to have a high Moral value. I thought it encouraged a grateful spirit. Instead of that charming child Jack Horner seizing the plum and promptly devouring it he cast up his eyes with a Saint-like expression exclaiming blest am I to be the fortunate possessor of such parents as do impart to me the high virtue of Godliness. On, On, went that female. She pulled down, and cast into the fire, all the little things that seem to be part of our childhood. And where the little rose-covered summer houses had stood for so long, she erected great dull stone buildings and parallel bars. O Mothers of this generation let us rise in a great body and blunt the tools of these women before it is too late. Let us, with renewed fervour, impart to the babes Little Jack Horner and all his contemporaries.

My beloved and I walked home in silence after that lecture. The rain was dripping on to my hat and I knew that my feet were soaking but I did not care. At the door I said "We will have the babies to tea tonight." They appeared at five o'clock and when they [had] eaten as much as they could and their cheeks were rosy and their eyes were bright with the fire they ran to their Daddy and begged for a story. Something seemed to come over my beloved. He sat down with his hands in his pockets and his feet on the mantelpiece, and began:- Once upon a time there was a dear little boy and his name was Little Jack Horner.

27/XII/03

New Years Eve. It is 12.30. All the bells in the village Churches are pealing. Another year has come. Now at the entrance of this New Year, my dearest,[22] I propose to begin my book. It will not be at all grand or dramatic, but just all that I have done. You, who are so far away, know so little of what happens to me, and it is selfish of me not to tell you more. I have just returned from a

---

[22]This passage is probably addressed to Tom Trowell who, with his brother Garnet, had left New Zealand to study music in Germany.

Midnight Service. It was very very beautiful & solemn. The air outside was
cold and bracing and the Night was a beautiful thing. Over all the woods
& the meadows Nature had tenderly flung a veil to protect from the frost, but
the trees stood out, dark and beautiful, against the clear starry sky. The church
looked truly very fit to be God's House, tonight. It looked so strong, so
invincible, so hospitable.

It was only during the Silent Prayer that I made up my mind to write
this. I mean this year to try and be a different person, and I want, at the end
of this year, to see how I have kept all the vows that I have made tonight.
So much happens in a year. One may mean so much good and do so little.
I am writing this by the light of a wee peep of gas, and I have only got on
a dressing gown - so décolleté. I am so tired, I think I must go to bed.
Tomorrow will be the 1st of January. What a wonderful and what a lovely
world this is. I thank God tonight that I am.    [J1-2]

# *Unbound Papers*

[MS-Papers-4006-14][23]

Dedicated to D _____

    "Ake, Ake, Aroha."[24]

      'The Countess'
      316

   "Little Fronds"
        Kass
        Kathleen M. Beauchamp.

    AKE AKE AROHA
           Kass.

           Night.
When the shadows of evening are falling
And the world is preparing for sleep
When the birds to their wee ones are calling
And the stars are beginning to peep

A peace steals into my heart
Which no one and nothing can break
And I from my old sorrows part
Till the morrow begins to awake.

O night, how I love and adore thee
Why dost thou so short a time stay
My sorrows come crowding back o'er me
When the shades of the night pass away.

I hope I may die in the darkness
When the world is so quiet & so still
And my soul pass away with the shadows
Ere the sun rises over the hill.

---

[23]This little notebook, which lacks a cover, has been cut through at centre page most of the way across the page. Its contents were, to some extent, copied into Notebook 37 (see p 16) but it contains a partly different contents page and 11 poems which are not in the other notebook and are given here. Some of them, at least, were written on board the SS *Niwaru* en route to London in early 1903.
   [24]Māori for 'love forever'.

### To M

For me, O love, thine eyes like stars are shining
For me, thy voice is all the sound I need
O love, dear love, dost know how I am pining
My heart to plead.

The world goes on, with tears & with laughter
I care not for the world, I care for thee
I care not for this life & what comes after
'Tis nought to me.

O love, dear love, thou art my soul, thy presence
Is aught that e'er can soothe my aching heart
Wilt thou not give me but one word of comfort
Before we part.

Thou'rt going, and the light from out my life is dying
It flickers & ere long it shall be dead
And I shall try to follow, blind with crying
Where thou hast led.

### Battle Hymn

Fight on, weary pilgrims, fight
Soon or late there shall be light
Struggle then, with main and might
Till the glass grows clear.

Be not weary, seek not rest
For to fight is to be blest
And your victories He shall test
When the glass grows clear.

Like your leader strive to be
Perfect, without fault is He
And his greatness we shall see
When the glass grows clear.

<Written on S.S. Niwaru –

### The Chief's Bombay Tiger.

Since leaving New Zealand
I grieve to say
A great Bombay tiger
Has come to stay.

He is kept by the chief
In the No. 2 hold
And is famous for doing
Whatever he's told.

And at night when the ladies
Have gone to bed
This great Bombay tiger
Prowls round overhead.

At six and seven, he's heard to roar>
At the ladies' porthole or cabin door
But the lady passengers venture to say
They never feel safe till that tiger's away.

Now your pardon I beg, dear chief, to intrude
And if you don't think me most horribly rude
Just keep your dear tiger in No. 2 hold
And your pardon I beg for being so rude.

## To Ping Pong by J.E.C.

Ping Pong, thy charms have captured ladies fair
Thou'rt spoken of by all the statesmen rare
Cupid and bow and arrows, these are thine
Ping Pong hast captured e'en this heart of mine.

I care not for the charms of playing whist
A game of billiards I can't well resist
But if I see a ping pong ball & bat
Why man, I cry, the game's not worth your hat.

Give me a table & a green baize net
A ball, a racquet, and a girl I met
I am content to play all day and night
Until I've lost my breath & lost my sight.

## To a Little Child

Sleep on, little one
All is well.
Better to die thus
Than go to Hell.

Life is but cold and hard
Death is sweet
Many the traps are set
For wandering feet.

Would I could die as thou
Hast done this day
In childish faith and love
Be ta'en away.

Rest, my little one
Flowers on your breast

Safe in the cold earth's arms
Ever at rest.

In the Darkness

I am sitting in the darkness
And the whole house is still
But I feel I need your presence
Since I've been ill.

It was different in the Springtime
Different then, when all was right
But when all the world is darkness
When all the world is night

O my darling then I want you
For I know you understand
And I yearn to feel your presence
And to feel you clasp my hand.

When I first was told my sorrow
Told that I could never more
See the gay world and the sunshine
As I always had before

O, I thought I could not bear it
Bear to live and to be blind
But the thought of your great absence
Drove all else from out my mind.

And I thought and thought about you
Would you sorrow? Would you care?
When you heard that I was blinded
And was left to linger here?

I am lonely in the darkness
All the world seems dull & still
And my friends have all forgot me
Since I've been ill.

Kia Ora
Ake! Ake! Kia kaha.
Huritia na awaka na
A _____ a E _____ e H _____ a
He hurahura te manu ka rere[25]

---

[25]'Be well. For ever and ever. Be strong. Turn the canoes back. Feathers make the bird fly.' The penultimate line is probably meant to suggest the verbal flourishes which occur in Māori speech making.

## The Springtime

O, a Queen came to visit our country
She was young, and was loved by us all
How we hailed the glad signs of her coming
When we first heard the merry thrush call.

And the flowers sprang up to peep at her
And the trees shook their young leaves with joy
And the daisies came out for her carpet
And she came to us, smiling & coy.

E'en the sun stayed to watch her and court her
How we wished she would stay here for aye
But, alas, she grew tired of our revels
And Queen Springtime soon vanished away.

## To Grace.

When shall I tell you it
Shall it be at night
When the soft wind kisses you
And the stars are bright

Or tell it in the twilight
When the shadows fall
And I still can see your face
Your face, loved best of all.

What matter when I tell you it
Though the fact is shocking
I'll tell you ere my courage fails
"There's a big hole in your stocking."

## Hope

Life is hard
But let us hope
And to live will bring less pain
Let us not in darkness grope
Hope again.

We are tired
But let us hope
And our rest will be more calm
Let us cling fast to life's rope
Safe from harm.

Farewell

Dear little book, farewell
I have loved thee long
Bright may your future be
Like a spring song.

Oft thou hast cheerèd me
When I was sad
When I was all alone
Thou made me glad.

Dear little book, farewell
I have loved thee long
With thee, my childish thoughts
Are ever gone.

Kass

[NL]

Verses of Little Q.

(1)
If you have never been a girl
You cannot know the sin
To wear just "dress material"
To keep your blouses in.

And I shall never quite forget
The rapture that I felt
When Mother went and bought for me
A Ladies' Leather Belt.

(2)
One dreadful day you came to me
And "O dear me" you said -
"The Smith's is runnin' after me
And say me hair is red."

The Smiths had been quite friends of mine
That feeling all was gone.
"It's just a halo, dear" I said
"God always had one on."

Whilst [...] always present this year, the last of the Queen's life [...] great heroic form - - -[26]

---

[26]This almost illegible sentence is written on the back of 'Verses of Little Q'.

[NL]

### Two Ideas with One Moral.

A. Once upon a time there was a nice, sweety, chubby little girl, and she did nothing at all except grow sweeter and chubbier and [her] hair more deliciously curly, each year of her life. She never worried about other people's affairs, she never bothered other people with wishing for wholly unnecessary knowledge, she had never heard of the verb 'to think' and as to 'reason' why it was Greek to her. At last she became so adorably chubby, so ridiculously light hearted that she fell down the stairs - and they made her a heavenly funeral, & the most warm snug little grave you can imagine - and even the undertaker said as he scraped the clay off his hands "Well, she <u>was</u> a dear ..."

Finis.

B. Once upon a time there was a nasty, thoughtful, thin little girl, and she did nothing at all except grow more thoughtful and thin - & her hair more obnoxiously straight - each year of her life. She always worried about other people's affairs, she always worried other people with wishing for unnecessary knowledge, she babbled solely of the verb 'to think' and as to 'reason', why it was life to her! At last she became so disgustingly thin - so preposterously wretched - that she fell up the stairs & they threw her into the darkest moistest little hole you can imagine - and even the undertaker said, as he put a handful of nails into his mouth, "Well, she <u>was</u> a horror."

Finis. 1903[27]

[NL]

### K _ _ Kathleen, Käthe, Kass, K, Kath, <Cass>

This is my world, this room of mine
Here I am living - - - & here I shall die
All my interests are here, in fine
- - - The hours slip quickly by.

Look on these shelves - just books, you would say
Friends I can tell you, one & all
Most of them sorrowful - - some of them gay - -
And my pictures that line the wall.

Yes, that is a Doré, from where I sit
At night with my books or my work, I see
The light that falls & glorifies it - - -
And I gaze & it strengthens me.

Ah! in this cupboard, my miser's store
Of music finger it sheaf on sheaf
Elixir of life - - it is something more
It is Heaven to me, in brief.

---

[27]On the back of this page KM has written 'To be perused at leisure.'

And that is my 'cello, my all in all
Ah, my beloved, quiet you stand
- - - If I let the bow ever so softly fall,
- - - The magic lies under my hand.

And on winter nights when the fire is low
We comfort each other, till it would seem
That the night outside, all cold & snow
Is the ghost of a long past dream.

This is my world, this room of mine
Here I am living - - - here I shall die
All my interests are here in fine
-    The hours slip quickly by.

# Notebook 29

## PART 1

[Notebook 29, qMS-1241][28]

### She[29]

He was but a child when he first saw Her. Such a wee child and ah, so ill, so very ill!!! It was night. The room was dark. Out of the window he saw the night, the stars, and the tall dark trees. And he lay in his little bed and gazed out at it. He had been in pain all day, and with the evening it had left him. "If he can but sleep", said the doctor, "sleep is his only chance." And he was lying there, hot and fevered, when She came to him. He saw Her, he saw Her!! And she was tall with a long white robe, that shimmered like the moonbeams, Her black hair streamed round her, Her white throat was bare. On her forehead shone a star, and there was another at her breast. She leant over him with a face full of tenderness and pity.

And he, not knowing, ah, the poor little child, not knowing stretched out his arms to touch her. For as he gazed at her his soul longed for her to take him in [her] arms and to soothe him and hold him to her breast. He was so tired, so very very tired. But she shrank back, before his fingers touched her robe, and she looked at him with such a look of compassion that the tears came to his eyes and he hid his face. When he looked again, she was gone. And he slept.

He did not see her again for many years. But Her memory haunted him always. He grew unlike other children. He did not play, or laugh, but sat alone and in silence, always thinking of her, always wishing for her. If she would only come again. Ah, if she would only come!!! One day when he was grown older, when many many years had passed and he had become a young man, he was thrown from his horse and was found unconscious. They found him on

---

[28]As mentioned in the introduction, Notebook 29 was not, originally, one notebook. At some stage someone—whether Murry or a subsequent custodian—took several pieces of notebooks which had the same page size, though different line spacing, placed them inside the cover of one of them, and tied the whole thing together. This item was given its own accession number and was subsequently labelled Notebook 29. Because its component pieces were written at widely differing times I have had, in this case, to break my rule about not dividing individual notebooks. The first part of Notebook 29 occurs, chronologically, at this point.
   [29]See note 6.

the road, with the blood streaming down his forehead, and they took him home and laid him on his bed. He moaned and tossed about for many days, and one day he sat up and in a strong voice cried out "I have seen Her. I have seen her!" They thought that the fall had injured his brain for ever after, for he grew more silent, more reserved, living quite by himself. He had seen her but she had not taken him with her although he had longed to go. Why should he wish to stay? She had shaken her head and gone without him.

One day, he walked by the river. The sun was hidden behind the clouds. The wind moaned as though in pain. The tall trees shook their branches in despair. Winter was at hand. But the river flowed on, calm and restful. And his heart was desolate. It moaned with the wind – Ah, for one sight of Her!!! Then a thought flashed across his brain. Why not go to the river and bury himself in its depths, and see her again, for always and for ever. And he gave one hoarse cry, and <u>then</u> ah, he saw her again. She stretched out her arms, with her lips parted, with her eyes luminous, and clasped him to her heart. She held [him] in her arms as she would a little child, but as her arms touched him, he felt all his sorrows, his tears and his bitterness fade away into the past, become buried with the past. Then he looked up at her. "Take me with you" he moaned, "take me with you." And she looked at him and smiled at him, and clasped him still more tightly in her arms and took him.

Death. Death. And her name was – ah! how well we know her you & I. She who came with our Forefathers, and will stay while this little universe will remain. Too often do we bar our doors against her, and watch her entrance with blinding tears. Her name was Death.
<beautiful – that has been with us since the beginning, and that will be with us to the end – Beautiful Death!!!>

Holiday Work and Reading.

---

(Private!)
Begun July 13th 1904.
Kathleen M. Beauchamp.

Books I have read.

| Name | Author | Date |
| --- | --- | --- |
| * Life & Letters of Byron v.I | Thomas Moore | B. J.14th F. J.17th |
| * Aftermath | J. Lane Allen | B. J.17 F. J.17th |
| * Dolly Dialogues | Anthony Hope | B. J.17th F. J.18th |
| Poems | Jean Ingelow | B. J.13th F. J.14th |
| * Life & Letters of Byron v.II | Thomas Moore | B. J.17th F. J.19th |
| * How Music Developed | Henderson | B. July 16th F. |
| * The Choir Invisible | J. Lane Allen | B. July 18th F. 20th |
| The Captain's Daughter | Sven Overton | B. July 20th F. J.20th |
| * Life of Romney | Rowley Clews | B. J.19th F. J.20th |
| * A Kentucky Cardinal | J. Lane Allen | B. J.23rd F. J.23rd |
| Life & Letters of Byron v.III | Thomas Moore | |

| | | |
|---|---|---|
| * Rupert of Hentzau | Anthony Hope | B. J.24th F. 24th |
| * My Japanese Wife | Clive Holland | |
| A Japanese Marriage | Douglas Sladen | |
| Captain Pamphile | Alexandre Dumas | |
| Vilette | Charlotte Bronte | |
| * Poems | E.A. Poe | |
| The Heart of Rome | F. Marion Crawford | |

N.B.  All books which I have enjoyed are marked thus:- *

### Music I have studied

| | | |
|---|---|---|
| Caprice | Noel Johnson | B. July13th F. J.17th |
| Warum | David Popper | B.13th F. |
| Le Désir (part only) | Servais | B.14th F. |
| Variations Symphoniques (part 2) Boëllman | | B. July 15th F. |

### Letters I have written.

Father
Mother
Aunt Li
Grannie
Gwen Rouse
Gwen Rouse
Marion Creelman
Gwen Rouse
Fraulein Petschtes

### Writing I have done

| | |
|---|---|
| Granz [?] (Prose) | B.J.13th F.J.13th(?) |
| Poem | B.J.16th F.J.16th |
| 'Alone' (Poetry) | B.J.14th F.J.14th |

18.VIII.04

Dear old George – I'm going to write you a letter. I guess you have forgotten all about me, and the times I had with you. Well, I haven't. I'll tell you who I am. Do you mind the red-haired boy with the big freckles who was in your form at school. One day you stuck wet varnish on his seat. God! how my Mother swore, and how you fellows laughed. Have you forgotten how you taught me to swim in the old bathing hole down in the 3rd meadow?
Don't say you have, old man – I mind it all as though it were yesterday.

# *Unbound Papers*

[MS-Papers-3981-105 ts]

### YOUR BIRTHDAY[30]

What! It can't be six o'clock. Dear, dear. how time flies. What about someone's bedtime? If I were you I should be just longing to go, for tomorrow is your birthday, and the sooner you get to sleep, the sooner the fun will begin. Well, if you have a story, it must be a "weeny" one. Snuggle up close ... quite comfy?

Once upon a time when you were quite small – only four years old – you had a birthday. You don't mean to say that you have forgotten? What a baby!

The day before Mummy and I went out and bought you a rocking-horse, and ordered you a cake with icing on the top, and four real candles, and a lovely frill of pink paper to go round it. Next morning, very early, I woke up feeling someone stroking my face and begging me to wake up. Why, I thought, it can't be that baby! It was. If it had not been your birthday, I would have made you go right back to bed, but you looked so excited, and jumped about so, I let you creep under the clothes and play 'rabbits'. I was the old father rabbit with a bone in my leg, and you were the mother rabbit, while the pillow was the shockin' baby rabbit. It would fall out of bed, and you had to jump down and rescue it and talk to it, while I lay still and told you what to do. Of course I could not move because of that bone in my leg. That's an awful thing some very old people have.

All the morning you went riding on the new rocking-horse, and when you were the milkman you even had a spot of real milk in the doll's saucepan. Oh, it was fun! In the afternoon, after you had been dressed for the party, Mummy and I let you play quite alone in the dining room. There was a big, big cupboard in there where all the birthday things were put ready for the tea.

You were very quiet for a long time, and then you came into the drawing room where we were sitting. "What a hot little girl" I said. You did not speak, but went to the window and began to sing 'Oh dear, what can the matter be'. But you could not get it right. Then you sat down very still with one finger in your mouth. The little clock on the piano struck three. You looked up.

---

[30]*Queen's College Magazine*, December 1904.

"When are they coming?" you said.

"Who, dear?"

"All the peoples!"

"Why, very soon. Have you got tired of waiting?"

You said nothing for a minute, and then you suddenly ran forward and buried your head in Mummy's lap.

"I don't want a party" you said.

For a moment Mummy and I could not say anything, we were so surprised. At last when I had got some breath back,

"Don't want a party?" I said. "Don't you want presents and games, and little friends to come and see you, and real tea? Don't you want birthday cake with pink and white icing? Wait until you see it!"

"No, no" you said. "Hate birthday cake." I really felt as though I was going to fall off the sofa. Mummy asked if you felt ill.

"Yes" you said, shakily. "Fink I've caught a measle."

Mummy asked if you would like to go to bed. You seemed so glad about it that I had to carry you upstairs right away. Poor Mummy had to go and tell Mary Ann to say to all of the party: Miss Baby's compliments, but she has suddenly become ill, and hopes that her little friends will be able to come again some other day.

We undressed you quickly and popped you into bed. Still you looked ill.

"Don't you feel any better, little one?" I whispered. You wiggled down under the bedclothes, and I heard you crying.

"Never mind" Mummy said, "we'll have the party another day just the same. The cake will keep." You cried much louder.

"Don't want any cake" you said.

"Oh, but you will when you are better" Mummy said.

A sudden thought struck me. I went out of the room, down to the dining room, and – opened the cupboard. Yes, there was the cake, but oh, where was the lovely pink and white icing off the top? Why was the frilly thing all torn, and the candles lying on the floor? Then, because I was a Daddy I understood. I went to the door and called Jane. "Please hide that cake somewhere or give it to the policeman" I said. I went back to the nursery.

"Baby," said I, "I have something to tell you." You grew hotter and hotter.

"The birthday cake is – lost" I said.

"It can't be" said Mummy.

"Well, it is," and I nodded my head like this.

"Poor darling, what a disappointment" said Mummy, kissing you ... About two minutes after you sat up.

"Funny thing" you said, "but all my pain's gone."

- - - - - - - - - - - - - -

That is all. So you say it may have been a little mouse? Well, may be. Sometimes (let me whisper) I think it was a baby. You don't think so?....

What, you say it was a Daddy!... I'm shocked...

Good-night, Little Precious. Say a monster big prayer for me.

---

[MS-Papers-4006-13]

> Dear friend, when back to Canada you go
> And leave old England far away behind
> When in the dark storms, in the bitter snow
> You hug your fire, with a quiet mind
>
> Think of the bathroom, warm and filled with light
> With strains of 'Orchid' and sweet music rare
> And Norway singing songs with all her might
> – Then wish that you could be transported there.
>
> Dear friend, when back to Canada you go
> And taste once more the sweet delights of home
> Do not forget us who have loved you so
> And think of us, wherever you may roam.
>
> > From
> > Kathleen M. Beauchamp
> > April 1904

[MS-Papers-3981-105 ts]

## One Day[31]

The sun streamed through the night nursery window, and woke them up, Jinks, Beggles, and Baby Luls. "Morning" they cried cheerfully, as they always did in the game called "Night" which they played in the nursery with the blinds down, all snugly tucked under the tablecloth.

Jinks sat up, the frills of her "nighty" perked up round her face like the petals of a daisy. "Where's Isabel Marion?" she said. She looked under the pillow and under the quilt, and then Beggles hopped out of his little white bed in the corner and joined the search. Baby Luls lay still placidly and looked on; "She was lyin' in my arms last night" said Jinks, a worried little maternal expression on her face. Beggles sat on the edge of the bed and swung his legs. Jinks turned to baby Luls. "You might help us" she said crossly, "Beggles is lookin' for her and he's only an uncle, so you might as you're an aunt and a godmother."

Baby Luls yawned, then sat up quickly. "O" she said, in a funny, little voice, "I'm sittin' on Isabel Mawion." Jinks' eyes grew big with horror. "A relation" she gasped, "I'll not let you be an aunt again, only a second removed cousin." Then in came mother. "Such a glorious day" she said nodding brightly. "Bath's ready, Jinks, hurry up and soap yourself well. Fly along, dear, if you only knew what it's like in the garden."

Jinks sprang to the ground, screwed up her plait into a tight little knob with one hairpin, seized her towel, and telling Luls to come in five minutes, she skipped off. Mother came and sat on Beggle's bed and smoothed his hair.

---

[31] *Queen's College Magazine*, July 1905.

"Let's all have a beautiful day" she said softly, "and be very very happy and good. I'll give you a surprise this afternoon."

"O" cried Beggles, cuddling her.

"Sweet mummy" said Baby Luls, as she ran to join Jinks. "I must go and finish dressing, sunbeam" said mother, never stirring however. "I wonder if all mummys is as good as you" said Beggles. "Do English chul'ren, an' French chul'ren, and little black chul'ren have the same kinds?" Mummy smiled happily. "Perhaps they have not got the same little girls and boy."

"Such a cold bath" cried Jinks and Luls, in chorus, performing a strange and wonderful dance in their "nighties". "I wented a - huh - a - huh - a - huh, every time Jinks squeezed the sponge on me neck" Luls shouted. They heard Beggles whistling "Down by the Swanee River" and splashing furiously. Beggles whistled like a blackbird in the bath. When he came back Jinks and Luls were at the petticoat stage.

"Funny thing, I can't find me shirt" he said sitting down despairingly. "All me other clothes is here, but mummy left it on the table 'cause she had to mend it." Luls suddenly turned pink and sat down on the floor to put on her socks. Jinks and Beggles had their second search party for that morning. "It's just 'systerious" they said. "Why Luls is cryin'" Beggles exclaimed. "O, O" said that wretched little mortal. "I've been and putted Beggles' shirt on meself." They laughed so much that Mummy came in to hurry them up. Beggles' hairdressing took a long time. "I don't know why" he said, "but mummy one hand shakes and the comb wobbles so, it won't go right . . ."

"Um" said Luls, "I kin smell hot scones." They took hands and raced down the stairs.

Daddy sat reading the paper in the nursery, and they rushed at him with enthusiasm.

"One game of engines before breakfast" they entreated.

"Well, just one" said daddy.

The garden was full of sunshine. The birds were all singing. Everything seemed to have blossomed in the night. "Now you hold on to the back of my coat" said daddy to Beggles. "Now Jinks hold Beggles' belt, and you hold Jinks' pinafore, baby. Ready - go - off. If anyone breaks this lovely train the game is over."

Oh how exciting it was. Father started quite slowly but got faster and faster, till they flew shrieking round and round the tennis court.

"Go on, daddy" they cried. "I feels like a tiger in 'Little Black Sambo'" Luls gasped.

Mummy came to the doorway.

"Breakfast at the next station" she said. They steamed majestically into the nursery.

After breakfast daddy had to go to office. They all stood on the front steps. Handkerchiefs and 'good-byes' were as fervent and numerous as though he was leaving home for a year.

"Bring me back a pony, daddy" Jinks cried.

"Me too" from Beggles.

"An' me barley sugar" piped Luls, hopping on one leg.

"Bring back yourself, dear" mother said smiling.

They watched till he was quite out of sight.

"Now let's go an' play shipwrecks" suggested Beggles. "There's a huge Apollinaris case in the back yard. We'll drag it round to the Dead Sea."

They found the case in the coal-house, and pushed, and pulled, and groaned till they reached their destination - a strip of waste ground where docks and long straggling grass grew in profusion.

"Now for provisions" said Jinks, climbing through the pantry window. Beggles and Luls followed. Mummy was baking buns. She gave them each one handful of currants, two lumps of sugar, and a water biscuit.

"That will keep us for months" they assured her. They slipped everything into Luls' sun-bonnet.

... A few minutes later, three Englishmen armed to the teeth were seen stealing round the Jungle. They seemed to be rather inconvenienced by numerous oceans, which they swam with great exertion and puffing. Suddenly, from behind a giant fuchsia bush they caught a glimpse of a tomahawk. A fierce battle ensued, ending in the complete victory of the English.

"One man wounded" said Beggles, with great satisfaction, viewing Jinks' knee.

"Wet me hanky under the tap, and bring a geranium leaf" said the victim.

She sat in the bottom of the boat and Beggles doctored her. First he laid on the cool leaf, which they believed was used by the ancient Britons for medicinal purposes, and then tightly bound round the handkerchief. The rest of the morning they cruised round Fiji, had a look at Queen Victoria, an unimportant fight off the coast of China, and arrived home in time for lunch.

They had fish for lunch and a great pineapple. Mummy thanked them fervently for having brought her back such useful presents from their wanderings. "I boughted the pineapple in India" said Luls, coaxing a piece into her spoon, with a fat little thumb.

"O, Luls, no," said Beggles, "I shot it off a tree in Ceylon."

"Both wrong" cried Jinks. "The Prince of Wales wrapped it in a bit of newspaper an' said 'there, take it to y'er mummy.'"

"Well, it's very good" said mummy. "And this afternoon we are going to the hills for a long walk."

"May I take Isabel Marion?" said Jinks hastily. Mummy assented.

"Not the pwam" Luls pleaded. "Please not the pwam, Jinks. You always wheels it over me feets."

"She's gettin' too old for the pram" said Jinks meditatively.

"Besides, I buried a poor little rabbit in the last babies' blanket, and the mattress has got no more insides left. Beggles and I will hold her hands."

Isabel Marion, decked in festive array, formed one of a very merry party. She literally swung along at a great pace several feet from the ground, supported by Jinks and Beggles, who held her by her little pink kid hands. They reached a hollow in the hill - "The City of Imagination" mummy called it - and there they sat and told stories. When her turn came, Baby Luls grew very fidgety, fanned her hot face with her pinny, carefully pulled up her socks, and then said:"Once there was a little girl, and her mummy gave her the slipper and she died, and was buried with flowers on her grave, Amen" she said breathlessly.

Tea was over. Daddy had come home. Mummy and he were having supper, and the babes were in the nursery, having a concert. Jinks had turned up the edge of the tablecloth, and was playing the piano with vigour. Beggles was playing the violin with a headless wooden horse (it had such a flat neck for his chin, he said), and bowing in a reckless and magnificent fashion with Isabel Marion's parasol. Luls was playing the organ on the verandah of the doll's house. It was exhausting work, but they entered into it heart and soul. Jinks' little hands twinkled up and down the keyboard, and she sang "Up into the Cherry Tree" with variations, and a violin and organ obligato, with distinct success.

Mummy and daddy came in and heard their last piece of poetry. They stood in a row. It was called "O think what George Adolphus did". It was a strong moral lesson, and they delivered it most gravely, with their eyes fixed sternly at mummy and daddy. One little polka round the table, with mummy playing "My mother said that I never should" and then daddy gave Luls a pick-a-back up to bed. They were so tired. Mummy came and tucked them up and cuddled them.

"Had a nice day?" she whispered.

"O, so lovely" they murmured.

"Pleasant dreams, my popsies" said daddy.

"Same to you" said the sleepy little voices.

Then a little squeaky voice piped "Doodnight, G'anny."

"That's that sweet little Isabel Marion" said Jinks.

---

[MS-Papers-4006-01]

### "LES DEUX ETRANGERES"

Fifi was in bed. She had been there so long that she had almost forgotten what being "up" was like. Day after day, night after night, she lay in the same room, with Mummy to hold her hand when the pain was very bad, and the nice "bow"y nurse to look after her. And every day the "gentleman with the little black bag" came - he seemed to grow kinder and kinder.

Fifi felt lonesome. Nurse had gone to sleep. The house was very quiet. Only the nursery clock went on doing arithmetic and the little dark lamp with its one bright eye had no conversational powers. She was not afraid of the dark - "it could not help itself" she told Mummy - but tonight a "bogey" feeling crept into the air. She said her prayers twice and then "Once in Royal David's City" - but she ended it "Jesus was that Father mild, Mary was his little child." and when she realised the enormity of her offence she was dreadfully shocked.

"Poor dear" she whispered "he <u>must</u> be blushing. I didn't mean it, Jesus dear, it was really quite a mistake - so please don't tell Mary." Then she lay very still. Bye and bye the darkness began to whisper softly. She shut her eyes and put her hands over her ears. Talking darkness is a very frightening thing; it creeps closer and closer and whispers more and more - till the next thing generally is somebody stroking your hair and giving you a drink - and a lovely "blinky" feeling from the candle.

But right suddenly the whispering stopped and she opened her eyes. Close by her bed stood two figures - one tall & dark, wrapped in a great flowing cloak with a grass cutter in his hand (she knew it was a grass cutter because Daddy had one in the Summer), and the other - very small and pale - with little wings wrapping him round.

"How do you do" said Fifi. She thought they must be visitors that Mummy had forgotten to tell her of - but in the night - <u>that</u> was funny. "I'm afraid there are no chairs, so will you sit on the bed?" The little pale one went and balanced himself on the railings at one end - the great tall & dark figure remained silent.

A pause ensued. Then Fifi began - "did you find your way to my room alright? I hope you did not get a s'prise at the looking glass on the stairs. People do, you know. When I was little once I had a bump as big as a n'egg." "We have come a long journey" cried the tall figure in a voice that made Fifi feel as though she was playing one note on the piano over and over - and very deep and sad.

"We have come a long journey in the dark and are very very tired. We have searched through all the rooms - but you are the smallest and you have the largest bed. Will you make room for one of us to sleep with you tonight?" Fifi looked at him meditatively. "You are too big" she said, shaking her head, but the little one - - - - "Oh" cried the sombre figure "I would fold you round in my great mantle - it is so soft and restful - and you would lie quite still, forget you had ever felt pain, and fall asleep."

Fifi considered. "The little one is so cold" she said. "You are really too big for my little bed." "I would carry you in my strong arms & show you wondrous things" cried the tall figure, advancing nearer. "But you might hurt me with your grass cutter", and her tears fell fast. "O I am so sorry to be so nasty" she sobbed, "but please, dear dark man, go away. I would like the little baby one."

So he folded his great mantle round him and strode softly from the room. Fifi stretched out her arms and the little pale one crept to her. She held him fast. "I shall creep into your heart" he whispered, "and stay there always, always." She smiled, then "are you <u>in</u> my heart, little thing?" "Yes, yes" he answered softly. "I am wrapping your heart round with my little wings." And Fifi was happy.

K. Mansfield Beauchamp

22.IV.06.

[MS-Papers-4006-16]

What, think you, causes me truest Joy.

What, think you, causes me truest joy
Down by the sea - the wild mad storm of waves
the fierce rushing swirl of waters together
The cruel salt spray that blows, that beats upon my face.
Wet grey sand, straight paths of it, leading far and away
And showing never a sign of where man's foot has trod
Till only the sky overhead peers at itself in the mirror
The flying clouds, silently screaming, shudder & gaze at
themselves - - -
The song of the wind as I stretch out my arms & embrace it
This indeed gives me joy.

ii.iii.06 K.B.

———————————

The Students' Room.

In the students' room the plain & simple beds
The pictures that line the walls, of various excellence thrown together
And the students with heads bent low, silent over their books.

ii.iii.06 K.B.

# Notebook 29

## PART 2

[Notebook 29, qMS-1241]

### My Potplants

April 1st. Today the weather has been very dull and gray. I woke this morning at four, and since then I have heard nothing save the sounds of the traffic, and felt nothing except a great longing to be back in the country, among the woods and gardens and meadows & the chorus of the Spring Orchestra.
All day during my work, I have found myself dreaming of the woods, and the little secret nooks that have been mine, and mine only, for many years. A girl passed under my window this morning selling primroses. I bought great bunches of them, and untied their tight chains, and let them stretch their poor little tired cramped selves in a sky blue dish that had been filled with primroses every year, but they were not like country primroses. As I bent over them, their weary pale faces looked into mine with the same depth of wondering strange fearful perplexity that I have sometimes seen on the face of a little dying child. It was as though Spring had entered my room but with her wings broken and soiled, and her song quiet - all quiet. This evening I have sat in my chair with my reading lamp turned low, and given myself up to thoughts of the years that have past. Like a strain of minor music they have surged across my heart, and the memory of them, sweet and fragrant as the perfume of my flowers, has sent a strange thrill of comfort through my tired brain.     [J2]

I thought of the time when I was quite a child and lived in the queer old rambling house that has long since been removed, and its place taken by other houses more useful but far less dear. That old house had an extraordinary fascination for me. I always thought of it as a species of ogre who controlled all the garden and the meadows and the woods. May I go and play in the hayfield today, I used to say, and gaze up timidly at its stern unblinking face, and it never failed to give me an answer. The great thing about it that puzzled me was that it never closed its eyes. Poor tired old house, I once remarked, perhaps if I was to lie you down on your back you could shut your eyes and go for a nice long nap. The day that we left that old house, after my Father died, all the blinds were down. I stared up at it. The old house had at last fallen asleep, yet its worn weather-beaten face seemed to gaze at me sorrowfully and gently.

Down at the bottom of our garden ran a little stream, and here I spent many happy hours. With my shoes and socks off, and my frock tucked high all round me, I used to wade, and attempt to catch certain very tiny fish that swam and played in its depths – or rather, its shallownesses. If I ever did catch one I always put it in a glass jam jar filled with water and carried it home to keep till it should grow into a whale. Alas, it never did grow at all though it was not for lack of care and attention.

During my childhood I lived surrounded by a luxurious quantity of flowers, and they were my only companions. My Mother died when I was very young and I had no brothers or sisters. How I loved my life. My greatest delight then was to find fresh flowers to love, and my greatest sorrow if they should die. I remember the year when Spring was very late in coming. I had stolen out in the garden in the dead of night to cover with a blanket the little snowdrop I had found the day before.

In the summer when the trees in our wood were in full leaf and the bracken was high and dainty and green, I used to linger for hours. One day, how well I remember it, I brought with me a tall lily I had found lying across the garden path, and I began to talk to it in a low dreamy voice. Suddenly I paused. Someone was coming towards me, singing a strange little French song. It was a woman, dressed all in a white soft gown open at the throat and with long loose hanging sleeves. In her hands she held roses – red red roses. I was so hidden in my little bracken nest that she could not possibly see me. My heart beat fast, and I felt the colour rush to my face. I never dreamed of her as an ordinary living woman. I thought her a fairy, or a Goddess of the wood. Nearer and nearer she came with her head held high and a strange sweet light in her eyes. Then I stretched out my arm and plucked at her dress. She looked down at me, startled. O you little child, she said, is this your wood? Why are you here all alone. My nerves were so unstrung I could do nothing, say nothing, but I hid my face in her dress and sobbed wildly, madly. In a moment she was down beside me. She took me on her lap and brushed my thick heavy hair from my hot face and kissed me and begged me to tell her what was the matter. Nothing, nothing, but they don't understand me, I answered. Who, little one? Nurse & the servants at home. But what about Mother & Father, she answered. Until that moment it had never dawned on me how utterly without people I was. I realised it then, and cried the more. Little by little I told her all that my life had been. She listened in silence, but at last she said would you like me to come here every day and talk to you and be your friend?

Yes, yes, I cried. Well, I will, she answered, and now, run home. Be good, and you will be happy. I went home slowly, wonderingly. That night as I knelt at my window with the star-lit sky above me, I cried God God, I love the beautiful white angel you have sent me. All through the summer days we lived together, she & I. I told her all my stories of my flowers and my trees, and she sang to me & read to me and talked to me. All my life seemed to begin anew in a wonderful beautiful way. In all I did, her hand seemed to lead me. At the end of the hot dry summer one day I said to her "Are you tired like the flowers. Are you tired of the sun?"

At the end of the Autumn when the bracken was golden brown, and trees were losing their leaves she told me she could not come to me again till the Springtime, till the first of April. When I do come back, she said, you must be here waiting for me.

When that day came I was there in the woods, but she did not come. At last someone came and said to me "Your lady cannot come, but you must come to her."

For what seemed to be miles we walked and at last we reached a little white beautiful house. Inside all was dim. I mounted the stairs with awe & dread. In a great white room she lay, my fairy of the woods, dressed in the old white gown with her sweet hair all about her, and her hands were filled with sweet dewy primroses. I bent over her & kissed her. "Are you the Queen of the Snow?" I whispered, "or one of my white white lilies?"

Stop! Why do I sit here and dream of all that is past, long past. Life is before. I must step in the ranks and fight with the rest of the world. Fight until Death shall come & hold me close, so close so close that I cannot breathe, that I cannot move, that I cannot cry. Then ah! then he shall fling me down in the tall sweet bracken of the woods, and I shall lie there dead quite dead and wait and wait till she comes to be once again.

- - - - - - - - - - - - - - -

Ah! my poor little primroses in the blue dish, they have withered & died!
FINIS[32]

Car j'ai dans mon coeur ...
<Once many years ago there lived a youth - he had great wealth and posit>

"I was never happy" Huia said, leaning back wearily and closing his eyes. Radiana laid her hand lightly on his eyelids. "That is because you do not know the secret" she said. "There is none" replied the young man. "Happiness is as vague, as indefinite as the scent of your [...] at night."
She suddenly rose and took a great spray of jasmine from the

Car j'ai dans mon coeur fleuri.

"I was never happy", Huia said, leaning back wearily and closing his eyes. Radiana laid her hand lightly against his face. "That is because you do not know the secret" she said. "There is none," answered the young man, in a dull toneless voice. The scent of the flowering jessamine clung round them with almost mystical sweetness. "O that flower," cried Radiana, breaking off a great

---

[32]At this point there is a series of drawings with the following captions: 'a Tom Brown tree; This is a "Liberty" field; this is very tasteful in blue grass with black poppies, brown butterflies & scarlet daffodils. (See Fashion Plate); a "blotting pad" field; Tom Brown clouds; One view of a Rose. (with many apologies to the original)'.

spray. "I literally feel it in my blood, Huia - literally." Huia opened his eyes and smiled languidly. "I like to think of your perfumed veins, but you are not like a jessamine - not at all. This flower never can be connected with joy, and tonight your happiness is too evident - it creates in me a profound melancholy." Radiana lay leaning back among the golden cushions, her eyes half-closed, her lips parted - her hair quivered with life. "I am half stifled with happiness" she murmured.

Huia caught her hands suddenly, roughly. "Give it to me" he said. "Withhold nothing from me Radiana." She twined her arms round his neck and raised her face to his. "Look in my eyes, Huia, listen, listen. I have a bird in my heart, deep down in my heart and it sings to me - and then I am happy - - - that is all. Look too, Huia, is there not a bird in your heart - and once it shakes one note from its golden throat, you cannot be sad."

The pain deepened in Huia's face. Silence fell between them, then the young man cried "I have looked into my heart and the bird is there - but it sleeps." "Call to it to awaken, Huia, cry to it that sleep is impossible." Deep down in his heart he saw the bird, still & slumbering, its beautiful plumage unruffled. A feeling of fierce anger overcame him. Why should this woman be capable of an emotion unattained by him."It must sing to me" he thought. "I shall force it to sing. I shall never rest day or night until the first note has shaken the very inmost visions of my soul." He released himself from the window and stepped out on to the balcony. It was a voluptuous night - powerful and yet yielding.

"Huia, Huia" called Radiana. "Give me my cloak" he said, "I shall go riding." "Riding, Huia." Radiana came and stood beside him - "no it is too late. You shall not go. You are not strong enough. I - I cannot be left alone - besides the roads are dangerous and the night is very dark - see - there is something almost cynical about the darkness, and the shadows." "You talk like a child - am I to be the companion of your unreasoning fancies. Hold, there" he called to a man who passed below. "Saddle my horse as fast as possible." He waited in the garden until the horse, a great powerful brute, was brought to him. By the light of the lantern Huia saw the servant's face. "What is the matter" he questioned.

"Nothing, sir - I am happy, I am well." He paused, the reins in his hands. "Define your happiness." "Ah it is as though the lark had got into my heart." "Even this fellow" thought Huia.

He rode on the cliffs beside the sea - the dreary lapping of the water and the soft thud of the horse's feet were the only sounds. Then he drew rein and stood looking over the water, and the lapping of the water beat in his brain - he felt the soft oozy water enfolding him - in his very hair.

Memories

December, cold, dark and dreary. The wind was blowing all round his house, the rain was pattering on the roof - and he was alone. He was old, his beard was white, he could hardly walk now. There was a fire in the little grate that flickered & died down, flickered again, & made strange shadows in the room, queer indefinable shapes. He sat beside the fire, one hand covering his face, the other grasping the arm of his chair. He was thinking, thinking, thinking. It was the eve of his birthday. Yes, he would die soon, everyone did. They would bury him in the little old churchyard and then pull his cottage down, and take away his things. They would forget all about him. It was very very quiet in the room. The storm raged outside, and the darkness came nearer and nearer.

Where would he be? Would he be in the old churchyard or - where? He huddled a little closer to the fire. If only he could blot out that one page, all might be well. It stood out amongst the others, some of which were white, some grey, but it was red, blood-red. As he thought of it, it seemed to grow bigger. It seemed to spread over all. God, God, how fearful. Quite dark now. The storm became less furious. He covered his face with his hands, the old lonely man, and he shook from head to foot. Suddenly he seemed to feel that there was something else in the room. Something that came nearer & nearer. He heard its garments rustle. He almost heard it breathe. He raised his head. The room became dimly lit. Before him was a figure clothed in a long grey garment. It was a woman. Her face was white as the snow. Her hair which fell over her shoulders was black and glossy, but he seemed to see streaks of grey in it. She looked old - very old - yet young. Suddenly he heard a faint cry. And the woman bent over something she held in her arms. It was a little child - such a wee thing, with flushed cheeks and great wistful eyes. It clung to the woman and it wailed again. She looked up at the old man and spoke. Her voice was full of despair. The tears rained down her face. "The baby is dying" she cried. "Dying of cold. You will let us stop here. You will not thrust us out as they have done." Unsteadily the old man rose to his feet and looked at the woman and pointed to his chair. "The fire is very low" was all he said.

Kathleen M. Beauchamp

French

Thème 51.

Cette chambre est longue de douze pieds, et large de six pieds. La rivière est profonde de dix pieds. Cette jeune fille a l'air très industrieuse. Cette princesse a l'air très fier. Je suis prêt à partir et j'en suis content. Soyez fidèle à et respectueu envers vos maitres. Ma maison est longue de soixante pieds, large de vingt pieds et haute de trente pieds. Mon oncle fut respecté et aimé de tout le monde. Soyons généreux pour nos semblables et bienveillant envers eux.

Thème 52.

Il avait son chapeau sur la tête tout le temps il était dans la chambre. Sa petite main et son petit pied sont d'un forme très aristocratique. J'étudie la langue française et toutes ses particularités, j'ai déjà parcouru les élements de sa grammaire. Ses amis et ses parents l'ont fait visit hier à l'occasion l'anniversaire de sa naissance. C'est mon bon ami et mon meilleur conseilleur. Que tenez-vous dans la main -

Thème 53.

Il me donnez pas les mêmes livres - Leurs amis eux mêmes les blâment de leur conduite. Mêmes les hommes les plus entreprenants hésitent à prendre part à cette entreprise. Tout est en sa faveur. Toute la maison fut brûlée. Toutes mes connaissances le bonté. Il eut quelques difficultés à être admis, en sa présence. Quelque patient qu'il soit, il fut obligé de mettre un terme à une telle ensolence. Quel qu'ils soient ces seront désappointés dans leur expectation (attente)

Thème 56.

Ils s'ennuient beaucoup dans cette petite ville - Il se flatte qu'il réussira. Elle se brûla. Tout le monde devrait parler de soi avec la plus grande modestie. Cette nouvelle a en soi, quelque chose de si extraordinaire qu'il est presque impossible d'y croire. Mon père parla toujours d'eux avec louange. Il en parle souvent, mais, je ne le croix pas. Je n'aime pas qu'on parle seulement de soi. Il alla dans sa chambre s'habiller pour nous accompagner au théâtre. Ce poème a en soi quelque chose qui touche et charme tous ceux qui le lisent.

Thème

Est-ce que je parle très vite? Est-ce que vous croyez je le reconterai? Est-ce que je le convirai? Est-ce que vous aimeriez à faire la connaissance de cet homme fameux?
Est-ce que je le [....] Est-ce que je sais ma leçon bien? Est-ce que je pars à sept heures ou huit heures le matin demain? Est-ce que vous parterai à la compagne loin sans connâitre une personne? Est-ce je pars avec vous ou avec votre cousin? Est-ce que je perds beaucoup

| box | = boîte (f) |
| corner | = coin (m) |
| fast | = vite |
| to kill | = teuer |
| remote | = éloigné |
| witty | = spirituel |
| yard | = cour |
| youth | = jeunesse |
| walnut | = noix |
| witty | = spirituel |
| To win | = gagner |
| worthy | = Digne |
| To wipe | = essuyer |
| wing | = aile |
| widow | = veuve |
| weigh (to) | = peser |
| Unless | = à moins que |
| Use (to) | = employer |
| Violet (c) | = violet |
| Violet (f) | = Violette |

| | | |
|---|---|---|
| Voice | = | voix |
| Tear | = | Larme |
| to throw | = | jeter |
| Truth | = | vérité |
| Tablecloth | = | nappe |
| Tap | = | Robinet |
| Threshold | = | Seuil |
| Trust | = | Se fier à |
| Tear | = | Larme |
| Thorn | = | épine |

# Notebook 1

[Notebook 1, qMS-1242][33]

Rough [Notes]

Chap I.     October 14th
Chap II.    The birth of the flame
Chap III.   The God
Chap IV

18.v. 06.

Chapter I
October 14th.

Juliet sat in front of the mirror brushing her hair. Her face was thoughtful and her hands trembled perceptibly. Suddenly she bent forward and stared at her own reflexion. Her hair, parted in the middle, fell in long straight masses of pale gold to her waist. Her forehead was high & square & very white, while there was an unusual fullness over her brows. Her eyes were a peculiar colour, almost approaching green, her nose very straight & fine, and her mouth was full of sensitive curves - the underlip decidedly too full for regular beauty. Her face was square in outline and her skin very white. The impression which

---

[33]KM's first piece of sustained (albeit autobiographical) fiction, usually referred to as 'Juliet', occurs in this notebook, interspersed throughout with other material. To facilitate reading, the scattered pieces of 'Juliet' have here been assembled, not into a continuous narrative but into the sequence of parts in the order in which they were written.

KM was still at school in London, aged 17, when she began 'Juliet', and eight or nine months later she abandoned it. It could fairly be described as 'Notes towards a novel' as it consists of a series of disconnected episodes (one assumes that the situations which appealed to her most were the ones she tackled first), and these are not written in the order that the chronology of the final narrative would demand. Nevertheless it is possible to piece together the main outline of a story, and to perceive the weaving in of themes which were to remain central to her for the rest of her life.

My own first transcription of 'Juliet' was published in *The Turnbull Library* Record in March 1970, and was, alas, imperfect. More time and work have enabled me to improve it.

In the original transcription I tagged each section with a letter of the alphabet for ease of reference. These tags are repeated here because they have now become part of the critical record. The pages of the notebook were numbered by Murry and the page numbers of each 'Juliet' piece are here supplied to convey an idea of the size of the notebook and the distribution of the 'Juliet' pieces within it.

There are inconsistencies and obscurities in the text which have, of course, been retained. Mr Wilberforce becomes Mr Night; David was once nearly written as Caesar (the name by which KM called Tom Trowell to whom she had long been romantically attached); Vere becomes Pearl; Juliet is at first the second of four children and later seems to be the youngest of three.

it caused was not by any means strictly beautiful. When in repose it conveyed an idea of extreme thoughtfulness - her mouth drooped slightly at the corners, her eyes were shadowed, but her expression was magnetic, her personality charged with vitality. She looked a dreamer, but her dreams were big with life - - -

But Juliet noticed none of these characteristics. Since her very early days she had cultivated the habit of conversing very intimately with the Mirror face. Her childhood had been lonely, the dream-face her only confidante. She was the second in a family of four. The eldest girl, Margaret, was now seventeen, Juliet was fourteen, and then two babies, Mary & Henry, aged seven & six respectively. The Mother was a slight pale little woman. She had been delicate & ailing before her marriage and she never could forget it. Margaret & she looked after the babies - and Mr Wilberforce,[34] a tall grey-bearded man with prominent blue eyes, large ungainly hands, and inclining to stoutness. He was a general merchant, director of several companies, chairman of several societies, thoroughly commonplace & commercial. The greater part of his life had been spent in New Zealand & all the children had been born there.

Juliet was the odd man out of the family - the ugly duckling. She had lived in a world of her own, created her own people, read anything & everything which came to hand, was possessed with a violent temper, and completely lacked placidity. She was dominated by her moods which swept through her and in number were legion. She had been, as yet, utterly idle at school, drifted through her classes, picked up a quantity of heterogeneous knowledge - and all the pleading & protestations of her teachers could not induce her to learn that which did not appeal to her. She criticised everybody and everything with which she came into contact, & wrapped herself in a fierce white reserve. 'I have four passions' she once wrote in an old diary - 'Nature, people, Mystery, and - the fourth no man can number.' Of late she had quarrelled frequently with the entire family, through pure lack of anything definite to occupy her thoughts. She had no defined paths ahead, no goal to reach & she felt compelled to vent her energy upon somebody, and that somebody was her family.

The large bedroom where she sat looked very dim and dark. There was a small fire in the grate and a big rocking chair before it, but these were the two positive luxuries which the room boasted of. Pictures were conspicuous by their absence, and all these little familiar things which make the sum total of so many girls' bedrooms found no place here. A long unvarnished bookshelf was nailed above the bed & a most miscellaneous collection of volumes found a resting place there. A glass of red roses stood on the dressing table and all her party clothes were carefully laid out on a chair. She dressed very deliberately in her white muslin frock - open at the neck & showing her full round throat - and tied her broad silk sash. Her hair hung in two great braids, unadorned

---

[34] KM's friend on whom the hero of this story, David, was based was Thomas Wilberforce Trowell. This exemplifies again her tendency to choose names she was already familiar with—or variations of them—for her not quite fictional characters.

with combs or ribbon. She put up her hands & patted the smooth heavy folds. Juliet's hands were as distinctive as any part of her. They were large, and exquisitely modelled. The fingers were not very long, and blunted at the tops, but no amount of work could change their beauty. She gesticulated a great deal & had a habit of sitting always nursing one knee, her fingers interlocked.

Before leaving her room she crossed over to the window. Outside a great pine tree was outlined against the night sky, and the sea, stretching far in the distance, called to her – 'Juliet, Juliet.' 'O night' she cried, leaning far out and turning her face up to the stars, 'O adorable night.' – – –

Then she picked up her long cloak and ran lightly downstairs. In the hall her Mother and Father were waiting, Mr Wilberforce wrapping up his throat in a great silk handkerchief with all that care & precision so common to perfectly healthy men who imagine they wrestle with weak constitutions.

'We shall drop you at Mrs Cecil's on the way, Juliet' said her Mother, carefully drawing on her long evening gloves, 'and then at ten o'clock you can call for us at Mrs Black's. And we shall come back together. You can wait in the hall if we're not ready. It's only a musical party.' The girl replied, and the three walked out of the house, down the broad stone steps, and into the long moonlit road. In the presence of so many stars and so many trees Juliet utterly forgot all the petty grievances of the day. She walked along beside her parents and 'let it all sink in' as she expressed.

'Do be careful of your clothes, child' the Mother said, as Mr Wilberforce held the gate open for her, 'and don't be late.' Then they left her. In front of her was the brilliantly lighted house. Sounds of merriment came to her, uproarious laughter, shrieks of excitement. And for two hours she played as vigorously as the rest of them, inwardly rebelling and very satisfied when the clock pointed to five minutes to ten. The 'party' stood and watched her from the door – cried to her not to be afraid, to remember 'Ghosts in the Garden', but she laughed & holding her coat tightly round her, ran the whole length of the way.

On the doorstep of Mrs Black's she paused to recover breath, and a faint, a very faint wave of Music was wafted to her. The drawing room seemed extraordinarily bright after the night outside. She was a little confused at first. The maid had said that they were all at supper, and she was to wait there. She went over to the table & bent over a bowl of flowers, but a sound of a chair being pushed back in the corner caused her to look up, startled. A boy of very much her own age was watching her curiously. He stood beside a great lamp & the light fell full on his face and his profusion of red-brown hair. Very pale he was with a dreaming exquisite face & a striking suggestion of confidence & Power in every feature. Juliet felt a great wave of colour spread over her face and neck. They stood staring into each other's eyes. Then he walked up to the table where she stood, a faint smile playing round his lips. 'If you are fond of flowers there are roses just outside the window' he said, 'and you can reach out your hands & touch them. The scent is perfect. Come & see.'

Side by side they crossed over to the wide opened window, & both leant

out. O, the late roses below them – thousands there seemed to Juliet.
She touched one, then another with her hands – they were all wet with dew.
'Heavy with tears' she said, looking up at the boy. He nodded appreciatively.
'Will you tell me your name?"Juliet – and yours?"David. I am a musician
& have been playing tonight – a 'cellist you know. I am going to Europe next
year."I too, but not for music – to complete my education, you know."Do you
want to go away?"Yes – and no. I long for fresh experiences, new places, but
I shall miss the things that I love here."Do you like nights Juliet'. His face was
transfigured. 'I feel like a chrysalis in the daytime, compared to my feelings
after sunset. For instance I should never have met you as I have if I hadn't just
come in from the stars. They make me all music. Sometimes I think that if I
could be alone long enough I should hear the Music of the Spheres. Think of
what would burst from those thousands of golden throats."I have heard so little
music' said Juliet sadly. 'There are so few opportunities. And a 'cello – I have
never heard a 'cello.' David's face was full of compassion & yet joy. 'Then I shall
be the first to show you what can be' he said. He stooped down & broke a
great flower off the branches & gave it to her. She fastened it in her dress, and
then the sound of the guests returning from the supper room put an end to
their conversation. Soon after, they left. Juliet purposely avoided saying
'goodnight' to David. She felt as though she could not, but she was conscious
of his eyes watching her as she left the room.

The walk home was silent. Margaret was awaiting their arrival and
immediately began telling Mrs Wilberforce how 'used up' the babies seemed.
'Henry has certainly a nasty little cough' she said, '& Mary looked so pasty.'
'Well, we shall all leave town in a couple of days' Mrs Wilberforce said.
'Tomorrow that young boy is coming here to play, and Father has asked a
number of men.'Juliet bade them goodnight & fled to her own room. Her
heart was beating furiously – she could hardly repress a feeling of the most
intense joy that bade her cry out. She sat on the side of her bed staring at the
darkness, her breath coming quickly. Sleep was impossible. The whole world
had changed & he was coming again tomorrow night, & she should hear him
play. She crept into bed and lay still, thinking. A curious sensation stole over
her – as though she was drifting in a great fiery sea of thoughts, & every
thought was sweet.

When she pulled up the blind next morning the trees outside were being
tossed to and fro, and the sea lashed into fury by a wild Southerly gale. Juliet
shuddered. The wind always hurt her, unsettled her. It was a Saturday, so there
was no thought of school. She wandered about all the morning, and in the
afternoon put on her reefer coat & tam-o'-shanter and went for a walk up the
hills that spread like a great wall behind the little town. The wind blew fiercer
than ever. She held on to bushes and strong tufts of grass, and climbed rapidly,
rejoicing in the strength that it required. Down in a hollow where the gorse
spread like a thick green mantle she paused to recover breath. The utter
loneliness of it filled her with pleasure. She stood perfectly still, letting the
wind blow cold & strong in her face and loosen her hair. The sky was dull

& grey, and vague thoughts swept through her – of the Future, of her leaving this little island & going so far away, of all that she knew and loved, all that she wished to be. 'O I wish I was a poet' she cried, spreading out her arms. 'I wish I could interpret this atmosphere, this influence.' She found a little bird fluttering near in a bush, its wing broken by the storm – and held it close to her, overcome with a feeling of tenderness. 'I am so strong' she said, 'and the strong are never hurt. It is always the weak who are pained.' (Foolish child! April 1908.)

She walked home more slowly. Now that the excitement of climbing had left her she felt tired & depressed. Clouds of dust whirled up the road – dry particles of sand stung her face. She longed for the evening to come, yet almost dreaded it.

When tea was over Juliet went back to her room, tried to read & failed, and walked up and down – nine steps one way – nine steps another. The feeling soothed her. She heard the front door bell ring and knew that the guests had arrived, but she stayed there till Margaret sought her out & brought her down with great indignation. The room seemed full of people, but Juliet was not shy. She held her head a little higher than usual & an expression of almost indifference came into her face. David stood by the piano unfastening his music case. She shook hands with him and shot him a keen quick glance of recognition. Then she curled herself up in a corner of the sofa & watched the people with amusement & interest. She liked to listen to little pieces of conversation, create her idea of their lives.

There was the usual amount of very second rate singing concerning Swallows and "Had I Known". Margaret played several nondescript pieces on the piano – & at last David's turn came. Juliet watched him with great pleasure & curiosity. A bright spot came into her cheeks, her eyes wide opened – but when he drew his bow across the strings her whole soul woke and lived for the first time in her life. She became utterly absorbed in the music. The room faded, the people faded. She saw only his sensitive inspired face, felt only the rapture that held her fast, that clung to her and hid her in its folds, as impenetrable and pure as the mists from the sea – – –

Suddenly the music ceased, the tears poured down her face & she came back to reality – – – She put her handkerchief to her eyes and when she looked round became aware of the amused glances of the company, and heard the steady, almost prophetic sounding voice of David's Father: "That child is a born musician."

The rest of the evening passed she knew not how. Something had come to life in Juliet's soul & it shone in her transfigured face. For that night she was brilliantly beautiful – not with the beauty of a child, but the charm of a woman seemed to emanate from her. David was conscious of this, conscious too that he had never played before as he was playing. They avoided each other strangely, but Mr Wilberforce praised the boy and said 'You might come & give my little daughter a few lessons, & see if she has any talent.' She never forgot their leave-taking. The wind was furious, and she stood on

the verandah and saw David turn round & smile at her before he passed
out of sight.      [(A) PP3-23]³⁵
'Know anything about these times that we have had - but whenever you come
to see us in London - I - I shall feel so utterly different.' David looked at her.
'Yet now you would not have it otherwise, Juliet. A secret is a glorious thing.'
She gave him both her hands. 'Goodbye, my friend' she said. 'I promise to
write to you - often - often.' He suddenly caught his breath. 'You would not
kiss me . . . Juliet', he said hoarsely. But she shook her head, and a moment
later the beach was deserted & the sea crept up & washed away their footmarks
from that place.      [(B) P23]

Chapter III

It was the close of a dark day - London was shrouded in fog. The streets
were wet and the long line of lampposts shone like dim ghosts of themselves.
A four-wheeler, laden with luggage, stopped at the door of an eminently
respectable house.      [(c) P24]
Juliet stumbled up the stairs - somehow she reached the door and let herself in
and locked it again. Then she groped her way into the sitting room. The fire
had gone out - she did not notice it. The wind had blown over the roses on
the table, & they lay in a crushed heap on the carpet. The room was flooded in
the cold light of the moon. She stood gazing at it all, then a long shudder
went through her and she fell heavily on to the floor. She was conscious as she
lay there. Why didn't I strike my head on the fender, she thought - I'm not
hurt a bit. I shall have to get up again and then it will be day. She shivered
incessantly from head to foot, and a wheel began to go round & round &
round in her head. 'Down & down & down & down & down' said the wheel
as it whirred, 'down & down & down & down & down.' Then it assumed
gigantic proportions, and she clung to it and it dragged her round. Round &
round & round & round & round in a great pit of darkness - and she fell.

[(D) P29-30]

It was certainly a very successful dinner party. Caesar was never so gay, so
irresponsible, so full of boyish spirits. He stood on his chair with a glass of the
1/3 claret in his hand & made interminable speeches till Rudolph seized him
by the coat & dragged him to earth. And then the four of them sat round the
fire and smoked, & laughed, & finally grew serious. Rudolph seized his fiddle
& played the Serenade Melancholique, and then they left Caesar. Their feelings
overcame them - "it was the claret" said Rudolph sighing heavily. "Gott sei
dank" said Caesar.      [P30]

---

³⁵The pages of the notebook were numbered by Murry and the page numbers of each 'Juliet' piece
are here supplied to convey an idea of the size of the notebook and the distribution of these pieces within it.
The other interspersed material, written at the same time, is presented here after 'Juliet', with page numbers
indicating its placement in the notebook. I have also repeated here the alphabetical identification I gave to
each of the sections in the original transcription because they have since been used in other people's critical
discussions.

<Juliet and Diana>

The Shudder of the Trees.

I am a lover of London Town.

"Keys with the caretaker." The street looked cheap. Juliet looked at it with tired eyes – dingy, forlorn, certainly this would be very near her standard. She found the caretaker & he conducted her up five flights of stairs. "Certainly not here" thought Juliet with an uneasy feeling that her legs might consider themselves as separate from her body & refuse to advance. And then – "Nonsense, perhaps it must be here." There was a passage and leading from it three rooms – one large 'living' room and a small bedroom and a minute kitchen. She looked round, noticed that the window had wide low ledges, that in the recess at either side of the fireplace there [was] a wide washed [white-washed?] cupboard doing up with a button. "O – I like it" she said, nodding seriously – and the rent was decidedly within her limit.          [(E) P52]

Das Geheimnis.

It happened when I was young but unconscious of Youth.

And dark crept into the room. Juliet, lying back in her chair, saw the sky a pale soft yellow, watched the steady outpouring of smoke from the chimneys opposite. A faint breath, like a sigh from the passing day, stirred the window curtains and blew on to her face. Sounds floated up to her – – – intensely individual yet blending into the great Chorale of Twilight. An extraordinary weakness stole over her. 'She was dying softly softly' like the day. Her arms hung straight on either side of her chair, her hair fell back among the cushions, her lips slightly parted.

– – – The horror of the long white day. She could not endure another. Here in this twilight, shaking off her great chains of Commerce, London shone, mystical, dreamlike. And Juliet too felt like a dream. She was floating, floating in the veil-like pale sky. Yesterday had never been, today had never been, tomorrow was not. This struggle for bread, this starvation of Art. How could she expect to keep art with her in the ugliness of her rooms, in the sordidness of her surroundings. Listlessly she raised her head & looked round. But the room was full of cool emptiness – nothing was apparent, everything suggestive and full of charm. "You will stay with me a little longer, while I can offer you this Magic hour" whispered –

The sky changed. Only a narrow strip of the pale yellow remained & above a thin blue on which the darkness of night sky was partially hidden. Patches of rich golden light shone in the houses. She felt her fatigue, her doubt, her regrets, slip off from her tired heart. "O - O", she said, "How weak I am. How I ought to be full of strength, & rejoicing all the day. Relations at the other end of the world who have, thank Heaven, cast me off and my wish fulfilled. I'm alone in the heart of London, working & living – – –" Then another thought came – she shook her head & frowned, but a great wave of bitter [...] memories broke over her & drowned all else – – – Where was he now. What was he doing. How did he live – married, single, rich, poor – nothing was known. She shook from head to foot with pain and anger with herself. Were those five years to haunt her always - would she never be strong enough to stand absolutely alone. Should the first thought at waking always be "Who knows" & the last thought at night "Perhaps tomorrow." She moved restlessly. "I say I am independent - I am utterly dependent. I say I am masculine - no-one could be more feminine. I say I am complete - I am hopelessly incomplete." Try as she would she knew that it was hopeless to attempt to change. "I must just put up with it" she said aloud.

Suddenly she listened. Someone was mounting the stairs quickly, lightly. She glanced at the clock, it was just half past eight. The steps came nearer. Outside her door they stopped. There was a momentary pause, then a knock, sharp, imperative. She sprang to her feet, and something within her seemed to spring to birth & laugh. She sprang to her feet, lit a small jet of gas, then opened the door wide. In the passage a man leaned against the wall, the intense black of his coat against the white wall, the broad sweep of his hat. Then he put out his hand. Terror seized her. "David" she whispered - she could scarcely articulate. Her mouth was parched. She leaned against the door for support. "David". "I have found you now" he said, seizing both her hands <& dragging her into the room & over to the light, his pale face full of a great peace.> (Nonsense)    [(F) PP53-56]

The Man.

When she reached the long tree-lined avenue, the rain had ceased and great splashes of sunlight lay across the road. As she neared the house she stopped & repeated the Dorian Grey. Her heart was beating almost unbearably. She pressed her hand against her hot face. "This is gloriously unconventional" said Juliet, "but I wish I was less frightened."

Walter opened the door. "Ha - you've come at last" he said, his voice full of intense hospitality. "Come along into the smoking room - second door to the right." She pushed aside the heavy purple portière. The room was full of gloom but vivid yellow curtains hung straight & fine before the three windows. Tall wrought-iron candle-sticks stood in the corners - the dead whiteness of the candles suddenly brought back a memory of Saint Gudule at dusk and Juliet caught her breath. There were prints of beautiful women on the walls, & the graceful figure of a girl holding a <great> shell in her exquisite arms stood on a table. There was a long low couch upholstered in dull purple, and quaint low chairs in the same colour. The room was full of the odour of chrysanthemums.[36] The blossoms were arranged in high glasses on the mantel shelf - - -

"I am afraid" said Walter, closing the door and speaking slightly apologetically, "it's not very - - -"

"Please I like it" Juliet said, smiling at him & pulling off her long gloves.

He pulled up a great armchair for her, then seating him[self] opposite so that

---

[36]This passage from 'Come along into the smoking room' to 'the odour of chrysanthemums' appeared, slightly reworked, in a story called 'The Education of Audrey' published in *The Evening Post*, Wellington, 13 January 1909.

he might watch her face - "Now tell me all about yourself." How revoltingly hearty his voice sounds, thought Juliet - - - She paused, then "There's not very much to tell."
"How about those complications."
"O they're quite gone, thank you. I - I took your advice."
"That's fine. That's fine. I knew you would my dear girl, I always said you had the grit in you."
O, the fearful paternal conceit.
"I - - I finally made up my mind to put an end to them. It was hard, you know - but - I have wished to thank you ever since."
"O that's alright, and as you grow older & see more cases of that very thing, you will realise better than you can now how right I was. Drifting is so dangerous."
"Yes - - you made me feel that."
"And don't you feel more comfortable in yourself. Of course you miss something."
"Yes I really do - intensely."
"Yes, naturally, but now the leaving [tearing?] part of the whole business is over, aren't you really very pleased?"
"Yes, I think I am." She sat very still & suddenly smiled slightly. "You have changed" said Walter. His voice had curiously altered.          [(G) PP63-65]

"We've told Father all about it, Juliet"[37] said Margaret. "And Father's fearfully angry" Mary added. Juliet slipped the Byron down in the front of her sailor blouse. She had no definite idea of what she had been reading but her head was full of strange unreasonable impulses. She was feeling slightly sorry for her absence of self control in that it incurred a long interview with her Father, and in all probability some degrading issue - no jam for a week, or to go to bed at seven o'clock until she apologised. She walked slowly to the house, up the broad stone steps, into the wide hall, and knocked at the morning room door.          [(H)]

At two o'clock in the afternoon Juliet had thrown a heavy book at her eldest sister Margaret, and a bottle of ink at her elder sister Mary. At six in the evening she was summoned to the morning room to explain these offences. After her two wholly successful acts of violence she had retired to a sloping lawn at the extreme end of the garden where she lay down comfortably & read Don Juan - - -
Margaret & Mary, still smarting from the shock to their sensitive little systems,

---

[37]On the page preceding this passage KM has listed chapter headings and names of characters in the story. The chapter headings are: 'i. Running away. B. night-meeting. ii. Sea chapter. iii. London. iv. College Influence. v. Vere. vi. Parents. vii. Project. viii. Fulfilment. ix. Truth & Illness. x. Marriage. xi. Vere & T. xii. Death.'
   The characters listed on this page who actually appear in the story are: Juliet Night, David Méjin, 'Margaret +', 'Mary +', Pearl Saffron. Those who make no appearance are: 'Mrs Dale mother-in-law to', Mr Dale, Mr Philip Dale, Mr Donald. Crossed out are: Kathie Schonfeld, Mark & David, Dr Cayton.

had rather rejoiced in the search for her, and more especially in the knowledge that Mr Night was pacing up & down, up and down. They were both virtuous enough to take a keen enjoyment in the punishment of others.       [(1) P72]
"Juliet – Juliet please sit still. You walked round & round this room till my pen is describing a hopeless & idiotic circle. I must get this off tonight, and I can't if you will be so restless."

There was a note of intense annoyance in Vere's voice. She looked up from the sheets of foolscap arranged in neat piles before her. The afternoon had closed in – Pearl[38] was writing by candlelight. Juliet had drawn down the blinds. The rain in the street hurt her. She had arranged all the odd books in a neat line on the mantelpiece. She had twice pulled the tablecloth straight, and then flung herself in a chair, tried to read & failed, tried to write & torn up the paper, sighed, tossed her hair out of her eyes, & finally started walking up & down the room, swiftly, quietly – – – She had a headache, felt tired, nervous – and longed to burst out crying.

For days the rain had been falling steadily monotonously over London until it seemed to be suffocating her, beating into her brain. She had slept very little at night and her face [was a] little worn and set. At Vere's remark she stopped walking and said "I – I beg your pardon. I did not quite realise what I was doing."

Vere laid down her pen & pushed back her chair. "Got a mood?" she said.
"Yes" said Juliet, "it's the very Devil. While it lasts I think it is going to be eternal & I'm contemplating suicide."
"It's sure to be something physical. Why don't you sleep better Juliet. Are you – you're not . . . repenting?"[39]
"Good Heavens, no. The truth is, my dear girl, well I hardly like to own it to myself even, you understand. Bernard Shaw would be gratified."
"You feel sexual."
"Horribly. And in need of a physical shock or violence – perhaps a good smacking would be beneficial."
"Don't laugh so much at yourself, Juliet. I'm sorry dear – you look wretchedly ill."
"It's the candlelight. Also I am in need of exercise. I shall go out, I think, for a walk, despite the fact that I shall become physically, mentally & psychically damped." "Do, dear."
"I feel a need of a big grey sky, and a long line of lights. Also a confused noise of traffic and the sense of many people – you know?"
"Yes, I understand, but I loathe the rain. It makes me irritable. I hate the slashing effect that it has – and it makes me 'fussy'."
Juliet went over to Vere & suddenly kissed her.

---

[38]Originally written as 'Vere' and subsequently altered to 'Pearl'.
[39]In my first transcription of 'Juliet', published in *The Turnbull Library Record*, I misread this word as 'expecting' and so missed the significance of KM's awareness of the possibility of regret at having cut oneself off from one's family, long before she herself experienced this.

"Think my dear" she said, one hand on Vere's shoulder, "if it had not happened I should be in the middle of Summer. Saturday night – helping the family to entertain a few friends to dinner perhaps, or hearing Father first snore & then yawn and finally tell me all he had for lunch, and all that everybody else had for lunch. The Evening would come to an end at ten o'clock with lemon & soda which Mother would refuse to drink because – quotation of course – it was so 'windy'. O Lord! Instead – I earn at least £1.0.0 a week, I live with the best friend that anyone could wish for in <u>London</u> and I am free! Voilà, by enumerating all these excellent fors & againsts I feel better, and inclined to kiss you again."

"Our friendship is unique" said Vere, folding her arms & staring at the light. "Nothing could separate us, Juliet. All the comforts of matrimony with none of its encumbrances, hein?"

"My word yes! As it is we are both individuals. We both ask from the other personal privacy, & we can be silent for hours when the desire seizes us."

"Think of a man always with you. A woman cannot be wholly natural with a man – there is always a feeling that she must take care that she doesn't let him go."

"A perpetual strain."

"Also I should inevitably want to fly very high if I was certain that my wings were clipped."

"Ugh" said Juliet, going over to the wardrobe & reaching for her coat & hat, "I loathe the very principle of matrimony. It must end in failure, & it is death to a woman's personality. She must drop the theme & begin to start playing the accompaniment. For me there is <u>no</u> attraction."

Vere suddenly laughed. "I was thinking of your past affaire de coeur with David Méjin," she said.

"Please don't" cried Juliet. "To think of it makes me feel overwhelmingly sick. When I think how he filled, swayed my whole life, how I worshipped him – only I did. How jealous I was of him! I kept the very envelopes of his letters for years, & he – to say the least – raised his hat & passed on." "What would you do if you met him now?"

"Broadly speaking – do as I had been done by. I should simply bow."

"I don't know that I would do that – – –"

"Well", she drew on her gloves, "I shall take the plunge dear, & bring you back a brown loaf for supper. There is something aesthetic in the substance of a brown loaf."

Once out in the streets Juliet walked very fast, her head bent. She was thinking, thinking. How absurd everything was. How small she was. She walked along Holborn and into Oxford Street. The restaurants were full of light, and the sound of laughter seemed to be in the air. <A curious helplessness took possession of her – an inability to speak or to stop walking.

Half way down Oxford Street she suddenly heard a hoarse cry in the street. There had been an accident. In an instant there had sprung up scores of people who were all hurrying forward. Juliet ran with them. As she neared the place she heard "'E's done for, poor feller. 'E caught 'im fair on the leg."

"Hit 'is head too - 'e was in the hansom.">      [(J) PP73-77]
(Let us linger no longer over these things. They are really very touching.)

David & Pearl were married as soon as I [ie they] reasonably could be after
Juliet's death, and a year & a half later, when a girl child was born, they both
decided she should be christened after 'poor Juliet'. Pearl gave up smoking
cigarettes & published a little volume which she called "Mother Thought" ...
somehow the title does not seem intensely original. Also, when they realised
the possibility of another extension to their family they bought a nice little
house near Cricklewood, and David achieved no small measure of success with
his gardening.

      *      *      *      *      *      *      *

Rudolf did not return to England after his tour in Italy but went further afield
to Spain & Portugal. So he knew nothing of Juliet's death until a long time
had passed - - - Mr Thring, the porter at No 65, gave him a most full, true
& particular account. In the Autumn season he brought out a very charming
little morceau "Souvenir de Juliet" It create quite a quiver[?] at the London
concerts. <So much so that he rearranged it for violoncello to be played with
muted strings.> It was reported on highest authority that the original MS was
stained with tears - - - -

(Let us linger no longer over these things. They are really very touching.)

                                                                 [(K) P78]

---

     The Triumph of Rudolph.

Juliet dressed with great care that afternoon. She had on a thin white muslin
frock with a square-cut yolk [sic] & short sleeves tied with ribbons. She
brushed out her long hair, & then braided it round her head. Pearl, sitting
huddled upon the lounge, smoking & read[ing] Zola's Paris, laughed. "How
do I look" said Juliet anxiously, slipping on a long coat & then taking a rapid
survey of her two possible hats. "Entirely irresistable my dear. Wear the black
one - it's so ingenuous-looking" said Pearl - - -
    "I want to make a really good impression. I've been looking hideous
lately I know - because I've been worried about the play - but now that it's
actually finished I shall grow a big conceit in myself. Do you know, Pearl" she
added, with mock gravity, "I never realised that Summer was here until today."
"Well run along or you'll be late dear. Kiss me first. Somehow I feel as though
I should like to take opium this afternoon."
    Juliet put her arms around her ... "Dearest & best" she said, & blushed
on saying it, "I should like to be staying with you but duty calls - you
understand." "Of course ... of course - by the way I shan't be in until after
eleven - I'm going to a Promenade." "Very well, I shall be waiting for you -
perhaps crushed to death by the criticism of David." "Who knows" said Pearl,
shrugging her shoulders.
    On her way to Canton Mansions Juliet bought 2 pink roses & tucked
them into her belt. Also she felt that the sunshine had got into her brain - - -

It was sparkling & golden & enchanting like champagne. She hugged her roll of MS as she mounted the stairs & then knocked quickly. Her heart was beating & she felt that her cheeks were crimson. She stood waiting for several seconds & then knocked again. Rudolf opened the door & swept her an extravagant bow.

"Bon jour, Mdlle" he cried in his mocking voice.

"Is David in" asked Juliet.

"He received your telegram Mdlle & a thousand apologies but asks me to amuse you for just thirty minutes as he has so important an engagement. It is just thirty minutes, Mdlle, and I am sorry for you – – –"

Juliet felt intensely annoyed. How could David have done such a thing, knowing as he did that she hated the very sight of Rudolf. Also for some inexplicable reason she felt afraid of him – he was so utterly at his ease, so lightly contemptuous, so recklessly impertinent. She stood by the table in the middle of the room, frowning slightly, & Rudolf leaned against the mantelpiece – and laughed. Then she turned to him.

"It is very kind of you to offer to entertain me. If I can sit here & read through my work I shall be quite happy, thank you" she said. On no account must she allow Rudolf to guess that her heart was beating violently, that she had to hold her hands under her long cloak so that he could not see how they were trembling. She drew up a chair & sat down.

"Dieu, Dieu, how hot it is" called Rudolf. "That coat is impossible Mdlle. Here – let me take it. Stand up – Voilà ... & your hat. Is it not heavy – – il faut souffrir – no, that cannot apply to you."

Juliet stood up & allowed him to take her coat & hat. She could not trust herself to speak to him. He is a fiend, she thought, a perfect fiend. How can he look at me like that. She did not know exactly what to do, and then suddenly thought – how idiotic I am. Really I am rude. Perhaps he is trying to be kind – & fancy being afraid of anyone.

Perhaps if I really can talk to him alone for 30 minutes we shall understand each other in the future. Perhaps – yes – I am sure that is why David has arranged this. She looked up & smiled suddenly.

"Après tout, I shall talk" she said – "Do you think I am rude."

"Not at all – perhaps you, if I might venture to say it, do not disguise your feelings very well, Mdlle." Rudolf sat down opposite to her, & leaning his elbows on the table watched her face – –

"Tenez" he said, "let us revive recollections. It is a charming thing that I love to do – – – My favourite word in the whole language is 'Souvenir', Mdlle."

"The first time I saw you" Juliet answered severely, "I heard you whisper to David 'but she is a curiosity', and I never forgave you. It sounded as though I edited the Family Herald."

"No. no, you misunderstood me. I was interested. You were so different from anyone else & you had known those tea coffee & cocoa creatures that we have seen – & also you did not like me. I saw it in your eyes."

"Did you expect me to. Did all the tea coffee & cocoa creatures 'cast down their golden crowns' straightway."

"Ah, you do not know the life of the musician" said Rudolf, sighing deeply
& casting his eyes heavenward.
Juliet laughed & said "Don't be affected. I don't like you, to tell you the truth
– you're forward, at least you appear so, and I feel that you despise me. I hate
that! I like you professionally, not personally."

She suddenly jumped up & looked at herself in the little glass that hung
over the mantelpiece.
"<u>How</u> my hair looks" she said, giving it a little pat all over. "Is it alright now?"
she appealed to him.
"Adorable" said Rudolf, "& the little white dress & the two pink roses & the
little black shoes – & the ribbon."
"Please stop" said Juliet. She was afraid again. Why would he not understand
when she was joking & when she was serious? It is his voice that is so
abominable, she thought. His voice & his eyes.

Rudolf tossed back his hair & opened the piano. He began playing the
overture to Tannhäuser, heavily & magnificently.
"Ah Mdlle" he said, raising his voice, "you do not understand me. We can
never be friends, I fear. There are too many obstacles. You are too
conventional."
"I am –" interrupted Juliet.
"Yes you are more conventional than a child from a convent school. Also you
never allow your feelings to run away with you – you have no core of
sensation."
"I haven't" cried Juliet.
"No you haven't. Also you are a bad actress & I am a wonderful reader of
charactère." He had come to the end of the Pilgrim's Song & began playing it
again. His tone was almost brutal. "It is the heritage from your parents" he
said. "You have fought against it, but voilà there it is, always conquering you.
You are afraid of everything & you suspect everybody. Dieu! how afraid you
are."
"I am not" said Juliet, shaking her head – but the colour rushed into her
cheeks.

He started the Venus Motif. "Here am I" he said "reckless, a lover of
all that you have desired to love, because my mother was a Danseuse and my
father an artist. Also there was no marriage – –" He ceased speaking but
the music filled the room. He repeated the wonderful Venus call. "Ah, it is
divine" he said. "That is what you should be, Juliet. What – how am I for
Tannhäuser."

The music was flooding Juliet's soul now. The room faded. She heard her
hot heavy impassioned voice above the storm of emotion – – –
"Stop, stop" she said, feeling as though some spell was being cast over her. She
shook from head to foot with anger & horror.
"Listen again" said Rudolf. It was a Chopin nocturne this time. "Live this life,
Juliet. Did Chopin fear to satisfy the cravings of his nature, his natural desires.
No, that is how[?] he is so great. Why do you push away just that which you
need, because of convention. Why do you dwarf your nature, spoil your life.

If you were a man you would be a teetotaller & then a Revivalist. You are the most beautiful girl I have ever seen - no don't interrupt - I shall never speak like this again. I shall go away tonight. But you are, Juliet. It is not regular beauty - it is fascination - some fearful attraction when you choose to appear fascinating. Yet you are a little timide, and you know nothing - absolutely nothing. You are blind, & far worse, you are deaf to all that is most worth living for."

Juliet sprang to her feet. "I shall <u>not</u> listen to you" she said, the tears starting to her eyes. "I shall go home now, this instant. How dare you speak like this Rudolf - how dare you. I am <u>suffocated</u>. Where did you put my coat & hat!" Her eyes were blazing.

Rudolf suddenly sprang up from the music stool & caught her by the arm. "It is not for nothing that I have such a tone" he said, speaking hoarsely. His face was mad with passion, white with desire.

"Leave me alone" said Juliet. She raised her eyes to his face, & his expression caused her to suddenly cease struggling & look up at him dumbly, her lips parted, terror in her eyes.

"You adorable creature" whispered Rudolf, his face close to hers. "You adorable creature - you shall not go now - -" She felt the room sway & heave. She felt that she was going to faint. "Rudolf, Rudolf" she said, & Rudolf's answer was "at last."      [(L) PP78–86]

It was eleven o'clock when David[40] entered the sitting room. He found Rudolf <clad in his pyjamas> at the piano composing. "Be quiet mon ami" he cried, "listen a moment." David stood still. Rudolf played madly, wildly, fiercely - the Music that was coursing through his brain seemed to intoxicate him. "It is my masterpiece" he shouted, closing the piano & falling on to David's neck.

"It was my masterpiece."

"What the Devil has come over you" cried David, bringing out of his pocket the program of the evening Promenade. "I'm still full of Wagner, & behold I find he is here incarnate in my room."

"Yes, yes" said Rudolf, pulling David's handkerchief out of his pocket and applying it to his eyes. "I am Wagner - I'm at the top of the whole world, & it is rather strange. Rejoice with me" he said, <running his hands through his hair.>

David lighted a cigarette & stood with his hands clasped behind his back. "Are you drunk?" he said thoughtfully. "Oui, oui, drunk I am - with the wine of Life, mon ami - - -"

"Well go and be drunk somewhere else. I've got an infernal headache & I want to smoke in peace."

"Ah excuse, mon cher" said Rudolf, laying his strong hand on David's arm. "I shall be like a sucking baby[?] if you will be kind. Where have you been."

"I took Pearl to the Promenade."

"Bon Dieu me garde!" ejaculated Rudolf. David turned to him sharply.

---

[40]'David' was written after 'Caes' had been firmly scored out with three strokes.

"Why not?" he said, "why not? What do you mean. We talked about Juliet the whole time."

"Did you take Pearl home."

"Yes. I didn't stay - Juliet was asleep on the sofa - - - & it was so late. Anyone been here?"

"Not a soul" cried Rudolf airily, waving his hands to express boundless emptiness & vast solitude - - -

"I suppose the rose leaves floated through the window" said David, stooping to pick up some pink petals.

"They were once a buttonhole" said Rudolf, "but it died & I threw it out of the window."

"That is a lie" was the answer. His voice was very quiet. "Juliet's been here, I know it. The remains of these blossoms[?] she was wearing ten minutes ago. Besides, I knew it the moment I came in." Rudolf grew suddenly confused & silent. Then he shrugged his shoulders.[41] "It is true" he said. "She left you this MS. I can't think why I invented that sweet little tale - - -" "Ah thanks" said David, taking the roll of paper from the table. "I can't think why you did either - you two fight like cat & dog." Rudolf frowned. "She hates me" he said. "She is impudent. This afternoon she insulted me. She is the only woman who has ever insulted me." "So you were ashamed to tell" queried David. "I wish that she hated me. It is an abominable position - - - I feel as though I ought to love her - to me she is an angel, she has always been an angel - but I do not. She is too like me. I understand her too well. We are both too moody, we both feel too much the same about everything. That is what I feel and so she does not attract me - do you understand?" "Perfectly - but Pearl?"[42] David paused, then "Need I tell you? I <u>cannot</u> help myself. I am madly in love with Pearl.[43] She is so inexplicable, so reckless, so unlike me - I cannot understand her. I cannot think how she feels about me. It attracts me - - - & she challenges me. The Lord only knows how all this will end" he added.

[(M) PP86A–89A]

And the winter came again. The rooms in Carbury Avenue began to look cold & cheerless.

"Don't for Heaven's sake start fires" said Pearl, "they stop me working strenuously - also the price of coal." So they kept the screen in front of the fireplace and resolutely refused to think of the long sweet drowsy evenings that might have been theirs. Juliet was sleeping badly again.

"I dream so much" she told Pearl. "Every night terrible dreams - all about when I was little & about people I'd quite forgotten - & then I wake & try not to sleep again - it is so heart-breaking." She had become intensely pale & the shadows were always under her eyes now. "You ought to feel more, & think less" Pearl would answer. "Write something stupendous, create a colossal scheme & then it will cure you." "Ideas keep coming to me - it is not for lack

---

[41]This last phrase begins p 88a at the top of which KM has written 'Trowell'.
[42]See note 38.
[43]See note 38.

of ideas that I have not written, but somehow that last play seemed to have stolen so much of my vitality."

They were both sitting in the half dark, talking thus, when Pearl suddenly looked at the clock & cried "Good Heavens - I must fly - I'm due for a sitting at half past six & it's nearly that now."

She went. Juliet listened to the sound of her steps going down down down, then along the corridor & then lost. She folded her hands in front of her & suddenly the tears poured down her face - - -

I wonder why I am crying, she thought - am I sad - am I am I. She crept over to the lounge & lay down, her head buried in the cushions. She was assailed with the most extraordinary thoughts. They seemed to be floating towards her, vast & terrible. I feel as though I was on a great river, she thought, & the rocks were all closing around me - coming towards me to sink me - and now & again Rudolf's face came before her - the broad low brow, the great sweep of hair, the fire of the eyes, the eager curve of his mouth - almost just a trifle mocking but also concerned, just a trifle concerned.

She saw the strong supple hands, hands such as Aubrey Beardsley would have given an Artist. It is Rudolf, & Rudolf & Rudolf she said to herself. Then suddenly a fierce thought sprang to birth in her brain - - - Did he ever think that there might be consequences to his act? Did he ever for one moment dream that Nature might cry to the world what was so hidden, so buried? Terror took possession of her. "O no, not that" she said, "never, never that. That would be diabolical & the world isn't diabolical - at least it can't be. Nothing would exist if it was." But if - if - then if she were certain she[44]

[(N) PP90–91A]

"How you've changed"[45] he said, half whispering. "Mightn't it have been better if you had just followed your destiny. For girls like Pearl it is of course different - she is made differently, Juliet, but - your guarded life. Perhaps by this time you would be - - -"

"Please be quiet" said Juliet. The tears were choking her now - the hopeless tragedy. O, yes, he was a fool, this David - why did she love him?

"But am I not right?" he went on, almost tenderly. She shook her head. "I have made my own bed - no, no I don't mean that. I adore this life, I worship it - it has been Heaven!" But she over acted her part. Suddenly he caught one of her hands.

"Listen" he said. "Listen. Go back, dear. We shall all help you, we have spoken so much of you lately. You are so changed - it is not right - you are wasting your life. And you have been dear & sweet to me always. How we change, Juliet. When we first knew each other, both so young, so full of quaint romantic impossibilities - but those two children are dead now & we are man & woman - all is different. You made a mistake - for the sake of your old view, Juliet, try & go back. We shall both help you - - - Pearl & I - - -"

---

[44]The passage which once followed, whether one page or more, was torn out prior to the numbering of the remaining pages.

[45]This sentence is preceded by 'her fears', which followed from a page now torn out.

Juliet looked up into [his] face. How very very heavy she had grown.
She could hardly hold up her head now - - - It is quite extraordinary -
like a dead body, she thought. All the six undertakers couldn't lift her now.
How curious - two Davids - how strange - two huge gigantic Davids - both of
them thundering "Pearl & I - - -" What colossal Davids. She must run away
& tell Grannie. She started to her feet - - - & fell - - -      [(o) PP92–93]

Day & night the rain fell. The sky would never be light again, it seemed. The
little bedroom was <full of bottles &> always dark but it did not matter - as
Pearl told David, Juliet did not need light now. <They nursed her together
now>
   When the doctor had first come & told Pearl how it was with Juliet the
girl was dismayed & horror stricken. She went into the sitting room where
David was waiting. "David" she said "this is awful - I had not the slightest idea
that Juliet - "
"What is the matter" he said.
"O our poor Juliet. She has been shockingly treated - you know - you
understand?"
"I'll not believe you" said David.
"It is perfectly true. David she is going to die."
"I'll not believe you."
"It is true. Come in and see her - she cannot know - - -"
They went back to her room. The doctor left as they entered, promising to
come again next morning. Also he would send a nurse immediately. Juliet lay
straight & still, her face twisted with horror. They stood & watched her. David
suddenly stroked her hand - - -
"Rudolf" she cried piteously, pleadingly - & then both of them knew.
   Day & night the rain fell & at last one afternoon the end came. <The
nurse had gone out for a few moments. Pearl & David stood by the bed.>
Juliet came back painfully. She was groping the dark, trying to feel her way
along. Out of the dark two voices came.
"It cannot be long now."
"But it is for the best. If she <u>had</u> lived what could have happened."
"I begin to believe there must be a merciful God."
"I, too."
She opened her eyes & saw the two beside her.
"Ought I to join your hands & say bless you" she whispered.
Suddenly she raised herself - "O - O I want to live" she screamed, but Death
put his hand over her mouth.      [(P) PP93A–95]

Juliet looked round her room curiously. So this was where she was to spend
the next three years - three years. It did not look inviting. She noticed two
texts ornamented with foxgloves & robins - - - & decided that they must
come down. The three large windows looked out upon the Mews below - the
houses built all round in a square. She wondered who would share this
sanctum. Some English girl, stiff & sporting, who would torture the walls with

pictures of dogs & keep a hockey stick in the corner. Heaven forbid, she thought. She sat down by the side of the bed & pulled off her long gloves. How strange & dim the light was.

She was alone in London - glorious thought. Three years of study before her. And then all Life to plunge into. The others were actually <u>gone</u> now. She was to meet total strangers. She could be just as she liked - they had never known her before. O, what a comfort it was to know that every minute sent The Others further away from her! I suppose I am preposterously unnatural, she thought, & smiled.

Then the porter brought in her two large boxes, and behind him Miss Mackay hovered & told Juliet she must have everything unpacked before teatime - it was quite one of the old customs. Did the glory of England rest upon old customs? She rather fancied it did. When to start overcoats & when to stop fires, hard boiled eggs for Sunday supper, and cold lunches. She knelt down on the floor and unstrapped her luggage. From the pocket of her suitcase she drew out David's picture & looked at it seriously, then bent forward & kissed it.

"Here we are, dear" she said aloud. "Boy of mine, I feel that life is beginning - write now."[46]

When the old custom had been sustained & she had undressed she suddenly longed to write just a few lines of her impressions. So she slipped into her kimono & drew out her notebook.

"If I could retain my solitude" she wrote, "I should be profoundly happy. The knowledge that sooner or later I shall be hampered with desirable acquaintances takes away much of the glamour. The great thing to do is to start as I mean to continue - never for one moment to be other than myself as I long to be, as I never yet have been except with David." She laid down her pen & began braiding her hair in two thick braids. There was a knock at the door and immediately afterwards Miss Mackay entered with a tall thin girl beside her.

"My dear" the old lady said, "Juliet", positive Maternity in her tone, "this is your roommate, Pearl Saffron - new like yourself so I hope you will be friends."     [(Q) PP95A–97A]

Because she was the youngest she expected the most. She had vague notions that it was always, would always be the third who was the favourite of the Gods. the fairy tales that she devoured voraciously during her childhood helped to stimulate the thought.     [(R) P98]

Juliet passed a sleepless night.[47] She lay still in the darkness staring at the dim outline of the roofs outside the window, thinking, thinking. Each moment her brain seemed more awake. If I do once go back, she thought, all will be over. It is stagnation, desolation that stares [me] in the face. I shall be lonely. I shall be thousands of miles from all that I care for & once I get there I can't come back. I can't do it. If they choose to behave like devils they must be treated as

---

[46]KM probably meant 'right now' but the word is clearly 'write' as she has it.
[47]At the top of this page KM wrote and crossed out 'Ake Ake Aroha'.

such. On one hand lay the mode bohème - alluring, knowledge-bringing, full of work and sensation, full of impulse, pulsating with the cry of Youth Youth Youth. Pearl with her pale eager face and smiling ripe mouth, crying to Juliet "Here I am - here we both are. Trust me dear, live with me. You and I to reach for things together, you and I to live and prove our new Philosophy."

On the other hand lay the Suitable Appropriate Existence. The days full of perpetual Society functions, the hours full of clothes discussions - the waste of life. The stifling atmosphere would kill me, she thought. The days - weeks - months - years of it all. Her father, with his successful characteristic respectable face, crying "Now is the time. What have I got for my money. Come along - deck yourself out, show the world that you are expensive. Now is the time for me to sit still and have my slippers brought for me. You are behaving badly. You must learn to realise that the silken cords of parental authority are very tight ropes indeed. I want no erratic spasmodic daughter. I demand a sane healthy-minded girl - <close the shutters upon your lopsided ambitions>. It is quite time for you to put up the shutters upon this period."
In the darkness Juliet smiled at the last expression. It was so exactly like him - an undeniable <u>trade</u> atmosphere.

Towards dawn she slipped out of bed, wrapped herself round in the quilt, and began pacing up and down. Her face was burning with excitement. It has been so easy to speak of taking the plunge when two years of student life lay definitely before me, but now that the moment has arrived, the water looked very cold. All their arguments passed sharply across her brain - a neat selection of platitudes, altruisms, aphorisms. Will they wear - will they hold good, she thought, and then cried "Yes, yes - I have the Key in my hands. Shall I unlock the door and get through & then shut it again, bang it again with all the old Life outside - & Pearl & I alone at last."

She sat down at the table & took up her pen, then wrote rapidly "Pearl I am coming. Understand I answer now for good & for all. I don't know why I have hesitated so long. Ought I to be grateful to you for taking me - - - I don't think I am, dear, because I would do exactly the same if the circumstances were reversed. You realise that I want to find out what everything is worth - & you too, my friend. What has held me back from coming has been I think principally the thought that we are not to be together for a week or a month or a year even, but for all times. It is rather immense & requires consideration. So to bed. I am lonely. J."

When the seven o'clock dressing bell rang [Juliet] woke to the full consciousness of a nervous headache. She knew from experience that it was of no earthly use to attempt to do anything except succumb & lie still. So she slipped into her kimono & went along the stone passage to Miss Grimwood's bedroom. That lady on a seat before the glass tastefully decorated[?] her head with her three soft switches, & when Juliet came in she enmeshed herself in a salmon pink fascinator[48] with no small measure of confusion & embarrassment. "I am afraid I shall have to stay in bed all day" said Juliet. Then in answer to numerous significant inquiries & nods - "No, nothing, thank you. Merely a

---

[48]A fascinator was a lace or crocheted head covering for women.

headache. Meals - no thank you. Yes, tea perhaps, if I might have it very strong. If I can just lie still. O, no, quite unnecessary - I shall take some phenacetin. If I might be left alone. Overwork - O, by no means. They are quite a common occurrence."

Then she went back to her room & pulled down the blinds & crept into bed.

The hours pulsed slowly on. After an immeasurable length of time she saw Pearl standing beside her, tall & grave in her black frock with a white feather boa round her throat.

"This is good" said Juliet sitting up with her hands clasped round her knees. "What is the time."

"Just four" Pearl smiled. "How do you feel."

"Rather damnable."

"Can you talk."

"My dear yes. I feel better for the sight of you. Give me that pink carnation you're wearing, & sit on the bed here."

"I got your letter this afternoon, Juliet, by the two o'clock post, & came straightway to your room, my dear."

They suddenly held each other's hand.

"To the devil with my relations" said Juliet.

"To the Devil with our Past Life" said Pearl. "All the way here I have been quoting Oscar's 'Relations are a very tedious set of people'. You know, it has been like a charm."[49]    [(s) PP106A–110A]

Chapter I

Behind the house the hills rose in a great sweep of melancholy grandeur. Before it lay the wide restless ocean. Juliet dreamed. She stood at the foot of a great bush-covered hill. It towered above her, and she had a curious sensation that it was alive and filled with antagonism towards her. On the very crown of the hill the sunlight lay, sheer golden. Juliet began to slowly climb. At first she followed a narrow sheep track for a short time, then lost sight of it & clung to brambles and trees, sometimes finding a firm foothold, sometimes stumbling or sinking ankle deep into a mass of rotting leaves. This will take me a terribly long time, she thought. Then a hand grasped hers and someone pulled her swiftly and carefully over the fallen tree trunks, across the narrow streams. She was out of the bush now. A long stretch of short grass was before her. The unseen guide disappeared.

Juliet resolutely walked on. The hill seemed to increase to an enormous size, the patch of sunlight at the top grew more intense, the air became full of sound. She was conscious of many people near her, of voices raised in anger or alarm. I must try & not look to the right or to the left, she thought, but only at the sunlight. Then she entered the bush again. The trees crowded round her, menacing, terrible. The fern trees waved their long green branches. They are like arms, thought Juliet. She walked faster, then began running, and suddenly tripped over a long thick supplejack[50] and fell.

---

[49]After this pencil written section KM subsequently wrote, in ink, 'I can wait no longer'.

[50]Supplejack: *Ripogonum scandens*, a name for various climbing and twining shrubs with tough pliable stems found in tropical and (as here) subtropical forests.

For some inexplicable reason she began to cry – loudly, like a little child – and made no attempt to get up. Then someone caught her by the shoulders and put her on her feet again and brushed the earth and twigs from her dress. She walked on, sobbing a little, and full of despair. On and on, until a river rushed across her path. Now it is all over, she thought. I shall have to stay on this side. She sat down on a flat rock and began throwing little pebbles into the water, and each pebble as it fell floated on the top of the water until there was a great bridge of the pebbles, and she walked across to the other side quite safely.

Now she found a road – a dusty much used road – and suddenly a great fog swept over all the land. Again she heard the sound of many voices, and suddenly in the darkness someone struck her in the face. A feeling of intolerable shame seized her – she ran faster & faster, and when the fog drew away it reminded her of the man at the circus. When he lifted the handkerchief off the flowerpot something beautiful was there. She was very near the end of the journey. Just a few more steps. But how heavy she had become! She could hardly walk. She was too tired to look for the sunlight – she only saw the dust on the road. So few more steps and then she could rest and feel that all the trouble was behind her. Her steps grew slower & slower – she seemed hardly to be moving.

Suddenly a gust of cold air blew on to her face. She looked up. She stood on the summit of the mountain. There was no sunlight, no sound, nothing.[51] Only the fierce wind that beat upon her face she could hardly stand against. She stretched her arms to cling to something – and fell.        [(T) PPIII–II4]

> The little boy went to sleep in the car
> The journey had been too long.
> He hadn't a notion that home was so far
> The little boy went to sleep in the car.

## Chapter I

### An Attempt.

Marina stood at the scullery door and called "Pat, Pat". The sun streamed over the courtyard – the pincushion flowers stood limply and thirstily against the wall of the feedroom.
"Pat – Pat" she called.
"Here Miss Marina" shouted a voice from the woodshed.
"Pat, I want to go riding."
"Daisy's in the paddock. The sheepskin I'll bring yer in a minute."
"Pat, I want to go now." She put her handkerchief over her head & walked over to the woodshed.
"Phew it's hot" she said, shaking back her long braid of hair. "I'll be a mass of freckles by the time I come back."
Pat put down the tomahawk & regarded her seriously.

---

[51] A sentence here, which has been crossed out, reads 'The shock of her falling woke her.'

"Wait for two hours, Miss Marina." But the girl shook her head.
"No, I'm off to see Farkey Anderson,[52] and it will be cooler in the bush."
Pat took up his big hat & together they walked across the yard, through the
great white gates, down the road and into the paddock.

Under the wattle trees Daisy regarded them seriously.
"I feel a bit of a devil to take her" Marina murmured. "Pat, make it alright
with the family if they kick up a shindy. I'm so dead sick of them all I must go
off." She laid her hand caressingly against the arm of his old blue shirt.
"Done, Miss Marina" said Pat, and he stood in the paddock & watched her
mount & ride straddle-legs out of sight. Riding was almost as natural as
walking to Marina. She held herself very loosely & far back from the waist,
like a native riding – and fear had never entered into her thoughts.

I like riding down this road with the sun hurting me, she mused. I'll love
everything that really comes fiercely – it makes me feel so "fighty", and that's
what I like. I wish I hadn't quarreled with Mother & Father again – that's a
distinct bore, especially as its only a week to my birthday.

> The sunlight shone in golden beams
> Across my lonely way
> But I was wrapped in youthful dreams
> And did not say them nay.
>
> If Mother & Father were left to themselves
> And hadn't a baby to play with
> Suppose now we left you alone on the street
> For someone to just run away with.
>
> I really can't think what we both would be at
> Two grumbly old nasty old cronies
> And never the sound of a young ladies feet
> To make us not feel by our lonies
>
> I think that we'd have to buy something instead
> A nice little dog or a kitten
> A nice little persian haired round little puss
> Not the family who would lose their mitten.
>
> But really we'd both of us feel very sad
> And quite wash our eyes out with water
> And sit very close and exclaim all the time
> If we only had that little daughter.

---

[52]Farquhar Campbell Anderson (1850–1926) was a farm labourer in Karori with a whiff of the exotic
about him. Born and educated in England, a son of Major-General Litchfield Anderson, Indian Army, who
was one-time Governor of Edinburgh Castle, Farkey had had some Indian Army experience himself before
coming to New Zealand prior to 1885. In New Zealand he was for some time in the Armed Constabulary
before becoming a farm labourer, mainly in South Karori. Unmarried, he was said to have been kind to
children who, in turn, liked and trusted him. KM would later (1916) write a poem about him titled 'The
Man with the Wooden Leg', employing a little poetic license because, although he was slightly lame, he did
not have a wooden leg.

A Young Ladies Version of
The Cards.
Diamonds are for grown up ladies
Clubs for Giants fierce & tall
Spades for digging the garden
But Hearts are meant for all –
O but Hearts are meant for all.

On waking next morning Käthie slipped out of bed, ran over to the window,
shook her hair back from her face & leaned out. "Good morning sea, sky,
trees, earth, blessed little island" she said, "for today the Mail comes in."
She sat on the window sill, her eyes half closed, a smile playing over her face,
and thought – <u>how</u> many years I have waited. How the days have begun and
ended – the long days – and never a word about him, and the life here flowed
on, and now it is Mail Day. "O Expectation, Expectation" she cried aloud,
her voice eager and high, & every pulse in her body beating with excitement.
"I feel [as] though my heart has run up a big flag and its blowing inside me."
     She dressed very slowly.
"My old green linen" she said, pulling it out joyfully. "Souvenir d'Angleterre.
I shall write an Orchestral Fantasie on that." Two roses for the front of her
blouse. She ran out into the garden – her heart suffocated her. She wished that
there were great thorns on the bushes to tear her hands.
"I want a big physical sensation" she said, and then she ran back to her room
and looked at herself in the long glass – the same Käthie of so long ago –
but yet not the same.

adoration & worship for ever & ever!

     What You Please

And another night was over, and another day came. Käthie lay still and
watched the light creep into her room, slowly and mournfully. "If the sun
shone I should go mad" she thought, "thank God that it is raining." Suddenly
she buried her face in the pillows. "O God, O God, O God" she cried, and
then "No you damned old hypocrite I won't shout at you." She laughed
suddenly. "Dear Mr Death, would you kindly send round a sheet this morning
as there is a large parcel awaiting your convenience."
     Then she lay with her face towards the window and cried – hopelessly,
madly. Long shudders passed through her, she grew icy cold – only her left
hand under its bandages seemed to burn into her like a white hot iron. "I shall
go mad – mad – mad" she moaned. "Hear me somebody. Is the whole place
dead. Listen – damn you all – I'm ruined, and there the devils lie in their beds
and dream & say 'Never mind, dear, you can always <u>write</u>.' O the simpering
brainless idiots – I shall commit suicide."
     She went through the whole scene again. The light in Leslie's[53] eyes –

---

[53]Leslie was the name of KM's brother who was 5½ years younger, and so only about 11 or 12 when
this piece was written.

the way his little hands had trembled when he showed her the great beautiful packet - all bought for two shillings, and most of them 'double-bangers'. How they two had crept round to the dining[room] window and looked in & seen all the dull quiet faces, and had to put their handkerchiefs into their mouths to stop all the laughter. How he had climbed up the fire escape ladder and into her bedroom, and come down with the box of matches in his mouth so he could hold on with both hands, and she had said "Good Rover - fetch it, drop it boy." She seemed to hear again his little agitated staccato voice. "You hold this big one in your hand & then light it and throw it away." And she had held the big one and lighted a match. A great noise came.
"<u>God</u> - my hand" she said - and fell into the great Dark.

Then there came the long long days, & the little voice always telling her to hold it in her hand. And at last the Doctor had told her that a very sad thing had happened. And she had said dear dear, couldn't he sew on five nice neat little crackers instead of the fingers, and she could live at the North Pole & be quite safe. He had left the room and closed the door loudly behind him. "More fireworks" she called, and lay still & laughed.

Käthie thought of it all quietly, calmly now. "I am well now" she thought, "if there is anything to be well for. I suppose they want to keep me here as long as possible because they don't know what is to happen next." Suddenly she flung back the covers and slipped out of bed. She felt as though she was walking on needles, & slowly, carefully, she dragged herself over to the dressingtable. Then she looked at her reflection in the mirror above. A long thin face, lines of suffering deeply engraved by the Artist Pain, an extraordinary pallor in her cheeks & lips.

"That is Käthie" she said hoarsely - "Käthie", & then suddenly realised the illness was over. Now she was looking back. "The fact that I have done this proves that it is over" she said. She looked curiously at her bandaged hand & then suddenly bent her head & kissed it. Then she crept back to bed, & when her Mother came, opening the door very softly, just poking her head in, Kathie said "Good morning. Can I see the paper?" & Mother, almost unbelieving, rushed into the girls' room & told them, & the three of them clung together & then went in to see her.

∧ ∧ ∧ ∧ ∧ ∧ ∧ ∧ ∧ ∧ ∧ ∧

She wondered why - what could have happened. Then she crept out of bed & ran to the head of the stairs. Leslie sat there whistling & plaiting a piece of flax. At the sight of her he stopped & uttered an exclamation.
"Dear little chappie" she said, "fly & bring me a paper - just for a secret - don't tell a soul darling." He shot down the bannister & in a moment he was back, the paper inside his sailor blouse.

Käthie sat down in her armchair. It was a difficult matter to manage a newspaper with one hand. She must lay it on the table. Bah! "Wool rising." "Fashionable Wedding." "Trouble in Russia." Surely all this was very harmless - - - She turned over the page - "Visit of Prominent Musician.

Recital tonight at Town Hall. Interview by our Special Correspondent" -
& then the name flared out, & she understood.

The paper lay at her feet now. "I shall go to that concert" she said.
She felt not the slightest emotion or surprise. She only wanted to lay her plans
carefully - but no inspiration came. At lunch time Chaddie brought in her tray.
"We're all going over to the Hutt[54] this afternoon till tomorrow" she said.
"You won't mind being here just with the Cook as you're so much better.
Dick[55] has asked us all & the Governor is going to be there."

When they had all gone it was already six o'clock. The recital
commenced at eight. She rang the bell & when the maid appeared she
motioned her to a chair.
"Now please listen" she [said] authoritatively. "Look what lies on the table."
Ten sovereigns were[56]

### The Tale of the Three.

<The first one was Vera Margaret. She was just ten - a tall thin child with
commonplace features, a great braid of light brown hair, and a rapt intensely
good expression in her hazel eyes and eager - - ->

Vera Margaret, Charlotte Mary & K.M. were cleaning out the doll's
house. There were three dippers of water on the floor, three little pieces of real
monkey brand[57] and in their hands they held three little rags - of various
degrees of dirtiness. They were being systematic thorough little souls and their
cheeks were flaming, their hands aching with the exertion.
"It's the chimleys" said K.M., polishing these articles with tremendous verve.
"All the dust seems to fly into them." "On them" corrected C.M. in her
careful cool little voice. "They haven't got any reglar insides you know."

Vera Margaret was working at the windows, trying to clean the little
square of glass without washing away the thin red line of paint which was the
dividing line between the bottom & top panes.
"How pleased all the family will be" she said "to find everything so fresh
and neat."

Outside the nursery window the rain was falling in torrents. They peeked
through & saw the long wet garden, the paddocks, and far away the
bush-covered hills were hardly to be seen - - - Early in the morning when
they had been allowed to put some sacking over their heads and run across the
courtyard into the feedroom to see Pat & get the clean boots, he had called the

---

[54]During KM's childhood Upper Hutt and Lower Hutt, now cities, were towns set in the valley of
the Hutt river, close to Wellington.

[55]'Dick' is possibly a reference to Richard Seddon, Prime Minister of New Zealand, who was connected by close friendship and by marriage to the Beauchamps. He died in office in June 1906 while the
Beauchamps were all still in England, and probably around the time this was being written.

[56]The following half page has been torn out, leaving some traces of script down the lefthand margin,
but the drama described here is explored further in another piece in Notebook 39 ('She unpacked her box')
to be found here on p 104.

[57]'Monkey Brand Bon Ami' is the proprietary name of a white domestic cleaner in block form.

day a 'Southerly busted'[58] and they knew that meant 'a big wetness and then a blow' as K.M. graphically described it.

- - - - - - - - - - - - - -

<Away beyond the line of the dark houses there is a sound like the call of the sea after a storm - passionate, solemn, strong. I am leaning far far out of the window in the warm still night air. Down below in the Mews the little lamp is singing a quiet song - - - it is the one glow of light in all this darkness. Men swilling the carriages with pails of water, their sudden sharp exclamations, their hoarse shouting, the faint thin cry of a very young child, and every quarter of an hour, the chiming of the bell from the church close by are the only sounds - - - impersonal, vague, intensely agitating.

It is at this hour and in this loneliness that London stretches out eager hands towards me, & in her eyes is the light of Knowledge.
"O in my streets" she whispers, "there is the passing of many feet, there are lines of flaming lights, there are cafés full of men and women, there is the intoxicating madness of Night Music - - - O the great glamour of Darkness, a tremendous Anticipation, and over all, the sound of laughter, half joyous, half fearful, dying away in a strange shudder of satisfaction and then swelling out once more. The men & women in the cafés hear it - they look at each other suddenly, swiftly, searchingly - - - then the lights seem stronger, the Night Music throbs yet more loudly.

Out of the theatres a great crowd streams into the street. There is the penetrating rhythm of the hansom cabs. Convention has long since sought her bed - with blinds down, with curtains drawn, she is sleeping & dreaming.
Do you not hear the quick beat of my heart. Do you not feel the hot rush of the blood through my veins? Your hand can pluck away the thin veil, your eyes can feast upon my shameless beauties. In my streets there is the answer to all your searchings and longings. Prove yourself. Permeate your senses with the heady perfume of Night. Let nothing remain hidden. Who knows but that in the exploration of my mysteries you may find the answer to your Questionings."

I lean out of the window - the dark houses stare at me, and above them a great sweep of sky. Where it meets the houses there is a strange lightness - - - a suggestion - - - a promise - - -

Silence. Now in the Mews below the cry of the child is silent, the chime of the bell seems less frequent - but away beyond the line of dark houses there is the sound like the call of the sea after a storm. It is assuming gigantic, terrible proportions - - - Nearer & nearer it comes - a vast uncontrollable burst of sound that springs consciously or unconsciously from the soul of every being. Yet it is one and the same as the faint thin cry of the very young child - the great chorale of Life - - -

The sobbing for the Moon. It is the old old cry for the Moon that rises forever into the great Vastness.>

---

[58]'Southerly Buster' is a colloquial (probably originally Australian) term for the cold, frequently wet, gales which assail the whole of New Zealand's long east coast.

Summer Idylle. 1906.

A slow tranquil surrender of the Night Spirits, a knowledge that her body was refreshed and cool and light, a great breath from the sea that skimmed through the window & kissed her laughingly – and her awakening was complete. She slipped out of bed and ran over to the window & looked out. The sea shone with such an intense splendour – danced, leapt up, cried aloud, ran along the line of white beach so daintily, drew back so shyly, & then flung itself on to the warm whiteness with so complete an abandon that she clapped her hands like a child, pulled the blinds high in every window & filled the room with brightness. She looked up at the sun – it could not be more than four o'clock & away in the bush a tui called. Suddenly she grew serious, frowned, & then smiled ironically. "I'd forgotten she existed" she laughed opening the door. She peered into the passage – the sun was not there, and the whole house was very quiet.

In Marina's room the scent of the manuka[59] was heavy and soothing. The floor was strewn with blossoms. Great sprays stood in every corner and in the fireplace and even over the bed. Marina lay straight and still in her bed, her hands clasped over her head, her lips slightly parted. A faint thin colour like the petal of a dull rose leaf shone in the dusk of her skin. Hinemoa[60] bent over her with a curious feeling of pleasure, intermingled with a sensation which she did not analyse. It came upon her if she had used too much perfume, if she had drunk wine that was too heavy & sweet, laid her hand on velvet that was too soft & smooth.

Marina was wrapped in the darkness of her hair. Hinemoa took it up in her hands & drew it away from her brow & face & shoulders. "Marina, Marina" she called, & Marina opened her eyes & said "Is it day" – and then sat up & took Hinemoa's face in her hands & kissed her just between her eyebrows. "O come quick, come quick" cried Hinemoa. "Your room is hot with this manuka & I want to bathe." "I come now" Marina answered, & suddenly she seized a great spray of manuka & threw it full in Hinemoa's face & the blossoms fell into her hair. "Snow Maiden – Snow Maiden" she said, laughing, "look at your hair. It is holding the blossoms in its curls." But Hinemoa filled her hands with manuka & they ran laughing out of the house & down to the shore.

And there it was before them. They stretched out their arms & ran in without speaking, & then swam swiftly & strongly towards an island that lay like a great emerald embedded in the heart of a gigantic amethyst. Hinemoa fell back a little to see Marina. She loved to watch her complete harmony – it increased her enjoyment.

---

[59]Manuka: *Leptospermum scoparium*, a flowering shrub also known as the tea-tree.

[60]I have standardised the spelling of this name (given by KM variously as 'Hinemoa', 'Hinemoi', and 'Hinemoia') to 'Hinemoa'. The Hinemoa of Māori legend was forced, for lack of canoes, to swim to an island to join her lover. 'Marina', although a name she used for herself in 'An Attempt', is here the name she gives to the Māori girl (who is probably based on her Māori schoolfriend Maata Mahupuku), while Hinemoa seems to be KM herself.

"You are just where you ought to be" she said, raising her voice. "But I like not that"[61], said Hinemoa, shaking back her hair. "I lack that congruity."
"It is because you are so utterly the foreign element - - - you see?"

They reached the island & lay on a long smooth ledge of brown rock & rested. Above them the fern trees rose, & among the fern trees a rata[62] rose like a pillar of flame.
"See the hanging beautiful arms of the fern trees" laughed Hinemoa.
"Not arms, not arms. All other trees have arms - saving the rata with his tongues of flame - but the fern trees have beautiful green hair. See, Hinemoa, it is hair, & know you not, should a warrior venture through the bush in the night they seize him & wrap him round in their hair & in the morning he is dead. They are cruel even as I might wish to be to thee, little Hinemoa."
She looked at Hinemoa with half shut eyes, her upper lip drawn back showing her teeth, but Hinemoa caught her hand. "[.....]" she pleaded.

"Now we dive" said Marina, rising & walking to the edge of the rock. The water was here in shadow, deep green, slumbering.
"Remember" she said, turning to Hinemoa, "it is with the eyes open that you must fall - otherwise it is useless. Fall into the water & look right down, down. Those who have never dived so do not know the sea. It is not ripples & foam, you see. Try & sink as deeply as [you] can - with the eyes open & then you will learn." Marina stood for a moment, poised like a beautiful statue, then she sprang down into the water. To Hinemoa it seemed a long bit of waiting, but at last Marina came up, & shook her head many times & cried out exultantly "Come - come."

A flood of excitement bounded to Hinemoa's brain. She quivered suddenly, laughed again, & then descended. When she came up she caught Marina's hands.
"I am mad - mad" she said. "Race me back, quickly, I shall drown myself."
She started swimming. Marina said "Little foolish one" but Hinemoa swam on, her eyes wide with terror, her lips parted. She reached the shore, wrung out her braid, & ran back into the house, never pausing to see if Marina would follow. She shut & locked the door, ran over to the mirror & looked at her reflection.
"What a fright you had, dear" she whispered, & bent & kissed the pale wet face. She dressed slowly & gravely in a straight white gown just like a child wears, then she drew on her stockings & shoes. Her hair was still wet.
She went to dry it on the verandah. Marina had dressed & prepared breakfast. She was standing in the sunshine, combing her hair, & catching hold of a long straight piece & watching the light shining through it.
"See how beautiful I am" she cried, as Hinemoa came up to her. "Come & eat, little one."

---

[61]What KM meant to write here may have been 'But I am not like that'.
[62]Rata: *Metrosiderus robusta*, a forest tree with spectacular red blossom.

"O I am hungry" said Hinemoa, going up to table. "Eggs and bread & honey
& peaches - & what is in this dish, Marina?"
"Baked koumaras - - -"[63]
Hinemoa sat down & peeled a peach & ate it with the juice running through
her fingers.
"Is it good?" said Marina.
"Very."
"And you are not afraid any more?"
"No."
"What was it like?"
"It was like - like - "
"Yes?"
Hinemoa bent her head.
"I have seen the look on your face" Marina laughed. "Hinemoa eat a
koumara."
"No, I don't like them. They're blue - they're too unnatural. Give me some
bread."
Marina handed her a piece, then helped herself to a koumara, which she ate
delicately, looking at Hinemoa with a strange half-smile expanding over her
face.
"I eat it for that reason" she said. "I eat it because it _is_ blue."
"Yes." said Hinemoa, breaking the bread in her white fingers.

> To those who can understand her[64]
> London means everything.
> Black buds in the Times[?] Square garden
> Can herald a glorious Spring.
> Oh the park! in the early morning.
> You can hear the robin sing.

jug and box for sweets for Godmother.

There are a more or less large number of weak minded looking females
waiting here - the slightly mushroom hat type, the flannel coat & skirt type.
I feel rather self-conscious so doubtless look arrogant. Not a man to be seen.
What must the feelings of Kreisler be. In two hours he will be playing.
Does that excite him - is he too blasé for excitement. Is he looking at his
fiddle calling to it, lifting the lid of the case - you know how - or he is eating
the proverbial sausage with his Frau - Pour quelque reason I am interested.
It is because one day Caesar shall be in the same position.

---

[63] The kumara (misspelt here and elsewhere by KM) is the New Zealand sweet potato which often
has a bluish tinge when cooked.
[64] At this point in the notebook there is a scene of a play about Radiana and Guido which has been
heavily crossed out and is omitted here because a fair copy of it, titled 'The Yellow Chrysanthemum', is
among the Newberry Library papers and is given on p 191.

Inside at last, we ate apples & chocolate while waiting & I read the book of
the lady in front. Flat to let opposite. Programs now.[65]

Quelque chose.[66]

1.X.06.

I walk along the broad almost deserted street. It has a meaningless forsaken
careless look, like a woman who has ceased to believe in her beauty.
The splendid rhythm of Life is absent. With tired white faces the people pass
to and fro, silently, drearily. All colour seemed to have lost its keenness.
The street is as toneless as a great stretch of sand. And soon I pass through the
narrow iron gate, up the little path and through the heavy doors into the
church. Silence hung motionless over the church, the shadow of her great
wings darkened everything. Through the gloom the figures of the Saints
showed dimly. The High Altar shone mystical - vision-like. Then I noticed
there were many people kneeling in the pews - their attitude strangely
pathetic, almost old world. A nun came & sat beside me. She raised a
passionless expressionless face, & the Rosary shone like a thread of silver
through the ivory of her fingers.      [J4]

At Sea.[67]

Swiftly the Night came. Like a great white bird the ship sped onward -
onward into the unknown. Through the darkness the stars shone, yet the sky
was a garden of golden flowers, heavy with colour. I lay on the deck of the
vessel, my hands clasped behind my head, and, watching them, I felt a curious
complex emotion, a swift mysterious realisation that they were shining steadily
& ever more powerfully into the very soul of my soul. I felt their still light
permeating the very depths, and fear & ecstasy held me still, shuddering.

There is some fearful magic in their shining, I thought. As the power of
the sunlight causes the firelight to become pale & wasted so is the flame of my
life becoming quenched by this star shining. I saw the flame of my life as a
little little candle flickering fearfully & fancifully, and I thought before long
it will go out and then. Even as I thought I saw there where it had shone -
darkness remained.

Then I was drifting, drifting - where - whence - whither. I was drifting
in a great boundless purple sea. I was being tossed to and fro by the power of
the waves, and the confused sound of many voices floated to me. A sense of
unutterable loneliness pervaded my spirit. I knew this sea was eternal - I was
eternal - this agony was eternal.

So, smiling at myself, I sit down to analyse this new influence, this
complex emotion. I am never anywhere for long without a like experience.
It is not one man or woman that a musician desires - it is the whole octave of

---

[65]This seems to have been written while waiting for admission to a concert by Fritz Kreisler
(1875–1962) the violinist, whose London debut was in 1901.
[66]At the top of this page are some experiments in spelling 'rhythm'—'rhythym'.
[67]Under this title are some drawings of flags.

the sex, & R. is my latest. The first time I saw him I was lying back in my chair & he walked past. I watched the complete rhythmic movement, the absolute self confidence, the beauty of his body, & that Quelque which is the everlasting & eternal in youth & creation stirred in me. I heard him speaking – he has a low full, strangely exciting voice, a habit of mimicking others, a keen sense of humour. His face is clean cut like the face of a statue, his mouth absolutely grecian. Also, he has seen much & lived much and his hand is perfectly strong and cool. He is certainly tall, & his clothes drape the lines of his figure. When I am with him a preposterous desire seizes me. I want to be badly hurt by him. I should like to be strangled by his firm hands. He smokes cigarettes frequently & exquisitely fastidiously.

Last night we sat on deck. He taught me picquet. It was intensely hot. He wore a loose silk shirt under his dress coat. He was curiously excitable, almost a little violent at times. There was a suppressed agitation in every look, every movement. He spoke French for the greater part of the time with exquisite fluency, and a certain extreme affectation – he has spent years in Paris. The more hearts you have the better, he said, leaning over my hand. I felt his coat sleeve against my bare arm. O one heart is a very pinched affair, I answered – in these days one must possess many. We exchanged a long look and his glance inflamed me like the scent of a gardenia.

Yesterday afternoon a game of cricket was in progress on the deck. R began bowling – I stood & watched. He took a few slow steps & then flung the ball at the wicket with the most marvellous force. Time & again he did it – each ball seemed to be aimed at my heart. I panted for breath - - -

We deny our minds to the extent that we castrate our bodies. I am wondering if that is true? & thinking that it most certainly is. Oh, I want to push it as far as it will go. Tomorrow night there is to be a ball. Thank Dieu I know that my dancing is really beautiful. I shall fight for what I want yet I don't [know] definitely what that is. I want to upset him, stir in him strange depths. He has seen so much, it would be such a conquest. At present he is - - I do not know – I think intensely curious & a little baffled. Am I to become eventually une jeune fille entretenue. It points to it. O God, that is better far than the daughter of my parents. What tedious old bores they seem. They are worse than I had even expected. They are prying & curious, they are watchful & cat-like, they discuss only the food. They quarrel between themselves in a hopelessly vulgar fashion. My Father spoke of my returning as damned rot, said look here he wouldn't have me fooling around in dark corners with fellows. His hands, covered with long sandy hair, are absolutely evil hands. A physically revolted feeling seizes me. He wants me to sit near, he watches me at meals, eats in the most abjectly blatantly vulgar manner that is describable. It is like a constant long offense, but I cannot escape from it. And it wraps me in its atmosphere. When I pass him the dishes at table, or a book, or give him a cushion, he refrains from thanking me. He is constantly suspicious, constantly overbearingly tyrannous. I watch him walking all the deck, his pale hideous speckled trousers, his absurdly antediluvian cap.

He is like a cat sometimes I think, except that his eyes are not like a cat's eyes – they are so pale, so frightfully offensive. When he is astonished or when he eats anything that pleases him I think they must start from his head. He watches the dishes go round, anxious to see that he shall have a good share. I cannot be alone or in the company of women for five minutes – he is there, eager, fearful, attempting to appear unconcerned, pulling at his long drooping red-grey moustache with his hairy hands. Ugh!

She is completely under his influence, suggestible & easily upset. Tells him what he must & must not do, looks constantly uneasy. They are both so absolutely idealistic – they are a constant offense to me. The sight of them causes me to feel utterly changed – I hesitate in my manner, appear constrained. They have no idea of the fitness of things. I shall never be able to live at home – I can plainly see that. There would be constant friction. For more than a quarter of an hour they are quite unbearable, & so absolutely my mental inferiors. What is going to happen in the future. I am full of a restless wonder, but I have none of that glorious vitality that I used to have so much. They are draining it out of me  - - -      [J4-7]

I attend a lecture of Thomas Moore.
Mrs Lightband - a woman a little over freely inclined to embonpoint. She has exceeding fair hair which bears evidence of much crimping & much back combing & many pads. It is poor [...] hair, all confined in a broad net. In the evening she wears extremely decolleté frocks, two tight rows of pearls.

> I constantly am hearing
> A cry, a muffled groan
> A voice deep & despairing
> Is Ethel all alone –
>
> All alone Ethel
> It sounds quite like a song
> You will be hearing Melisand[?]
> Before so very long
>
> But is the heart of every man
> Become so like a stone
> That he[68]
> While Ethel's all alone?
> I constantly am hearing.

If Tom Moore was aboard the Corinthic[69] I fancy his Muse would be inspired to sing

---

[68]The rest of this line is obliterated by a large ink-blot which KM has embellished with legs to turn it into a spider.

[69]SS *Corinthic* was the ship on which the Beauchamp family returned to New Zealand in October–December 1906.

Oft in the stilly Night
Ere slumbers chains have bound me
My sleep is put to flight
By all the noise around me.

Along the corridor
Strange gurgles, many a sound.     [J7]


          The [...] Child of the Sea.
Here in the sunlight wild I lie
Wrapt up warm with my pillow & coat
Sometimes I look at the big blue sky

Damn!

The wide grey sky, the wide grey sky
And ever the clouds move slowly by
The fierce shrill note of the sea-birds cry
<Quiet I lie, quiet I lie>
Here in my strange bed.

The endless sea, the endless sea
And the song that is sung repeatedly
In every rhythm & time & theme
Till I shriek aloud ... but it deafens me.

The changing light, the changing light
Purple and gold change to the night
A wide strong blue when the sun is bright
A riot of colour - a wonder sight.

Valley & hill, valley & hill
I am swept along - I never am still
I have cried, I have cursed, I have prayed my fill.

It carries me near the loved one.

Here we
And the shivering song of the poplars
And away in the distance the sea.


Edgar Allan - Atmosphere - untidiness of landscape - Height, river, small boat, Italy, colour purple - the result of fire - manuka - Ai. Hotel man with daughter - willows the yellow transparent effect.

When N[ew] Z[ealand] is more artificial she will give birth to an artist who can treat her natural beauties adequately. This sounds paradoxical but is true.

                                                                    [J10]

A long strand of rope attached to a railway carriage flapped forlornly in the rain.

Three men in blue shirts all lifting the strong plank[?], the dull horses standing by.

toi toi grass.[70] Copper colour & black. bracken – dead valley of bracken.

Feb. 26th.

Kathie Schonfeld.

> Twilight walkers with sand – out building roof tops 5.
> 22 Poets Cottage – sombre – mysterious – good colouring.
> 2. From Lambeth Bridge – London Atmosphere – Every object in smoke
> – Street scene St Ive's superb colouring – bright – lustrous[?] signboard.
> 10. Distance – Immensity & age – London.
> 19. Chelsea & [...] by Whistler – composition pleasing.
> English Village The absolute effect.
> St Ives Rackham [Packham?]-like colour – almost grotesque – grey day –
> English Village –
> –
> 9 St Ives – water so good – stones gorse colouring.
> 25. Sympathy.[71]

> 1 drawers
> 2 vest
> 1 night
> 4 blouses
> 1 stockings
> 2 hand.
> 1 pill bot.

> association of ideas.                    24.V.07.
> General Analysis of the Mind.
> F.P. analysis.
> F.P. synthesis.
> First beauty – then [....]
> Heredity – inherent physical tendencies when a certain
> tendency[?] comes – the mind has its tendency to act in like
> manner.
> consciousness.
> Bundle of Habits.
> Seeing the object in perspective – cognisance of an object.
> Pass from image to language –
> Illusion hallucination delusion.

---

[70]Toi toi is an alternative spelling of Toetoe: *Cortaderia toetoe*, a plant with tall, pale, feathery fronds.

[71]These, although almost impossible to read, appear to be notes on an exhibition of paintings, or, possibly, reproductions of paintings in a book or catalogue.

In these – illusion – the thing to be [...] if your nerve is
set going – when the object is there. Byron & Scott.
the danger of hallucination. It is a step from the [....]
From sensation to Perception – mental image of the thing –
the after image – then from an image into an idea – –[72]

> Fair Water Nymph, I pray of you
> Dont splash the water so
> Although I'm sure its lovely to
> Make big waves with your toe.
>
> Six o'clock is bathing time,
> Bring the tub & bring the water
> Spread the big mat on the floor
> Run & fetch the little daughter.
>
> When youve got on your party frock,
> We really think you sweet
> And even in a pinafore
> You're very clean & neat.
>
> But O the time we love you best
> Is – by the Nursery hearth
> With just your little nakeds on
> And splashing in the bath.
>
> It's quite the most important thing
> That happens in the day
> When you have sat on Daddy's knee
> And quite forgot to play
>
> And feel your head go noddy nod
> And almost 'clined to cry
> Then Mummy says – come precious one
> It's time for bedy bye.
>
> <All babies know that Daddies are
> Quite specially useful things
> For while the Mummy gets the tub
> He undoes all the strings.>
>
> She takes you from your comfy place
> Your warm & cosy nest
> And pops off all your clothes until
> You've only just a vest.

---

[72]The extreme difficulty of reading the above passage, and its fragmentary nature, make the resulting transcription less than satisfactorily coherent. At most, it is suggestive of some of the ideas which KM was entertaining at the time. Similar ideas are explored towards the end of Notebook 2.

So back you creep to Daddykin
He gives your toes a rub
While Mummy puts the bath mat down
And fetches in the tub.

And sponge & soap & powder box
(The dear soft fluffy puffs)
And Mummy ties her apron on
And pushes up her cuffs.

The towels are spread before the fire
And Mummy pins your hair
And then she does your hair on top
In one big wobbly curl
And says now run along jump in
O <u>what</u> a lucky girl.

To get in right all by yourself's
The hardest thing of all.
The water looks so big & hot
And O – you feel so small.

But when you're soaped from top to toe
All lovely frothy white
You feel you never can get out
But just stay there all night

And [she] puts the sponge right in your mouth
And makes the waves go by
[…] takes you, rolls you up
You haven't time to cry.

It seems to you she rubs too hard
You cry O that's enough.
And then the cloud of powder comes
You love the powder puff.

And while she pops your Nighty on
And puts away your clothes
You pull your Daddy down quite close
And powder all <u>his</u> nose.

I am full of Ideas, tonight. Now they must, at all costs, germinate. I have seen enough to make me full of fancy. I should like to write something so beautiful and yet modern and yet student–like – & full of Summer. Here is a shot. Now truly I ought to be able, but I don't feel by any means confident.     [J21]

De ta linge[?] detachée.
Pauvre Feuille […]
Ou va tu?

To a White Rose.

biddi–biddis

Oh, do let me write something really good, let me sketch an idea & work it
out. Here is silence and peace and splendour, bush and birds. Far away I hear
builders at work upon a house, and the broom sends me half crazy. Let it be a
poem. Well, here goes. I'm red hot for ideas. More power to your elbow, my
dearest Kathie. That is so, and I shall do well.
Fitful sunshine now – I am glad, it will be a beautiful afternoon. But I pray
you, let me write.     [J12]

H   Yvonne walked slowly through the gardens. She was tired,
A   unhappy. Kathie dear do write me something. I can't take
R   my hat off my face – I'll freckle so, said Yvonne, but do
P   give me advice. What can happen to me – for goodness sake
E R S M A G A Z I N E – – – – – – – – –
say something. But the Dwarf was silent. She heard him quietly walking.
It's the old complaint, he said, I'm so dashed tired of it. You all say the same
& you all want the same. No I dont said Yvonne – she had no idea what
he meant. I want Oh, I hardly know. I can't put it into words – but the
want's there.
      Blissfully, blissfully down the golden hillside the broom waved
& beckoned. Swinging their hands as children do, a little song bubbling in
their lifted throats and they walked slowly. Evening is coming, said Phyllis.
Below them lay the sea. They stood still a moment watching it. The little
waves ran along the white beach so daintily, drew back so shyly, then flung
themself along the smooth strong sandy stretch with such delicate abandon
that Phyllis smiled.
      "Evening is coming", she said, looking up at Corydon. The wind had
blown a little curl of hair across her cheek. A pulse in her throat beat
flutteringly. And above them – in the opaque sky – the pale star heralded the
night. " And the darkness is coming" said Corydon – – – – –
      Across the vivid blue sky floated one solitary white cloud. That is a fairy
boat, said Phyllis. She lay on her back among the flowering broom. It was
difficult to distinguish which was blossom & which her sweet hair. A dainty
china-like little figure in her white pink-sprigged skirt, her bodice laced with
blue, her blue stockings & ridiculous fascinating pink slippers. By her side was
a long white crook – gay with a posy of pink roses and ribbons.
      Who are you, O Little Man of the yellow eyes, said Phyllis. Why do you
cry Oh Phyllis,[73]

---

[73]The dwarf with the yellow eyes appears again in a Newberry Library piece. It is entitled 'In
Summer', and was presumably written contemporaneously with this (p 174).

Lying there, with her face buried in her hands, shuddering from head to foot with grief & rage at this Inexplicable Something which seemed to guard the door to Everything, Kathie had her terrible hour. She could not think connectedly. Outside in the fierce wind she heard the [....] sound of the

I feel passionate & mad. Why not write something good. Here's a thought. Of course it may be nothing.

My hands clasped idly in my lap. Sitting in my room I watch the window curtains blow to & fro.

"The Romance of Woman's Influence" Alice Cochran.
Coninsby Disraeli.

And London is calling me the live long day.

Out here it is the Summer time
The days are hot and white
The gardens are ablaze with flowers
The sky with stars at night.
And [?] past my [?] bed
I watch the sparkling bay - - -
With London ever calling me
The live long day.

The people all about our place
They're meaning to be kind
They drive around to visit me
From miles & miles behind.
But I had rather sit alone
Why can't they stay away.
It's London ever calling me
The live long day.

I know the bush is beautiful
The cities up to date
In life, they say, we're on the top
It's England, though, that's late.
But I, with all my longing heart,
I care not what they say
It's London ever calling me
The live long day.

When I get back to London streets
When I am there again
I shall forget that Summer's here
While I am in the rain.
But I shall only feel at last

The wizard[74] has his way
And London's ever calling me
The live long day.
5.X.07.

London London I know what I shall do.
I have been almost stifling here
And mad with love of you
And poverty I welcome, yes –

Kathleen M. Beauchamp.

Dear Dr Tudor-Jones –[75]
I want to write you a few words only – of thanks

Macdowell[76]

She sat on the broad window-sill, her hands clasped loosely in her lap.
Just below her in the garden a passion flower twined round a little fence –
in the half-light the blossoms were like pale hands among the leaves.
In the distance a little belt of pine trees, dark & motionless against a saffron
evening sky.

Inside the room she could see dimly the piano, the two tall pewter
candlesticks and a shallow bowl full of hill crimson carnations. The Australian
Student was playing, and turning round & round on the revolving music stool,
and talking excitedly. They were both smoking beautiful cigarettes. It gave
Rana such pleasure to sit there in the gloom smoking and listening that she felt
languid with delight. "Well, here's a pretty kettle of fish" said the Monkey,
"he's done for himself rather considerably."

He jumped from his perch on to the floor & ran to the man, dragging
his silver chain after him. He felt in the man's pockets – lo, in the waistcoat
one, a little silver pencil & a lump of sugar . . . nothing else. "Neither of these
possessions can make much tangible difference to the gentleman's future
welfare" said the monkey, nibbling the sugar & scratching his head with the
little silver pencil.

And through the uncurtained window the moon shone in upon the
Broken Things. High & white & sweet was the moon & the sky like black

---

[74]The reference here to London as a 'wizard' should be noted as it illuminates an excessively difficult
and debated passage in the Urewera camping trip material in Notebook 2. (See note 145)

[75]The Rev Dr William Tudor Jones, DPhil, FRGS (1865–1946) was a Presbyterian Minister in Wales
until he became a Unitarian in 1899. In 1906 he was posted to New Zealand by the British & Foreign
Unitarian Association for the propagation of liberal religion, where he was the Preacher at the Unitarian Free
Church in Wellington. He was the author of many books and articles on religion and the philosophy of
religion. In a letter to her sister Vera on 17 January 1908 KM wrote about him rather disparagingly.

[76]MacDowell, a name KM uses several times in these early manuscripts, was in her mind because she
admired the work of the American romantic composer Edward Alexander MacDowell (1861–1908) which
was popular at that time.

velvet. The monkey finished the sugar & carefully licked his paw – then, glancing up, he saw the man. With one bound he fled into the shadow, & then, crouching, whimpering, shivering, he crept into his corner.

= = = = = = =

Everybody spoke of the dark man as a crank. Some went even so far as to say he followed a cult, and that is sufficiently damning for an archangel in these days. His entire establishment consisted of the terracotta plastered room.

The Man, the Monkey and the Mask.

He had lived there a very long time – ten years – twenty years – even more – he himself was astonishingly vague. And it was a small terracotta plastered wall on the fourth floor, but undoubtedly there was a balcony quite three feet long that was the great attraction. The man had few possessions – a bed, a chair, a wide cupboard, and a grand piano. He had no pictures, but directly opposite the piano a little black velvet curtain hid the Mask. And in one corner he kept the monkey tethered by a thin silver chain to a white perch.

Everybody spoke of the Man as a crank. Some even whispered that he followed a cult, and that is sufficient to damn the reputation of an archangel. Small wonder that he had few friends. He was tall & thin – emaciated even – but in his face shone that divine, never-to-be-mistaken light of Youth.

Poems of the Apostle of Youth.
1. Late in the night. I lie in my bed & press my face into the pillow. Oh, how strong I feel – like a giant even, and far too happy to sleep.
2. Now is the Winter gone, and the first crocus lights its wan lamp upon the barren earth.
3. Kneeling by the stream I watch a brown leaf float down the shining water. Oh, little brown leaf – whither – whither?
4. Often at midnight I open my window and there wanders in my room many a ghostly visitant's welcome. I love to feel your icy kisses upon my hot mouth.
5. A briar rose is swinging in the blue day. But a wind comes & the blossom is shattered. Strange that it should be far more beautiful as it trails in the dust.

Here, then, is a little summary of what I need – power, wealth, and freedom. It is the hopelessly insipid doctrine that love is the only thing in the world, taught, hammered into women from generation to generation which hampers us so cruelly. We must get rid of that bogey, and then they come – the opportunity of happiness and freedom.     [J37]

The long day pulsed slowly through. Late in the afternoon the Man crept out of bed and over to the window. He pulled it wide open and leaned out. From the street came a muttering confused nightly sound but he looked over the shining silver roofs of the houses <opposite to where the sunset burned in the sky>. There was a jagged scarlet wound in the pale sky. The wind blew towards him – he stood motionless, hardly thinking, yet some dark ghost seemed to be confronting his inner self, shrieking why, why, and wherefore.

Then the night came – the sky was filled with the gold of stars. Lights woke in the houses opposite. He felt curiously remote from it all – the sole spectator at some colossal stupendous drama. He looked down into the street. A girl, slight & very shabbily dressed, was walking up the area steps of the house opposite. She had a blue gingham apron over her dress. In one hand she held a letter. She looked so astonishingly young that he felt glad she was not forced to cross the broad – the pillar box stood in the shadow a few yards away.

Then he noticed a man standing on the pavement waiting. The girl noticed him too. She put her hand up to her hair, anxiously pulled her apron straight & almost ran forward. She lifted her hand to drop the letter, & the man waiting on the pavement suddenly caught hold of her & kissed her – twice. The girl slipped her arms round his neck, kissed him on the mouth.

The watcher left the window. He staggered across the room, wrenched the black velvet curtain from the mask.
"Damn you damn you damn you" he screamed & struck her thrice on her smiling mouth. (In the corner the monkey was very methodically searching for fleas.)

But the mask crashed down upon the floor in a thousand pieces & the man fell too, silently. He looked like a bundle of worn out rags.

Cher Monsieur,
   J'ai recu une lettre de mon ami Mere St Joseph Aubert.[77]
Elle me dit que, quand vous

I shall never I shall never be able to change my handwriting.[78]

Cigarettes. In the room below me a man is smoking a cigaret. The perfume floats through my window, and I am besieged by so many memories that for a little space – I forget – to remember. Outside in the evening sky there is a wide lightness – in the garden next door the lawn is being mowed. I hear the sharp monotonous clattering sound of the machine.

It is the 31st of December – very cool and quiet. The sounds of the lawn mower emphasise my rustic surroundings. And that cigaret!   [J34]

   When They Met After Parting.
At Gravesend she received a letter from
        April 1908.

<That style of risqué after dinner conversation which is all the world over supposed to be so essential to the happiness and digestion of men.>

---

[77]Mother Mary Joseph Aubert (1835-1926) was born Marie Henriette Suzanne in France and came to New Zealand as a young woman (1860). Renowned for her work as a Māori missioner, teacher and healer, she is currently a candidate for canonisation. This fragment is the only clue to any connection between KM and Mother Aubert.
 [78]The above piece of French was written in an attempt at copperplate.

Criticism of Pure Reason

257. Kant.

Life of Kant.
Hegel.

Ah! never more again
Never more again
Cries my soul in pain
Elëanore.

- - - - -

Ah! never more again
Falls the winter rain
Where thy head is lain
Elëanore.

- - - - - -

Ah! my life is dead with sorrow
Ah for me there is no morrow
Thou from me my life didst borrow
Elëanore.

- - - - - -

All the world is dark & dreary
E'en the sea is very weary
And the wind is wild & eerie
Elëanore.                                    Seddon

- - - - - -


Lo I am standing the test.
Laughing I go to my doom
Crushed on the great Earth's breast
And the Night for Shroud & tomb.

---------------

I betwixt Heaven & Earth
I on the window sill
Sitting here shaken with mirth
For I have lived my fill.

---------------

These are the words that I write
Scribble & just let them lie
While I pass into the night,
Take a great leap & die.

---------------

Riding alone is the moon
Through the great black starlit space
I shall look like her quite soon
I with my dead white face.

---------------

Far far below the court
Search for me there O my friend
I – I shall not count for aught
Yet I alone choose my end.

———————————

Haunted by night & by day
By shadows that cry to me – flee
Loose the great bonds leave your place
Learn what Existence can be.

———————————

# *Notebook 29*

## PART 3

[Notebook 29, qMS-1241]

\<Rosamind Wiggs of the Cabbage Patch. Mrs Wiggs of the Cabbage Patch by an American author. Poor unfortunate. Rosamind.\>

In The Tropics.

How I love to wake in the morning
And know I am far out at sea
That night has gone, day is dawning
And I am with thee, with thee.

And I go out on deck in the sunshine
And the sea is as calm as a lake
See the flying fish far on the starboard
There is no sound the silence to break.

Save the lazy flap-flap of the mainsail
And the voice of the men at their tasks –
O Sea, how I love to be with thee
'Tis all that my tired spirit asks.

And we pace the ship, forard in silence
Your hand clasped in mine, and our eyes
Gazing far on the distant horizon
To the place our future home lies.

And at night, when the stars come out slowly
And we glide ever on in the dark
And the phosphorus floods past like fireballs
There is no sound our silence to mark.

O the peace, and the hush, and the beauty
I would that my sea life would last
And I left all my Soul in the Tropics
And my heart 'tis bound up in the past.

# *Unbound Papers*

[MS-Papers-4006–12]

A Common Ballad.
Sabbath Afternoon. – 13.v.06

Outside is the roar of London town
But we have pulled the sun blinds down
And are as snug as snug can be
Chaddie[79] and me.

She lying on the empty bed
Her book half covering up her head
And very much "en déshabille"
Chaddie - not me.

I – sitting here to write to you
And looking like a stocking blue
We both are longing for our tea
Chaddie & me.

But we're not really learned tho'
This poem sounds as if we're so
And with our grammar we're most free
Chaddie & me.

Our sister – with her face all red
Has gone to see her Ma instead
Well – she is she, & we are we
Chaddie & me.

Far better here to quietly stay
And eat & yawn away the day
We'll end by going to the d - - -
Chaddie & me.

She now is very fast asleep
God grant her hair in waves will keep
But no one is so sweet as we
Chaddie and me.

-----

[79]Chaddie is KM's sister Charlotte Mary Beauchamp (1887–1966).

# Notebook 39

[Notebook 39, qMS-1243]

To Kathleen Beauchamp
from
Clara F. Wood[80]
In very affectionate remembrance of 41 Harley Street
July 14th 1906

Ka nui taku aroha ki a [...][81]

Die Wege des Lebens.

To be premature is to be perfect.

O.W.[82]

Greek dress was in its essence inartistic. Nothing should reveal the body but the body itself.

O.W.

Genius in a woman is the mystic laurel of Apollo springing from the soft breast of Daphne. It hurts in the growing and sometimes breaks the heart from which it springs.

M.C.

Through the tense silence came floating a long sweet passionate cry of pain – a shivering moan that touched the edge of Joy. The ceaseless craving of the finite for the infinite which is and ever shall be – the great chorale of Life.

M.C.

To acknowledge the presence of Fear is to give birth to Failure.

K.M.

Me marier et avoir des enfants! Mais quelle blanchisseuse – je veux la gloire.

Marie Bashkirtseff. Russian.

---

[80] The compounders (boarders) at Queen's College lived with and were in the charge of Miss Clara Wood at 41 Harley Street. This inscription is in Miss Wood's hand.

[81] Māori for 'With much love to'. The name is illegible.

[82] In the following quotations and observations 'K.M.', 'A Woman', and 'A.W.' are all KM herself. These, with the Oscar Wilde quotes, comprise more than half the total quotations. KM probably enjoyed the similarity of the attributions 'A.W.' and 'O.W.'

It is one of Nature's general rules – and part of her habitual injustice – that "to him that hath shall be given – but from him that hath not shall be taken even that which he hath."

> J.S.M.

"The dark lantern of the Spirit which none see by, but those that bear it."
The mere cessation of Existence is no evil to anyone; the idea is only formidable through the illusion of imagination which makes one conceive oneself as if one were alive and feeling oneself dead.

> J.S.M.

It is possible to have a strong self-love without any self-satisfaction, rather with a self-discontent which is the more intense because one's own little cover of egoistic sensibility is a supreme cover.

> G.E.

Genius itself is not en règle; it comes into the world to make new rules.

> G.E.

A man who speaks effectively through Music is compelled to something more difficult than parliamentary eloquence.

> G.E.

Among the heirs of Art – as at the division of the Promised Land – each has to win his portion by hand fighting. The bestowal is a matter of prophecy – and is a title without possession.

Any great achievement in acting or in music grows with the growth. Whenever an artist has been able to say "I came, I saw, I conquered" it has been at the end of patient practise. Genius is at first little more than a great capacity for receiving discipline. Your muscles, your whole frame must go like a watch – true, true, true, true to a hair.[83]

> G.E.

Il est plus aisé de connaître l'homme en général que de connaître un homme en particulier.

> La Rochefoucauld.

If anyone should importune me to give a reason why I loved him, I feel it could not otherwise be expressed than by making answer 'Because it was he; because it was I.' There is beyond what I say, I know not what inexplicable and inevitable power that brought on this union.

> Montaigne.

The strongest man is he who stands most alone.

> Henrik Ibsen.

It is only <u>men</u> who can hear of death without thinking of mourning and the blinds.

> Merriman.

---

[83]Slipped under the binding thread of this page is a newspaper cutting in which 'our London correspondent' writes that 'Arnold Trowell, a clever young New Zealand 'cellist, who has won fame all over Europe, is to make his debut before a London audience in April.' ('Arnold Trowell' was the stage name of KM's friend Tom Trowell.)

Happy people are never brilliant. It implies friction.

K.M.

Be as one that knoweth, and yet holdeth his tongue.

In nature there are no rewards or punishments; there are consequences.

The future comes not from before to meet us, but streams up from behind – over our heads!

Sound can create colour and atmosphere.

H.V.

What mankind thinks venial it is hardly ever supposed that God looks upon in a serious light - at least by those who feel in themselves any inclination to practise it.

J.S.M.

It is not naturally, or generally, the happy who are most anxious for a prolongation of this present life - or for a life hereafter; it is those who have never been happy.

J.S.M.

- - - it is no unnatural part of the idea of a happy life that life itself is to be laid down, after the best that it can give has been fully enjoyed through a long lapse of time, when all its pleasures, even those of benevolence, are familiar, and <u>nothing</u> <u>untasted</u> & <u>unknown</u> is left to stimulate curiosity and keep up the desire of prolonged existence.

J.S.M.

Push everything as far as it will go.

O.W.

The old despise everything, the middle aged believe everything, the young know everything.

O.W.

To love madly, perhaps, is not wise, yet should you love madly it is far wiser than not to love at all.

M.M.

People who learn only from experience do not allow for intuition.

A.H.H.

No life is spoiled but one whose growth is arrested.

O.W.

We are not sent into the world to air our moral prejudices.

O.W.

If you want to mar a nature you have merely to reform it.

O.W.

The only way to get rid of a temptation is to yield to it.

O.W.

Conscience and cowardice are really the same things.
Conscience is the trade mark of the firm. That is all.

O.W.

The value of an idea has nothing whatever to do with the sincerity of the man who expresses it.

O.W.

To realise one's nature perfectly - that is what each of us is here for.

O.W.

The mind of the thoroughly well informed man is a dreadful thing. It is like a bric-a-brac shop - all monsters and dust & everything priced above its proper value.

O.W.     [J2-5]

Let us bathe - on our brows let us twine
The roses & sup
No water to temper the wine
Though deep be the cup.
For Desire is a pleasure that ends
And when it is past
Old age & the parting from friends
And death at last.

From the Greek of Paton[84]

"That which lies deepest is the longest sought,
"That which lies highest is the latest found,
"That which lies dearest is the dearest bought,
"That which is truest is the hardest taught
"That which is noblest has the widest bound.     1907.

I am that which is.
No mortal man dare lift the veil.
He is alone of himself & to him alone do all men owe their being.
Religion of Beethoven - August 1905.

Realise your Youth while you have it. Don't squander the gold of your days listening to the tedious, trying to improve the hopeless failure, or giving away your life to the ignorant, the common or the vulgar, which are the aims, the false ideals of our Age. Live! Live the wonderful Life that is in you. Let nothing be lost upon you. Be always reaching for New Sensations . . . Be afraid of nothing.

O.W.

Ambition is a curse if you are not armour-proof against everything else, unless you are willing to sacrifice yourself to your ambition.

A Woman.

---

[84]WR Paton (d 1921) was the editor and translator of *Anthology of Love Poetry of the Greek*, 1898.

It cannot be possible to go through all the abandonment of Music – and care humanly for anything human afterwards.

A Woman.

All Musicians, no matter how insignificant, come to life emasculated of their power to take life seriously. It is not one man or woman but the complete octave of sex that they desire …

A.W.

You feel helpless under the yoke of creation.

A.W.

Nature makes such fools of us! What is the use of liking anyone if a washerwoman can do exactly the same thing? Well, this is Nature's trick to ensure population.

A.W.

To have the courage of your excess – to find the limit of yourself!

A.W.

Most women turn to salt, looking back.

A.W.

Big people have always entirely followed their own inclinations. Why should one remember the names of people who do what everyone else does? To break a law with success is to be illustrious.

A.W.

And wealth is for brains & the brave; for those who can get it its there to be got. Those who haven't got it are – generally speaking – fools.

O.W.

I do not want to earn a living, I want to live.

O.W.

You suspend yourself from the heights of an inspiration and rebound in sickening jolts from cathedral pinnacles to the mud on the street.
A.W.

It will be a hideous world when everything is permitted. Our nerves can't supply all the dynamics. We need laws to break in order to give our vitality exercise.

A.W.

A woman really cannot understand Music till she has had the actual experience of those laboriously concealed things which are evidently the foundation of them all …

A.W.

The translation of an emotion into act is its death – its logical end … But […] this way isn't the act of unlawful things. It is the curiosity of our own temperament, the deliberate expression of our own tendencies, the welding into an Art of act or incident some raw emotion of the blood. For we castrate our minds to the extent by which we deny our bodies.

O.W.

Comme une fleur que le veut chasse
Et qui vient à nos pieds mourir,
Aussi tout passe - tout s'éfface
Excepté le souvenir.

March 30th 1907.
Selections from Dorian Gray.
Being natural is simply a pose, and the most irritating pose I know.
- - - I like persons with no principles better than anything else in the world.
The worst of having a romance of any kind is that it leaves one so unromantic.
Those who are faithful know only the trivial side of love; it is the faithless who
know love's tragedies! All influence is immoral - immoral from the scientific
point of view. Nothing can cure the soul but the senses - just as nothing can
cure the senses but the soul.     [J10-12]

June 1st 1907. Day's Bay.[85]
And another change. I sit in the small poverty stricken sitting room - the one
and only room which the cottage contains with the exception of a cabin like
bedroom fitted with bunks, and an outhouse with a bath, and wood cellar,
coal cellar, complete. On one hand is the sea stretching right up the yard,
on the other the bush growing close down almost to my front door.     [J12]

Sunday night.
I am here, almost dead with cold, almost dead with tiredness. I cannot sleep
because the end has come with such suddenness that even I who have
anticipated it so long and so thoroughly, am shocked & overwhelmed. She[86] is
tired. Last night I spent in her arms, and tonight I hate her - which being
interpreteth meaneth that I adore her, that I cannot lie in my bed and not feel
the magic of her body. Which means that Sex seems as nothing to me. I feel
more powerfully all those so termed sexual impulses with her than I have with
any men. She enthrals, enslaves me, and her personal self, her body absolute, is
my worship. I feel that to lie with my head on her breast is to feel what Life
can hold. All my troubles, my wretched fears, are swept away. Gone are the
recollections of Caesar & Adonis, gone the terrible banality of my life.
Nothing remains except the shelter of her arms. And of course a week ago
I could have borne all this because I had never known what it truly was to love
& be loved, to adore passionately - but now I feel that if she is denied me I
must - the soul of me goes into the streets and craves love of the casual
stranger, begs & prays for a little of the precious poison. I am half mad with
love. She is positively at present - above my music even - everything. And now

[85] While the girls were at school in London their father arranged for a cottage to be built on a rocky
promontory (Downes Point, Day's Bay) across the harbour from Wellington. It was the Beauchamps'
holiday retreat, and today, extended and modernised, it is still lived in.
[86] 'She', referred to here, is KM's friend Edith Bendall ('EKB') (1879–1985).

she is going. Anticipation has become Realisation – the Bubble has proved its fairy origin. And this is really my last experience of the kind – my last – I cannot bear it any longer. It really kills my soul, each time I feel it more deeply, because each time the wound is stabbed afresh and the knife probes new flesh and reawakens tortures in the old.

Beside me burns the steady flame of the candle – golden and like a blossom – but if I sit here long enough it will shrink down and flicker & die. And so is Life, and so, above all, is Love – a vague transitory fleeting thing, & Pessimism gaunt & terrible stares me in the face, & I cling to old illusions. I am in love with rainbows & crystal glasses. The rainbow fades & the glass is splintered into 1000 diamond fragments. Where are they scattered – in the immensity of the sky, to the four winds of heaven – gone – – –

In my life – so much Love in imagination, in reality 18 barren years. Never pure spontaneous affectionate impulse. Adonis was – dare I seek into the heart of me – nothing but a pose. And now she comes, and pillowed against her, clinging to her hands, her face against mine, I am child, woman, and more than half man.[87]    [J12–13][88]

Outside the sea is washing fully with the sound of perfect harmony the barren waste of grey sand & heavy rock. So she has done. I have felt the cool healing flowing on the water, the smoothing of the rough parts, the white foam, the green coolness, and now again blazing sun & a frantic barrenness. I cannot sleep, I shall not sleep again. This is madness, I know, but it is too real for sanity, it is too swiftly incredible to be doubted. Once again I must bear this changing of the tide – my life is a Rosary of Fierce Combats for Two, each bound together with the powerful magnetic chain of Sex. And, at the end, does the emblem of the crucified hang – surely – – – I do not know & I do not wish to look, but I am so shocked with grief that I feel I cannot continue my hard course of loving and being unloved – of giving loves only to find them flung back at me, faded, worm eaten. Bah! What is the next move I wonder – my death, my resignation, or my Passivity. It will not last. I snap my fingers at Fate. I will not dance to the Music of the Marionettes. Damn it all! I suppose it ends. I cannot remain tragic?

And then, noises began to creep so close that I went back to the bedroom, & in the darkness leaned out of the window. She slept peacefully. I could not wake her – I tried to but without avail, and each moment my horror of everything seemed to increase. In the yard the very fence became terrible. As I stared at the posts they became hideous forms of Chinamen[89] – most vivid and terrible. They leant idly against nothing, their legs crossed,

---

[87]KM wrote 'I am a child, a woman' (as in Murry's transcription) but then immediately crossed out the two 'a's.

[88]Murry's note in his edition: 'After an indecipherable page the journal becomes legible again.' In fact, the pages he omitted here are less indecipherable than many he tackled and published.

[89]Under the racist policies of the New Zealand Government in the late 1890s and early 1900s it was not unusual for children to have superstitious fears of 'Chinamen'.

their heads twitching. It was fearfully cold. I leaned further out and watched one figure - he bent & mimicked & wriggled, then his head rolled off & under the house - it rolled round & round: a black ball - a cat perhaps - it leapt into space. I looked at the figure again - it was crucified, hung lifeless before me, yet sneering. Silence profound - this was too awful. I took off my dressing gown & slippers & sat on the edge of the bed, trembling, half crying, hysterical with grief. Somehow silently she woke, & came over to me, took me again into the shelter of her arms. We lay down together still silently, she every now & then pressing me to her, kissing me, my head on her breasts, her hands round my body, stroking me lovingly, warming me, [...]-ing to give me more life again. Then her voice whispering "Better now darling?" I could not answer with words. And again "I suppose you could not tell me. . ." I drew close to her warm sweet body, happier than I had ever been than I could ever have imagined being, the Past once more buried - clinging to her & wishing that this darkness might last for ever - - -

Never is the feeling of possession so strong I thought. Here there can be but one person with her. Here by a thousand delicate suggestions I can absorb her - for the time. What an experience, & when we returned to town small wonder that I could not sleep but tossed to & fro, & yearned, & realised - a thousand things which had been obscure - - - O Oscar! Am I peculiarly susceptible to sexual impulse? I must be I suppose, but I rejoice. Now each time I see her I want her to put her arms round me & hold me against her. I think she wants to too, but she is afraid, & Custom hedges her in, I feel. We shall go away again & more weekend [...]

i.vi.07.     [J13–14]

This afternoon a man is coming to see me, to bring his 'cello, to hear me play, and now that the moment est arrivé I do not want to see him. He is bloated, lover of a thousand actresses, roamer of every city under the sun, wealthy, bachelor, and yesterday when I met him I behaved like a fool - simply for no reason. He traded[?] by asking to call today - now he comes. Kathie you are a hideous lunatic. He has such a miserably unintellectual head. No - I'm glad about the whole affair. I shall pervert it - - - make it fascinating.

June 25th. I hate everybody, loathe myself, loathe my Life and love Caesar. Each week - sometimes every day, tout dépends - when I think of that fascinating cult which I wish to absorb me I come to the conclusion that all this shall truly end. Liberty - no matter what the cost, no matter what the trial. I begin hideously unhappy, make God knows how many resolves - and then break them! One day I shall not do so - - - I shall "strike while the iron is white hot" - and praise Myself and my unconquerable soul. From the amethyst outlook my situation is devilishly fascinating, but it cannot be permanent - the charm consists mainly in its instability. It has existed long enough - I must wander. I cannot - will not - build a house upon any damned rock. But money - money - money is what I need and do not possess. I find a resemblance in myself to John Addington Symonds.[90]

The day is white with frost - a low blue mist lingers daintily among the pine avenue. It is very cold, and there is a sharp sound of carts passing. Quite early, too. A train whistle sounds, a tram passes at the end of the street, the maids are putting away crockery. Downstairs in the Music Room the 'cello is dreaming. I wonder if it shall be under the hand of its Maestro. I think not.

Well a year has passed. What has happened. London behind me, Mimi[91] behind me, Caesar gone. My music has gained, become a thing of 10000 times more beauty & strength. I myself have changed - rather curiously. I am colossally interesting to myself. One fascinating Day has been mine. My friend sent me Dorian.

And I have written a book of child verse - how <u>absurd</u>. But I am very glad - it is too exquisitely unreal. And while my thoughts are redolent of Purple Fancies and the white sweetness of gardenias, I present the world "with this elegant thimble" - - I have been engaged to a young Englishman for three weeks because his figure was so beautiful. I have been tediously foolish many times - especially with Oscar Fox and Siegfried Eichelbaum[92] - but that is past. This year coming will be memorable. It will celebrate the culmination of the cult - the full flowering of the Gardenia. This time next year I shall have been [with?] Mimi again.

Evening. All the morning I played - very difficult music - & was happy. In the afternoon came Caesar's Father & Mother & Sister. Caesar's Father[93] & I played. I was unhappy. I did not play well - my hand & wrist hurt me horribly and I did not feel that glorious hidden well of Music deep in me. I was - too - sad - Caesar's Father depressed me. I felt that something was making him suffer, & I knew what it was, so I suffered too, but thought of, spoke of this strange Master of me, all the time. I gave them a great bouquet of camelias to take home. I played a whole Bach concerto by sight, and Mr T. had copied for me something beautiful. I am glad that it came into my life today. Then in the Abenddämmerung I went out in to the streets. It was so beautiful - the full moon was like a strain of music heard through a closed door - mist over everything, the hills mere shadows tonight. I became terribly unhappy, almost wept in the street, and yet Music enveloped me - again -

---

[90]John Addington Symonds (1840–1893) was an aesthete, essayist, Renaissance historian, critic and poet *manqué*. His energies were dissipated first by his long tormented struggle to conceal and deny his homosexual nature, and, second, by the tuberculosis with which he was diagnosed at the age of 25 and which compelled him to spend his last years in the Swiss Alps. It is unlikely that KM knew of his homosexuality since Horatio F Brown's two volume biography of Symonds (1895) suppressed it.

[91]Mimi was the nickname of Vere Bartrick-Baker, a close friend at school in London.

[92]Oscar Fox has not been identified. Siegfried Eichelbaum (1886–1952) was a student at Victoria College of the University of New Zealand who was noted for his gift of witty repartee. Although he was later admitted as a barrister and solicitor of the Supreme Court he spent most of his working life in business. What part he played, if any, in the tedious foolishness of 1907 is not known, but he did possess, keep for many years, and proudly display, a dance programme from those days on which KM had written her name.

[93]Caesar's father, Thomas Trowell senior, was the music teacher from whom KM took 'cello lessons.

caught me, held me, thank Heaven. I could have died. I should be dead but for that, I know. I sent Mr T. a beautiful book - something that I truly treasure.

It is just eight o'clock. Perhaps, somewhere in the world, he is waking or dressing, or playing or eating breakfast - and I am here. Well, greetings, Caesar, and a happy day to you. A letter from me arrives in London today. It is extraordinary to live so far away from one's other self, and yet each day to feel nearer - so I feel. Everything about him seems to be made plain - now. I think of him in any every situation, and feel that I understand him too. He must always be everything to me - the one man whom I can call Master and Lover too, and though I know I shall have many fascinating connections in my Life none will be like this - so lasting, so deep, so everything - because he poured into my virgin soul the Life essence of Music - - Never an hour passes free from his influence. I love him - but I wonder, with all my soul - And here is the kernel of the whole matter - the Oscar-like thread.

I want to practically celebrate this day by beginning to write a book. In my brain, as I walk each day, as I dress, as I speak, or even before playing my 'cello, a thousand delicate images float and are gone. I want to write a book - that is unreal yet wholly possible because out of the question - that raises in the hearts of the readers emotions, sensations too vivid not to take effect, which causes a thousand delicate tears, a thousand sweet chimes of laughter. I shall never attempt anything approaching the histrionic, and it must be ultra modern. I am sitting right over the fire as I write, dreaming, my face hot with the coals. Far away a steamer is calling, calling, and - God God - my restless soul.

Here, my Friend it is Winter.
June 29th.
I do not think that I shall ever be able to write any Child Verse again. The faculty has gone - I <u>think</u>. What a charming morning I have passed! with the Violinist & the Singer. She has a curious resemblance to Mark Hambourg[94] - the completely musical face - - We sat in the Violinist's room - the curtains blew in and out the window, & the violets in a little glass, blue & white, were beautiful. And I am sure they both loved me. But this afternoon has been horrible. E.K.B. bored me. I bored her. I felt unhappy, and I think so did she - but she never took the initiative.      [J14-17]

And now E.K.B. is a thing of the Past, absolutely, irrevocably.[95] Thank Heaven! It was, I consider retrospectively, a frantically maudlin relationship, & one better ended - also she will not achieve a great deal of greatness. She has not the necessary impetus of character.

Do other people of my own age feel as I do I wonder so absolutely powerful <u>licentious</u>, so almost physically ill. I alone in this silent clock filled room have become powerfully - - - I want Maata. I want her as I have had

---

[94]Mark Hambourg (1879–1960) was a Russian born pianist who had become a British subject and whom KM much admired.
[95]This piece, down to 'Russian novel' occupies one page in the top margin of which Murry has written 'I omitted this – deliberately. 11.3.54.'

her – terribly. This is unclean I know but true. What an extraordinary thing – I feel savagely crude, and almost powerfully enamoured of the child. I had thought that a thing of the Past. Heigh Ho!!!!!!!!!! My mind is like a Russian novel.

Sunday 11.viii.07.[96]
Beloved – tho' I do not see you know that I am yours – every thought, every feeling in me belongs to you. I wake in the morning and have been dreaming of you, and all through the day while my outer life is going on steadily, monotonously, even drearily, my inner life I live with you – in leaps and bounds – I go through with you every phase of emotion that is possible – loving you. To me you are man, lover, artist, husband, friend – giving me all, & I surrendering you all – everything. And so this loneliness is not so terrible to me because in reality my outer life is but a phantom life – a world of intangible meaningless grey shadow. My inner life pulsates with sunshine and Music & Happiness – unlimited vast unfathomable wells of Happiness and You. One day we shall be together again and then – and then only – I shall realise myself, shall come to my own. Because I feel – I have always felt – that you hold in your hands just those closing final bars which leave my life song incomplete – because you are to me more necessary than anything else. Nothing matters, nothing is while you usurp my life. O let it remain as it is. Do not suddenly crush out this one beautiful flower. I am afraid, even while I am rejoicing.

But whatever happens – tho' you marry another, tho we never meet again – I belong to you, we belong to each other. And whenever you want me, with both my hands I say – unashamed, fiercely proud, exultant, triumphant, satisfied at last – "take me". Each night I go to sleep with your letters under my pillow & in the darkness I stretch out my hands & clasp the thin envelope close to my body so that it lies there warmly, & I smile in the darkness and sometimes my body aches as though with fatigue – but I understand.

Kätherine Schönfeld.     [J17–18]

August 15th.
She unpacked her box[97] and then went into the sitting room. She was in a curious vague mood, wandering about the room, opening the piano, striking a chord and shutting it again, taking up the books from the table and putting them back, staring out of the window at the heavy grey rain and the poor draggled line of houses, then staring at her own reflection in the glass over the mantelpiece. She leant both her elbows on the mantelpiece and spoke to the face. "Well" she said, "are you feeling better – less insufferably bored, less

---

[96]Draft of a letter to Thomas (Arnold) Trowell.
[97]See note 56.

hideously foolish. And in a week's time you will be married to him. How does
that appeal to you now. Yes, my dear, I know it seemed inevitable out there -
away - out there, but now - are you glad you came or are you still haunted
with the idea of that miserable David." Bah! She tossed back her hair.
"I despise you - do cease being a child and look things in the face.
What matter if you do love him so much - he does not care a ½ stamp for
you, and Philip does - or for what he thinks is you." She laughed, bitterly,
and the tears rushed into her eyes. "I'm ruining my life - that's the long and
short of it" she said. "My beautiful Ideals, Resolutions, theories, are as dead
as my fiddle playing - - - & I am wrapt up in conventional feminine
thoughts - - -" The face in the glass was sullen, the brows drawn together,
yet the mouth quivering - - - "O how I hate it" she said, in a curiously dull
even toneless voice - "how I hate myself and - and my head aches. Poof! I feel
suffocated. I want cigarets. After all this exquisite respectability - to smoke
again, and read again, and sit over the fire until I like, and no maid -
or anything."

She ran into the bedroom & put on a long coat & fur cap - no gloves
she decided, and no veil, no umbrella, but just a fine fresh poverty-stricken
feeling. She ran down the narrow stairs, along the passage, and into the street.
The wind blew in great gusts. There was a pungent smell of sea water.
Her hair curled darkly round her face. "O" she said, almost running a little,
"O how fine this is." She took in great draughts of the fresh air. It seemed to
intoxicate her. With her hands in her pockets and her head thrown back she
walked with the wind full in her face. The sense of physical struggle seemed
such a blessed relief - such a beautifully simple thing after all this mental
fighting. "I'm alive again" she said, and laughed aloud. There were few people
in the streets. She found a tobacconists & bought a packet of State Express
Cig. & a copy of the evening paper. Coming back to her rooms the sky ahead
was banked with purple clouds. Yet to her it was full of suggestion and promise
- - She felt almost too strong - capable of anything - capable of pushing down
the houses if she stretched out her hands - like a giant, and O the friendly
buffeting wind, the laughing splashing rain.

Up the stairs again and back into the sitting room. The blinds had been
pulled down & a lamp stood on the table. A little tea was spread - a boiled egg,
a teapot to herself, a little roll of bread. It looked so delicious and homely
Anna could hardly wait to take off her hat & coat & wash her hands. "The
teapot allures me" she said "and the egg beckons & the roll calls & cries, and
O I am hungry, and I'll read the paper while I'm eating." She spread out the
crisp white sheet, and suddenly a wave of colour seemed to rush over her
whole body. Something within her, some numbed part of her, woke to fierce
life. "O God" said Helena [sic], crushing the paper in her hands. Then she read
it again - David Rositter - only Violin Recital - in the Assembly Hall tonight
at 7.30. Anna glanced over at the clock - it was barely seven. I shall get ready
now, she said. In the dark bedroom while she was feeling for her outdoor
clothes she whispered to herself. "David, David" said Anna, "here we are

again, dear, you see – thrown together. It's all in the lap of the Gods David,
and I promise this shall truly be the last time. But before I die, dear, I'm going
to have a fling – I must <u>hear</u> you. I don't want to, but I must & nothing
matters at all but – <u>beloved</u>." She groped her way over to the window,
& kneeling down, her chin in her hands, peered out into the darkness.
Silence at first, and then faintly, but fully – a wonderful agitating sound –
the call of her savage lawless Mother – the sea. She listened – it came again
and again, and each time it seemed to sweep over her and carry away all the
shifting clinging hypocrises which had wrapt her round – and she, Anna,
was living again – understanding – <u>feeling</u>. How she felt! In my heart, she said,
I am praying, praying – I'm sick of everything, but I belong to you now.

August 20th 1907.
Rain beating upon the windows, and a windstorm violent & terrible. I came
up into my room to go to bed and suddenly, half undressed, I began thinking
& looking at Caesar's portrait, and wondering. And I felt that I could have
written:"Beloved, I could bury my face in the pillow & weep & weep
& weep. Here it is night & winter rain. You are in a glory of Summer and
daylight, the thunder of traffic, the call of life. I must possess it too. I must
suffer & conquer. I must leave here – I cannot look ahead into the long
unutterable grey vastnesses of Misty Future years. Do you know that you are
all in all – you <u>are</u> my Life. I am tired & miserable tonight, so forgive me –
I am sick of Winter darkness & I want to laugh & I want to listen."
    Words will not be found, but how I <u>felt</u> – & now to bed, hopefully to lie
& look into the darkness & think & weave beautiful scarlet patterns, & <u>hope</u>
to dream. My 'cello is better, but I fancy Mr Trowell is annoyed with me.
That must not happen. What is to become of us <u>all</u>. I am so eager – & yet –
that is all. Buon riposo.

August 27th. A happy day. I have spent a perfect day. Never have I loved
Mr Trowell so much, or felt so in accord with him, and my 'cello expressing
everything. This morning we played Weber's Trio – tragic, fiercely dramatic,
full of rhythm and accent and close shade. And then this afternoon I became
frightened. I felt that I had nothing to play, that I could not touch the
Concerti, that I had not improved. How horrible it was – yet the sunlight lay
on the music room floor, and my 'cello was warm to touch. He came, and in
one instant we understood each other and I think he was happy. O joyous
time – it was almost inhuman, and to hear that "Bravely done – you've a real
good grip of it all – very good." I would not have exchanged those words for
all the laurel wreaths in existence. And to end with a Weber Fugue passage for
first violin and then 'cello. It bit into my blood. Après we had tea and currant
buns in the Smoking Room and ate to the accompaniment of the Fugue.
And discussed – Marriage and Music – the mistake that a woman makes ever
to think that she is first in a musician's estimation – it must inevitably be first
His Art. I know I understand. And also – talk of sympathy. If I marry Caesar –
and I thought of him all the time – I think I could prove a great many things.

Mr Trowell said she must share his glories and always keep him on the heights.
Curiously Christian[?] [...] came before me - - - and Adelaida[98] & edelweiss.
He could not infuse enough Love into his voice this afternoon, nor I for
him - - - Good evening, my beloved - tonight I shall speak through
your Music.

Aug 28th. I had a letter from Adelaida today about Arnold Trowell, and at
present I have no idea how I felt. First, so sorrowful, so hurt, so pained,
that I contemplated the most outrageous things; now only <u>old</u> and angry
and lonely, & as though everything except my 'cello had lost its interest
for me. Now which is it to be. Shall I applaud him in his manner of living.
Shall I say - do as you please, live as you like, see Life, gain Experience,
increase your outlook. Or shall I condemn it. This is how I think - it's a great
pity that Artists do live so, but as they do - <u>well</u> - - but I shall not.        [J18-19]

Talk of Art!! Ah! I am in Heaven. I have been with Fritz Rupp[99] the Opera
Singer. He has played, sang, acted, spoken. My sadness is gone,[100] is a thing of
the past. While such men live I am happy. O Man you give me life. I felt my
body vibrate to his singing. He is a true Musician. His eyes, his face, his look,
he plays everything - Rigoletto, Wagner, Walkure, Saint-Saiens. Life - Life - it
is playing past me in a torrent of divine melody. Keep me at it. Keep me at it.
Let me too become a great Musician. They are my people, by a glance we
understand each other. There is fresh impetus. I adore them.

2nd Sep.
O let me lift it - even ever so slightly. It hangs before me - even, heavy,
motionless - this curtain, this which holds the Future. Let me just hold a
corner up & peep beyond, then maybe I shall be content to let it fall.
    They[101] leave N.Z., all of them <u>my</u> people, <u>my</u> Father - it has come of
course. I used to think - as long as they are here I can bear it - & now? I shall
somehow or other go too. You just see!

6th. I am frightened and trying to be brave. This is the greatest and most
terrible torture that I have ever thought of enduring, but I can have courage,
face him bravely with my head high, and <u>fight</u> - for Life, absolutely. O what
can happen. Help, support.[102] Here at least I am standing terribly absolutely
alone. What can I do. O what can happen. Shall it be Heaven or shall it be
Hell. I <u>must</u> win - but I first must face the guns resolutely. It is no good
shrinking behind these hedges and great stones, remaining in the shadow.

---

[98]'Adelaida' was one of KM's names for Ida Constance Baker (LM), her school friend and life long
companion.
    [99]The George Musgrove Grand Opera Company had a 12 night season in Wellington from the 19th
of August 1907. Reviews were mixed and of the only two singers who were consistently praised Herr Fritz
Rupp was one. 'A singer of first rank'. 'An artist never at fault'.
    [100]In the top margin here Murry wrote 'I omitted this because I did not understand a crucial
word. 11.3.54.'
    [101]ie the Trowell family.
    [102]Murry put brackets round 'O what can happen. Help, support.' and wrote in the margin '? O what
can happen. Omitted. 11.3.54.'

In the full glare I must go to Death or life. Now is the time to prove myself.
Now is the fulfilment of all my philosophy and my knowledge. Think only
what it means for a moment, think of that and then do not mind if the enemy
fire and fire again. You have the magic suit of mail. Belief in the outcome
clothes you but be firm and rational and calm - & at last learn that you must
go forth into the great battle with a strong heart. I cannot longer stay in the
shadow tho. My heart is <u>hurting</u> me with FEAR. Here is the supreme crisis -
here is the 9th wave. If it goes over my head I must rise & shake the water out
of my eyes and hair - and plunge in. O - Victory must be mine. With both
hands I embrace the thought. Help Help - stand firm & let the music crash
& deafen. It cannot hide the beating of my heart.

 O Kathleen, I pity you, but I see that it had to come, this great wrench.
In your life you are always a coward until the very last moment, but here is the
greatest thing of your Life. Prove yourself strong. Dearest I hold your two
hands & my eyes look full into yours - trustingly, firmly, resolutely, full of
supreme calm, hope, and illimitable Belief. You must be a woman now & bear
the agony of creating. Prove yourself. Be strong, be kind, be wise, and it is
yours. Do not at the last moment lose courage - argue wisely & quietly.
Be more man than woman. Keep your brain perfectly clear. Keep your
balance!!!! Convince your Father that it is "la seule chose". Think of the
Heaven that might be yours, that [is] before you after this fight. They stand
& wait for you with outstretched hands, & with a glad cry you fall into their
arms - the Future Years. Good luck my precious one - I love you.   [J19-20]

We really <u>must</u>.
O I have a glorious subject for a Vignette. Have you the Smart Set,[103] asked the
girl in the bookshop.

21.X.07.
Damn my family - O Heavens, what bores they are. I detest them all heartily.
I shall certainly not be here much longer - thank Heaven for that! Even when
I am alone in a room they come outside the door and call to each other -
discuss the butchers orders or the soiled linen, and, I feel, wreck my life.
It is so humiliating. And this morning I do not wish to write but to read
Marie Bashkirtseff. But if they enter the room & find me <u>merely</u> with a
book their tragic complaining looks upset me altogether.

 Here in my room I feel as though I was in London. O London - to write
the word makes me feel that I could burst into tears. Isn't it terrible to love
anything so much. I do not care at all for men - but <u>London</u> - it is Life.
These creatures, May N.[104] & E. K. who try to play with me, they are fools
and I despise them both. I am longing to consort with my superiors. What is it
with me? Am I absolutely nobody but merely inordinately vain. I do not know
- but I am most fearfully unhappy, that is all. I am so unhappy that I wish I was
dead - yet I should be mad to die when I have not yet lived <u>at all</u>.

---

[103]'The Smart Set', was an American literary periodical with an English edition published in London.
[104]Murry has pencilled 'May Newman' above this on the manuscript.

Well, I have sat here for two hours and read – my right hand is quite cold. She is a young fool, and I detest her. As she comes into the room I put down Marie & seize my pen. She leans against the door rattling the handle and says – are you writing a colossal thing or an ordinary thing or anything exciting. How completely inane! I tell her to leave the room <u>at once</u>. Now if this door would open & Mimi walk in – Mimi or Ida or my charming Gwen[105] – how happy I should be – with all three I can be myself. Outside the window there is a lumbering sound of trams and an insipid sound of birds song. Now here comes tea & I yield to the temptation – <u>as usual</u>.

I am so eternally thankful that I did not allow J– to kiss me – I am constantly hearing of him, and I feel to meet him would be horrible. But why? It is ridiculous – I used him merely for copy. I am always so supremely afraid of appearing ridiculous. The feeling is fostered by Oscar who has so absolutely the essence of savoir faire. . I like to appear in any society entirely at my ease, conscious of my own importance – which in my estimation is unlimited – affable, and very receptive. I like to appear slightly condescending, very much of la grand monde, & to be the centre of interest. Yes, but quelque fois to my unutterable chagrin, unmistakable shyness seizes me. Isn't it ludicrous – I become conscious of my hands and slightly inclined to blush.

22nd. I thank Heaven that at present, though I am damnable, I am in love with nobody – except <u>myself</u>.        [J21–22]

> My dear Mr Trowell,
>     I cannot let you leave without telling you how grateful I am, and must be all my life, for what you have done for me, and given me. You have shown me that there is something so immeasurably higher and greater than I had ever realised before in Music, and therefore, too, in Life.
>     Do you know – so many times when you have been with me I have felt that I must tell you that when I came from England, friendless and sorrowful, you changed all my life – – – And Music which meant much to me before in a vague desultory fashion, is now fraught with inner meaning.
>     Please I want you to remember that all my life I am being grateful & happy and proud to have known you. Looking back I have been so stupid and you so patient. I think of that little Canon of Cherubini's as a gate – opened with so much difficulty & leading to so wide a road. I wish you – Everything with both hands and all my heart, & what I look forward to as the greatest joy I can imagine is to share a program with you at a London concert.

Feb 10th.
I shall end of course – by killing myself.

---

[105] Gwen Rouse was a London school friend.

March 15th. I purchase my brilliance with my life. It were better that I were dead, really. I am unlike others because I have experienced all that there is to experience - but there is no one to help me. Of course Oscar - Dorian Gray has brought this S.S. to pass.

May 1st. I am now much worse than ever. Madness must lie this way. Pull yourself Up.      [J36]

May 1908. I have just finished reading a book by Elizabeth Robins "Come & Find Me". Really a clever, splendid book; it creates in me such a sense of power. I feel that I do now realise, dimly, what women in the future will be capable of achieving. They truly, as yet, have never had their chance. Talk of our enlightened days and our emancipated country - pure nonsense. We are firmly held in the self fashioned chains of slavery. Yes - now I see that they <u>are</u> self fashioned and must be self removed. Eh bien - now where is my ideal and ideas of life? Does Oscar - and there is a gardenia yet alive beside my bed - does Oscar still keep so firm a stronghold in my soul? No! Because now I am growing capable of seeing a wider vision - a little Oscar, a little Symons, a little Dolf Wyllarde, Ibsen, Tolstoi, Elizabeth Robins, Shaw, D'Annunzio, Meredith. To weave the intricate tapestry of one's own life it is well to take a thread from many harmonious skeins, and to realise that there must be harmony. Not necessary to grow the sheep, comb the wool, colour and brand it, but joyfully take all that is ready and with that saved time go a great way further. Independence, resolve, firm purpose and the gift of discrimination, <u>mental clearness</u> - here are the inevitables. Again, Will - the realisation that Art is absolutely self development. The knowledge that genius is dormant in every soul, that that very individuality which is at the root of our being is what matters so poignantly.      [J36-37]

Vignette:-
They are a ridiculous company in this brown holland world[106] - an elephant, a white poodle playing the 'cello, a blue jug, agnome in a red cap, a handkerchief [box], a box of matches, and the whole flanked by two gigantic blazing candles - [...] blossoms in a green setting. Tonight I sat in a low chair, smoking, and by and bye I was so silent they forgot me & took life. The dog shook back its braids and started vigorously bowing, the elephant trumpeted wildly, the blue jug settled herself with a great exhibition of snugness, the gnome took off his red cap and fanned himself with it, the handkerchief box yawned, the box of matches shook himself with a crisp vigour that half startled half charmed me, & the candles blazed & flamed & cast strange evil patterns over the brown holland world.

But then, shouted the elephant to the dog "Cease this foolish scraping." He rushed to the unfortunate animal, clasped him and his 'cello in his trunk, shook them & deposited them on the top of the handkerchief box who shrieked feebly & blushed a vivid rose. The blue jug spoke with a compressed spout. "At least attempt to conduct yourselves as gentlemen" she said.

---

[106]'Brown holland' was an unbleached linen fabric.

"This ridiculous nonsense takes place every evening." And the elephant, utterly discomforted, ambled away behind the match box. Heavens how the gnome laughed, stuffing his red cap into his mouth, leering at the dog in a Quilp-like[107] manner. But the matchbox, her palmy days long over, her body scratched & worthless, whispered soft nothings to the elephant. Once when the breeze almost blew out the light of the candles I saw him bend over & kiss her with his trunk - it was an intensely novel proceeding. The dog was playing hey diddle carefully, with one finger. The H.B., a martyr to obesity, was snoring. The gnome was digging the blue jug in the ribs. The elephant sat holding the matchbox in his trunk. The candles blazed when Yvonne entered. She ran across the room and flung a great bouquet of white lilac & roses on the table. "Oh the darkness" said Yvonne, pressing the clicking light button. She sat down, her elbows planted firmly in the brown holland world, her long loose sleeves sweeping to right & to left the dog, the elephant, the handkerchief box, the blue jug, & the matches. "That is so like you" I said, flinging away my cigaret - "You have smothered a whole world with your roses."

---

9 p.m. Sunday Night.   May 17th.   Full Moon.
<u>Now to plan it</u>.
O, Kathleen, do not weave any more of these fearful meshes. You have been so loathsomely unwise. Do take wisdom from all that you have and must still suffer. I really know that you <u>can't</u> stay as you are now. Be good - for the love of God - be good, & brave and do tell the truth more & live a better life. I am tired of all this deceit - and the moon still shines, and the stars are still there. You'd better go & see the Doctor tomorrow about your heart, and then try & solve all the silly drivelling problems. Go anywhere - don't stay here - accept work - fight against people. As it is, with a rapidity unimaginable, you are going to the Devil. PULL UP NOW YOURSELF. It is really most extraordinary that I should feel so confident of dying of heart failure - and entirely Arthur's[108] fault.   [J36]

October 12th. This is my unfortunate month. I dislike exceedingly to have to pass through it - each day fills me with terror.   [J37]

December 21st 1908.
I should like to write a life much in the style of Walter Pater's 'Child in the House'. About a girl in Wellington; the singular charm and barrenness of that place, with climatic effects - wind, rain, spring, night, the sea, the cloud pageantry. And then to leave the place and go to Europe, to live there a dual existence - to go back and be utterly disillusioned, to find out the truth of all,

---

[107]Daniel Quilp was the evil, deformed dwarf in Dickens' *The Old Curiosity Shop*.

[108]Murry's published note stated 'I can trace no character of that name in the hectic drama of Katherine's life at this period.' However, the reference may be to a connection between heart failure and one of KM's forebears—possibly her grandfather, Arthur Beauchamp.

to return to London. to live there an existence so full & so strange that Life itself seemed to greet her, and, ill to the point of death, return to W. & die there. A story, no, it would be a sketch, hardly that, more a psychological study of the most erudite character. I should fill it with climatic disturbance, & also of the strange longing for the artificial. I should call it 'Strife', & the child I should call – Ah, I have it – I'd make her a half caste Maori & call her Maata. Bring into it Warbrick the guide.[109]     [J37-38]

1889                    The Story of Pearl Button.[110]

Life was a very vague scheme of things until Pearl Button went to school in the Spring of 1897 – the 14th of October – her birthday.
Hop Hop.
The door of the class room opened and a little child stepped in. "I think please, Mr Dyer, I'll marry you when I've finished marrying Mr Lee. Will you wait please?" "Oh, yes, I'll wait" said Mr Dyer. "Thank you very much" said P.B. "Mr Dyer" said Pearl Button, "is it afternoon." "Quite late afternoon, Pearl". " Aren't they going to have the singing." "Teacher thought maybe you'd like to be quiet." "Oh no – because – I simply love the singing & its only through the window." Mr Dyer turned to Bridget. "Tell the children little P.B. would like them to sing."
    The child lay silent, watching the shadows chase each other across the ceiling. Mr Dyer noticed a transfer stuck to the little wrist he held & a bead ring on her fourth finger. Her hands were so small – [...] for even a child of her age, & soft. He suddenly remembered the supplejack whipping & almost groaned aloud. Far away Mr Atkinson was mowing the front paddock – the swishing of the scythe seemed to fill the empty sunlit air. Then the sound was lost in the high clear voices of the children that floated through the windows into the room where little Pearl Button was lying so quietly. The child did not move but tears poured down her face. "Oh, Mr Dyer" she said, "That's the song I came to school with. It's my favourite song Mr Dyer."
    Oh Forest green & fair
    Oh Pine trees waving high
    How sweet their cool retreat
    How full of rest.
In the pause which followed the first verse Mr Dyer heard the sharpening of the scythe. "It was rather wobbly[?]" said the child. "I hope they'll sing it again – ah there it is." Once more, but softer, they seemed to be singing to the rhythmic swishing of the scythe. The child closed her eyes & suddenly clung to Mr Dyer's hand. "Isn't it heavingly". And forth into those forests green & fair, in whose bounds no foot has trod, whose pine trees waving high ruffle the

---

[109]Warbrick was the guide on the Urewera camping trip which took place in the previous year and is described in Notebook 2.
    [110]This is not to be confused with KM's published story 'How Pearl Button was Kidnapped' written some years later. In this piece, the date at the beginning, 1889, one year after she herself was born, and 'the 14th of October – her birthday', KM's own birthday, suggest that she had herself in mind.

darkness in their heavy hands, into the forests green & fair [one line illegible] held by the children's voices, wandered the dream-child soul of little Pearl Button & was lost among the shades of that cool retreat.

Oh, Forest green & fair etc.

The door of the class room opened & a little child entered. She stood quite still, soberly staring[?], her pink sunbonnet pushed back from her placid face, in her hands two great paua[111] shells.
"Well" said Teacher, gravely, "have you come with a message." "No" said the child. The class began to laugh but the child did not smile. "You must run away" [Teacher] said. "This is only a place where little girls learn lessons." "Please I've come to school" said the child. "Oh, who sent you." said Teacher. "I – I sent myself." The children screamed with laughter. Here was an extraordinary state of affairs - a child who came to school all by her own self – no Mother to promise her honey for tea if she'd stop holding on like grim death to the gates of the schoolyard, no Father to give you a bit of blue pencil if you walked in like a man hanging your hat on the peg, first time. "What is your name?" asked Teacher.
"Pearl"
"Pearl who? Speak up."
"Pearl Button." This time Teacher smiled.
"What does Mother do?"
"Mother washes."
"And Father?"
"Father – " she paused a moment – "Father doesn't wash."

Expenses.[112]

| | £ | s | d |
|---|---|---|---|
| Tarts | | | 6 |
| Luggage carrier | | | 6 |
| buns | | | 6 |
| Luggage carrier | | 2 | 0 |
| bread & buns | | | 9 |

---

[111]The paua is a large edible mollusc (in the USA, abalone) with an iridescent inner shell.
[112]At the back of the notebook.

# *Unbound Papers*

[NL ts]

## THE GREEN TREE [113]
### A Fairy Tale.

Once upon a time the Boy planted a seed in a little plot of ground that his Father had given him for his very own. And because he shielded it from the rough winds, watered it every evening, built a little glass frame so that it might have the benefit of each ray of sunlight, it sprang out of the warm earth in less time than it takes to tell, a sturdy green twig.

"Come" said the Boy, "this is bound to be Exceedingly Special. I truly believe it will grow into a tall tree." But his Father and Mother and the Neighbours and the Village People laughed and shook with laughter.
"It's a weed, you greenhorn" they cried. "Leave it alone and play football."

The Boy scarcely heard them. Hours he spent each day tending it. At night he dreamed of it, waking sometimes in an agony of fear that a wind had arisen and blown upon it, that a hailstorm had spattered upon its green leaves. But the Tree grew strong and green and beautiful.

The house where the Boy lived was mean and tumble-down, and his Father and Mother had lived there so long that they had grown mean and tumble-down too - the spirit of the Cottage seemed to have grown upon them as a lichen upon an old stone. Indeed, the Boy standing in the garden by his tree and looking at the outside of the house could trace a most curious resemblance - the shrunken door, so like their withered mouths - the blank, uncurtained windows, so like their vacant eyes. Even the projecting porch like the peak of his Father's nose.

"It's quite as good as an enlarged photograph" mused the Boy, nodding gravely.

One summer night, he could not sleep, but lay tossing to and fro upon his narrow bed. The blankets seemed to weigh him down, even the roof, he felt, was pressing upon his forehead. He was like the brown seed longing to burst through all these coverings and out into the cool air, and stretch up and

---

[113]This story cannot be dated but is likely to belong with this early material.

up and up. A little breeze swung the window blinds to and fro, and the tassel tapping on the glass was to him a secret knocking from the garden – a call to come out. He sprang up in his little white nightdress, feeling his way out of the room along the narrow passage, unbolting the low door, and so reaching the splendid magic of the night garden.

Ah, his tree. The boy stood beside it, flung his arms round it, kissed it with his young mouth again and again. It bruised his lips, there was a strange bitter taste in his mouth, and he looked so young and small in his white night-shirt that two stars shot from Heaven into his eyes, and the Moon who was walking through the garden laid her white hands upon his brow, and the nightingale singing upon a rose bush for one moment nestled against his little bosom.

"This is a fairy child" said the Moon. "He belongs to us now." The Boy slept in the garden, and when he woke in the morning on his pale face gleamed the dew like tears, and his heart sang over and over the song of the Nightingale.

That night seemed to be the beginning of his mysterious life with the Green Tree. All the love of his young soul, all the strength of his young body he spent upon it. He grew pale and thin, sleeping but little, speaking hardly at all. His parents at last grew tired of jeering at him. They agreed with the Neighbours and Village People that he was mad and let him be.

"Yet it seems a criminal shame" said the Village people, "that he is not supporting his aged parents instead of growing a tree. Of course it may be beautiful, but that's no reason to spend his life over it. There are forests of trees – so what's the good of that."

But about this time a terrible thing happened. It was winter, and the ground was smothered in snow. The Boy sat by the fire with his parents. He was looking into the fire and thinking, thinking – he did not know of what. Suddenly he listened to his parents speaking together. "We have no money" they said, "no hope of any money, and what shall we do? It is Winter; there is only one thing – to cut down the boy's tree, and sell it for firewood in the village."

He gave a great cry and started up, his face aflame. "You shall not touch a leaf or a twig, I tell you it is mine, you shall not." Words choked him. He looked out of the window; the snow seemed to fall upon his cold heart; terror gripped him with an icy hand. And his beautiful strong tree – bare now, but full of sap – stood outlined against the winter sky. He flung out his arms towards it. "Not a twig shall you touch."

In the early afternoon of the next day the Boy went to the village. Hardly had he left the house when his mother flung on her long cloak and, trembling with excitement, went to the Neighbour's house and told her story.

"You have two strong sons" she said, "who have supported you these many a year. I pray you send them to cut down the branches of this Tree while my son is away. My husband and I are old and our arms are weak."
"Dear God, what a creature!" cried the two young men, "we shall come immediately." They snatched up ropes and an axe and a saw.

"Go you inside" they said to the Boy's mother, "and stay by the fire. You shall have some fine wood soon."

So she went. The two great hulking fellows climbed up a branch, balancing themselves firmly they began to cut at a great bough that spread very high and strong beyond the tree. "This is short work, Brother" one said, cutting and sawing. "Work for men like us, and not for boys."

The branch swayed and bent and shivered like a live thing, and the old people inside, hearing the noise, smiled together. Soon it creaked and groaned, then swung from one side to the other.

"Steady does it, Brother, we must find our rope. Climb down." But it was too late. Hardly had their feet touched the ground when the great bough, a tree in itself, crashed down, not straight to the ground, but right through the cottage.

Crash! The Cottage fell into a thousand pieces, and the old people, buried underneath, were killed by the weight of the falling timber.

The Neighbour's sons, shrieking like demented children, rushed back to their father and mother, and stammered out their tale. Soon a crowd assembled, the women all shrieking and wringing their hands.

They dug out the bodies of the old people, covered them decently, and took them to the vicarage.

"It is all his cursed tree" said the Village People, "his cursed tree. First he has ruined them with it, and now he has killed them ... Where is the Boy?"

They found him lying as though dead, upon the village street. No one dared to take him in, but the village lads built a little shelter under the Green Tree, filled it with food and water and a straw pallet and left him, crossing themselves, and praying as they went.

"This is very strange" said the Boy. "At first I felt a terrible pain in my arm, and now this numbness ... I cannot move my arm and – this weakness of my body ..."

He did not know of what had happened, but he saw that the cottage was pulled down and said "That is good. Now the branches can grow longer and the roots more deeply. It is as it should be."

All day long he lay still, watching the light come through the opening in the top, faint, then clear, then golden, and then fading. It seemed to rise and fall like the song that the Nightingale had sung in his heart so long ago. And, lying there so long, he began almost unconsciously to fashion songs of the Green Tree – of its growth, of the colour of its leaves, how it looked in the morning, how it moved at night. And he sang of how it clung to its last golden leaves, as though afraid of the subtle beauty of nudity, and of how the golden leaves had floated into his bosom and lay there, fairy gold, always shining. Song after song he made, and sang to himself through the Winter and the Spring.

As the bough of the Tree had healed so he was well again, but had no wish to leave his shelter. He could watch the Green Tree and tend it – that was all he cared for ... except that in this Spring weather he was haunted by a thought that ran hot in his veins like the sap in the budding tree.

"Who will tend the Tree when I am gone. Now if I only had some sons who would promise me - alas - alas - I am alone."

So the thought haunted him, and the songs that he made grew passionate and restless. Flinging his arms round the Green Tree he sang as though his heart would break.

One night a Wandering Minstrel who was passing through the Village heard his passionate songs and amazed at the beauty of them, he unlatched the gate and came through the Garden.

"Who is he that sings in the night to the Green Tree" he cried, and the Boy, crying out, "It is the Green Tree's Lover."

"I pray you write down the songs that I may bear them with me into all lands and to all people."

"Alas" answered the Boy, "I have no parchment."

"That is easy" said the Wandering Minstrel, "for I have a scroll in my pack. But yet no ink and no pen."

"Those I can supply" said the Boy, and taking the parchment from the Wandering Minstrel he went into his hut and found his knife. He pierced himself with it on the wrist and dipping the sharpened end of the twig into the blood he wrote down the First Song.

For all that Summer the Wandering Minstrel stayed with the Boy, learning his songs, and then when they were all written, he journeyed far and away into the country, singing the songs of the Green Tree, until all the world knew and loved them. They were sung in castles and concert-halls, and played upon the barrel-organs in the street - that is Fame indeed! But the Writer's name the Wandering Minstrel told to nobody, except to one girl who had promised him a kiss for it and her red mouth tempted him to distraction.

It was not long after this that the Boy, one fine morning, saw the Girl with the Red Mouth leaning over his garden fence. She nodded and smiled at him.

"Why are you come" he said, "I live alone."

"I wanted to see for myself the Green Tree" she said, " I have heard your songs, and they seem to call to my heart. Was it of a Tree that you wrote, or a Maid, or ... " She smiled.

And suddenly the same thought which had haunted the Boy in early Spring, thrummed in his blood. In her smile he seemed to know her as the mother of his strong sons, she so tall and slim, so like a young tree herself.

"It was to the Green Tree that I wrote these songs" he said, "but, Girl with the Red Mouth, I wrote them that you might hear. Go not back the long way you have come, but stay here with me, and I shall write you many songs."

So she stayed, and at first they were happy together, but when the strangeness of it had worn off, when she had tired of the Boy's young strength, she said to him one day "Boy, I am tired of living under the shadow of this great Green Tree. Let us travel."

"Travel" he said, "but I go journeys every day, seeking and seeking. Every day I find something strange and wonderful. Look up among the branches - see among the boughs ..."

"Nothing" she said, "but leaves, and leaves, and leaves. Boy, let me travel,
I hate this damp Green Tree."

Then he left her. "Go" he said, "you are spoiling my songs."

She told one of the neighbour's sons of what had happened with so
many tears and her red mouth trembling that he took her to wed instead. At
first the Boy did not notice her absence, he was busy with a new song, but
lying down at night, he found her place empty and cold, and all that he had
wished for in her smote his heart.

"Alas" he cried, "I seem curiously fated."

Again, as so many years ago, it was a hot night. Again the Boy rose.
He had not eaten all that day, and felt dizzy and light-headed. Out of his hut
he crept. The Green Tree waved above and around him. Looking up in the
branches it was like looking into a great Sea Cavern, cool and deep.
"You would not leave me" he said, love in his heart. "Oh Green Tree, you
would not leave me ... Have you nothing to give." He looked up among the
branches and, lo, on the topmost bough, a golden flower, a great golden fruit.

"At last" said the Boy, "my Green Tree has borne fruit."

It was easy for the Boy to climb – he knew every step, every foothold.
Higher and higher he swung, until it seemed that the stars were tangled just
above him and the earth, a mist, miles away. Higher and higher still – the
yellow fruit was just above him. He reached out his hands for it – what –
nothing there... He fell and lay still on the grass.

"The young Greenhorn has done for himself at last" said the Village
people, "he always was looking for the Moon."

And they cut down the Green Tree and sold it in little bundles of
firewood, so that next Winter children clapped their hands and cried "See, see
what wonderful colours. See, see what is in the fire."

But even that wood was burnt away and, at last ... a little handful of
ashes was thrown to the four winds.

# *Notebook 29*

## PART 4

[Notebook 29, qMS-1241]

April 1907

Night came swiftly.

Pearl had ridden far out of the town, along the road that crept like a white
ribbon by the side of the sea. She had a fierce longing to escape from people,
to find herself alone. And when the last house had disappeared she reined in.
She felt as wild as the sea that thundered against the rocks and threw up
exquisite passionate curves of white spray - as troubled - as full of agitation as
the sky, a riot of flame colour, and purple, and scarlet - as profoundly
melancholy as the purple hills. The wind blew the bitter salt-laden air into her
face - she flung back her head, & half shut her eyes. What was happening to
her. She felt terrified yet triumphant, exultant yet cowed. He was coming to
see her that evening - he, the very soul and spirit of her. More than a year had
passed since she had received a letter, since she had heard anything from him,
and now just this note which she had slipped under her loose suede gloves.
I must try & realise it, she thought, I must decide what I am going to do or
say. I am a fool to expect anything. A visit from a friend, that is all. He may be
married - he certainly does not care for me - O look it in the face. And the
thought was more bitter & strong than the fierce salt air. She could think of
nothing consecutively. Her mind had got beyond control. For so many weeks
Life had been a little thing of [...] and simplicity. Now something magnificent
and fierce seized her, & shook her.

I think I have been dead, she thought. I <u>must</u> have been dead. Would he
have changed - had <u>she</u> changed - grown older looking, sadder, thinner.
She kept trying to gain mastery over herself but in vain. An absurd fancy came
to her that she was conducting an Orchestra that would not heed her signals to
them to stop but continued playing more and more fiercely some Hungarian
Fantasie, some Dvorak Serenade. She wheeled her horse round and lashed at it
brutally, savagely, with her whip. The animal took fright and cantered in the
direction of home. O faster she called to it - faster, faster. Some terrific energy
had sprung to birth in her brain. When she reached the town the streets were

lighted, rain was falling, and the reflections in the silver streets were lurid. She took the horse to the stables. Outside the front door she paused a moment to feel for her latchkey. There was a great cabbage tree growing in the front garden and the shadow it cast on the door looked like a many-armed monster waving her away - the action was fantastic & real. She stood still, fascinated. In the hall she took off her gloves & hat & looked at herself in the glass. Her face was pale, her eyes shining, her mouth scarlet. From the half-open drawing room door she saw the reflection of fire dancing on the walls & felt very pleased. She would have some tea, change her dress & then wait for him. She pushed open the door. Before her, standing by the fireplace, stood Max. Pearl shut the door and stood leaning against it. For one moment every pulse in her body seemed to have stopped beating then a wave of scarlet rushed over her. "Is it you" she whispered. "It is I." He suddenly came forward & caught her two cold hands in his. "I'll [...] for a moment" he said - his voice shook oddly. Pearl suddenly raised her eyes to his face - the same yet not the same - new lines of suffering & strength and courage.

Then their eyes met. He caught hold of her & kissed her mouth, her eyes, her throat, her cold hands. She felt as though a wild sea storm was sweeping over the sandy wastes of her nature. And then, his arms still round her, she heard him saying "Pearl, Pearl, I have been dead and now I am alive. I cannot exist without you. I need you - you are Life to me. Pearl, Pearl, hear me. I have come to tell you just this - that I must have you - Pearl, answer me."

The long year was swept away & had become as nothing. Nothing mattered - if she would but listen & feel his strength. "I am yours" she whispered. Then Silence fell. "Max, let me go. I want to know a great deal." She walked over to the fire and kneeling on the floor spread out her hands to the blaze. M flung himself in to an easy chair.

"There is nothing to tell you, Pearl." "O but there is - twelve months to account for." "They don't exist now Pearl." He leant forward. "Pearl look at me. Don't let us bother each other about the Past. It has been hell - but let us live in the present & future only." "Very well" she said - "I am too glad to have you to be horrid today. Max would you like some tea - I've had nothing to eat since breakfast this morning." "I should. Shall I ring." "Please." "Tea please, and a lamp, & light the candles in the music room.

---

Enough 1 to 6 [?]
Very Faible

By dint of hiding from others the self that is in us we may end by being unable to find it ourselves. (Act ii Scene ii)

The things that we really wish to say can never be put into words. (Act ii Scene iii)

Les hommes ont je ne sais quelle peur étrange de la beauté (Maurice Maeterlinck)

There danced before his eyes a vision of the wonderful Spring of 1893, marching through the city in green robes, with nodding plumes of lilac and a great retinue of laburnums bearing lanterns, and chestnuts swinging tapers in their hundred arms.

I have read enough for this afternoon. Now I want to write. Shall I be able, I wonder? Here is the attempt.     [J8]

It was late in the afternoon of an Autumn day. I stood at the street corner waiting for a tram car. The rain was falling, and the houses were like the sudden fearful eye of Fear. Wind in the town, and the cold wet rain

> This is just a little song
> That a child once sang to me.
> (O the bitter years and long
> Since she sat upon my knee.)
> Mother when we take a walk, you and I along the
> Shore I can scarcely ever talk.

I can write nothing at all. I have many ideas - but no grip of any subject. I want to write verses - but they won't come. I cannot rhyme but that is not all[?]. I cannot get a charming effect any way. It is hatefully annoying, and disheartening. Still there is nothing like trying so I shall make a further attempt. I should like to write something just a trifle mysterious - but really very beautiful and original.     [J8]

> O Mother Mine, O mother mine
> Snuggle me close and hold me fast
> When will the weather again be fine
> Shall I really get well at last?

In the room next to mine a little boy is ill. He is a strange little fellow - very quick, very forward, with the intense curiosity of childhood strongly developed. I met his Mother on the stairs this afternoon and she told me he had burnt his hand in the fire. All through the evening as I have sat here alone, studying, I have heard the steady creak of a rocking chair, and each time that the sound came - a little voice crying O Mother, O Mother. She is holding him in her arms, maybe, rocking him to sleep. His face is pillowed against her, his tangled curls against her cheek.

Vignette.

I groped my way up the dark stairs and down the stone passage into my little room. Lights from the street outside streamed across the floor and showed the great piles of books in common dull bindings on the table, and a small pile of letters, and a tray with tea and bread. Outside the wind called, shrieked. The rain flung itself over everything, furiously, passionately. I looked out of the window. Below me in the shining street was mirrored another London - a drowned city - and I shuddered and drew the curtains. There was much work to be done - proof sheets to be corrected, letters to look over and answer. I lit my candle and sat down at the table. Deep in my work then - but a curious persistent sound kept coming to me -

The Growing of Wings.

Try & make some sort of sketch of the whole - it will be far simpler, so to speak, block it in. For instance place your characters carefully and completely. Yvonne is born in New Zealand. At the death of her Father she is sent to London to Miss Pitts who keeps a boarding house for young girls who wish to study at the various Colleges. Here is the opportunity for sketching in, say, Opal Vedron, Constance Foster, and Mrs Manners. She is taken by Mrs Manners to see her nephew Paul Harding - author.     [J8]

Although there were no God, God would remain the greatest notion man has had. Evolution is eventually God - nicht?

Vulgarity is the affectation of the manners of a class to which one does not belong.

- - - Browning. Prophet of the morbidly healthy all- inquiring intellect that never quite grasped the idea of intelligence. "I was ever a fighter."

Is Hope only the subtlest form of cowardice?

deletion

The first stage of the passionate pilgrimage to intelligence is ennui Personality.

Mummy's Garden Frock[114]

> Shadow children thin & small
> Now the day is left behind
> You are dancing on the wall
> On the curtain on the blind.
>
> On the ceiling children too
> Peeking round the nursery door
> Let me come & play with you
> As we always played before.
>
> Lets pretend that we have wings
> And can really truly fly
> Over every sorts of things
> Up & up into the sky
>
> Where the sweet star children play
> It does seem a dreadful rule
> They must stay inside all day
> I suppose they go to school.

---

[114]This title has no text following.

And tonight dears - can you see
They are having such a race
With their Father moon - the tree
Almost hides his funny face.

Shadow children - once at night
I was all tucked up in bed
Father moon came - such a fright!
Through the window popped his head

I could see his staring eyes
O my dears I was afraid
That was not a nice surprise.
And the dreadful noise I made!

Let us make a Fairy ring
Shadow children hand in hand
And our songs quite softly sing
That we learnt in Fairy land.

Shadow children thin & small
Look the day is far behind
And I kiss you - on the wall
On the curtains, on the blind.

28.4.07.

Songs from Fairy land.
Daddy's Picture.[115]

There is, I think, Mr Trowell. Definitely I have decided not to be a musician -
its not my forte, I can plainly see. The fact remains at that - I must be an
authoress. Caesar is losing hold of me. Edie is waiting for me - I shall slip into
her arms, they are safest. Do you love me?     [J8]

116

I have a little garden plot
That Daddy gave to me
And there I grow forgetmenot
And radishes for tea.

And pansies for my Mother dear
<Sweet williams in a row>
Grace before meat.

---

[115]Two more discarded titles.
[116]The poem 'Rain and Wind' which occurs here is omitted because there is another copy of it, titled
'Winter Song', in Newberry Notebook 1. See p 180.

# *Unbound Papers*

[NL ts]

### SHE & THE BOY; or, THE STORY OF THE
### FUNNY-OLD-THING.

Well. The Thoughtful Child and The Boy ("Yes, silly names, I quite agree with you" … "No, I can't possibly change them") had been a little crabby together. And you know that really means "pinching", which is an awful terrible thing that even well brought up little crabs don't think of doing.

It all happened because The Boy said he had nine currants in his bread-and-butter pudding at dinner, and the Thoughtful Child said she had more, and he didn't believe her. Oh, such a quarrel. And, at the end, there they were singing the song of the Little Horrors - you know:-

"You didn't"

"I did"

"You didn't"

"I did"

If the Thoughtful Child hadn't started washing her eyes out, they might have been doing it still. But she washed them out so much that The Boy got nice and kissed her. ("Yes, it was a very wet kiss"). After that they both lay down on the lawn and put their hats over their faces, and baked. Oh, that is such a lovely thing to do. There is a nice little hot "hatty" smell after a while like nothing else. ("The bits scratch your nose? Oh, that must be awkward"). And then, you know what I mean, because you still belong to the Secret Society, they found themselves walking along a white road. Very nice it was, too - hand in hand, which is the only proper way. And by and bye they came to a little house called "Step-Inside-and-Find-Out". The Thoughtful Child said "Isn't that a sweet name? Let's". And The Boy said "Let's" too, so they lifted the latch ("No, it's not the same door quite - Yes, it just opened the same way") and walked in. Oh, my Goodness. It was the queerest little room, full of machinery that thumped and bumped and jumped all the time. Such a noise there was too. And fussing about with her head tied up in a "hanky" and felt slippers - red - on her feet, was a Funny-Old-Thing. ("You know what that means, don't you? Yes - I beg your pardon for being so insulting.")

"If you please" said The Boy, "where are we?" The Funny-Old-Thing turned round and stared at them. "I know" said the Thoughtful Child giving a jump, "it's the Heart of the World." "Correct" said the Funny-Old-Thing, wiping the oil off her hands with a corner of her skirt, and still staring. "Now where <u>in</u> earth did you come from?" The Thoughtful Child and The Boy looked puzzled, and had perfect railway lines round their foreheads. "Well" said the Thoughtful Child, "we were both lying <u>flat</u> in the sun." "Oh, I understand, don't explain, Child, I see" said the Funny-Old-Thing. "The sun's caught you. That don't happen so often to folks in these days as it used to. Sit down and be quiet a moment. I've just got to attend to this volcano - it's boiling over."

They sat down on a narrow bench, and presently the Funny-Old-Thing sat opposite to them.

"Attention, please" she said, and took the hanky off her head, and blew her nose with it hard. ("Yes, with the same hanky ... Very nasty habit, dear, you're quite right.") She looked so particular and so solemn that the Thoughtful Child felt that she was in Sunday School and began whispering "The Lord is my Shepherd" to see if she remembered the verses.

"Never whisper in public" cried the Funny-Old-Thing. "If you have anything sensible to say, you may depend upon it everybody wants to hear you. And if you haven't, there's no sense in whispering. You look far too young to talk nonsense." The Thoughtful Child screwed up a corner of her "pinny" and put it into her mouth. ("You like the taste? Well, may be, I've forgotten").

"What are you doing, Funny-Old-Thing" asked The Boy.

"Making the wheels go round, young man, and keeping grown-up people awake, but letting them see what I can do when I like."

"How old are you?" said the Thoughtful Child.

"How many babies have you got?" said The Boy.

"Are you married?" said the Thoughtful Child.

"What's your favourite vegetable?" said The Boy.

Now these are really most important questions, as everybody knows. The Funny-Old-Thing didn't pay the slightest attention to them. She started talking to herself, and this is what she said:-

"People are so careless about their youth. They leave it behind just like you do hankies at parties, and toothbrushes when you're visiting, and umbrellas in hansoms. And there's no Scotland Yard for lost youth, and you only have one, so nobody else's fits you at all. How sad it does seem. Bear that in mind."

"What is youth" asked the Thoughtful Child.

"Something that you only have once - and sometimes don't have at all, but it's hard to escape."

"Oh, Whooping Cough" said The Boy. "The loud sort that makes a great deal of noise and means treacle in teaspoons."

There was silence then for a minute while the Funny-Old-Thing got up and stirred the Bay of Biscay, and made it as rough as rough. She came back to her chair with a queer little smile round the corners of her face humming "Heigh-ho, blow the man down". "Now you can talk" she said.

"We are going to get married" said the Thoughtful Child.

"And have babies" cried The Boy.

"Oh, such babies" said the Thoughtful Child, "dozens and dozens of <u>such</u> babies." And both of them raised their hands and wagged their heads so hard that the Funny-Old-Thing grew quite giddy watching them.

"What do you eat" asked The Boy

"Oh, that's a mystery" said the Funny-Old-Thing, licking her lips in a mouth-watery way. ("Mystery? Oh it means curtains and keys – to tell you a secret, very often a great deal of rubbish.")

"When we pay calls, we always have something to eat" said The Boy. The Funny-Old-Thing looked rather ashamed, and got up and skimmed them two little cups of creamy foam from the Bay of Biscay, which, by this time, was very excited. They found it very "tasty", with just that nice little "salty" flavour which you have sometimes at the seaside when you suck your thumb.

"Now, I think we'd better go home" said the Thoughtful Child, getting up and trying to smooth the place where she had screwed her pinafore.

"Goodbye Funny-Old-Thing, don't you feel a little lonesome here?"

"Goodbye" said the Funny-Old-Thing. "I guess you're a real sweet little girl." And The Boy kissed her. She was very hard and "cornery", but after he had done that she was pink.

They went out at the door, and then, very far away, they heard someone calling "Children, children." And they tried to run, and couldn't, and fell down and sat up on their very own lawn. There stood Daddy. They flew at him, and he lifted up the Thoughtful Child, and she snuggled close to him. And when he had said "My little blossom" and she "My precious Dads" and he "My blooming rosebud" and she "My blessed Farves" and he "My blithesome wench", and a great many other things which belong to the Secret Society language, which you know I never can tell, Daddy cried "My, what hot cheeks." "I've been on a travel" said the Thoughtful Child. When she had said that, she and The Boy had a sudden awful feeling that they were going to burst because they couldn't tell "all through" at the same time. But they both explained and described, and when it was all over both had terrible "tea cups" and their eyes shone like new pennies – so bright. "Dear me" said Daddy, "dear, dear me. To think." And he rolled his eyes so awfully till the spots went right up into his head.

"Here comes the lamp, precious. Well, did you like it? Give me a "really truly" kiss. No, not on the very back of my ear, Cherub."

K. Mansfield.[117]

[NL ts]

## THE THOUGHTFUL CHILD

They had lived together for a very long time – Father, Mother and she, in the white house on the Hill. Other people lived a great way off, and seemed a

---

[117]This manuscript is a typescript but carries an autograph signature.

little unreal to the thoughtful child. She had no time for them, and so many "really truly" friends with her always. After tea time you always might come across "The Bhong with the Luminous Nose" on the gravel path, and "Little Johnny Head-in-Air" wandered somewhere near the pool in the back-yard - not to mention the animals. It is always a difficult question as to who are changed Princes and Princesses, and who not, and thousands of Fairies.

The thoughtful child knew 'most everything about Fairies. She had been one herself once, and lived in a crocus on the lawn. Oh, the dear house it made, and one day Father "peeked" out of the window and saw the crocus and cut it with his penknife, and carried it ever so carefully to Mother. "Oh, how charming" said Mother, "Thank you, dear husband." She put her face close down to smell the fresh "snowy" smell, and the thoughtful child couldn't help it - she put her arms round the Mother's neck. Now, it always happens that, if a fairy does that, she is not a fairy any more. The thoughtful child knew that, but she was not sorry. It was such a beautiful feeling.

So they lived together. Sometimes she was naughty. That was when the black monkey crept down the chimney and perched on the second button of her pinafore, but Oh, the lovely, sad time that came after the monkey had got hungry and crept back to nibble a bit of soot. The "beg-your-pardon" moment when Father took her on his knee and said, "I knew it wasn't my little daughter" and Mother let her paint some ladies' dresses out of a Fashion Book - it always gave her a "creepy" feeling down her back.

Wonderful things were happening all day to the Thoughtful Child. From the moment when she woke and watched "Jack-on-the-Wall" doing a dance all by himself for her to the time when she found the barley sugar on her pillow - all in the dark - while Mother was looking for the bed candle. Through the days Father drove away to find bread and butter, and Mother looked after the house, so she played there ever so many games. One nice one was "paying calls". She tucked her hair under her sun-bonnet, held up her dress "like a train" and visited all the houses in Box Hedge Street. There was the Pansy School where dear children with clean faces sang "Gentle Jesus" and other songs that she taught them very carefully - the long words slowly - the Violet Family, who played "Hide & Seek" all the day long, the rich "Lady Hollyhock" and Sweet William - a little common - she had heard him say "'andsome" - but still very friendly.

Some days there was no lawn at all, but only a great big sea, and she lived in a "teeny weeny" house all by herself, and was a mermaid. Very fresh it was to swim about for as long as she liked, and dive and do "leg stroke", and when she was tired creep back under the wheelbarrow - into her house I mean.

Then there were Dinner Parties under the Fuchsia bush on the pink seat, when she'd do the cooking and make cakes of rich brown flour and water, and sliced geranium stalk for "leming" peel. Truly it was easy to give dinner parties, the garden was so full of cooking things. Pepper in pepper pots at Mr Poppy's, Eggs - ready poached - at Mr Daisy's, and Caraway Seeds at Grandfather Dandelion's.

But the best times she had were with the Shadow Children in the wood at the bottom of the garden. When she went into the wood, somehow she never felt "jokey", but almost like Church time. It was quite different to sit on the ground and look right up and listen to the trees talking, talking to each other. They always had so much to say, and she understood it, but she could not "say it back" to anyone, not even to Father and Mother, because they would not understand now. They had stopped being Fairies for so long.

Nobody ever said "Good morning" or "Nice day" or "don't wet your shoes" or "out loud" things in the wood, yet the Thoughtful Child understood all these, and answered them inside her. Also if she had talked the Shadow Children would never have crept out of their little places and come to her, so she was quiet, and they came, all of them, and smiled at her. They taught her how to kiss a tree, where it could feel, how never to tread where the primroses sleep, how to make the bluebells ring, and, most of all, how to catch the sunbeams, and pop them into her mouth, and then jump till they shook down, down, right into her heart. She was always good at these times. Who could have been naughty when there were no chimneys to hold monkeys, and only a sunbeam lighting a fire in her heart.

The Shadow Children were very thin. Oh, very thin indeed, but, as they always said in their "inside talk" – "Who could be fat and still slip about as they did?" Also, very often they jumped through key holes, in fact, the Thoughtful Child knew that keyholes were front doors to them, and no fat person ever could come through a keyhole "unsticked".

But the day It happened, the Thoughtful Child had been very happy with them, playing and dancing and sunbeam-catching, when, suddenly, she called out loud, like a person "Who are you, Shadow Children?" She looked round and they were gone. She called and cried, but they did not come back. So at last she ran out of the wood across the garden, and right into Father's room. It was late, so he had finished finding bread and butter. "Father, Farves," she sobbed, "they're all gone, gone, my Shadow Children." Father's face was very serious, yet glad, too. "Never mind" he said, "Mother has found a real brother for you." "Oh" she said, "let me see him, do." And she did. So small he was, and sunburnt, she thought. "I like my Shadow Children best" she said, shaking her head gravely.

So the days passed, and brother began to grow and stretch out his arms. The Thoughtful Child watched him with a quiet face, but most of the time she spent in the wood calling and whispering the sweetest "inside" things, but the Shadow Children never answered. Brother used to be carried on to the lawn, never into the wood – it was too shady, but often when the Thoughtful Child looked at him, she saw his eyes looking that way, looking, looking, and she wondered about it. It was Summer when he came, so by the Winter he was really getting big, and thinking about "sitting up," so Mother told her. She smiled at that, but even smiling seemed like going to cry, now everything was funny – she was lonesome, lonesome, with almost a real pain.

The Winter seemed to come very soon, when the Thoughtful Child stayed in the house all day, and looked out of the nursery window across the garden at the wood. And the garden was all white with snow, and the wood all still and soft looking. Everything was asleep, she thought. Perhaps the Shadow Children, too, were cuddled under the blanket and would pop their heads out when it was all gone.

Brother got something the matter with him. He cried all the day until the Thoughtful Child was cross. Mother was with him always, and Father, too. She wandered about from room to room and looked carefully at all the keyholes. She wished Brother had never come. He could not play or talk inside him, and – and – Mother – Father – – –

One night she woke up and heard someone crying in her room. It was Mother. Father held a light and Mother took the Thoughtful Child to her arms, and said "You are all that we have now, baby, baby". Her face was very wet.

She did not see Brother again, though Mother and Father were always with her now. They were sad, and never played, but just sat and looked at her, and did not even smile. All the house seemed quiet, even the furniture looked different. There was a "party-all-over" feeling. The Thoughtful Child tried to walk on the carpets always, so as not to make a noise ever. Oh, how lonesome she was, till at last she went to Mother and said "I think I would like to go to bed", and it was nicer there.

But when the doctor came one day, he said "There is no snow in the garden now, Thoughtful Child. Would you like to get up and take a little walk?" She grew hot all over her face. "Please" she whispered. Mother put on her clothes and her fur coat and her cap. She went slowly down the stairs out of the front door across the garden and into the wood. No blanket now, but trees with little green babies. They waved at her. She stood still, and then someone caught hold of her hand. She looked down and saw it was brother smiling at her. "Brother," she said, in the "inside" voice, "are you a shadow child?" "Yes," he answered, "I've come to play. Let's go sunbeam-catching." All round her in a ring she saw the Shadow Children hand in hand, she and Brother together in the middle, and they danced round them and sang the Fairy Song.

The Thoughtful Child went back to the house, still singing a little. In the hall, she called "Father – Mother" and they came to her. She was laughing and dancing on one leg. "Don't be sad, dears" she said, "Brother's here. I've been playing with him in the garden. He lives in the wood and he sends his love."

And the sunbeams that she had swallowed grew so big that when she started laughing they flew out – all except one, and filled the whole house.

---

[NL ts]

It is evening, and very cold. From my window the laurestinus bush, in this half light, looks weighted with snow. It moves languidly, gently, backwards and forwards, and each time I look at it a delicate flower melody fills my brain.

Against the pearl sky the great hills tower, gorse-covered, leonine, magnificently savage. The air is quiet with thin rain, yet, from the karaka tree comes a tremulous sound of bird's song.

In the Avenue, three little boys are crouched under a tree smoking cigarettes. They are quite silent, and though terrified of discovery, their attitudes are full of luxurious abandon ... And the grey smoke floats into the air - their incense, strong and perfumed, to the Great God of the Forbidden.

Two men pass down the Avenue, talking eagerly ... in the house opposite are four beautiful squares of golden light. ... My room is almost in darkness. The bed frightens me - it is so long and white. And the tassel of the window blind moves languidly to and fro. I cannot believe that it is not some living thing ...

It is growing very dark. The little boys, laughing shrilly, have left the Avenue.

And I, leaning out of my window, alone, peering into the gloom, am seized by a passionate desire for everything that is hidden and forbidden. I want the Night to come and kiss me with her hot mouth, and lead me through an amethyst twilight to the garden of the White Gardenia ...

The laurestinus bush moves languidly, gently, backwards and forwards. There is a dull, heavy sound of clocks striking far away, and, in my room, darkness, emptiness, save for the ghostlike bed. I feel to lie there quiet, silent, passively cold would be too fearful - yet ... quite a little fascinating.

[NL ts]

## VIGNETTE - WESTMINSTER CATHEDRAL.[118]

Did we ever climb that tower, Vere, you and I? Is it all a charming romance?

Very languidly and dreamily we wandered through Westminster Cathedral. A faint blue perfume of incense filled the air. In one chapel a woman was kneeling, the rosary falling - a little stream of silver through the ivory of her fingers.

Then we came to the heavily locked gates and stood before them, smiling at each other. An old man - I wonder if you remember his hands, they were rude, knotted, gnarled hands - opened the gates and we passed through.

Looking back, those stairs seem to me to have been endless, an eternity of stone steps, then a great ascent of wooden ladders, and a dark, narrow staircase, twisting upwards. And sometimes, Vere, you were first, and sometimes I led the way. Often we walked together or rested, a little breathless, on a stone parapet, saying "Can we go further? ...

Always the thin blue perfume of the incense enveloped us. It filled the whole incident with dream atmosphere.

So, at last, we reached the dome. A balcony had been built east and west, north and south - a little shrine to each of the four winds of Heaven. With a

---

[118]There are two typescripts of this vignette in the Newberry Library. One of them has, at the top, in a hand other than KM's, 'Vere Bartrick-Baker, Paradise Farm, Chobham, nr Woking.'

sensation of extraordinary relief, of lightness, we stepped out upon the balcony, and, below us, London was spread out like a charming, intricate tapestry ... I think of it now, Vere, as a wonderful fusion of amethyst and silver.

And laughing, laughing childishly, with our hands on each other's shoulders, we watched the little people walking in the streets, like flies in the folds of some gigantic tablecloth. The sky was filled with grey clouds. They floated by like a flock of silent birds. And I remember far away the Crystal Palace shone, a moonstone pearl in an emerald setting.

We leaned far over the parapet, and the four winds of Heaven seemed to beat upon us both. A long strand of your hair blew across my face, and the voice of London thundered out some stupendous, colossal, overwhelming fugue to the whole world – to us, clinging together outside the little tower.

"Do you think," I said, "in the evening when they have trimmed their lamps and set them in the blue dome of the sky, the ghosts may lean out, shoulder to shoulder, and point down to London and whisper 'This is where I lived; in the Spring we walked there together'. Do you think, sometimes, sometimes, when there is no light in the sky darkness, they have drowned their little flame in a passion of tears ..."

"Look," you said, "that is our street. Perhaps, years hence, we shall look out and say 'In the third house, on the right-hand side, we kissed each other.'"

Out of the wind, down the stairs, down the wooden ladders, we went together. The iron gate clanged to after us. A service was being held in one of the chapels. While the people knelt, a great wave of music broke over, flooded the whole building. A boy in a long gown walked slowly up the aisle. He held in his arms a great spray of flowering lilies.

But you and I, Vere, passed out into the streets.

[NL]

Prose.[119]

1) Now a certain young man of the city fell sick. And he could find no cure for his sickness; it was as though a flame burnt by day and by night in his heart, & all his strength was gone out of him.

And he went unto his friends and told them of his ill, but they mocked at him and laughed at him with their mouths and cried:- "Verily, thy cure is not hard to find. Thou must fain seek a nurse whose lips are golden with wine and who weareth a little Order of the Garter from the Burlington Arcade. Fie upon thee! Tush! We will have none of thee."

But he was sore troubled. And the women whom he had loved left him for there was no more light in his eyes, neither was there any sound of laughter in his speech. And his days were as stale as the Buttonhole of Yesterday; his nights were barren of beauty.

But, beloved, certain of his Pater's Friends heard of his sickness and came

---

[119]This exercise in biblical style, with its Oscar Wilde overtones, cannot be dated by anything other than the handwriting which is 'early', although the mention of 'Bavaria' might be an echo from the period KM herself spent there in 1909.

unto him with fair words and spake with him softly. "Why goest thou not unto the Country House of thy Pater and tarry there awhile? Perchance the tumult of thy days and the burden of thy life has wearied thee. The full flower of thy manhood thou canst not wantonly fling away, and the treasures of thy youth thou canst not count as nothingness. For lo, thy oats are yet as seeds to be sown. Haply the Vicar hath a daughter or thy sister hath a Confidential Friend ..." But he cried out and spake against them. Bitter words issued out of his mouth. "Go ye your ways," he commanded, "as for me I am sick unto death of your fox faces."

And he arose and went into the street and took a Taxi unto Harley Street - yea unto the Hives of the doctors fared he sorrowfully. And he went to one and to another and stamped his feet upon their Expensive Velvet Pile Carpets when they spake unto him of young girls and Happy English Homes. "Now verily," he cried, "I am about to die. Ye stand before me in your rich apparel - yea even unto the bald crowns of your heads are ye polished. Yet there is nothing beneath this polish. Ye are Old Boots in New Blacking." And his heart was angered against them. Even the Taxi he dismissed with loud words. For he said unto himself "all men are robbers."

2) And as he journeyed towards Piccadilly Circus he met a goodly procession of Sandwich Men bearing placards covered with Cryptic Signs and strange lettering. "Alas," said the young man, "would that I could change places with one of these. For though their appearance speaketh of long fasting, a Sick Heart is heavier to bear than an Empty Belly."

But they marvelled to see him standing at that hour and alone in such a place, and certain of the more Flagrant Spirits among them made obeisance giving unto him one of the scrolls which they carried ...

> Consult Dayêésha Keephfâ
> Central Africa's Only Mud Diviner.
> For Many Years Confidential Advisor to All the Provincial
> Harems.
> Complete Diagnosis of Your Heart and its Needs in One Interview.
> <u>Mascot Motto</u>:- 'A Cracked Heart Never Breaks.'
> 10-1 New Bond Street.

Save for the timely presence of the Traffic a strange cry would have fallen upon the ears of the multitude.
"Lo," said the young man, pulling out his watch, and seeing that he had yet an hour to wait before the Desert of the Piccadilly Circus Tube Station blossomed with his Last Rose, "this is the hand of Fate. Behold I will hie me thither." And he girded up his loins and he went. And he journeyed swiftly unto That Place.

3) Now when he had come thither he climbed up a flight of stairs that were narrow and uncarpeted, neither was there any linoleum to cover their nakedness. And on the first floor he tarried and knocked upon a door that bore the marks of many fingers - yea, the marks of the Fingers of Secrecy and

the marks of the Fingers of Suède saw he upon that door. And it was opened unto him.

And he entered a little room that was hung with red draperies and the skins of wild beasts and the skins of rabbits were upon that floor. And seated before a table he saw a little man having a Red Quill behind his ear. "At last," said the Old Man, "is my fame noised abroad in the market places of the Great City." "It was in Piccadilly Circus that I read of thee."
"What seekest thou?"
"I am sick of a sore disease, yea, verily, my heart is sick and not all the wise men who dwell in the valley of the shadow of Harley Street can cure me of my ill. I pray ye, comfort me. For my cigaret is as hay in my mouth. Yea, even though I pay a guinea a Bundle for my Asparagas it is but as a green herb that must be swallowed."

And the Old Man took a Flat Dish and spread upon it a mixture of water and earth. From the red pot of a geranium flower took he the earth and from the window box of the Masseuse next to him, stole he yet further. And he mixed it and placed it in the hands of the young man.

"Now, by Livingstone, thou shalt see what thou shalt see" he cried, turning up his eyes until they were like unto eggs that have been poachèd. And he began to speak but the words were in a strange tongue.
"Speak the more clearly." demanded the young man, "for thy mouth is so full of false teeth that I cannot hear what thou speakest unto me." But he heeded him not.

Now as the young man sat there silent and weary, a square patch of sunlight lay upon the floor & he saw suddenly the shadow of a bird that flew across it - once and then again. "Ah," he cried, "I know. It is the bird only that can cure my ill. It is the bird that I have seen in the sunlight on thy floor. Could I but hold that bird upon my heart and I were well again."
"Behold," spake Dayêésha Keephfâ, "thou hast consulted the oracle and it is made plain unto thee. It is so. But thou canst never find the bird, for it flies by night across the world, neither does it brood in any tree. Thou art doomed to wander over the face of the globe and find it not. No hearthstone shall know the sight of thy slippers. Thou shalt not be aroused from bed to make warm the food of thy children."
But the Young Man laughed him to scorn and cried unto him with a loud voice:-
"Fool, I shall find the bird; thou art little better than the rest of them." And he arose, knocking over the table of the Old Man in his flight so that the ink well spilled upon the floor.
"Now indeed it is well," said the Old Man, "for he hath left behind him his cigaret case studded with diamonds and my rabbits hath he turned into leopards."

4) On the evening of That Day the Young Man gathered together into a waterproof mackintosh the Vital Necessities of Life - one pair socks and a handkerchief and toothbrush and a safety razor, and a little packet of seasick

cure, folded he up together. And when evening was come, ere yet the voice of the diner was heard in the land he fared forth from that city upon his quest.

5) Now concerning the details of that Pilgrimage I shall not speak save to say that for three years he searched all the cities of the world, the secret places and the solitary deserts – yea, even the Fashionate Watering Places knew his presence. But no sight or sound of the bird was vouchsafed him – neither did he hear speech of it in the market places of Brighton or of Bruges. But it came to pass one night as he sat in a little café in Bavaria, he heard two men speaking together.

"If it be millinery which has tempted thee, Brother, go you to the old man who dwells in the city over the mountains. For he keeps many Strange Birds. There are not so many birds in all the land as he keeps, and they are in cages of gold and silver work. Fine strings of pearls hath one – and another he has snared with a ruby as red as the mouth of thy mistress. There is a bird with a white breast so soft that it can only sleep upon … another breast." And they laughed.

But the Young Man thought:– I must go swiftly & see what this thing is. Haply this man will gain his destination before me.

Now in the early morning as he journeyed he heard a soft sound of weeping, and he saw, sitting under a tree, a little maid. She was clad in a brown garment that fell from her round throat to her ankles; her hair leapt round her body like a ruddy flame.

"Why weepest thou," he said. She pushed back her long hair, and moved away from him, yet could she not hide her sobbing.

"Why weepest thou." he said, "for it is not comely for a maid to weep."

# Notebook 2

[Notebook 2, qMS-1244][120]

Rien n'est vrai que le [beauté]
K. Mansfield November 1907
4 Fitzherbert Terrace
Wellington
N.Z.

Rough Note Book

A woman never ever knows when the curtain has fallen.

O.W.

Urewera - Kaingaroa Plains.
On the journey the sea was most beautiful - a silver point etching and a pale sun breaking through pearl clouds. There is something inexpressibly charming to me in railway travelling. I lean out of the window - the breeze blows, buffeting and friendly against my face, and the child spirit, hidden away under a thousand and one grey City wrappings, bursts its bonds & exults within me. I watch the long succession of brown paddocks, beautiful with here a thick spreading of buttercups, there a white sweetness of arum lilies. And there are valleys lit with the swaying light of broom blossom; in the distance grey whares[121] - two eyes & a mouth with a bright petticoat frill of a garden creeping round them. On a white road once a procession of patient cattle wended their way, funereal wise - and behind them a boy rode on a brown horse - something in the poise of his figure, in the strong sunburnt colour of

---

[120]A large part of this notebook is taken up with KM's quickly pencil scribbled impressions of her camping trip in the Urewera district of the North Island in 1907. Murry tackled it and published his transcripton in the *Journal*. Many parts of it defeated him, however, and these he omitted. In what he did use there are inevitably many misreadings. This part of Notebook 2 was also tackled by Ian A Gordon who published it together with an interesting and useful introduction and route map, as *The Urewera Notebook*, OUP, Wellington, 1978. Gordon also made decisions about the order in which the pieces were written, and presented them accordingly, whereas I have transcribed the pages in the order in which they occur. My transcription differs in very many details from those of both of my predecessors; although in building on and improving their work I am, of course, much indebted to them.

[121]Whare: a Māori dwelling.

his naked legs reminded me of Walt Whitman. Everywhere on the hills great masses of charred logs - looking for all the world like strange fantastic beasts, a yawning crocodile, a headless horse, a gigantic gosling, a watchdog - to be smiled at and scorned in the daylight, but a veritable nightmare in the darkness. And now & again the silver tree trunks, like a skeleton army, invade the hills.

At Kaitoki the train stopped for 'morning lunch' - the inevitable tea of the New Zealander. The F.T. [Fellow Traveller] and I paced the platform, peered into the long wooden saloon where a great counter was piled with ham sandwiches & cups & saucers, soda cake and great billys of milk. We did not want to eat & walked to the end of the platform & looked into the valley. Below us lay a shivering mass of white native blossom, a little tree touched with scarlet, a clump of toi-toi waving in the wind & looking for all the world like a family of little girls drying their hair. Late in the afternoon we stopped at Jakesville. How we play inside the house while Life sits on the front door step & Death mounts guard at the back.

After brief snatches of terribly unrefreshing sleep I woke and found the grey dawn slipping into the tent. I was hot & tired and full of discomfort - the frightful buzzing of the mosquitos, the slow breathing of the others seemed to weigh upon my brain for a moment and then I found that the air was alive with birds' song. From far and near they called & cried to each other. I got up & slipped through the little tent opening on to the wet grass. All round me the willow still full of gloomy shades, the caravan in the glade a ghost of itself - but across the clouded grey sky the vivid streak of rose colour blazoned in the day. The grass was full of clover bloom. I caught up my dressing gown with both hands & ran down to the river, and the water flowed on, musically laughing, & the green willows - suddenly stirred by the breath of the dawning day - swung softly together. Then I forgot the tent and was happy - - -

- - - - - - - - - - - - - - -

So we crept again through that frightful wire fence which every time seemed to grow tighter & tighter, and walked along the white soft road. On one side the sky was filled with the sunset - vivid, clear yellow and bronze green & that incredible cloud shade of thick mauve. Round us in the darkness the horses were moving softly with a most eerie sound. Visions of long dead Maoris, of forgotten battles and vanished feuds stirred in me - till I ran through the dark glade on to a bare hill - the track was very narrow & steep. And at the summit a little Maori whare was painted black against the wide sky. Before it two cabbage trees stretched out phantom fingers, and a dog, watching me coming up the hill, barked madly. Then I saw the first star - very sweet & faint - in the yellow sky, and then another & another like little holes - like pinholes. And all round me in the gathering gloom the wood hens called to each other with monotonous persistence - they seemed to be lost and suffering. I neared the whare and a little Maori girl and three boys sprang from nowhere & waved & beckoned. At the door a beautiful old Maori woman sat cuddling a cat. She wore a white handkerchief round her black hair and [a] vivid green & black cheque rug wrapped round her body. Under the rug I caught a

glimpse of a very full blue print dress, with native fashion, the skirt over the
bodice.    [J22–24]

Petane Valley
Monday morning

Bon jour, Marie dearest.[122] Your humble servant is seated on the very top
of I know not how much luggage - so excuse the writing. This is a most
extraordinary experience.

Our journey was charming. A great many Maoris in the train - in
fact I lunched next to a great brown fellow at Woodville. That was a
memorable meal. We were both starving, with that dreadful silent
hunger. Picture to yourself a great barn of a place, full of pink papered
chandeliers and long tables, decorated with paper flowers, and humanity
most painfully en évidence. You could cut the atmosphere with a knife.

Then the rain fell heavily, drearily on to the river & the flax swamp
& the mile upon mile of dull plain. In the distance, far and away in the
distance, the mountains were hidden behind a thick grey veil.    [J24]

Monday. The Manuka and sheep country - very steep & bare, yet relieved here
and there by the rivers & willows, and little bush ravines. It was intensely hot -
we were tired & in the evening arrived at Pohue where Bodley has the
accomodation House, and his fourteen daughters grow peas. We camped on
the top of a hill, mountains all round & in the evening walked in the bush - to
a beautiful daisy pied creek - ferns, tuis, & we saw the sheep sheds - smell
& sound - 12 Maoris - their hoarse crying, dinner cooking in the homestead,
the roses, the Maori cook. Post letters there - see Maoris.

Tuesday morning start very early - Titi-oKura[123] - the rough roads & glorious
mountains & bush. The top of Taranga-Kuma[124] - rain in the morning & then
a clear day - the view - mountains all round & the organ pipes. We laugh with
joy all day. We lunch past the Maori pah[125] & get right into the bush. In the
afternoon more perfect bush & we camp at Tarawera Mineral baths - the old
man, the candle in a tin, the scenery, the old shed, the hot water, the falling,
the road - how we sleep.
Next day walking and bush, clematis & orchids, meet Mary by the ploughed
field & at last come to the Waipunga falls - the fierce wind, the flax & manuka,
the bad roads, camp by the river, & then up hill - the heat - to Rangitaiki.
Post letters. Came on a peninsula, the purple, the ferns, the clean house,
evening, the cream, the wild pigs.

Woman and daughter, the man, their happiness. Solemn word - Facial[?]
                                                                    [J25]

---

[122]KM's sister Charlotte Mary was known sometimes as 'Chaddie', sometimes as 'Marie'.
[123]The high Titiokura Saddle.
[124]The Turangakuma Mountain Range.
[125]'Pah' refers to pā: a Māori fortified village.

<u>Thursday</u> the plain, rain, long unending purple mountains, river ducks, one clump of broom, wild horses, the great pumice fire, lambs in the sun, orchids, fluff in the manuka, snow berries. After a time manuka & a tree or two, more horses, it rains violently, the fearful road. No water. Night in the tent, the rain, climbing to see where anything is, the quivering air, the solitude. Early bed, the strange sound, the utter back blocks. Fear as to whether this was the rain, the close[?] breakfast, the kitchen - at night & at morning, the wet clothes.

In the morning rain first, the chuffing sound of the horses - we get up very early indeed and at six o'clock ready to start, the sun breaks through the grey clouds. There is a little dainty wind, and a wide fissure of blue sky. Wet boots, wet motor veil, torn coat, the dew shining on the scrub. No breakfast. We start, the road grows worse & worse. We seem to pass through nothing but scrub covered valleys, and then suddenly comes round the corner a piece of road. Great joy, but the horses sink right into it - the traces are broken, it grows more & more hopeless. The weather breaks & rain pours down. We lose the track again and again, become rather hopeless, when suddenly far ahead we see a man on a white horse. The men leave the trap & rush off. By and by through the track we met two men Maoris in dirty blue ducks - one can hardly speak English. They are surveyors. We stop, boil the billy & have tea & herrings. Oh! how good.

Ahead the purple mountain, the thin wretched dogs - we talk to them - <u>thin</u>. We drive the horses off but there is no water, the dark people, the conversation - E ta, Haeremai te kai[126] - it is cold. The crackling fire of manuka, walking breast high through the manuka, lily of the valley, the ti tree as we approach Galatea. We lunch by the Galatea River - there is an island in the centre and a great clump of trees, the water is very green and swift. I see a wonderful huge horsefly, the great heat of the sun and then the clouds roll up.

"Mother's little lamb isn't 'e" she said, tossing the baby up in the air. "When 'e's asleep" cried the girl, bringing a clean pinafore and a little starched bib. "Hold the horses or they'll make a bolt for the river". My fright.

Encounter one man surveyor on white horse, his conversation, raupo whare[127] in distance. Picture. At the city gates we pull up & walk into the 'city'. There is one store, an Accomodation House, and a G.P.O. Mrs Prodgers is here with the baby and the Englishmen - it is a lovely river, the Maori women are rather special, the Post boy, the children, an accident to the horses - very great, the Maori room, the cushions. Then a straight road in a sort of basin of stony mountains. Far away in the distance a little cloud shines in the sunlight. Through the red gate there were waving fields, a fresh flax swamp, the homestead in the distance - tree encircled, a little field of standing willow & cabbage trees, & away in the distance the purple hills in the shadow. Sheep in for shearing.

Here we drive in and ask for a paddock. Past the shearing shed, past the homestead, to a beautiful place with a little patch of bush, tuis, magpies, cattle,

---

[126]E ta, Haeremai te kai: Māori for 'Come and have some food, friend!'
[127]Raupō whare: a small Māori dwelling made of raupō (bulrush).

and water running through. But I know from bitter experience that we shall
be eaten with mosquitos. Two Maori girls are washing. I go to talk with them.
They are so utterly kids. While the dinner cooks I walk away, and lean over a
giant log. Before me a perfect panorama of sunset – long sweet steel-like
clouds against the faint blue, the hills full of gloom, a little river with a tree
beside it is burnished silver like the sea, the sheep, and a weird passionate
abandon of birds, the bush birds cries[?], the fanciful shapes of the supplejacks
– – Then the advent of Bella, her charm in the dusk, the very dusk incarnate.
Her strange dress, her plaited hair & shy swaying figure. The life they lead
here.

In the shearing sheds, the yellow dress with huia feathers[128]on the coat
jacket with scarlet rata blossom. The speed, heat, and look of the sheep.
Farewell. The road to Te Whaiti. Meet the guide. Wild strawberries. The pink
leaved ferns. Matai.[129] Lunched at a space in the bush cut through a tree, and
then by devious routes we came to the pah. It was adorable. Just the collection
of huts, the built place for koumara & potato. We visit first the house.
No English, then a charming little place, roses & pinks in the garden, through
the doorway the kettle & fire & bright tins, the woman, the child in the pink
dress & red sleeves in all this vast[?] glory. How she stands gathering her pleats
of dress – she can say just 'yes'. Then we go into the parlour – photos, a
chiming clock, mats, kits,[130] red table cloth, horse hair sofa. The child saying
"Nicely thank you", the shy children, the Mother & the brown baby – thin
& naked, the other bright children, her splendid face & regal bearing. Then at
the gate of the P.O. a great bright coloured crowd, almost threatening looking
– a follower of Rua[131] with long Fijian hair & side combs, a most beautiful girl
of 15, she is married to a patriarch, her laughing face, her hands playing with
the children's hair, her smiles. Across the bad river, the guide, the swimming
dogs – it flows on. He stands in the water a regal figure then his <u>alight</u> & we
are out, the absolute ease of his figure – so boneless, he speeds our parting
journey, his voice is so good. He speaks most correctly and yet enunciates each
word. We see him last stopping to rub his horses near a mound of tutu[132] –
amazingly emerald in colour. The sun is fearfully hot. We camp by the guide's
whare, the splendour of the night, the late fire, broken snippets. Then the birds
calling through the night.

<u>Sunday</u> A splendid morning. Washing in the creek. Leave early, leaving some
luggage, on the way to Matatua, the silver birch, thick white flowers, that
Elysian valley of bush, the redtipped ferns, the sound of the chocks, then
almost a bare hill among green hills, winter bare tree trunks & a stone colour
sky. We saw a little flock of white sheep, such a whare on a hill, carved too, but
no one is at home though there is a suggestion of fire lately. From this saddle

---

[128]Huia feathers: large ornamental tail feathers of the huia, a native bird (now extinct).
[129]Matai: *Prumnopitys taxifolia*, a common forest tree.
[130]Kits: kete, baskets made of plaited flax.
[131]Rua Kenana Hepetipa (1869–1937) was a Māori prophet who reached the zenith of his influence
over a section of the Urewera Māori in 1908 and 1909. He wore, at that time, a profusion of hair and a beard.
[132]Tutu: *Coriaria arborea*, a small poisonous tree, commonly known as 'toot'.

we look across mile upon mile of green bush then brown bush russet colour, blue distance and a wide cloud flecked sky. All the people must doubtless have gone shearing. I see none -- - - Above the whare there is a grave, a green mound looking over the knob whare down into[?] the valley - the air, the shining water, the sheep quite terror stricken flee before us, while at the head of a great valley the blazing sun uplifts itself like a gigantic torch to light the bush - it is all so gigantic and tragic & even in the bright sunlight it is so passionately secret. And in here[?] the entirely thoughtful[?] look. We go again to reach the valley-road. A green red & brown butterfly, the green hill a river superb & then a vault of green bush, the sunlight slanting in to the trees, an island in this river decked with tree fern. And always through the bush this hushed sound of water running on brown pebbles. It seems to breathe the full deep bygone essence of it all - a fairy fountain of golden rings - then rounding a corner we pass several little whares, deserted & grey. They look very old and desolate - almost haunted - on the door there is a horse collar or a torn or scribbled notice - flowers in the garden, one clump of golden broom, one clump of yellow irises. Not even a dog greets us. All the whares look out upon the river & the valley & the bush gloried hills. These trees smothered in cream blossom.      [J25–29]

Oh, what a comfort[133]

Blue skirt, great piece of greenstone, black hair, beautiful bone ear rings.
    We plunge back into the bush & finally reach a whare, several whares, deserted now but showing signs of recent habitation - a white cow & her calf are tethered to the side of the road, a brown cow & a brown calf, a grey mare & a preposterous looking little foal are the sole inhabitants. There is a great open clearing here and we decide to pitch our tents.
Bright and[?] Early. The wet bushes brush against my face, like sunflecked avenues. This new bracken is like H.G. Wells dream flowers, like strings of Beads. The sky in the water is like white swans in a blue mirror.
    We pluck 'nga maui'[134] with the Maori children - in the sunshine. Their talk & their queer droll ways. They laugh very much at us, but we learn, too, tho' it is difficult and tedious, too, because our hands are so stiff. One girl is particularly interesting with auburn hair and black eyes. She laughs with an indescribable manner and has very white teeth. Also another Maori in a red & black striped flannel jacket. The small boy is raggedly dressed in brown, his clothes are torn in many places, he wears a brown felt hat with a 'koe-koea'[135] feather placed rakishly to the side. Here, too, I meet Prodgers - it is splendid to see once again real English people. I am so tired & sick of the third rate article. Give me the Maori and the tourist but nothing between. Also this place proved utterly disappointing after Umuroa which was fascinating in the extreme. The Maoris here know some English and some Maori - not like the

---

[133]This underlined phrase is written in the top margin of the page.
[134]Ngā mauī: string games.
[135]Koekoeā: *Urodynamis taitensis*, the long-tailed cuckoo.

other natives. Also these people dress in almost English clothes compared with
the natives [t]here, and they wear a great deal of ornament in Umuroa &
strange hair fashions. I found nothing of interest here.

Johanna Hill        Warbeck

Galatea             Longfellow

So we journey from their whare to Waiotapu. A grey day & I drive - long
dust-thick road & then before us Tarawera with the great white cleft.
The poverty of the country, but the gorgeous blue mountain - all round is a
great stretch of burnt manuka.

We lunch and begin to decide whether to go to the Wharepuni - the
men folk go but eventually come back and say that the walk is too long, also
the heat of the day, but there is a great pah 1½ miles away. There we go. The
first view - a man on the side of the road, in a white shirt and brown pants
waits for us. Opposite is a thick bark[?] Maori fence - in the distance across the
paddock several whares clustered together like snails upon the green patch.
And across the paddock a number of little boys come straggling along from the
ages of twelve to three - out at elbow, bare footed, indescribably dirty, but
some of them almost beautiful, none of them very strong. There is one great
fellow, Isaiah[?], who speaks English. Black curls clustering around his broad
brow, rest almost languor in his black eyes, a slouching walk & yet there
slumbers in his face passion might and strength. Also a little chap in

On Monday night we slept outside Warbrick's whare - rather sweet.
Mrs Warbrick is such a picture in her pink dressing gown, her wide elastic hat,
her black fringe. Her hands are like carving. She gives us a great loaf of bread,
leans swaying against the wire fence & in the distance I see the niece Johanna
watering her garden with a white enamel teapot. She is a fat well made child
in a blue pinafore, her hair plaited & most strange eyes. Then she milks the
cows & Wahi brings us a great bowl of milk & a little cup of cream. Also a cup
of curd. She dines with us, teaches me Maori & smokes a cigaret. Johanna is
rather silent, reads Byron & Shakespeare & wants to go back to school.
W. teaches her fancy work. At night we go & see her - the clean place, the
pictures, the beds, Byron & the candle-like flowers in a glass - sweet - the
paper & pens, photos of Maoris & whites too. Johanna stays by the door.
We see her jewelery, her clothes. I got a Maori Kit. W thinks the old people at
Umuroa so dirty. Yes. Would I like to sleep there? Hot water. Home in the
dark. Johanna more silent - there is something sad about it all - she is so lonely.
Next day they see us off. I hear the guide's horse coming in the night. She has
been up very early. J. is shyer today. She talks to the little boy from over the
road. Now the boy's Mother comes - a worn but rather beautiful woman who
smiles delightfully. Yes, she has five children tho she looks so young. The girl is
shearing now. It is in Winter that it is so cold, all snow & they sit by the fire,
never go out at all, just sit with many clothes on & smoke. Farewell. Johanna
again waters the flowers. Soon she will go to milk the cow, & then begin
again, I suppose.    [J29-30]

Sunday                                        Nowhere
Dear Mr Millar –

I have to thank you for keeping my none too small amount of
correspondence – I went to the Bank yesterday afternoon, foolishly
forgetting that it was closing day. Would you kindly address any letters
that may arrive for me c/o Bank of New Zealand, Hastings – I shall be
there on Saturday –

This paper is vile, but I am once more on the march.

Once more thank you –
                        Sincerely yours
                        K.M. Beauchamp


                        Tuesday.
<u>Thursday</u> – on the lake. A beautiful day – the people – Rotorua is not what I
expect.
Friday – A quiet day in the grounds – reading, & watched[?] afternoon – baths,
Priest & Rachael.[136] Feel fearfully low.
Saturday – Rain, letters, Tom's hotel, Rain, bad night.[137]
Sunday leave, fine day.

<u>On the journey to Waiotapu.</u> In the distance these hills – to the right almost
violet, to the left grey with rain. Behind a great mount of pewter colour and
silver. And then as we journey a little line of brilliant green trees, and a mound
of yellow grass. We stop at a little swamp to feed the horses and there is only
the sound of a frog. Tense stillness, almost terrible. Then the mountains are
more pronounced – they are still most beautiful and by and bye a little puff of
white steam. We pass the Forest Tree plantations and by turns & twists the road
pass[es] several steam holes. Perfect stillness, and a strange red tinge in the cliffs,
the naked ribbing of the earth showing through. We passed over oily thick
green rape,[138] round the sides the manuka clambered in fantastic blossoming.
The air is heavy with sulphur, more steam, white & fine. Camp by a great
sheet of water, here the frogs croak dismally – it is a grey evening. Bye & bye
we go to see the mud volcano – marvellous – oh, so different, mount these
steps, all slimy & grey & peer in. It bulges out of the bowl in great dollops of
loathsome colour like a boiling filthy sore upon the earth, and a little boiling
pool below, a thin coating of petroleum, black ridged. Rain began to fall –

---

[136]Priest and Rachael Baths are hot mineral springs in Rotorua.

[137]Tom Seddon, MP, a son of the late Prime Minister, Richard John Seddon, was connected by
marriage to the Beauchamps in that his sister Phoebe married KM's uncle Frank Dyer. Tom happened to be
staying in Rotorua at this time and has related how he accidentally came upon KM weeping on a park bench
in the rain and endeavoured to console her.

[138]Rape: *Brassica napus*, a turnip-like crop grown to fatten sheep. IA Gordon, who reads 'We passed
one oily bright green lake' for my 'We passed over oily thick green rape' has pointed out to me that rape, a
winter crop, would be unlikely to be green in November. This, I concede, throws doubt on my reading
which nevertheless still looks correct to me.

she is disgusted & outraged. Coming back the horrible road, the long long distance & finally soaking wetness & hunger. Bed - & wetness again.

The morning is fine but hot - the nearer they get to the town the more she hates it - perhaps it is smell.[139] It is pretty hot, a rise to see the blue lake. They pass Whaka - ugly suburban houses, ugly streets, old shaking buses, crowds of the veiled tourists. But letters are good, & they camp in a paddock behind the puffing trains. How nice the old lady is next door & her flowers, her white piccotes & briar roses - that evening she has a bath. Thursday the loathsome trip. Friday so tired that she sits in the Sanatorium grounds all the morning & that evening - horrid - the people - bores[?] Morning & Afternoon in Whaka - the [...] seem good & the cerise handbags. Also the little naked boys & girls but the coy airs - bah! Rain again, Saturday letters - far more - & lunch with Tom & the quiet afternoon - <u>fearful</u> rain, up to the ankles, the wet camp, the fear of having to move. She thinks Rotorua is loathsome & likes only that little Hell.[140]

Sunday morning, the early start, it seems at each mile post her heart leaps. But as they leave it the town is very beautiful & Whaka full of white mist, strangely fanciful. She almost wishes - no - Oh, it is too hot where they lunch - she feels so ill, so tired, her headache is most violent. She can hardly open her eyes but must lean back - each jolt of the cart pains her, but the further they go the load begins to lighten. They meet a Maori again, walking along barefooted & strong. She shouted Te nakoto[141] & [...]      [J30-31]

Rotorua.                                    Friday.
Mother dearest[142]
     Thank you for your wire which I received today and for Chaddie's lovely letter. So Vera has definitely left. I can hardly realise it. What a strange household you must be feeling. You sound most gay, at home. I am so glad. I wrote to Chaddie on Wednesday. Yesterday was very hot indeed. A party of us went a Round Trip to the Hamurana Spring, the Okere Falls, across Lake Rotoiti to Tikitere, and then back here by coach. I confess frankly that I hate going trips with a party of tourists - they spoil half my pleasure - don't they yours? You know the lady who is the wit of the day and is 'flirty', and the inevitable old man who becomes disgusted with everything, and the honeymoon couples. Rotorua is a happy hunting ground for these. We came back in the

---

[139]Rotorua is, to this day, pervaded by a strong sulphurous smell.

[140]Murry has 'Hell', Gordon has 'Hill', thus giving rise to a good deal of conjecture. The word itself could be either: one's reading of it depends on the sense. Murry has 'She thinks Rotarua [sic] is loathsome and ugly – that little Hell.' Gordon, quite correctly, read 'She thinks Rotorua is loathsome and likes only that little'. He then felt, not unnaturally, that 'Hill' made more sense than 'Hell'. My own reading of the word is 'Hell' on the assumption that it refers to the boiling mud so feelingly described in the preceding paragraph.

[141]This is a slightly wrong usage in that 'Te nakoto' should be written 'Tēnā koutou' and is a greeting to a group rather than to a single person.

[142]KM wrote another long letter to her mother in this notebook and then tore the pages out, presumably to post them. The fact that the letter survived and is now among her papers in the Turnbull Library suggests, however, that she did not post it. It can be found after Notebook 2, on p 168.

evening grey with dust – hair and eyes and clothing, so I went and soaked in the Rachael bath. The tub is very large – it is a wise plan to always use the public one, and there one meets one sex very much "in their nakeds". Women are so apt to become communicate on these occasions that I carefully avoid them. I came home, <u>dined</u>, and went into town with Mrs Ebbett. We ended with a Priest Bath – another pleasant thing, but most curious. At first one feels attacked by Deepa's[143] friends – the humble worms. The bath is of aerated water, very hot, and you sit in the spring. But afterwards you [.....] is warm again – there is no maudlin affectation

Sunday
I am tired to death with a headache & a thoroughly weary feeling.
Like stones grey & blue hills, the great basins, the birds, the wonderful green flax swamp, and always these briars. Mist over the distant hills, the fascinating valleys of toitoi swayed by the wind. Silence again, and a world full of the loneliness and the sweetness of the wild places. Kathie in the morning in the manuka paddock saw the dew hanging from the blossoms & leaves, put it to her lips & it seemed to poison her with the longing for the sweet wildness of the plains, for the silent speech of the Silent Places, the golden rain of blossom.

Rotorua
The first evening – the yellow sky – she lies in the grass tired, & hears the X[144] bell. It sounds across the darkness ineffably tender and touching like the touch of a child's hand in the dark.

The Hamurana Spring
The still rain, the colourful tangle of willow & rose & thorn – like Millais' Ophelia, the undergrowth & then the spring – like Maurice Maeterlinck.

Monday. All Sunday the further she went from Rotorua the happier she became. Towards evening they came to a great mountain – Pohataroa – it was very rugged & old & grim – an ancient fighting pah. Here the Maoris had fought, and at the top of this peak a spring bubbled. In the blue evening it was grim, forbidden, silent, towering against the sky – an everlasting monument. Then rounding a corner they saw the Waikato river, turbulent, muddy, rushing below them, & in a little hollow, girt about with pine & willow trees, the Atiamuri Hotel. As they neared the house the persistent barking of dogs, the people hanging over the fence, the red sedately ridiculous turkeys. They camp in a paddock by the river, a wonderful spot. On one side the river, on the opposite bank great scrub covered mountains. Before them a wide sheet of swift smooth water, and a poplar tree & a long straight guerdon [sic] of pines. The willow tree, shaggy & laden, dips lazily luxuriously in the water. Just upon the bank ahead of them a manuka tree in full flowers leans towards

---

[143]'Deepa' was the family nickname for KM's great uncle Henry Herron Beauchamp, father of Mary Annette (Elizabeth) who wrote *Elizabeth and her German Garden*.
[144]'X' was KM's shorthand for 'church'.

the water – the paddock is full of manuka – two grey horses are outlined against the sky. After dinner they are happy & tired – the man comes from the hotel – yes, there are rapids to be seen, and a good track. They are not very far – she is gloomy & fidgety – they start, go through the gates, always there is a thundering sound from afar off. Down the sandy path & then branch off into a little pine avenue – the ground is red brown with needles. Great boulders come in their path, the manuka has grown over the path. With head bent, hands out, they battle through. Then suddenly a clearing of burnt manuka and they [...] cry aloud – There is the river. Savage, grey, fierce, rushing, tumbling, thrashing[?], sucking the life from the still placid flow of water behind – like waves of the sea, like fierce wolves. The noise is like thunder & right before them the lonely mountain outlined against a vivid orange sky. The colour is so intense that it is reflected in their faces, in their hair. The very rock on which they climb is hot with the colour. They climb higher, the sunset changes, becomes mauve, & in the waning light all the stretch of burnt manuka is like a thin mauve mist around them. A bird, large and widely[?] silent, flies from the river right into the flowering sky. There is no other sound except the voice of the passionate river. They climb on to a great black rock & sit huddled up there alone – fiercely almost brutally thinking – like Wagner. Behind them the sky was faintly heliotrope, & then suddenly from behind a cloud a little silver moon shone through. One sudden exquisite note in the night terza. The sky changed, glowed again, and the river sounded more thundering, more deafening. They walked back slowly, lost their way and found it, took up a handful of pine needles and smelt it, greedily – & then in the distant paddock the tent shone like a golden poppy. Washing outside, the stars, & the utter spell – magic.

Next morning – mist over the whole world. Lying, her arms over her head, she can see faintly like a grey thought the river & the mist – they are hardly distinct. She is not tired now – only happy. Goes to the door of the tent, all is very grey, there is no sun first thing, she can see the poplar tree mirrored in the water. The grass is wet, there is the familiar sound of buckets. As she brushes her hair a wave of cold air strikes her, clamps cold fingers about her heart – it is the wizard London.[145] Gradually the sun comes, the poplar is green brown, the dew shines in everything. A little group of geese and goslings float across the river, the mist becomes white, rises from the mountain ahead. There are the pines & there, just on the bank, the flowing manuka is a riot of white colour against the blue water, a lark sings, the water bubbles, she can just see ahead the gleam of the rapids. The mist seems rising & falling – here comes the theme again for the last time, & now the day fully enters with a duet for two oboes – you <u>hear</u> it. Sunshine had there ever been such sunshine. They walked down the wet road through the pine trees, the sun gleamed golden, locusts crunched in the bushes, through her thin blouse she felt it scorching her skin & was glad.     [J31-33]

---

[145]London is referred to as a wizard also in KM's poem 'Out here it is the summer time' in Notebook 1.

<u>Monday</u> on the road to Orakei Koraka. The rainbow Falls in a great basin.

We surmount[?] the hill – at the summit we look below at mile on mile of brown river winding in & out among the mountains, the banks fringed with toi toi. All the plains & hills are like a mirror for the sky. We 3 climb to a great height. Then there came rapids – great foaming rushing torrents – they tore down among the mountains, thundering, roaring. We drew rein & there was a wide space of blue forget-me-nots.

The quiet bush, & mist is in the golden moss. The silent river, the ducks, the mint, the quiet, & then through the leaves & trees, the water. Then the climb, the rocks, the uncertain foot walk, higher & higher, clinging to the trees, the shrubs, till at last on the grey rock we fling ourselves – blue as the Tropical sea where the rapids commence, & then a tumultuous foaming torrent of water, leaping, crashing, snow white, like lions fighting, thundering against the green land, & the land stretches out ineffectual arms to hold it back. It seems there is nothing in the world but this shattering sound of water – it casts into the air a shower of silver spray – it is one gigantic battle. I watch it and am one with it.

Aratiatia Rapids. The almost purple

    1 nightdress
    3 petticoat bodices
    2pr drawers
    dress shields
    handkerchiefs
    2pr stockings
    3 vests
    2 blouses[146]

then through more bush, the ferns are almost too exquisite, gloomy shades, sequestered deeps, & out again, another rock to climb, another view – here the colouring is far more intense, the purple, the blue, the great green lashed rock. The water thunders down, foam rushes, then pours itself through a narrow passage & comes out in a wide blue bay. And floating on the water are the canoe[?] remains, & more rushing white & wider passage, more eddying, & at last, far in the distance, a wide shining stretch of shadowed sweetness. Peace. We plunge back again, there is a last view. Very near the water the sound is far louder & under it all I hear the dull

<u>Monday night</u>
<Dear Man>
I am a vagrant – a Wanderer, a Gypsy tonight booming sound – it rises half a tone about each minute but that is all – it never ceases – – – & where the water catches the light there is a rainbow pink, blue and white – But it is all too short –

---

[146]This laundry list and the line of text above it occur in the middle of the preceding paragraph which was written around them.

<u>Orakei-Korako</u> Round a bend of the road & the river we see poplars tall
& strong, and a suggestion of a fence. Then more poplars & then in the
distance a great patch of flowering potatoes, mauve,[147] blue & white.
There is no sign of people, nor the sound of a dog, but we hear from among
the manuka the deathlike thudding like a paddle wheel. We go down to the
dragon's Mouth - it is a most difficult walk down a scrambling path, holding
on by bushes and trees, then there is one fierce jump & we are there. It belches
filthy steam and smoke, there is green slime and yellow scale like appearance,
infinitely impressive, and always that curious thudding engine like sound.
We walk on a broad flat terrace & there is so thin a crust that one would
[have] thought it almost dangerous to move. We see a very small geyser by the
river & mud & sulphur holes. Across the road & in the manuka is a pink mud
pool. The other side of the river are many steam holes & signs where geysers
have been. And signs where terraces might be. It is too brazenly hot for words
- we hear the whole time the noise -

Monday Night
<u>In Bed</u>.

    Dearest Baby -
    This will, I think, be my last letter to you - before I reach home - I
    wrote last to Chaddie from Rotorua - I must say I hated that town - it
    did not suit me at all - I never felt so ill or depressed - It was, I

    <u>Tuesday</u>
We drive through Wairakei through the hot day to the Huka [...] Falls.
Here the river is the colour turquoise (peacock blue) the falls utterly superb -
frothing and foaming - the foam drops for a long way down the water - again
that sound. Great poplars at the side, in the distance the gleaming river. But I
was not so impressed at first sight. We drove into the bush, then got on to a
bridge, stood there, and were silent[?] all the shuddering wonder was below us!
In the afternoon we climbed down the bank, first a ladder then rough steps,
another ladder, catching, swaying, laughing, bush to one side, and a fern
grotto, pale green, like Tannhauser - green ferns hang from the top all round in
dampness & beauty and we are below the falls, the mountain of water, the
sound - the essence of it a peculiar green. So we drove[148]

We come over the hill to Taupo. Before us the lake - in the foreground blue,
then purple, then siiver. On this side the pines, the gum trees, the clustering
houses, and a fringed yellow meadow. In the lake the little Motutaiko, and
beyond that silver watèr mountains until at last Ruapehu, snow covered,
majestic, God of it all, towers against the steel sky, already behind us Tohara is
under a cloud - all the clouds are so vivid white, grey blue. On one side there
is a little jutting promontory of green flat land. In the bracken the broom.
We approach Taupo across a white bridge - the peacock blue river along a

---

[147]'Leslie Heron Beauchamp' is written in the top margin of this page.
[148]In the top margin of this page KM has written 'waitapu = sacred water, wairaki = hot water'.

white road to the Lake Hotel. There are the Maoris lounging in the sun, one in a black & white blazer, blue pants. In the shade an old Maori drunk & a little child is crouched. Soon other Maoris come out, help the old man into a ramshackle cart where a white boney horse is very lamed. The child cries & cries, the old man sways to and fro - she holds on to him with a most pathetic gesture. They drive out of sight.

<pre>
hiko rere   =   blouse
pare kote   =   shirt
te mata kuru boots      te putu
potai       =   hat
te ata      =   breakfast
te awatea   =   dinner
te [...]    =   the [...]
</pre>

## Vignette

Sunset Tuesday.
I stand in the manuka scrub, the fairy blossom. Away ahead the pines black, the soughing of the wind. On my right the lake is cold, grey, steel-like, the quiet land sleeps beside it. Away ahead in the silver sea lies the island, then the wild sky. Everywhere the golden broom tossed its golden fragrant plumes into the evening air. I am on a little rise - to my right a great tree of mimosa laden with blossoms bends & foams in the breeze.

And, before me, the lake is drowned in the sunset. The distant mountains are silver blue, and the sky, first vivid rose, thins & spreads into a pale amber. Far away on my left the land is heavily heliotrope, curving & sharply outlined, and fold upon fold of grey sky. And far far ahead a little golden moon daintily, graciously dances in the blue floor of the sky. A white moth flutters past me. I hear always the whispering of the water.

I am alone. I am hidden. Life seems to have passed away, drifted, drifted, miles & worlds on beyond this fairy sight. Very faint & clear the bird calls & cries, and another on a little scarlet touched pine tree close by me answers with an ecstasy of song.

Then I hear steps approaching. A young Maori girl climbs slowly up the hill - she does not see me, I do not move. She reaches a little knoll and suddenly sits down native fashion, her legs crossed under her, her hands clasped in her lap. She is dressed in a blue skirt & white soft blouse. Round her neck is a piece of twisted flax & and [sic] a long piece of greenstone is suspended from it. Her black hair is twisted softly at her neck, she wears long white & red bone earrings. She is very young. She sits silent, utterly motionless, her head thrown back. All the lines of her face are passionate, violent, crudely savage, but in her lifted eyes slumbers a tragic illimitable Peace. The sky changes, softens, the lake is all grey mist, the land in heavy shadow, silence broods among the trees. The girl does not move. But very faint

& sweet and beautiful, a star wakes in the sky. She is the very incarnation of evening, and lo - the first star shines in her eyes.

Taupo. December 1907.

Taupo 10.
The road winds by the lake, then we mount through great avenues of pines & acacias to the Terraces Hotel. Here are lawns and cut trees, little corners, long hidden walks, shady paths, all the red brown pine needle carpet. The house is not pretty but poppies grow round it. All is harmonious & peaceful & delicious. We camp in a pine forest - beautiful - there are chickens cheeping, the people are so utterly benevolent, we are like children here with happiness. We dine, then the sunset, then supper at the Hotel, and the night is utterly perfect. We go to the mineral baths. The walk there down the hill is divine, the suggestion of running water and cypresses - it is very steep. And a fine bath though very hot, and a douche, so pleasant. Then home, tired, hot, happy, blissfully happy. We sleep in the tent - the wind is our lullaby. We wake early and wash & dress & go down to the bath again. Honeysuckle, roses pink & white, periwinkles, syringas, red hot pokers, those <u>yellow flowers</u> - the ground is smothered. Fruit trees with promise of harvest, the hot lake & pools, even the homely clothes-prop in the lush grass - & more mimosa. The birds are magical. I feel I cannot leave but pluck the honeysuckle, & the splashes of light lie in the pine wood.

Then goodbye Taupo and here are more plains. I feel quite at home again & at last we come to Opipi, the scene of a most horrible massacre. Only 2 men were saved - one rushed through the bush, one was cutting wood. We stop to look for water and there are 2 men - one seems the most perfect Maori - like bronze, the new pink shirt, printed images[?], his horrible licensed walk, his cigaret. Then we are in a valley of broom - such colour - it is strewn everywhere. I have never dreamed of such vivid blossom. Then lunch at Rangataiki. The store is so ugly - they do not seem glad or surprised to see us, give us fresh bread, all surly & familiar and they seem troubled[?]. And again the plain. We say goodbye to [...] and at nightfall rounding the bend reach our copse. It is a threatening evening, the farm child, the woman, her great boots - she has been digging. How glad she is to see us, her garrulous ways, the child's thoughtful fascination. Then at night among the tussocks.

Then to the Waipunga falls - river, and rain falls[?] Wound in a rolled[?] tarpaulin like a kitten, sheltering, young thing in wet clothes, bathing face neck & hands in a bucket of water. Then in the full glory of the morning, the dew on the grass & warrata, a lark thrilling madly, drinking a great pannikin of tea and a whole round of bread & jam.

December 14th. My last morning. Oh what a storm last night. And a crimson dawn, with the willows lashing together - the hollies[?]

Youth.

O Flower of Youth!
See in my hand I hold
This blossom flaming yellow & pale gold
And all its petals flutter at my feet
Can Death be sweet?

Look at it now!
Just the pale gleam is heart
Heart of the flower see is white & bare
The silken wrapping scattered on the ground
What have I found?

If one had come
On a sweet summer day
Breathless, half waking, full of youth I say
If one had come [...] from the glen
What happens then?

Sighing it dies
In the dawn flush of life
Never to know the terror & the strife
Which kills all summer blossoms when they blow.
Far better so
Ah! better better so.

K. Mansfield
December 15th 1907.

Baby                    Albert Mallinson
  send for my camera

    Timetable
    6-8    technique
    9-1    practise
    2-5    write
           Freedom

In the train – December 17th. Has there ever been a hotter day – the land is parched, golden with the heat. The sheep are sheltering in the shadow of the rocks. In the distance the hills are shimmering in the heat. M & I sitting opposite each other. I look <u>perfectly charming</u>. And I read a little book called The Book of Tea[?]. It is wholly adorable.    [J33]

December 28th. Once more I am in the train with May Gilmer this time. I am rather amused and very happy. I know or rather feel that I shall have a good day, and that is worth travelling 5000 miles. But I wonder how May Newman will feel. I rather have a suspicion that she is 'off' me, but I like me so I am happy. I have spent since returning an idle week full of nothingness.

Now before next Sunday we must be absolutely definite. Oh, the sea and
Wagner together - O thank God that I have written five poems.

Evening. So I spent it in the bush with her. She is extremely graceful,
dressed in white - she floats along. We sit in the bush, she with the sunshine
making her brown hair a lovely auburn - how fascinating. But I feel quiet -
there are poppies & sweet peas, faded coves and broken walls, poppies in the
grass - tainui[149] and cabbage trees lining the path. Salmon & potatoes and
cherries - & later - sitting in a brown tree trunk - milk & thin slices of pale
yellow cake. It is like a dream. The sea is tropically blue - there is a little island
Mana Island. At whiles through the bush we see a flax swamp, burnt to a red
black & then beyond it the sea. In the bush there is a great deal of fern.
My little pipi-wharoua[150] is heard again and again. How hot the sand is -
it burns my feet through my brown shoes. I take off my hat & put on, rather
like a Spanish lady, a little brown veil. We talk MUSIC. Chiefly Macdowell[151]
& Chopin, and I, alas, feel a little superior.

And that one solitary tree - how aged. I ought to make a good author.
I certainly have the ambition and the ideas but have I the power to carry it all
through? Yes - if I get back but not unless I do - but after all <u>why not</u>.     [J33-34]

The year has dawned.    My Year.
          1 9 0 8
And a Happy New Year to you. O the sky, the great star, the light, the sound,
the little Xes, the drunkards, the cool air, the hootings.[152]
Well - I have the brain and also the inventive faculty! What else is needed?

                                                                          [J34]

23rd January.  I wait for Clara Butt and Kennerly Rumford.[153] Now there is
Kathleen Smith's sister - a pale slender girl with long black hair brushed back
from her face - a most childish figure. She is with her Mother & sister.
She wears a cream satin opera coat with long lace in the sleeves. The dull quiet
house, the arum lilies on the balcony, the heavy furniture, the library full of
dust, the faded photographs of her Father, her Mother's feebleness, her quaint
manners, insufficient food & no daylight. Such is the life to this Althea.
Dickens of course. Thackeray & Stevenson. Some letters, a great many old
diaries. So she grows older, put into all this silence. The old servant & two
decrepit terrible dogs with impossible names, the walks - very sedate -
occasional rides in a tram car, & the feeble music - she plays on the piano -
it has pleated satin let in at the rosewood back. Meagre fires, no visits, and a
small bedroom with a little white china angel holding holy water. The church,

---

[149]Tainui: *Pomaderris apetala*, a shrub with greenish flowers.
[150]Pipi-wharauroa: shining cuckoo.
[151]See note 76.
[152]The noises of New Year's Eve in Wellington included (and still do), 'the little Xes'—church
bells—and 'hootings'—the midnight horns and salutes of all the ships in the harbour.
[153]Clara Butt (contralto) and her husband Kennerley Rumford (baritone), undergoing an Australasian
concert tour, gave three concerts in Wellington on the 21st, 23rd and 25th of January 1908 which were
described in the *New Zealand Free Lance* of 1 February 1908 as 'the greatest events in our musical history
so far.'

the romantic influence. How one day she puts two roses in her hair and stands in front of a mirror and sees that she is beautiful.      [J35]

A wet afternoon in the Library[154] – in March. I have read most strange books here – one on the Path to Rome, one of Maori Art – – – Through the long avenue of pine trees, where the shadow of Night crept from tree to tree. The Autumn afternoon it really would be better to call it so. This is what I want – the little asphalt path like a mauve ribbon, the great fragrant warm sweetness of the pine needles massed & heaped together, ruddy with perfume. Then the trees – hundreds there seem in the dull light, a vast procession of gloomy forms. Now here, now there, the shades of night are trooping softly, the air is heavy with a faint uneasy sound, a restless beating to & fro, a long unceasing sigh, & far away in the distance there is a dreary waste of grey sea – a desert of heaving water.

Grey, grey – there is no light in it at all, & the autumn air is cold with the coldness of drowned men. And Night is rising out of the sea – a ghastly broken form, & the autumn world sinks into that broken embrace, pillows its tired head upon that pulseless heart.

There is a little asphalt path like a mauve ribbon, and it is fringed with a vast procession of pine trees. In this dull light there seem to be hundreds of them. They are huddled together and muffled in their gloomy shadows.

On the earth a fragrant sweetness & pine needles, massed & heaped up, ruddy with perfume. And through the black lace-like tracery of trees a pale sky full of hurrying clouds. Far away in the distance a dreary waste of grey sea, a desert of heaving water.

Grey, grey . . . there is no light at all, and the autumn air is cold with the coldness of traceless spaces. Out of the grey sea creeps the ghastly, drowned body of Night. Her long dark hair swam among the branches of the pine trees, her dead body walks along the little mauve ribbon of an asphalt path.
She stretches out her arms and the autumn world sinks into that frozen embrace, pillows its tired head upon that pulseless heart.

And the long procession of pine trees, huddled together, are ghostly fearful snowmen at the wedding with Death.

January 23rd. Morgen habe ich sehr viele Glück gehabt, auch Herr Weston hätte Mittagessen mit uns gehabt.[155]

Nau i waka ana te kakahu he taniko taku.[156]
You wove the garment, I put the border to it.

---

[154]During this time KM had reader's privileges at the General Assembly Library, usually referred to by her as 'the Parliamentary Library', in Molesworth Street.
[155]'This morning I was very lucky, Mr Weston also had lunch with us.'
[156]This is a slightly incorrect rendering of a Māori proverb 'Nāu i whatu te kākahu he tāniko tāku' which means, literally, 'By you is woven the garment, the decorative border is mine.' Less literally it can mean 'The cloak is woven before the ornamental border is added' or 'It is the parents who are responsible for the character of the child' or 'You had the story, I supplied the words for it.'

Outside the Town Hall
January 23rd

Mein lieber Freund -
Die letze woche hat Dr Crosby mir - Ihre "Reverie du Soir" -
mitgebrocken - So muss ich etwas schreiben - Iche finde diese Werk so
wunderbar schön - so träumerisch - und auch so sehnsuchtsvoll.
Hoffenlich, diese Jahre - höre ich Ire die Reverie du Soir in einer
Konzert spielen! Meine gute Freundin Ida Baker hat mir mehrerere
Blätter von den Zeitunge gegeben - Was für eine succès merveille.
Oftenmals in meinen Gedanken habe ich Ihnen kongratuliert. Ich
komme nach England früh in March - Ich hasse Wellington - und -
naturlich sehne ich nach London - Haben sie mehrere Journaux von mir
gehabt? Und was denken sie von dieser? Warum haben sie mir nicht
erzählt! Wie geht Ihren Vater - und auch die Mutter und auch Ihren liebe
würdige Schwesterchen? Das Haus - achtzehn Buller Strasse - steht so
einsam aus! Mit vielen Grüssen fur diese Jahre 1908.
                                        Ihre Freundin
                                                K.
Muss aber Deutsch schreiben. Es giebt so vielen Leuten - der gar nicht
diese Sprache kennen![157]

January 28th 1908.
Books selected for study:-
Charles Dickens      G.K. Chesterton
Literary Geography      William Sharp.


          Charles Dickens 1812.
egalitarian - the egalitarian French Rev. idea - tends to produce great men.
Our meals, our manners and our daily dress are random symbols of the soul.
p.16. By simply going on being absurd a thing can become godlike; there is
but one step from the ridiculous to the sublime! p.21. Dream for one mad
moment that the grass is green. 23. It is from the backs of the elderly
gentlemen that the wings of the butterfly should burst. p.35. His soul was a
shot silk of black and crimson, not a mixed colour of grey and purple. Youth is

---

[157]The translation of this draft letter to Tom Trowell is as follows
My dear friend -
Last week Dr Crosby brought me – your "Reverie du Soir" - So I have to write something – I find this
work so wonderfully beautiful – so dreamy – and so full of longing too. I hope I shall hear you play the
Reverie du Soir in a concert this year! My good friend Ida Baker has given me several pages from the
newspapers – What a succès merveille. Often in my thoughts I have congratulated you. I am coming to
England in early March – I hate Wellington – and – of course I long for London – Have you had several
journaux from me? And what do you think of them? Why haven't you told me? How is your father – and
your mother too, and also your dear worthy little sister? The house – 18 Buller Street – stands so lonely!
With many greetings for this year 1908.
                    Your friend
                            K.
But must write German. There are so many people – who don't know this language at all.

almost everything else but original.
pragmatical =
de minimus non amat lex =
<u>Manners</u> those grand rhythms of the social harmony. p.127.

### Juliette Delacour

It happened that on Juliette Delacour's fourth birthday she played on a wide
balcony with her Father. It was a golden day – from the garden below floated
the scents of flowers innumerable – roses and lilies, mignonette, and the faint
mystic sweetness of carnations.

Juliette was never still. She had received a little book & a china tea pot
full of chocolates – a charming tea pot painted all over with a design of cats
and babies. She held up her white frock & danced to & fro, to & fro. Her
father lay in a long cushioned chair, a coloured rug about his knees, and she
had given him to make him better her tea pot. "Hold it carefully, dear Papa"
she cried, "hold it carefully". Sunshine streamed upon them both – upon the
man's pale face, upon the child's wildrose tinted cheeks. A dainty wind stirred
the flowers in the garden below – it blew Juliette's black silk-like hair across
her face.

And at the same moment – Oh, terrible, unforgettable horror – the tea
pot fell to the ground where its silver paper spoils scattered here & there.
The child uttered a little cry of mingled disappointment & astonishment.
Her Father's head was sunk upon his breast, the rug had slipped on [to] the
balcony floor. She thought he had fallen asleep, ran to him & shook him by
the arm, beat upon his cheeks – roughly, with her child hands. "Papa Papa
wake up, don't be frightened dear, about the tea pot." Juliette knelt on the
floor and stripping a chocolate of its silver paper she held it close to him, tried
to force it into his mouth. "See Papa, just one. I'm not angry." Suddenly she
burst into a frightful passion of weeping, and so they found her, & carried her
to her room.

And the next day she was led into a dark room. Looking back upon it in
after years, the room seemed to assume gigantic proportions – a vast gloomy
cavern. She was told to kiss the white face upon the little bed. For a moment
she shrank back, frightened, but then leaned forward – & so they lay a little
space, warm cheek against cold cheek, & the lilies smothering both.

In after years it seemed to Juliette that never again was there so much
sunlight. The great brown house was partially closed, shutters were drawn
across the windows, the furniture was enveloped in ghostlike hideous shapeless
coverings. There were never any flowers on the tables and shelves, and her
Mother dismissed all the servants except an old Frenchwoman – she cooked
for and waited on them all – her Mother, her sister, and she.

While the Summer flowers were still sweet in the garden her Mother
taught her to read from an old red book used years ago by her tall pale sister
who sat so placidly sewing all day long, and embroidering grapes & leaves
upon a square frame. Her Mother in her dull dress, her faded face, curiously
calm, awed & terrified the child. But she learnt with ease & rapidity, reading

aloud the little old world foolish stories with such passionate eagerness that her Mother was amazed. The brown house stood far back from a narrow tree lined road. But the garden was so full of trees & lawns, flowers & hedges, little overgrown paths, deserted arbours, that Juliette never passed out of the gates. And no people ever disturbed their solitude.

The Unexpected Must Happen.

Guy Gaythorn knocked the ash from his cigar end into the fire behind his back, restored the comfort to his lips, tilted his head further back if that were possible, & balancing himself on his toes for half a second, proceeded – "You are half witch, Judith, and half pussy cat my dear – that subtle combination which is so essentially feminine, but if you were not so young, so completely childish – it is no use denying the fact – I should be seriously annoyed."

The lady upon the opposite side of the table plucked a feather from her fan & blew it across the polished surface where it lay like a tiny swan on a dark miniature lake. "Allow me to assure you, sir, that under the circumstances I feel my action in this matter to be beyond reproach." She suddenly rose, stretched out her white arms and looked at him, half laughing, half angry, from under her long lashes. "Why on earth, because in a weak moment I became engaged to you, am I to regard you as the only Adam. Why, the Garden of Eden now a days is simply stocked with them and they are like Penny-in-the-slot machines, Guy – they all fascinate me, and I want to find out about them all. So for Heaven's sake don't develop the middle aged, vulgar, jealous husband attitude, but leave me my adorable Macdowell – the boy needs a woman – his Father's history you know – in peace.

The man made no reply for a moment. Then with a sudden movement, almost with fierceness he took his wife in his arms, kissed her passionately, then pushed her gently back into her seat. "We have argued quite long enough, & quite often enough upon this – to me – painful subject, Judith. I will have no more of it. Let us now spend a quiet evening together." She was surprised, satisfied, soothed with the spontaneous passion of the man, but a frightful fear had crept into her very blood. Why would he not leave her as he had intended, and meet his friends at the Admiralty Club. God! What would he say or do if the door were to open, as in a few moments it would open, and Cecil, eager, living, excitable, burst into the room. She could not forgive herself for her foolish action in giving him the duplicate key to her flat – it was so lacking in dignity, it <u>looked</u> so bad, even though she knew it meant nothing. She clasped her hands convulsively. What could she do, how could she <u>make</u> Guy go.

It was strongly evident that her husband would not leave her. To get him away from their room she must go with him. This <u>must</u> be done. <u>How</u>! Suddenly a thought seized her & the relief that it brought lighted her face with what Guy interpreted as love. Moving quickly to the window she lifted the blind, & the moonlight flooded the room & killed the firelight. "Guy it is moonlight again, just as it was that happy night. Let us walk for a while" & her voice was full of trembling persuasion. "Do you want to Judith" he said. "Let us go. Life is too short for you and me to quarrel. Run and get on your coat & hat."

Swiftly she left the room & ran along the passage. She was standing in front of the mirror buttoning her jacket when - was it fancy - it could not be reality - she heard the front door open & close, steps across the hall, then her husband's voice, loud and commanding. "Your[e] Cecil Macdowell."

She stood motionless, helpless, listening intensely for further sounds. The painful throbbing at her temples suggested some long forgotten melody which repeated & repeated itself maddeningly. But there came no sound from the sitting room. Then suddenly the door opened, the two men came out - talking excitedly, her husband paused to put on a coat & hat & the next moment the hall door had clicked behind them & she was alone!

- - - great white hungry lions, tumbling over each other, screaming, roaring, shaking back their long manes, fighting, foaming to reach the long stretch of sweet warm sand. They are full of an eternal desire, they are miserable with the Misery of Eternity. Have I ever been so happy before. Across the blue sea floated a boat with an orange sail, a butterfly on a blue blossom. Now the Italian fishermen are sailing in, their white sail bellying in the wind. Far away a man is rowing in a little boat. On the beach a group of fishermen in blue jerseys, thick blue trousers rolled to the knees. The sun shines on their crisp black hair, it shines on their faces so that their skins are the colour of warm amber, it shines on their bare legs & firm brown arms. They are drawing shoreward a little open boat - the Napoli - the long black wet rope running through their fingers & falling in a mystic pattern on the foam blown sand. And there are long delicate golden brown sprays of beautiful seaweed, a

[158]
The partisans of analysis describe minutely the state of the soul, the secret motive of every action as being of far greater importance than the action itself. The partisans of objectivity give us the result of this evolution sans describing the secret processes. They convey the state of the soul through the slightest gesture - i.e. realism, flesh covered bones, which is the artists method for me. In as much as art seems to me <u>pure vision</u> I am indeed a partisan of objectivity. Yet I cannot take the simile of the soul and the body for the bone is no bony framework. Supposing ones bones were not bone but liquid light - which suffuses itself, fluctuates - well and good, but the bones are permanent and changeless - .˙. - - that fails.

<u>Thursday</u>. I am at the sea - at Island Bay[159] in fact - lying flat on my face on the warm white sand. And before me the sea stretches - miles, after all, the

---

[158]KM has turned the book upside down to write the following paragraph, and then turned it back again.

[159]Island Bay, in Wellington, is on the southern coast of the North Island. The snow covered peaks of the South Island's Kaikoura Ranges are often spectacularly visible.

horizon looks. To my right, shrouded in mist like a fairy land, a dream country, the snow mountains of the South Island. To my left, fold upon fold of splendid golden hills, two white lighthouses like great watching birds perched upon them. A huge yellow dog lies by me; he is wet & ruffled, and I have no boots or stockings on. A print dress, a panama hat, a big parasol.
Adelaida I wish that you were with me.

Where the rocks lie their shadow is thickly violet upon the green blue. You know that <u>peacock</u> shade of water. Blue it is with the blueness of Rossetti, green with the greenness of William Morris. Oh, what a glorious day this is. I shall stay here until after dark, walking along the beach, the waves foaming over my feet, drinking a great deal of tea & eating a preposterous amount of bread & apricot jam at a little place called The Cliff House.

Across the blue sea a boat is floating with an orange sail. Now the Maori fishermen are sailing in, their white sail bellying in the wind. On the beach a group of them, with blue jerseys, thick trousers rolled to their knees. The sun shines on their thick crisp hair, & shines on their faces, so that their skins are the colour of hot amber. It shines on their bare legs & firm brown arms. They are drawing in a little boat called "Te Kooti", the wet rope running through their fingers and falling in a mystic pattern on the foam blown sand.     [J9-10]

Evening.   By the sea.   Lying thus on the sand, the foam almost washing over my hands, I feel the magic of the sea. Behind the golden hills the sun is going down, a ruby jewel in a lurid setting, and there is a faint flush everywhere over sea & land. To my right the sky has blossomed into vivid rose but to my left the land is hidden by a grey blue mist lightened now here now there by a suggestion of the sun- colour - it is like land seen from a ship a very long way away - dreamland, mirage, enchanted country. Two sea birds high in the air fly screaming towards the light. It beats upon their white breasts, it flames upon their dull wings. Far away a little boat is sailing on the sweet water, a golden butterfly upon the dainty bosom of a mystic blossom.

And now the Italian fishermen are sailing in, their white sail bellying in the breeze - several come rowing in a little boat. They spring ashore. The sun shines on their crisp black hair. It shines on their faces, so that their skin is the colour of hot amber, on their bare legs & strong brown arms. They are dragging towards them the boat, the long black wet rope running through their fingers & falling in a mystic pattern on the foam blown sand. They call to one another. I cannot hear what they say but against the long rhythmic pulsing of the sea their voices sound curiously insignificant, like voices in a dream.

And there are exquisite golden brown sprays & garlands of seaweed set about with berries, white and brown. Are they flowers blown from the garden of the sea-King's daughter - does she wander through the delicate coral forest seeking them, her long hair floating behind her, playing upon a little silver shell? And near me I see a light upon the blue coast - steadily tenderly it beams - a little candle set upon the great altar of the world. The glow pales in the sky, on the land, but the voice of the sea grows stronger. Oh, to sail & sail into the heart of the sea. Is it darkness and silence there or is – a Great Light. So the grey sand slips – sifts through my fingers. Night comes swiftly.

February.

Vignette.
Outside, the carts rattled past through the hot street. Some woman outside my window was talking loudly, shrieking with laughter. A little breath stirred the window curtains – they moved languidly to & fro.

The pursuit of experience is the refuge of the unimaginative.

<u>Vignette</u>   Summer in Winter.
Through the wild Winter afternoon Carlotta[160] at the piano sang of love. Standing by the window I watched her beautiful passionate profile. The walls were hung with daffodil silk – a faint golden light seemed to linger on her face. She wore a long black frock & a hat with a drooping black feather. Her gloves, her great ermine coat, her silver purse were flung over the lounge beside her. The air was faintly scented with the perfume she loved that Winter – peau d'Espagne. There was a little fire of juniper wood burning in the grate & the flames cast into the room strange grotesque shadows that leapt upon the walls, the curtains, that lurked under the chairs, behind the lounge, that hid in the corners, & seemed to point long shadow fingers at Carlotta. She sang & sang and the room seemed warm & full of sunshine & happy flowers.

"Come" her voice cried to me "and we shall wander in a mystic garden filled with beautiful nonexistent flowers. And I alone possess the key, I alone can search out the secret paths. Lo! there is a bower lit with the pale light of gardenia blossom, & the fountains are filled with laughing water." I drew back the heavy curtains from the window – the rain was splashing against the glass. The house opposite repelled me – it was like the face of an old old man drowned in tears. In the garden below rotting leaves were heaped upon the lawns in the walls, the skeleton trees rattled together, the wind had torn a rose bush from the ground – it sprawled across the path, ugly & thorn-encrusted. Heavily, drearily fell the winter rain upon the dead garden, upon the skeleton trees. I turned from the window & in the warm firelit room, with almost a noble defiance in her voice, Carlotta at the piano sang passionately of love.

9.11.07.

[161]
<u>Vignette</u>.
This is Angelica
Fallen from Heaven
Fallen from Heaven
Into my arms.

---

[160]'Carlotta' was one of KM's names for Maata Mahupuku.
[161] At this point in the notebook there are several pressed and dried blossoms.

Will you go back again
Little Angelica
Back into Heaven
Out of my arms.

"No", said Angelica
Here is my Heaven
Here is my heaven
Here in your arms

Not out of Heaven
But into my Heaven
Here have I fallen
Here in your arms.

In the pocket of an old coat I found one of Ariadne's[162] gloves - a cream suède glove fastening with two silver buttons. And it has been there two years. But still it holds some exquisite suggestion of Carlotta - still when I lay it against my cheek I can detect the sweet of the perfume she affected. O, Carlotta - have you remembered. We were floating down Regent Street in a hansom, on either side of us the blossoms of golden light, and ahead a little half hoop of a moon.   [J35-36]

[163]
      1799-1850
<u>Balzac</u>. "La passion est toute l'humanité."
In him, as in all great artists, there is something more than nature - a divine excess, <u>an over plus</u>.
His supreme passion is the passion of <u>Will</u>. His creations are full of fire - each man & each woman called by name responds as does King Lear or Hamlet.
He is concerned with the senses through the intellect. His style is by no means perfect - the stylist sees life through coloured glasses. Balzac deals in the elemental passions & desires, and <u>money</u> is with him a symbol, not an entity. Here is the thesis of the Human Comedy.
<u>First</u>       effects
<u>Second</u>     causes
<u>Third</u>       Principles
Essai sur les forces humaines.
Filled with the joy of creation he lived most vividly. He loved 2 women, the second whom he married, Madame de Hanska, was the Beatrice to his Dante. Balzac is colossal.

<u>Prosper Mérimée</u>. attendissement une fois par an. "In history I care only for anecdotes." There is always with him this union of <u>curiosity</u> with <u>indifference</u> - student curiosity; the indifference of the man of the world.

---

[162]'Ariadne' was another of the names bestowed upon Maata.
[163]The next page carries two outline pencil sketches which look like a Māori sleeping house and a food storehouse. KM would have drawn these when she was on her Urewera trip and not as late as their position in the notebook would suggest.

De Quincy - a tangled attempt to communicate the incommunicable - his narrative like a worm turning back upon itself as it moves. His prose is shouted from the platform.

Nathaniel Hawthorne - he is with Tolstoi the only novelist of the soul. He is concerned with what is abnormal- "was plucked up out of a mystery and had its roots still clinging to him." His people are dreams, sometimes faintly conscious that they dream. He too often substitutes fancy for imagination. "His feeling for flowers was very exquisite & seemed not so much a taste as an emotion." Writes with his nerves - White Magic.

Walter Pater - an exquisite fineness. "rêve le miracle d'une prose poétique musicale sans rhythme et sans rime." "Philosophy is a systematic appreciation of a kind of music in the very nature of things" (Plato & Platonism)

R.L.S. A literary vagrant. True style is not the dress, but the flesh of the thought. "He awakens the eternal spirit of romance even in the bosom of the conventional."

Flaubert. Nous ne suivons plus la même route, nous ne navignons plus dans la même nacelle. Moi je ne cherche pas le port, mais la haute mer.

### Leves Amores[164]

But in the night, lo every bird upon the bulging screen broke into song, lo every flower upon the tattered paper budded and foamed into blossom. Yes, even the green vine upon the bed curtains wreathed itself into strange chaplets & garlands, twined round us in a leafy embrace, held us with a thousand clinging tendrils.

I can never forget the Thistle Hotel.[165] I can never forget that strange Winter night. I had asked her to dine with me and then go to the Opera. My room was opposite hers. She said she would come but could I do up her evening bodice - it was hooks at the back. Very well. It was still daylight when I knocked at her door and entered. In her petticoat bodice and a full silk petticoat she was washing - sponging her face & neck. She said she was finished, that I could sit on the bed & wait for her.

And I looked round at the dreary room. The one filthy window faced the street - she could see the choked cobwebbed dustgrimed windows of a warehouse opposite. For furniture the room contained a low bed draped with revolting yellow vine-patterned curtains, a chair, a wardrobe with a piece of cracked mirror attached, a washstand. But the paper almost hurt me physically

---

[164]'Leves Amores' ('casual loves') has given rise to a good deal of speculation. Either it describes a lesbian encounter or it is a piece of narrative fiction in which the narrator is male. KM said of it in a letter to her father's secretary who typed it for her 'I can't think how I wrote it – it's partly a sort of dream.' (CLKM I, p35). There is a typescript of it in the Newberry Library which, although it carries the autograph signature 'K Mansfield', differs in several respects from this manuscript version and is the only version so far published. In this manuscript it can be seen that KM wrote the finale of the story before writing the story itself.
[165]The Thistle Hotel was a small Public House in Mulgrave St, half a mile from where the Beauchamps lived in Fitzherbert Terrace. It is still flourishing today as the oldest extant hotel in New Zealand.

– it hung in tattered strips from the wall, in its less discoloured & faded patches I could trace the pattern of roses – birds & flowers – and the frieze was a conventional design of buds – of what species the good God knows.

And this was where she lived. I watched her curiously. She was pulling on long thin stockings & saying damn because she could not fasten her suspenders. And I felt within me a certainty that nothing beautiful could ever happen in that room, and for her I felt contempt, a little tolerance, a little pity. A dull grey light hovered over the room yet seemed to accentuate the thin tawdriness of her clothes, the squalor of her life. She looked, too, dull & grey & tired. And I sat by the bed and thought – come, this is old age. I have forgotten passion. I have been left behind in the beautiful golden-voiced procession of Youth. I am seeing life in the dressing room of the theatre now.

So we dined somewhere & went to the Opera. It was late when we came out into the crowded night street, late and cold. She gathered up her long skirts – silently we walked back to the Thistle Hotel, down the white pathway fringed with beautiful golden lilies, up the amethyst staircase. Was Youth dead. Was Youth dead? She told me as we walked along the corridor to her room she was glad that night had come. I did not ask why. I was glad to[o]. It seemed a secret between us. So I went with her into her room to undo those troublesome hooks. She lit a little candle on an enamel bracket. The light filled the room with darkness. Like a sleepy child she slipped off her frock & then suddenly turned to me & flung her arms round my neck.

And Youth was not dead.

– – – – – – – – – – – – – – – –

Rewa[166] felt that she had entered upon a new life, that she was purified, reborn. She slipped off her blouse, drew on a white jersey & short blue skirt, and went for a walk. The rain had ceased, the sea thundered against the brown rocks in the brown sand. The sky was faintly mirrored in the yellow puddles. On both sides of the road the toi toi branches bent in the wind to shake out their fluffy golden hair. She had never seen the bush more exquisite. Each separate tree fern seemed to take new life. Great bushes of briar berries heavy with silver rain drops flashed against the green hills, & once, listening intently, Rewa heard the sweet wild song of the pipiwharauroa. She walked rapidly, her head thrown back. She tore off a great branch of briar berries & swung them in one hand. The sea sounded sturdy, resolute, full – – It seemed to call upon her to live a boundless free glorious life, to revel in her physical strength, her mental fitness, to keep[?] the world.

The cottage stood upon a great ledge of brown rock that stretched out to sea.

Now it would be colossally interesting if I could only write a really good novel. Something unusual that would surely catch on – a trifle outré in the

---

[166]This fragment seems to be the beginning of an idea which KM developed further in Notebook 8, to appear later in this edition (p 220). In a letter to her sister Vera, of May–June 1908 (CLKM 1, p46) KM refers to it as 'a novel entitled The Youth of Rewa'.

main - something that would make me really famous. Let's see!!!
K sat on the rug.

High in the dingy tenement house
the sick lay
So my poor Aunt Harriet is dead with Bright's disease and heart failure. I am
so sorry, but what is to be done?

In the train. Liverpool.[?]
I am in a carriage with fier [ie vier?] männe. An old [...] with a look of a Will
Owen[167] bargee, a blue & white striped necktie - he is stamped with the
impress of labor. Opposite, a younger one - great square ears, a stupid receding
chin, a nose like an ill-bred dog. Both men carry baskets covered down with
black American cloth. One is quite talkative, the other relegates his
conversational powers to 'ay'. At Hereford a man & a woman enter & sit
opposite me & never do I see them without bundles [of] violets & maiden
hair and a little asparagas fern. What I notice most of them is their unfinished
look, a half formed look, a lack of curse or grace. His enormous tan boots
& purple hands, a cut finger bound with a soiled cloth. His tiepin a horseshoe
with a racing whip through the centre. The woman blushes - her hair is
shockingly overdressed; he has presumably suffered from boils on the neck.
Both have very bad [...] What can she talk of - they are to me hardly human.
I know I repel them - I feel it. Now they go out & a woman comes in with
two children, a plain woman with scraped back hair & a pink silk scarf. The
boy is Jo. The little girl, her face burnt red in the sun - she has hand knitted
socks & little leather boots & smiles - such a merry face. She bosses & drives
the little boy. And a man enters the carriage, very fair & full blooded - he reads
a book of Meat Inspection, I the poems of Dante Gabriel Rossetti - the
Fleshly School of Poetry.

Night. J'attends pour la première fois dans ma vie le crise de ma vie. As I wait,
a flock of sheep pass down the street in the moonlight. I hear the cracking [of]
the whip & behind the dark heavy cart - like a death cart, il me semble. And
all in this sacrificial light. I look lovely. I do not fear, I only feel. I pray the
dear Lord I have not waited too long for my soul hungers as my body all day
has hungered & cried for him. Ah come now - soon. Each moment, il me
semble, is a moment of supreme danger, but this man I love with all my heart.
The other I do not even care about. It comes. I go to bed.[168]        [J35]

It is the evening of Good Friday; the day of all the year surely the most
significant. I always always feel the nail prints in my hands, the sickening thirst
in my throat, the agony of Jesus. He is surely not dead and surely all whom we
love who have died are close to us - Grandmother and Jesus & all of them.
Oh, lend me your aid - I thirst too, I hang upon the cross. Let me be crucified
so that I may cry "it is finished".

---

[167]Will Owen was a cartoonist for *Punch* magazine who specialised in comic drawings of inshore
fishermen, 'old salts', bargees etc.
[168]The juxtaposition of this entry with the following one made Murry uncomfortable. He pencilled a
note: 'These entries do not belong to the same time', and he omitted the second of them.

I could find no rest
Tossed & turned, and cried aloud, I suffer.
In my tortured breast
Turned the knife, & probed the flesh more deeply.

Up against it – Life seemed like a wall
Brick and fouled & grimed.

Oh delicate branches reaching out for the sun
The plants – on tiptoe stretching up [to] the light.

I cannot say it now. Maybe I shall be able to, much later.
In an agony I shall suddenly express myself – it is the joy
of self expression  –  –  –

Do you see him?

Look, in the half light here,
High behind the curtain hanging there
See how it swings & trembles
Oh woman do not cry upon him so
It is the wind that makes the curtain blow
Pillow thy head upon my barren breast.
The child! he comes & stands beside my chair
Then claps his hands upon my eyes – "who's there
Motherling." "Ive no notion[?] – its not you."

The child he came into this room tonight
Groping his way – Why havent you a light
Mother. My eyes were tired with weeping dear
I'm not afraid of dark if you stay here
(Oh the thought in heart & brain
He cannot see the light again.)

The child – he came & stood beside my chair
Then pressed his hands before my eyes. "Who's there
Motherling – guess." It never could be you.
Oh no – three guesses – wait then that's too few  –  –  –
The only hands to bring her calm
Folded closely, palm to palm.

The child – he shyly stood in front of me
Am I too big to sit upon your knee
Motherling? I'm too tired for any fun
If I'm too heavy – "No my little son."
(The blood within her veins ran cold
Light he was – so light to hold)
The child – he hid his face against my breast
Crying "Oh Mother let me rest."        [J38-40]

In the train to Harwich.[169] I am afraid I really am not at all myself – so here I am – I took a drug this afternoon & slept until after five – then Ida woke me – Still half asleep & terribly tired I packed – had some supper – M.[170] most excited at the prospect of me going away again & still on the spur of the moment, I take the train to Liv.S.S.[171] bought a 2nd class ticket & here I am – tired out still but unable to sleep. The carriage is full – but Garnie I feel that I am going <u>home</u>. To escape England it is my great desire – I loathe England. It is a dark night full of rain. There is a little child opposite me in a red cloak sleeping. She shakes her hair much as Dolly[172] did when I was a girl in Brussels so many years ago – Everybody sleeps but I – The train shatters through the darkness. I wear a green silk scarf & a dark brown hat with a burst of dull pink velvet. I travel under the name of Mrs K. Bendall –

Morning in the Bruxelles – I have slept splendidly – taken a small brandy & soda before turning in – and now feel almost better, though I have still that intolerable headache which has haunted me – I sit in the ladies cabin on my hat box washed & dressed & very evidently amused – at everybody – I have just washed & brushed my hair. The people. Oh the fat lady in pink wool – ye Gods – & the other pious old English governess – who intends staying at a convent just outside Brussels – Everybody thinks I am French – I must go to Cooks & see about everything.

29th April – In this room. Almost before this is written I shall read it from another room and such is Life. Packed again I leave for London. Shall I ever be a happy woman again. Je ne pense pas, je ne veux pas. Oh to be in New York. Hear me, I can't rest – that's the agonizing part.

'Tis a sweet day, Brother, but I see it not. My <u>body</u> is so self conscious – Je pense of all the frightful things possible – "all this filthiness" – Sick at heart till I am physically sick – with no home – no place in which I can hang up my hat – & say here I belong – for there is no such place in the wide world for me. But attendez – you must not eat, & you had better not sleep! No good <u>looking</u> 'fit' & <u>feeling</u> dead.

<u>In the train to Anvers</u>. I love Belgium for I love green & mauve. I wonder when I shall sit & read aloud to my little son.     [J40-41]

"Whatever actually occurs is spoiled for Art." Wilde – in his essay on Wainwright says "It is only the Philistine who seeks to measure a personality by the vulgar test of production. Life itself is an Art."
"A truth in art is that which [is] contradictory is also true." Wilde, as Symons so aptly says, was the "supreme artist in intellectual attitudes." To the Italian,

---

[169]KM was still using this notebook in 1909 when, on her way to Brussels, she scribbled into it this draft of a letter to Garnet Trowell to whom she had switched her affections from his twin brother Tom.
[170]'M' was Margaret Wishart, a music student who, with KM, lived at Beauchamp Lodge in London, and with whom KM had been to Brussels a few months earlier.
[171]Liverpool Street Station.
[172]Dolly was the younger sister of the Trowell twins. KM is referring here to a visit made by the Beauchamp sisters with their aunt Belle Dyer when the girls were at school, to Brussels where the Trowell twins were studying music.

Love "comes from a root in Boccaccio, through the stem of Petrarch, to the flower of Dante." And so he becomes the idealist of material things, instead of the materialist of spiritual things - like Wilde - and after Beardsley the spirit is known only through the body - the body is but clay in the shaping or destroying hands of the spirit. "Soul & senses, senses & soul" - here is the innate spirit of Henry Wotton, here is the quintessence of Wilde's life, <of Dowson, and of Arthur Symons two most vitally interesting books of Poems. To Pater this did not so exactly apply>,[173] yet there is a very real sensuousness in his earliest Portraits - a certain voluptuous pleasure in garden scents. "Well, nature is immoral. Birth is a grossly sexual thing - - - Death is a grossly physical thing."

The Renaissance cultivated personality as we cultivate orchids - striving after a heightening of natural beauty which is not nature - a perversity which may be poisonous - -
    - "K.M. says the <u>intensity</u> of an action is its truth." "Not everyone can become the artist of his own life, or have the courage to go his own way." D'Annunzio cannot imagine beauty without a pattern. <u>Is a thing the expression of an individuality?</u>

Mallarmé.
"La chair est triste, hélas! et j'ai lu tous les livres."
For the principles of Art are eternal - the principles of Morality ebb and flow even with the <u>climate</u>. Whatever I find in Humanity is part of the eternal substance which nature wears for Art to combine into a beautiful pattern.

<u>The Moods of Men</u>. Whatever has existed has achieved the right to artistic existence. But experience is not everything. Much depends on the experimentalist. Formal art is so apt to be the enemy of artists - Symons.

Mérimée has les idées très arrêtées. The artist becomes an artist by the intensification of Memory - extraneous. It is the clear sighted sensitiveness of a man who watches human things closely, bringing them home to himself with the deliberate essaying art of an actor who has to represent a particular passion in movement!

Now I really do want to write. Here is silence - peace - save for the dull murmur of the sea - the sea, almost as Little Paul knew it.
There is the island - the sea ripples up against the beach so passive, so beautiful. Ah! Quelle joie.

<u>Zola</u> defines Art as nature seen through a temperament (drives in a victoria to see the peasants).

<u>Maupassant</u> - his abundant vitality. Great artists are those who can make men see their particular illusion. (That is true with limitations.)

---

[173]KM has written in the margin beside this crossed out passage 'Good God! What a creature!'

<u>Balzac</u>. <u>The partisans of analysis</u> describe minutely the state of the soul – the secret motives of every action – as being of infinitely greater importance than the action itself.

<u>The partisans of objectivity</u> give us the result of the evolution without describing the secret processes. He makes his characters so demean themselves that their slightest gesture shall be the expression of their souls. So there is more colour. It is a portrait, but the flesh covers the bones. He was trained under the severe eye of Flaubert.

"The light soul of the champagne flew off in tiny bubbles."

<u>Philosophy of George Meredith</u>
<u>Memoirs of the 18th Century</u>. Paston

I wish indeed that I had a fountain pen. I won't be able to write anything else all day because I feel like an exhausted being. As though all the energy has left me after that one splendid <u>burst</u> of it.

> ½ lb flour
> ¼ lb sugar
> ¼ lb walnuts
> 2 eggs
> 1 teaspoon baking powder
> ¼ lb of butter.
> Bake in a moderate oven for 20 minutes.   Mrs Webber.[174]

> enohora – a goodbye to you who are staying[175]
> haerera – goodbye to you leaving
> tamaiti – child
> tangata – man
> raupo – flax
> e ta haeremai te kai – I say come to eat
> Hau Hau pai marere – peace and goodwill
> pipi wharuroa – a bird of good tidings and good news. Size of a skylark.
> It has a green striped head.
> te hoiho – the horse
> te hipi – the sheep
> te rori – the road
> korero pakeha iakoi – do you speak English
> rangi te wera – hot day
> te rangi pai – fine day
> kaha – strong

---

[174]Mrs Webber was one of the party on the Urewera camping trip in 1907.

[175]The faint pencil in which this list of Māori vocabulary was written has been pored over too often and is now no longer adequately legible. I have taken it (with his kind permission) from IA Gordon's *The Urewera Notebook* which was prepared 20 years ago when the writing was more accessible than it is now.

rewai – potatoes
In this part of the Island[176] 'wh' is 'f'

| | | |
|---|---:|---:|
| Tea | | 3 |
| Lunch | 2 | 0 |
| […] | | 6 |
| milk | 1 | 0 |
| wire | | 6 |
| wire | | 7½ |
| | | 6½ |
| | 12 | 0 |
| | 1 | 6 |
| | 1 | 3 |
| | 1 | 6 |
| | 1 | 0 |
| | | 9 |
| | 1 | 0 |
| | | 7½ |
| | 3 | 9 |
| | 3 | 4 |
| | 2 | 0 |
| | 3 | 0 |
| | 2 | |
| £1 | 17 | 7½ |

Julian Mark[177]

---

[176] ie the Urewera.
[177] 'Julian Mark', written inside the back cover of this notebook, was one of KM's pseudonyms of that time.

# *Unbound Papers*

[MS-Papers-4026-1]

Waipunga Riverside
Wednesday

Dear my Mother,[178]

I wrote you my last letter on Monday - and posted it at Pohui in the afternoon. I continue my doings. We drove on through sheep country to Pohui that night past Maori 'pahs' and nothing else, and pitched our camp at the top of a bare hill above the Pohui Accomodation House - kept by a certain Mr Bodley - a <u>great</u> pa-man[179] with 14 daughters who sit & shell peas all day! Below the hill there was a great valley and the bush I cannot describe. It is the entrance to the Ahurakura Station, and though we were tired & hungry Millie, Mrs Webber & I dived down a bridle track - and followed the bush. The tuis really sounded like rivers running - everywhere the trees hung wreathed with clematis and rata and mistletoe. It was very cool & we washed in a creek - the sides all smothered in daisies, the ferns everywhere, and eventually came to the homestead. It is a queer spot - ramshackle & hideous, but the garden is gorgeous. A Maori girl with her hair in two long braids, sat at the doorstep shelling peas, & while we were talking to her the owner came & offered to show us the shearing sheds. You know the sheep sound like a wave of the sea - you can hardly hear yourself speak. He took us through it all - they had only two white men working - and the Maoris have a most strange bird like call as they hustle the sheep. When we came home it was quite dark & <u>how</u> I slept.

Next morning at five we were up & working, and really looking back at yesterday I cannot believe that I have not been to a prodigious biograph[180] show. We drove down the Titi-o'Kura, and the road is one

---

[178]See note 142.

[179]'Pa-man' was a Beauchamp family expression denoting a slightly eccentric paterfamilias who is amusing, lovable, and trustworthy.

[180]A biograph (projector) show was one in which a series of images was projected from slides on to a large screen.

series of turns – a great abyss each side of you – and ruts so deep that you
rise three feet in the air, scream & descend as though learning to trot.
It poured with rain early but then the weather was very clear & light,
with a fierce wind in the mountains. We got great sprays of clematis and
konini,[181] and drove first through a bush path. But the greatest sight I
have seen was the view from the top of Taranga-kuma. You draw rein at
the top of the mountains & round you everywhere are other mountains,
bush covered, & far below in the valley little Tarawera & a silver ribbon
of river. I could do nothing but laugh – it must have been the air, & the
danger.

 We reached the Tarawera Hotel in the evening & camped in a little
bush hollow.
Grubby, my dear – I felt dreadful – my clothes were white with dust –
we had accomplished 8 miles of hill climbing, so after dinner (broad
beans cooked over a camp fire and tongue & cake and tea) we prowled
round and found an "agèd aged man" who had the key of the mineral
baths. I wrapt clean clothes in my towel, & the old man rushed home to
seize a candle in a tin. He guided us through the bush track by the river,
& my dear I've never met such a cure. I don't think he ever had possessed
a tooth & he never ceased talking – you know the effect?

 The Bath House is a shed – three of us bathed in a great pool, waist
high, and we of course in our nakeds. The water was very hot, & like oil
– most delicious. We swam & soaped & swam & soaked & floated,
& when we came out each drank a great mug of mineral water – luke
warm & tasting like Miss Wood's eggs at their worst stage. But you feel
inwardly & outwardly like velvet. This morning we walked most of the
journey – and in one place met a most fascinating Maori – an old
splendid man. He took Mrs Webber & me to see his 'wahine'[182] & child.
It is a tropical day – the woman squatted in front of the whare. She, too,
was very beautiful – strongly Maori – & when we had shaken hands she
unwrapped her offspring from under two mats, & held it on her knee.
The child wore a little red frock & a tight bonnet – such a darling thing
I wanted it for a doll – but in a perfect bath of perspiration. Mother
couldn't speak a word of English & I had a great pantomime.

 Kathleen – pointing to her own teeth & then to the baby's – "Ah!"
Mother – very appreciative – "Ai!" Kathleen – pointing to the baby's long
curling eyelashes "Oh!"
Mother – most delighted "Aii!"
And so on.

 I jumped the baby up & down in the air, and it crowed with
laughter & the Mother & Father, beaming, shook hands with me again.
Then we drove off, waving until out of sight – all the Maoris do that.
Just before pulling up for lunch we came to the Waipunga Falls – my first

---

[181]Konini: *fuchsia excorticata*, a shrub or small tree with blue pollen flowers.
[182]Wahine: woman, wife.

experience of great waterfalls. They are indescribably beautiful – three – one beside the other & a ravine of bush either side. The noise is like thunder & the sun shone full on the water. I am sitting now, on the bank of the river just a few bends away – the water is flowing past, and the manuka flax & fern line the banks.

Must go on. Goodbye, dear. Tell Jeanne I saw families of wild pigs & horses here, & that we have five horses, such dear old things. They nearly ate my head through the tent last night.

I am still bitten & burnt, but oil of camper, Solomon solution, glycerine & cucumber, rose water, are curing me, & I keep wrapt in a motor veil. This is the way to travel – it is so slow & so absolutely free, and I'm quite fond of all the people – they are ultra-Colonial but thoroughly kind & good hearted & generous, and always more than good to me. We sleep tonight at the Rangitaiki & then the plains & the back blocks.

Love to everybody. I am very happy.

Your daughter
Kathleen.

Later. Posting at country shed. Can't buy envelopes. Had wonderful dinner of tomatoes – Ah! he's found me an hotel envelope.   K.

[MS-Papers-4067-2 ts]

## Vignette[183]
### In the Botanical Gardens.  New Zealand.

They are such a subtle combination of the artificial and the natural – that is, partly, the secret of their charm.

From the Entrance Gate down the broad Central Walk, with the orthodox banality of carpet bedding on either side, stroll men and women and children, a great many children who call to each other lustily, and jump up and down the green wooden seats. They seem as meaningless, as lacking in individuality, as the little figures in an impressionist landscape – here, only, because they "tone in" – the children's red hoods, the bright dresses of the women, the sombre clothing of the men.

Above the carpet bedding on one hand there is a green hedge, and above the hedge a long row of Cabbage Trees. I stare and stare up at them, and, suddenly, the green hedge is a stave, and the Cabbage Trees, now high, now low, have become an arrangement of notes – a curious, pattering, native melody.

In the Enclosure the Spring flowers are almost too beautiful – a great stretch of foam-like cowslips. As I bend over them, the air is heavy with their yellow scent, like hay and new milk and the kisses of children, and, further on, a sunlit wonder of chiming daffodils.

---

[183] This vignette, slightly trimmed, was published in *The Native Companion*, December 2, 1907, signed Julian Mark.

Before me two great rhododendron bushes. Against the dark, broad leaves the blossoms rise, flamelike, tremulous in the still air, and the pearl rose loving-cup of a magnolia hangs delicately on the grey bough.

Everywhere there are clusters of china blue pansies, a mist of forget-me-nots, a tangle of anemones. Strange that these anemones – scarlet and amethyst and purple – vibrant with colour, always appear to me a trifle dangerous, sinister, seductive but poisonous.

And, leaving the Enclosure, I pass a little gully, filled with tree ferns, and lit with the pale virgin lamps of arum lilies.

I turn from the smooth swept paths, and climb up a steep track where the knotted tree roots have seared a rude pattern in the yellow clay.
And, suddenly, it disappears, all the pretty, carefully-tended surface of gravel and sward and blossom, and there is bush, silent and splendid. On the green moss, on the brown earth, a wide splashing of yellow sunlight.
And, everywhere that strange, indefinable scent. As I breathe it, it seems to absorb, to become part of me – and I am old with the age of centuries, strong with the strength of savagery.

Somewhere I hear the soft rhythmic flowing of water, and I follow the path down and down until I come to a little stream idly, dreamily floating past. I fling myself down and put my hands in the water. An inexplicable persistent feeling seizes me that I must become one with it all. Remembrance has gone – this is the Lotus Land – the green trees stir languorously, sleepily ... there is the silver sound of a bird's call. Bending down, I drink a little of the water. Oh is it magic? Shall I, looking intently, see vague forms lurking in the shadow staring at me malevolently, wildly, the thief of their birthright?
Shall I, down the hillside, through the bush, ever in the shadow, see a great company moving towards me, their faces averted, wreathed with green garlands, passing, passing, following the little stream in silence until it is sucked into the wide sea ...

There is a sudden restless movement, a pressure of the trees – they sway against one another ... It is like the sound of weeping ...

I pass down the Central Walk towards the Entrance Gates. The men and women and children are crowding the pathway, looking reverently, admiringly, at the carpet bedding, spelling aloud the Latin names of the flowers.

Here is laughter and movement and bright sunlight – but, behind me ... is it near, or miles and miles away ... the bush lies, hidden in the shadow.

---

[MS-Papers-3981-105]

## IN A CAFE[184]

Each day they walked down Bond Street together, between the hours of twelve and one, and turned in at the Blenheim Cafe for lunch and conversation. She, a pale, dark girl with that unmistakeable air of

---

[184]Published in *The Native Companion*, December 2, 1907, No. 5.

"acquaintance with life" which is so general among the students in London, and an expression at once of intense eagerness and anticipated disillusion. Life to a girl who had read Nietzsche, Eugene Sue, Baudelaire, D'Annunzio, Georges Barres, Catulle Mendes, Sudermann, Ibsen, Tolstoi, was, in her opinion, but a trifle obvious. He, was slightly taller than she with the regulation "stoop" and heavy walk, and the regulation wide hat and soft tie. But to her he walked in a great light, and she knew that genius had traced the laurel wreath round his brows.

Each day they sat at the same table in the left-hand corner - she with her elbows on the table, her chin in her hands, watching him while he talked. And sometimes he criticised the people. Then she would throw back her head, and make the most keenly witty remarks; but for the most part it was Art, Art, Art, and youth, scarlet youth, and morality, and life, and the Ten Deadly Conventions - with a glorious irresponsibility, an intoxicating glamour.

"Life in its fullest sense is granted to artists only" he would say, running his white hands through his hair, "and in our brains we create the most eloquent, the most fertile images. I can derive exquisite pleasure from the simplest things - the very soot on my dressing table, a heavy morbid tone on the white."

"Oh, now, oh!! now - nonsense" she would interrupt, her voice full of affectionate remonstrance. "My dear, you are viewing life from a hyper-sensitive aspect ... Can we afford one portion of red currant jelly between us? I have ordered it so you must ... Look at the colour - nom d'un chien, how beautiful. How much better to have it for two-pence instead of possessing a wife in an apron to cook it for you. And you would have to "stone" the currants, and then, perhaps, the result would not "jell". Listen to my technicalities - domestic instinct, you see. I shall marry an English clergyman yet, and have you to stay for the weekend to compose voluntaries for the Early Service."

He shouted with laughter. "My dear girl, you won't do that. I always connect the Church with dispensing tea and buns on a lawn, and festooning graves, and making little shawls for you and the parishioners to wear on your respective heads in the passages. No, I assure you, it is not your vocation."

And one day, when they had talked together in this strain, she leaned across the table, her face flushed suddenly. "Do you think that I shall ever marry?" she said. For a moment he sat silent, staring into the mirror opposite. Then he turned to her, and she imagined she read in his face all that had never been there for her, and never would be.

"I am sure you will" he said, "why?"

"Question not the prophetic answer." She pulled the little bunch of violets from the front of her coat, and began playing with the flowers, shaking them out, and loosening the threads. She knew the danger of the conversation, but suspense was sickening her. If she could feel a little more certainly ...

"Do you think I should make a good wife?"

"That depends." He stirred his coffee thoughtfully. "Yes; why not?

Interesting, certainly, beyond doubt; and who could do better than marry a problem? Misunderstanding keepeth Love alive."

"I believe that, too" she said, "and yet, somehow, it's abominable. Oh! how I want and want things which are out of the question."

"But not a husband, surely?"

"I hardly see myself settling down to sentimental domesticity and discussing the price of mutton."

"Ah, now you are being foolish. You know that marriage need not mean that. Mine won't. And I certainly shall marry." "Oh, oh, oh - then there are years of bachelorhood ahead of you, extravagant and reckless one." A sudden tremendous happiness seemed to have sprung to birth in her heart. "Oh! this adorable life" she said. "Oh! the infinite possibilities. Listen; can't you hear London knocking, knocking?"

He looked at her and suddenly found her beautiful, with her intensely magnetic expression and the violets against her face. He bent forward and whispered the simplest request; yet it seemed to carry a subtle, unmistakeable, joyous significance.

"May I have your violets to keep?"

"They are yours" she said, and the touch of his fingers thrilled her. They sat in silence for a few minutes. He was annoyed at having yielded to a sudden sentimental impulse, and felt, somehow, that she had expected it of him. He felt a light hand on his shoulder and, looking up, smiled at the Fellow Student. "Well?"

"There is a rehearsal of your Fantasie at the Aeolian Hall at two o'clock. Come, quickly."

He sprang up and shook hands with her across the table.

"Till tomorrow" he said, "au revoir", and took the Fellow Student's arm. Once outside the wind was bitterly cold. "Nice weather for playing" said the Fellow Student. "Keep your hands warm." He dropped the violets on the pavement and thrust his hands into his coat pockets. The Fellow Student began relating an adventure of a slightly unscrupulous character, and he laughed and continued laughing all the way down the street.

- - - - - - - - - - - - -

When the two men had left, she took a slip of paper from her pocket, and wrote a date. She was conscious of never having felt so entirely happy before. So, in a dream, she threaded her way past the tables. The little violinist, who had so often played the Wienawski "Legende" for her, smiled as she passed, and she had a sudden impulse to shake hands with him. Out in the cold street - what did the cold matter? A great fire was hugging her heart.

It had been raining. She looked down at the wet pavements, and saw the violets. She knew them immediately - realised swiftly what had happened. She felt herself grow white to the lips. Then, very delicately and deliberately, she kicked the flowers into the gutter; and she, too, laughed, and continued laughing all the way down the street.

- - - - - - - - - - - - -

Thus is the High Torch of Tragedy kindled at the little spark of Sentiment, and the good God pity the bearer.

———————————

[NL ts]

## IN SUMMER[185]

And for the first time in her short life, Phyllis wept.

She lay on the hillside among the flowering broom, her head pillowed, childlike, on her arms. "Oh, I think I am going to die" she said. Phyllis did not look like Death in her white, pink-sprigged skirt, her blue laced bodice, her pink stockings, and ridiculously small, red-heeled, pink slippers. By her side was a long white crook, gay with a posy of roses and ribbons, and near by, her wide rose-wreathed hat, and a little straw basket full of barley sugar.

"Oh, I have never been so unhappy before" sobbed Phyllis. "I have a curious pain somewhere."

Suddenly she heard a bee buzzing very close to her ear. She sat up hastily. And there, standing before her, laughing softly, was the Yellow Dwarf. His hair was yellow, he had yellow eyes, his skin was the colour of hot amber. He wore a tight fitting yellow silk garment, and long, soft, yellow suede boots.

"Who <u>are</u> you" said Phyllis, shaking her hair out of her eyes.

"Why are you crying?" said the Yellow Dwarf.

"Who are you?" said Phyllis. Her flowerlike face, her long eyes, her rose mouth, excited the Yellow Dwarf curiously. With charming grace he leant against a spray of broom blossom.

"I" he said, "I am the child of the gorse and of the broom - of the wild gorse, my Father, and of the dainty broom, my Mother. And I live upon dewdrops fried in sunshine and the spoil of honey bees. By day I lie on the warm hillside, and smile at the blue sky, and count the little flocks of white clouds that pass so gently, so dreamily above me. And at night. Oh" - he bent forward, took one of Phyllis' curls in his hand and pulled it gently, teasingly - "you're too young to know."

"Tell me" cried Phyllis eagerly.

He laughed, and Phyllis fancied - was it fancy? - that, at the sound, every blade of grass on the warm hillside quivered and took new life.

"Oh, perhaps" he said, "<u>later on</u>. First you must tell me all about yourself, why you came here, why you have been weeping, what you want. Spread out your skirt, little Phyllis, that I may sit upon a piece of it, and hand me, I pray you, ever the slightest suspicion of that barley sugar."

She did as he asked her. Then, "why should I tell you" she asked.

"Look" said the Yellow Dwarf.

In his hand he held a very perfect, languishing golden rose. "Bend down,

———————————

[185]See note 73. This typescript carries an autograph signature.

little Phyllis. Oh what perfume, what perfume." His voice was like a caress, and, as she bent over the rose, "This is a magic flower" he said.

Looking at him anew, Phyllis saw in his yellow eyes, perfect understanding, unbounded sympathy, and, too, command.

"I will tell you now" she said, "it is this."

"I am listening."

"Well, long, long ago, my Mother sat alone in her cottage, and it was Summer. In the garden, she told me this, all the roses were like nodding, perfumed bells. There had never been so many flowers before, she said, in any garden. But she sat in the little house, dreaming, and by and bye, a white butterfly drifted through the open window - Oh a beautiful wonderful butterfly, and there, curled up between its two wings, I lay a baby, fast asleep."

"How infinitely delicious" murmured the Yellow Dwarf. "And then, Phyllis?"

"Oh, she was so happy, my Mother. She wrapped me in her fine embroidered handkerchiefs until I was big enough for clothes, and then she spun me little things - they were too lovely. So I grew old enough to walk and talk, and, every night, she sat beside me until I slept, and sang softly, softly, "Little Bo-Peep." She called me Phyllis, but she said 'You must always remember that you are a Fairy Child, and that one day, the Great Pedlar, Fate, will come knocking at the door, and you must not say him nay.' So I remembered. I was never unhappy. I learned a great many songs, and drank milk out of a little white cup, and my Mother curled and uncurled my hair, and we looked at each other in the looking glass. Then, one day, my Mother was in the fields. I sat by the table threading a necklace of glass beads. Somebody knocked at the door.

'Come in' I said. The door opened, and there stood a great black man. Oh, so big, I can never say how big" said Phyllis. "He was dressed in the richest silks, red as roses, yellow as buttercups, blue as periwinkles. He had round gold earrings in his ears, and, on his shoulders, he carried a great carved chest.

'Little Phyllis' he said, and his voice was like the wind up the chimney, 'I am Fate'. Then he set down the great carved chest, and opened it. Within lay my shepherdess dress, my tiny shoes, and silk stockings, even my little straw basket of barley sugar. And I remembered what my Mother had told me, and put on the clothes. He gave me, too, a silver whistle, and when I blew upon it I heard a pattering sound in the garden. I looked out, and saw a little flock of white sheep."

"This comes of lullabies" interrupted the Yellow Dwarf. Phyllis did not listen.

"I forgot my Mother, and my white cup, and my necklace of glass beads, but I followed where the white sheep led, far away, far away."

"How long ago did this happen, Phyllis?" asked the Yellow Dwarf. "I do not know" she said. Again the tears fell down her face. "I think it must have been a thousand years ago."

"Perhaps so, go on."

"There is really nothing else, except, except" ... a tiny blush stole up her face, her brow ..." somehow everything is changing. My clothes, they are too small for me, my slippers hurt my feet, my stockings are torn by brambles, and I am tired of barley sugar, and, Yellow Dwarf, I have lost my silver whistle, so all my sheep have strayed. And I want something, I do not know what, but I think I shall never cease weeping."

The Yellow Dwarf smiled.

"Tut, you girls, you're all alike" he said, taking her hand and patting it softly. "Now wait here one moment, look, what is this in my pocket?" He took out a tiny packet, shook it in the breeze, and it was a yellow frock, straight and fine, like sunshine, like Summer. "This is what you ought to be wearing, Phyllis."

But Phyllis was already slipping out of her skirt and bodice. She bent down and he popped the new frock over her head. "Oh, how nice" she said.

He eyed her slippers doubtfully. "It is Summer, child, why not bare feet?"

So she took off her shoes and stockings, and her feet were like little white birds on the warm hillside. "I have grown out of my child clothes" she said, gravely.

The Yellow Dwarf caught her hands. "You are to walk over the hillside" - his voice was like running water, like the soft sound of Summer leaves - "you will come to a tree, and under the tree, your Happiness sits, waiting."

Dreaming, she left him. By and bye, she came to a laburnum tree, a bower of beauty, and under the tree sat Corydon, playing on an instrument with seven silver strings. He was dark and strong. He wore a garland of roses, and <u>very little else</u>.

"Oh, at last" he said, and took her hand.

As their fingers met, as they stared at each other, fascinated and happy, a lark rose suddenly and mounted singing, singing into the Summer sky.

"That is my unhappiness" said Phyllis, nodding to Corydon, "it has flown away, singing, at your touch."

Blissfully, blissfully, down the warm hillside, swinging their hands as children do, the broom waving and beckoning, they walked slowly.

"Evening is coming" said Phyllis.

Below them lay the sea. The little waves ran along the line of white beach, so daintily, drew back so shyly, then flung themselves along the smooth, strong sand stretch with such absolute abandon that Phyllis smiled.

"It is telling me something" she said - then looking up at Corydon - "Evening is coming." The wind had blown a curl of her hair across her face, a pulse at her throat beat flutteringly. Above them, in the opaque sky, one pale star heralded the night.

"Darkness is coming" said Corydon, catching her in his strong arms.

And somewhere, in the tangle of broom, the Yellow Dwarf shook with laughter.

Julian Mark.

[NL]

L'Incendie.

A stretch of gorse clothing the hillside has caught fire.
From my window I see the blue smoke spreading afar in twists and turns and curves of thin exquisite loveliness. I see, too, the fierce red glow of the flames. I watch their mad hungry progress. There is a steady, strong destructive sound. The flames rush forward, crying "See, see, can we <u>ever</u> be satisfied?"

Above the hills the sky is widely luminous. Below the hills is a street of little wooden houses. From the yards come the piercing incoherent sounds of children at play, and at this evening hour their voices sound thin and old, their crying seeming full of protestation.

Each moment the fire on the hills is gaining strength. From my window I watch it, eagerly, fascinated and horrified. Shall it be always <u>from my window</u> that I must watch the fire burning? May I not hold the flames in my hand, if only for a little while, and hold them against my heart - and laugh as they fiercely attack it?

Karl Mansfield
21.1.1907.

# *Newberry Notebook 1*

### Song By The Window Before Bed

Little star, little star
Come down. Quick.
The Moon is a Bogey-man
He'll catch you certain if he can
Little star, little star
Come down quick.

Little star, little star
Whisper "Yes".
The trees are just niggers all
They look so black, they are so tall.
Little star, little star
Whisper "Yes".

Little star, little star
Gone - all gone -
The Bogey-man swallered you
The nigger trees are laughing, too
Little star. little star
Gone - all gone.

---

[186]Notebook 1 in the Newberry Library's holdings consists of poems and 'The Yellow Chrysanth-emum'. Most of the poems in it were used by Murry in the 'Child Verses 1907' section of his *Poems by Katherine Mansfield*, Constable, London, 1923. They have been ignored since but are interesting for the flavour they convey, with its Robert Louis Stevenson influence, of KM's conception of a Victorian childhood.

The Funeral

It was Mr Lun's "At Home" day
So of course he never came
But it didn't make much difference
We <u>was</u> happy all the same.

And just sittin' by the window
With what Mummy calls "the blue"
When we saw a lovely funeral
Comin' up our own street, too.

All the horses wore a bonnet
With a wobbly curly feather

A Little Boy's Dream

To and fro, to and fro
In my little boat I go
Sailing far across the sea
All alone – just little me
And the sea is big and strong
And the journey very long
To and fro, to and fro
In my little boat I go.

Sea & sky, sea & sky.
Quietly on the deck I lie
Having just a little rest.
I have really done my best
In an awful Pirate Fight
But we captured them alright.
Sea and sky, sea & sky
Quietly on the deck I lie.

Far away, far away
From my home and from my play
On a journey without end
Only with the sea for friend
And the fishes in the sea
But they swim away from me
Far away, far away
From my home and from my play.

Then he cried "O <u>Mother</u> dear"
And he woke and sat upright.
They were in the rocking chair
Mother's arms around him – tight.

Winter Song

Rain and wind, and wind and rain
Will the Summer come again?
Rain on houses, on the street
Wetting all the people's feet
Though they run with might & main
Rain and wind and wind and rain.

Snow and sleet and sleet and snow
Will the Winter never go?
What do beggar children do
With no fire to cuddle to
P'raps with nowhere warm to go?
Snow and sleet & sleet and snow.

Hail and ice, and ice and hail
Water frozen in the pail
See the robins brown and red
They are waiting to be fed
Poor dears! battling in the gale
Hail and ice and ice and hail.

On a Young Lady's Sixth Anniversary

Baby Babbles - only <u>one</u> -
Now to sit up has begun.

Little Babbles quite turned <u>two</u>
Walks as well as I and you.

And Miss Babbles <u>one</u> <u>two</u> <u>three</u>
Has a teaspoon at her tea.

But her Highness at <u>four</u>
Learns to open the front door.

And her Majesty - now <u>six</u>
Can her shoestring neatly fix.

Babbles, Babbles - have a care
You will soon <u>put</u> <u>up</u> <u>your</u> hair!

Song of the Little White Girl

Cabbage Tree, Cabbage Tree - what is the matter -
Why are you shaking so, why do you chatter?
'Cause it is just a white baby you see -
And it's the black ones you like - Cabbage Tree?

Cabbage Tree, Cabbage Tree - you're a strange fellow
With your green hair and your legs browny-yellow
Wouldn't you like to have curls, dear, like me?
What! no-one to make them - O <u>poor</u> Cabbage Tree!
Never mind, Cabbage Tree - when I am taller
And if you grow - please - a little bit smaller
I shall be able by that time - may be -
To make you the loveliest curls, Cabbage Tree.


### A Few Rules for Beginners

Babies must not eat the coal
And they must not make grimaces
Nor in party dresses roll
And must never black their faces.

They must learn that "pointing"'s rude
They must sit quite still at table
And must always eat the food
Put before them - if they're able.

If they fall they must not cry
Though it's known how painful this is
Lo - there's always Mother by
Who will comfort them with kisses.


### A Day in Bed

I wish I had not got a cold
The wind is big and wild.
I wish that I was very old
Not just a little child.

Somehow the day is very long
Just keeping here - alone
I do not like the big wind's song
He's growling for a bone.

He's like an awful dog we had
Who used to creep around
And snatch at things - he was so bad -
With just that horrid sound.

I'm sitting up and Nurse has made
Me wear a woolly shawl
I wish I was not so afraid
It's horrid to be small.

It really feels quite like a day
Since I have had my tea
P'raps everybody's gone away
And just forgotten me.

And O – I cannot go to sleep
Although I <u>am</u> in bed.
The wind keeps going "creepy creep"
And waiting to be fed.

## Opposites

The Half-Soled-Boots-With-Toecaps-child
Walked out into the street
And splashed in all the puddles till
She [had] such shocking feet.

The Patent-Leather-Slipper-child
Stayed quietly in the house
And sat upon the fender stool
As still as any mouse.

The Half-Soled-Boots-With-Toecaps-child
Her hands were black as ink
She would come rushing through the house
And begging for a drink.

The Patent-Leather-Slipper-child
Her hands were white as snow
She did not like to play around
She only liked to sew.

The Half-Soled-Boots-With-Toecaps-child
Lost hair ribbons galore –
She dropped them on the garden walks
She dropped them on the floor.

The Patent-Leather-Slipper-child
O – thoughtful little girl
She liked to walk quite soberly
It kept her hair in curl.

The Half-Soled-Boots-With-Toecaps-child
When she was glad – or proud –
Just flung her arms round Mother's neck
And kissed her very loud.

The Patent-Leather-Slipper-child
Was shocked at such a sight
She only offered you her cheek
At morning and at night.

O - Half-Soled-Boots-With-Toecaps-child
Her happy laughing face
Does like a scented summer rose
Make sweet the dullest place.

O Patent-Leather-Slipper-child -
My dear, I'm well content
To hold my daughter in my arms
And - not an ornament.

VI[or XI?].07


### Song of Karen the Dancing Child

(O little white feet of mine)
Out in the storm and the rain you fly
(Red red shoes the colour of wine)
Can the <u>children</u> hear my cry?

(O little white feet of mine)
Never a child in the whole great town
(Red red shoes the colour of wine)
Lights out and the blinds pulled down.

(O little white feet of mine)
Never a light on a window pane
(Red red shoes the colour of wine)
And the wild wet cry of the rain.

(O little white feet of mine)
Shall I <u>never</u> again be still?
(Red red shoes the colour of wine)
And away over valley and hill.

(O little white feet of mine)
Children - children open the door!
(Red red shoes the colour of wine)
And the wind shrieks "never more".


### A Joyful Song of Five!

Come let us all sing very high
And all sing very loud -
And keep on singing in the street
Until there's quite a crowd.

And keep on singing in the house
And up and down the stairs
Then underneath the furniture
Let's all play Polar Bears

And crawl about with doormats on
And growl and howl and squeak
Then in the garden let us fly
And play at "Hide & Seek"

And "Here We Gather Nuts & May"
"I Wrote a Letter", too
"Here we go round the Mulberry Bush"
"The Child Who Lost its Shoe"

And every game we <u>ever</u> played
And then - to stay alive -
Let's end with lots of Birthday cake
Because Today You're Five.

### The Candle Fairy

The candle is a fairy house
That's smooth and round and white
And Mother carries it about
Whenever it is night.

Right at the top a fairy lives
A lovely yellow one
And if you blow a little bit
It has all sorts of fun.

It bows and dances by itself
In such a clever way
And then it stretches very tall
"Well, <u>it</u> grows fast" you say.

The little chimney of the house
Is black and really sweet
And there the candle fairy stands
Though you can't see its feet.

And when the dark is very big
And you've been having dreams
Then Mother brings the candle in
How friendly like it seems!

It's only just for Mothers that
The candle fairy comes
And if you play with it - it bites
Your fingers and your thumbs.

But still you love it very much
This candle fairy, dear
Because, at night, it always means
That Mother's very near.

The Last Thing

Now the Dustman's reached our door
Now the blinds are all pulled down
Everything is growing quiet
Even noises in the town.

You - all ready for your bed -
First - kneel down by Mummy's chair
Fold your hands upon her lap
Learn to say a little prayer.

First, just "thank you, God", and then
"Gentle Jesus meek and mild"
Last "I lay me down to sleep
Make me please a better child."

Very solemn, very grave
Then you get up from your knees
And you rush to Daddykins
"Now the Barley-sugar - <u>please</u>"

The Quarrel

We stood in the vegetable garden
As angry and cross as could be
'Cause you said you would not beg pardin'
For eatin' my radish at tea.

I said "I shall go an' tell Mummy
I hope it is makin' you ill
I hope you've a pain in your tummy
And then she will give you a pill."

But you cried out "Goodbye then - for ever -
Go and play with <u>your</u> silly old toys
If you think you're so grown-up and clever
I'll run off and play with the Boys."

A Song for Our Real Children

We sang "Up In the Cherry Tree"
Both sittin' on the lawn
And then we sang "The Busy Bee"
And "Jesus Chris' was born".

O dear, we had a lovely time
An' when the tea bell rang
All by ourselves we made a rhyme
To tell Nurse how we sang.

So when we both is old and wise
With babies six and seven
We'll say "We made this for a s'prise
When you was all in Heaven."

### Grown-up Talks

Half-Past-Six and I were talking
In a very grown-up way.
We had got so tired with running
That we did not want to play.

"How do babies come, I wonder"
He said, lookin' at the sky
"Does God mix the things together
An' just make it – like a pie?"

I was really not quite certain
But it sounded very nice
It was all that we could think of,
'Sides the book said "sugar and spice".

Half-Past-Six said – he's so clever
Cleverer than me, I mean –
"I suppose God makes the black ones
When the saucepan isn't clean."

### You won't understand this – 'cause you're a Boy

If you have never been a girl
You cannot know the sin
To wear just "dress material"
To keep your "bodies" in.

An' I shall never quite forget
The feeling that I felt
When Mummy went and bought for me
A Ladies Leather Belt.

### The Lonesome Child

The baby in the looking glass
Is smiling through at me
She has her teaspoon in her hand
Her feeder on for tea.

And if I look behind her I
Can see the table spread
I wonder if she has to eat
The nasty crusts of bread.

Her doll – like mine – is sitting close
Beside her special chair
She has a pussy on her cup
It must be <u>my</u> cup there.

Her picture book is on the floor
The cover's just the same
And tidily upon the shelf
I see my Ninepin game.

O baby in the looking glass
Come through and play with me
And if you will I promise, dear,
To eat your crusts at tea.

Evening Song of the Thoughtful Child

Shadow children – thin and small
Now the day is left behind
You are dancing on the wall
On the curtains – on the blind.

On the ceiling, children, too
Peeking round the nursery door
Let me come and play with you
As we always played before.

Let's pretend that we have wings
And can really truly fly
Over every sort of things
Up and up into the sky.

Where the sweet star children play
It does seem a dreadful rule
They must stay inside all day
I suppose they go to school.

And tonight, dears, do you see
They are having <u>such</u> a race
With their Father Moon ... the tree
Almost hides his funny face.

Shadow children – once at night
I was all tucked up in bed
Father Moon came – such a fright!
Through the window poked his head.

I could see his staring eyes
O my dears – I was afraid
<u>That</u> was not a nice surprise
And the <u>dreadful</u> noise I made.

Let us make a Fairy Ring
Shadow children, hand in hand
And our songs quite softly sing
That we learnt in Fairy land.

Shadow children, thin and small
See - the day is <u>far</u> behind
And I kiss you - on the wall
On the curtains - on the blind.

### Autumn Song

Now's the time when childrens noses
All become as red as roses
And the colour of their faces
Makes me think of orchard places
Where the juicy apples grow

And tomatoes - in a row.
And today - the hardened sinner
Never could be late for dinner
But will jump up to the table
Just as soon as he is able
Ask for three times hot roast mutton
O the shocking little glutton!

Come then, find your ball and racquet,
Pop into your winter jacket
With the lovely bearskin lining
While the sun is brightly shining
Let us run and play together
And just <u>love</u> the Autumn Weather.

### Spring Wind in London

I blow across the stagnant world
I blow across the sea
For me, the sailor's flag unfurled
For me, the uprooted tree.
My challenge to the world is hurled
The world must bow to me.

I drive the clouds across the sky
I huddle them, like sheep,
Merciless shepherd's dog am I
And shepherd's watch I keep
If in the quiet vales they lie
I blow them up the steep.

Lo! In the treetops do I hide
In every living thing
On the moon's yellow wings I glide
On the wild rose I swing
On the sea-horse's back I ride
And what then do I bring?

And when a little child is ill
I pause, and with my hand
I wave the window curtain frill
That he may understand
Outside the wind is blowing still
It is a pleasant land.

Oh, stranger in a foreign place
See what I bring to you,
This rain is tears upon your face
I tell you - tell you true
I came from that forgotten place
Where once the wattle grew.

All the wild sweetness of the flower
Tangled against the wall
It was that magic, silent hour ...
The branches grew so tall
They twined themselves into a bower
The sun shone ... and the fall

Of yellow blossom on the grass!
You feel that golden rain
Both of you could not hold, alas,
Both of you tried in vain.
A memory, stranger. So I pass ...
It will not come again.

K. Mansfield 1909.


A Fairy Tale

Now this is the story of Olaf
Who, ages and ages ago,
Lived right on the top of a mountain
A mountain all covered with snow.

And he was quite pretty and tiny
With beautiful curling fair hair
And small hands like delicate flowers
Cheeks kissed by the cold mountain air.

He lived in a hut made of pine wood
Just one little room and a door
A table, a chair, and a bedstead
And animal skins on the floor.

Now Olaf was partly a fairy
And so never wanted to eat
He thought dewdrops and raindrops were plenty
And snowflakes – and all perfumes sweet.

In the daytime when sweeping and dusting
And cleaning was quite at an end
He would sit very still on the doorstep
And dream – O – that he had a friend.

Somebody to come when he called them
Somebody to catch by the hand
Somebody to sleep with at night time
Somebody who'd quite understand.

One night in the middle of winter
He lay wide awake on his bed
Outside there was fury of tempest
And calling of wolves to be fed.

Thin wolves, grey and silent as shadows
And Olaf was frightened to death
He had peeked through a crack in the doorpost
He had seen the white smoke of their breath.

But suddenly over the storm wind
He heard a small voice, pleadingly
Cry "I am a snow fairy, Olaf
Unfasten the window for me."

So he did, and there flew through the opening
The daintiest prettiest sprite
Her face and her dress and her stockings
Her hands and her curls – were all white.

And she said: "O you poor little stranger
Before I am melted, you know,
I have brought you a valuable present
A little brown fiddle and bow.

So now you can never be lonely
With a fiddle, you see, for a friend
But all through the Summer & Winter
Play beautiful songs without end."

And then – O – she melted like water
But Olaf was happy at last
The fiddle he tucked in his shoulder
He held his small bow very fast ...

So perhaps, on the quietest of evenings,
If you listen you may hear him soon
The child who is playing the fiddle
'Way up in the cold lonely moon.

KMB 24.VI [or XI?].07

The Yellow Chrysanthemum[187]

KMB

Radiana.

Scene: A circular room with dull purple hangings. Four Roman candles set in heavy wrought-iron holders shed a pale thin light. Across the windows yellow curtains are hung – straight and fine. On a couch below the window a woman is seated, holding a little mirror up to her face, and shaking the petals of a yellow chrysanthemum over her hair.

Radiana: Ah! how beautiful! They are like little pieces of perfumed gold falling over my hair ... They are like little drops of pure amber falling, falling into the darkness of my hair ... They are like flakes of golden snow ...
(she leans far back among the purple cushions) O, I am wrapt in the perfume of the chrysanthemums. The air is full of the perfume ... It is as though there had been a dead body in the room ... It is the body of Summer who is lying dead in the room – and all her beautiful gold is spent ... My fingers burn with the scent of her dead body ...
O, I thirst, I thirst. My soul is like a great stretch of sand on which the sun has shone all the long day. I am dried up, parched, hot. I am waiting for the waves to beat upon me, to hold me in a green, strong embrace ...
        (Guido enters)
Guido: Radiana ... Radiana! No – stir not ...
Ah! how beautiful you are – golden and white like the heart of a water lily ...
The petals in your hair are like little stars in the Night sweetness ... Your face in the depths of your hair is like a pale flower in a deep forest ... Never have I seen you so beautiful! Your gown is the colour of a cloud of narcissus blossom and your hands are like strange white moths.
        (He seats himself beside her)
Look at me – speak to me – Radiana! Last night I woke from a dream, fearful and overpowering. It hovered round my brow – vague, shadow-like. And as

---

[187]See note 64. There are some minor changes of word order, but the only new material in 'The Yellow Chrysanthemum' which was not in the crossed out draft in Notebook 1 is 'Ah! how loathsome!' in Guido's final speech.

I lay still and stared into the purple darkness your face, Radiana, came before me ... the sweetness of your eyelids, and the shadows that lie under your eyes ... In the intensity of my longing I cried aloud, and beat upon the pillows of my couch ... I shook from my hair to my feet and shuddered with the strength of myself ... I was drowning, suffocating in the heart of a purple sea ... and the light of your face was as the light of the moon above the waters ... In the topaz of the morning sky I rode forth towards the mountains. All the day I have journeyed through the emerald of the forests, and when Twilight fell I saw the white towers of your castle far ahead of me ...

Radiana:  O - I am afraid - I am afraid ... Somewhere under these hangings, know you not, Summer lies dead ... Ah! the perfume of her dead body stifles me! Loose my girdle, Guido ... I cannot breathe ...

Guido: Radiana, you dream ... you have been too much alone ... See, see, I am weeping! The tears all falling down my face, and on to your silver throat. You are so beautiful that you are tragic ... tragic ... One cannot possess so much beauty - and yet live.

Radiana:  (in a stifled voice) Take off your cloak and wrap me in its folds ... I am so cold and weary ... tired of passion, weary of love ... In the night hours I have called and cried for you. I have wept in the long darkness. My hair has become heavy and damp with my tears ... Through the days I have leant against my balcony in the hot sunlight, and pulled the petals, one by one, from the roses that grow there so passionately and beautifully ... I have watched the petals fluttering to my feet, one by one, till my feet were covered with the crimson of them ... And I have felt that I was standing in a pool of blood ... At the fall of each petal I have whispered your name ... I have been like a virgin telling her rosary ... my beads were rose petals ... beautiful drops of blood ... It is gone ... my desire ... my strength is gone ...

Guido: Radiana, Radiana your brow is so hot - it is burning beneath my hand ... Speak to me again. Your breath is as sweet as the perfume of incense. Your body is like a shell - white and cool - that has been cast up by the sea on to the dull shore ... Look, I will raise you to your feet ... My arms are round you ... I am very strong ... here in the darkness of this room ... let me feel your body leaning against me ... Can I give you my strength? It is as though I had a great torch in my heart that leaps up and flames and burns all over my body. I feel as though my hair were on fire ... Radiana, Radiana! Let me give you my strength ... Let me pour into you the fire that is coursing through me ...

Radiana:  Ah! Ah!

(A cold wind blows through the room. The light of the candles is quenched. The yellow curtains blow in and out from the windows, silently, heavily. Guido, in the darkness, lifts Radiana in his arms and lays her upon the couch.)

Guido: (whispering) I spread all your hair around you. It is so dark ... I can only see your face and your hands and your little white feet ... Your face is like a little moon ... a wan moon in the fierceness of a storm night.

Radiana: O, O, the perfume of the dead body ...

Guido: It is the smoke from the candles ... The night air has blown their light out ...

Radiana: O the dead body of the Summer.

Guido: (fiercely) Why are you so pale? Why are you so pale? Why are you shuddering? Close your eyes ... close your eyes ...

Radiana: Guido!...

Guido: Hold me! Hold to me! I shall hold your little hands against my face ... Feel how hot I am ... and you so cold ... Your fingers are damp ... and there is a strange scent ... Radiana! Radiana! Horror! Horror! I am holding a dead body ... It is the perfume of your dead body ... and I am afraid. Ah! how loathsome!... I shall wrap you round in your hair ... shut out your face ... hide your hands, cover your pale feet ...
(Suddenly he rises from the couch where he has been kneeling, and wrenches one of the yellow curtains from the windows. He flings it over her body.)
                    CURTAIN.

[NL ts]
                    Vignette - By the Sea[188]
Lying thus on the sand, the foam almost washing over my hands, I am spellbound by the sea.

Behind the golden hills the sun is going down, a flaming jewel in a lurid setting, and there is a faint flush everywhere, on sea and land. To my right the sky has blossomed into a vivid rose, but, to my left, the land is hidden by a grey blue mist, lightened now here, now there, by the sun colour ... it is like land seen from a ship, very far away, dreamland, mirage, enchanted country.

Two sea birds, high in the air, fly screaming towards the light. It beats upon their white breasts. It flames upon their dull wings. Far away, a little boat is sailing upon the sweet water, a golden butterfly upon the dainty bosom of a mystic blossom.

And now the Italian fishermen are sailing in, their white sails bellying in the breeze. Several come rowing in a little boat. They spring ashore, the light shines on their crisp black hair, it shines on their faces, so that their skin is the colour of hot amber on their bare legs and strong brown arms. They are dragging towards them the boat, the long black, wet rope running through

---

[188]This typescript is a fair copy of the manuscript in the Turnbull's Notebook 2 (p 156). The differences between the two versions are of interest.

their fingers and falling in a bold pattern on the foam-blown sand. They call to one another – I cannot hear what they say – but against the long, rhythmic pulsing of the sea their voices sound curiously insignificant, like voices in a dream.

And there are exquisite golden brown sprays and garlands of sea weed, set about with berries, white and brown. Are they flowers blown from the garden of the Sea King's Daughter? Does she wander through the delicate coral forests, seeking them, playing upon a little silver shell, her long hair floating behind her?

And near me there is a light upon the blue coast, steadily, tenderly it burns, a little candle set upon the great altar of the world.

The glow pales in the sky, on the land, but ever the long, rhythmic pulsing of the sea. Oh, to sail and sail into the heart of the sea. Is it darkness and silence there, or is it a Great Light?

So the grey sand slips, drifts through my fingers.

Night comes swiftly.

# *Unbound Papers*

[MS-Papers-3981-105 ts]

Study: The Death of a Rose[189]

It is a sensation that can never be forgotten, to sit in solitude, in semi-darkness, and to watch the slow, sweet, shadowful death of a Rose.

Oh, to see the perfection of the perfumed petals being changed ever so slightly, as though a thin flame had kissed each with hot breath, and where the wounds had bled the colour is savagely intense ... I have before me such a Rose, in a thin, clear glass, and behind it a little spray of scarlet leaves. Yesterday it was beautiful with a certain serene, tearful, virginal beauty; it was strong and wholesome, and the scent was fresh and invigorating. Today it is heavy and languid with the loves of a thousand strange Things, who, lured by the gold of my candlelight, came in the Purple Hours, and kissed it hotly on the mouth, and sucked it into their beautiful lips with tearing, passionate desire.

... So now it dies ... And I listen ... for under each petal fold there lies the ghost of a dead melody, as frail and as full of suggestion as a ray of light upon a shadowed pool. Oh, divine sweet Rose. Oh, exotic and elusive and deliciously vague Death.

From the tedious sobbing and gasping, and hoarse guttural screaming, and uncouth repulsive movements of the body of the dying Man, I draw apart, and, smiling, I lean over you and watch your dainty, delicate Death.

[NL]

Vignette.

Through the Autumn afternoon - I sat before the fire in the Library - and read - almost a little wildly. I wanted to drug myself with books - drown my thoughts in a great violet sea of Oblivion. I read about Youth - how the Young and the Strong had gone forth into battle - with banners of golden and blue and crimson. Of the sunshine that turned their processions into a river of colour - and the songs that, mellow and sweet, rose in their round throats.

---

[189]Published in *Triad*, July 1908.

I read of the young Painters – hollow eyed and pale – who paced their studios like young tigers – and with stupendous colossal ideas. How they sat together at night, in sweet companionship, round a fire – their cigarette smoke mystical, ethereal. And in the glowing coals was shadowed the beautiful flame – like body of Art.

And deeply I pored over the books of Youthful Musicians.
Splendid – and tragic – and prophetic their faces gleamed at me – always with that strange haunted look. They had taken Life to them, and sung a Scarlet Song that had no ending and no beginning. And I read of all their resolves – and of their feverish haste, and the Phantastic Desires that sang themselves to birth … This and much more I read in my books.

Then all in a fever myself I rushed out of the stifling house – out of the city streets and on to the gorse golden hills. A white road ran round the hills – there I walked. And below me, like a beautiful Pre-Raphaelite picture, lay the sea and the violet mountains. The sky all a riot of rose and yellow, amethyst and purple.

At the foot of the hill – the city – but all curtained by a blue mist that hung over it in pale wreaths of Beauty. No sound at all – and yet – the Silence of that Phrophetic Atmosphere – that is created by the Twilight only. I leaned against a low paling fence – in my brain thoughts were clashing with the sound of cymbals. I felt Myself – by the power of my Youth – alone – God of it all.

Love and Fellowship – work and Delicious Fascinating Pleasures – must exist for me – if I only search for them. Away out in the harbour lights shone from the ships, and now in the city too – golden beckoning flowers.

There came a sound of slowly moving horses. I saw coming towards me a heavy carriage – slowly, slowly, coming towards me. And I stood still – and waited. The horses were hot and strained, the driver muffled up to the eyes… it was very cold. As it passed me I saw, inside, an old man, his head fallen back among the cushions, the eyes closed, the mouth half open, and hands of Age crossed before him. He was muttering to himself – mumbling, muttering.

Slowly it passed, and I watched it wind round the hill out of sight.
I turned again towards the sea and the mountains – the City and the golden lights – but Darkness had rushed across the sky.
      K. Mansfield. 4.x.07.

---

[NL]

On the Sea Shore.[190]

Hull. Nov.5.08.

    Deafening roar of the ocean
    The wild waves thunder and beat

---

[190]The first six of the following poems in the Newberry Library have 'Hull, Nov. 5, 08' ('Nov. 4' in two cases) in another hand, presumably that of Garnet Trowell who must have received these poems in Hull while he was travelling as a violinist in the Moody-Manners Opera Company. Murry's acquisition of them was apparently after KM's death since none of them appear in his 1923 edition of the *Poems*.

Sea weed, fragments of wreckage
They fling them up to her feet.

She, her pale face worn with waiting
Stands alone in the shuddering day
And watches the flight of a sea–gull
Wearily winging its way.

"Why do you scream, oh sea bird,
And why do you fly to me?"
"I am the soul of your lover
Who lies drowned far out at sea."

### A Sad Truth

Hull. Nov. 5. 08

We were so hungry, he and I
We knew not what to do
And so we bought a sugar cake
Oh, quite enough for two.

We ate it slowly, bit by bit
And not a crumb was wasted
It was the very best, we said
That we had ever tasted.

But all this happened years ago
Now we are rich and old
Yet we cannot buy such sugar cake
With our united gold.

K. Mansfield. 1908.

### A Song of Summer.

Hull. Nov. 4. 08

At break of day the Summer sun
Shines through our windows one by one
He takes us by his great warm hand
And the world is changed to Fairyland.
He gives us fairy bread to eat
And fairy nectar, strange and sweet
While a magic bird the whole day long
Sings in our hearts his mating song.

### The Winter Fire.

Hull. Nov. 4. 08

Winter without, but in the curtained room
Flushed into beauty by a fluttering fire
Shuttered and blinded from the ugly street
A woman sits - her hands locked round her knees

And bending forward ... O'er her loosened hair
The firelight spins a web of shining gold
Sears her pale mouth with kisses passionate
Wraps her tired body in a hot embrace.
Propped by the fender her rain-sodden boots
Steam, and suspended from the iron bed
Her coat and skirt, her wilted, draggled hat.
But she is happy, huddled by the fire
All recollections of the dingy day
Dwindle to nothingness, and she forgets
That in the street outside the rain which falls
Muddies the pavement to a greasy brown,
That in the morning she must start again
And search again for that which will not come.
She does not feel the sickening despair
That creeps into her bones throughout the day.
In her great eyes - dear Christ - the light of dreams
Lingered and shone. And she a child again
Saw pictures in the fire. Those other days
The rambling house, the cool, sweet-scented rooms
The portraits on the walls, and China bowls
Filled with 'pot pourri'. On her rocking chair
Her sofa pillow broidered with her name -[191]
She saw again her bedroom, very bare
The blue quilt worked with daisies white and gold
Where she slept dreamlessly...
... Opening her window, from the new-mown lawn
The fragrant, fragrant scent of perfumed grass
The lilac tossing in the shining air
Its purple plumes. The laurustinus bush
Its blossoms like pale hands among the leaves
Quivered and swayed. And, oh, the sun
That kisses her to life and warmth again
So she is young, and stretches out her arms ...
The woman, huddled by the fire, restlessly stirs
Sighing a little, like a sleepy child
While the red ashes crumble into grey.

Suddenly, from the street, a burst of sound
A barrel organ turned and jarred & wheezed
The drunken, bestial, hiccoughing voice of London.

1908

---

[191]A rough draft of this poem in the Turnbull's Notebook 29 includes, after 'broidered with her name' a passage which has been crossed out:
She saw again her mother in a muslin-spotted gown,
The sleeves turned back, and in her fine young arms
Great bowls of rowan berries for the hall.

### The Lilac Tree

Hull. Nov. 5.08

The branches of the lilac tree
Are bent with blossom - in the air
They sway and languish dreamily
And we, pressed close, are kissing there
The blossoms falling on her hair -
Oh, lilac tree, Oh, lilac tree
Shelter us, cover us, secretly.

The branches of the lilac tree
All withered in the winter air
Shiver - a skeleton in minstrelsy[?]
Soon must the tree stand stripped and bare
And I shall never find her there
Oh, lilac tree, Oh, lilac tree
Shower down thy leaves and cover me.

### In the Church

Hull. Nov. 5.08.

In the church, with folded hands she sits
Watching the ivy beat upon the pane
Of a stained glass window, until she is fain
To shut her eyes - - - yet ever hears it tapping.

"Come out" says the ivy
"I spring from the mound
Where your husband lies buried.
You, too, in the ground
(The hour is at hand)
You must lie down beside him."

In the church with folded hands she sits
Seeing a bride and bridegroom, hand in hand
Stand at the altar, but no wedding band
Crowns the young bride - save a chaplet of ivy leaves.

### The Trio

Out in the fog stained, mud stained street they stand
Two women and a man ... Their draggled clothes
Hang on their withered bodies. It is cold
So cold the very rain and fog feel starved
And bite into their scarcely covered bones.
Their purple hands move restlessly, at first
They try to sheild them with their thread-bare cuffs
Then thrust them in their coats, and then again

Blow on their fingers, but to no avail.
The women wear a strangely faded look
As though the rain which beat upon them both
And, never ceasing, always dripping down
Had worn away their features ... In their eyes
Hunger had lit a pallid, wavering torch...
The man is like a seedy, draggled bird
He frowns upon the women, savagely...
Opposite them a warehouse, huge and grey
And ugly - in the ghostly light of fog
It looms gigantic - through the open doors
Men and more men are passing out and in.
... Then, at a signal from the draggled man
The women sing - God, from their withered mouths
A tragedy of singing issues forth
High pitched and wandering, crazy, tuneless tune
Over and over comes the same refrain
"Say, shepherds, have you seen my Flora pass this way..."
The simple words hang trembling in the air
So strange, so foreign, if the filthy street
Had blossomed into daisies; if a vine
Had wreathed itself upon the warehouse wall
It would have been more natural - they sing
Shivering, staring - on their withered mouths
The winter day has set a frozen kiss...
Coldly impassive, cynically grim
The warehouse seems to sneer at them and cry
"My doors are shut and bolted, locked and barred
And in my bosom nurture I my spawn
Upon the blackened blood of my stone heart
I blind their eyes. I stop their mouths with dust
I hypnotise them with the chink of gold
They search and grope - but ever out of reach
I keep it, jingling. They can never hear
Your Floras and your shepherds..." Through the fog
The quavering voices fall and rise again...
Are silent - and the trio shuffles on.

                                        K. Mansfield. 9.XII.08.


Vignette

I look out through the window. A rhododendron bush sways restlessly, mysteriously, to and fro... The bare trees stand crucified against the opalescent sky.

In the next room someone is playing the piano. The sun shines whitely, touches the rhododendron leaves with soft color. To and fro the branches sway, stretching upwards, outwards, so mysteriously; it is as though they moved in a dream.

Through the open window, the cold air, blowing in, stirs the heavy folds of the curtains ... What is being played in the next room ... Does the music float through this room - and out of the window to the garden? Does the plant hear it, and answer to the sound? The music, too, is strangely restless ... it is seeking something... perhaps this mystic, green plant, so faintly touched with sun color ...

... I dream ... And there is no plant, no music - only a restless mysterious seeking, a stretching upwards to the light - and outwards - a dream like movement.

What is it?

I look out into the garden at the bare trees crucified against the opalescent sky... The sun is smothered under the white wing of a cloud - in the shadowed garden the plant is trembling.

K. Mansfield. 11.xii.08.

Revelation.

All through the Winter afternoon
We sat together, he and I...
Down in the garden every tree
Seemed frozen to the sky

Yes, every twisted tree that bared
Its naked limbs for sacrifice
Was patterned like a monstrous weed
Upon a lake of ice.

It was as though the pallid world
Was gripped in the embrace of Death
He wrapt the garden in his shroud
He killed it with his breath.

So through the Winter afternoon
We sat together by the fire
And in its heart strange magic worlds
Would build, would flame, expire

In an intensity of flame -
Our books were heaped upon the floor
Fantastic chronicles of men
Of cities seen no more

Of countries buried by the sea
Of people who had laughed and cried
And madly suffered - who had held
The world - - and then, had died.

A faded pageant of the past
Trooped by us in the gathering gloom
And we could hear strange, muffled cries
Like voices from the tomb.

And sometimes as we turned a page
We heard the shivering sound of rain
It trickled down the window glass
Like tears upon the pane.

We two, it seemed, were shut apart
Were fire bound from the Winter world
And all the secrets of the past
Lay, like a scroll unfurled.

As through the Winter afternoon
We dreaming, read of many lands
And woke ... to find the Book of Life
Spread open in our hands.

K. Mansfield. 4.XII.08.

[MS-Papers-4006-15]

Red as the wine of forgotten ages
Yellow as gold by the sunbeams spun
Pink as the gowns of Aurora's pages
White as the robes of a sinless one
Sweeter than Araby's winds that blow
Roses. Roses I love you so.

It cannot be possible to go through all the abandonment of
Music and care humanly for anything human afterwards.

K. Mansfield. 1908.

[MSI-Papers-3988-11]

October. (To V.M.B.)[192]

Dim mist of a fog-bound day ...
From the lilac trees that droop in St Marys Square
The dead leaves fall, a silent, shivering cloud.
Through the gray haze the carts loom heavy, gigantic
Down the dull street. Children at play in the gutter
Quarrel and cry; their voices are flat and toneless.
With a sound like the shuffling tread of some giant monster

---

[192]VMB—Vera Margaret Beauchamp (1885–1977), KM's eldest sister (later Mrs Mackintosh Bell) pasted this poem into a scrapbook of 'Mansfieldiana' which she subsequently gave to the Turnbull Library. The poem was published in the 'Table Talk' column of the *Daily News* on 3 November 1909.

I hear the trains escape from the station near, and <u>tear</u>
their way into the country.
Everything looks fantastic, repellent.  I see from my window
An old man pass, dull, formless, like the stump of a dead
tree moving.
The virginia creeper, like blood, streams down the face of
the houses.
Even the railings, blackened and sharply defined, look evil
and strangely malignant.
Dim mist of a fog-bound day
From the lilac trees that droop in St Mary's Square
The dead leaves fall, a silent fluttering crowd.
Dead thoughts that, shivering, fall on the barren earth ...
Over and under it all the muttering murmur of London.

K. Mansfield
22
IX
08
London

[NL]

### Youth and Age

Youth and Age walked hand in hand beneath the trees. A strange, half-frozen
day, yet the air was drenched with thin sunshine, and the blue sky full of white
winged clouds... The garden beds were smothered under a mauve mist of
Michaelmas daisies, burning with the dusky fires of chysanthemum blossoms.
In the dew pearled grass white daisies, like butterflies, quivered and shone.

Age walked slowly. The riotous Autumn wind blew her black skirt about
her shapeless body; her strange face gleamed like ivory in the silver setting of
her hair. And she stared with faded eyes at the blackened boughs of the trees,
at the leaves, falling in a fluttering crowd upon the dew pearled grass. One leaf
touched her cheek - God! it was like a kiss from the withered mouth of
Death! And in the bare trees she saw her naked soul, to be tossed, defenceless,
in the fury of a thousand tempests, to be torn, limb from limb, by Winter, by
her last lover, by Death ... Her heart beat in her body like a frightened bird -
a caged bird that beat its wings - in vain - in vain -

Youth suddenly stood still, her laughing child face lit with sunlight, and
stretched out her white arms, her rosy tipped fingers to the blackened boughs.
Ever the leaves fell in a shining shower upon her radiant face and bosom. Her
heart beat in her body like a restless bird, like a <u>strong</u> bird that if it did but
spread its wings would fly away - away - "See," she cried to Age, "see the kisses
of Summer, the golden leaves from the fairy book of Spring."

————————\\————————

K. Mansfield
1.X.08

[NL]

### The Thoughtful Child. Her Literary Aspirations.
### (To E.K.B.)[193]

In a very short time now the Thoughtful Child is going to take to pothooks. In fact she had one lesson the other day and she made an 'A' - "a sort of gate, Father" - and a 'B' - "two little rooms' - and a '1' - "just a long, Father - and a '2' - "a 'long' with a bag at one end and a piggy tail." After that she washed the faces of her family with the slate sponge and found it far more fascinating. "But I will learn" she says, nodding and smiling, when I'm turned some more, dear" - her way of expressing birthdays.

You see we are so very anxious to write a book for all those Poor Things who have no babies of their own to look after but other people's children - for 'Aunt Emilys' who wipe their feet on two doormats, for Uncle Peters who "nearly blow their noses right into their hankeys - so hard" - that they may therein read about the private and particular language of the Secret Society - to which every respectable child belongs - their customs and their demands.

As it is they are always being misunderstood. I remember the last time Uncle Peter came to stay with us. It was in the smoking room after tea ... "Father always 'snugs' me in the evenings, Uncle Peter" announced the Thoughtful Child, climbing up my chair.
"Eh, what!" said Uncle Peter.
"We have such nice snuggles."
"Eh, what!" said Uncle Peter - and we really thought his eyes were going to drop right over the carpet - they were so surprised.

Then the next day at dinner - there was apple tart. "Won't you have some of the friendly cow, Uncle Peter" asked my daughter, waving her teaspoon airily at the cream jug. "Bless me, you're a very smart young lady." "Oh, it's not me, Uncle Peter - Mr Stevenson, you know." But he did not know - and she was amazed. "Oh, I knew that years ago," she cried. "Years and years before I was born even. Why I remember -" "Yes, dear, that's enough" said Mother, looking at me and I smiled back at her. Was Mother thinking of those Winter evenings when she sat sewing, sewing, and I read to her from the "Child's Garden", and showed her the pictures that peeked and ran out at you from every corner. Small wonder the Thoughtful Child remembers that - small wonder ...

And there are times when you cannot be called 'young lady', or 'child' or 'little girl', when there is a pain in you that will not get better until someone says 'Chick-a-bidee' or "Toodle-ums' or 'Precious Poppet', or 'Dear-my-sweet'. Uncle Peters and Aunt Emilys do not realise one half of the importance of these things ...

We never say we have cried - we "wash our eyes out". When we want to whisper we tell people "please shut your ears". When we are tired of the house

---

[193]Edith K Bendall (1879-1986) was KM's friend Edie, who was to have been the illustrator of a projected book of child verses and stories by KM. This story was no doubt one of them.

"my feet are so <u>walky</u>". When we lie flat and look up there is no blue sky and white clouds – those are the sweetest pet lambs roaming through fields of forgetmenots.

They must learn, too, that there are no such things as dolls – they are fairy babies living for a little time with Thoughtful Children to be treated ever so kindly – and dressed and undressed and buttoned and tied – never sewn. And the day you wake and find one gone – she is carried off in the night to a real Mother who will wake and find her curled up in her arms like a little pink flower. Why, one day, when we were out walking and a little girl passed with her nurse – "why <u>there's</u> my Arabella Susan, Father" cried the Thoughtful Child, "she's got just the same fat legs." The little girl did not look at all pleased but some children are quite 'blushy' about it. My daughter is not – she remembers perfectly well being Janet Maria and having biscuit crumbs popped into her mouth with a hair pin …

And what is the use of a waistcoat pocket if it does not contain a chocolate button – one with little white seeds all over. You take them carefully off and put <u>one</u> back into the pocket so another button can grow there. And then you eat the brown part and sometimes it sticks to the top of your mouth – tongue or no tongue it won't come down again.

In so many families a boiled egg is a "higgledy piggledy" in remembrance of the black hen who laid hers for gentlemen only. "Fathers are always gentlemen" – and you say "Father, some bread, please." "Plain or coloured, Miss," answers Father, smiling at you across the jam pot, "half a yard cut on the cross, I take it, with as little selvedge as possible." You do not understand at all but it is the 'jokey' voice and you expect to be talked to that way…

There is another thing. When you are staying away and bedtime comes – "Can I have a candle, please Aunt Emily" – and your voice seems to come from your poor little pink toes quite lost 'way down in the cold sheet. It is different at home – where Mother holds your hands and sings – but Aunt Emily's hands are cold and knobbly like the bath tap, and Aunt Emily, shaking out your clothes until the wonder is that a button is left to tell the tale says "Nonsense, child – spoilt girls – wrong[?] days – bad habits."

So you lie there, quiet, until a piece of the dark creeps under your bed and hides there and <u>begins to come out</u>, nearer and nearer and nearer and nearer and <u>nearer</u> – until there you are sitting up in bed, your curls standing up round your head like a regiment of soldiers and Aunt Emily – who comes so quickly she must have been waiting round the corner with a glass of water in her 'bath-tappy' hand. Now if she had only known to have nice hands and a song – none of that need have happened …

About having your hair washed – This is a ceremony which ought to be the right of Mothers only, the Thoughtful Child tells me. No Aunt, be she ever so 'Auntie', no Godmother, no dear old friend must trespass here. It is Mother alone who keeps the soap out of your eyes, it is only Mother who gives you 3d if you do not splash through the bathroom floor on to the dining room ceiling, who dries you very very gently – all the others make you feel as if your head was coming off in the towel – and who kisses that little place at the back of your neck that comes with leaning ...

The Thoughtful Child would like the point made very clear. People – the right sort of people – must expect children to sit on them. "Now, there's <u>no</u> place to sit on Uncle Peter" she says, "and Aunt Emily is so cracky. Now, you, Father dear, why I'm sitting on <u>you</u> now, and Mother." I put an arm round her to hold her there, tightly, shuddering at the thought that one day I shall be so Uncle Peterish and she so old that maybe we shall sit sedately in two chairs and talk about the newspaper.

"The book would be very big, Father dear."

"Oh very, indeed."

"There are such lots and lots more. I'll have to begin quite soon and make billions of books for Aunt Emilys and Uncle Peters." She slips down from my knee and pushes the curls back from her face, looking a little flushed and puzzled.

"Perhaps, Father dear," the voice is distinctly wobbly, "perhaps I'd better make pothooks before I've turned."

"Oh, not yet, Babbles. I've got a bone in my arm. <u>Soon</u>."

She is all joy again – let it rest at that.

———————————\\ ———————————

K. Mansfield

IV.08

# Notebook 29

## PART 5

[Notebook 29, qMS-1241][194]

29/10/08.

You ask me for a picture of my room.

And through the wood he lightly came
And lightly caught me by the hand
He called me by my childish name
How could I understand?

He led me by a secret way
A little path that seemed to wind
And lose itself – the shining day
Was very far behind.

For here the trees so thickly stood
The sunlight could not filter through
Dear Christ it was a magic wood
And magic boughs that grew.

And I have waited long for thee
He scorched me with his fiery breath.
I am the one eternity
Not – love – not love – but Death.

The very silence seemed to break
And quiver with a thousand things
The bird of passion seemed to wake
I felt it spread its wings

And fly from his head into mine
He led me to a little bower
All smothered with the creeping vine
And purple passion flower.
And there we kissed & passionately
We clung together – all the past
Blotted from out my memory
I knew I had found love at last.

---

[194]The final part of the ubiquitous Notebook 29.

# *Unbound Papers*

[MS-Papers-4006-13]

Kâthie Schônfeld.[195]

I am quite happy for you see
My books & music stay with me
My days and nights are melody.

And in the morning the great sun
Climbs through the windows one by one
Calls to me, laughs that the day's begun.

Late in the night - when I'm awake
Comes the quiet moon to sweetly make
Delicate lamplight for my sake.

And from my window - down below
There is a box where the Spring flowers grow
Daffodils golden breathe & blow.

I do not know why things touch us so, she said - "Home Sweet
Home" - you know I think of all the maudlin, piteously inane,
foolishly insipid songs, and its pauses are perpetually
punctuated with vociferous nose-blowing - people are fools.

Neither do I.

[MS-Papers-4006-15]

Out to the glow of the sunset, brother[196]
Come with me
The wild waves play and embrace one another

---

[195] This poem is written on a page with the printed heading 'Consulat de France à Smyrne.' One can only guess at where KM got it from—perhaps the house of a school friend with diplomatic connections. On the back of the page is the comment which follows here: 'I do not know why ...' 'Neither do I', at the end, is written later and in different ink.

[196] Whether this poem is (strangely prophetically) addressed to her brother or whether she is using 'brother' as one might say 'friend' (a common usage in George Borrow's popular Romany tales of that time) is not known.

Let us join their play my brother
Far away out at sea.

The sky is wondrous fair O brother
(Let us go)
The great sad Ocean shall be our Mother
We are tired & she will rock us brother
Gently to and fro.

Why do you linger here, my brother
(The sunset dies)
The sun & the sea say goodbye to each other
Come away, soon will be too late, my brother
Hark to the sea birds' cries.

Ah! all the glory has faded brother
The sea is still
She is waiting for us to creep under the cover
Of her great blue wings O brother, brother
Peace, we shall soon be still.

We stood together on the shore
The wind was moaning the sun was dying
And the sea was crying crying crying
For ever more.

We knew we should part on the morrow
We looked towards the sea and sky
And dared not move, and could not cry
For sorrow.

We did not know when we should meet
We only knew we had to part

# Notebook 8

[Notebook 8, qMS-1245][197]

Kathleen M Beauchamp
Beauchamp Lodge[198]
Warwick Crescent
Maid Hill
London N.W.
October 1908.

How tired I am. It is I think because this Aunt of mine[199] has been talking and talking until she has dragged all the vitality out of me - endless conversation about endless families & dead people - twelve children but seven were carried away. And then the men & the long long pieces of ugly linen & ugly thread. Oh how tired I was!!!

October 17th
Came here at Forest pour un rest[?] in a motor. Felt damned tired and more than damned hungry. Have an appetite that I would not sell for £100. It is damp and misty. I walked into the village & bought pencil & paper & postcards. Saw what especially attracted me, a square, the church in the centre, the [...] à l'autre coté the little village houses - it was very sweet. These people amuse me to the very last degree - they are shriekingly funny, but happy too, I'm sure - wealthy people and every possible wish gratified - they look so funny[?] & dear. Miss A. the cigaret lady smokes all the time - plays a rattling good game - and old women but do you know they object to my smoking - shut the door you - fool women [?] they can't stand the smoking. R.S.L. I was sure.

---

[197]Notebook 8 was page numbered by Murry, starting at the back, and consequently accessioned at the back. It is reproduced here, of course, from the front.
[198]Beauchamp Lodge, a hostel for music students, was where KM lived on her return to London, until she disqualified herself by marrying George Bowden and had to leave.
[199]'this Aunt of mine' was KM's aunt Belle Dyer who stayed in England to be near the Beauchamp girls during their schooling at Queen's College, married Harry Trinder, and so settled there. KM visited her in Surrey from 14–19 October 1908.

Oct 19th. Feel frightful & can't think why. Met Martin today. Feel awful, shocking, terrible. What is to be done, I <u>wonder</u>.[200]

Naturalising the Supernatural. Frank Podmore.[201] The highly [....] attitude of the world - to ask what is the "commercial use" of everything. Sir William [...] declares that
Chaddie - stocks. But Mrs Rayner V - picture. Maata - light coat & skirt. Rippy[?] - Doris. Eric - Music. Jeanne - books. Martin[?] P.C.s. Doris

In a bus outside Victoria Station. Left Belle today - very happy & well for her home & child are delightful. She seems

I wonder if I will ever be happy again - that's the question sans [...]. It seems my brain is dead. My soul numbed with horrid grief. A man in the bus is blushing - a vivid purple hue. This Hand on my Heart again. <u>The Shadow of the Hand</u>.
<u>3 o'clock</u> this afternoon.

Wednesday 21st. 20 after three.[202]
Well, after a day of most turbulent packing Margaret and I drove off to Victoria 20 after seven. London looked garish, festive, alluring, only in the Park there were vague [...] crowds huddled together at the Marble Arch - a body of Police waited by their horses. Victoria - the huge station seemed alive with police and passengers. Already by the Continental train strange foreign types of people gathered - a Pole, tall, thin, smoking a long narrow cigar, a Turk, scarlet fez topping his sombre face. We four filled a compartment. There were wide fat English seats with a neat little white antimacassar buttoned across the top. And the doors were slammed - a last view of the wide platform and we had rushed our way into the country. I read a little and then huddled up in the corner, half sleeping, half waking. I thought of you. To open my eyes and find you beside me - if it was we two together going abroad. I felt, mainly, wrapped in a great cloak of thought. And so on and on. Every now & then, out of the window peering, I saw a signal box loom up in the darkness.
We shattered through the tunnels - then a halt at Lewes, ten minutes off Newhaven. Packets of corn beef sandwiches were produced and black grapes in frilled white paper - we have one of those extraordinary little meals that English people indulge in travelling. And then Newhaven: all change.
Tired sleepy people, children crying fretfully, the Pole again - and again the cigar - the Turk weighed down with huge white wicker baskets, stream along the platform up the damp gangway to the damper boat.
    I have a confused impression of rain and [...] lights and sailors in greatcoats & boots, like Flying Dutchman mariners. We go aft to the Ladies

---

[200]At this time KM feared she might be pregnant after a shipboard adventure on the way to England.
[201]Frank Podmore (1855–1910), writer on psychical research, wrote *The Naturalisation of the Supernatural* in 1908.
[202]KM was invited by her friend Margaret Wishart and her parents to accompany them to Paris for a few days for a naval wedding. This passage appears to be a draft of a letter to Garnet Trowell to whom she was by this time romantically attached.

Cabin where a little French woman is in attendance, her white face peering curiously at us over billows & billows of apron. Such wide blue velvet couches, such hard bolsters for tired heads. We slip off boots and skirts & coats, wash, and wrapped round in my big coat & a rug tucked round my toes I settled down for the night. It was amusing, you know, all round these same huddled figures, smothered in the same little brown rugs, like patients in a hospital ward. And the little French woman sits in the middle knitting a stocking. Beside her on a red table a lamp throws a fantastic wavering light. All through the hours, half sleeping, half waking I would open my eyes and see this little bowed figure & the wavering light seemed to play fantastic tricks with her - the stocking in my fancy grew gigantic, enormous. It seemed almost symbolical - the sleeping figures and in the light the little quiet woman knitting an eternal stocking. At last I really slept only to be wakened - deux heures et demi. My shoulder & hip ached, my hand had gone to sleep. I stretched wearily - still the strong thudding vibration of the boat, the swishing of the water. Then suddenly - how can I describe it, beloved - it was as though I lay in your arms. For a moment I turned my face to the wall, could not look at people feeling as I did. I was strong, refreshed, waked to such full life that I got up laughing, plunged my face into the glad cold water - & booted & spurred - ran up on deck to find Dieppe - the landing stage like the mouth of some giant monster, and a little crowd of officials groaning a gangway on board.

We disembark, hustle up the sanded stairs to the luggage room where the flaring posters on the walls - Normandy, Bretagne, Paris, Luxembourg - are like magic hands stretched out in invitation. See what I hold - come here. In the buffet we have rolls and strong coffee out of thick white cups. In the centre of the table there is a little flat strong peasantware bowl of berries. I think - dear me, he wouldn't believe that. Next table to me a honeymoon couple - she with a new wedding ring, and all blatantly new luggage. I look at them and think dear me how much happier we should be, how at ease we would feel where these two only look nervy, ashamed & apologetic to the waiters. And again into the high padded carriage. A porter runs along the platform shaking up the darkness with a jangly bell, shrill whistles sound, & now we are finally to Paris. At first on one side the street of rain-washed cobblestones, on the other the harbour full of lights - the darkness. I slept but woke at Rouen - it was bitterly cold. An official with a bell about the size of a 3d bit[203] dashed along the platform. Opposite in a buffet 2 gens d'armes were drinking. We started again and next I remember blue light flooding the windows of the carriage. I rubbed one - a little peephole for myself - and saw green trees white with frost. Then little by little dawn, a sky like steel - on both sides of us quaint small grey blue villages, houses, [...], fields girt with Noah's Ark trees. And now and again the moon, like steel, slipped through the streets. At last Dawn came - in the sky hung a pink banner of cloud. It grew and widened until at last it touched the houses & fields - peered into the

---

[203] A '3d bit' was a three-penny coin—a quarter of a shilling.

mirror. Dawn sat up in bed with a pink fascinator[204] round her head. At the station sleepy officials shouted French French French, & then St. Lazare at last - a great platform - cold with the coldness of more than Winter.

Observe me then dearest on the Newhaven platform wrapped in two coats and wooly gloves & furs, and eating a sugar bun as big as myself almost with the joy of the world. A rough sea journey is a strange conglomeration of sensations. I, in a moment seem caught by a thousand memories - am a child again, sitting on the deck in my Grandmother's lap - and me in a red riding cloak - going over to Nelson, to Picton,[205] to England for the first time & the second - - -

It was frightfully rough. I lay still, perished with cold, & felt dreadful. Eventually Margaret & I succumbed to the fearful agonies of mal de mer, & the few hours seemed an eternity of time. What joy to reach Newhaven, to come up into the air & see the pale shadowed town, the lights shivering in the cold harbour, the gangway leading to land. I began to laugh & observe.

<u>Thursday week</u>. <u>Sylvia</u>[206] to tea with me.
October 29th. Went to Mrs Charley Boyd & at last put my mind at rest.[207]
Now I must more definitely arrange my life. I'm being <u>bad</u>, Must send Sidney's books. Must write Woodie.[208]

> And through the wood he lightly came[209]
> And lightly caught me by the hand
> And called me by my childish name
> How could I understand.
> He led me by a secret way
> And overhead the thicket branching wild
> Shut out the [...] day.

Kiwi

Arthur Symons.[210]
I wish to make a little selection for future reference - - -
He drew the melody from the violin as one draws the perfume from a flower, with a kind of slumbrous ecstasy.
Misunderstood isolation reading them like a cryptogrammatist he shuts me in upon a house of dreams, full of intimate & ghostly voices.

---

[204]See note 48.

[205]Nelson and Picton were the two northernmost ports of the South Island of New Zealand to which ferries from Wellington sailed. They gave access to the Marlborough Sounds where the Beauchamps sometimes had summer holidays.

[206]Sylvia Payne, a daughter of KM's mother's cousin Frank Payne, had been at Queen's College with the Beauchamps and had become friendly with them all.

[207]Presumably this was the end of KM's worries about pregnancy.

[208]'Woodie' refers to Miss Clara Wood. See note 80.

[209]A more complete version of this poem is in Notebook 29, on p 207.

[210]This is not a heading but just the jotting down of the name of someone KM happened to be reading at the time or was planning to read. It is often difficult in these notebooks to distinguish between headings (or titles) and stray jottings.

In the music of Wagner there is that breadth & universality by which emotion ceases to be personal & becomes elemental. He stood, as the music seemed to foam about him, as a rock against which the foam beats.

The music of Wagner has human blood in it. What Wagner tried to do is to unite mysticism and the senses, to render mysticism through the senses. That is what Rossetti tried to do in painting - that insatiable crying out of a carnal voice.

And that trilling of Chopin - the dew as well as the rain has a sound for him.
Parsifal - light
Tristan - sea
Ring - fire
It is a sea change - the life of the foam on the edge of the depths.
Caress you like the fur of a cat.
We have blind vengeance, aged and helpless wisdom, we have the conflict of passions fighting in the dark, destroying what they desire most in the world.

Strauss. Don Juan - passion & [...]. All the notes of the music evaporated like bubbles. Oscar was a philosopher in masquerade. K.M.
Memory is a garden and the flowers in it are imitation immortelles - everlasting flowers - dry as dust & leafless. K.M.
It seems that every S. evening at nine o'clock I must go & meet you, my beloved. The sea cry is the desire of more abundant life, of unlimited freedom, of an unknown ecstasy.
You do not necessarily get to your destination by taking the right turning at the beginning of the journey.

Even the American daughter might take her Mother to see it without compromising[?] the innocence of old age.

The thought had taken fire & become a kind of passion.
Mozart music sans le désir, content with beauty. It has the fine lines of a Durer picture or of Botticelli, compared with the Titian splendour of Wagner. There is the romantic suggestion of magic in this beauty.

- - - - - - - - - - - - - -

Maeterlinck

Was this the face that launched a thousand ships
And burnt the topless towers of Ilium.

Mes mains dans les votres.

Words for T.W.T.

And which do I love most my dear
The substance or the shadow.

Out in the fog stained mud stained street they stand.

Seems to peer out at them, to sneer & cry
My doors are closed and bolted, locked & barred

And in my bosom nurture I my spawn
From the blackened blood of my stone heart.
I blind their eyes, I stop their mouths with dust
I hypnotise them with the clink of gold.
They search & grope, but ever out of reach
I keep it jingling, they can never hear
Your Flora & your Shepherdess
Through the fog
The quavering voices fall & rise again, are silent.
And the trio shuffle on.

---

Out in the fog stained, mud stained street they stand
Two women and a man, their draggled clothes
Hang on their withered bodies. It is cold
So cold the very rain & fog are starved
And bite into their scarcely covered bones.
Their purple hands move restlessly – at first
They try to shield them with their threadbare cuffs
Then thrust them in their thin coats, & then again
Blow on their fingers but to no avail.
The women wear a strangely faded look
As though the rain which beat upon them both
And never ceasing, always dripping down
Had worn away their features – in their eyes
Hunger had lit a pallid wavering fire.
The Man is like a seedy draggled bird
He frowns upon the women savagely.
Opposite them a warehouse huge & grey
And ugly in this ghostly light of fog
It looms gigantic – through the open doors
Men and more men are passing in & out.
Then at a signal from the draggled man
The women sing. God, from their withered mouths
A tragedy of singing issues forth
High pitched & wandering, crazy tuneless tune.
Over & over comes the same refrain
Say, shepherds have you seen my Flora pass this way?
The simple words hang tiredly in the air
So strange, so foreign – if the filthy street
Had blossomed into daisies, if a vine
Had wreathed itself upon the warehouse wall
It would have been more natural – they sing
Shivering, staring up at the great wall.
Coldly impassive, cynically grim
The warehouse seems to sneer at them & cry

Les Lettres Mortes

<I am in love with love.>

### Song of the Camellia Blossoms.

Dark dark the leaves of the camellia tree
The flowers of the camellia tree
Are whiter far than snow.
I could drown myself in you
Lose myself in your embrace.

### A God, one day on Mount Olympus.

Cupid one day grew tired, & fell asleep, his head pillowed against the barren breasts of Minerva. Looking down upon his loveliness she dreamed. When he woke & begged her to play with him, dreams still hunched against her barren

So strange it is that I could smile
So sweet that I could weep
Our hands had fallen in love dear while
Our souls were still asleep.

burst - she blew a bubble for him

Long time before we
To fall & to rise again - laughing
To catch it - to reach out an arm[211]
Oh, there is its only charm.

Cupid one day grew tired and fell asleep, his golden head pillowed against the barren breast of Minerva. Looking down upon his loveliness she grew sorrowful & then dreamy, & when he woke & begged her play with him, beating upon her with his child hands, she borrowed a reed that Pan had fashioned for a pipe, & dipping it into the shadowed water of Lethe that flows out but remains always, shadowed, silent, she blew a bubble into the shining air & coloured the heart of it with her dreams.

And Cupid, laughing, clutched at it with his child hands but it blew up & away into the air - tremulously lovely - blew away away over the world. Cupid & Minerva watched it fascinated. "See, see" said Minerva, "the little people - how they fly after it, see - they forsake their houses & fields, their wives & children, [...] their women from them & heed them not - & all run after my bubble." She clapped her hands & laughed. "I do not like such games" said Cupid, plucking out a wing feather & sticking it jauntily into his golden curls. "Such games are never for people."

Why can I not write a happy story, very much in the style of The Love Episode or The Soul of Milly Green. Let me think out a really fine plot and

---

[211]The line following this is illegible.

then slog at it and get it ended today. It would do me worlds of good & Sidney
would be so delighted. Come, surely that is not hard! Something a little
sonoro, for, why I cannot tell, I'm rather good at that style of thing.
Have a child in it - a wunderkind. Have a coffee stall in it.

"sleepy eyes and a poisonous voice." He met her again on the Pier at
Eastbourne[212] - the wind had blown her hair in soft curls round her face,
wild rose colour stained her neck, her red mouth trembled - - - The wind
was terribly strong. She was trying to hold her skirts down, laughing in a
childish eager way - - - That is how Tim saw her after four years. Her letter
was forgotten, his suspicions he pitched from him as one throws a pebble far
into the sea - the fact of her, the reality of her, the beauty of her made his
strong heart tremble - he almost stumbled forward holding out his hands -
Miriam -
    "Life what a gale" said Miriam. "You haven't changed a day Tim, except
you're look ....."
And one day when he bought her a bunch of daffodils she burst out crying,
holding the flowers up to her face. "Oh what a fool I am" she said, "and the
sticky stuff in the stems will stain all this white lace."
She stood under a lamp, the yellow shade made her hair & face & body shine
like gold - like a daffodil herself. "Well whats the price" said Miriam, laughing
softly, taking a little bottle of perfume from the table & sprinkling her
handkerchief. "4 2/4 and a packet of pins thrown in." She looked at him over
her bare shoulder & Howard[?] sprang up & caught her in his arms.
"My God" he said, "So much beauty - my God, I could kill you."

Now I really must continue with this its not so hard as it at first sight appears,
at least I dont think so. Come let me start.

In the cool of the evening when Twilight had softly entered the garden, the
shadow of her presence lingering upon every tree & shrub and plant, Miriam
could remain indoors no longer. She got up stiffly from her knees and strapped
and corded the tin box that she had been packing so laboriously, with so many
eager hopes, vague half regretful desires and memories folded among the plain
linen and simple childish treasures. In the faded light the pink wallpaper,
stripped now of her christmas cards and Pictorial Supplements, of her Bible
Class certificates, and paper fans, looked hideous - blotched, like the face of
her Father when he was angry. She shuddered and walked over to the window.
The trees waved to her, she smelt the wild sweetness of the wallflower growing
by the gate, the soft musky perfume of the little white pansies that spread
down the garden like moths - - - I'll pick a big bunch and take them with me,
she said, nodding gravely.
    In the kitchen her Mother was bathing her younger children. Miriam
heard their laughing voices - "Can't I splash, look, Mum, look at me
swimming", but as she passed through Silence fell - the children looked up in

---

[212]Eastbourne is a beach settlement on the opposite side of the harbour from Wellington City.

sudden awe of this tall black sister playing with them it only seemed yesterday
& now going to London all alone and with her hair up - - - The Mother
raised her hot face & looked anxiously at Miriam. Going out for a spell, she
asked. No Mother,
I thought I'd get some flowers to take with me tomorrow. Oh alright. Take the
pertater knife - its on the plate rack - there. You wont mess yer hands then.
Expect anybody along Mirrie.

At the question her tired face relaxed, a little smile hovered round the
corners of her mouth. Miriam blushed faintly. "Oh I don't know Mother."
She stepped out of the house quickly, down the narrow path to the wall
flowers. So strong the scent it almost seemed to drag her into it. She knelt
down on the grass border and cut a great spray of them, then a pink full blown
rose, some mignonette, a handful of sweet william. Twilight had deepened into
darkness. She gathered the flowers up in the skirt of her dress & stood upright.
In the dark someone quite close beside her called her - "Mirrie".

Miriam turned round sharply, the colour flooding her face & throat.
She had been waiting all the time - the flowers were only an excuse - and yet
now that he came she wanted to fly back into the house - her heart beat in
her body like a frightened bird.
"How quietly you came."
"I went first to the house, through the back way but your Mother told me you
were out here, so I walked through, over the grass - that's why you didn't hear.
I wanted to surprise you." She laughed awkwardly. All the time they stood
facing each other, M. holding the flowers gathered up in her skirt, Tim[213]
clasping and unclasping his hands & kicking a stone which was firmly wedged
into the pathway. He seemed to regard that a far more important item than the
fact of Miriam, so few yards away. She bit her lip. The silence seemed to hang
trembling, a thin veil between them, a breath at any moment to be torn apart
by something new & strange. Miriam looked down too, at the stone in the
path.

Ah, at last he kicked it out of the path, sent it flying out of the garden.
Miriam smiled[?], for something had happened to her [...], yet trembled
- - - In the dark garden Tim came nearer to her. "Mirrie" he said, "Mirrie".
The rough passion of his voice startled her so much that she dropped her
flowers - they lay heaped about her feet. Tim caught her by the arms.
"Oh girl" he said "I've been in a Hell all day, thinking what might happen to
you in London. It's no joke for a girl like you, Mirrie. You're young and you're
innocent. Why you don't know any more about real Life than a lamb in
Spring." He shook her roughly as though it was her fault. "Oh" he said,
"I'd like to take you up in my arms & carry you away right now & never let
you see anything else." "Don't Tim" said Mirrie. Tears started to her eyes, ran
down her cheeks.[214]

---

[213]At the top of the next page KM wrote 'Milford Lane, Arundel Street'.
[214]Several lines hereafter are obliterated by ink blots.

It was his thorough good sense, his innate spirit of gentleness, his unfailing patience and self-sacrifice which angered Miriam more than anything else. Perhaps if he had shown her less regard she would have felt for him a tolerance if nothing else, but as it was - - - Miriam was a child still - one of those women who go through Life's greatest experiences and remain children still. She loved to drift with the current but the current had to be <u>strong</u>. Till the world ends - vote or no vote, sexual equality or no sexual equality, that will be the type of woman who considers herself cheated of her rightful position if her husband does not throw the fire irons at her - the E.V. attitude, the Jane Eyre passion will be upon the sex while women are women. Sacrifice is her primary and fundamental attribute. She is given to and does not give. Man must take the initiative - they are as uncommon now as they were 1909 years ago, but Miriam had been spoiled & had drunk of wine so strong that she craved it ever, that all else sickened her. She had warmed herself by a fire so fierce that anything less passionate chilled her. When Tim took her tenderly in his arms, kissed her brow & chin & hair, it seemed a wild beast fought & tore - - - ravaging with hunger, it smelt meat & was denied it, & beat against the bars in vain. Her mental state of mind affected her physically. She grew tired easily & was querulous - upset by the least unexpected noise or excitement. [...] to go [...]. Hypercritical of Tim. Noticed the way he walked, held his head, put on his clothes. Was offended by all that he did.

Golden Tulips.

### The Last Lover

And so she lay upon her bed
And waited through the night.
He will be coming soon she said
And Oh, his step is light.

How cold you are, how very cold
Cling closely then to me
[One line illegible]
Why do you lie so pale & still
Never a word spoke he.

On her warm bosom his cold head
&lt;Drooped like a fallen thing&gt;
Im afraid, afraid, she said.

### Scarlet Tulips

Strange flower, half opened, scarlet
So soft to feel and press
My lips upon your petals
Inhaled restlessness

A fever and a longing
Desire that burns in me
A violent scarlet passion
Stirs me so savagely.

Strange flowers half opened, scarlet
Show me your heart of flame
Do you keep it in silken wrapping
I shall find it all the same
I shall kiss your scarlet petals
Till they open your heart for me
And a beautiful tremulous passion

Shall bind us, savagely.

It is only interesting in that I make it psychological & place the school say at Harley Street.

Oh, Käthe, je veux ecrire quelque chose d'immense mais c'est bien difficile – even so. Death is preferable to barrenness. Much in your idea of a good book.

Born in New Zealand in Wgtn,[215] describing the storm, the esplanade, the bedroom, then old Mrs Macpanaty[?] the M. dies at birth so the child is brought up by the grandmother. The Father a shrewd man of business – no other children. The journey to the country & cousins, Aunt Miriam. Private school life, and journey to England with the Father. Left there at college, meeting with Beatrice. His Mother's house in Carlton Hill and he lives there alone with an old servant, a man who knows them both.
I must really formulate some more of this plan – it seems that I can go no further which is manifestly absurd.

I am beginning to find myself. I am coming back, she said.
She woke on Sunday morning chilled through, and raising herself on her elbow looked out over a grey waste of sea.[216] The sky was full of hurrying grey clouds. Wind had risen during the night – it took the little cottage in a gigantic grip, shook it as a dog shakes a rat. A loose sheet of corrugated iron in the back yard kept banging against the outhouse – the persistent sound at last got on Rewa's nerves. She thought she must get Jennie to hold it down with a large stone. She got out of her bunk and dressed rapidly, all the time staring out at the angry sea – it moved heavily, lumbering against the rock – just a glint of white teeth showing, just a suggestion of what it could do – – –
She heard Jennie unlock the back door, saw her stumble across the yard, her apron round her head, & come back from the outhouse laden with manuka. Presently there was a strong clean smell of the wood burning, a crackling sound. Rewa slipped into a blue jersey and rough blue skirt, she brushed out

---

[215]KM made a start on this piece in Notebook 2. (See note 166).
[216]The setting here is the cottage at Downes Point. (See note 85)

her hair and plaited it in a long braid, slipped her feet into red mocassins
& went into the living room. Jennie, setting the table, looked up anxiously.

"You look fair done up Miss Rewa" she said, "its this atmosphere that
does it, Miss. There's going to be a terrible storm – the seagulls have all come
close to the land Miss, regiments of them are on the wharf poles, Miss.
Did you hear me get up in the night and bring in the tea towels Miss?
They were tied to the line like and all twisted up like tape measures. I was
lying awake Miss & I kept thinking of them till I got up. The wind was that
bad I felt it would have torn my hair off and it was so scary Miss Rewa,
to hear it getting up more & more."
"There's going to be a storm Jennie" said Rewa. "We must keep up a good
fire, and I shall be in all day. You had better have the little stove in your
bedroom – when you are sewing."
"Oh yes thank you Miss, and there are plenty of books you can read."
"Here let me make the toast Jennie – Oh, how good it smells."
She knelt down before the fire, the light on her face and the short curls of her
hair round her forehead. Jennie looked across at her, a little smile hovering
round the corners of her mouth.
"Oh Miss Rewa beggin your pardon but you don't look more older than
when you were twelve & used to come into the kitchen for buttered crusts."
"Oh Jennie I'd forgotten" cried Rewa, "and sometimes it was dripping & salt
& pepper you remember." "Yes Miss I remember. Your breakfasts ready
Miss Rewa. Have it while it's hot."
"We've still got some [...] strawberry," said Jennie
"I'll walk over to the store this evening, Miss – Oh, it won't be open –
Sunday."
"You can get in at the side door " said Rewa. "What do we need."
"Carbonated soda, Miss, and some monkey brand."
"Can't they wait till tomorrow."
"Well I don't like feeling they're not there, Miss Rewa."
The table cleared, the red cloth straightened, Rewa went into the bedroom,
pulled out her old trunk from under the bunk & found her writing case.
She took it into the sitting room & sat down on the floor before the fire.

> The New Zealander
> K. Mansfield

My dear Friend,
I wonder where you are and what doing? London England seems to me almost
another planet. I cannot realise that only a few months ago we talked in your
cool room & outside saw the leaves turning in the chestnut tree at the corner.
That Life seems dead for me – buried surely. After my terrible sorrow London
seemed to lose all her reality. I had thought of her as a gigantic Mother in
whose womb were bred all the Great Ones of the earth, & then, suddenly she
was barren, sterile – her body the burial ground of all who counted in the
world. I could not have stayed there any longer. I'd rather be a frightened child

lost in a funeral procession – yes, as bad as that – and came home – each day bitterly eager for your – and here I am.

It is Summer. You I suppose are abroad or in London – I wish I knew. But today there is a storm threatening each moment to burst upon us. It is as though the shadow of its giant form is even now upon the sea, & the waves know & move restlessly, yet fiercely. Wind raises great pillars of sand up in the road, in the bush, the trees lashing together, and the long leaves of the flax bushes stream like ribbons of green & silver.

How like me to have not told you even where I am but your fatal gift of divination [...] assures me that you know, that I never need explain. I see you now in this quiet room, scented with the manuka wood that burns so brilliantly. It is dull indeed except for the firelight. Quite plainly I see you, standing, your back to the fire, and saying "Rewa" – the name was always a little foreign on your lips.

Dear Friend, from my life I write to you in your life – and yet it seems that we never meet on any definite ground, that I found you in the borders of Nomans Land, that our hands met & knew each other there. The Future is quite in darkness but I know now that I am on the road again, back again, and that [this] time I journey with a fuller knowledge – a child no longer.

Rewa pushed back her chair, went over to the window, knelt on the little pink couch, pillowed her arms on the sill, & looked out over the sea. And it suddenly seemed to her that all those miles upon miles of leaden water were held together, were banded together, shepherded – to separate her from him. I shall never cross them again, she thought. I shall always be standing here on the rocks looking out over the water. Yet turning back into the room his warm presence seemed to fill it. In love surely, she thought, time is not, time never was, time cannot be. And does not the sun teach me that more than all else. Ebb and flow maybe, light & darkness, calm & storm, yet always such depths to discover, such treasures to find – – –

And nothing is ever lost – cast up on the beach one moment, thrown on the barren rocks, but taken back again with the tide turning, surely, surely, into its great bosom. Not all the fires of the earth could quench the sea – but such helplessness – it was bitter in the mouth. I must give myself tomorrow, she thought – I am too much like my wild lawless Mother, and my baptisms of sea water – my baptisms & sacraments – it is in my blood now. I can promise nothing. She went back to her letter.

You know, dear Friend, what store I set on your Friendship – so alone am I. Perhaps you are the only human being whom I love. This is not by nature of a confession – rather it is an affirmation – I am going to dedicate myself to my own, to my trees, my mountains, my solitary places, my little rivers – for in them it seems, I have my being.

We shall not meet again but I shall keep the thought[?] of you in my heart until I die. That is all ...

She addressed the letter, sealed it. Pausing a moment, the wind seemed to have increased in violence & again as in those past years she heard the strange overtone & undertone as though it were crying and then it gathered together the voices of all those who had died, and the crying of all those who were not yet born. And it seemed that the wind called her and the children of the wind - the sea itself cried her name. She put on a pair of sandshoes, a long cloak - head covering was out of the question. In the quiet bedroom Jennie was stitching at a long holland cloth, her comfortable stockinged feet pressed against the bars of the stove, & singing to herself as she stitched "Come to Jesus" - a pacification to the Almighty for her breaking of the Sabbath.

Said Rewa "I shall be out for some hours Jennie." Said Jennie "Very well Miss Rewa - I'll keep up the fire." At her touch the door burst open. With great difficulty she closed it again. And then the wind seemed to her like a giant child, waiting, watching for a moment's peephole to rush in - to invade the cottage, to blow it off the very face of the globe.

There were no flowers left in the garden & storm-beaten, her carnations & marigolds sprawled across the path. She did not [know] exactly where she was going but held to the fence a moment & looked up and down the road. Nothing to be seen. She suddenly started almost running in the direction of the yellow clay bush path that so many years ago she had found and loved. Once in the bush it was easier - she was more sheltered, though the sound was more violent. It seemed that every tree had found voice. Rewa looked round her - the living[?] green, the wild sweet scented [...] tasted of the Forest leaf she bit in her mouth - all these entered in to her - - - She climbed quickly, catching at trees & branches, wrenching her hand. A long arm of lawyer[217] pulled her skirt - the leaves brilliantly scarlet, the plant looked as though it had fed on blood. Sticking to the supplejacks, almost swinging herself upwards. And at last the top was reached & the bush behind. She slipped on to the grass plateau, the great ledge overhanging the sea - here unprotected[?] the wind spent its fury. I have had a [...] it cried and now lo you are the sacrifice. She didn't have time to stand up but crawled on hands & knees to the top of the land. Looking round she saw the whole depth down bush covered, and below her lay the sea - right out to the open ocean it spread, leant against the sky, dead cheek against dead cheek.

But clumps of manuka grew upon the cliff and Rewa lay down in it. The plant was strongly sprung and thick with leaf & flower so that it pillowed her. She was warm & dry and tried with her long climbing to laugh silently. The sea looked swollen with agony - it broke against rocks & sand-shelters [?] with a harsh shattering sound. And then suddenly the rain fell in great gouts. The sky seemed let loose upon the earth. Rewa did not move - the rain beat upon her, drenched her thin clothes - but she looked out at the swirl of waters almost smiling. "You must satisfy me now, Oh my Mother" she said, "I have come back to the heart of Nature - take me, take me."

As she lay there, rain-beaten, wind-tossed, on her frail body even to the roots of her hair, she felt the thundering of the sea.

---

[217]Bush lawyer: *Rubus cissoides*, a forest plant whose long probing midribs, armed with sharp hooked prickles, enable it to climb up or along other vegetation, and to catch painfully at the flesh of unwary walkers.

Nature spoke.

"I am desire" said the sea, "I crave all, insatiably I long, untiringly I hold."

"I am breath" said the wind. "I blow over all the waste places of the earth & make them filled with my voice."

"I am that which holds seed" said the earth. "I am that which receives & gives back again, ever more bountifully, from the life in the plant, and so I justify my being."

"I am healing" said the rain, "the ugliness & sorrow that has been before I wipe away with my tears. I fill the barren valleys with running water."

"I am love" said the bush, "for I am blown hither by the breath of the wind, conceived in the womb of the earth, roused by the rain. And I bloom in great waves like the waves of the sea."

"I am desire" said the sea. "Insatiably [I] crave, hold all & give all, I sink myself in all that I possess, and yet I am I and changeless & untouched by the sinking. I am drawn up to the sky by the sun, & yet I return and am the same."

Rewa stood upright, stretched out her arms. Darkness shrouded the world. Through the storm she heard footsteps behind her, wheeled round sharply, her terror distorting her face. But he came forward & caught her in his arms. "You" she said, "you". Their voices were carried away by the wind; the bush & sea seemed to thunder all that [they] said. "I have come for my own" he said, holding her, her long braids of hair blown across his face. She clung passionately. "I am desire" said the sea, "I crave all, insatiably I long, untiringly I hold."

------

P.A. Vaile, 29a Charing Cross Road, W.C.

6–6.30 130 Fleet Street.

Friday - Bath[?]

Saturday –

Sunday 3, Albert Hall.

Monday

Tuesday - Aunt Annie[?]

Wed:

Thursd:

Friday:

Saturd: Dr Saleeby.[218]

Sunday:

Write Mrs Galloway, and Edith […] letters. Send one copy.

Veronal.

It was the freedom of those days - the knowledge that an she would she could shake from her all the self-forged chains & banish all, & pillow her head in her Mother's lap. All that irretrievably gone now.

------

[218]It was at the home of Dr Caleb Saleeby, the well-known popular-science writer, that KM first met George Bowden to whom she was briefly married.

Song of the Cabbage Tree. The knot of Flax.
Then All the [....] the world let come in. Eta Eta Eta.[219]

> She has thrown me the knotted flax
> It lies concealed in my bosom
> It twists about my heart
> Sapping the life blood from me
> As the rata saps the kauri
> As the little clinging tendril
> covers the giant kauri
> So is the flax on my heart
> So would her arms round my body
> Cling & crush & enfold me.
> Like the flowering rata
> Is her young mouth's scarlet.

I have a perfectly frantic desire to write something really fine, and an inability
to do so which is infinitely distressing, as you may imagine. However let's
make the attempt even though it should come to nothing at all great ...
To long for chains, and once securely bound

> This woman calls the      [J44]

March 14th
This almost mad hunger to work is gnawing at me. It was as though some
insidious & terrible worm ate & ate at my heart - a frightful & intolerable
agony overcomes me. I feel that I must be alone or die, that a book has got to
be conceived & written. But the difficulty is that I am not yet free enough to
give myself uninterrupted hours. Oh how damnable it is - for at last I shall be
able to write quelque chose worth writing. I want to realise a far Horizon -
it's not so tremendously difficult, & I could surely do it excellently well.      [J44]

February 29th 1912.
I left in daylight. Biggy B[220] came as far as the muddy part of the road in her
brown blanket, then I sang & saw the cottagers - got skeered and half ran -
very nasty. Now for it.

Gypsies have been here: there's a bit of colour they have left hanging to
a thorn hedge, and a broken pail, and the bracken trodden. We passed a farm -
five asses in a green field, and a boy with a pink dusky face gave us a glass of
water to drink.

At the bottom of a field there was a tree with curiously interlaced
boughs & branches, they very black, the tree silver against a sky that was silver
and folded with a strange blue. In the tree sang a bird.

The feeling of dark strength in pictures, like the pull of savage hair[?]

---

[219]E tā e tā e tā is a Māori form of address. It can also mean friend, or an expression of surprise. What
exactly KM meant here is not known.
[220]'Biggy B' was a nickname for Beatrice Hastings.

– damp, [...] I crush it against my breast as I would hold a lost love –
with passion & terror & the melancholy of memory.

Memory is the rain in the mirage of the desert.

> And Mr Wells has got a play upon the English stage.
> Now – Arnold Bennett comes from where
> They make their pretty songs[?]
> I was a draper in my time
> And now I am all the rage
> My name is Mr H.G. Wells
> And Kipps is on the stage.
> Im Arnold Bennett L.S.D.

"Ooh er there's the pond, isn't it nice but very dutch looking."
It was a round basin of water with shallow banks bright green & set with
young willows. "Um – Holland – very" said B, and balanced herself on a fence
rail. A cart lumbered past driven by an old man with a face like a tree stump,
thought K. She smiled at him. "Maand them [...]" said the old man. "There's
a fearful lot of them thar aboot."
"Look" cried B, pointing with her stick, and then they saw the pond was alive
with frogs – with frogs at their nuptials – too revolting a sight – they were like
Nietzsche with the lid off. B. found five glued together and try though she
would she found it impossible to separate the horrors. K. screamed every
moment.

"Pot of tea please and a penny bun."

her thrills in the memory. I am like a harp – if one listens eyes shut and deeply
enough one hears that strange ringing which with years of sweeping waves
grows fainter and more forlorn, and yet is there. I am like a shell murmuring
of the restless tides and the troubled passion of the deep sea.[221]

---

[221] Notebook 8 ends with some rough sketches of birds, and the first three verses of the poem 'In the
Tropics' which occurs in a more complete form in Notebook 29 (p 92).

# *Unbound Papers*

[MS-Papers-4006-01]

A.C.F. Letter.[222]                                        Night

It is at last over - this wearisome day, and dusk is beginning to sift in among
the branches of the drenched chestnut tree. I think I must have caught cold in
my beautiful exultant walk yesterday, for today I am ill. After I wrote to you
I began to work but could not - and so cold. Fancy wearing 2 pairs of
stockings and 2 coats - & a hot water bottle in June and shivering ... I think
it is the pain that makes me shiver and feel dizzy. To be alone all day, ill, in a
house whose every sound seems foreign to you - and to feel a terrible
confusion in your body which affects you mentally, suddenly pictures for you
detestable incidents - revolting personalities - which you only shake off - to
find recurring again as the pain seems to diminish & grow worse - Alas! I shall
not walk with bare feet in wild woods again - not until I have grown
accustomed to the climate ... The only adorable thing I can imagine is for my
Grandmother to put me to bed - & bring me a bowl of hot bread & milk &
standing, her hands folded - the left thumb over the right - and say in her
adorable voice:- "There darling - isn't that nice." Oh, what a miracle of
happiness that would be. To wake later to find her turning down the
bedclothes to see if your feet were cold - & wrapping them up in a little pink
singlet softer than a cat's fur ... Alas!

Some day when I am asked - "Mother where was I born" and I answer -
"In Bavaria, dear", I shall feel again I think this coldness - physical mental -
heart coldness - hand coldness - soul coldness. Beloved - I am not so sad
tonight - it is only that I feel desperately the need of speech - the conviction
that you are present ... that is all.

Sunday morning. Yet another Sunday. What has this day not brought us
both. For me it is full of sweetness and anguish. Glasgow - Liverpool - Carlton

---

[222]Beside this Murry has written '?meaning'. One can only guess. The letter seems to be to Garnet
Trowell, written in June 1909 when KM was in Bavaria awaiting the birth of their baby. But since Garnet
had by this time cut himself off from her it seems likely that this was a 'fantasy' letter—an exercise in wish-
fulfilment.

Hill - <u>Our Home</u>. It is raining again today - just a steady, persistent rain that seems to drift one from one memory to the other. When I had finished my letter to you I went down to supper - drank a little soup, and the old Doctor next me - suddenly said "Please go to bed <u>now</u>" & I went like a lamb & drank some hot milk. It was a night of agony & when I felt morning was at last come I lighted a candle - looked at the watch & found it was just a quarter to twelve! Now I know what it is to fight a drug - Veronal was on the table by my bed - oblivion - deep sleep - think of it! But I did not take any. Now I am up and dressed - propping          [J41-42]

[NL]

Being the list of Virtues & Vices appertaining to
Miss Bartrick-Baker[223]

I.    a supreme sense of justice gained by careful and unbiased reflection on all things.
II.   A capacity for feeling very deeply.
III.  A tendency to be a little too hard on the average faulty creature.
IV.   A great tendency to underestimate her merits.
      She is a little too inclined to taking so great an interest in the truly Great of the World that she forgets to be great herself, & she would be if she had determined to.

V.    She is jealous, yes very jealous.
      She is broad minded, very, & decidedly clever.
      She is sympathetic, very much so in theory & practise, but the theory is greater than the practise.
      She is altogether very different to this old Black Sheep of a creature, who breaks promises & is altogether a great bore!!

Here endeth this list. Que pensez-vous? Moi, je ne sais pas.
                                                   Kathie.

[NL ts]

## HIS SISTER'S KEEPER[224]

The girl came up on deck to find Dieppe like the mouth of some giant monster and a little crowd of officials groaning a gangway on board. Then up the sanded staircase to the luggage room, where the flaring posters on the walls - Normandy, Brittany, Paris, Luxembourg - seemed like magic hands stretched out in invitation - "See what I hold, come here."

    Her one small bag was passed without comment. There was still half an hour to spare before the train left. She was cold and tired, and went into the

---

[223] Vere Bartrick-Baker, also known as Mimi, was one of KM's closest friends at Queen's College. She features as 'Pearl' in KM's unfinished novel 'Juliet', found on p 57.

[224] This typescript, unlike most typescripts in these collections, does not seem to be sprinkled with misreadings. That, together with the fact that it is signed and dated in her hand, suggests that KM typed it herself and that it can be relied on as accurate. It has many points of interest, particularly, perhaps, her idealised and romantic view of her young brother expressed six years *before* his death.

Buffet for a cup of coffee. Glancing at her watch she found that it was barely three o'clock. Three o'clock in the morning ... and Dieppe ... when she had only made up her mind at six o'clock the evening before, and at seven she had been at Victoria, debating still, still safe, and now ... well, anything to live. She was sick of existing. If she had spent another day of the frightful monotony it would have driven her mad, and after all so many would only have jumped at the opportunity when it was first offered. This idiotic habit of drawing back would never take her anywhere at all. She sipped her coffee slowly out of a thick, white cup, noticed the little fern-filled dish of Hungarian peasant ware on the table, and at the table next to her, a honeymoon couple - she looked half-smilingly, half-sneeringly at the blatantly new wedding-ring upon the woman's finger, their new clothes, and yellow leather handbag. They looked ridiculous - abashed, self-conscious and almost apologetic towards the waiter. Heaven preserve her!

Then out again on to the cold platform to climb into the high, padded carriage. A porter ran along smashing up the darkness with a jangling bell - shrill whistles sounded. She was settling her bag and hat and umbrella in the rack when the door was thrown open and a woman half fell, half jumped into the carriage, seizing her suitcase from a porter. She threw him some money, he banged the door to, and they were off.

"That was a case of all but," said the Fellow Passenger, panting a little, holding her handkerchief up to her lips, "I hadn't an idea..."

She tugged at the buttons of her coat collar. The girl smiled and watched her curiously. The Fellow Passenger was a woman, obviously young still, but over dressed, her childish face covered with rouge and powder, her pretty brown hair curled and puffed against her hat. She wore a scarlet blanket coat over a pale blue cloth dress, her high-heeled shoes were cut low enough to show her blue clocked stockings. She sat down in one corner, putting her feet on the opposite cushion, and began peeling off her suede gloves, a little smile still curving her red mouth; her eyes, serious. Out of the window on one side the girl saw a street of rain-washed cobble stones - on the other side the harbour full of lights - then darkness ...

She wrapped her cloak round her and took out a little copy of "The Shropshire Lad" from an inside pocket but could not read. The Fellow Passenger was never still. She opened a red leather bag, took out a powder puff, a mirror, looked at herself critically, put out her tongue, wet her finger and carefully smoothed her eyebrows, found a hairpin and put her curls in position. Then she recklessly applied the pink powder to face and throat and even the bosom of her dress. "Gilding refined gold and painting the lily" she said, glancing up and catching the girl's eye. "But lilies have no right to go journeying in railway carriages, my dear, even they can't be exempt from smuts. My name's Lily - a series of remarkable coincidences."

She flung back her head, laughing like a child, and showing her little white teeth like seeds in a red fruit. Then suddenly serious "I say that to everybody I meet travelling. It's the greatest point. Came on me like an inspiration one day when I was in the same carriage with a Salvation Army

Officer. You see it puts one on such a charming footing, such a delicate flower-like intimacy. What are you reading ... Oh, don't tell me, it's poems. And you wanted to be alone in the carriage, to curl up and look out of the window, then read a little verse, then remember how he smiled at you in the last verse of the hymn on Sunday evening. It's a good thing I came in to chaperon you ... you're too pretty for empty railway carriages. Are you going to stay in Paris with grandma in rooms conveniently near the Louvre. I am." As she spoke she laughed so much, spread out her little white hands with such a friendly gesture that the girl caught the infection.

"Do go on" she said. "Of course I'm going to grandma. I felt somehow you must be going to yours."

"Oh, what a surprise" said the Fellow Passenger, sobering a little, "your voice isn't at all what I had hoped and expected of you - and now I see that your eyebrows too - no, not gênée at all, my dear, you don't tell me ... Do you want to go to sleep?"

She suddenly stood up, stretching herself like a little kitten, yawning and rubbing her eyes. "I'm not sleepy."

"Neither am I" said the girl. "I slept on the boat."

"I am feeling queer" said the Fellow Passenger. "Could howl with crying or put my head out of the window and wave my hanky at nobody at all, or shoot myself or read a love poem. Hand me the book."
The girl gave it to her in silence.

"Hallo" said the Fellow Passenger, "got a fit of the tarradiddles - your hands are on the jump."

"I am tired" said the girl, blushing faintly.

"I know, my dear, the heaviness that endures for a night ... Good Lord. Now you go bye-bye while I read."

She curled up in the railway carriage, pillowed her head on her arm, the little book in her hand. It was bitterly cold. The girl felt suddenly exhausted. It was the Fellow Passenger's comment upon her nervous shaky hands. She had not quite got command of herself. She could not quite see the future. Felt suddenly that she had plunged into a sea without the slightest idea as to whether she was swimming towards land or quicksand, or mirage. Now this Fellow Passenger, her assurance, her laughter, the very way she powdered her face, all seemed to speak of success and experience. The girl felt crude beside her, longed suddenly to speak of a dozen vague fears. But she fell asleep and did not wake until the train stopped at Rouen. It certainly was bitterly cold. The Fellow Passenger was tugging a long fur out of her rug-strap.

"Felt I couldn't do without my little piece of dog" she said.

"Have I been asleep?" said the girl.

"Asleep, my dear, like a baby, with your eyelashes curled on your nice little pink cheeks - most fascinating to a 'Young Lady's Companion'. That's a neat way of expressing a fact, isn't it. I've got a gift that way." She picked up the red book that she had been reading. "I say, there's a photo pasted in here of a kiddy - who is he?" And the girl answered "Oh, that's my brother."
A wave of colour seemed to flood over her whole body. She did not want this

woman to look at him, to speak laughingly of him. Felt almost ashamed for one moment of her sentimentality, that she could snatch away the little photograph and hide it in her bosom. But the Fellow Passenger did not laugh. She spread the page out on her lap.

"Oh, so that's your brother. My word he looks fine – a regular boy, and yet ... there's something so sensitive and splendid in his face – spiritual, my dear."

"Yes, that's just it." The girl sat upright, her hands clasped on her knees, "he's a marvellous child." Her heart warmed to this other woman, she could have kissed her.

"Well, nurse, your night-duty now" said the Fellow Passenger, her voice regaining its flippant tone. "I'm going up the wooden lane. Send me to sleep with a story – about your little brother." The girl smiled but the Fellow Passenger nodded gravely. "Across my heart" she said, "I'd really love to hear anything, it's so refreshing." She wound her fur twice round her throat and lay down to sleep.

"When I last saw him" said the girl, "he was thirteen – very young, you see, but tall and splendidly made, broad shoulders and slight of hip – you know." She was speaking to nobody really, only thinking aloud, her head raised, in her eyes almost a prophetic sweetness. The light fell upon the yellow braids of her hair. "I felt maternal towards him. As a baby he clung to me, and all the years after – I could still when I looked at him, feel those little hands round my neck, on my face, blindly feeling. And through all the sadness of my girlhood that child brought me light and sweetness. He had a little habit of bringing me flowers – a rose, some violets, a spray of apple blossom – yes, he was always coming to me with his hands full of flowers. I have so many pictures of him" said the girl, "in my mind you know. He will be the finest man on earth. Oh, I see him as a little child sitting on the table while I scrubbed his grubby knees, and after his bath in my room in the morning in his pink pyjamas, his hair curling all over his head, standing on one leg and flicking the towel and crying 'It's a lovely day, dearest'. And at night after he had gone to bed we had a mysterious game called 'Pyjama arm'. I used to go in the dark and lie down on his bed, my head pillowed on his arm while he told me all his thoughts, his growing ideas, his strange little fantastic conceptions, questioned me, implicitly believed in me. In the dark even now sometimes I hear that little high voice. And then, particularly after he had been playing cricket, I could hear him stumbling up the stairs, hot, out of breath, his shirt collar unbuttoned, his hair on end, damp with perspiration, and mopping his face with an indescribable handkerchief."

The girl laughed suddenly. "He was so absent-minded, too. Often I would go into his room when he was half an hour late for breakfast – 'I can't find my braces anywhere, sister, I've been looking and looking' and they'd be buttoned to his trousers all the time, trailing on the floor. Then he used to stand on a chair and part his hair before my mirror, called it a 'bug-track' after he'd been to school. He read too, everything I gave him, good things you know, the very best always. Oh dear, what didn't he exact and demand of me

in those days. I remember very well saying Goodbye to him. He was going to
school, and we kissed for a moment and then I leaned out of my window.
It had been raining – the air was very cool and clean. He waved to me from
the gate and I listened, hearing the glad little footsteps die down the street,
fainter and fainter, so fast … out of my life." She stopped speaking a moment.
The Fellow Passenger was lying with her hands over her face. Blue light
flooded the windows of the carriage and the girl, rubbing a place in the glass,
saw in the gloom a green tree white with frost.

"He is going to be a splendid man" she said suddenly, "Oh, one of the
best – a wonderful man. Yes, you were right – spiritual is the word. He needs
the very best influences … Are you laughing?"

She thought the Fellow Passenger stirred. No answer. The train throbbed
on and the girl, tired out, lay down in the corner. Then, the Fellow Passenger
suddenly sat up, and to her amazement the girl saw that her face was wet with
tears. She was twisting her handkerchief in her hand, dabbing her eyes with it,
the powder and rouge smudging her face, and she suddenly slipped down to
the floor of the carriage and pillowed her head in the girl's lap.

"Oh, listen" she said. "I, too, had just such a brother, just. The world to
me, you understand. We lived just so together. I was his sister and his mother.
On him I based all the hopes and aspirations of my life. Unhappy at home,
too, you know, and he my ideal – but we did not part – oh no. We were twins,
that was the great difference to you, so although I felt older and he always
came to me I had not felt him as a child in my arms. That does make such a
difference – absurd how we love the helplessness, but we do … I gave up my
life for him. Put him, if you like, upon a pedestal, made him perfect man,
and he you know took such care of me, watched over me so. We decided that
when I was old enough we should live together. I did not wish to marry, he
filled my life, and I was sound asleep, really, you know. Well, one day I had to
go to London. We lived in the country and at that time my brother was living
in London sharing a small flat. I was to stay several days with an aunt of mine.
My train was very late, and when we reached the station Aunt was not to be
found. I waited on the station – all alone – and by and bye a woman quietly
dressed came up and asked me if I was waiting for anybody. You know I was
young. All I said to her was 'Have you come from my Aunt, Mrs –' oh well,
the name's nothing – and she said 'Yes, there's a cab waiting.' My aunt was
engaged and would meet me at the house. So we walked along the platform,
it was six o'clock, a winter day and quite dark. I remember several people
looking at us closely – I had my hair down still you know, in a long plait.
A carriage was waiting, we got in. The woman gave no address, but we drove
a long distance. During the drive she was silent, and I, thinking her a maid of
my aunt's, looked out of the window. We drove for what seemed an
interminable distance, and then at last the carriage stopped in a quiet street,
a large grey stone house before us. Though I had never been to stay with her
before, the house did not look at all as I had expected, but still I was
unsuspicious. The woman had a key, and I remember standing on the steps and
looking down the lighted street as she fitted it into the lock. Then she turned

round. 'Well, come in Miss, your aunt will be waiting for you.' So I walked into the hall and the door was shut to. I wonder if you can imagine my feelings at seeing a great heavily furnished hall with a gilt mirror and in the glass visiting cards - the names most curious to me. The woman with me took off her hat and cloak.

'I'll have your things taken to your room, Miss' she said. 'I'm afraid your Aunt won't be able to see you tonight. You will find some supper ready - this way.' I followed her up the stairs along the passage and into a bedroom. She turned on the light, the room was large and ugly, but I was too tired and hungry to care about anything except that there was some supper on a table by the fire. The woman stood by me while I ate, and, I cannot tell you why, I think it was the strange silence of the house, of this woman - even the room seemed curiously expectant - I was frightened and after all I could not eat. If you will send up my boxes I will go to bed, I told her.

'Yes' she said, moving towards the door, the supper tray in her hands. 'I'd go to bed now, if I were you, and have a nice long sleep.'

Something in her voice ... I turned round, but she was out of the room, the door shut and I heard the heavy key grate in the lock. Locked in! I ran to the door, pulled it, shook it, beat upon it with my hands - it was no use. Silent a moment, terror choking me, I heard in the passage outside a woman laughing - such stupid, senseless laughter - it rose and fell ... Who was laughing like that - why? I cried out and screamed - nobody came. Stories I had overheard from the servants, newspaper reports that I had half read, vague transitory thoughts I had imagined almost obliterated - they trooped before me now, a hideous procession of hideous realities. There was a bell push in the room above the electric switch - I rang and rang - still silence.

Then I thought of him - my splendid brother. What would he think or say to know his sister ... And he was in the same city, visiting Aunt, maybe. His horror and terror at learning the awful truth. I remembered our conversations together - his high ideals - his reverence for women.

At the thought I cried anew, flinging myself down upon the bed, my hands over my face. Finally, do you know, I fell asleep tired out - and woke, to find the room in darkness - someone was kissing my neck and throat, someone was whispering to me to ... think of it, my dear, his arms round me, a country girl, filled with a white heat of reserve and terror - " The Fellow Passenger laughed bitterly, her voice full of tears.

"I struggled like a little wild cat, shook him off me, rushed to the bell push, and groping for it, in the darkness my hand touched the electric switch instead. I turned round - and it was he - the idol, my brother. Sic transit gloria me." said the Fellow Passenger. "We both left that room, but I went into another."

The girl stared, sat up, and rubbed her eyes. The carriage was full of light. Out of the windows a sky like steel, and on both sides quaint, small, grey-built villages, miniature fields girt with Noah's ark trees. And now and again the river, like a silver ribbon through the green tapestry of the fields.

At last dawn came. In the sky hung a pink banner of cloud. It grew and widened until at last it touched the houses and fields and peered into the silver mirror of the river. She looked across at the Fellow Passenger who lay still as before, her hands over her face. A strange, terrible dream, thought the girl.

They were nearly there. The girl gathered together her wraps, pulled down her hat, then tapped the Fellow Passenger on the shoulder.

"We're there" she said, "nearly."

"Oh all right my dear, half a shake." She sat up and felt again for her powder puff – applied it with renewed vigour. They did not speak again until the station was reached. The Fellow Passenger got out first, greeted gaily a man whom she called Bertie. As she stepped from the carriage the girl saw her drop her handkerchief – it lay on the floor. The girl picked it up – a little damp ball – and handed it to her.

"Oh thanks" said the Fellow Passenger carelessly. "Bye bye dear."

In the cold of the winter morning the girl stumbled out of the train, her bag and rug and umbrella in her hand. A man came up to her gladly, quickly, but she almost ran past him and out alone into the street.

K. Mansfield

1909.

[MS-Papers-4729 ts]

Whit Monday.

Hotel Marquardt,

Stuttgart.

Dearest,[225]

There is so much to tell you of, and yet all my impressions seem to be put into a lolly bag and jumbled up together – sticking together, even, yet – the yellow against the green! You know. Take one? And here is Holland green with meadows gilt-edged with buttercups, with children in wooden shoes, with cows, with windmills, and Rotterdam – full of canals and bridges – of light and sweetness. And even arriving – this is one on the top – at the Hook of Holland, seeing the dawn break into the sky in a wave of gold. Take another – Wiesbaden 4.30 p.m. We are at the station. I am remembering Rudy. Ah, how <u>hot</u> it is! We drink something red that foams out of a bottle in an ice-pail. And did you realise that to arrive here one must pass through the Rhine valley – see the castles –

---

[225]In 1972 Mary Middleton Murry's secretary, Ruth Baker, sent me a group of about half a dozen typed copies of Mansfield letters to various people. In due course the originals of all except this one turned up and were incorporated into The Collected Letters. All of the typed copies when compared with the originals were found to be very faulty transcripts, and I have no doubt that this one, were its original available, would also be seen to be very inaccurate. Inadvertently omitted from *The Collected Letters*, it is now part of the Turnbull's collection, and so finds its way into this edition.

If it was addressed to Garnet Trowell, as seems most likely, it must have been written in 1909. Whit Monday in 1909 was 31 May. Since Mrs Beauchamp arrived in London from New Zealand on 27 May and whisked KM off to Bäd Worishofen in Bavaria in time to take ship again in London on 10 June, we may confidently suppose that this letter describes KM's journey with her mother to Bavaria. It was probably not sent, nor even written to be sent, since by this time Garnet had cut himself off from KM, and this letter is not among those he kept which are now in the Library of the University of Windsor, Ontario, Canada.

river – Lorelei – all – all. I have heard many people cry their disappointment over the Rhine. Maybe that accounted for my joy in it – in vineclad hills – in pink Nussbaüme – in the castles high up on the rocks, and the river seeming to unroll before you like an old faded tapestry – all set in and wrought with medieval charm. It was 'beautiful beyond compare' – the villages at the river-side – you see the patterned roofs – you see a certain painstaking patching of the hills – mauve, green, dully blue. You see the woods – the rivers – the gardens, blossomful – you hear the people.

And here is Frankfort – Mainz – Coblenz – Cöln (Nach Kevlaar) – Bonn and Heidelborg, where a real live Carl Heinz boarded our train – all sword-slashed and be-ribboned and feeling very lovely.

At the German frontier, where all the baggage was examined – after it was done I went out of the station and ran down a little path and looked over a fence. Lilac filled the air – it seemed almost <u>smudged</u> with lilac, washed in with it – laburnum tantalizing, fairy purses of it – may – and a child with a brown neck and a little blue overall – so checked that I felt he must have some connection with a railway official and, on account of his size, got muddled with the railway tickets – Oh, but a beautiful child! – peeked through the railings.

[MS-Papers-4006-13]

The Grandmother.

Underneath the cherry trees
The Grandmother in her lilac printed gown
Carried Little Brother in her arms.
A wind, no older than Little Brother,
Shook the branches of the cherry trees
So that the blossom snowed on her hair
And on her faded lilac gown.
I said: "May I see?"
She bent down and lifted a corner of his shawl.
He was fast asleep.
But his mouth moved as if he were kissing.
"Beautiful" said the Grandmother, nodding and smiling.
But my lips quivered.
And looking at her kind face
I wanted to be in the place of Little Brother
To put my arms round her neck
And kiss the two tears that shone in her eyes.          [J43 S5]

[NL]

## THE SEA CHILD

Into the world you sent her, mother,
    Fashioned her body of coral and foam,
Combed a wave in her hair's warm smother,

And drove her away from home.
In the dark of the night she crept to the town
And under a doorway she laid her down,
The little blue child in the foam-fringed gown.

And never a sister and never a brother
To hear her call, to answer her cry
Her face shone out from the hair's warm smother
Like a moonkin up in the sky.
She sold her corals; she sold her foam;
Her rainbow heart like a singing shell
Broke in her body:she crept back home.

Peace, go back to the world, my daughter,
Daughter, go back to the darkling land;
There is nothing here but sad sea water,
And a handful of shifting sand.

[MS-Papers-4006-01][226]

Just as she was making some tea he came in & she called, going to the door
& seeing him standing in the passage. 'Hullo' they said - he came in. She said,
like some tea? Yes he would: he'd met Joe Simpson out - she must meet Joe.

They drank tea out of bowls & started talking & smoking. He told her his life
- she told him hers. She went over to the window & leaned out. Come over
here. He saw the sea & a ship - yes, so did she - it moved: with sails. They
leaned from the window & talked - a great deal. Then she said - I'm going to
bed - goodnight. Goodnight. You would like a big coat? No, thanks - at any
rate I've got mine. But how charming he looked! With his great umbrella
furled - and walking like a God.      [J48]

[MS-Papers-4028]

## FLORYAN NACHDENKLICH[227]

Floryan sits in the black chintz chair,
An Indian curtain behind his head
Blue and brown and white and red
Floryan sits quite still - quite still.
There is a noise like rising tide
Of wind and rain in the black outside.
But the fire light leaps on Floryan's wall
And the Indian curtain suddenly seems
To stir and shake like a thousand dreams.

---

[226]'This fragment is written on a page torn out of an old diary—April 1909—which, according to
Murry's pencilled note, 'is not the real date. ?1911'.
    [227]The title means Floryan Pensive, and the poem is about Floryan Sobieniowski, the Polish writer
KM met in Bäd Worishofen in 1909. It was published in the *Dominion*, Wellington, 3 March 1913.

The Indian flowers drink the fire
As though it were sun, and the Indian leaves
Patter and sway to an echo breeze.
On the great brown boughs of the Indian tree
Little birds sing and preen their wings.
They flash through the sun like jewel rings.
And the great tree grows and moves and spreads
Through the silent room, and the rising tide
Of wind and rain in the black outside
Fades - and Floryan suddenly stirs
And lifts his eyes, and weeps to see
The dreaming flowers of the Indian tree.

Katherine Mansfield.

[MS-Papers-4006-02][228]

57 Chancery Lane, London W.C.
### EPISODE
"The Child" in Love.

<She arrived at the house at half past six. T. sat at the piano striking vague empty chords with> the soft pedal down & watching with narrowed brilliant eyes like a malicious elf. She pushed open the iron gate that jarred on the loose pebbles as it swung back. The house was in darkness, but standing on the doorstep she heard the faint voice of T's <piano> violin. Sadder than her heart the sound, and like her heart speaking so faintly from behind closed doors in a darkened house. She paused on the step, her hand touching the doorbell. Even then it was not [too] late to run away - yes it __was__ too late. He might not

---

[228]KM made several attempts at her novel *Maata* which became dispersed, ending up some in the Turnbull and some in the Newberry. They are brought together here. Maata is based not on the real life Maata, KM's New Zealand friend, but on herself, and the story is largely autobiographical. It is concerned with the time when, having left New Zealand for the last time at the age of 19, she returned to London and renewed relationships with Ida Baker and the Trowell family. Having been for a long time romantically interested in one of the Trowell twins—Tommy—she now fell in love with the other—Garnet. For a time, while he was touring the provinces as a violinist in a theatre orchestra, they pretended they were married until, inevitably, she became pregnant and the relationship came to grief. There was no heroic suicide, as in the fictionalised version, but there probably was betrayal, rejection, anguish and disillusion.

Rhoda Bendall is clearly based on Ida Baker and indeed this manuscript represents KM's only surviving attempt to describe Ida's feelings for her. 'Bendall', the surname of KM's Wellington friend 'E.K.B.', is a name she also used elsewhere. 'Rhoda' and 'Rhody' are suggested by 'The Rhodesian Mountain', one of KM's names for Ida Baker. 'Philip', who owes a lot to KM's brother Leslie, has a name which is also used in 'Toots' (see Volume Two, p 101). 'Hal' is the name by which KM's father was known to his wife. 'Ellie' in the list of characters seems to have become 'Mally' in the text. Rachael West's first appearance in the 'plan' is as Marion West.

'Evershed' is also the name of a similar anti-hero in 'Brave Love' with which this story has a number of other affinities. In 'Brave Love' (see Volume Two, p 35) there are two South American young men who have no function at all in the story, and in the list of characters for 'Maata' there are 'The Greek boys' who make no appearance. In both stories the heroine is beautiful, cynical, self absorbed, drawn to the innocent young lover, but destructive of him too. In both cases the young man is not only betrayed but also punished. The uncommon name 'Evershed' was the middle name of James Evershed Agate, 1877–1947, essayist and dramatic critic. It seems likely that Evershed in both stories was suggested by George Bowden, and that Mildred in one and Rachael West in the other were suggested by Beatrice Hastings.

love her, might not have need of her, but she loved him – she had terrible need of him – he understood. By his presence and quiet gestures, by that almost tragic dignity that wrapt his youth in its folds, by that mysterious vibration in his quiet voice, by his childish laughter and his quaint delight and wonder in the simplest things, by his hair & hands, his very clothes – oh God, by everything about him, every atom, every particle. What on earth was she doing? She looked up at the dark house, shivering. How long had she been standing there. What was the use of this absurd litany? Had anybody seen her – had she spoken aloud? She rang the bell sharply. O believe me he does not care for you. You are nothing to him – now or ever. Grant your sorrow worthy in accepting it with dignity. Be brave – courage! So the poor child, standing pale and cold in the gathering dusk, all the youth drained out of her face.

Jenny opened the door smiling & voluble[?], and at the same moment Maisie danced into the hall, her wild curls flying about her, and flung herself into Maata's arms. "You're late, you're late, you bad wicked child – you said you'd be here at five and I'm angry & offended with you, you darling." Maata felt half suffocated by the strain of the child's little eager body, her smothering kisses, her fumbling[?] hands – & yet it comforted her – – it was something real & human and safe. "I couldn't get here any earlier" she said. "O Maisie, how wonderful your hair is, dear. You've been washing [it]." The child flushed with joy, urged at a little blue ribbon & shook her curls into wilder confusion.
"I washed it this afternoon & it's not dry yet. I'm finishing it by the kitchen fire. Come downstairs, mummy's there, she's making an apple pie for dinner & I'm going to prick your name in the pastry with a fork. Can't take your arm going down the stairs, it is too narrow – I'll go first though – it's one of my <u>flying</u> days. I can jump for steps at a time in the dark even." "O be careful" said Maata. The child's happy laughter answered her

In the bright hot kitchen Mrs Close, an apron tied over her black dress, shook the rolling pin at Maata.
"No" she said, "you shan't kiss me. Don't come near me, you bad girl. You've broken your promise – you said you'd come early. Get away. Go & play with Maisie in the dining room. We won't speak to you will we Jenny."
But Maata made a dive forward, caught her round the waist & hugged her. "O you blessed angel, I'm glad to be here. I've been such a cross grumpy miserable pig all day – nearly sat on the doorstep & put my coat over my head & cried before coming in this evening. Be nice to me – give me a little bit of the apple before it's cooked." She looked round the room, a bright colour grew in her cheeks. "I <u>love</u> this kitchen – I'm all cured."

And she believed it. The tide had turned with a swing that turned her up breathless. She looked at the big black stove, shedding so bright a light from behind the open bars, at all the homely cooking things on the table, at the blue dinner set on the dresser, at Jenny peeling potatoes with a penny book of fortune-telling propped against the water bowl, at everything – so real & simple and human.

"Perhaps you've caught a little chill on the liver" suggested Mrs Close, dusting the squat lump of dough with the flourcaster & kneading it smoothly with her quick little hands. "A nice hot dinner will put you right, won't it Maisie. Now Jenny, my girl, hurry up with the spuds & hide your book before Miss Maata gets hold of it or we won't hear a word more out of her - - - what have you been doing all day dearie - - - Maisie, take a peep at the joint. Use the oven cloth, child."

"I" - Maata sat on the table edge and nibbled her quarter of apple. She had done nothing at all, she reflected, except go deeper & deeper. Aloud: "O, working out a story, dabbling and worrying my foggy little brain. Is Father in?" "No, he and Hal have gone for a walk. They won't be back till seven. I made the boy take the old man out for an airing, they were both getting so snappy, but he did not want to go because you were coming." "Bless his heart. How many miracles has he performed since yesterday." "He finished his quintet this morning" cried Maisie, "and do you know who he's dedicated it to - you & Philip." "Not really, Maisie."

At his name, spoken so carelessly, her heart quivered in her breast. "True as death. Pip said it was an en-ig-matical honour. What does that mean Mummy?" "Don't know, my dear - ask Maata. Maata, you mustn't sit about in your coat. Go upstairs and take your things off in my bedroom - there is a peep of gas and a clean brush on the dressing table."

"I'll go with you and turn it up" said Maisie. Half way up the stairs Mrs Close called to the child. "Come back here Maisie. You haven't time. You must set the table, there's a good girl. You'll have Maata all the evening." "O Mother." "Do as you're told, darling" whispered Maata, only half [wondering] why she did not plead for the child. "Well, well don't be long. I've got such lots to tell you."

At the corner of the staircase the plaster figure of Penelope holding the red gas globe in her hand. The face seemed to be smiling at Maata, seemed to guess her secret, to know quite well why she wished to run upstairs alone. And in the bedroom with the flickering gaslight on wall & ceiling Maata smiled too - the blind smile of the plaster figure - she saw the resemblance in the glass. Why not? She would surprise him just for one moment, would say "Good evening" and run down to the others. Louder now the voice of the violin from the room above & miles away the warm bright kitchen - the staircase a dark journey separating her from the others leading him up to her. Even in that moment alone her sorrow returned, she saw herself playing a game with Maisie & the Mother, she knew that under her laughter - give it one moment's being - her heart still cried and was lonely. Lightly, on tiptoe she crept up the stairs. She stood a moment outside his door, she heard him pacing slowly up & down as he played, she turned the handle of the door, slipped in, stood her back against it. Philip started - she heard his quick breath. Then he nodded & went on playing a moment, never looking at her. The wailing music filled the room. There was no light except a pale gleaming

from the window space, and his long shadow on the ceiling like a cross.
She could see the outlines of the pictures on the dark walls, some flowers in a
glass on the mantelpiece. With the frightened eyes of a little captive child, with
the eager eyes of a lover she strained to see more of the room. The violin case
lying open on the white bed was like a little coffin. On the table by the
window she saw his books heaped. She was leaning against his coat that hung
on the door peg. All these vague thing seemed clearer than his figure - he was
just the shadow of herself, pacing up & down - the shadow she had lost or
never found that cried her sorrow.

Suddenly he took his violin from his chin, wrapped it in a silk
handkerchief, laid it in the case, clipped the bow through the loops, locked it
up & stood the case in a corner. He came over to her, running his hands
through his hair as though to free his thoughts, and stood before her smiling.
Still she did not speak or move. He fingered her coat, and his smile deepened.
"I thought you were a real ghost, girl" he said. "Come over to the window
& sit down."
"Pip, have I disturbed you?"
"No - I've finished. Have you been here long."

She sat down, leaned her elbows on the table & cupped her chin in her
hands. He took a pillow from the narrow bed, propped it behind him and sat
down, knees crossed, one hand on the table beating a finger exercise. They
were quiet again. She looked out at the dark street and the tree branches that
grew along the wall of the house opposite & seemed to grow outwards instead
of upwards as though they strained to hold one another in the dark. She heard
the ticking of his watch in his waistcoat pocket & [at] that she looked up at
him and laughed.
"What a very loud watch."
"Only just now" he said gravely. "There's a sort of secret conspiracy between it
and the heart it beats over. What have you been doing all day?" She turned
slightly away from him. She meant to speak quite lightly, to prevaricate. But
the truth trembled against the gates of her lips - forced its way through.
"I - have been unhappy."
"So have I." He spoke very simply. "I knew you had been." The words came
from her in a breathless broken voice. "You know sometimes I feel I am
pursued by a sort of Fate - you know - by an impending disaster that spreads
its wings over my heart - or maybe only the shadow of its wings - but it's so
black & terrible I can't describe it. Sometimes I think it is [...], foreboding,
telling me that what I am facing in the future - is - " she shrugged her
shoulders - "just <u>darkness</u>."

His hand on the table lay still - he clenched it. She saw the thin
pale hand & to that she spoke as though it held her in its grip & forced from
her . . .
"It seems so ridiculous, so childish, to say with the countless thousands - I am
misunderstood - and [...] - my youth I suppose - there the fact is. I feel like a
prisoner condemned to penal servitude, without the option of - anything

more sudden. I do not know who has condemned me, tried me, and so I –
to all intents & purposes – walk abroad with people who love me & are good
to me – <u>miserable</u> myself. Whenever I remember that I am quite quite apart
from them – the real me I mean, Pip – there aren't any words. I can't explain
myself." He got up, leaned against the window frame & looked down at her.
"Don't trouble" he said. "I can tell you – in your words in my own expression
– 'a lonely prisoner' – that is what I am, that is what you are." She nodded.
"But" she said, comforted, inexpressibly comforted by him, "don't think
I always feel this way. I think that when I am happy I am more happy than
anybody. The rareness of my depression does not make it any the less terrible
though." "I know, I know, Maata."

In the pause that followed she felt that their speech had sunk into a deep
unknown gulf that had separated her from him – that the confused words had
filled up the gulf. The door burst open. Hal came in, flicking his table napkin
in his hand.
"Dinner bell's rung three times. Jenny has called you. Mother is in a wax,
meat's cold. What are you two birds doing? Out with it, Pip, you sly dog."
"O I must fly down" said Maata.
"No – no" Hal spread out his arms to catch her. "Not until I know what you
two have been up to."
"Don't be absurd, Hal. Let me go. Pip, your hair's wild even in this light –
they'll be so angry."
"Not so fast, my sweet sister."
"Don't be a fool Hal" said Philip, laughing, "we've been looking at the trees
on the house wall opposite – that's all."
"What!" laughed Hal. "The ones that Maata said yesterday were holding each
others hands in the dark. Shame on you. Go down to your betters, Miss."
"O you baby" she said, running down the stairs. Hal went up and nudged
Pip in the ribs.
"Lucky fellow" he said & shouted after them all the way to the dining room
"I <u>knew</u> it, I <u>knew</u> it."

[MS-Papers-4006-01]

Maata knelt by the dining room fire helping Maisie roast chestnuts. They had a
packet of the little hard nuts beside them and a hat pin to prick them with an
old Daily Mirror leaf to hold the charred peelings. In the rosy glow of the fire
the two children, leaning against each other, laughed and whispered, very
absorbed, very intent. By the table sat Mrs Close, darning whole new feet into
a pair of Hal's socks. Her skirt was turned back over her lap, her little slippered
feet curled round the chair legs. Now and again she leant forward and opened
her mouth for Maisie to pop in a 'beautifully soft one', but she was, for the
most part, pale and tired. With a drawing board propped against the table,
sheets of manuscript surrounding the big untidy inkstand, some pink blotting
paper, the old man busied himself copying out Hal's latest score. Sometimes he
whistled, sometimes he heaved great windy sighs, scratched his head with the

pen end, rapped the rhythm of the score on the table. The room was warm
and all pleasantly scented with the roasting nuts. The window curtains in the
flickering light looked heavier, and quite profound their ugly red colour,
as though they wished for a little space to hold these four together ...

Now and again, in the hush, they heard Hal's piano. He was busy with
something - a theme that had seized him at dinner and made him refuse
pudding but carry an apple with him to the drawing room. Very strange it
sounded. He played it over and over in different keys, varying the tempo,
suddenly and wonderfully enriching the accompaniment. And sometimes it
sounded uneasy and terrified, cried that it was being tortured in his hands,
did not want to yield him its secret, and sometimes it sounded as though it
were in love with itself and could not give him enough of its treasure.

"Mum" said Maisie suddenly, "where's our Philip."
"Don't know, dearie - ask Maata," Mrs Close, doubling a strand of wool and
laboriously threading the needle.
"Do you know where he is - he'd love some of these chestnuts. O, do you
remember how he used to love chestnuts when he was a little thing, Mum,
and roast them in the bonfire in the back yard, and dirty his handkerchiefs
with them?"
"That I do - - Do you know Maata I'll never forget one day finding the
boys after they'd been having a bonfire, washing their handkerchiefs and their
little white 'duckies' at the garden tap on the front lawn. For everybody to
see - - - you know. I didn't keep a girl then - did all the washing myself,
and I had to give them what for if they dirtied their clothes. I couldn't bear
ironing, & children make enough work. There were little Maisie's pinafores
then too... But to see these kids with a bit of soap and some pumice stone
they'd found on the esplanade, scrubbing their hankies and hanging them
to dry on a flax bush - I thought I'd have died laughing."
"O, the darlings. I can see them" laughed Maata. "So serious, you know."
She shook her skirts, crept over to Mrs Close and sat leaning against her, her
bright hair between the older woman's knees. "Tell me about when they were
little" she coaxed - "Anything". "O do Mother. About the time they had their
photo taken and Philip lost the hairpin out of his [...] curl and cried so
awfully" Maisie pleaded, standing a row of four fat soldiers on the second
fire bar.

Mrs Close put her darning on the table, settled herself, and rested her
hands on Maata's hair. The tired dragged look left her face - it sweetened and
grew happy - - "Well that's all there is of that story" she said, "except that
being twins and feeling everything together, you know, Hal started crying too,
and they made such a dreadful noise that people stopped in the street and
looked in at the shop. O, I did feel ashamed. And the photographer - a fine
fellow he was, with a game leg, unfortunately, said 'Well, Mrs Close, at any
rate your children know how to attract a public' and I would not have thought
twice about the remark if I hadn't taken them to a phrenologist the week
before who told me crowds and crowds of people all listening to them -"

"Just what they will do, of course" interrupted Maisie.

"– and my boys being very famous. Well, thought I, as I tied the string of Hal's white muslin hat – the one you had afterwards Maisie,[229] with the lace frill – they've begun early enough, and a little too early for me." "Do you mean old Wrigglesworth the photographer" asked Mr Close, not pausing in his work, speaking slowly and half to the rhythm of his work. "He went bust he did – the same year and set fire to his own shop to get the insurance money, so they say. Had a fine bass voice in his time and sang 'Vittoria' in the Town Hall at a charity concert." "That's the man. His wife was a flashy woman – she ruined him. I never saw another woman wear the clothes she put on her back on Sundays."[230]

A voice from the door. Phil had slipped quietly in and stood against the lintel, hands in his pockets, looking at them with laughter.

"O I remember her, Mother – Hal & I used to shout at her – compliments of the season, where did you get that hat!"

"Pure little wretches" said the Mother, "come to the fire & warm your hands, dear. Where have you been?"

"Up in my room" said Phil. "Maisie – give me one. I came down to steal Maata. It's such a beautiful night. Do you want to go for a walk, dearest?"

"No" said Mrs Close, answering for her, "she's not to be disturbed, she's just got comfy. You go & talk to your brother, my son." She was eager with recollection – she had her little audience about her, sympathising – she did not want them to get up and leave her with the old man and that sock to be darned by gaslight. She was tired with a dragging tiredness of middle age, and the feeling of Maata pressed up so closely seemed to relieve some pain – no definite pain – just a sensation. But Philip was restless and not to be denied. He went over to the window, parted the curtain and blind and looked out. Maata from her comfortable place, watching him, saw his eyes lift to the stars – and understood.

"Fine night darling?" she asked softly.

"Wonderful! There are clouds, you know, hurrying, and stars above them shining in pools of still light. I think there is a warm wind blowing – the leaves are shaking in the bushes out here. It's the sort of night for Primrose Hill – just because of the name – you know that sort of night?" He turned round from the window, speaking almost indifferently.

"Well, if you don't want to, I'll go by myself. I must get some air – –"

"Maata was longing to go – knew she was going – but just how to leave Mrs Close <u>happy</u> worried her.

"Mother, I suppose it's my duty to go out with this bad boy" she said, in her baby voice. And Mrs Close knew the spell was over, her battle lost, drew away her knees & took up the torn sock.

---

[229]Here KM started to write 'Dolly', crossed it out and substituted 'Maisie', thus confirming that it was the Trowells she had in mind.

[230]The foremost photographer in Wellington during the last 30 years of the 19th Century, and into the 20th Century was James Dacie Wrigglesworth (1836–1906). In 1901 his premises were destroyed by fire, although there was no published suggestion of fraud.

"Well go if you want to" she said, "don't stay here talking about it and interrupt your father."

"Me too, me too" from Maisie.

"No" replied the Mother firmly - she still had the whip hand here. "You go off to bed my girl, and don't sit any longer scorching your face & getting indigestion with all that rubbish. <u>Off</u> you go!" Maisie made a face and shrugged her shoulders.

In the hall Maata unhooked Hal's greatcoat and pulled it on. It was immense for her, the astrakhan collar half way up her head. From a pocket she took out a torn pair of gloves, two empty cigaret boxes & some cherry stones. She left them in a pile on the hall chair. "O the child" she breathed. But Phil did not answer. He took her arm, half dragged her down the steps, through the little gate and on to the forsaken, half-lighted road. Then he walked slowly. She said, lightly "We're in Mother's bad books you know, my darling." His hand tightened on her arm, he turned his grave intense gaze to her. "O I can't help it" he said, with a sort of desperation in his voice. "I <u>wanted</u> you tonight, terribly - just you to myself. I've been in my room ever since dinner, without a light, sitting on the side of the bed. I took out my fiddle and went to play but couldn't - just thought. And - do you know that sensation, beloved - the darkness seemed to close about me, utterly engulf me. I couldn't get away from it, or fight it, or move, lift a finger - it was like being drowned in a dream, but unlike a dream were my Thoughts. They were like most sure arrows winged into my heart from the dead past and tearing open the old wounds, poisoning the present. I felt -" his voice sank to a whisper "- too ugly for words. And something outside myself and yet the essence of me, seemed to point and sneer, saying 'Yes look - there you are. You're nothing but a dummy figure set up as a target for these most sure arrows. It's your own fault - you provided the weapons yourself, and now you're surprised they should be used against you, you [...] fool. And whatever you try to do you are helpless. Everything you hold will pass at last, be turned and twisted into one of these arrows, and winged against you. For that is the Law of your life. You are one of those for whom  - - -'"

Maata, listening, now raised her head to the sky where around the hurrying clouds the little bright stars shone fantastically - like arrows, thousands of arrows - under which they walked like lost children, close together & yet not safe. The fear entered her heart, the wind blew about them both. She heard their footsteps on the paving stones. They quickened their pace, pressing forward. She wanted terribly to run away with him to some secret place and hide him as a brooding bird so that if one of them had to be struck it must be her. Intolerable the thought that Philip was sad. She began to pray to nobody and nothing as they half ran up the hill - "If one of us has to bear anything let that one be me. Not that I'm stronger or anything like that, but it's easier for me, I would rather have it. It doesn't hurt me - anything passes off me like water off a duck's back. My nature's different. I don't need so much - but he needs everything. O give him everything. O make & keep him

happy, he flowers in happiness, he can only work when he is happy.
His greatness is not the kind that needs grief. Help! Help!"

They turned into a street of irregular large houses with gardens full of
autumn flowers. She saw michaelmas daisies pressing through a white fence
& there was a great bush of chrysanthemums growing by quite a country gate.
Lights shone in these houses - the glow of fire and shaded lamps. From one
came the voice of a woman singing. Maata stopped and whispered "Listen".
It was not because of the music she paused, but that house had a beautiful
garden. She wanted Philip to see it. There was a round lawn like a great pool
and a very big tree of dark leaves curling & drooped over the grass - the voice
of the woman might have floated to them out of the tree! It was a deep voice,
secret and full. They waited until her song had ceased and then walked further.
By and bye he said "We shall have just such a house one day." "Of course"
she replied, smiling wistfully. Then "Philip - isn't Patience a dreadful thing.
Well - I just <u>haven't</u> any, where you are concerned. And I don't want to have
any. Everything must happen now, here. We ought you know to have walked
through that gate & in at the front door, & found - " "Maisie sitting on the
stairs waiting for us." He laughed. "O, my blessed darling what a beast I am.
I don't know how I dared to come into the diningroom, take you out like this,
and talk all that <u>rubbish</u>. Heaven knows it seemed true enough, but now -
laughable. I'll explain it. I hadn't seen you for <u>at least two hours</u>. Now do you
wonder I cried instinctively like a baby - a very young baby who's been too
short a time with you to be left alone yet. But I promise & promise, Maata, it
won't happen again!" "What do you suppose I was doing in the diningroom"
she said, "making Mother talk about you. I was worse than a crying baby -
I was a starving one. And never make promises to me, sweetheart. I refuse to
take them - I have no need of such things."

On Primrose Hill there were many lovers, wandering aimlessly through
the tousled grass, sitting on little benches, pressed against the trees. Curious
the silence of these people - the children were silent too. It was like walking
into the middle of a service, thought Maata, and felt ashamed, as though she
& Philip had arrived a little too late & were disturbing the others. But the
others did not appear disturbed - they were as indifferent as the trees.
She & Philip found a little place against some railings and looked out over
London. Mist floated over the streets and houses. The lights shone silver with
fanlike wings - it was all most perfectly unreal.
"These people are ghosts - there is only you and me" whispered Philip.
"And that city - nothing but a mirage from which they have floated - flung up
in the tide of it and plain for us to see just for one moment, and then drawn
back again ... Can't you hear the mirage wave."
"O yes, I hear it. I love it. What friendly ghosts, little brother."
"They wouldn't be if they knew we were here. They'd turn upon us, darkly
powerful. Don't be afraid. That is only a ruse of mine to get your other hand
as well. Do you suppose I dare to kiss you?"
"You have to, it's part of the service" she laughed.

On the way home she had a beautiful idea. They found a little grocer's shop still open and bought a bottle of stout for Mother & some Kola for Hal and themselves - - - The light still burned in the diningroom but Mr Close was not there. His work was put away. Hal lay full length on the green sofa. Mrs Close poked viciously at the little dusty fire. She raised her head as they came in and looked up rather glumly. But Maata produced the stout bottle. Philip took some glasses from the table. It was impossible to resist the gaiety of the 2 children. Mrs Close & Hal who had been talking 'money worries' drew up to the table.

"What a colour you've got from the air" said Mrs Close, holding the glass to Philip. "That's enough, my boy - don't fill it too full - I only want a sip."

"The air. I like that." said Hal, drinking out of the bottle. "Look at old Pip's hand shaking. You've been giving that hand too much exercise, my lad. Which side does she walk on? Don't pour any out of mine - I'll have the bottle."

"No you won't" cried Maata. "Fair does, my child. There are only 2 bottles of kola between the three of us!" "O Mum aren't they pigs. Here have I been sitting at that cold cold piano playing for hours & hours - to them - and now they won't even let me have a bottle of kola. O, aren't they sneaks - aren't they beasts. And they pretend to be in Love."

"O let the infant play with it then" said Phil. "We'll share a bottle & you can have a whole one. Don't swallow the marble unless you really want to, old Horse. Have some more stout, Mother & I'll promise you the best dream in the dream book tomorrow morning." "Well I don't mind - just a drop. I hope your Father's asleep - I feel so lively I could kick him out of bed. How a drop of stout in the evening perks me up - like nothing else. When you get to my age you'll need it, Maata, though I must say you don't look as if you did just now. I always did have a fondness for stout. I remember the first nurse I had when the twins were born started me off. And there is nothing like it when you're that way. Just wait till my first grandchild begins to come along!"

Hal adored his mother in this vein. He ran over to her with the bottle in his hand & began kissing her face & neck and hair.

"She's in her cups" he laughed. "Now's the time for confidential intimacies, my friends. Give her her head. Philip - run out and get her 6d of gin."

But Phil was taking off Maata's shoes & whispering to her.

"Let's get them to bed, and I'll make up the fire. Come down again."

So Maata yawned & smiled across at Mrs Close.

"If you popped into bed now, Mummy" she said, "you'd sleep like a top, while you're warm."

"I'm going, I'm going." The little woman got up, set down her glass & gave Hal a great hug. She pulled down his head & murmured something.

Hal winked at the others.

"Yes" he said. "I suppose we'd better. They'll drive us away from our own fireside, but we'll go, won't we, little Mummy, & come down in half an hour & look at them through the keyhole."

"You little silly, come & kiss me goodnight" said Maata.

"What were you playing this evening?"

"Shan't say. O how nice your face feels - so cool. I wouldn't mind betting you my collection of apple cores that in half an hour ..."

"Mother take him away."

Maata & Philip listened to the others going up the stairs. To Hal pretending to be a baby & asking to have his hand held, & saying he was frightened - could he be tucked up, & where did the dark go in the daytime. To Mrs Close in answer, scolding and loving, and then laughing as Maisie laughed. Then the sound of the two doors closing.

Philip put out the gas & gathered the beloved Maata into his arms.

[MS-Papers-4006-01]

Chapter X.

They did not fall like leaves - they fell like feathers, fluttering and floating from the trees that lined the road where Mally lived. Who was it used to say that every leaf you caught meant a happy month? Rhody of course. She saw Rhody, the tall schoolgirl, break from the 'crocodile' when they walked in the Park, and run after the leaves, with big, far too big, gestures, as though she expected the whole tree to fall into her arms. Rhody used to keep the leaves in her bible & take them out & hold them up to the light and gaze at them in scripture lessons. And she always said she knew each one apart. Well, if she said so, she did. Just like her.

The clock in the big church opposite Mally's flat struck five. But Maata did not hurry. Idle and happy she walked under the falling leaves. A sharp sweet scent was in the air, and a stronger more wintry smell of damp earth. She could feel the mist on her eyelids & lips. That sensation of boundless strength and happiness flowed over her again. It was almost physical - her lungs felt like wings - she could fly away on a deep breath, light and strong - but I am glad I am going to Mally. Tonight I can

Now I am myself again, now I am quite safe, she said, like a little child that was in its bed after a nightmare. And she thought - if I could only remember always that under everything there is only this; that everything that is not this is on the surface & will not really matter in the end. What is life really? What is real & unreal. Oh God.

& troubled sounds familiar yet unreal like the memory and the promise of sadness. They shook her heart. She did not want to listen. She could have listened for ever. Standing there in the dark she drifted away to that shadowy loneliness which sometimes seemed to her to be her only true life, the only changeless truth - the thing that she was never really certain was not reality after all. How extraordinary! She saw herself all these last weeks, playing a part - being Maata, being herself, caring for things that after all don't matter at all. Why, only that afternoon, a minute or two ago, she had believed in it all - & it was all nothing, nothing.     [s26-27]

# *Newberry Notebook 2*

[Newberry Notebook 2]

### MAATA: PLAN

1913.

Maisie 14, Philip 19, Maata 19, Hal 17, Rhoda 19, Max 18.

Chapter I. <Rhoda Bendall wakes up in the rain and remembers that it is the day of Maata's arrival. A sort of a song of songs from Rhoda to Maata. A day of waiting. The past reviewed and Maata brought up to date. Ending with Rhoda at the station.>

√ Aug 13th

<Chapter II. Philip and Maisie are waiting for Maata. She arrives. She sees them first. She is radiant, eager - her lovely voice like water. She goes off with Rhoda in a hansom through the wet sunshiny street to a room in the house by the canal. She half undresses and curls up on the bed. Sends Rhoda out for food. She is alone in a dusky room. The lights from the street come in. She rolls & stretches & flings out her arms ... laughing & chuckling.>

√ November 16th

Chapter III. Evening at the Closes. The old ghost wandering up and down. Ma, so excited. Father very flushed, and wheezing. Hal malicious and Maisie romping. They watched her run up the steps. The door flew open. She was in Janey's arms. She is introduced to May and Debussy. A tour of the house. Supper and stout and ale in the dining room. Before they go Hal plays his latest. She sits against the window curtain in the blue chair, her arms along the sides, a bunch of violets falling from her fingers. Philip leans against the mantelpiece watching her, breathing to the rise and fall of her breath.

Chapter IV. The arrival of the piano. The room transformed. The blue bed cover stitched with gold towers & minarets & a border of leopards. Chrysanthemums. A tiny fire. Maata in a grey and pink gown, in a <u>cur-ious</u> mood. She had spent yesterday shopping. She felt like she used to when she was a little girl & spoke her name & address outside the sweet shop. She pokes

up the fire and sits down at the piano. 'Mon coeur s'ouvre à ta voix.' "I had
no idea. I did not dream – and that you should need anything – you with your
voice." "Listen, listen a moment, darling." 'To the Forest'. She ran forward
& took Rhoda's hand & her arm. "But that is <u>nothing</u> to what my voice is
going to be like – nothing. Just wait. I promise, promise –" She reverts always
to money. "But you have some haven't you?.. I can't explain but my spirit
seems to need luxury. I can only expand among beautiful things." "I
understand – of course – it must be so." "And the absurd thing is that it's only
a question of time … and when I do have it I'll have no more need of it."
Rhoda left her. On the canal bridge for the first time she refused a beggar.

Chapter V. Sunday at the Close family. Hot and fine. The boys are late to
breakfast – they do not wear collars & ties. Maisie in mignonette green. Be it
known … that they have hereby decided to envelop the capillary substance of
our illustrious craniums in the folds of the pellucid aqua purissima! The great
event dinner. A joint and greens and plum pie. Debussy wears a bow tie.
May's strange dream. The knock at the area door. Maata is very fine in a wine
dark cloth dress with an astrakhan coat... Afterwards she goes up & puts on
a big apron & washes Hal's hair. A walk to the Heath, Hal, Maisie, Maata
& Philip. And after tea, while Mum & Dad are playing Halma[231] & Maisie
reads Dickens, she and Philip play cribbage. In the evening, Music. The old
man holds her 'trembling with life'.

Chapter VI. The singing lesson and the concert. In the middle she leaves and
wanders about, exhausted, unhappy. It is cold and windy. Why hadn't she said
she could not afford to pay so much. She arrives home draggled. Rhoda is
there. She tells Rhoda. Rhoda persuades her to allow her to pay.

Chapter VII. Maata at the Closes. Only the Mother is in. They have a long
talk in the ugly dining room with the darning basket. The family come in for
tea. It brightens. She & Philip have another game and Maata is persuaded to
stay for dinner. Hal sees her home. "What do you think of my brother?"
The letter from Rhoda.

Chapter VIII. Philip surveys his life and his prospects. His loneliness – his lack
of faith in himself. He hears Maisie singing in her room. He goes in to her.
"No, I can't go on with you listening." "Don't be such a baby, kid." In his
desire to stamp out the image of Maata he sits on Maisie's bed with her curled
up in his arms & plans her gorgeous life. She is happy beyond words. "And
we'll have a little house, girlie, on the shores of the Mediterranean & travel all
over the world." "Just you & I, Pip." "Yes, yes, just you and I." He denies
Maata. He hugs & kisses her. "Not enough, not enough."

Chapter IX. Maata meets at the flat the dark strange boy, Max Castello. Mally
does not arrive. They sit and talk among the garden baskets of artificial flowers.
Passion is the only thing in life. It is to dare everything. They are bitter and
cold. His eyes shine as though by candlelight. They arrange to meet.

---

[231]'Halma' was a board game invented about 1880—a forerunner of Chinese Checkers.

Chapter X. What rubbish is this what rubbish, she stammered, clenching her little hands in her astrakhan muff. It grows foggy. Outside the house Rhoda stands like a forlorn tree with a big box in her hands. She lights the fire for Maata & the box is opened. "How could you know – you fairy godmother?" A black astrakhan coat lined with silver brocade sprigged with mignonette. It had little side pockets & a high collar. "I wanted to give you one that would cover your whole precious body but the pennies would not be found. You can wear this in the house too." Maata puts it on. "Yes", very satisfied, "that is <u>you</u>." She protests. "No, it is my Xmas present." She is sweet, sweet to Rhoda. Maisie & Hal arrive, Hal very jolly. She is to go home to dinner. The fog deepens. They go out, arm in arm, coughing, and Rhoda disappears. "Extraordinary girl."

Chapter XI. For three days the fog hung thick. Maata stayed in her room. She would see nobody. A hatred of the place & the people was on her. She told Mally she had a cold. She denied Rhoda. Walked up and down, up and down, staring in front of her. On the afternoon of the 3rd day Mally came. She had a lesson in her room, and all her burdens somehow changed. She sang. Mally. "No, you need not look at me. Start where you like." She sings. "Ah, you're in love. Go on." She sang, lifting, lifting in song. Her colour came back. She went over to Mally, put her arm round her neck & hugged her, & when she had gone she ran up to the Closes. Janey was in the kitchen making an apple pie. Maata bubbled with joy. She inspected the whole house. Philip's gratitude and adoration wrapped her. They played cribbage again, laughing. They walked home together arm in arm. "Hook on, dear girl," said Philip. They lost their way and she held close to him, under cover of laughter and cold. It took them a long time to get home. He left her on the doorstep. She promised faithfully to go again tomorrow at <u>three</u>.

Chapter XII. When Maisie came in next morning to wake Philip, she found he was already up and dressed. He was sorting his music. Maisie had a duster in her hands & a blue handkerchief like a turban on her head. She was dusting the drawing room. She was amazed to see Pip dressed & sat down on the floor to help him. He was rather quiet, very pale, with shaking hands. "Well, you are queer – what's the matter?" There was nothing. He says "When Maata comes this afternoon tell her to come straight up to my room. I'm going to work all day – & Pussy – see that nobody else butts in. I want to see her alone." Maisie makes big eyes of surprise. Then she blushes & says "Oh alright. I think it's rather mean of you though." She won't help him any more. All day she watched her brother. He does not eat, he laughs stupidly, his hands shake. He roams up & down his room, up & down. Seven times during the morning he tiptoes downstairs to look at the clock. Maata is very late coming. It is five o'clock. She goes straight to Philip. His room is in dark. He is practising. The violin case on the bed is like a tiny coffin. They comfort the loneliness in each other, she sitting at the table by the window, Philip on the bed. They grow very peaceful and quiet. He lights the gas for her to look at the shell he found when he was tidying up. They stand close together. Her hands shake. She holds it & turns it over. They look up at each other. He puts his arm round her shoulder. They smile timidly & kiss. He puts his arms round her & she lays her hands upon his cheeks & gazes at him. He says "I worship you girl" & she nods & says breathlessly "I too, I too." "Maata - do you love me?" Still with that mysterious smile she says "Of course I do." Hal interrupts. They tell the delighted family. Only Maisie bursts into tears & rushes to her room. "I can't understand Maisie" said Philip, puzzled. "Oh well, it will be a great change for her" said the Mother. "But why, Mum. How?" "Oh well, least said spoils the broth, my son. You'll understand some day." They have a merry dinner with Kola and stout. Mrs Close gets very confidential. Hal, too. "Wait till you see the old ghost's big toe, Maata." The family leave them the dining room. They turn the gas low & lie down on the little green sofa, their bodies touching.

Chapter XIII. Rhoda spends the night with her Mother. "I never seem to see you at all. You are always out or creeping about the staircase like a thief. What about that friend of yours? Why hasn't she been to see me? Why can't you be like other girls?" She spends a dreadful night. When the Mother sleeps she creeps into the drawing room & pulls up the blind and sees the night clear with stars. Life seems empty and horrible. She cries out for Maata. The moon comes through the window. She lies flat on her back with her arms wide and stares up at the big round moon. I wish I was a spirit. Why have I got this body - - I would like to be a spirit and watch near my darling. Maata you are not happy, some danger is near you. Maata what are you doing now? I shall draw some more money tomorrow and buy her that black scarf with moonstones. This moon is like me - so white and cold. Maata will wrap us round her little breast - in the black night of her scarf.

Chapter XIV. She was at the bank before it opened & with Maata before 10. Maata was dressing. Leaning forward to tie her shoes. "I've something to tell you. You'll be surprised. I'm going to marry Philip." Rhoda is opposite a mirror. She watches herself. "Oh when was it arranged." "Late last evening." Rhoda: "I knew." Maata is intensely annoyed. "How could you <u>know</u>." They walk together to the Closes. But something has happened. "No, I won't come in. When shall I see you again?" "Oh, I don't know. Sometime next week - - or come to tea on Sunday. Do."

Chapter XV. The two children in love. Playing ball in the garden, in Pip's room, going for walks. Raspberry Nose & old Winter. It seems that everybody loves us. They cannot bear to be separated. He tries for and obtains a position in a theatre orchestra. Steak sandwiches. They all prepare for Christmas. Maata is to spend it with them. Maisie is not well. She gets very thin.

Chapter XVI. Mally goes to Rome until February to give singing lessons. At Maata's last lesson Max is there. They have lentil soup with pieces of sausage in it. She wears her engagement ring. She is very happy but Mally shakes her head. "You couldn't be poor." "But why not? I'll make money with my singing, Mally." "You are not made for such a marriage, my dear. You want a man who would throw you across the room and beat you. Nobody else will ever keep a woman like you." Max listens. "Where would you be without your fine clothes now." "I - I haven't got any." "Pooh! I've been watching. Look at your coat - £10.10.0. Your hat - £5.5.0. Your shoes & gloves & today a gold purse. Monsieur ton mari won't be able to provide such luxuries. Better stay as you are." "But surely you aren't suggesting ..." "Nothing at all, my dear, except that your own money does not buy them." Maata bristled. She was defiant. "I need these things. They help me. I can't sing if I'm draggled & poor." "Tell it to somebody else - Pooh! What do you know of such things. What has money to do with it. Fine feathers don't make fine artists, my dear." Mally gets into a terrible rage. Max leans back and laughs. Maata goes, half crying. Max & Mally are left alone. He soothes her, and strokes & strokes her, maliciously smiling.

Chapter XVII.  Christmas Eve leading to Xmas day. By the gas fire in Maata's room, wrapped in a rug. Low wind outside. Christmas Day. Happy fooling and a sad, lovely evening. Rhoda comes in the afternoon. Maisie fondles Rhoda. The two seem like friends. It is arranged that Maata shall go & stay at the Closes.

Chapter XVIII.  Next day Rhoda packs for her. They spend the day together in the old happy way. They go out to tea & it is not until evening that they say goodbye. "Now I shall see even less of you. May I write?" "Of course." Her room is very clean with mats everywhere. "Now I won't even be surprised if you & Philip sleep in that very bed after you're married." "Oh Mother, dear." "Well, there's no need to blush about it." She & Maisie make it up.

Chapter XIX.  The visit to Covent Garden. The return, heaped with flowers. Philip is asleep. They cover his bed. She gets frightened & wakes him & kisses & kisses him. Invitation to the wedding. Mrs Close doesn't want to accept. Hal to go too & Father.

Chapter XX.  The departure of the three. The three are left in the house. Their happiness. It is early spring, and the sun shines on the drawing room carpet. Philip goes out, comes in late. They are lovers.

Chapter XXI.  Maisie discovers them, but says nothing - she thinks they have been secretly married. She is full of the secret, and she can afford now to be nice to Maata & kiss her & hug her & help her to make Pip's bed.

Chapter XXII.  The old people return, very crochety. Everything goes wrong & Philip goes away. She begins taking lessons again. Max Castello sees her home. She feels shaken. Hal disapproves utterly of Max Castello. "I don't think you're fair on the old ghost, Maata." "Oh how absurd you are. What a baby you are!" They start quarreling. An uneasy gloom settles on the house. May is dismissed. They are sick of Maata's fine ways. And she is sick of their commonness. She goes away for the weekend & comes back to find Ma wants the money for the washing. No, she won't give it. How silent they are all growing. Only Maisie looks better & turns from Maata to her Mother.

Chapter XXIII. Maisie tells of their love episode. The silence explodes. They are violent, hysterical, half mad. She is denied the house immediately and she goes away to Rhoda who finds her a horrible little poor room.

Chapter XXIV. She cannot stand it & goes to Philip, to the theatre. He comes in & stands resining his bow, looking over the house. He sees her. They go back to the dirty ugly house & are wonderfully happy.

Chapter XXV. The morning he goes she finds his Mother's letter. There is a scene. He leaves her early in the morning & on the train journey back to London she meets Marion West. They become very intimate. High falutin, false, & talk as the train shatters through the dark.

Chapter XXVI. Rhoda prepares for her home. Soothing sentimentality[?] Her children. The fire. The white lilac in a jar. Maata is cold and abstracted. Very beautiful. Before she goes to bed she writes Pip a letter. She wants him, wants him. Pip I'm frightened.

Chapter XXVII. Next morning after the post has come & brought her no letter she leaves for Rachael West. What a fine house! And the jolly people. In the evening she sings 'I met my love'. She wears a yellow chrysanthemum in her hair. Rachael fusses & pets her to the hilt. She meets Mr Evershed.

Chapter XXVIII. I cannot come to London. Come here if you can. We have very good digs & Ma cooks poached egg O.R. She shows the letter to Rachael who poisons her mind. But go. I would if I were you - you need to go this time & see just how you stand. Rachael is smoking, her head thrown back, the lovely lines of her milky throat in the light. Mr Evershed sees her to the station. Books, flowers - everything she wants.

Chapter XXIX. But it is raining, pouring with rain as Philip sets out to meet Maata. He is suspicious & cold, his heart eaten with fatigue. She is changed. Only when they are going to bed that night & her young husband takes her into his arms ... I think my heart will break for joy. They spend the week in gloom - what is the matter with you. On the morning of going away she wakes early & sees the sheep. She is cruel. "You're your Mother's boy. And Maisie's. What's the good of pretending. I am not made to be poor." She scolds, scolds all the way home from Charlies Aunt in the soaking rain.

Chapter XXX. Rhoda loses her. Writes to Pip. She has gone back to Mrs West's. Please to go & see her. He writes, pleads. But she will not answer his letters. Then he is ill & there is silence. She goes for a walk & meets Maisie in the park. The sheep again. "I'll not tell you - not I." Maisie is with Rhoda. She goes straight home. She & Rachael drink port. They sit on the sofa in Evershed's room. He proposes. She accepts. They are married next afternoon.

Chapter XXXI. Rhoda gains admittance. She sees the wedding ring. She is terribly hurt. She explains. Maata buries her head in the cushions. Did you ever hear of a broken heart. She promises to arrange a meeting. Does he know? Of course – he saw it in the paper. He had some sort of a breakdown. But better now. Says it is for the last time.

Chapter XXXII. The meeting in the spring. The walk on the heath. I want to tell you something. I have never lived with Evershed as his wife – never. Their rapture at last. They arrange to go to America. She will get the money. She can. He leaves her & Max Castello speaks to him & tells him the truth & gives him the letters.

Chapter XXXIII. She goes to Rhoda. It is all made plain. She is going to spend the night with Rhoda. And tomorrow the money can be had. She confides all her plans & hopes. She falls asleep at last like a lovely little child. Rhoda lies on the floor by the dying fire – the supreme sacrifice made.

Chapter XXXIV. He did not know how he reached home. Yes he had had supper. He goes upstairs to his room & burns his papers & tidies up – then downstairs – first to the kitchen – sees them all & the brightness. Hal is in the drawingroom playing. Hallo old ghost. Going into the garden. There is a high white moon & the plane trees stand up in the blue air. He thinks they are very beautiful. His heart bursts with grief. He listens to Hal & by & bye he takes out the revolver & puts the spout in his mouth & shoots himself.

Chapter XXXV. Rhoda sees Max & Maata & a lot of others after a concert. Maata speaks to her. There is only one thing. Are you happy. Life is not gay. Life is never gay.

End of plan: August 2nd 1913.

Characters.

Maata Nelson

Rhoda Bendall
Mrs Bendall (her Mother)

William Close
Mrs Close
Hal Close
Maisie Close
Philip, Pip Close

Elena (Ellie) Thal
Max Castello
Rachael West
Evershed
The Greek boys
Old Mrs Freeman (R.W.'s Mother)
Mrs Banks (M's landlady)

Bessie Banks (daughter)
Raspberry Nose
Old Wintergreen
May (Mrs Close's servant)

## Chapter I

The sound of rain woke Rhoda Bendall. It fell, quick and sharp, through the open window on to the polished floor. "Dear me", she thought, "it's raining", and she lay still, mild and sleepy, listening to the quick patter. Every morning the effort to get up seemed greater and more dreadful. She dropped asleep like a tired beast dropping into a dark soft pit and her heart turned faint before the struggle to raise up this long, heavy body once again. "I must wake up. I must. It's raining. The curtains will be quite wet, and so will the floor." She opened her eyes and stared into the dusky room. Her clothes lay in the middle of the floor, fan-shaped, white and grey. "They are like the plumage of some great bird" she thought, staring at the untidy bundle. "I am going to get up now and shut the window." But she did not move. Nothing helped her. There was no sound from the house. Her room, at the very top, and overlooking garden strips and the backs of other houses, was remote as an empty nest in a bare tree. "I wonder what the time is. I ought to have a clock in this room: that would be a great help. It's dark but I'm sure it's late." A little puff of damp air blew in with the rain, making her shiver. She turned, sighed and sat up, shaking back <the loose mane of fair hair.>

At the moment of raising herself Rhoda Bendall remembered. She flung out of bed, her eyes dilated, her nostrils quivered. Stretching out her arms, smiling in ecstasy, she staggered forward. "Maata, my beloved, Maata, my adored one. It is your day – today we meet again." She leaned out of the window, feeling the rain whip up her sleepy blood. <Clumsily she pulled at the buttons of her nightgown and bared her dead white throat and breast.> "A-ah", she breathed, in a surge of ecstasy. "I am baptized. I am baptized into a new day." Down in the garden the ivy wall gleamed like bronze; some birds fluffed their feathers in the broken fountain bowl. She could see each shining spear of grass. She saw herself walking down there in her white gown, with flowing hair – a saint in a holy picture of a garden, glorying and triumphant. Maata! Maata! Can you hear me? My treasure, my beloved one, the day is beautiful with you. Your breath is in this <sweet> wind and the same rain falls on us both. <u>On us both</u>. Oh God, bring her quickly. Bring her quickly, God. Yes; I think you must, crooned Rhoda Bendall, walking up and down, "for she is of you. She is your spirit, your essence. She is God in woman." In rapture she stopped before the mirror and stared in to it, dreamily smiling. "I wish you could see me now, Maata mine. I am almost beautiful. I look – I look –" and she parted her hair, holding it tight to her face with her large hands "– like a Botticelli. Very nearly worthy of you. I have changed very much. I think, my soul, I am more what you would have me – a strong, silent force of Love."

A picture of Maata stood on the writing desk and before it a shell with some incense dust. Rhoda kneeled down, her arms along the desk, her chin in her hands. "Good morning, beloved" she whispered, rocking to and fro on heavy unbreaking waves of love. "Why - so - sad? There is a shadow on your brow and eyes, and your mouth" she said, drawing her lips along the backs of her hands, "has kissed sorrow." She crouched back. "Maata has never kissed me on the mouth, but I know what her lips feel like - they feel like carnations. I can see them", she fluttered her eyelids - "exquisite, exquisite, every little curve. Do not be sad, my darling. Let me keep away from you everything that is not beautiful and fitting. You are perfection. How can you help being hurt by this world, Maata. It is my destiny to serve you. I was dead when you found me and without you I am nothing. Let me serve." While she pleaded a strange sensation of blind, tireless strength filled every particle of her. "Yes, Yes" she stammered, "I know you are near me, beloved. And I am here, waiting. Let me serve. Oh, Maata, I can tell you now. there is only one thing left that has any terror for me ... it is that you have grown too strong to need me. You are so terribly strong."

She cringed before the picture and opened her hands <like a beggar>. "I cannot follow you on to the heights. Stoop sometimes to me. I know you cannot belong wholly to me - the great world needs you - but I am all yours." She sat quiet while the ecstasy ebbed away, leaving her cold and hungry, with all the long hours to wear through, somehow, until the late afternoon when Maata would arrive. "I must go and find the time" she decided. But she did not move. <I see you Rhoda. Now you look like your normal self and you will sit there a long time making up your mind to dress and go slowly down all those gloomy stairs into the breakfast room.>

"I don't feel strong enough to bear the ordinary world today - I shrink from it. Not until I have seen you again, Maata. You see, Maata, it's two years. What a long breath of you I had to take to last me two whole years!" Her slow mind began rebuilding the parting with Maata. They had taken a four-wheeler to the station because of the luggage. Maata's voice: "The old ramshackle, Rhody. It's like sitting on the lap of an old clothes woman." It had been a lovely day. Virginia creeper moved over the houses. "Look at my flags, Rhody - all bloody." And a great many people at the station - crowds and crowds - such noise and confusion. And through it all Maata had laughed. "I shall always be the same, Rhody - I can't help it. Don't be angry with me. It's just at the last moment anything makes one happy - just at the moment of jumping you aren't frightened any more - only terribly happy. Happy. And I'm coming back. Listen." She put her little warm hands on Rhoda's shoulders. "I'm coming back. Yes, believe me. I'll be back in 2 years - you do believe me." And she had answered "I have faith, beloved, but I can't believe. I'm too broken just now."

Remembering, Rhoda struck her right palm with her clenched fist. "Fool. What weakness!" She got up from the floor, dressed in the grey & white clothes & braided her hair round her head, burning with scorn for herself. "And I've forgotten to shut the window - the floor is soaking. Oh, well - it doesn't matter." She hesitated, stepped to the window, stopped and turned to the door. "No - it's no matter. Little, little trivial things. And besides, why shouldn't rain come in through the windows. It has as much right as wind or scent, surely - surely."

All the way down the gloomy stairs, past her Mother's bedroom door, past the deserted silent rooms, she carried the silly thought as a weapon against her dread. In the breakfast room the clock pointed to half past eleven. So late! She hovered over the untidy breakfast table & wished, as she always wished, that she had the courage to ask for some fresh tea. But it was unreasonable to be two hours late. "I will drink all the milk instead" she decided, "and <u>eat</u>. Yes - eat." She cut some rounds of bread, buttered them thickly & spread them with jam, and ate, stuffing her mouth full, washing it down with milk. "Dare I go on, dare I?" The same battle was fought each morning between her violent bodily hunger & a wavering sense of shame. "I wonder why I have to eat so much. I suppose it is because I am so big & heavy. I never have enough to eat - never." She dropped some lumps of sugar in the milk jug & ate them with a spoon. "Now I shall just have one more round of bread & butter to take away the taste of the sugar."

As she finished the last crust the housemaid came in. "Telegram for you, Miss Rhoda." "Thank you, Nellie." She tore it out of the envelope. "Pouring with rain. Arrive Charing X 4.30. Love. Maata." A-Ah! It had come. How like her to have put pouring with rain first - just like her. She read & reread it, walking up the stairs, thrust it into her blouse, took her hat & gloves & purse & walked out of the house to spend the day buying flowers for Maata's new room & walking about & idly and slowly, slowly dragging through the hours until it was time to go to the station.

## Chapter II

They walked up & down the platform - a curious couple. Philip very tall & thin in a buttoned frock-coat & top hat; Maisie very short & fat in a blue sailor suit & a wide straw hat with a wreath round it. She held her brother's arm & half danced & gazed up at him with big eyes of admiration. "Oh Pip, you do look fine - you look simply ripping. Much the handsomest man here. Ah! I wish you always wore a frock coat. And that blue tie. It makes your eyes all blacky." He gave her arm a squeeze and laughed at her. "Don't, kid - you're making me blush. People'll think we're a newly married couple." "Pip!" Maisie shrieked with joy. "Don't be so absurd. I haven't even got my hair <u>tied back</u>. And look at my skirt! Very short. I wish you could make Mum lengthen my skirts. She won't realise I'm fourteen. It's awful to wear these short things." "Well you are a Miss Blinge. If you could see your knees you wouldn't want to wear any skirt at all." "What do you mean? My knees are different to other people's are they?" "Aren't they. You look at most girls - they're pigeon-kneed. Knees turn in like this." He stopped & showed her. "A fright. You've got knees like a little boy statue." "Have I?" said Maisie, very pleased. "Well, fancy! I never knew."

The station platform was crowded with people waiting for the boat train to come in. They stood together in little groups, the women talking with a great show of animation, the men silent & bored looking. In and out among them trundled the porters. "By your leave. By your leave. IF you please!" The clarion of voices that seemed to resolve curiously, if you listened, into one insistent strident voice, was broken by the sound of bells & whistles & the shuffling blaring noise of the trains. White smoke floated up from somewhere & hung below the station roof like misty fires, dissolved, came again in swaying wreaths. Wonderfully beautiful, thought Philip, & so full of life. He pointed it out to Maisie. "Look, girlie, look at that smoke. <That is how the high note on a fiddle played pianissimo ought to sound.>" But Maisie was tortured with impatience. "What's the time, Philip, what's the time. Why doesn't that stupid old train come in. I'll never come & wait for anybody again - as long as I live - never." "It won't be long now" and he said, to distract her, "Bet you won't know Maata again!" "Do you mean I'll have forgotten what she looks like. You can't mean that!" "Yes I do. It's five years since you saw her. If you jump back five times it makes you only nine." They stood still together & he put his hand on her soft little shoulder & rubbed his fingers against her neck & tiny ear. "You can't think what a sweet you were then, kid." "Tell me" she said, basking like a kitten in his warm love. "Well, you were only about up to your own shoulder, and your hair was fairer than it is now - not half so apricotty - more like butter beans. Mum used to tie it back with two yellow bows. And you had a white cashmere dress with a yellow sash & tan stockings & tan shoes & a paper umbrella with canaries flying round it. And you used to walk up & down Kitchener Road & then Hal & I knew to come strolling up pretending to be 2 photographers." "Yes, go on" said Maisie. "Oh, I remember."

The platform was getting very crowded. The train was expected. The pitch of the excited voices rose higher and stronger. Some broad beams of late sun struck through the glass roof of the station. Philip's heart began to beat quickly. "Go on" said Maisie. "We would come up to you & then suddenly start back - like this - " He started & put his hand to his heart, staring at Maisie. "And then we would take off our hats & say 'Pardon Mamselle. May we 'ave ze honour of photographing you. We are ze court photographers of ze Kaiser of Chermany on tour.' And then we'd set up the camera. Three clothes props & a soap box & the bit of black velvet off the top of the piano, & you would pose against old Mr Williams' gate that had 2 stone jars on top of it. I took the photographs & Hal used to arrange you. 'Ver' good, ver' good'" said Philip, acting the part. "'A leetle to the left foreground. Ze parasol oblique to foreshorten ze elbow - '"

A bell clanged. There was a cry of "Here comes the train." "Philip, Philip - the train - look, look." She jumped up & down, tugging his arm. A huge express swung into the station, slowed down, stopped. There were heads at every window - hundreds it seemed to Maisie. "We'll never find her" she wailed, "we'll never find her, Phil." "Yes we will. Here, take my hand. We'll run up & down. I've got an idea. Take off your hat. She'll see your hair." Up & down they ran, dodging the greeting, kissing groups. No sign, no sign. Suddenly Maisie felt 2 hands round her neck. She turned & was caught up tight, trembling, into Maata's arms. "Maata, Maata, is it <u>really</u> you?" & a laughing voice between kisses stammered "You darling, you darling, I knew you by your hair."

For ever afterwards Philip had only to shut his eyes & he saw the two again - in a world of people - Maata stooping & Maisie given to her - he felt again that furious unbearable expectation until Maata straightened up and turned to him her warm beautiful face. She was dressed in grey. She wore a little hat with a wing in it and a dark silky veil pushed up just above her eyebrows. A bright colour shone beneath her brown skin, her lips were trembling, but her eyes laughed. Simply from access of amazement he could say nothing but "Yes, you've come, you've come" & press her hands & laugh back at her. He had never in life imagined anyone could look so radiant and so triumphant. "Are you really Phil?" she said, in a shy voice, speaking very slowly. "I - I wouldn't have known you. Oh - yes I would. When you smile - oh yes - but you've changed - changed - . He's very nearly frightening, isn't he Maisie?" But Maisie had turned aside & seen Rhoda Bendall, standing apart, very pale, with a thin smile on her lips, waiting. She determined to capture Maata before Rhoda could speak to her. "Maata you're coming home with us now, aren't you? They're all expecting you - we promised to bring you." "Look here, dear girl, what about your luggage" asked Philip, grave and practical all of a sudden. At that Maata's laughter bubbled up again, so sweet & delicious to hear that it started Pip & Maisie off, & the three, looking at each other, laughed like little children. "Of course, my luggage. I'd forgotten all about it. I'm a nice person to travel about all over the wicked world. It's in the van I think. Which is the van - back or front - I can't remember." "Why" said Philip, waving his hand, "here's Miss Bendall."

What an extraordinary thing! How could it have happened. From the moment she had found Maisie & Phil Maata had quite forgotten Rhoda - forgotten all about her. "Rhody dear", kissing Rhoda's cold cheek. "Where <u>have</u> you been. Have you been looking for me all this time. I'd - I'd forgotten all about you." At the gay cruel words Rhoda grew paler & when she spoke it was in a rising[?] affected voice to hide her horrible agitation. "I didn't see you at first & then - you had found Maisie and Mr Close. So I ran after your luggage. Two big yellow boxes & a hat box & a roll of rugs - I had them put in a hansom. It's waiting. Was there anything else?" "No, that was all. Oh Rhody dear how wonderful of you to have found them. Let me see. Now what had I better do - -" "Come to us, come to us" said Maisie, "& let Miss Bendall take your luggage." "What do you want to do" said Pip. She looked at him while she spoke. "I really ought to go off with Rhoda now & see my new rooms & unpack a little & come to you for supper if I may? Otherwise I shall have to go back late at night into a strange room, not even knowing where the matches are kept, Maisie. Yes, that's my best plan." "But the cake" said Maisie. "There's a cake with your name on it for tea." "We'll hide it till supper" Philip consoled her. "Yes, that's best. You'll - come as soon as you can, Maata." "As soon as I can" she answered. "Where's the hansom, Rhoda." "Here quite close."

Rhoda & Maata were alone, side by side in the jolting, swaying hansom. "We have a long way to go" said Rhoda. "Have you enough room. Are you quite comfortable?" Fearing to touch Maata she squeezed up [in] a corner & tried to stop the exhausted trembling of her body. Those moments at the station hurt her still. Her throat ached & tears pressed in her eyeballs. Courage, courage, she said to herself. You have her - she is here. "Ah" breathed Maata, lying back & folding her hands. "It's good to be here at last, Rhody, & look - the sun's shining. Has it been raining all day?" "I'm - I'm not quite sure. I think it has." Rhoda frowned at herself, but Maata did not seem to notice the stupid reply. She went on questioning Rhoda. Had Rhoda found her a nice room, was there a piano, how much did it cost, was the landlady pleasant, what did it look out on? And her manner and voice were so composed - almost languid - that Rhoda became calm. Her heart lifted & began to feed on joy. She wanted to be out of the hansom with Maata in her room. To help Maata off with her coat & hat, to do all the little things for her, to see her, to watch her move. All the while she drank that lovely voice.

"We are nearly there now. Look, here is the river", as though she had put the river there so that Maata might care for it. "Your sitting room faces the river. In the winter the birds come right up to the window - sometimes they fly through, so Mrs Banks your landlady told me." Maata said "I like rivers." The hansom slowed down before a big grey stone house. "This is your key" said Rhoda. "Your rooms are on the first floor. Will you go straight up & let me settle with the man & see about the luggage." Maata gave Rhoda her purse. On the first floor, when she had finished with the boxes she knocked at the sitting room door. "Come in." Maata stood at the window. She had not even raised her veil or taken off her gloves. "You - you do not like it" stammered Rhoda. "You're disappointed." For answer, Maata stepped forward & laid her hands on Rhoda's shoulders. "Thank you my friend" she said. The sitting room was a studio, scantily furnished, with brown paper walls & black paint. It was very pleasant in a detached, unlittered way. A little fire burned in the grate & some pots of flowering heath, pink & white, gave it a still, chaste charm. A bedroom, a kitchen, <a lavatory> completed the tiny flat. Each bore evidence of Rhoda's devotion. There was even hot water in the wash basin covered in a pink & white towel., and a tea tray was ready in the kitchen & the kettle sang on a pinch of gas. "Yes, oh yes" said Maata, walking about, "I shall be happy here. This is quite right, Rhody. It's all lovely. And when I have my piano in the studio & cover the couch & have my books & pictures about it will be a good room to work in. There - take my bags - undo their locks & give me what I want. I'm going to wash & change into that green dress near the top."

Rhoda knelt on the floor & handled her darling's possessions as though these were all - every one - more precious than gold. Then she crouched back watching Maata step out of her grey skirt, slip off her blouse, &, standing before the mirror, let down her torrent of black silky hair. There was not very much light in the bedroom & Maata's skin flamed like yellow roses. The scent of her, like musk & spice, was on the air. When she brushed her hair she talked to Rhoda, to that silent adoring image crouched on the floor with wide eyes & pale lips. At last Maata, shaking her powder puff, noticed. "What is the matter dear" she said, & smiled at Rhoda who clasped her hands & smiled back. "I never dreamed - no I never ever dreamed that you were so beautiful, Maata. I never ever dreamed that your voice was so wonderful nor your movements - every supple movement - nor your skin so gleaming nor your hair - your - your [...] hair. I'd forgotten or just dimly remembered the way your little hands move, so sure & dainty, my little angel - everything about you - - -"

But Maata sat forward & took Rhoda's heavy head in her hands & laughed. "You mustn't flatter me so, darling, really not" and she said, still laughing, "Oh, it's so good to be spoiled, Rhody! But help me to dress now & bring me some of those violets out of the sitting room. I'll wear them." "Yes, dear." "Thank you. How nice to feel your capable hands again. Were you surprised that Maisie & Philip were down at the station." "Yes, perhaps a little" said Rhoda. "I telegraphed them from Plymouth. I don't know <u>why</u> exactly but you know they are such darlings - all of them - & they & you are my only people in London." "Of course, dear, I quite understand."

"And then, at Plymouth today, England suddenly stopped being Queen Victoria & turned into a most unworthy creature & I got homesick for some of my own people." Rhoda brought her the violets. "I suppose you're dreadfully disappointed that I'm going out tonight" said Maata. "But I can come with you to the gate can't I" said Rhoda. "Of course you can. But tell me - <u>are</u> you disappointed." Rhoda looked down into Maata's half shut eyes. "I do not allow myself to be disappointed. You are not to bother your wise head over me & my concerns. I am here to make you happy & to be with you when you want me, but I am not here to be like any other member of the world - just <u>considered</u> - because -" Her eyes brimmed & an expression of tragic caresses came into her face. "Don't you understand, little sweetheart, I love you - - - That merely to see you, to be able to - to put my hand on your coat like that & know it is warm with you - - -"

Chapter III

---

Young Country[232]
Chapter I. Mrs Preston sits at the window waiting for Rachael to return from school. It is a cold, windy afternoon. She is tired and sad. As the shadows fall in the room she sits thinking of her past life - of her married life and of her son & grandchild. R. comes home, is very happy. She does her homework while the grandmother knits. Then she sets supper. Fred comes home drunk & upsets the hash in his rage. "God damn hash!" R. in a furious temper curses him & runs away - out of the house & down the road to the sea. Finally she returns. She comes in at the back door. Her father is asleep. The grandmother is waiting for her. The two go up to bed.

---

[232]See Volume Two, note 46 for the reference to another piece of this story in Volume Two, p 63.

Chapter II. Hawk Street. The Houses. Mrs Bead and Tui. Ray & Tui go to the same school & are sworn friends. They keep themselves to themselves. Tui is idle & vain but Ray is clever.

Mrs Preston sat at the window waiting for Rachael to return from school. The day was cold & loud with the South wind. She sat in the rocking chair with a piece of pink knitting in her lap - her feet rested on the blue hassock and she was very still. Rachael was late and Mrs Preston felt vaguely anxious. Behind her crouched the little house - quite silent except for the kitchen clock & the dripping of the scullery tap. She thought "I must go & turn off that tap" but she did not move. "Oh dear" she thought mournfully, watching the scrubby garden bushes beat in the wind, "I wish that child would come. I wish this wind would go down. Tch! Tch! What a day. I wonder if the kitchen fire is alight. I ought to go & see". But she was too heavy & tired to go. On days like this she knew that she was old. Her heart beat in a faint, muffled way, and sigh as often as she might she could not fill her body with enough breath to make it beat faster. "Yes I am an old woman." "Old" hooted the wind, shaking the wooden house like a matchbox. And her thoughts recalled again the image that kept such stern vigil with her - her husband lying in his coffin, with the grey hair brushed off his brow & his face pale & watchful, pressed between the banks of wet clay - and waiting for her. She drew her heliotrope shawl closer with fingers that trembled.

The window where she sat looked out upon the road & then on to a street that ran sheer up the side of a hill. It had houses on either side - ugly houses with concrete walls covered with terrible nasturtiums. The town was on the other side of the hill & beyond the town the wharfs & the harbour with its two humped islands. Hawk Street was a poor ragged edge of the blowy place. The houses were built alike & painted alike - brown with red fittings. Each had a little front garden & an asphalt yard with clotheslines strung across it. Beyond the yards another hill & a wilder reared up like a huge wave. A queer yellow light flickered over Hawk Street and over Town, Hills, like the light of windy candles, & dark shadows blotted out the room where Mrs Preston sat. Suddenly, on the brow of the hill she saw Rachael. Ah, there she was. Mrs Preston got up & nodded & waved her knitting. How the child ran - with her blue cape flying about her she swooped down upon the little house, kicked open the gate, over the crunchy gravel & into Mrs Preston's arms. "Oh my little Gran" she cried, dropping her kit & pushing her hat on to her neck. "Did you think I was lost. I was kept in. I got nought for arithmetic again, my darling girl, & I've sat in that horrible cold classroom waiting to come home till I nearly burst." "You are a little late" said Mrs Preston mildly, "but I thought it was something like that. Come into the kitchen & get warm, child. Your cheeks are like ice." "Oh, don't you pretend" said Rachael, swinging on to the kitchen table, "that you haven't been waiting & waiting here for me & listening to the wretched old wind, & making up your mind that you're an old woman now & that nobody loves you. I know you too well by this time, Miss." "Nonsense" said Mrs Preston, turning with the lamp, "nothing of the kind." Warm bright lamplight painted the kitchen, and

Rachael leaned forward unlacing her boots, with her curls a red shower over her shoulders. "I'm so hungry - starving. Ugh - they're off. Pull up my stockings at the top. Grannie can I have something to eat. She was simply starving[?]. Let's have a quiet cup of tea together - I'll make it." "No, you go & fetch the gingerbread out of the tin in the pantry" said the grandmother, fitting her darling's little thin feet into woollen slippers. "Alright, & give me a candle. I want to go upstairs a minute."

While Mrs Preston made the tea, laid a cloth across a corner of the kitchen table, she heard Rachael running about upstairs, pulling open drawers, & Rachael's voice floated down – "What sort of a day have you had?"
"Oh quite ordinary."
"Haven't you hated this old wind."
"Yes, it has been dreadful."
"I suppose Queen Victoria or His Excellency the Governor didn't drop in this afternoon."
"No, dear, nobody's been."
"Grandma, where are my clean handkies."
"In their usual place."
"That's a clever answer, isn't it. Can I have some of your lavender water?"
The house was alive with her.

(24 pages per day i.e. 5,000 words for 15 days - 75,000 words.)
Day 1st.

<Across the pale grey sky above the houses there floats a grey cloud shaped like a poodle, and now it is a mountain and then it is a bird with wings outspread, flown away. What is this strange white light that comes from the street & from the pavement?>

Rose Eagle

It was wonderful how quickly Rose Eagle forgot the first fourteen years of her life. They were nothing but a dream out of which she wakened to find herself sitting on her yellow tin box in the kitchen of her 'first place', with a queer shaking in her hands and knees and the hot blood burning and lightening her cheeks. She and the yellow tin box might have been washed through the back door into Mrs Taylor's kitchen on the last wave of a sea-storm - so forlorn and unfamiliar they appeared, and she turned her head from side to side as though she were sensing quiet and stillness for the first time ...

It was late in the afternoon of a hot December day. The sun shone through the drawn blind in long pencil rays of light over the floor and the face of the dresser and a church calendar picture of a dreamy young Jesus with an armful of lambs, and facing her sat Mrs Taylor, changing the baby who sprawled on her lap waving his hands and blowing bubbles. Mrs Taylor kept on talking to Rose in a vague, singing voice, the clock on the mantelpiece ticked sharply and a tap in the scullery tip-tipped like stealthy footsteps.

"Yes m'm" said Rose Eagle, and "no, m'm", to all that Mrs Taylor said.

"You will share Reggie's room, Rose. Reggie is my eldest boy. He is four and he has just started school. And now that you have come I'll give up having baby at night – he keeps me awake so. You're used to babies."

"Oh yes, m'm!"

"I really don't feel well enough to tell you your duties today", said Mrs Taylor, languidly sticking safety pins into the gurgling baby. Rose Eagle got up and bent over Mrs Taylor.

"Here" she said, "give 'im to me", and as she straightened herself with the warm, fat lump in her arms she felt frightened no longer. Baby Taylor was to Rose Eagle the saucer of milk to the stray cat – the fact of acceptance proved resignation.

"My word! What 'air 'e's got!" said Rose Eagle, cuddling, "it's like black feathers." Mrs Taylor rose with her hands to her head. Tall and thin in her lilac cotton dress, she pushed back from her forehead the heaping black hair, with eyes half shut and quivering lips.

"My! You do look bad", said Rose, relishing this performance. "You go an''ave a lie down on your bed, m'm, and I'll bring you a cup of tea in a minute. I'll manage best ways I can." She followed her mistress out of the kitchen, along the little passage into the best bedroom.

"Lie down! Take yer shoes off!" Mrs Taylor submitted, sighing, and Rose Eagle tiptoed back into the kitchen.

This story seems to me to lack coherence and sharpness. That's the principal thing: it's not at all sharp. It's like eating a bunch of grapes instead of a grain of caviare... I have a pretty bad habit of spreading myself at times, of overwriting and understating – it's just carelessness. Now there is this novel – of Valentine by Grant Richards. A novel which is constructed with fastidious care and excellent taste is bound by its own nature to be something of a charming rarity for it requires a skill and lightness of touch    [J117-118 S57-59]

# Notebook 33

[Notebook 33, qMS-1246][233]

WEEKLY ACCOUNT

January 17th 1914
31 Rue de Tournon, Paris.

| | | Frcs | centimes |
|---|---|---|---|
| 17th | In hand | 101 | 50 |
| | cakes | | 40 |
| | eggs | | 40 |
| | stamp | | 25 |
| | ironmongery | 1 | 15 |
| | wood | 1 | 50 |
| | butter & bread | | 80 |
| | dinner | 1 | 85 |
| | cigarettes | | 65 |
| | | 6 | 80 |
| | jug and basin | 7 | 50 |
| | enamel jug | 5 | 90 |
| | curtain material | 4 | 5 |
| | bill with sewing woman | 3 | 00 |
| | ham | | 55 |
| | eggs | | 80 |
| | bread | | 20 |
| | felt | 2 | 50 |
| | fares | | 20 |
| | | 25 | 75 |

[233]Some 20 pages have been torn out of the beginning of this notebook prior to Murry's page numbering of it. Some of the verso pages carry bits of arithmetic which, because they are unrelated to anything and therefore meaningless, have been omitted.

Tea, the chemist & marmalade
Far indeed today I've strayed
Through paths untrodden, shops unbeaten
And now the bloody stuff is eaten
The chemist the marmalade & tea
Lord how nice & cheap they be!     [J49 S12]

| | | |
|---|---|---|
| tea | | 75 |
| chemist | I | 50 |
| marmalade | | 85 |
| eggs | I | 10 |
| cake | | 40 |
| honey | | 45 |
| ham | | 55 |
| bread | | 40 |
| butter | | 55 |
| sardines | | 35 |
| cigarettes | | 65 |
| screws | | 10 |
| oranges | | 40 |
| biscuits | | 30 |
| | 8 | 35 |

Tips and fares and silly femmes
Have skipped about my day like lambs
And great their happiness increased
Since I am the one who has been fleeced!     [J49 S12]

| | | |
|---|---|---|
| Femme de menage | 13 | 00 |
| fares | | 30 |
| coffee | | 95 |
| veal | | 55 |
| cake | | 40 |
| tips | | 40 |
| | 15 | 50 |

To M.O.P.[234]
Blast you for a mingy churl
You stop a baiting of a girl!
Just you try and pick my pocket
I'll put you into <Hell> & lock it!

| | |
|---|---|
| bread | 40 |
| butter | 85 |
| eggs | 80 |

---

[234]A possible meaning of these initials is 'Master of the Purse'.

| | | |
|---|---:|---:|
| veal & ham | | 80 |
| cake | | 65 |
| slippers | 1 | 95 |
| | 4 | 75 |
| | | |
| Total | 6 | 80 |
| | 25 | 75 |
| | 8 | 35 |
| | 15 | 50 |
| | 4 | 75 |
| | 62 | 25 |

| frc. | cens. |
|---|---|
| 62 | 25 |

| | | |
|---|---:|---:|
| cake | | 40 |
| ham | | 80 |
| eggs | | 80 |
| bread | | 40 |
| butter | 1 | 10 |
| sugar | | 65 |
| eggs | | 40 |
| liqueur | 6 | 50 |
| oranges | | 50 |
| cake | | 60 |
| glasses | 1 | 00 |
| sardines & tea | 1 | 50 |
| | 14 | 65 |

Jack

| | |
|---|---|
| 3.25 | liqueur |
| 1.40 | petit fours |
| 1.0 | cigarettes |
| 2.90 | coal |
| 8.55 | |

| | |
|---|---:|
| honey | 65 |
| bread | 40 |
| eggs | 50 |
| ham | 65 |
| cigarettes | 65 |
| stamp | |
| | 3.35 |

| | | |
|---|---|---:|
| Monday | eggs | 80 |
| | Montmartre | 3 00 |

|  |  |  |  |
|---|---|---|---|
| dinner | | 2 | 10 |
| laundry | | 7 | 50 |
| | | 13 | 40 |

| | | |
|---|---|---|
| milk | 8 | 85 |
| hair | | 30 |
| eggs | | 50 |
| café | | 50 |
| | 10 | 15 |

| | | |
|---|---|---|
| eggs butter sugar | 1 | 90 |
| Femme de menage | 12 | 00 |
| | 13 | 90 |
| | 10 | 15 |
| | 13 | 40 |
| | 3 | 35 |
| | 14 | 65 |
| | 62 | 25 |
| | 117 | 70 |

### 119 Beaufort Mansions  Feb 28th

| | | | |
|---|---|---|---|
| In hand | 1 | 0 | 0 |
| Odd stores | | 4 | 7 |
| Fruit & vegetables & eggs | | 6 | 3 |
| steak ordered rib | | 4 | 2 |
| coal and wood | | 3 | 6 |
| Butter cheese | | | 11 ½ |
| cigarettes | | | 6 |
| Veda bread | | | 3 |
| Soap and senna | | 1 | 1 |
| Cullens[235] stores | | 4 | 8 |
| Fares & postage | | | 10 |
| bacon | | | 7 |
| | £1 | 1 | 4 ½[236] |

### 119 Beaufort Mansions Chelsea  March 1st

| | | | |
|---|---|---|---|
| In hand | 2 | 10 | 0 |
| Bacon | | | 6 |
| eggs | | | 9 |
| O.W. | | 1 | 0 |
| bread | | | 2 |
| Bacon | | 1 | 0 |

---

[235] A high class grocery store with several branches in London.

[236] This total does not accord with the items. The number of shillings beside 'Fruit & vegetables & eggs' has been altered from 3 to something that looks like 6 but may be 1.

| | | |
|---|---|---|
| butter | | 6 ½ |
| bread | | 5 |
| boot polish | | 6 ½ |
| butchers bill | 4 | 6 ½ |
| safety pin for Jack | | 9 |
| hat pins | | 6 |
| lunch | 1 | 6 |
| Fares | | 8 |
| cigarettes | | 6 |
| Jack | 3 | 0 |
| | 16 | 4 ½ |
| Brought forward | 16 | 4 ½ |
| servants wages | 10 | 6 |
| grater (9d) steel (1/-) | 1 | 9 |
| Biscuits & cigarettes (Thursd.) | 1 | 0 |
| Fresh canterbury eggs | 1 | 3 |
| Flowers | | 6 |
| spats | 2 | 6 |
| stockings & handkerchief | 2 | 9 |
| £1 | 16 | 8 ½ |

237

Hotel Beau Rivage, Bandol-sur-Mer, Var. December 1915.

| | Frcs | cents |
|---|---|---|
| In hand | 90 | |
| paper | | 5 |
| oranges | | 20 |
| biscuits | | 40 |
| cigarettes | | 75 |
| matches | | 10 |
| paper | | 5 |
| stamp | | 25 |
| writing paper | | 30 |
| paper | | 5 |
| casserole | | 60 |
| methylated spirit | | 95 |
| stamps | | 85 |
| exercise book | | 20 |
| paper | | 5 |
| stamps | | 50 |
| | 5 | 30 |

---

[237]At this point Murry has written 'O Tig you are a little cod. And yet.'

| Brought forward | 5 | 30 |
|---|---|---|
| stamps | | 35 |
| tips | | 30 |
| paper | | 5 |
| borax | | 25 |
| laundry (!) | 3 | 15 |
| paper | | 5 |
| | 9 | 45 |

| Hotel Bill for J.& me | 62 | 50 |
|---|---|---|
| Tip to maidservant | 3 | 0 |
| stamps | I | 10 |
| | 76 | 05 |

| stamps | I | 10 |
|---|---|---|
| matches | | 10 |
| stamps | | 35 |
| | 86 | 60 |

December 20th 1915

| In hand | 349.55 |
|---|---|
| 20th cigarettes | 75 |
| stamp | 25 |
| telegrams (!) | 6.60 |
| | 7.60 |
| In hand | 341.95 |
| 21st stamp | 25 |
| […] | 75 |
| 22nd stamps | 85 |
| | 1.85 |
| In hand | 340.10 |

| 23rd letter paper + envelopes | 55 |
|---|---|
| stamps | 85 |
| tip | 2.0 |
| 24th stamps | 50 |
| bill | 59.80 |
| | 63.35 |
| 276.75 | |
| In hand | 276.75 |

| 25th | roses | 35 |
|---|---|---|
| 26th | stamps | 75 |
| 27th | cigarettes | 75 |

| 28th | telegrams | 9.0 |
| | stamps | 75 |
| | material | 3.50 |
| | | 15.5 |
| 30th | In hand | 261.40 |
| | apartement | 105.0 |

cristaux
lion d'or brun & noir

Higher Tregerthen, Zennor, St Ives.
May 8th 1916.   1 pkt self-rising flour
2 " cigarettes
½ lb lard
May 24th    3 lbs potatoes
[238]

bread 3. standard [...]
bacon 1/–
potatoes
onions
½ lb butter
1.40 milk
.55 butter
1.25 bread
2.00 eggs
3:50 meat & sundries
2.10 mirror
.70 tea
.30 sugar
.70 coffee

13.30

2 francs a day
300 in 12 weeks at 25 frcs a week.

| jug and basin | Vera |
| curtains | Marie |
| see about policies | Kay |
| see about tables | Mother |
| | Gibson |
| | Gilbert |
| | [...] |
| | Vere |

---

[238]It is necessary, here, to turn to the end of the book and work backwards. One page at the end of the book is torn out.

## LEMON PUDDING

6 ozs bread crumbs
3 ozs moist sugar
½ pint milk
2 eggs
4 ozs stoneless raisins
1 oz flour
4 ozs 'Atora'[239]

Strained juice & grated rind 2 lemons
Pinch of salt
1 teaspoonful Baking Powder
Ornament a well greased basin with the raisins. Mix dry ingredients together, add lemon juice, milk and eggs. Steam 2½ hrs.

## MARMALADE PUDDING

4 ozs bread crumbs
3 ozs Atora
1 egg
½ lb marmalade
2 ozs flour

Shred Atora. Put it in a basin with the flour and breadcrumbs. Beat the egg, add it to the marmalade. Pour on to the dry ingredients & mix thoroughly. Put into a greased basin, cover with greased paper, and steam for 2 hours.

## FIG PUDDING

4 ozs Atora
4 ozs flour
¾ lb figs
1 large apple
4 ozs brown sugar
4 ozs Bread crumbs
1 egg
1 teaspoonful baking powder.

Chop figs and apple fine. Mix flour & baking powder, add all the dry ingredients & then the egg well beaten, with enough milk to moisten. Pour in greased basin and steam 2½ hours.

---

[239]'Atora' was the brand name of a suet sold in packets for baking.

## CHILDRENS PUDDING

4 ozs flour
2 ozs sugar
1 egg
pinch of salt
1 teaspoonful Baking Powder
3 tablespoons milk
4      "       jam
2 ozs ATORA

Mix dry ingredients together with egg and milk. Put jam at bottom of basin, pour in mixture and steam 1½ hours.

# *Notebook 19*

[Notebook 19, qMS-1247][240]

Notes. February 1914.

There is in genius itself an unconscious activity: there is genius in the man of genius. S.T.C.

<u>dumbell poetry</u>.

"A calm irresistible well-being – almost mystic in character, and yet doubtless connected with physical conditions."

<u>Writes Dorothy</u>:

> William (P.G.) is very well
> And gravely blithe – you know his way
> Talking with woodruff or harebell
> And idling all the summer day
> As he can well afford to do.
> P.G. for that again. For who
> Is more Divinely Entitled to.
> He rises and breakfasts sharp at seven
> Then pastes some fern fronds in his book
> Until his milk comes at eleven
> With two fresh scones baked by the cook.
> And then he paces in the sun
> Until we dine at half past one
> God and the cook are very good
> Laughs William relishing his food
> (Sometimes the tears rush to my eyes
> How kind he is – and oh, how wise!)
> After he sits and reads to me
> Until at four we take our tea

---

[240]Many pages have been cut out of this notebook, both at the front and at the back.

My dear, you hardly would believe
That William could so sigh and grieve
Over a simple childish tale
How 'Mary Trod Upon the Snail'
Or 'Little Ernie Lost his Pail'
And then perhaps a good half mile
He walks to get an appetite
For supper which we take at night
In the substantial country style.
By nine he's in bed and fast asleep
Not <u>snoring</u> dear, but very deep
Oh deep asleep indeed!
And so on ad. lib. What a Pa-man!     [J49-50]

I am going to read Goethe. Except for a few poems I know nothing of his –
well. I shall read Poetry & Truth immediately.

'When all is done human life is at its greatest and best but a little froward child
to be played with and humoured a little, to keep it quiet until it fall asleep,
and then the care is over.' Temple.
That's the sort of strain, not for what it says and means but for the 'lilt' of it
that sets me writing.     [J50]

'Will you touch me with the child in my arms' is no mere pleasantry. Change
the 'will' into 'can' and its tief, sehr tief!²⁴¹ I was thinking just now . . that I
hardly dare give rein to my thoughts of Jack and to my longing for Jack.
And I thought – if I had a child I would play with it now, and <u>lose myself in it</u>
and kiss it and make it laugh. I'd use a child as my guard against my deepest
feeling. When I felt – no I'll think no more of this, its intolerable and
unbearable – I'd dance the baby. Thats true I think of all all women – and it
accounts for the curious look of security that you see in young mothers – they
are safe from any <u>ultimate</u> state of feeling because of the child in their arms.
And it accounts also for the women who call men 'children'. Such women fill
themselves with their men – gorge themselves really to a state of absolute
heartlessness. Watch the sly, satisfied smile of women who say "men are
nothing but babies".

"The irritable refinement of her mind."

"They were neither of them quite enough in love to imagine that £350 a year
would supply them with all the comforts of life." Jane Austen's Elinor and
Edward.
My God! say I.     [J51]

I went into Jacks room and looked through the window. It was evening, with
little light, and what there was very soft – the Freak Hour when people never
seem to be quite in focus. I watched a man walking up the road – & he looked

---

²⁴¹German for 'profound, very profound'.

like a fly walking up a wall, and some men straining up with a barrow – all bottoms and feet. In the house opposite at a ground floor heavily barred window sat a little dark girl in a grey shawl reading a book. Her hair was parted down the middle & she had a small oval face. She was perfectly charming so set in the window with the shining white of the book. I felt a sort of Spanish infatuation …

It is as though God opened his hand and let you dance on it a little and then shut it up tight – so tight that you could not even cry. The wind is terrible tonight. I am very tired – but I cant go to bed. I cant <u>sleep</u> or <u>eat</u>. Too tired.

[J51]

'It was the touch of art that P. was suffering, the inexorable magic touch that still transforms in spite of us; that never hesitates to test & examine the materials it has to transmute, but never fails to transmute them.'[242]     [J52]

to 'lay the child at the right door.'

To change habitations is to die to them.
Cut off in the flower of - - - To KMM & JMM of a flat 31 Rue de Tournon – stillborn –

But they adopted [an] infant, with all its pretty wardrobe & previously warmed toes takes kindly to us. We hope to keep it <u>some months</u>.

Lamb on country:-

In the ruins of Palymyra I could gird myself up to solitude, or muse to the snoring of the […] – sleepers, but to have a little teasing image of a town about one; country folks that do not look like country folks, shops 2 yds square, half a dozen apples & 2d of overcooked gingerbread for the worthy fruiterers of Oxford Street.

My flesh tingles at such caterpillars.[243]

---

[242]KM left the following pages but started writing again at the back of the book.
[243]There follows a page of isolated words: 'J.M. Murry, Poison, that's them, arrogant, Steamship.' This book also contains some notes in Murry's hand.

# *Notebook 23*

[Notebook 23, qMS-1248][244]

K.T. and her sister were walking down a road that was bounded on one side by a high hill and had on the other a deep ravine. So deep was the ravine that the cliffs at its base shone like the points of teeth, sharp and tiny. Her sister was very frightened and clung to her arm trembling and crying so K.T. hid her terror and said "It is alright. It is perfectly alright." She had a little black fur muff slipped over one hand. Suddenly there came driving towards them a chariot like the one in her blue Latin book, drawn by six stumpy horses and driven by a charioteer in a skull cap. They came at a furious gallop but the charioteer was calm, a quiet evil smile dyed his lips. "Oh K.T. Oh K.T. Im frightened", sobbed her sister. "Its quite alright, its perfectly alright" scolded K.T. But as she watched the chariot a strange thing took place. Though the horses maintained their tearing gallop they were not coming towards her and her sister <u>but were galloping backwards</u> while the charioteer smiled as though with deep satisfaction. K.T. put her little black muff over her sisters face. "They're gone, they're quite gone." But now the deafening clatter came from behind them like the sound of an army of horsemen in clashing armour. Louder and louder and nearer and nearer came the noise. "Oh K.T. Oh K.T." moaned the sister, and K.T. shut her lips, only pressing her sister's arm. The noise was upon them - in a moment - <u>now</u>.

And nothing passed but a black horse as tall as a house with a dark serene rider in a wide hat gliding past them like a ship through dark water and gliding importantly down the hill. The sight was so fearful that K.T. knew she dreamed. "I must wake up at once", and she made every effort to shut her eyes and shake away the scene - but it would not go. She tried to call and she felt her lips open but no sound would come. She shouted and screamed without a sound until at last she felt her bed and lifted her head into the burning dark of the bedroom.     [J52-53]

---

[244]On the front cover KM has written 'Commenced March 6th 1914.'

The Toothache Sunday.

Ah, why can't I describe all that happens! I think quite seriously that L.M. and I are so extraordinarily interesting. It is not while <u>the thing</u> is happening that I think that but the significance is near enough to bite its heels & make me start, too. Have I ruined her happy life - am I to blame? When I see her pale and so tired that she shuffles her feet as she walks when she comes to me - drenched after tears - when I see the buttons hanging off her coats & her skirt torn - why do I call myself to account for all this, & feel that I am responsible for her. She gave me the gift of her self. Take me Katie. I am yours. I will serve you & walk in your ways, Katie. I ought to have made a happy being of her. I ought to have 'answered her prayers'- they cost me so little & they were so humble. I ought to have proved my own worthiness of a disciple - but I didnt. Yes, I am altogether to blame. Sometimes I excuse myself. 'We were too much of an age. I was experimenting & being hurt when she leaned upon me. I couldn't have stopped the sacrifice if Id wanted to -' but its all prevarication. Tonight I saw her all drawn up with pain & I came from Jack's room to see her crouched by my fire like a little animal. So I helped her to bed on the sofa & made her a hot drink & brought her some rugs & my dark eiderdown. And as I tucked her up she was so touching - her long fair hair, so familiar, remembered for so long, drawn back from her face, that it was easy to stoop & kiss her - not as I usually do, one little half kiss, but quick loving kisses such as one delights to give a tired child. "Oh" she sighed "I have dreamed of this" (All the while I was faintly revolted.) "Oh" she breathed, when I asked her if she was comfortable, "This is Paradise, beloved." Good God! I must be at ordinary times a callous brute. It is the first time in all these years that I have leaned to her & kissed her like that. I don't know why I always shrink ever so faintly from her touch. I could not kiss her lips.

Ah, how I long to talk about It, sometimes - not for a moment but until I am tired out and I have got rid of the burden of memory. It is ridiculous in me to expect Jack to understand or to sympathise and yet when he does not & is bored or hums I am dreadfully wretched - mainly perhaps because of my own inability to enchant him.     [J53-54 S12-14]

The view from my window this morning is so tremendously exciting. A high wind is blowing & the glass is dashed with rain. In the timber yard beside the cemetery there are large pools of water and smoke blows from     [J54 S12-14]

The workmen came in to the middle of my thinking [....] lighted a fire in the yard.

I really have a faint idea that it might send me mad.     [J55]

... lifted her poor face all stained and patched with crying. Her body was obedient but how slowly and gravely it obeyed as though protesting against the urge of her brave spirit. There was no sound in the room but her quiet breathing & the fluttering rush of the fire and the sting of rain on the glass.

Outside lights appeared at one and then another window. The sky was grey and folded except for one lane of pale red fringed with little clouds.

    Content to stand outside & bathe & bask in the light that fell from Katie's warm bright windows, content to listen to the voice of her darling among other voices and to look for her darlings gracious shadow.    [J54 S14]

The Last Friday. Today the world is cracking. Im waiting for Jack & Ida. I have been sewing as Mother used to with ones heart pushing in the needle. Horrible! But is there really something far more horrible than ever could resolve itself into reality and is it that something which terrifies me so? In the middle of it I looked out & saw the workmen having lunch. They had lighted a fire & sat on a board balanced by 2 barrels. They were eating & smoking & cutting up sandwitches.    [J54-55 S15]

Raven

# *Notebook 18*

[Notebook 18, QMS-1249][245]

Katherine Mansfield Murry.
Private use.

MARCH

19 THURSDAY Dreamed about N.Z. Very delightful.

20 FRIDAY Dreamed about N.Z. again - one of the painful dreams when Im there & hazy about my return ticket.

21 SATURDAY Travelled with 2 brown women. One had a basket of chickweed on her arm, the other a basket of daffodils. They both carried babies bound, somehow, to them with a torn shawl. Neat spare women with combed and braided hair. They slung talk at each other across the bus. Then one woman took a piece of bread from her sagging pocket & gave it to the baby, the other opened her bodice & put the child to her breast. They sat and rocked their knees and darted their quick eyes over the bus load, busy and indifferent they looked.

22 SUNDAY Went to Albert Hall with B.C.[246] A bad dull concert. But I thought all the while that I'd rather be with musical people than any others and that they're mine, really. A violinist (miles away) bent his head & his hair grew like Garnie's:[247] that made me think so, I suppose. I ought to be able to write about them wonderfully.

A.M.[248]

23 SUNDAY Mother and Jeanne.

When I get by myself Im always more or less actively miserable. Nobody knows or could know what a weight L.M. is upon me. She simply drags me

---

[245]'W. Straker's Diary for 1914.'
[246]Probably Beatrice Campbell. See note 256.
[247]ie Garnet Trowell's.
[248]'A.M.' or 'Aunt Martha', was KM's euphemism for her menstrual period. Sometimes, to euphemise it further, she referred to it as 'Tante Marthe'.

down & then sits on me, calm and huge. The strongest reason for my happiness in Paris was that I was 'safe' from her. If it were not for Jack I should live quite alone. Its raining. I have a cold and my fire has gone out. Sparrows outside are cheeping like chickens. Oh heavens what a different scene the sound recalls, the warm sun and the tiny yellow balls, so dainty, treading down the grass blades, and Sheehan[249] giving me the smallest chick wrapped in a flannel to carry to the kitchen fire.

24 TUESDAY Mother's birthday. I woke at 2 o'clock and got up & sat on the box by the window thinking of her. I would love to see her again & the little frown between her brows and to hear her voice. But I don't think I will. My memory of her is so complete that I dont think it will be disturbed.[250] The Polinsons[?] dined with us last night. It was dull. They are worthy and pleasant but Mrs P is a weight and P makes me feel <u>old</u>. He only likes me because of what I used to be like, and he thinks the 'normal' me abnormally quiet and a bit lifeless. I don't want to see them again. Thank God! Theres a sprinkle of sun today. The river tonight was low and the little walls and towers & chimneys on the opposite bank black against the night. I keep thinking of <u>Paris</u> and <u>money</u>. I am getting all <u>my</u> spring out of the sunsets.

25 WEDNESDAY Ida and I travelled miles today. we sat in a bus talking and now and again when I looked up I kept seeing the squares with their butterfly leaves just ready to fly. We met near the old haunts - Queen Anne Street - and walked in one of the little lanes and short cuts that we know so well- side by side, talking. Let me tie your veil, & I stop, & she ties it and we walk on again. In the persian shop she leaned against a red and black silk curtain. She was very pale & her black hat looked enormous, and she kept wanting to buy me "these things - feel how soft they are" and smiling & speaking just above her breath for tiredness.

26 THURSDAY New Moon 6h 9m p.m.[251] (I didnt see it, though.) Ida & I took the tram to Clapham. She left at about 9 p.m. having dressed me. When I leave her hands I feel hung with wreaths. A silly unreal evening at Miss Royde Smiths.[252] Pretty rooms & pretty people, pretty coffee & cigarettes out of a silver tankard. A sort of sham Meredith atmosphere lurking. Amber Reeves[253] has a pert, nice face - that was all. I was wretched. I have nothing to say to 'charming' women. I feel like a cat among tigers. The ladies left to themselves talked ghosts & childbeds. I am wretchedly unhappy among everybody - and the silence . . .

---

[249]Pat Sheehan was the handyman at Chesney Wold, Karori, in KM's childhood.

[250]It was not. Annie Beauchamp died in 1918 without seeing KM again.

[251]This information about the New Moon is printed in the diary.

[252]Naomi Royde Smith (1875–1964), literary editor of the *Westminster Gazette* from 1912–1922, was also a novelist, playwright and biographer.

[253]Amber Reeves, daughter of William Pember Reeves, a prominent New Zealand politician, was one of the series of remarkable women with whom HG Wells had love affairs.

27 FRIDAY  Jacks P. Exam.[254] He went off half crying because he'd not sent the urgent work that kept him all yesterday to the post. I am waiting for Ida to come. She's very late. Everything is in a state of suspense – even birds and chimneys. Frightened <u>in private</u>. At the last moment Ida never said goodbye at all but took the fiddle and ran.[255] I walked away down some narrow streets, large drops of rain fell. I reached some packing warehouses and the delicious smell of fresh wood and straw reminded me of Wellington. I could almost fancy a saw mill. In the evening the Campbells[256] & the little parrot swinging on a wire.

28 SATURDAY  Put my clothes in order.
The crocuses in B.P. [Battersea Park] reminded me of autumn in Bavaria. The ground is wet and it looks as though winter were dying – the grass long and green among the trampled flowers. Birds are far more savage looking than the wildest beasts. Think of a forest full of <u>wild</u> birds – or if the birds 'turned' even here. I want to get alone. The magnolia conspicua is in bud.

29 SUNDAY  Jack would really think me important if I brought him L.S.D.[257] He thinks he's far and away the first fiddle. How he'd love to boast of what I got out of a play. Thats why Im going to start one today. Ill sweat my guts out till I bring it off too. A hideous day.

30 MONDAY  'I am afraid you are too psychological Mr Temple.'[258] Then I went off and bought the bacon.

31 TUESDAY  A splendid fine morning but as I know I have to go out and change the cheque & pay the bills I can do nothing & I feel wretched. Life is a hateful business, there's no denying it. When G. & J.[259] were talking in the park of physical wellbeing & of how they still could look forward to 'parties' I nearly groaned. And I am sure J. could get a great deal of pleasure out of pleasant society. I couldnt. Ive done with it & cant contact it at all now. I had so much rather lean idly over the bridge & watch the boats & the free unfamiliar people & feel the wind blow. No, I hate society. The idea of the play seems perfect tripe today.

APRIL

1 WEDNESDAY  Spent another frightful day. Nothing helps or could help me except a person who could guess. And Jack is far too absorbed in his own affairs poor dear to ever do so. Also, he doesn't consider the people within his reach, psychologically speaking. As long as ones mood isnt directed

---

[254]Jack's public examination at Oxford.
[255]This was the day Ida left for Rhodesia where she remained for two years.
[256]Gordon and Beatrice Campbell, Lord and Lady Glenavy were close friends of the Murrys at this time.
[257]'L.S.D.' refers to pounds, shillings and pence—ie money.
[258]Murry's note: 'An allusion to Maurice Temple, a character in a novel I was writing at this time, called *Still Life*.'
[259]Gordon Campbell and Jack.

towards or against him hes quite unconscious and unsuspicious. Very sane, but lonely and difficult for me to understand. Saw Campbell and talked L.S.D. Went for a walk & had some vague comfort given by some children and the noise of the water, like rising waves.

2 THURSDAY I have begun to sleep badly again and I have decided to tear up everything that I've written and start again. I am sure that is best. This misery persists and I am so tired under it. If I could write with my old fluency for <u>one day</u> the spell would be broken. Its the continual effort - the slow building up of my idea and then before my eyes and out of my power, its slow dissolving.

3 FRIDAY Written to L.M. and to Mother & Father. Went for walk by the river this evening and watched the boats. Two had red sails and one had white. The trees are budding almost before ones eyes in this warm weather - big white buds like birds in the chestnut trees, and round trees just sprinkled with green. The world is exceedingly lovely. My letter to L.M. was a great effort - she seemed somehow 'out of the running' but then so does everybody. I feel a real horror of people closing over me. I could not <u>bear</u> them. I wish I lived in a barge with Jack for a husband and a little boy for a son.

4 SATURDAY Won a moral victory this morning to my great relief. Went out to spend 2/11 & left it unspent. But I have never known a more hideous day. Terribly lonely. Nothing that isn't satirical is really true for me to write just now. If I try to find things lovely I turn pretty pretty. And at the same time I am so frightened of writing mockery for satire that my pen hovers and wont settle. Dined with Campbells & Drey.[260] Afterwards to Café Royal. The sheep were bleating and we set up a feeble counterpart. Saw a fight. One woman with her back to me, her arms crooked sharp at the elbows, her head thrust out like a big bird. Drey is frightened.

5 SUNDAY No bird sits a tree more proudly than a pigeon. It looks as though placed there by the Lord. The sky was silky blue & white and the sun shone through the little leaves. But the children pinched and crooked made me feel a bit out of love with God. I realised last night, more than ever, when I tried to explain myself to Jack and saw his incredulity, how profoundly I love him. Not for what I'd have him & in spite of himself sometimes he is really my mate. I love him to the inmost.

6 MONDAY I went out with Jack to find a shop but instead we came to Swan Walk and passed and remarked the delightful houses, white with flowering pear trees in the gardens and green railings and fine carved gates. I want a little house very much. I am afraid this house is haunted. At any rate trouble[?] is embedded in it like a lump of fat. And after dark the kitchen crawls. Drey came tonight. He's evidently in some kind of trouble with

---

[260]O Raymond Drey (1885–1976) was a journalist, drama critic and art critic. In 1913 he married the American painter Anne Estelle Rice who was a close friend of KM.

Anne:[261] I don't know what. Hes a silly fellow in talk, uneasy and Kosherheaded.[262] J x K W L last night and I deceived.[263] My mind is full of embroidery but there isn't any material to hold it together or make it strong. A silly state! Lesley Moore seems to be simply fading away. I can hardly remember her objectively - subjectively she is just the same.

7 TUESDAY The heavens opened for the sunset tonight. When I had thought the day folded and sealed came a hint of heavenly bright petals. I sat behind the window pricked with rain, and looked until that hard thing in my breast melted and broke into the smallest fountain murmuring of aforetime, and I drank the sky and the whisper. Now who is to decide between let it be or force it. Jack believes in the whip - he says his steed has plenty of strength but it is idle and shies at such a journey in prospect but I feel if mine does not gallop and prance at free will Im not riding at all, but swinging from its tail. For example today . . . & tonight he's all sparks.     [J55-60]

AUGUST

30 SUNDAY We go to Cornwall tomorrow, I suppose. Ive reread my diary. Tell me, is there a God! I do not trust Jack. Im old tonight. Ah, I wish I had a lover to nurse me - love me - hold me - comfort me - to stop me thinking.

NOVEMBER

3 TUESDAY Its full moon with a vengeance tonight. Out of the front door a field of big turnips and beyond a spiky wood with red bands of light behind it. Out of the back door an old tree with just a leaf or two remaining & a moon perched in the branches. I feel very deeply happy and free. Colette Willy is in my thoughts tonight. I feel my own self awake and stretching - stretching so that Im on tip toe; full of happy joy. Can it be true that one <u>can</u> renew oneself. Dear dear Samuel Butler![264] Just you wait. Ill do you proud. Tomorrow at about 10.30 I go into action.     [J61]

15 SUNDAY Its very quiet. Ive reread L'Entrave. I suppose Colette is the only woman in France who does just this. I don't care a fig at present for anyone I know except her. But the book to be written is still unwritten - I cant sit down & fire away like Jack.

---

[261]Anne Drey was born Anne Estelle Rice in the United States in 1879. She became a painter, settled in Paris, and in 1913 married O Raymond Drey. Anne developed a close friendship with KM, and painted the well-known portrait of her which hangs in the NZ National Gallery in Wellington.

[262]'kosher' is a variant of kosh or cosh—a short blunt instrument.

[263]Murry underlined this sentence in pencil and wrote beside it, on the facing page 'I don't understand this (1938)'. The initials almost certainly mean 'Jack and Katherine were lovers'. This was the somewhat de-energised term she used to refer to what she once (in connection with Francis Carco) called 'the act of love'.

[264]Samuel Butler (1835–1902) English man of letters, spent four and a half years in New Zealand from 1860–1864. Of his two best-known works, *Erewhon*, 1872, and *The Way of All Flesh*, 1903, the former was about his experience of running a New Zealand sheep station.

16 MONDAY  A letter from Francis Carco.[265] I had not expected it and yet when it came it seemed quite inevitable – the writing – the way the letters were made, his confidence and his warm sensational life. I wish he were my friend – he's very near me. His personality comes right through his letters to Jack – & I want to laugh and run into the road.       [J62]

---

[265]Murry's note: 'A letter from Francis Carco to me.' Francis Carco (1886–1958), a French writer and friend of Murry, became the focus of KM's wish for a romantic adventure in 1915. The affair was short lived and disillusioning. In 1918 she used him as a model for Raoul Duquette in 'Je ne Parle pas Francais'.

# *Unbound Papers*

[MS-Papers-4006-02]

I have not told Jack that I have heard again from Francis. Jack is not really interested in fact – when after that struggle I showed him a letter which had given me such a shock he thought it <u>funny</u> & wasn't sure that it was a love letter. I decided that I made a fool of myself by running to Jack with quelqu'un m'a donné <u>ca</u>. So, though its been hard, Ive refrained. F. may be leaving Besancon soon for the front, he told me, & he said – je vous aime chaque jour davantage – & he told me that all the while we had been in Paris he had loved me. Well, he thinks so <u>now</u>, and that he would like to love in a little hut on the edge of the world where no one would ever come, and that at times now he has merely an awful sensation of <u>emptiness</u>, he would like to lie in the road & let the world pass over him et quand je m'endors je vous prends dans mes bras et j'eprouve ma triste affreuse – and – ever so much more. The day after this letter he sent me another, very short – Chere Katherine je ne veux que vous. Vous etes et vous serez toute ma vie. Je suis        [J62]

[MS-Papers-4006-02]

December 18th. That decides me – that frees me. I'll play this game no longer. I created the situation – very well – Ill do the other thing with <u>moderate</u> care, & before it is too late. Thats all. He has made me feel like a girl. I've lived, loved just like any girl – but Im not a girl, & these feelings are not mine. For him I am hardly anything except a gratification & a comfort. Of course Gordon doesn't know me through him. He doesn't know me himself – or want to. I submit – thats true – but I'm not Colette not even Lesley. Jack – Jack – we are not going to stay together. I know that as well as you do. Dont be afraid of hurting me. What we have got each to kill is my <u>you</u> & your <u>me</u>. Thats all. Lets do it nicely & go to the funeral in the same carriage & hold hands hard over the new grave, & smile & wish each other luck. I can. And so can you. Yes – I have already said 'adieu' to you now.

 Darling, it has been lovely. We shall never forget – no never. Goodbye.

When once I have left you I will be more remote than you could imagine.
I see you & Gordon discussing the extraordinary <u>time</u> it lasted. But I am far
away & different to what you think.     [J62-63 S18-19]

[MS-Papers-4006-02]

> Given the [...]
> Henry in the K[?] Sixpence
> Farkey Anderson
> The Aloe
> Mothers Guitar

December 28th.
The year is nearly over. Snow has fallen and everything is white. It is very
cold. I have changed the position of my desk into a corner. Perhaps I shall be
able to write far more easily here. Yes, this is a good place for the desk, because
I cannot see out of the stupid window - I am quite private. The lamp stands
on one corner & <u>in</u> the corner. Its rays fall on the yellow & green indian
curtains & on the strip of red embroidery. The forlorn wind scarcely breathes.
I love to close my eyes a moment & think of the land outside white under the
mingled snow and moonlight - white trees, white fields, the heaps of stones by
the roadside white, snow in the furrows. Mon dieu how quiet & how patient!.
If he were to come I should not even hear his footsteps.     [J63]

[MS-Papers-4006-15]

### The Meeting.

> We started speaking
> Looked at each other; then turned away.
> The tears kept rising to my eyes
> But I could not weep
> I wanted to take your hand
> But my hand trembled.
> You kept counting the days
> Before we should meet again
> But both of us felt in our heart
> That we parted for ever and ever.
> The ticking of the little clock filled the quiet room
> Listen I said: it is so loud
> Like a horse galloping on a lonely road.
> As loud as that - a horse galloping past in the night.
> You shut me up in your arms -
> But the sound of the clock stifled our hearts beating.
> You said 'I cannot go: all that is living of me
> Is here for ever and ever.'
> Then you went.
> The world changed.. The sound of the clock grew fainter

Dwindled away, became a minute thing.
I whispered in the darkness:'If it stops, I shall die.'

---

[MS-Papers-4006-12]

These be two
Country women
What a size!
Grand big arms
And round red faces
Big substantial
Sit down places
Great big bosoms
Firm as cheese
Bursting through their country jacket.

Wide big laps
And sturdy knees
Hands outspread
Round and rosy
Hands to hold
A country posy
Or a baby or a lamb
And such eyes!
Stupid, shifty, small & sly
Peeping through a slit of sty
Squinting through a neighbour's placket.

---

Most merciful God
Look kindly upon
An impudent child
Who wants sitting on.
This evening late
I went to the door
And then to the gate
There were more stars - more
Than I could have expected
Even I!
I was simply amazed
Almighty, August
I was utterly dazed
Omnipotent, Just
In a word I was floored
Lord God of Hosts, Lord!
That at this time of day

They should still blaze away
That thou hadst not rejected
Or at least circumspected
Their white silver beauty
. . Was it spite . . Was it duty . . ?

[MS-Papers-4006-13]

### Deaf House Agent[266]

That deaf old man!
With his hand to his ear
His hand to his head stood out like a shell
Horny and hollow. He said "I can't hear"
He muttered "Don't shout
I can hear very well!"
He mumbled: "I can't catch a word
I can't follow."
Then Jack with a voice like a Protestant bell
Roared "Particulars. Farmhouse. At 10 quid a year!"
"I dunno wot place you are talking about."
Said the deaf old man.
Said Jack "What the HELL"
But the deaf old man took a pin from his desk, picked a piece
of wool the size of a hen's egg from his ear, had a good look
at it, decided in its favour & replaced it in the
aforementioned organ.      [J60]

[MS-Papers-4006-16]

Toujours fatiguée Madame
Oui toujours fatiguée
Je ne me lève pas Victorine et le courier
Victorine smiles meaning Pas encore passé.      [J129]

---

[266]There are two manuscript copies of 'Deaf House Agent'.

# Notebook 10

[Notebook 10, qMS-1250]²⁶⁷

Henry IV
Henry V

<u>O sovereign mistress of true melancholy</u>

And there is nothing left remarkable
Beneath the visiting moon.

So find we profit by losing of our prayers.
-   -   -   -   -   -   -

The April's in her eyes: it is love's spring
And these the showers to bring it on.
-   -   -   -   -   -   -

<u>Enobarbus:</u>        Yet he that can endure
To follow with allegiance a fallen lord
Does conquer him that did his master conquer
And earns a place i' the story.
-   -   -   -   -   -   -

                Tis one of those odd tricks
That sorrow shoots out o' the mind.
-   -   -   -   -   -   -

                And then what's brave; what's noble
Let's do it after the high Roman fashion
And make death proud to take us.
Come away: this case of that huge spirit now is cold.
Ah, women, women, come we have no friend
But resolution & the briefest end.
-   -   -   -   -   -   -

---

²⁶⁷Murry's note at the beginning of this notebook: 'These Shakespeare quotations, copied sometimes by K.M. & sometimes by me, were made at Villa Pauline, Jan 1916. We used to read part of a play of S. every night. And the one who was not reading aloud would copy the lines which particularly struck us. (Jan.1924, JMM).' Most of them are in his hand. I have put [KM] after those in hers. Apart from these 1916 Shakespeare entries, which were written at the end of a partly empty book, this is a 1914 notebook.

Nay, it is but the finer part of love …

    –  –  –  –  –  –

<u>Eno</u>. The tears live in an onion
Should water this sorrow…

    –  –  –  –  –  –

On the Alps
It is reported thou didst eat strange flesh
Which some did die to look on – and all this
Was borne so like a soldier that thy cheek
So much as lanked not.

    –  –  –  –  –  –

Cleo:  If thou with Caesar
Paragon my man of men

    –  –  –  –  –  –

The demi-Atlas of the earth, the arm
And burgonet of men

    –  –  –  –  –  –

"Where's my serpent of old Nile?" – for so he calls me.

    –  –  –  –  –  –

            Great Pompey
Wd stand & make his eyes grow in my brow.

    –  –  –  –  –  –

           Our courteous Antony
Being barbered ten times o'er, goes to the feast
And, for his ordinary pays his heart
For what his eyes eat only.

    –  –  –  –  –  –

           A rarer spirit never
Did steer humanity; but you gods give us
Some faults to make us men.

    –  –  –  –  –  –

Worth many babes and beggars.

    –  –  –  –  –  –

Or I shall show the cinders of my spirits
Through the ashes of my chance.

    –  –  –  –  –  –

I have immortal longings in me.

    –  –  –  –  –  –

The stroke of death
Is as a lover's pinch
That hurts & is desired

    –  –  –  –  –  –

           Now from head to foot
I am marble constant; now the fleeting moon
No planet is of mine.

    –  –  –  –  –  –

<u>As You Like It</u>.

Touchstone. Or by destinies decreed.
Well said that was laid on with a trowel.

- - - - - -

Thus men grow wiser every day (the rib-breaking sport.)

- - - - - -

(K) When I was at home I was in a better place
But travellers must be content.

- - - - - -

(K)            I like this place
And willingly would waste my time in it.

- - - - - -

I can suck melancholy out of a song
As a weasel sucks eggs.

- - - - - -

'dry as the remainder biscuit after a voyage.'
Touchstone on Country Life. Act III.ii

- - - - - -

I was seven of the nine days out of the wonder.

- - - - - -

When I was an Irish rat and that I can hardly remember.

- - - - - -

But all's brave that youth mounts & folly prides

- - - - - -

III.iii.
When a man's verses cannot be understood, nor a man's good
wit seconded with the forward child Understanding, it strikes
a man more dead than a great reckoning in a little room.

- - - - - -

It is good to be sad & say nothing.

- - - - - -

But men have died from time to time and worms have eaten them
– but not for love.

- - - - - -

24 Jan. 16.     Henry IV. Part 1.

as much grace as wd go before an egg with butter.

- - - - - -

Thou hast the most unsavoury similes.

- - - - - -

The poor abuses of the time want countenance

- - - - - -

Oh the blood more stirs
To rouse a lion than to start a hare.

- - - - - -

It were an easy leap
To pluck bright honour from the pale-faced moon.

\-  \-  \-  \-  \-  \-

Henry IV.

Out of this nettle danger
We pluck this flower safety.          [KM]

\-  \-  \-  \-  \-  \-

But a Corinthian, a lad of mettle . . .

\-  \-  \-  \-  \-  \-

Buckram-men

\-  \-  \-  \-  \-  \-

Falstaff, you carried your guts away as nimbly . . .

\-  \-  \-  \-  \-  \-

I was coward on instinct.

\-  \-  \-  \-  \-  \-

A plague of sighing & grief: it blows a man up like a
bladder.

\-  \-  \-  \-  \-  \-

For I must speak in Passion & I will do it in King Cambyses'
vein.

\-  \-  \-  \-  \-  \-

O Jesu – he does it as [like]
One of those harlotry players, as ever I see.

\-  \-  \-  \-  \-  \-

(Hotspur and Glendower's grandiloquence)
(mincing poetry) (scimble-scamble stuff)

\-  \-  \-  \-  \-  \-

I had rather live
With cheese and garlic in a windmill far
Than feed on cates, and have him talk to me
In any summer house in Christendom.

\-  \-  \-  \-  \-  \-

Henry IV. III. ii.

They began
To loathe the taste of sweetness, whereof a little
More than a little is by much too much.

\-  \-  \-  \-  \-  \-

Every beardless vain comparative.

\-  \-  \-  \-  \-  \-

III.iii

I will repent while I have some liking.

\-  \-  \-  \-  \-  \-

I live out of all order, all compass . . .

\-  \-  \-  \-  \-  \-

Theres no more faith in thee than in a stewed prune ...

I have more flesh than another and therefore more frailty.

IV.

To set so rich a main on the nice hazard of one mortal hour.

ii Food for powder – food for powder

mortal men, mortal men.

V.

F. I would it were bedtime Hal & all well.
H. Why thou owest God a death.

The fox – however cherished & chained up
Will have a wild trick of his ancestors.

But thought's the slave of life and life's Time's fool;
And Time that takes survey of all the world
Must have a stop.

F. (met by Harry & Lancaster, with Hotspur on his back)
Lord, lord, how this world is given to lying!

Two stars keep not their motion in one sphere.

Henry IV. II

It was always yet the trick of our English nation; if they
have a good thing to make it too common.

I'll tickle thy catastrophe!

Commit the oldest sins the newest kind of ways

O Westmoreland thou art a summer bird
That ever in the haunch of winter sings
The lifting up of day.

I may justly say with the hook-nosed fellow of Rome:
I came, I saw, I overcame.

Under which King, Bezonian, speak or die!

Henry Vth

But that the scambling & unquiet time ...      [KM]

But when he speaks
The air a chartered libertine is still.      [KM]

The law Salick that they have in France

– – – – – – –

That make such waste in brief mortality.

   –   –   –   –   –   –

Surveys
The singing masons building roofs of gold.

   –   –   –   –   –   –

if you would walk off Id prick your guts a little in good
terms as I may; and thats the humor of it.     [KM]

Why the devil should we keep knives to cut one another's
throats.    [KM]

Holdfast is the only dog, my duck.

Nym: I cannot kiss; that's the humour of it, but adieu.     [KM]

And that's the plainsong of it.

   –   –   –   –   –   –

(For Nym he hath heard that men of few words are the best men.)

   –   –   –   –   –   –

I have built
Two chantries, where the sad & solemn priests
Sing still for Richard's soul.

   –   –   –   –   –   –

IV. v.

But I had not so much of man in me
And all my mother came into mine eyes
And gave me up to tears.

   –   –   –   –   –   –

For there is figures in all things.

   –   –   –   –   –   –

For maids well summered & warm kept, are like flies at
Bartholomew-tide, blind, though they have eyes: and then they
will endure handling, which before would not abide looking on

   –   –   –   –   –   –

Twelfth night.    the whole.          IV

Clo.   What is the opinion of Pythagoras concerning wild fowl.
Mal.   That the soul of our grandam might happily inhabit a bird.
Clo.   What thinkest thou of his opinion.
Mal.   I think nobly of the soul & no way approve his opinion.

This is the air, this is the glorious sun
This the pearl she gave me.

This to give a dog & in recompense desire my dog again.

That very envy & the tongue of loss
Cried fame upon him.

A very devil incardinate.

Nor can there be that deity in my nature
Of here and everywhere.

Finish his mortal act.

That orbed continent of fire
Doth sever night from day.

I was one sir in this interlude
One Sir Topas sir; but that's all one.

Troilus & Cressida.     Feb. 4. 1916.

Ajax. I.ii.
Porridge after meat.     [J112-113 s51]

August 17.

I simply cannot believe that there was a time when I cared about Turgenev.
Such a poseur! Such a hypocrite! Its true he was wonderfully talented but
I keep thinking what a good cinema film On the Eve would make.     [J61]

To Beauty. Why should you come tonight when it is so cold & grey and
when the clouds are heavy, the trees troubled in their swinging?

Paul Moorhouse          George Coorie[?]
          John Long 6/-

& winter a peacock blue     [?]   [?]

Then I put my hand over it & felt for a latch & then through the bars.
I suppose one isnt expected to vault over it, I thought – or to ride a bicycle up
this side & dive into a fountain of real water on the other.     [J60]

| July 22nd [1914] | |
|---|---|
| curtains | 3.6 |
| Bread | .2 |
| Spirits salts | .3 |
| Salmon | .6½ |
| beans | .6½ |
| vinegar | .3 |
| hairpins | .1 |
| stud | .2 |
| bread | .2 |
| tomatoes | .3 |
| tips | .2 |
| | 6.1 |
| petits fours | .6 |
| flowers | .6 |

| kidneys | 9 |
| currants | 5 |
| Fares | 4 |
| Dairy & Cullen[?] | 10.0 |
| bath tray | 1.6 |
| Braid | 3.10 |
| fares | 5 |
| | £1.4.1 |

cigrets
bread
½ lb steak

I wish I could have a second family 3 boys to match the girls - all to be born just at the age when they are most tiresome[?] - with strong round heads & bright eyes & hands & feet much too big for them.

hydrangeas.

She lay in bed,[268] still, straight, her hands clasped above her head, her lips faintly parted and her eyes wide open. Now all the doors were shut in the house, and now Mr Derry had wound up his watch, leapt into his side of the bed, lying down straight, the sheet to his chin beside his frail wife. Her little face framed in springing light hair lay pressed in the pillow, her hands half hidden in the long frilled sleeves were folded over the quilt. Ready? Yes dear. He turned out the light and was asleep 'like a shot'. She would have fallen asleep too, but her heart was a little 'dicky'. It would not go quite fast enough and that made breathing so difficult. "If I could only take a long deep breath". She closed her eyes & a tiny line appeared between her brows & she drank the air in little sips. And its not worth while disturbing Henry to get my heart mixture. Hes been so wonderfully good & patient, loathing these affairs as I know he does. Full of love she listened to his strong even breathing - the Darling. In some strange way the sound of Henrys breathing eased her. Oh, soothed her wonderfully . .

Now Vera read the last verse appointed for that night by the Bible Society "For he mightily convinced the Jews & that publickly, showing by the scriptures that Jesus was Christ", & put the hand-painted Jerusalem-lily book mark in her bible & blew out the candle & tried not to remember "La Faute des Roses" but to think over what she had read until she fell asleep, & Mary decided not to bother about plaiting her hair that night but curled up & hugged her & began to dream almost before she fell asleep. In fact she answered "Yes very exciting" out loud in the dream & it woke her & she had to go to sleep again.

In his little room at the back Hans sat in his shirt on the edge of the bed, eating some patties, a leg of chicken & a chunk of almond icing out of a napkin stained with claret spread on his knees. He had had supper with the

---

[268]Murry supplied the title 'Sleeping House' to this piece in *The Scrapbook*.

women servants but these were his pickings. "Ha Ha! das war lustig."
He munched & licked his fingers & he felt an oily glow all over him. Then
he too lay down, & began to snore, thrashing about in his sleep. His toes stuck
out from the blanket like a comic picture.

The servants lay side by side in the narrow iron beds. Cook blew out the
candle & sighed & settled. I must say I do feel that lively, said Zaidee & tittered
a bit. "You know that young feller brought the champagne. He is a farm boy,
I think. Gave him the rough side of my tongue I did. See is tie stud! Flashy,
I called him. Keep off it Flashy, I said. He did look <u>silly</u>." But Cook hadnt seen
his tie. She had been too busy bending over the oven. Yes that was her job.
She never got a sight of anything & small thanks too. Where would they be
without her she'd like to know. And she saw herself bending over the oven,
stooping over the table, cutting things, bringing things out, stirring, never
looking up & everybody laughing & having jokes round her. But she was
frightened of answering Zaidee crossly. If you answered a person crossly
& they died in the night youd be blamed for ever afterwards. She was always
believing things like that. "Oh Life, I am tired" said Cook & turned to
the wall.

Now everybody in the house was [asleep] except Eleanor. I shall never
go to sleep again. She clasped her arms over her head - she had a strange
feeling that she floated floated in the dark. Her eyes shone, she could not stop
smiling & she could not grow calm. Calm - yes, I must grow calm. But it was
impossible. I shall never grow calm again. Her heart beat Philip plainly Philip
like a bell ringing in the alarm of battle. Yes, love was a battle. All confusion
and excitement - a breathless, desperate thing. Looking into the future Eleanor
saw only Philip & she, young & strong and shining, fighting the whole world,
& turning & crying to each other we have won. No, that didn't matter - it was
the fighting that counted. I have been a dark feeble thing like a house lighted
with one candle - but now there is a fire in every part of me and I am strong,
my love, my dear.

There was no sound in the house any more <nor any light except the
white beams of moonlight shining on the carpets and in the [...] the flowers
that were yesterday night in the garden, the hydrangeas, the silvery waxy
branches of syringa flowers, the red roses that grew singly on long stems & the
little round roses that fluttered their petals on to the grass at a breath.
Serene & majestic stood the house, filled with its brood of sleeping people.
The air blew through it, lifting the curtains & filling it with the scent of the
earth and grass and trees.> nor any light save where the moon shone on the
floors & ceilings, on the stairs, on the dismantled supper table, gleaming on
the mirrors and the fading flowers. <The music and the dancing and the night
have happened hundreds and hundreds of years ago. All the sleeping people, so
still and mysterious, appeared [in the] house under this old, changeless light of
moon - you could not believe that they who lay so quietly in the bosom of the
house would ever wake again.>

Silence hung over the garden, but the garden was awake. Its fruit and its
flowers filled the air with a sweet and a wild scent. White and grey moths flew

over the silvery mantle of the syringa bushes. On the dark camellia trees the flowers were poised like white and red birds. The tall trees hung their boughs over pools that were shadows. So still and mysterious appeared the house under this old, changeless light of moon, it seemed that the music and the dancing night had happened hundreds & hundreds of years ago. They who lay so quietly in its bosom might never wake again.[269]      [s15-18]

Today is Sunday. It is raining a little and the birds are cheeping. There's a smell of food & a noise of chopping cabbage.

Oh, if only I could make a celebration & do a bit of writing. I long & long to write & the words just won't come. Its a queer business, yet when I read people like Gorky, for instance, I realise how streets ahead of them I be ...

| | |
|---|---|
| cigarettes | 6 d |
| butter | 3 ½ |
| bread | 1 |
| | 10 ½ |

KMM 23.V.14.

---

[269]After the above piece there is a drawing of a boat containing one person, on a river surrounded by trees, with a hill in the background. The last part of this notebook is taken up with drawings of faces and figures, some obviously of Jack—one labelled 'surprised', and another 'Jack in the boat'. Murry has noted 'These drawings were made on the river Arun between Pulborough & Amberley.' Finally, on what was originally the first page Murry has noted 'This end. JMM. May 1914. Sketches at Pulborough.'

# *Unbound Papers*

[NL]²⁷⁰

The brilliant sunny weather, & spring weather. The pansies in the Kasino grounds, the lilac bushes. I see her walking under a parasol. The little sick boy. His death. The whole peasant family in mourning – that night Peter goes to see her & they kiss.

It was evening. The lamp was lighted on the round table. The frau tapped, came in and took away the supper tray. "Shall I draw the curtains gnadige frau?" she whispered. Her face very scarlet from cooking & her eyes burnt by the fire made her look like a little girl who has been playing in the wind.

"No" said Elena, "I will draw them later. The light is so lovely." The frau smiled at her & went out setting down the tray in the hall that she might close the door more quietly. Elena heard her steps on the stairs, heard the eager babble that greeted her as she opened the kitchen door, that always greeted her. She is like a bird flying back to her nest, thought Elena, and then the house was quiet again. The lovely light shone in the window. She loved to think of the world outside white under the mingled snow & moonlight. White trees, white fields, the heaps of stones by the roadside white, snow in all the furrows. Mon Dieu how quiet it was. There is nobody except the moon, she thought, & she saw the moon walking over the snow, walking slowly through the heavy forests like a hunter, landing upon the tops of hills as though she stood upon a wave crest, bending over the sleeping gardens, gathering from the sleeping gardens white and green roses, slipping through the frozen bushes & looking into tiny houses, smiling strangely. She had a feeling that 2 wings rushed to open in her breast.

"Oh I want to sing."

She got up quickly & walked across the room to Peter's bed. She sat down on the edge of it. Peter was not asleep. Propped up against the pillows, his arms along the sheet, he looked as beautiful a little boy as ever ran away from

---

²⁷⁰The main story in this notebook, though it harks back to KM's time in Germany and her care of the sick little boy from London in 1909, was not written until 1914.

Heaven. His straight black hair was tumbled. There were 2 little spots like
cherry stains on his cheeks, his red lips were parted, the collar of his cream
flannel nightgown stood up in 2 peaks to his chin.
"Sleepy?" asked Elena, smiling. He shook his head. Of course he was not
sleepy. How could he have been sleepy with eyes like that. Oh how she longed
to sing!
"What are you thinking about Peter?"
"Nothing my Mother" said Peter, giving the lie to his imploring
beseeching eyes.
"Really nothing?" She bent down the better to see him.
Suddenly he lifted his hands & then clasped them and let them fall – so –
but still he did not speak. Only his eyes implored her – troubled terrified eyes.
How strange he looked – he must be feverish. She put her pretty caressing
hand on his forehead & brushed his fringe to the outside. Yes he was feverish.
A little web of sweat hung on his face.
"Do you feel quite well?" she asked tenderly. He nodded "yes" and at the same
time she knew what his eyes were saying.
"Mother, do not sing. Mother I could not bear you to sing tonight."
She never doubted his feeling for an instant. She knew, more plainly than if he
had spoken, whether he were conscious of it or not, Peter was imploring her
not to sing.
     But the knowledge did not take away her longing – her longing pushed
in her breast. It was wild, it would not be denied. Free me, free me!
"Mother" implored Peter's eyes, "do not sing tonight." But I must sing, Peter.
The longing is far stronger than I. And when she had asserted the fact to
herself it became so, it leapt up, cruel and eager. If he did not want me to sing
he would say so, she thought – he is not a baby – not such a baby as that. She
took his hand between hers – tenderly, tenderly she stroked. She carried it to
her eager bosom as though to make him feel how her desire pressed. A
mysterious fascinating smile parted her lips, her nostrils quivered. She breathed
deeply & with the breath her beauty flowered.
Rich[?] she was & powerful.
"You ought to be asleep" she whispered fondly. "It's long past your sleeping
time, darling. Would you like Mother to sing you to sleep Peter?" Her words
flew, explaining. Deliberately she veiled her eyes & did not meet his. "But not
really sing. Just make up as I go along – a song for a sleepy boy – about the
moon, darling, about the moon." The hand she held did not quiver. She put it
down. She looked about her at the shadowy room, at the window where the
strange light beckoned. As in a dream she saw the dark head on the white
pillows. Beautiful! Beautiful! & she lifted her bosom to those urgent wings.
But she would only sing gently, only softly, Peter. Listen – snow is falling, out
of the sky falls the snow, like green & white roses and nobody sees but the
moon. From her cloud pillows the moon arises & floats with the falling snow
& gathers the green & white roses, the little white buds of snow, in her
gleaming fingers. Softly, softly.
     As she sang she stood up and singing still she went to the window & put

her arms along the frame. Peter shut his eyes. He floated into his mother's singing bosom & rose & fell to her breath. His wonderful mother had wings. Yes, yes, she could fly. She flew with him out of the window to show him the snow and to give him some of the roses. He felt the snow on his chest & creeping up to his throat it formed a little necklace round his neck. It crept up.

"But not to my mouth Mother. Mother, not over my eyes."

     In the middle of her singing there came a knock at the door. Two sharp knocks, they were like a blow on the heart to her. Still half under the spell of her singing, like a queen she flung the door open. The doctor stood on the landing in his big driving coat. He was beating his fur hat against the stair rail. "I am afraid I am interrupting" he said, & from his voice she thought he was accusing her. Her lips curled.

"Not at all" she said coldly. He strode into the room pulling off his big coat. She shut the door & leaned against it.

"The young man's never asleep, is it?" said the doctor.

Still the same tone.

"Yes he is asleep" said Eleanor [sic], and she felt her glow ebb away from her like a retreating wave. The doctor went over to the bed. He parted the sheets & caught hold of Peter's arm to raise him. Suddenly she saw an extraordinary alertness in his face, in his movements. He dropped on one knee & put his arm under Peter's shoulder. "Bring over that lamp" he commanded, "& take off the globe. Quick now!" She held the lamp in her two hands. She felt the blood creep creep away from her body. She saw the doctor give Peter a long searching glance, & then put him back on the pillows & straighten the sheet. "So that's it" he said, shooting out his lower lip & frowning.

"What?" The word dropped from her lips like a pebble. The young doctor barely glanced at her. This time the sneer was unmistakeable.

"You know as well as I do" he said. "Here, give me that lamp." And as he took the lamp from her he said quite calmly "He is dead of course."


There is always something wonderfully touching in the sight of a young mother with a delicate child, and when the mother is beautiful and radiant, and when the child is like her but terribly unlike - a little shadow page carrying with bird-like hands his mother's glory - then the sight is enough to melt the most frozen heart. Not a heart had withstood Elena and Peter throughout the Journey. Arms had shot out to lift little Peter up and down steps, in and out of railway carriages, eyes had caressed them, Peter had been offered flowers and cakes - even some silver cachous from a minute flask dragged out of her red pocket by a French baby wearing long yellow boots. Now it was the end of the day & the last stage of their journey. They had only 1 hour more, one town more. From her dressing case Elena took out a bottle of eau de cologne, shook some on to her handkerchief, & raising her veil slightly she held the handkerchief to her lips & nostrils. She did not really want the eau de cologne. She was not really exhausted but her perfect sense of the

dramatic fitness of things prompted the action. She could not bear that even so
small an audience – half a dozen people in a railway carriage – should go away
indifferent or unsatisfied. She felt bound to play exquisitely for them. Why she
even took the trouble to play exquisitely for Peter when he and she were alone
together. Sometimes in front of her mirror she played most exquisitely of all.
She quite realised it, she would have acknowledged the fact frankly. You see,
as a singer I am more or less a public woman & I find it really frightfully
difficult to keep my private & my public life apart. Also – I feel so much myself
on the stage that perhaps I only act when I am off. Yes, well there was some
truth in that.

It was sunset. They were going through fields of tall gleaming flowers.
In the deep bright light they looked more silver and gold than white & yellow.
There were blue flowers like lapis lazuli, and a tall red plant with flowers like
plumes. In the distance the horizon was banked by forests of fir and pine black
against a glittering golden sky. The sun sets to a fanfare of trumpets, thought
Elena & she longed to compose a hymn to the departing sun – in french.
Soleil – it was lovely – it has a wonderful [...] sound.

Suddenly she felt a soft pressure on her arm. Peter was leaning against
her, his head lying on his chest. There was hardly anything to be seen of him
but the charming back of his white neck & the faint V of hair between the
2 neckbones. She bent over him – and just for a moment she caught the tender
glance & smile of the old woman opposite. He has gone to sleep. I know.
I have had them too. Many many children this old lap has carried, said the
glance & the smile. "Asleep darling?" asked Elena. Peter looked up, his
wonderful grey eyes blind, hidden by the curly lashes. She said "Come, come
on to my lap." With a long graceful supple movement she gathered up her
little son & held him in her arms. Like all children he was not merely asleep,
he was drowned in sleep. Helpless, his arms & legs dangling, his head jerking
to the train. She put his head in the hollow of her neck & rested her own on
his silky black hair. "That's better, isn't it" she whispered. Peter gave a sigh, and
again Elena caught the glance of the old woman opposite – kindly, envious.
The old woman looked sadly at her hands as though she asked – remembrance.

Again she looked out of the window. A breeze flew among the daisies,
ruffling their petals – she fancied she could smell their bitter scent. And
suddenly she remembered a year in her childhood when the hills & the valleys
of her home had been smothered under these same flowers, and the school
children had dragged a toboggan to the top of the tallest hills & made a slide.
She heard again their shrieks & screams of excitement. They had been too
excited to wait their turn in the toboggan. They had rolled and tumbled
among the feathery snow, & jumped up & down, running through the daisies,
pulling each other, until all the side of the hill lay in green tatters.
She remembered now the agony she had felt & been ashamed to show.
Yes, to this very day she regretted her part in it. It had left a wound for life.
<She sighed – yes, that was the first time I deliberately sinned against myself.>
Ugh! What little men & women children are! thought Elena – and she turned

from the window & wondered how on earth she could bear any more of this journey. Really the last moments of a journey are intolerable. If she could only share the state of apathy that these people were sunk in. The noise of the train seemed to act upon them like a drug. They were content to be carried away. But their stupid country faces, so lulled, so soothed, revolted her faintly as she watched them.

No, she would rather suffer these strange pangs of excitement that set upon her at the end of a journey. Any journey – it was always the same. Though more than half her life had been spent in travelling the thrill remained. The unknown place to which she travelled had in her head a fanciful image. It was a town. Ah, it was always the poor quarter that she saw first. The narrow streets, the tall houses teeming with careless unruly life. Footsteps ran through them ceaselessly, they ran through the narrow dark vein of the houses. Strange doors banged open, banged shut. In the basements lived the dregs of humanity – old men who kept birds in tiny cages or bought rabbit skins or sold little paper bags of coal & wood. On the roofs there were lean cats & pigeons & vulgar clothes hanging out to dry. And the shops, the little shops that she loved brimmed over on to the pavement. They were lighted with long whistling flares of gas – or stalls lighted by candles in round glass globes, or by lamps benign in spreading shades like haymakers' hats. And then there were the cafés and the little […] bars. The swing doors opened, the sound of a gramophone rushed out mingled with the clink of glasses and girls' laughter & men's voices very loud. I will go there, I will go there.
To the fringe of the town, to the new roads sticky with clay where the railways thrust out roots of iron, where new houses, dark & blind, reared up in the air as though for the first time or the last. Yes, there she was walking, her coat collar turned up, her hands in her pockets. A little fox terrier dog rooted in the gutters full of dead leaves. Or it was a village of white & green houses with red geraniums at the windows and lilac bushes in the garden. She was leaning out of the window in the evening. Below her the hay carts were passing and the air smelt of hay. Behind the haycarts came the girls with scarlet cheeks. One of them carried a cornflower bush in her hands, one of them carried poppies.

And although these things never came to pass it did not matter. Faced with reality she did not even regret them. They faded out of her mind until they were forgotten, then on the torn web of the old dream the new dream began silently to spin. But what was the quality in them that excited her so, that [made] her tremble. Her mouth burned. Her heart beat so powerfully she had scarcely room in her body for her quick breath. Like a woman on the way to her lover who stifles her own despairing impatience by crying to him "Yes, yes, I am coming, I am coming as fast as I can. I am on my way now, I am hurrying, hurrying to you" – so Elena cried out to herself. And Peter, the unfamiliar burden, did not see the gold burn out of the sky. He did not see the forest rush to surround the train like an army, and then fall back leaving fields again, and more fields threaded with streams and spanned with wooden bridges. Not even the shrill toy-like whistling of the engine waked him as the train drew up at the station. Then he rubbed his eyes & staggered as Elena set him down like a bird fallen out of a nest. "Try & wake up for a little while Peter" she said. "You shall go to bed

Paul Deroulede. J & Jean Tharaud.

le pêle mêle the armenian silk shirt, the black frilly[?] man in a fez, the hoards[?] of [...] flocking into the street, the cards of braid, the large pictures of his brother & the armenian dressed like Prussian princes sitting on little carpets.
His teeth under his moustache & the rings on his podgy[?] fingers.
Boris is in love with Jacques. That terrible walk home when they did not touch each other - the horror of it, the wonder of it & then the shadows mingled.

While he talked he put his hand upon the back of her neck. She tilted back her head & smiled at him. When I was a very little girl, she said, my nurse used to put me to bed very early - before sunset - & I never could sleep. I used to lie with my eyes closed & the sun & the flowers still danced on my eyelids. Now, she said, when I go to bed & shut my eyes it is your smiles that dance on my eyelids, your image that floats & dances. Oh, I long, as I used to long then, to spring out of bed & run back into the brightness - I love you - I love you.

One night when Jack was with Goodyear[271] & I had gone to bed and he said that what he really wanted was a woman who would keep him - yes, that's what he really wanted - & then again, so much later, with Campbell, he said I was the one who submitted. Yes I gave way to him & still do, but then I did it because I did not feel the urgency of my own desires. Now I do and though I submit from habit now it is always under a sort of protest which I call an adieu submission. It always may be the last time.

Mais pourquoi faites vous ce?
Pour moi-meme d'abord et puis pour vous.

on the torn web of the old dream the new dream began silently to spin.

envelloppée
enveloppée

I cannot get a move on today. I feel rather horribly dry.

Elena Bendall
Peter Bendall

---

[271]Frederick Goodyear (1887–1917) was a gifted young man towards whom both the Murrys felt very warmly. He was in the army and did not survive the war. Later, in a letter to Murry of 19 May 1921 KM wrote 'Your mention of Grundy gave me Goodyear again—living, young, a bit careless and worried—but enjoying the worry, in the years before the war, when a pale moon shone above Picadilly Circus and we three stood at the corner and didn't want to separate or go home.'

1.  0.0 bed
  10.6 chair
  8.6 washstand
  6.11 screen
  10.0 table
  5.0 lamp
  5.0 crocks
  10.0 stain floor
  5.0 shelves

———————

  £4.  0.11
  mirror    3.0
  chair    4.6          7.6

To be without books and to be alone are the 2 essentials to my writing –
<u>endless time</u> no fires to attend to, no-one to wait for – days and nights on end.
I'd better find a room in London quickly – and £5 with which to furnish it.

I'm simply dreaming this afternoon and all the while I know that my dream
can come true only by Balzacian methods – that is by the absolute sticking
to work.
j'ecris
j'ecrivai
What idiocy!

The only one who sang ill was the cripple. One would think it were rather
his crutches that sang and not he for the voice was so hard and wooden,
it dragged so, it swung so heavy.
    There were 2 blind men with lean shanks and red noses. One of them
had a spotted snake-like stick with a sharp end, the other walked with his hand
on the fiddler's shoulder. The cripple was a little short[?] fellow with a tiny
round head, broad shoulders, long arms, & legs that seemed to end in a couple
of big knots. He wore black spectacles too, that tied to his head by a black
cord fastened in a bow behind. All the more difficult pieces of money – the
sous that dropped down the drains or over the palings, or were lost – he it was
who swung to find them & this seemed to be agreed between them for the
fiddler & the leader made no effort to help.

The sweet small notes of the robin sang in

Out popped the beads & down rained the ha'pennies. Round them in a ring
stood the small audience. Little girls in black pinafores with their hair tied up
in ribbons, little boys in blue pinafores that buttoned on their shoulders[?],
their hands behind their backs, their legs wide.
    Below the terrace there is a great pother. Four men are engaged with a
long tangled rope. They are stretching it across the road – for what reason I do
not know & I am sure they don't – & tying one end to a blue gum tree, the
other to a large palm by the shore. There are four sacks of grain one side of the
road & a cart upturned, and beside the palm a bundle of green peas[?]. Some
tiny white & blue boats are drawn up to the shore.

# Index

## NAMES, FICTIONAL AND PERSONAL

### Volume One

*Note: A name is indexed the first time it appears in a passage or section.*

The Katherine Mansfield Notebooks

Volume Two

*Katherine Mansfield, 1917.*
*From the journals of John Middleton Murry.*

*The*
# Katherine Mansfield
*Notebooks*

Volume Two

*edited by*
MARGARET SCOTT

are this teaches me with sharpness the 21st this point of view clear medicine seems to me just completely right. It will let me take off my head work in ordino popitom efficio of he thinks it would astonish future generations. Once the you man to have at ones dying brook — had put me at any rate so in Krester in the process — gradual loss of sensitiveness — coldness in the joints etc. It lie there pucking. This is very valuable to know. I must make a note of this. As he closed all the box teeking with is in knots, it all a grahm of this the seems so useless today may just be that Bink Ceel life with there all pleto a future generation ... Has a sense of the eager breath — of the a plenious limes in this bricks. and the egyptian parasite tegrip its new cycle of viery in a wate juaice afputes me like a just work of Art. No, thats with neither; in made nofue this perfect me noves is. with its

*Manuscript page from Notebook 20, 1922, reproduced actual size.*
*For the transcription see page 313 of this volume.*
ALEXANDER TURNBULL LIBRARY, NLNZ


PREVIOUS PAGE:
*Manuscript page from Notebook 16, 1919, reproduced actual size.*
*For the transcription see page 173, lines 1–12, of this volume.*
ALEXANDER TURNBULL LIBRARY, NLNZ

# Contents

## ABBREVIATIONS

| | |
|---|---|
| S | *The Scrapbook of Katherine Mansfield*, ed J M Murry, Constable & Co Ltd, London, 1939 |
| J | *Journal of Katherine Mansfield: Definitive Edition*, ed J M Murry, Constable & Co Ltd, London, 1954 |
| CLKM | *The Collected Letters of Katherine Mansfield*, ed Vincent O'Sullivan and Margaret Scott, Clarendon Press, Oxford. Vol 1, 1984; Vol 2, 1987; Vol 3, 1993; Vol 4, 1996; Vol 5, forthcoming |
| ts | typescript |
| ATL | Alexander Turnbull Library |
| NL | Newberry Library |

# *Notebook 4*

[Notebook 4, qMS-1251][1]

Katherine Mansfield.

I shall be obliged if the contents of this book
are regarded as my private property.[2]

What a vile little diary. But I am determined to keep it this year. We saw the
old year out and the new year in. A lovely night, blue and gold. The church
bells were ringing. I went into the garden and opened the gate and nearly -
just walked away. Jack stood at the window mashing an orange in a cup. The
shadow of the rose tree lay on the grass like a tiny bouquet. The moon and the
dew had put a spangle on everything. But just at 12 o'clock I thought I heard
footsteps in the road & got frightened & ran back into the house. But nobody
passed. Jack thought I was a great baby about the whole affair. The ghost of
Lesley ran through my heart her hair flying - very pale, with dark startled eyes.
And I thought of Francis. Deja dans la petite piece de l'hotel de Cluny j'etais
sur de vous etre attaché - and then je suis jaloux de vous comme un avare.
I live within sound of a rushing river that only I can hear. It is a curious sort
of life ... more real than this three year idyll, more natural to that which I
suppose I really am.

For this year I have two wishes  to write  to make money. (Yesterday I
heard someone discussing Laura Grey.) Consider. With money we could go
away as we liked, have a room in London, be as free as we liked and be
independent & proud with nobodies. It is only poverty that holds us so tightly.
Well, J doesn't want money & wont earn money. I must. How? First, get this
book finished - that is a start. When. At the end of January. If you do that you
are saved. If I wrote night & day I could do it. Yes I could. Right O.

I feel the new life coming nearer. I believe just as I have always believed.
Yes it will come. All will be well.     [J63-64]

---

[1]'Home Diary for 1915'—a diary with printed dates and days for 1915. An entry for 21st January was
squashed in at the front of this diary, its own place having been taken by an entry made earlier on the 21st. I
have moved it to its chronological position.

[2]Written on fly-leaf of the notebook, under the name Katherine Mansfield.

1 FRIDAY [January]

A LETTER.

To London. It was raining and very cold. I posted my letter at the G.P.O. Saw Kotilianski.[3] The setting was very good for a story some time. I felt depressed et inquiète a cause de ses … Hardly slept at all and dreamed a terrible dream about Mother. J. read me some of his book. He must beware of a kind of melodramatic intellectual sentimentality. 'A little crack'

2 SATURDAY

A horrible morning and afternoon. Je me sens incapable de tout and at the same time I am just not writing very well. I must finish my story tomorrow. I ought to work at it all day - yes, all day & into the night if necessary. A vile day. J'ai l'envie de prieur au bon Dieu comme le vieux pere Tolstoi. Oh Lord make me a better creature tomorrow. Le coeur me monte aux levres d'un gout de sang. Je me deteste aujourd'hui. Dined at Lawrences and talked the island.[4] It is quite real except some part of me is blind to it. Six months ago Id have jumped. The chief thing I feel lately about myself is that I am getting old. I don't feel like a girl any more, or even like a young woman. I feel really quite past my prime. At times the fear of death is dreadful. I feel so much older than Jack and that he recognises it I am sure. He never used to but now he often talks like a young man to an older woman. Well, perhaps, its a good thing.

3 SUNDAY

A cold ugly day. It was dark soon after 2. Spent it trying to write, and running from my room into the kitchen. I could not get really warm. The day felt endless. Read in the evening and in bed read with J. a good deal of poetry. If I lived alone I would be very dependant on poetry. Talked over the island idea with J. For me I know it has come too late. Wrote & posted Mother.

4 MONDAY

V.A.F.[5] Woke early and saw a snowy branch across the window. It is cold, snow has fallen & now it is thawing. The hedges & the trees are covered with beads of water. Very dark, too, with a wind somewhere. I long to be alone for a bit. I make a vow to finish a book this month. To write all day & at night too & get it finished, I swear. Told Jack who understood. But did not start that night for we were lovers & at 12 oclock I was dead tired and what Anatole calls 'sèche'. Dreamed of Lilian Shelleys legs.

5 TUESDAY

Saw the sun rise. A lovely apricot sky with flames in it and then a solemn pink. Heavens how beautiful! I heard a knocking & went downstairs. It was Benny cutting away the ivy. Over the grass lay the fallen nests - wisps of hay

---

[3]Samuel Solomonovich Koteliansky (1882–1955), 'Kot', a Russian Jew living in London, became an important friend whom KM felt she could trust. He and KM collaborated in translations of Russian writers into English, mainly Tchekov and Dostoevsky.

[4]Murry's note: 'A plan of making a settlement in some remote island. It was probably of the same order of seriousness as Coleridge's pantisocratic colony on the Susquehannah.' Lawrence called it 'Rananim'.

[5]'VAF' is presumably a private code in which the third initial refers to Francis.

& feather. He looked like an ivy bush himself. I made early tea & carried it up
to Jack who lay half awake with crinkled eyes. I feel so full of love today after
having seen the sun rise.

Eve. Have written a good deal. He is very near today. I suppose he has got my
letter for I keep thrilling to the thought of him.

### 6 WEDNESDAY

A LETTER, rather 2. We went to London. I took the letters. He has haunted
me all day. I have seen for him and with him all day long. As I went to
Piccadilly in the evening on top of a bus I nearly got up & called out his name.
I longed for him so, & yet I dare not push my thoughts as far as they will go.
Had my hair washed & hands done. Went to Hippodrome. The audience -
their heads & hands - were the only things worth watching. In the gloom
they seemed so remote, so infallible in movement. Went to Pantomime.
Very interesting. Began to think of Panto tradition. Would like to write in it.
Had my photo taken for him.

### 7 THURSDAY

Out with Jack in the morning. A wet day. Saw a cinema in the afternoon.
Tea with Kot. at the Russian Law Bureau. He was quiet & unhappy. He cut
his finger. There was something very desperate about him. Jack sat & plucked
his fingers. On the way home in the carriage he put his hand in my muff
& the other between us I started talking about Love. How sensible Jack was.
Yes I love Jack, but all the while my heart says Too late Too late. Adieu. I know
I shall go. I thought of him all day again. Mrs Hearn had made the house clean
and nice. Dreamed of Lesley.

### 8 FRIDAY

Had letter from Lesley. She has been ill. Worked a little this morning. Less this
afternoon (Oh God a train is passing) Will sit up all night & work. It is windy,
dark and soul-killing sunless weather. He is like poison in my blood. Jack and
I were lovers after supper in my room. I nearly 'cut across his line of male'[6] by
talking of Francis. After I worked & wasted time and went to bed wretched
with myself. It was terribly cold. Jack interrupted me all day with my work.
I did practically nothing. Wrote and sent a piece of my hair.

### 9 SATURDAY

Jack went to town. I worked a little - chased the fowls - one brown fowl
refused to leave the garden. Long after it knew there was no gap in the wire
netting it kept on running up and down. I must not forget all that, nor how
cold it was nor how the mud coated my thin shoes. In the evening
Lawrence & Kot. They talked plans but I felt very antagonistic to the whole
affair. After they had gone Jack & I lay in bed, deeply in love - strangely in
love. Everything made plain between us. It was very wonderful. We gave
each other our freedom in a strange way. I had such a longing to kiss Jack

---

[6] A phrase of Lawrence's.

and say Goodbye Love - I don't know why exactly. I pressed his cheek against
mine & he felt small & I felt an anguish of Love. Then I said suddenly
what are you thinking and he said I was thinking that you had gone away
& Campbell & Frieda came to tell me - & I was not a bit upset or surprised.
(When Lawrence mentioned F's name by chance tonight it cut me like
a knife.)

### 10 SUNDAY

Windy & dark. In the morning Frieda, suddenly. She had had a row with
Lawrence. She tired me to death. At night we went to L's leaving her here.
It was a warm night with big drops of rain falling. I didn't mind the going but
the coming back was rather awful.[7] I was not well & tired and my heart could
scarcely beat. But we made up a song to keep going. The rain splashed up to
my knees & I was frightened. L. was nice, very nice, sitting with the piece of
string [in] his hand, on true sex.

### 11 MONDAY

No letter. I had counted on one. I got up in the dark to be ready for my
little maid & watched the dawn coming. It wasn't up to much though.
I am wretched. It is a bright winking day. My God My God let me work.
Wasted   Wasted.[8]

### 12 TUESDAY

Quarrelled with J. in bed. A <u>letter</u> written in pencil, when he was wet to the
skin. I have sent an answer today, rather written it. Now I can get on. I am
determined to take a flat in Surrey Lodge. Have been in more of a state of
virtue today. Actually finished the story Brave Love and I don't know what to
think of it even now. Read it to Jack who was also puzzled. Violent headache
but rather happy.

### 13 WEDNESDAY

Sent it. From today Jack has got his own room. The coal has come. I set great
store by that. (So far my little maid is simply excellent.) A vile & misty day
with a cold wind.

### 14 THURSDAY

I had a letter from F asking me to come - the most wonderful letter he has
ever sent me. I carried it with me to London. I thought of nothing else all day
- it tired me out & refreshed me & then I was tired again. Saw Palliser[9] & saw
Gordon. The day was far too short. Bought Jack's banjo. Came home in the

---

[7]It was a three mile walk from Rose Tree Cottage, The Lee, near Great Missenden, to Lawrence's
cottage at Chesham.
[8]'Wasted Wasted'. Between these two words is a small ink sketch of a figure hanging on a crucifix.
[9]Charles Palliser, a New Zealand banker friend of KM's father, was then living in London. Some
three years later KM wrote to Anne Drey 'If you should meet a tall man with a pointed grey beard and a
voice like the sky at evening, salute him from me. His name is Charles Palliser, and he was a love of my salad
days.' (CLKM Volume I, p354.) He was also the father of Eileen Palliser with whom KM shared a room at
Queen's College.

carriage. I imagined he was with me. Yes, I was in love all the day long and in the night too & tired out. Jack kicked the banjo.

### 15 FRIDAY

Heard from Lesley and Lawrence. Today it was worse. A tremendous wind blew. The sky was like zinc. I tried to write to him but my letter broke the bounds of my letters & I couldnt. So I told Jack a little. In the evening we went to the Lawrences. Frieda was rather nice. I had a difficulty in not telling her so dreadful did I feel. Came home busy & tired with thought but could not work so went to bed immediately & dreamed of N.Z. Heard from Clayton[10] & Palliser.

### 16 SATURDAY

A letter. He has left Besancon. He had left the [...]. Oh, God, let me work today. Its all I beg. I must write today & post it. He has my money. Raining & pouring with wind as usual. A dreadful depressing day. My hands are like ice. (And now Jack has gone to Chesham & Rose has taken his letter to the post.) Now, Ah bliss, I am alone for a little. I can write. What shall I write. What is there to say. Just to somehow to tell him that I love him and that I am his for life. That is all there is to say. If I stop loving him before the year is out what shall I do with his book. I do not mean stop loving it. I mean if our love should be wounded and should die or be lost or taken prisoner. When I think of him at the front I am simply numb. It has no meaning for me at all. While we were waiting for tea Gordon came - we were glad. A moment when we were alone Gordon asked about him. Jack was in the kitchen cooking. I felt bitterly ashamed. Walked to Lawrences. They were horrible & witless and dull.

### 17 SUNDAY

Jack told me about Queenie. A fine day. Went for a walk & saw some plovers in a field. But the wind was dreadful. I could have walked a million miles. Yesterday I read Gordon Brave Love. He gave me an enormous kick about my work. Was far away from J all day with the other. At night we were lovers in his room. When I shut my eyes & leaned my cheek against his for a moment I dreamed. It was horrible. I felt I betrayed F & slept hardly at all.

### 18 MONDAY

MSS & letter from Cooks. It is morning and a new week. I have my work to do. I am very unhappy - life feels so poor. I tried to write, but it came scrappy and dreary. All day I was possessed by my hate of England. It is after him my one passion - a loathing for England. At night we took the fur rug down in front of the fire & I tried, quite vainly, to forget. I told Jack a lot about him. Jack was rather amused than otherwise. He said he'd have to tell Gordon!

### 19 TUESDAY

No letter - the morning a sheer waste. Got on slowly with Cinema, but badly. Sat on the divan & saw rather than wrote. Still it all was better. Lawrences to

---

[10]Douglas Clayton, a professional typist, was recommended to KM by Lawrence.

dinner. They came late. Jack made a currant pudding. Lawrence arrived cross but he gradually worked round to me. We talked of the war and its horrors. I have simply felt building in me my unhappy love and all to no purpose. Wrote to him just a little note. Jack was horrid at times. Letter from Mary[?].

### 20 WEDNESDAY

No letter. A man outside is breaking stones. The day is utterly quiet. Sometimes a leaf rustles and a strange puff of wind passes the window. The old man chops chops as though it were a heart beating out there. I waited for the post as of old today – but no letter. In the afternoon there came a violent storm, but we walked over to Cannans,[11] dined with them & the Lawrences & the Smiths & had a play after. Later we went to the L.s to sleep – very untidy – newspapers & faded mistletoe. I hardly slept at all, but it was nice.

### 21 THURSDAY

Proofs rec. & sent back. Letter Mr Polinson[?]. No letter. A stormy day. We walked back this morning. J. told me a dream. We quarrelled all the way home more or less. It has rained & snowed & hailed & the wind blows. The dog at the inn howls. A man is far away playing the bugle. I have read and sewed today but not written a word. I want to tonight. It is so funny to sit quietly sewing while my heart is never for a moment still. I am dreadfully tired in the head & body. This sad place is killing me. I live upon old, made up dreams, but they do not deceive either of us.

21st Jan. I am in the sitting room downstairs. The wind howls outside but here it is so warm & pleasant. It looks like a real room where real people have lived. My sewing basket is on the table, under the bookcase are poked J's old house shoes. The black chair, half in shadow, looks as though a happy person had sprawled there. We had roast mutton & onion sauce & baked rice for dinner. It <u>sounds</u> alright. I have run the ribbons through my underclothing with a hairpin in the good home way – but my anxious heart is eating up my body, eating up my nerves, eating up my brain, now slowly, now at tremendous speed. I feel this poison slowly filling my veins – every particle becoming slowly tainted. Yes love like this is a malady, a fever, a storm. It is almost like hate, one is so hot with it & never, never calm – never for an instant. I remember years ago saying I wish I were one of those happy people who can suffer <u>so far</u> & then collapse, or become exhausted – but I am just the opposite. The more I suffer the more of fiery energy I feel to bear it. Darling Darling!

### 22 FRIDAY

No letter. Weather worse than ever, culminating at teatime when I surprised myself by breaking down. I simply felt for a moment overcome with anguish & came upstairs & put my head on the black cushion. After that I deliberately drugged myself with Jack and made it the more bearable by talking french. In the evening read & pretended to write but did not write a line worth a 1d. Reread Jésus la Caille. My longing for cities engulfs me.

---

[11]Gilbert Cannan (1884–1955) was a novelist. His wife Mary was the ex-wife of Sir James Barrie.

23 SATURDAY

A LETTER.

No letter. The old man breaking stones is here again. A thick white mist reaches the edge of the field. I have spent hours waiting for the post. Jack went to Chesham. I did nothing. After tea Rose went out & came back with a letter and a photograph. I came up here & simply felt my whole body go out to him as if the sun had suddenly filled the room, warm and lovely. He called me 'ma petite cherie' – my little darling. Oh, God save me from this war and let us see each other soon. I talked with Jack, playing with the fringe of his lamp. But he refused to take it at all seriously. The dinner was good, the fire burned. The rain stopped. I sat after in the corner by the fire on a black pillow and dreamed. His photograph I put in the corner of the landscape picture, leaning against a wattle tree, his hands in his pockets.

24 SUNDAY

Washed my hair and worked and read a little. In the evening came the Smiths, a pleasant little pair, if only just something in him did not remind me of Bowden. Jack was nice to them. They were 10000000 of miles away. After J talked to me of the early days. Yes, it is all in the past. It was a rainy indefinite day, a silly shivery sort of day, not worth seeing.

26 TUESDAY

Went to London. We found Beatrice C. had arrived so Drey put us up. Drey's flat looked lovely to me. Had tea at the Criterion with Campbell & Drey. Had my hands done. In the evening went to the Oxford and saw Marie Lloyd who was very good. Slept on the big divan in Anne's Rooms. In the afternoon it was very foggy in London but the relief to be there was simply immense. Thought of Francis all day. He haunted me. Drey had a whig[?] bonnet

27 WEDNESDAY

To Chancery Lane with J. to the bank. Saw in the Strand a man in a blue coat who walked like F. Ever since, I cant get him out of my mind. Met a woman who'd been in the cinema with me – her old yellow teeth & pink roses in her hat & [...] lovely eyes & battered hair. I shall not forget her – no no. She was wonderful.[12] Kot for lunch at the Dieppe café among the singing canaries. Posted F. my photograph. Had supper with Kot and went to Pavillion after. Mlle Devanter[?] sang. She is very good.

28 THURSDAY

A LETTER. He is as wretched as I. I wrote and posted to him at this new address. I read & reread the letter until it was all crumpled. Bridget[13] half ate it in her mouth. I loved her for that. She is the only person who has come anywhere near us just like that. I sat on the sofa & watched her little hands

---

[12]Murry's note: 'She was probably the original of Miss Moss in "Pictures". In 1913 K had acted as a super in a few cinematograph productions.'

[13]Hon Beatrice Columbine (Brigid), daughter of Gordon and Beatrice Campbell (Lord and Lady Glenavy) was born on 25 June 1914, and so would have been eight months old at this time.

crunching the letter and felt she understood all about us and found us delicious! Went to dinner and to the Chelsea Palace.

### 29 FRIDAY

A cold day. Still at Dreys. Looked for rooms all the morning but found none. Lunched with Jack and then met Drey and went to Curtis Brown. He was nice but I feel so extremely ugly that I couldn't even be intelligent. But I like him and the woman there too. Campbells again. <u>Dadda</u> <u>Hallo</u>. Saw Koteliansky at the station. He was very nice. I rather cling to him. He brought me a skirt and some cigarettes & some chocolates. Home[?] was[?] house with fire and a drive in milky moonlight.

### 31 SUNDAY

Jack rode over to Marys to get my work. I read all day. I felt rather ill. It came on to rain in the evening and the wind was furious. We talked of London. Jack understands that I want to live there and apart from him. It is time. I felt quite impotent to write all day and I read and smoked, feeling ill physically a bit and dreadfully ugly. I shall not speak of him.

### FEBRUARY 1 – MONDAY

No letter. I had expected one. A slight attack of flue is bowling me over. There is a glimpse of sun - the trees look as though they were hanging out to dry. My cold gained on me all day. I read the Lonely [?] Nietzsche but I felt a bit ashamed of my feelings for this man in the past. He's, if you like, "human all too human". Read until late. Felt wretched simply beyond words. Life was like sawdust and sand. Talked short stories to Jack.

### 2 TUESDAY

V.A.F.
A Letter. He is very unhappy. His letter did not bring us nearer, but I feel a bit more cheerful today because I dont look quite so revolting as I have done. No the day ended in being as bad as ever. For one thing my illness is really severe & I am worried beyond endurance by the length of time that letters take and by the silence. I have been embroidering my kimono with black wool. Bah! What rot! What do I care for such rubbish. Francis Francis I cannot stand the war any longer.

### 3 WEDNESDAY

A cold day with a strong wind. I can do nothing. Have tidied my desk and drunk some quinine and that is all. But I know I shall go because otherwise I'll die of despair. My head is so hot but my hands are cold. Perhaps I am <u>dead</u> & just pretending to live here. There is at any rate no sign of life in me. I cant write to him either. I want another, a warmer letter.

### 4 THURSDAY

A.M. Today the sun began to shine & my cold is better - only my cough remains. Gilbert & Mary came to tea and supper. Mary looked very sweet but we were dull. Rose did everything very well. I sent her in the afternoon to beg a letter for me from the post but none came. I felt anxious all yesterday for a letter. Finished C[rime] & P[unishment]. Very bad I thought it too.

5 FRIDAY

A LETTER. It is morning. The men[?] are plunging[?] through the green hills. Far away a dog barks. Its still & clear. And a little photograph - very like. God I am happy!! Now to read it again.

6 SATURDAY

Today I had an urgent letter. He had just got my photograph - and he wants me to come immediately. This is going to be a very difficult business I can see that.

15 MONDAY

Went to London with Jack.

16 TUESDAY

Came to Paris.

19 FRIDAY

Came to Gray.[14]
<u>One night</u>.     [J64-74]

20 SATURDAY

I am waiting for my déjeuner. Beside me on a chair is a thick leather belt and his sword. He left at nearly eight oclock. I am just up. It is a quite clear day: my heart feels rather heavy. Ive got a feeling about this prison business which frightens me. I cant bear to think of him in prison - and another feeling, very profound, that he does not love me at all. I find him wonderful. I don't really love him now I know him, but he is so rich and so careless - that I love. We spent a queer night. The room - the room. The little lamp, the wooden ceiling, the bouquets of pink daisies that unfolded at dawn, the picture of the man bringing the rabbit. And F. quite naked making up the fire with a tiny brass poker - so natural and so beautiful. F. again dressing - en petit soldat - his shirt, knickers, socks, little tie, jersey, black puttees, jacket. Washing & brushing his hair with my ivory hair brush, & then just for a moment I saw him passing the window - & then he was gone. That is a terrible moment for a woman.     [J75]

> I seem to have just escaped the prison cell, Jaggle[15] dearest, because I find this place is in the zone of the armies, and therefore forbidden to women. However, my Aunt's illness pulled me through. I had some really awful moments. Outside the station he was waiting. He merely <u>sang</u> (so typical) "Follow me but not as though you were doing so" until we came to a tiny toll house by the river against which leant a faded cab. But once fed with my suitcase and our two selves it dashed off like the wind - the door opening and shutting to his horror as he is not allowed in cabs.

---

[14]Gray, in the Zone of the Armies, in France, was where Francis Carco was stationed and where KM travelled to meet him.

[15]'Jaggle' was one of KM's diminutives for Jack.

We drove to a village nearby, to a large white house where he had taken a room for me - a most extraordinary room furnished with a bed, a wax apple and an immense flowery clock. It's very hot. The sun streams through the blind. The garden outside is full of wallflowers and blue enamel saucepans. It would make you laugh, too.

---

England is like a dream. I am sitting at the window of a little square room, furnished with a bed, a wax apple and an immense flowery clock. Outside the window there is a garden full of wallflowers and blue enamel saucepans. The clocks are striking five and the last rays of sun pour under the swinging blind. It is very hot - the kind of heat that makes one cheek burn in infancy. But I am so happy I must just send you a word on a spare page of my diary, dear. I have had some dreadful adventures on my way here because the place is within the zone of the armies and not allowed to women. The last old pa-man who saw my passport, 'M. le Colonel' - very grand with a black tea cosy and gold tassel on his head and smoking what lady novelists call a 'heavy Egyptian cigarette' nearly sent me back. But Frieda, its such wonderful country - all rivers and woods and large birds that look blue in the sunlight. I keep thinking of you and Lawrence. The French soldiers are 'pour rire'. Even when they are wounded they seem to lean out of their sheds and wave their bandages at the train. But I saw some prisoners today - not at all funny - Oh I have so much to tell you. I had better not begin. We shall see each other again some day, won't we, darling. 'Voila le petit soldat joyeaux et jeune' he has been delivering letters. It is hot as summer - one only sits and laughs.

> Your loving
> Katherine.

The curious thing was that I could not concentrate on the end of the journey. I simply felt so happy that I leaned out of the window with my arms along the brass rail & my feet crossed and watched the sunlight and the wonderful country unfolding. At Chateaudun where we had to change I went to the buffet to drink. A big pale green room with a large stove jutting out and a buffet with coloured bottles. Two women, their arms folded, leaned against the counter. A little boy very pale running from table to table taking the orders. It was full of soldiers sitting back in their chairs swinging their legs & eating. The sun shone through the windows. The little boy poured me out a glass of horrible black coffee. He served the soldiers with a kind of dreary contempt. In the porch an old man arrived with a panier of brown spotted fish. Large fish - like the fish one sees in glass cases swim through forests of beautiful pressed seaweed. The soldiers laughed and slapped each other. They tramped about in their heavy boots. The women looked after them & the old man stood humbly waiting for someone to attend to him, his cap in his hands - as though he knew that the life he represented in his torn jacket with his

basket of fish – his peaceful occupation – did not exist any more & had no
right to thrust itself here.

The last moments of the journey I was very frightened. We arrived at
Gray & one by one like women going in to see a doctor we slipped through
the door into a hot room completely filled with 2 tables & two colonels, like
colonels in comic opera. Big shiny grey whiskered men with a touch of burnt
red in the cheeks, both smoking, one a cigarette with a long curly ash hanging
from it. He had a ring on his finger. Sumptuous & omnipotent he looked.
I shut my teeth. I kept my fingers from trembling as I handed the passport
& the ticket. It wont do, it wont do at all, said my colonel, & looked at me for
what seemed a long time in silence. His eyes were like 2 little grey stones.
He took my passport to the other colonel who dismissed his objection,
stamped it & let me go. I nearly knelt on the floor. By the station stood
F. terribly pale. He saluted, smiled, and said turn to the right & follow me as
though you were not following. How fast he went towards the suspension
bridge. He had a postmans bag on his back and a paper parcel. The street was
very muddy. In the toll house by the bridge a scraggy woman, her hands
wrapped in a shawl, peered out at us & against the toll house leaned a very
faded cab. Montez vite vite, said F. He threw my suitcase, his letter bag, the
parcel & the rack on the floor. The driver swung into activity, lashed the bony
horse & we tore away, both doors flapping & banging. Bonjour ma cherie said
F. and we kissed one each very quickly & then clutched at the banging doors.
They would not keep shut & F. who is not supposed to ride in cabs had to try
to hide. Soldiers passed all the time. At the barracks we stopped a moment
& a crowd of faces blocked the window. Prends ca mon vieux said F. handing
over the paper parcel. Off we flew again. By a river, down a long strange
white street with houses on either side very gay & bright in the late sunlight
F. put his arm round me. I know you will like the house. Its quite white
& so is the room, & the people are. At last we arrived. The woman of the
house with a serious baby in her arms came to the door. It is alright.
Yes alright. Bonjour Madame. It was like an elopement. We went into a room
on the ground floor & the door was shut. Down went the suitcase the letter
bag the rack again. Laughing & trembling we pressed against each other a long
long kiss – interrupted by a clock on the wall striking five. He lit the fire.
We sighed together a little, but always laughing. The whole affair seemed
somehow so ridiculous and at the same time so utterly natural. There was
nothing to do but laugh.

Then he left me for a moment. I brushed my hair and washed & was
ready when he came back to go out to dinner. To dinner. The wounded were
coming down the hill. They were all bandaged up. One man looked as though
he had 2 red carnations over his ears, one man as though his hand was covered
in black sealing wax. F. talked & talked & talked. When I was little I thought
this sin was the most terrible thing in the world but now it is quite pale.
The restaurant nearby, the soldier with the strange eyes. We ordered sausages
& cotelettes and fried potatoes. The [...] at the little <u>Vive la Belgique</u> shop.

Then the long lazy dinner. I hardly said a word. When we came out stars were shining, through wispy clouds, and a moon hung like a candle flame over the ponte church spire. There was a fire in our room and a tiny lamp on the table. The fire flickered on the white wood ceiling. It was as though we were on a boat. We talked in whispers overcome by this discreet little lamp. In the most natural manner we slowly undressed by the stove. F. swung into the bed. Is it cold, I said. "No, not at all cold. Viens ma bebe, dont be frightened. The waves are quite small." His laughing face & his pretty hair, one hand with a bangle over the sheets,he looked like a girl. But seeing his puttees, his thin black tie & the feel of his flannelette shirt - & the sword, the big ugly sword, but not between us, lying in a chair.

The act of love seemed somehow quite incidental, we talked so much. It was so warm & delicious lying curled in each others arms, by the light of the tiny lamp le fils de Maeterlinck, only the clock & the fire to be heard. A whole life passed in the night: other people other things, but we lay like 2 old people coughing faintly under the eiderdown, and laughing at each other and away we went to India, to South America, to Marseilles in the white boat & then we talked of Paris & sometimes I lost him in a crowd of people & it was dark & frightening, & then he was in my arms again & we were kissing. (Here he is. I know his steps.)

I remember how he talked of the sea in his childhood, how clear it was: how he used to lean over the pier & watch it & the fish and shells gleaming[16] - and then his story 'Le lapin blanc'. At last the day came & birds sang & again I saw the pink marguerites on the wall. He was tres paresseux. He lay on his stomach & would not get up. Even at my 1.2.3 and then he shivered & felt ill and had fever and a sore throat and shivers. All the same he washed scrupulously and dressed & finally I had the blue & red vision again over mon bébé - & then a blurred impression of him through the blind. I did not feel happy again until I had been to the cabinet and seen the immense ridiculous rabbits. By the time he came at 12.30 I felt awfully happy. We went off to lunch at the same little restaurant & had eggs we dipped the bread in & peas and oranges. The soldiers there. The garden full of empty bottles. Saw the little boy - the same boy who had smoked the long cigarette the night before. (It is just struck three. He cannot be here before five.)

<u>18 March</u>. Came to Paris again.

<u>19 March</u>. In Paris.

<u>24 March</u>. Kick off.    [J75-79]

Cet heros aux cheveux longs qui des heures entieres, gratte avec son canne dans le sable, or, ayant besoin de vivre crache un peu de sang, et avec un long regard larmoyant mais satisfié ecrit le mot finis sur le meme sable gratté.

[J79 s20]

---

[16]Francis Carco (1886–1958) was born in Noumea, New Caledonia.

# Unbound Papers

[MS-Papers-4006–03]

I did not tell you that I dreamed all night of Rupert Brooke.[17] And today as
I left the house he was standing at the door, with a rucksack on his back & his
broad hat shading his face. So after I had posted your letter I did not go home.
I went a long very idle sort of amble along the quais. It was exquisitely hot -
white clouds lay upon the sky like sheets spread out to dry. In the big
sandheaps down by the river children had hollowed out tunnels and caverns.
They sat in them stolid and content, their hair glistening in the sun. Now and
then a man lay stretched on his face, his head in his arms. The river was full of
big silver stars, the trees shook faintly, glinting with light, and I found
delightful places - little squares with white square houses - quite hollow they
looked with the windows gaping open. Narrow streets arched over with
chestnut boughs - or perhaps quite deserted with a clock tower showing over
the roofs. The sun put a spell on everything. I crossed and recrossed the river
& leaned over the bridges & kept thinking we were coming to a Park when
we weren't. You cannot think what pleasure my invisible, imaginary
companion gave me. If he had been alive it would never have possibly
occurred, but - its a game I like to play - to walk and to talk with the dead
who smile and are silent - and <u>free</u> quite finally free. When I lived alone
I would often come home, put my key in the door, & find someone there
waiting for me. "Hallo! have you been here long?" I suppose that sounds
dreadful rubbish to you.

    I am sitting on a broad bench in the sun hard by Notre Dame. In front
of me theres a hedge of ivy. An old man walks along with a basket on his arm
pinching off the withered leaves. In the priests garden they are cutting the
grass. I love this big cathedral. The little view I have of it now is of pointed
narrow spires, fretted against the blue, and one or two squatting stone parrots
balanced on a little balcony. It is like a pen drawing by a Bogey. And I like the
Saints with their crowns on their collars and their heads in their hands.

---

[17]As a heading to this piece KM has written 'Paris Xmas 1914'. Murry has crossed this out and
written under it 'May 1915'. In fact, the piece was clearly written after Rupert Brooke's death which
occurred on April 23 1915.

Like the old saints in some cathedral, decoupé but with their crowns hanging over their collars.      [J79-80 s20]

[MS-Papers-4006–03]

… England that I wrote twice I should return on Tuesday. I nearly told the concierge – I was half ready. Today it does not seem to matter. Perhaps the fact that Jack never says once that he longs for me, is desolate without me, never calls me – He has been to me the being that in a solitary world held my hand, and I his, was real among shadows. And ready to laugh and to run, but tonight he is <u>not quite so real</u>. Pour sûr he is very well without me. My impatience et mon douleur must seem exaggerated to him. Shall I go back? It depends entirely on him. I will not write so often or so much. I have been a little absurd. (This old habit of 'jotting' has come back.)      [J82 s20]

Yes I am a widow, said Miss Edith Barnet sadly laying down the P.D.M. [Paris Daily Mail] My husband died just one month before my little one came.

Evening.[18]
<u>October 1915</u> they are walking up and down the garden in Acacia Road. It is dusky; the michaelmas daisies are bright as feathers. From the old fruit-tree at the bottom of the garden – the slender tree rather like a poplar – there falls a little round pear, hard as a stone. Did you hear that, Katie? Can you find it?
By Jove – that familiar sound. Their hands move over the thin moist grass.
He picks it up, and, unconsciously, as of old, polishes it on his handkerchief.
Do you remember the enormous number of pears there used to be on
that old tree.
Down by the violet bed.
And how after there'd been a southerly buster we used to go out with clothes baskets to pick them up.
And how while we stooped they went on falling, bouncing on our backs & heads. And how far they used to be scattered – ever so far, under the violet leaves, down the steps, right down to the Lily Lawn we used to find them trodden in the grass. And how soon the ants got to them – I can see now that little round hole with a sort of fringe of brown pepper round it.
Do you know I've never seen pears like them since.
They were so bright – canary yellow, & small. And the peel was so thin and the pips jet – jet black.
First you pulled out the little stem & sucked it. It was faintly sour & then you ate them always from the top – core & all.
The pips were delicious.
Do you remember sitting on the pink garden seat.
I shall never forget that pink garden seat. It is the only garden seat for me.
Where is it now. Do you think we shall be allowed to sit in it in Heaven.

---

[18]The following passage was written in the month of the death of KM's brother, Leslie Heron Beauchamp.

It always wobbled a bit & there was usually the marks of a snail on it.
Sitting on that seat, swinging our legs & eating the pears.
But isnt it extraordinary how <u>deep</u> our happiness was - how positive - deep,
shining, warm. I remember the way we used to look at each other & smile -
do you? Sharing a secret - what was it?
I think it was the family feeling. We were almost like one child. I always see
us walking about together, looking at things together with the same eyes,
discussing. I felt that again - just now - when we looked for the pear in the
grass.
I remembered ruffling the violet leaves with you. Oh that garden!
Do you remember that some of the pears we found used to have little teeth
marks in them.
Yes.
Who bit them.
It was always a mystery.
He puts his arm round her. They pace up and down. A thin round moon
shines over the pear tree & the ivy walls of the garden glitter like metal.
The air smells chill, heavy, very cold.
We shall go back there one day, when its all over.
We'll go back together.
And find everything.
Everything.
She leans against his shoulder. The moonlight deepens. Now they are facing
the back of the house. A square of light shows in a window.
Give me your hand. You know I shall always be a stranger here.
Yes, darling, I know.
Walk up & down once more & then we'll go in.
Its so curious - my absolute confidence that I'll come back. I feel its as certain
as this pear.
I feel that too.
I couldn't not come back, you know that feeling. Its awfully mysterious.
Their shadows on the grass are long & strange. A puff of strange wind whispers
in the ivy and the old moon touches them with silver. She shivers.
You're cold.
Dreadfully cold.
He puts his arm round her. Suddenly he kisses her.
Goodbye darling.
Ah why do you say that!
Darling goodbye - goodbye - - -     [J83-85]

October 29th 1915:
Awake awake! my little boy.
A misty, misty evening. I want to write down the fact that not only am I not
afraid of death - I welcome the idea of death. I believe in immortality because
he is not here, and I long to join him. First, my darling, Ive got things to do
for both of us and then I will come as quickly as I can to you. Dearest heart,

I know you are there and I live with you - and I will write for you. Other people are near, but they are not close to me - to you only do I belong just as <u>you</u> belong to me. Nobody knows how often I am with you. Indeed I am always with you and I begin to feel that <u>you</u> know - that when I leave this house and this place it will be with you & I will never even for the shortest space of time be away from you again. You know I can never be Jack's lover again. You have me, you're in my flesh as well as in my soul. I give Jack my 'surplus' love but to you I hold and to you I give my deepest love. Jack is no more than - - - anybody might be.      [J85-86]

Brother.
I think I have known for a long time that life was over for me, but I never realised it or acknowledged it until my brother died. Yes, though he is lying in the middle of a little wood in France and I am still walking upright, and feeling the sun and the wind from the sea, I am just as much dead as he is. The present and the future mean nothing to me: I am no longer 'curious' about people; I do not wish to go anywhere and the only possible value that anything can have for me is that it should put me in mind of something that happened or was when we were alive.

'Do you remember, Katie?' I hear his voice in trees and flowers, in scents and light and shadow. Have people, apart from those far away people, ever existed for me? Or have they always failed me, and faded because I denied them reality? Supposing I were to die, as I sit at this table, playing with my indian paper knife - what would be the difference. No difference at all. Then why don't I commit suicide? Because I feel I have a duty to perform to the lovely time when we were both alive. I want to write about it and he wanted me to. We talked it over in my little top room in London. I said: I will just put on the front page: To my brother - Leslie Heron Beauchamp. Very well: it shall be done.

The wind died down at sunset. Half a ring of moon hangs in the hollow air. It is very quiet. Somewhere I can hear a woman crooning a song. Perhaps she is crouched before the stove in the corridor, for it is the kind of song that a woman sings before a fire - brooding, warm, sleepy and safe. I see a little house with flower patches under the windows and the soft mass of a haystack at the back. The fowls have all gone to roost - they are wooly blurs on the perches. The pony is in the stable with a cloth on. The dog lies in his kennel, his head on his forepaws. The cat sits up beside the woman, her tail tucked in and the man, still young and careless comes clinking up the dark road. Suddenly a spot of light shows in the window and in the pansy bed below & he walks quicker, whistling.

But where are these comely people? These young strong people with hard healthy bodies and curling hair. They are not saints or philosophers. They are decent human beings - but where <u>are</u> <u>they</u>?

Sunday: 10 minutes past 4. I am sure that this Sunday is the worst Sunday of all my life. Ive touched bottom. Even my heart doesn't beat any longer. I only keep alive by a kind of buzz of blood in my veins. Now the dark is coming back again – only at the windows there is a white glare. My watch ticks loudly and strongly on the bed table, as though it were rich with minute life while I faint – I die.

It is evening again. the sea runs very high. It frets, sweeps up and over, hangs, leaps upon the rocks. In the sharp metallic light the rocks have a reddish tinge, above them a broad band of green mixed with a rich sooty black, above it the cone of a violet mountain, above the mountain a light blue sky shining like the inside of a wet sea shell. Every moment the light changes. Even as I write it is no longer hard. Some small white clouds top the mountain like tossed up smoke. And now a purple colour, very menacing and awful is pulling over the sky. The trees tumble about in the unsteady light. A dog barks. The gardener, talking to himself, shuffles across the new raked paths, picks up his weed basket and goes off. Two lovers are walking together by the edge of the sea. They are muffled up in coats. She has a red handkerchief on her head. They walk, very proud and careless, hugging each other and bearing the wind.

I am ill today. I cannot walk at all & in pain.

Wednesday. Today I am hardening my heart. I am walking all round my heart and building up the defences. I do not mean to leave a loophole even for a tuft of violets to grow in. Give me a hard heart, oh Lord. Lord harden thou my heart.

This morning I could walk a little. So I went to the Post office. It was bright with sun. The palm trees stood up in the air, crisp and shining. The blue gums hung heavy with sun as is their wont. When I reached the road I heard a singing. A funny thought . . 'the english have come'– but of course it was not they.    [J89-91]

Et in Arcadia ego.[19]

To sit in front of the little wood fire, your hands crossed in your lap and your eyes closed. To fancy you see again upon your eyelids all the dancing beauty of the day, to feel the flame on your throat as you used to imagine you felt the spot of yellow when Bogey[20] held a buttercup under your chin . . . When breathing is such delight that you are almost afraid to breathe – as though a butterfly fanned its wings upon your breast. Still to taste the warm sunlight that melted in your mouth, still to smell the white waxy scent that lay upon the jonquil fields and the wild spicy scent of the rosemary growing in little tufts among the red rocks close to the brim of the sea . . .

The moon is rising but the reluctant day lingers upon the sea and sky. The sea is dabbled with a pink the colour of unripe cherries, and in the sky there is a flying yellow light like the wings of canaries. Very stubborn and solid

---

[19]Murry's note pencilled beside this title: 'Bandol Dec.24 1915. See Letters'.
[20]'Bogey' was a nickname for KM's brother when they were children. Later she used it as a nickname for Jack.

are the trunks of the palm trees. Springing from their tops the stiff green bouquets seem to cut into the evening air and, among them, the blue gum trees, tall and slender with sickle shaped leaves and drooping branches half blue, half violet. The moon is just over the mountain behind the village. The dogs know she is there; already they begin to howl and bark. The fishermen are shouting and whistling to one another as they bring in their boats; some young boys are singing in half-broken voices down by the shore, and there is a noise of children crying, little children with burnt cheeks and sand between their toes being carried home to bed.

I am tired, blissfully tired. Do you suppose that daisies feel blissfully tired when they shut for the night and the dews descend upon them?     [J92-93]

This afternoon I did not go for a walk. There is a long stone embankment that goes out to the sea. Huge stones on either side and a little rough goat path in the centre. When I came to the end the sun was going down so, feeling extremely solitary and romantic, I sat me down upon a stone & watched the red sun which looked horribly like a morsel of tinned apricot sink into a sea like a huge junket. I began, feebly, but certainly perceptibly, to harp 'Alone between sea & sky etc.' But suddenly I saw a minute speck on the bar coming towards me. It grew, it granded. It turned into a young officer in dark blue, slim, with an olive skin, fine eyebrows, long black eyes, a fine silky moustache.
You are alone, M.
Alone M.
You are living at the hotel, M.
At the hotel, M.
Ah, I have noticed you walking alone several times.
It is possible M.
He blushed & put his hand to his cap.
I am very indiscreet, M.
Very indiscreet, M.     [J91-92]

[MS-Papers-4006-03]

Unfinished.
### The Dark Hollow.
"You're a sweet creature, aren't you," said Nina, getting on to a chair so that she could see her waist in front and behind in the little mirror. "What are you staring at the ceiling for? Money wont fall through the ceiling on to the quilt, you know." She got off the chair and suddenly such a flame of rage leapt up in her that she trembled all over. "And you bloody well won't milk me any longer" she muttered. He did not move even his eyes. "Ive done with you." She jerked open a drawer and grubbing among the bits of finery for a little black lace veil - "done with you," she repeated. Just as she was going out of the door there came a sort of chuckle from the bed. "Toodle-oo!" said the voice. She flounced round and tossed her head. "What's that? What's that you say." But he was staring at the ceiling again. She turned to go and the chuckle was

repeated. "Toodle-oo!" mocked the voice. Her knees trembled so horribly that she could hardly walk down the five flights of dark winding stairs.

It was dusk in the streets and a fine misty rain was falling. The lights from the cafés and street lamps showed like great blurred splodges of blue and yellow. The traffic trailed up and down the greasy road and people, muffled up to the eyes, passed and repassed Nina, all going quickly to - somewhere or other. She too walked quickly, copying them, pretending. It was very cold. She felt the rain on her face and hands and then on her shoulders and knees. "And I havent even an umbrella!" Good God, that seemed the last straw. Not even an umbrella! She walked faster still, holding her handkerchief up to her lips. Where she was going to or what she was going to do she had not the slightest idea. She would walk until she was tired and then - her thoughts dropped into a dark hollow. But a faint voice came from the hollow. "This has happened to you before and will happen again and again and again." Oh, how tired she was! "I wonder <u>where</u> I am." She stopped under the awning of a flowershop and peered into the road. But how could she tell. "Its a street, ma cherie, and thats all there is to be said for it." With a faint smile on her lips she turned and looked in at the flowershop window. As she watched an arm was thrust among the flowers and a hand hovered over some bunches of violets, closing finally on the very smallest. "Someone's busting the bank. I wouldn't mind betting you the money I haven't got - thats a woman." She was quite silly with tiredness. "Right, of course!" At that moment a girl came to the shop door with the violets tucked in her jacket and stood fumbling with the catch of her umbrella. Nina's eyes widened. She moved nearer, staring. Was it? . . it couldnt be . . yes it was! "Louise!" she cried. "Nina!" cried the girl in a charming happy voice. "How extraordinary! Is it really Nina?" "Yes, really" and Nina nodded, her eyes very big and black behind the lace veil. "But," said Louise, "are you living here? Where are you going to, now?" She wanted to answer "Nowhere in particular" but somehow her voice had gone and she could only point to her throat with a strange, quivering smile. "What's the matter? Are you ill?" She managed to whisper "A little bit tired" and Louise saw big bright tears falling down her cheeks. "Come home with me," she said quickly. "Come home with me, now. I live quite close here." She put her arm round Nina. "Child, you're wet through. Dont tremble so, you poor little thing. Its just down this road and across the court - in here." She half carried Nina up the stairs to the door of her flat. At the door Nina held back a moment. "Is there anybody . ." "No", said Louise, "no, dear, you needn't see anybody. Come," and she opened a door at the end of a narrow passage into a room half alight with an open fire. "Take off your things while I go and get the lamp," said Louise. But Nina crouched down by the fire and her weeping changed to sobbing, to a dreadful half sobbing half coughing that she could not stop. Without a word Louise knelt down. She took off Nina's hat, raised her a little and pulled off the wet jacket. She slipped down beside her and took Nina's dark head on her lap and stroked her hair and her cheeks with firm, loving fingers. Ah! How good that felt! Her sobbing changed to long sighs and finally she lay still with her eyes shut, her head pressed against Louise. "And she doesn't even wear a corset. Quel courage!" thought Nina.

"Now you're better aren't you. Are you feeling warmer?" said the kind, charming voice. Nina nodded and under her sleepy content her brain began to be busy with . . what to tell Louise. She sat up, half opened her eyes and smiled shyly. "I'm dreadfully ashamed" she said. Louise got up and leaned against the mantelpiece & looked at the fire. "Dont bother to apologise" she said, "and don't bother to explain. You'd only - make up a story - you know, and neither of us would be any the wiser." "Oh no" said Nina, "no I shouldn't, not to you. Why should I make up stories to you? But there's nothing to tell," she said - nothing. Louise put out her foot and kicked a piece of wood into sparks. In the quiet they heard the rain threshing against the window. "What I mean is," said Nina, "there's no sort of a story." Louise was still silent and unseen by her Nina made a little grimace. "She thinks it will do me good to get it off my mind," she thought, slyly. "Louise," she put her hand lightly on the other's arm. "Let me tell you." Louise nodded but did not look up.

"Well, you know, after I left school," said Nina, speaking in a low rapid voice, "I hadn't any home to go to - you remember I never really knew who my people were - someone paid for me, c'était tout. And - you heard, didn't you? - I went on the stage."

"Yes, I heard that," said Louise.

"I had - pretty good luck at first" said Nina, "but then I got ill and my voice went - and - a hard time came," she said. "And then you know out of pure cowardice - yes really - I couldn't fight any more and I hadn't the courage to - I married." Louise turned her grave glance to her. "I didn't love him a bit" said Nina, shaking her head, "just because I was afraid." "Alright. I understand" said Louise. Nina looked away from her - her voice hardened. "And then - oh well it served me right - he was a brute and my" she just hesitated a second, "my baby died and I left him." "Ah," whispered Louise. "And I went on the stage again, and worked and had a bigger fight than before, because - I was - lonely in a different way - until -" She walked right away from Louise & over to the window and lifted the curtain & looked out - "until now," she said and laughed shortly. "How do you mean?" said Louise. "Oh, my dear," said Nina, very flippant "I've been out of work six weeks - I've not got a sou. I'm so tired that the agents won't look at me and now this afternoon the crisis came. The landlady told me she'd let my room. She kept all the clothes I had left to pay for my rent, and turned me out with one shilling which I gave to the poor little chambermaid as I walked down the stairs. Pretty - isn't it?" and she looked out into the rainy court. "Mon Dieu! have I overdone it," she thought. "Was the shilling a mistake?" Said Louise, very thoughtfully "I say Nina, how old are you?" "Twenty two" said Nina. "Why?" "Well, you left school when you were sixteen and you've been married to a beast and had a baby and been earning your living for six years. Not exactly gay, is it?" Thank God she had believed it all.

"No I don't suppose it is" said Nina.
Another pause.

"Well, what are you going to do now" said Louise, and she came up to Nina & put her hand on the back of Nina's neck and ruffled up her short black hair. "Stay with us for a while, will you," she said, "and see how things turn out. Us is I and a man called David Field. We've been living together for the last three years." She was very cool. "But - but how can I" said Nina. "I don't believe you realise Louise. I haven't anything at all. No clothes" she said, "no money. I'm just as I am. I might be a kitten." "Yes I do realise that" said Louise, "and I can quite understand you don't want to be a charity child. Well you needn't. But I've got a little money put by - there's a tiny room here with a campbed in it and you can pay me back whatever you cost me when you're in luck again. That's simple enough. Its no good being sentimental when one is really in a tight place - is it? And, quite apart from that" said Louise, "I'd like to have you. I think you've had a rotten time. I'd like to feed you up and make you happy and spoil you and turn you into the old Nina again." "But Mr ..." Nina hesitated. "Oh, David?" laughed Louise, "David's alright. Don't bother about him. Tell me what you want to do." Nina said, very frankly, looking straight into Louise's eyes "I want to stay. You know I'll pay you back. Yes I want to stay." "Good" said Louise, "I'm glad. Now we needn't talk about it again. Come away from that rainy window. I don't know what you feel like but I want some tea." "Oh, look" said Nina tragically, "look at my dress." Her little dark blue silk frock was stained with black patches of rain. "Take it off" said Louise. "I'll go and find you something to put on. Bother!" She looked at Nina standing in her short petticoat by the fire. "I'm too staid for you. You're such a little beauty. You are a lovely little being." "Oh," Nina protested. "I'd like to wrap you up in David's chinese silk portière. Well - wait - I'll find you something."

## II

They were spreading over the camp bed a red and white indian cover when they heard the front door open and steps in the hall. "That's David" whispered Louise, smiling. "Stay here while I go and explain - you don't mind?"
"Of course not." Nina curled up on the bed. She heard voices. "Hallo Davy." "Hallo Lou. Hasn't it been a rotten day." "Yes, there's a lovely fire in your room." "Good, come on in and talk." Then the sound of a door shutting. Quiet as a little cat crouched Nina. She scarcely seemed to breathe but her eyes were busy, taking in every detail of her room - the low chair with its pretty striped pillows, the gold paper screen hiding the washstand, the black chest of drawers covered with a strip of indian embroidery, the books, the long blue curtains drawn across the window. A lamp stood on the table by the bed. It had a green shade with tiny red apples painted on it, and she looked at her hands lying small and rosy in the ring of soft light. "I must come of a good stock," she decided. "My wrists and my ankles are so fine." A mysterious sense of wellbeing filled her. It did not matter how long this lasted. At any rate for the time she had dropped out of her own world and all its beastliness, and that

was enough. Never look to the future or you will find the future is looking at
you. The funny thing was that Louise had believed her story - had taken it all
so simply and naturally that Nina began to have a faint feeling that it was true.
She saw herself, little and brave, going to agent after agent. Quite plainly she
saw the brute of a husband. There wasn't any difficulty in imagining him -
but even the baby was there, pale, with big solemn eyes, lying across her lap.
"But the crying. I did not put that on. No, I could not help that. How I
sobbed!" she thought admiringly, and yawned and stretched herself thinking
of nothing at all until Louise called "Come and show yourself, Nina."

### III

David sat down at the piano and struck a succession of quick light chords.
He looked at Louise. "What shall I play?" he said, half petulantly, in the voice
of a spoilt child. "Play the Sibelius Sonata." "Do you want that?" She nodded,
and he smiled at her, and began to play. Louise lay back in her chair, her arms
stretched along the sides and her hands drooping. In the dim light her face
with half shut eyes was like a beautiful soft mask. But although she wanted to
listen to David her thoughts would not attend her wishes. They beckoned her
with strange sweet smiles to half remembered places. She was very lovely lying
and listening, but - I am happy. I am at peace with myself. I am safe. In the
very way she breathed one could tell that of Louise. "It is love" thought Nina.
Of course it is love that gives her that air. But what sort of love? What can
there be in that conceited boy to keep one satisfied three years. She doesn't
mother him and no he's not the grand bébé type. Is Louise frightfully
passionate? Do those two when they are alone - oh no, it isn't possible.
And besides Louise has not the chic and the uncertainty for a really great affair.
I do not understand them at all - at all - thought Nina, half angry, folding
herself up in a corner of the sofa. David had come to the second movement -
the slow movement that is based on a folk-song and is so sad and so lovely.
His proud head was tilted back a little the better to listen      [s28-37]

[MS-Papers-4006-04]

### Afternoon in Spring

It is raining. Big soft drops splash on the peoples hands and cheeks; immense
warm drops like melted stars.

"Here are roses. Here are lilies" caws the old hag in the gutter - but the
lilies, bunched tight in a frill of green look more like faded cauliflowers. Up
and down she drags the creaking barrow. A sad, sickly smell comes from it.
Nobody wants to buy. You must walk in the middle of the road; there is no
room on the pavement, for every single shop brims over: every shop shows
a tattered frill of soiled lace and dirty ribbons to charm and entice you. And
there are tables set out with toy cannons and soldiers and zeppelins and
photograph frames complete with ogling beauties, and hideous tin brooches
with bébé or chèrie written on them, and strings of

Femme Seule.

Hope! you misery - you sentimental faded female. Break your last string and
have done with it - I shall go mad with your monotonous plucking. My heart
throbs to it - every little pulse beats in time. It is morning. I lie in the empty
bed, the huge bed - big as a field and as cold and unsheltered. Through the
shutters the sunlight comes up from the river and flows over the ceiling in
trembling waves. From outside comes the noise of a hammer tapping and
down below in the house a door opens and shuts. But all about me I hear the
solitude spinning her web. Is this my room. Are these my clothes folded over
the arm chair. Under the pillow - sign and seal of a lonely woman - ticks my
watch. The bell jangles. Ah, at last. I leap out of bed and run to the door in
my chemise.

"Voici votre lait Madame" says the concierge gazing severely at my knees.

"Merci bien Madame" I cry, smiling gayly & swinging the milk bottle.

"Pas de poste pour moi."

"Rien Madame."

Shut the door, stand in the hall a moment & listen listen for her hated
twanging. I implore her once again to play you that charming little thing
for one note only - coax her - court her      [J82-83]

Ninon de Long Clothes.[21]

---

[21]'Ninon de Longclothes': a pseudonym of Beatrice Hastings.

# *Notebook 45*

[Notebook 45, qMS-1253][22]

        Saunders Lane.
Our house in Tinakori Road stood far back from the road. It was a big white painted square house with a slender pillared verandah and balcony running all the way round. In the front from the verandah edge the garden sloped away in terraces & flights of concrete steps - down - until you reached the stone wall covered with nasturtiums that <kept us so "beautifully private"> had three gates let into it - the visitors' gate, the Tradesman's gate, and a huge pair of old iron gates that were never used and clashed and clamoured when Bogey & I tried to swing on them.

        Tinakori road was not fashionable, it was very mixed. Of course there were some good houses in it - old ones like ours for instance, hidden away in wildish gardens, & there was no doubt that land there would become extremely valuable, as Father said, if one bought enough & hung on. It was high, it was healthy, the sun poured in all the windows all day long, and once we had a decent tramway service, as Father argued

        But it was a little trying to have ones own washerwoman living next door who would persist in attempting to talk to Mother over the fence - & then just beyond her 'hovel' as Mother called it there lived an old man who burnt leather in his back yard whenever the wind blew our way. And then, just opposite our house, across the road, there was a paling fence & below the paling fence, in a hollow, squeezed in almost under the fold of a huge gorse-covered hill, was Saunders Lane. And further along there lived an endless family of halfcastes who appeared to have planted their garden with empty jam tins and old saucepans and black iron kettles without lids.

T.B.M.R.:[23] Jinnie Moore was awfully good at elocution. Was she better than I? I could make the girls cry when I read Dickens in the sewing class - and she

---

[22]This is the 'Massilia' notebook, used predominantly for writing 'The Aloe' in. On the front cover KM has written: 'The Aloe VI. Commencé March 12th'.
[23]'TBMR'—probably 'The Beautiful Miss Richardson', the heading below.

couldn't, but then she never tried to. She didn't care for Dickens. She liked something about horses and tramps and shipwrecks and prairie fires - they were her style, her reckless, redhaired dashing style.     [J106-107]

My dear they are like the bundles that stewards arrange in water bottles on second class salon tables of coastal boats.
I keep waiting for the postman. Every step in the road I feel is his step.

Who is he whom I seek? It is a warm, loving, eager companion in whose Love there are no horrible dark gulfs, none of those terribly beetling cliffs and thick[?] peaks that frighten me in my dreams. Neither shall he shut at evening like a jealous flower. He will be open all night long to me - but he is not.

The Beautiful Miss Richardson.
Why can't I change my hair ribbon on Wednesday afternoons. All the other girls are allowed to - and it can't be because Mother really thinks I shall lose my best one. I know a way to tie a hair ribbon so that it simply can't possibly come off - and she knows I do because she taught me herself. But 'No' says Mother - you may put on your threadwork pinafore, but you may not put on your blue satin hair ribbon. Your ordinary brown velvet one is perfectly neat, suitable and unobtrusive as it is. (Mother loves sentences like this) I can't help what all the other girls do. Have you got your thimble?
Yes Mother, in my pocket.
Show it to me, dear.
I said, Mother, it was in my pocket.
Well, show it to me so that I can be perfectly sure.
Oh Mother, why do you treat me like a baby. You always seem to forget on purpose that I'm in my teens. None of the other girls' Mothers ...
     Oh well, I'll take my blue satin hair ribbon in my pocket & change when I get to school. It serves Mother right. I don't want to deceive her but she makes me deceive her & she doesn't really care a bit - she only wants to show her power. Its Wednesday afternoon. I love Wednesday afternoons. I simply adore them. We don't have any real school - only sewing class and elocution in the drawing room for the girls who take private lessons. Everything is different on Wednesdays. Some of the older ones even wear Japanese silk blouses, & we change into our slippers & we all wash our hands at the lavatory basin in the passage. The inkpots are put away by the monitors, the desks pushed against the walls. There is a long table down the middle of the room with 2 big straw baskets on it, the chairs are arranged in little groups, the windows are opened wide. Even the garden outside with its beaten paths & its flowery bushes tumbled & draggled because the little ones will root under for their balls - seems to change, to become real on Wednesdays. When we lift our heads to thread our needles & look out through the windows the fuchsia is wafting & the camellias are white & red in the bright sun.
     We are making cheap flannelette chemises for the Maori Mission. They are as long as nightdresses, very full, with huge armholes and a plain band

round the neck - not even a lace edging. Those poor Maoris. They can't all be as fat as these chemises! But Mrs Wallis, the Bishops wife, said when she gave the newspaper pattern to the headmistress "It is wiser to reckon on them being fat." The headmistress laughed very much & told Miss Dunston[?] our class mistress but Miss Dunston is very fat herself, so she blushed frightfully - of course it was pure spite on the headmistress's part. Skinny little thing! I know she thinks she's got a lovely slim figure - you should see her pressing her little grey alpaca hips when she is talking to the curate before Scripture lesson - - - -

But even she is not the same on Wednesday afternoon. Her grey alpaca dress is adorned with a black tulle bow, she wears a tall comb in her hair. When she is not inspecting the sewing she sits at the end of the long table, her gold- rimmed eyeglasses hooked on her long peaked nose that has such funny little red veins in the end of it, and she reads Dickens aloud.

Our classroom is very big. The walls are pale, so are the window sashes & the doors - & all the girls sit on their little cane chairs, their faces hanging above a froth of cream flannelette. On their heads their best hair ribbons perch & quiver. Their hands lift and fall as they sew those Maori Mission seams. Sometimes they sigh or Mary Swainson sneezes. Ever since she had an operation on her nose she is always sneezing. . or Madge Rothschild who wears a glacé silk petticoat gets up & rustles to the table for the scissors or some more thread, or to ask if she has to turn down a selvedge.

But all the same it is quiet in the room, it is very quiet, & when the headmistress reads Dickens aloud there is something so fascinating in her voice that I could listen for years & years. She is reading David Copperfield. When there is a full page illustration she passes the book round for us to look. One by one we put our sewing down. "Quickly girls - don't dawdle over it." How funny! The headmistress herself is exactly like one of these illustrations - so tiny, so spry. While she waits for the book to come back she sits polishing her eyeglasses on a handkerchief that is tucked between 2 hooks of her grey alpaca bodice. What does she remind me of. She reminds me of a bird and a donkey mixed. Bring me that hem to look at, will you Katherine?

[J114-117 S54-57]

Nastasya Filippovna Barashkov.[24]
page 7. She is first mentioned by Rogozhin in the train and she is immediately 'recognised' by a man with a red nose and pimpled face who 'knows all about her.' "Armance and Coralie & Princess Patsy & N.F." "We'll go and see N.F." Prophetic words.

page 9. Why did she accept the earrings from a man she never had seen? She was not greedy for jewels. She had plenty & she was extremely particular in her conduct towards other men. Is that a kind of russian custom? To accept the earrings as a kind of recognition of her beauty. Then you get a glimpse. She flung them [...]. This you old grey beard.

26–27. The portrait "dark & deep, passionate & disdainful."

---

[24] Notes on Dostoevsky's 'The Idiot'.

33. Her face is cheerful but she has passed through terrible suffering, hasn't she? . . . Its a proud face, awfully proud, but I don't know whether she is goodhearted. Ah! if she were! That would redeem it all.

page 37 The story of Nastasya. That change in her when she appears at Petersburg – her knowledge almost 'technical' of how things are done in the world is not at all impossible. With such women it appears to be a kind of instinct. Maata was just the same – she simply knew these things from nowhere. Her action, when Dostoievsky says 'from spite', is to show her power, & now that he has jerked out the weapon with which he wounded her she feels the dreadful smart.     [J109-110]

It is a strange fact about Madame Allegre.[25] She walks very well - quite beautifully. I saw her just now go down to the bottom of the garden with a pail in one hand & a basket in the other.

Prepare charcoal fire every night before turning in. Then one has only to go down, put a match to it, stick on the funnel, & its ready by the time you're dressed! How clever!

I must break through again. I feel so anxious and so worried about the Sardinia[26] that I <u>cant</u> write. What I have done seems to me to be awfully, impossibly good compared to the STUFF I wrote yesterday. I believe if I had another <u>shock</u>(!), if for instance Mlle Marthe turned up, I might manage but at present je veux mourir. I ought to write a letter from Beryl to Nan Fry.[27] This is all too laborious!

Beryl Fairfield.
What is it that I'm getting at? It is really Beryl's 'Sosie'. The fact that for a long time now, she really hasn't been even able to control her second self: its her second self who now controls her. There was [a] kind of radiant being who wasn't either spiteful or malicious of whom she'd had a glimpse whose very voice was different to hers who was grave who never would have dreamed of doing the things that she did. Had she banished this being or had it really got simply tired and left her. I want to get at all this <u>through</u> her just as I got at Linda <u>through</u> Linda. To suddenly merge her into herself

Robin sends to Beryl

> Lives like logs of driftwood
> Tossed on a watery main
> Other logs encounter
> Drift, touch, part again
> And so it is with our lives
> On life's tempestuous sea
> We meet, we greet, we sever
> Drifting eternally.

---

[25]Madame Allègre and her husband owned the Villa Pauline in Bandol where the Murrys spent a happy three months at the beginning of 1916.
[26]The *Sardinia* was the ship on which KM's sister Chaddie was travelling to Marseilles where KM planned to meet her.
[27]Several ink sketches of a person playing a 'cello, a violin, and a piano.

Shatov & his wife.
There is something awfully significant about the attitude of Shatov to his wife,
& it is amazing how, when Dostoievsky at last turns a soft but penetrating full
light upon him, how we have managed to gather a great deal of knowledge of
his character from the former vague sidelights and shadowy impressions. He is
just what we thought him - he behaves just as we would expect him to do.
There is all that crudity & what you might call shock[?]-headedness in his
nature & it is wonderfully tragic that he who is so soon to be destroyed himself
should suddenly realise - & through a third person, through a little squeaking
baby - the miracle just being alive is.
       Every time I read these chapters about his new born happiness I
cherish a kind of tiny hope that this time he will escape - he will be warned -
he won't die.
       How did Dostoievsky know about that extraordinary vindictiveness, that
relish for bitter laughter that comes over women in pain? Its a very secret thing
but its profound, profound. They don't want to spare the one whom they love.
If that one loves them with a kind of blind devotion like Shatov did Marie,
they long to torment him & this tormenting gives them real positive relief.
Does this resemble in any way the 'tormenting' that D. describes so often in his
affairs of passion? Are his women ever happy when they torment their lovers?
No. They too are in the agonies of labour - they are giving birth to their new
selves, and they never believe in their deliverance.       [J110-111]

Why won't he go once more to the door to look for something from the post.
It really is rather absurd to be in such a position with anyone: I am ashamed of
myself. I'll go alone. And now he comes asking me what the time is.[28]

I must not go on thinking like this. My thoughts are all of Chaddie - of our
meeting on Monday, of what we shall [say] & how we shall look. I keep
wondering what I shall do if the boat arrives in the middle of the night or
what I shall do if someone robs me while I am there. A thousand different
thoughts. And what she will say & if she will expect me. These things fly
through my head like mad things. They never finish and then there is always
the idea that I may by some awful error miss her. It isn't possible. And what we
shall do when we <u>do</u> meet. This is sheer sin for I ought to be writing my book
& instead I am pretending here. But all these various things are really very
difficult to keep up the fight against. And the desire for midday and an
omelette is really awful. I'm hungry beyond words. An omelette, hot coffee,
bread & butter and jam - I could cry at the very thought. Only you see, fool
who is reading this, I went out awfully early before eight o'clock. I was down
in the village with my filet[29] in my hand agetting of the lunch & the dinner./
And although it pleuvéd cats and dogs/ I marched about the land/ and came
back home a kind of hardened sinner./[30] For the petit pois/ I really must

---

[28]Murry's note: 'This does not belong.'
[29]The French word 'filet' means 'net', ie 'string bag'.
[30]The words 'hardened sinner' are actually quite impossible to read. They are Murry's inspired guess.

confess/ were sinfully expensive/ & I couldn't have bought less./ I <u>had</u> to buy
a demi–livre/ and that's by no means ample./ By the time that they've been
shelled and cooked/ Il ne reste plus qu'un sample./ Twenty to twelve says our
old clock/ It seems to talk and slyly mock/ My hunger and my real distress/ At
giving way to wickedness/ Oh say a 1/4 say ten to/ Whirr in the whirring way
you do/ Before you strike/ But no, as I have oft observed/ All clocks are deaf –
this hasn't heard/ And as it is – grace a my doigt the brute is fast beyond all
divining. It is really only seven/ Minutes past a pale eleven./ Now Jack has got
up & made a move/ But only to the shelves above/ He's settled again/ Oh
what a blow/ I've still a good fifteen to go/ But once the brute has chimèd
well/ I may be dead and gone to hell.

But it wasn't as bad as all that after All. I struck work and we had no end of
a good feed and now it is 2 (by our clock). So I'll knock off this rubbish
& really settle down.     [J113-114 S52-53]

> To L.H.B.[31]
> 1894–1915
> Last night for the first time since you were dead
> I walked with you, my brother, in a dream.
> We were at home again beside the stream
> Fringed with tall berry bushes, white and red.
> "Don't touch them: they are poisonous," I said
> But your hand hovered, and I saw a beam
> Of strange bright laughter flying round your head
> And as you stooped I saw the berries gleam
> "Don't you remember? We called them Dead Man's Bread!"
> I woke and heard the wind moan and the roar
> Of the dark water tumbling on the shore.
> Where – where is the path of my dream for my eager feet
> By the remembered stream my brother stands
> Waiting for me with berries in his hands
> "These are my body. Sister, take and eat."
>                                  Katherine Mansfield

> how cross Grandmother was –
> green lichen moss.

> The trees will toss their little leaves
> To mourn the loss of the new goldfinch.

Jack's application is a perpetual reminder to me. Why am I not writing too?
Why, feeling so rich, with the greater part of this to be written <u>before</u> I go
back to England do I not begin? If only I have the courage to press against the
stiff, swollen gate all that lies within is mine. Why do I linger for a moment.

---

[31]Another version of this poem is in MS-Papers-4006-13 and may be found on p 66.

Because I am idle, out of the habit of work and spendthrift beyond belief. Really it is idleness, a kind of immense idleness - hateful and disgraceful.

I was thinking yesterday of my <u>wasted</u> <u>wasted</u> early girlhood. My college life, which is such a vivid and detailed memory in one way might never have contained a book or a lecture. I lived in the girls, the professor, the big lovely building, the leaping fires in winter & the abundant flowers in summer. The views out of the windows, all the pattern that was - weaving. Nobody saw it, I felt, as I did. My mind was just like a squirrel. I gathered & gathered & hid away for that long 'winter' when I should rediscover all this treasure - and if anybody came close I scuttled up the tallest darkest tree & hid in the branches.

And I was so awfully fascinated in watching Hall Griffin[32] & all his tricks - thinking about him as he sat there - his private life, what he was like as a man (he told us he & his brother once wrote an enormous poem called The Epic of the Griffins) etc etc. Then it was only at rare intervals that something flashed through all this busyness - something about Spenser's Faery Queene or Keats Isabella & the Pot of Basil. Those flashes were always when I disagreed flatly with H.G. & wrote in my notes - this man is a fool.

And Cramb - wonderful Cramb! The figure of Cramb was enough, he was 'history' to me. Ageless & fiery, eating himself up again & again, very fierce at what he had seen but going a bit blind because he had looked so long. Cramb, striding up & down, filled me up to the brim. I couldn't write down Cramb's thunder. I simply wanted to sit & eat him. Every gesture, every shifting of his walk, all his tones and looks are as vivid to me as though it were yesterday - but of all he said I only remember phrases - "he sat there & his wig fell off". "Anne Bullen a lovely <u>pure</u> creature stepping out of her quiet door into the light and clamour", & looking back & seeing the familiar door shut upon her with a little click as it were - final.

But what coherent account could I give of the history of English Literature? Or what of English History? None. When I think in <u>dates</u> & <u>times</u> the wrong people come in - the right people are missing. When I read a play of Shakespeare I want to be able to place it in relation to what came before & what comes after. I want to realise what England was like then - at least a little - & what the people looked like (but even as I write I feel I can do this at least the latter thing) but when a man is mentioned, even though the man is real I don't want to set him on the right hand of Sam Johnson when he ought to be living under Shakespeare's shadow. And this I often do.

Since I came here I have been very interested in the Bible. I have read the Bible for hours on end & I began to do so with just the same desire - I wanted to know if Lot followed close on Noah or something like that. But I feel so bitterly I should have known facts like this: they ought to be part of my breathing. Is there another grown person as ignorant as I? But [why] didn't I listen to the old Principal[33] who lectured on Bible History twice a

---

[32]Hall Griffin and Cramb were two of KM's teachers at Queen's College—of English Literature and History respectively.
[33]Canon G C Bell.

week instead of staring at his face that was very round, a dark red colour with a kind of bloom on it & covered all over with little red veins with endless tiny tributaries that ran even into his forehead & were lost in his bushy white hair.

He had tiny hands, too, puffed up, purple, shining under the stained flesh. I used to think looking at his hands - he will have a stroke & die of paralysis. They told us he was a very learned man, but I could not help seeing him in a double-breasted frock coat, a large pseudo-clerical pith helmet, a clean white handkerchief falling over the back of his neck staring and pointing out with an umbrella a probable site of a probable encampment of some wandering tribe - to his wife, an elderly lady with a threatening cerebral tumour who had to go everywhere in a basket chair arranged on the back of a donkey, & his two daughters in thread gloves & sand shoes smelling faintly of some anti-mosquito mixture.

As he lectured I used to sit, building his house, peopling it, filling it with curious ebony & ivory furniture, cupboards like tiny domes & tables with elephants legs presented to him by grateful missionary friends ... I never came into contact with him but once when he asked any young lady in the room to hold up her hand if she had been chased by a wild bull & as nobody else did I held up mine (though of course I hadn't). Ah, he said, I am afraid you do not count. You are a little savage from New Zealand - which was really a trifle exacting - for it must be the rarest thing to be chased by a wild bull up & down Harley Street, Wimpole Street, Welbeck Street, Queen Anne, round & round Cavendish Square.

And why didn't I learn French with M. Huguenot. What an opportunity missed! What has it not cost me! He lectured in a long narrow room that was painted all over - the walls, door & window frames a charming shade of mignonette green. The ceiling was white & just below it there was a frieze of long looped chains of white flowers. On either side of the marble mantelpiece a naked small boy staggered under a big platter of grapes that he held above his head. Below the windows, far below, there was a stable court paved in cobblestones - one could hear the faint clatter of carriages coming out or in, the noise of water gushing out of a pump into a big pail, some youth clumping about & whistling. The room was never very light & in summer M. H. liked the blind to be drawn half way down the window ... He was a little fat man        [J103-106]

| Congreve[34] | Dryden | Donne |
|---|---|---|
| Addison | Thomas Arnold | Duvel |
| Steele | Marvel | [?] |
| Gay | Milton | Webster |
| Swift | | |
| Pope | | |
| Defoe | Shakespeare | |

---

[34] These lists of names are written on the page facing the one where KM speculates on how much she knows of the history of English Literature.

| | |
|---|---|
| Richardson | |
| 1715–1780 | Marlowe |
| Walpole | Peel |
| Gray | Greene |
| Austen | Nash |
| Dr Johnson | Surrey   Chaucer |
| Goldsmith | Wyett |
| Smolet | Speare |
| Fielding | |

Spring comes with exquisite effect in England. A.B.B.[35]     [J114]

Now, really, what is it that I do want to write? I ask myself: Am I less of a writer than I used to be. Is the need to write less urgent? Does it still seem as natural to me to seek that form of expression. Has speech fulfilled it? Do I ask anything more than to relate to remember to assure myself? There are times when these thoughts half frighten me and very nearly convince. I say: You are so fulfilled now in your own being, in being alive, in loving, in aspiring towards a greater sense of life and a deeper loving that the other thing has gone out of you. But no, at bottom I am not convinced for at bottom never has been my desire so ardent. Only the form that I would choose has changed utterly. I feel no longer concerned with the same appearances of things. The people who lived or who I wished to bring into my stories don't interest me any more. The plots of my stories leave me perfectly cold. Granted that these people exist and all the differences complexities and resolutions are true to them. Why should I write about them? They are not near me. All the false threads that bound them to me are cut away quite.

Now – now I want to write recollections of my own country.
Yes I want to write about my own country until I simply exhaust my store – not only because it is a 'sacred debt' that I pay to my country because my brother & I were born there, but also because in my thoughts I range with him over all the remembered places. I am never far away from them. I long to renew them in writing.

And the people, the people we loved there. Of them too I want to write – another 'debt of love'. Oh, I want for one moment to make our undiscovered country leap into the eyes of the old world. It must be mysterious, as though floating – it must take the breath. It must be 'one of those islands'... I shall tell everything, even of how the laundry basket squeaked at '75' – but all must be told with a sense of mystery, a radiance, an after glow because you, my little sun of it, are set. You have dropped over the dazzling brim of the world. Now I must play my part  –  –

Then I want to write poetry. I feel always trembling on the brink of poetry. The almond tree, the birds, the little wood where you are, the flowers

---

[35]Murry misread this in the *Journal* as 'Spring comes with exquisite effort in England.' In that form it has been much quoted and commented on by critics. The initials ABB are those of Annie Burnell Beauchamp, KM's mother.

you do not see, the open window out of which I lean & dream that you
are against my shoulder, & the times that your photograph 'looks sad'.
But especially I want to write a kind of long elegy to you - - - perhaps not
in poetry. No, perhaps in Prose - almost certainly in a kind of special <u>prose</u>.

And lastly I want to keep a kind of <u>minute note book</u> - to be published
some day. That is all. No novels, no problem stories, nothing that is not
simple, open. Any of this I may start at any moment.

K.M. 22.I.1916.     [J93-94]

Having read the whole of the Idiot through again, & fairly carefully, I feel
slightly more bewildered than I did before as regards Nastasya Philippovna's
character. She's really not well done - she's badly done, & there goes [sic] up
as one reads on a kind of irritation, a <u>balked</u> fascination which almost succeeds
finally in blotting out those first & really marvellous impressions of her. What
was Dostoievsky really aiming at?     [J110]

| | |
|---|---|
| belgian dress | a dark blue |
| purple coat and skirt | a flowered one or check |
| black silk dress | russian blouse |
| chinese | blue jacket |
| Belts[?] for occasional | red jacket |
| travelling coat and skirt (2) | bulgarian jacket. |

well say this [?]
I love you I love you. The words are like flowers. The more often I run into
the garden & pluck them for you the more plentifully they grow.

I've just got the idea of being run down or over à la the good soul in Lady
Frazer's book.[36]

Hotel Beau Rivage Bandol Var. VII.XII.1915.
I shall keep a strict account of all monies while I am here.

| | |
|---|---|
| In hand | 90 francs. |
| oranges | .20 cent. |
| biscuits | .40 |
| stamps | .35 |
| cigarettes | .75 |
| matches | .10 |
| paper | . 5 |
| stamp | .25 |
| writing paper | .30 |
| paper | . 5 |

——————
2.45

---

[36]Possibly Lady Lilly Grove Frazer (d 1941), wife of Sir James Frazer who wrote *The Golden Bough*.
She was a prolific writer and translator from the French, specialising mainly in fairy tales and scenes of French
life and child life written in colloquial French. Which of her books is referred to here is unknown.

|            |      |
|------------|------|
| casserole  | .60  |
| methylated | .95  |

as soon as we reach home.

I am too cold to move a pen.[37]

(The old man could not get over the fact that he was still strong enough to lift such a lump of a boy. He wanted to do it again and again. Even when the little boy was awfully tired of the game the old man kept putting out his arms and smiling foolishly and trying to lift him still higher. He even tried with one arm ...)      [J106]

(In the scurely as Lottie says.)      [J98 s38]

---

[37]On some of the verso pages of 'The Aloe' manuscript KM has written this and the following two notes.

# *Unbound Papers*

[NL]

### BRAVE LOVE [38]
#### I.

As Mitka turned into Wyndham Square he heard a beautiful clock strike ten. The sound seemed to come from far away, from high up in the air. Mitka stopped to listen and to look up and about him. It was a warm, still night. The sky was studded with big stars and moonlight lay on the white houses and on the trees and little lawns of the square. Some of the houses had pink and white awnings spread over the balconies. The windows of all of them were filled with boxes of flowering plants, and through the open, lighted windows there came the sound of voices and laughter. Under the warm, white light the place looked strangely gay and lovely, but not quite real. It was like a place in a dream with a dream's aloofness and security in its own unreality. But then, thought Mitka walking on in the steps of his sharp shadow, the land is always like a dream to me. I shall long all my life to live on the land and while I am longing my life will pass in little ships and big ships ...

As he came to number "34" he heard the sound of a piano and then Mildred West's voice floated to him. "It is all in vain - I implore thee." Ah, thought Mitka, she is singing to my brother. My brother is there - my darling

---

[38] 'Brave Love' is, strictly, outside the scope of this edition in that it is a complete story and it has been published. However, its history puts it in a special category. KM refers to it in a diary entry for 12 January 1915 where she says, 'Actually finished the story Brave Love and I don't know what to think of it even now. Read it to Jack who was also puzzled. Violent headache but rather happy.' Murry's footnote to this is, 'Of this story only the opening pages survive.' In fact the story was in Ida Baker's possession and when she sold it to a dealer he allowed her to keep a rather primitive photocopy of it. She gave this to me in 1971 and my transcription of it was published in *Landfall*, the New Zealand Literary Quarterly, in March 1972. That version—full of gaps and hesitancies—was picked up and republished, once in Germany (in German translation), once in Japan, and once in New Zealand where a reprint by Golden Press of Constable's *Collected Stories* tacked this one on to the end. The Oxford University Press *The Stories of Katherine Mansfield: Definitive Edition* omits 'Brave Love' on the grounds that it is 'a tedious, confusing story never published by KM'.

The manuscript of the story eventually came to light in the Newberry Library where I was able to work on it and produce a more complete and accurate transcription than that published in *Landfall* in 1972. It can hardly be denied that the story is, on the surface, tedious and confusing, but it nevertheless has its own importance and should be studied. It would seem, then, that this, the better of the only two transcriptions of this story so far, should find a place in this edition.

Paddy! And he ran up the steps and gave the bell a pull that sent the German
waiter rushing up from the dirty bowels of the house. Before Mitka had time
to ask for his brother he heard Mildred's voice from the drawing room landing.
"Who is there? Hans, who is it?" Mitka ran into the hall past the German
waiter and shouted gaily, "It is I, Mitka."

"Mitka!" Mildred sounded very pleased. She came rustling down the
stairs. "Really Mitka!" and into the hall. "Where have you come from?"
She put her bare scented arms round his neck and kissed him and then held
him away from her. "Let me look at you." Which meant at the same time -
"You may look at me, I am as lovely as ever." She wore a black dress and no
ornaments except a pair of black pearl ear rings and a black rose dropping from
her pale coloured hair. Her red lips and her beautiful painted eyes smiled at
Mitka and he recognised the perfume that always clung about his brother -
the perfume like sweet dry wood. "Heavens, child, how brown you are!
You are brown as a nut," said Mildred. She put her hand under his chin and
tilted his face. "Grown a moustache, too. But I can't quite believe in it, Mitka.
You look as young as ever."

He crinkled up his eyes. "Ah, you are going to push fun at me again,"
he said. "But I do not mind now. Since I leave here - for three years nobody is
pulling my leg. I am quite forgetting how it feels."
"Come up to the drawing room," she said, laughing at him. "You speak worse
English than ever. Come up to the drawing room. Paddy is there.
He'll be amazed at seeing you."

Mitka hesitated. "Couldn't I see him in some more private spot first,"
he suggested. But Mildred was firm. "No, you're not to be let off. We'd love to
see you kiss Paddy. There is no one to be afraid of. Come along," and she took
his hand and ran upstairs with him crying "Paddy, Paddy, guess who's here?
Look who I've brought you."

For the moment Mitka forgot everything but his beautiful tall brother,
all black and white, moving across the room to him. Tears started to his eyes.
He ran and embraced Paddy and squeezed his arms.
"Why didn't you let me know, little one," said Paddy, almost as touched as
Mitka. "Ah," he said, "I wanted to be a surprise for you. If I come back so
suddenly it's as though I'm never quite gone."
"Listen to him." Mildred put her arm round his shoulder and pinched his ear.
"Now you must be a little gentleman and say 'Good evening' to Mother and
be introduced to your audience."

The drawing room was just as he had remembered it - all pink and
white, with lamp shades like swollen roses and dozens of photographs in silver
frames. Old Mrs Farmer, Mildred's mother, sat in her accustomed corner, with
a ravel of wool and needles on her lap and just as before the little table beside
her holding the parrot's cage, covered in a red and white check cloth.
She looked withered and trembling as he bent over her tiny yellow hand.
"Well now!" she quavered. "Well, well, well! I know you, young man,
I know you," and peeped up slyly at him out of her puzzled eyes.
"Miss Valerie Brandon," and Mitka bowed to a tall girl who stood at the grand

piano, playing chords with the soft pedal down. She was wrapped in a gauze scarf and her neck and hair were steeped in candlelight. "Colonel Foster" - an old man at the fire place, his feet towards the empty grate, and his plump, purplish hands, folded over his round stomach. "And these are my two boys." Mildred pointed, mocking, to two very dark young men playing cards in a corner. They grinned at Mitka, shuffled their feet, half rose, then subsided. "That's all over." Mildred gave an affected sigh, put her hand in Paddy's waistcoat pocket and took out his cigarette case. "Sit down on the sofa and hold Paddy's hand." She stood by the tall lamp looking down at them and each time she blew the smoke from her lips she lifted her head and seemed to offer to them her milky throat and breast.

"First thing of all," said Mitka, watching her in his naive admiring way, "I must deeply apologise for my clothes. But you know, being so seldom on land I have not got an evening dress. I know - it's a shocking confession."

"We'll forgive you," laughed Mildred. "It's a very nice blue serge dress, anyhow. Where have you come from? How long are you staying?"

"I came from Alexandria," he said, "and I am staying five days. Then I go to Marseilles, and," he shrugged, "Alexandria again. Back and forward, you know, all the time." "And have you had any wonderful adventures?" teased Mildred.

"Oh, no," said Mitka simply. "It's very quiet at sea, you know." He rubbed his hands together. "Very quiet indeed." In the little pause they heard the soft muffled chords from the piano and the sound of the parrot walking over the roof of his cage.

"Stay with us, won't you," said Paddy. "Stay the five days here. There's an extra bed in my room that you can have."

"What! May I really - Oh, Paddy how sweet of you." Mitka longed to embrace him again. He wondered if Paddy had really changed or if it was only the people and the English room that made him feel so far away and so foreign.

"I'll lend you a nightdress for tonight," said Mildred. A snigger came from the dark young men in the corner and the hop-hop-hop of the ivory cribbage pegs. But nobody paid any attention. The Colonel was asleep, his baggy chin settled in his collar, Mrs Farmer's little eyes flew from Mildred to the brothers and back to Mildred, her face screwed tight in the effort to hear what they were saying, and Valerie Brandon sat down on the piano stool and began to play as softly as ever - she was all wrapped up in a gold net of quivering candle light.

"Oh," said Mitka, "how glad I am to be here. How beautiful it is. How full of peace." He smiled at Mildred & Paddy. "You're easily satisfied, my son," said she and made a little grimace.

"He's young," shrilled Mrs Farmer, suddenly. "Let him be, Mildred. He'll learn soon enough. He's young." Her lace cap trembled to her talking and she clicked open a large black fan and beat the air with it. "Dear me, Mother," drawled Mildred. "We are a-going it tonight, aren't we?" Mitka saw Paddy frown and heard him whisper, "Let her alone, Mildred." "Well, she's got no

right to interfere." Mildred shrugged her shoulders as Mrs Farmer gathered up
and burst out again. "You wait, young man," she said. "You just wait a bit
before you're so pleased with the outside of the glass." Mitka felt very
uncomfortable. What a fool I am, he thought. My silly happiness always makes
a scene. Now Paddy will be cross with me. I know he will.

But Paddy, as if he read Mitka's thoughts and wanted to reassure him,
put his hand on Mitka's knee and said kindly, "So here's my little brother
again." Mildred leaned back in her chair and smoked with half shut eyes.
"Oh, Val," she drawled, "do stop that melancholy stuff. You're melting all my
bones, darling. Do stop." Mitka looked over at the piano. The girl stopped
playing. She folded herself in her white gauze scarf and wheeled round on the
piano stool, facing them. "Very well," she said, "I'll stop. I've been crying
myself for the last half hour." As she spoke she smiled faintly, her head a little
on one side. She looked very slim and young perched on the little stool.
She had black hair and long grey eyes. "I wonder," she said, still mocking,
"if the parrot's asleep." She slipped off the stool with a little rustle of silk and
went over to the cage and raised the cloth. "Polly - Polly -" she called and the
parrot answered, copying her low voice. "Polly, Polly."

"Valerie, don't. He'll pull you to pieces," protested Mildred. But the girl
opened the cage and put her hand in and drew it out with the red and grey
parrot on her finger. Crouching back on her heels she held the bird up in her
hand and stroked it and raised its wings. "Does he hate his silly old cage,"
she said, "and does the silly old light make him blink?" The parrot walked up
her arm on to her shoulder and flapped its wings. "There, I told you so.
He'll ruin your scarf," said Mildred. "No, he won't," said Valerie Brandon,
"and I rather like the feeling of his sharp old claws in my shoulder. It amuses
me," she added slowly and slowly turned and smiled at Mitka, who sat quite
still watching the curious girl. "Would you like to nurse the pretty parrot?"
she asked.
"Oh, Val, don't be a little fool."
"Who'd like to dandle our pretty Poll?" and she laughed and bit her under lip.
"Oh, shut up," said Mildred. But Valerie did not take her eyes off Mitka.
The room and the lamps and the people all faded before the girl with the
parrot who looked and looked at him so strangely that his heart shivered.
"Pretty Polly," she mocked, coaxing the parrot.
"He'll muss her in a minute," shrieked Mrs Farmer with infinite relish.
"It's your bed-time, Mother," said Mildred. "Come along."
Paddy took out his watch. "I'm going too, and so is Mitka."
Mildred nodded. "I'll wake the old C. and toddle him off. Now, boys,"
she said to the two dark young gentlemen, "off with you. And leave your
windows open." Valerie put back the parrot and dropped the check cloth.
She stood smiling, her finger on her lips as though she were listening to
something going on inside the cage until Mildred went up and put her arm
round her. "Come up to my room and let's have a drink - the four of us,"
she said.

The rooms on the top floor of the house belonged to Mildred and

Paddy. When the two brothers entered she was sitting on the side of the bed in a blue silk kimono embroidered in white wings. Valerie Brandon was beside her and they were smiling at each other. On a little table stood a bottle of wine and four glasses. "In honour of Mitka," said Mildred. "Open it, Paddy." For some silly reason Mitka felt shy. He could hardly bear to look at the two women and at the room which seemed so full of an unknown Mildred.

Her slippers and her dress lay on a couch. A powder puff was on the table with the glasses, the big, soft bed was half turned down. "I'll tell you something," said Mildred. "Mitka feels shy. Don't you? You're rather frightened, aren't you, Mitka? You think we're improper."

"Don't tease him," said Paddy. "You're horrid tonight, Mildred."

"Am I?" said Mildred, and as he handed her a glass she put her fingers round his. "Am I really, Paddy?"

"Well - no - not <u>really</u>," and Mitka heard the strange laugh of content that Paddy had for his woman. By slow degrees and scarcely knowing why he avoided her and yet wanted to look, Mitka glanced at Valerie. She was looking at him again but now her eyes were changed. She only looked kind and sweet and gentle and she seemed to be saying "Don't be shy. We're only playing." She drank her wine in tiny sips, and he drank from his glass when she did and felt quite free and gay again.

Suddenly there was a sound of steps on the stairs. Someone whistled. "That's Evershed home," said Mildred lightly, looking at Valerie. The girl put down her glass.

"Bon soir, mes amis," she said.

"Who's Evershed?" asked Mitka.

## II

When Mitka came down to breakfast next morning there was nobody in the dining room except Mildred and old Colonel Foster. The Colonel sat in the sunny window with a copy of the morning Post spread across his knees, but Mildred was just pouring out her tea.

"Hallo, you nice child to wait for me," she said.

"Why, has everybody gone?" asked Mitka.

"Yes, thank the Lord. Breakfast is a baleful time in this house. The boys have to be off to the office early and Paddy has to go to the city. Later Evershed wants things specially cooked & -" she nodded in the direction of the window " - has to be fed with a spoon, nearly. I wait till they're gone & then feed in peace. Help yourself, dear. Did you sleep alright?"

"Like tops," said Mitka.

"Good," said Mildred absently. She looked tired and pale. "Don't stare at me, my child," she said. "I always look a rag in the mornings. I loathe mornings - especially ones like these - indecently bright, when the sun changes into a housepainter."

Mitka looked at her anxiously. "I think you must be suffering from a nerve," he said. "Really, frankly, the morning is lovely, but you do not feel strong enough to dress yourself up in it like you do the night."

"What do you mean?"

"Like this," said Mitka. "When I see you at night I always think this woman she wears the night as though it were her covering. She smells of it and her eyes are full of it and her voice has a thrill … you know how exciting the night is, and how unknown. That is how you look too. I told Paddy that in bed last night & he said yes – I was right. He said he had never lost that feeling of you too. Well," he shrugged his shoulders & crinkled his eyes at her, "you ought to wear the daytime in the same way. You know I have an idea that women, beautiful women, are the spirits of nature in that way. I mean that nature reflects herself in them as she does in ponds or flowers."

As Mildred listened to him she laughed. "How absurd you are," said she, but grace flowed back in her gestures and her smile and she looked very sweetly at Mitka. "Mitka, tell me something."

"What?"

"Have you ever been in love?"

"This is no place for me," said a voice at the door and Valerie Brandon strolled to the table & leaned her hands on it. "Good morning," said she, and leaning forward she kissed Mildred's hair.

"Good morning. How interesting you look in that white dress with the black lace shawl."

"Don't I" she said. "Like a Spanish waitress in a café chantant! Isn't it hot. Hot already." She sat down at the table and put her hands up to her cheeks.

"Can I get you some breakfast?" said Mitka politely.

She shook her head. "No, I don't eat it. What on earth were you talking about, Mildred, with Mr –" she hesitated " – Mr Mitka over the toast and bacon – the difference between Love and passion, or should women be as free as men? I don't know what I didn't hear as I came in."

"No." Mildred pushed back her chair. "Got a cigarette, Mitka? Thank you. They smell delicious. They're the sort you had before."

"Give me one too," said Valerie and she took the case from Mildred.

"I was having a good look at him in the morning light," went on Mildred. "And I thought there is really something awfully attractive about Mitka. I mean, although he does look young in spite of the moustache, he looks as though extraordinary things might happen to him. Don't you think …"

"I'm not sure," said Valerie, considering him seriously.

Mitka looked up at her & smiled. "Ah," he said, "Mildred is pulling my leg again. She loves to tease me. Really her opinion is this is not a bad little fellow. I put up with him for a few days."

"I expect you're right," answered Valerie. "Here! What am I doing? I'm pinching your cigarette case."

"Go and smoke up in the drawing room," said Mildred. "I must get all this cleared away. Go on both of you." She went to the door and called, "Hans, Hans."

"Madame," said the German waiter appearing from nowhere with a thick bandage round his neck.

**Katherine Mansfield** (1888–1923) was born in Wellington, New Zealand, as Kathleen Mansfield Beauchamp. After she moved to England in 1908, she never returned to her native country. Among her publications are *In a German Pension, Prelude, Bliss and Other Stories, The Garden Party and Other Stories, Poems, The Dove's Nest and Other Stories,* and *Something Childish and Other Stories.* After her death from tuberculosis, her husband, John Middleton Murry (1889–1957), edited selections from her notebooks and published many of her works and letters.

**Margaret Scott** transcribed "The Unpublished Manuscript of Katherine Mansfield" for six installments in the *Turnbull Library Record* in 1970–74, and she has coedited five volumes of *The Collected Letters of Katherine Mansfield.* She is the author of *Recollecting Mansfield.*

"What is the matter now?" said Mildred in a disgusted voice. "More boils again, Hans. Ugh! How dreadful you look."

"Come along," said Valerie.

"Ah, Madame, please to excuse," mumbled the German waiter.

"No I won't excuse you Hans. I'm sure it's because you don't wash."
She scolded him in a hard angry voice that Valerie and Mitka heard all the way up the stairs.

"No one could stand this room in the daytime," said Valerie. "Come on to the balcony." There she unfolded a canvas chair and lay back, one arm behind her head. Mitka sat on a little stool, smoking. They were quiet. Then Valerie spoke. "I like being with you," she said. "You make me feel so good. No, I'm not joking. I mean it quite seriously. You can't think" - she snapped off a geranium from the balcony rail and bit the stalk - "what a relief you are, how rare it is to see someone like you who isn't either false or - ugly."

Mitka opened his eyes very wide. "Are you really not making jokes?" he said. "No of course I'm not." She sounded quite cross, & began to bite the head of the flower. "Why should I bother to? But if you only knew what the whole crowd of us was like - my heavens you'd welcome someone like yourself for a change. It's not that we're bad or wicked," she said, throwing away the geranium stalk, "but we're ever so dull - so out of the way of real life."

"What does that last mean?" asked Mitka softly.

"We're not alive," she said. "Ugh! What a houseful we are! What a crew! You can't imagine," she turned to Mitka again & smiled, "how absurd you looked in the drawing room last night with Mrs Farmer & the Colonel & the 2 South Americans & Mildred & I. I shall never forget the way you ran in with your eyes dancing - nor the way you looked round & said 'How beautiful it is here'. I nearly screamed!"

"But," said Mitka in a puzzled voice, "what's the matter with the house? Isn't it like other houses?"

"Oh, I <u>suppose</u> so," she said. "Like heaps of others suppose. Yes, I'm sure it is. I can feel the dust of hundreds of them in the hem of my skirt."

"But why do you stay here if you hate it so," asked Mitka, more and more astonished.

"Ah," Valerie laughed, that's quite a different story. Ask me another. Yes, why do I? I wonder - " and she got up out of her chair & leant against the rail looking down at Mitka. "After all, it's rather an easy question. Why does anyone do anything. Because they can't help it, I suppose. You get caught in a wheel & round & round you go."

"I don't think that," said Mitka. "I don't believe in wheels. If you really look yourself in the open face and say what you want to do you can do it. Otherwise, why not jump off the balcony? What's the good of anything else."

"Do you really think that people can do what they like" asked Valerie slowly. "Oh dear, I'm afraid Mildred's right in calling you young. I believed it once - & acted on it, too. That <u>really</u> was funny."

Mitka said wisely, "That depends, doesn't it, on what you want to do."
"No," she said, "there is only one thing. To get free & to keep free. Oh well,
she said, bitterly, I see myself doing it. But that's what I noticed about you,
I think. You looked really & truly free."
Mitka nodded. "That's quite true," he said. "Yes, I am."
"But supposing," she began, & then stopped. "Oh dear, what's the good.
What on earth am I talking like this for. It's such nonsense, such hopeless
nonsense," she cried desperately. "There's old Mrs Farmer down there going
tata in a bath chair. She's seen us. Wave your hand to the baby."
"Don't," cried Mitka in a troubled voice. "Please, please don't. You make me
dreadfully sad." He took the ends of her scarf & fingered them while he
talked, his head bent. "I cannot bear to think of anyone being so dreadfully
unhappy. Perhaps I am, as you say, young – a 'silly boy' – but I would do
anything in my power to help you. Believe me – I would." If he had looked
up he would have been amazed to see her face. There was such a strange
mingling of relief and scorn and amusement painted upon it. But he did
not look up.

"Then be my friend," she said in a low, reflecting voice. "I don't know
why but immediately I saw you I wanted you for my friend. I knew that
somehow or other you could help me infinitely – infinitely – & that I – in a
way – don't misunderstand me – had been waiting for your help. Be my friend,
my –" her voice dropped, "– my secret friend. Will you?"

Ah God, what bliss is this! thought Mitka. At last someone is asking for
the gift of my friendship. I who have never had a friend, who have never had
anyone to wholly love. He took her hand kissed it eagerly, humbly. "I will be
yours to my heart," he said.

### III

"Val. Are you there. Can I come in?"
"Yes do. I'm manicuring. What's the time, Mildred."
"About half past three. Paddy's just rung up from the city. He wants me to
go for a run into the country with him. He's hired a motor."
"Dear me, what extravagance," said Valerie putting a little dab of red on
each nail.
"Isn't it, my dear. I think it's for Mitka chiefly. Will you make a fourth? We'll
be back for dinner."
"Yes, I'd like to," said Valerie slowly.
"You & Evershed aren't going out this evening are you" asked Mildred.
The girl shook her head. "No, not that I know of. Yes, I'd like to come.
What time?"
"Well, he's starting now. He'll be here in about half an hour, I suppose. You'd
better get dressed. I know the hours it takes you. How frightfully hot it is still.
You lucky little creature, I believe you've got the coolest room in the house."
"Well I boiled in it last night," said Valerie &, looking up from her polishing,
she and Mildred burst out laughing.
"What do you think of Mitka" asked Mildred. "Here, lend me those things.
I'll have a go at my hands while you get dressed."

"He's a nice little boy," said Valerie lightly.

"Yes, isn't he. Paddy's devoted to him. He's amusing too – don't you think?"

"Yes, he is rather."

"You've made an extraordinary impression on him," said Mildred.

"I have? Oh rot!"

"My dear, it's perfectly true. I watched him at lunch today. He couldn't keep his eyes off you."

"You'll be pairing off the Colonel with your dear Mother next," said Valerie, powdering her neck and arms.

"Not a bad idea either. But I'm quite serious about Mitka. I'd tell you anything."

"Oh well, what does it matter. He'll be gone in five days. I'll draw him on, I've half a mind to. What shall I wear. I never have a rag to put on. I'm frightfully wild with Evershed."

"That's all very well," said Mildred. "But you're a fool to talk like that. Where on earth would you be without Evershed? I don't say he is particularly fascinating but he's worth any amount of money & he's mad about you and he's awfully decent – and talk about spoiling you! Don't you quarrel with your luck, my dear. Eversheds don't grow on trees."

"But Mildred I'm so bored bored bored! You know as well as I do I've never been in love with Evershed & he knows it too. That's what keeps him so keen on me I suppose. But – perhaps it's the hot weather's brought things to a crisis with me. I'm seeking for a romantic passion…"

"And Mitka's to be sacrificed," said Mildred shrewdly.

"Merci Madame." Valerie made a little face. "<u>Je n'aime pas les petits bébés</u>."

"I don't believe you. But you won't listen to me."

"Yes I will, darling." Valerie kissed Mildred very lightly on the eyelids. "I always listen to you, especially when you wear that blue veil and look like a Parisian madonna."

"Oh get along with you."

"Catch hold of his coat, Paddy. Don't let him stand on the seat," said Mildred. "Mitka, you ought to be ashamed of yourself. People will say you've never been in a motor before. Just look at him, Valerie."

Do what he would Mitka could not stop smiling. He did not mind Mildred teasing him. Nobody could upset his happiness. He sat very still beside Paddy. He felt rather than saw his friend opposite to him, her little gloved hands clasped in her lap. This wonderful change in a few hours, he thought. Who am I? Am I the same man who came here last night? I am not at all the same. I belong to someone – the woman who sits opposite to me has asked me to be her – her secret friend. Now when I am at sea I shall always have someone to talk to in my thoughts & to look at the stars with me & to share my sadness. But I cannot be sad <u>like that</u> any more – I can have that precious lovely feeling. Wherever I go my friend is thinking perhaps of me, & whenever I come back there is she to come to. I will come running up from my ship. One thing I must learn – how to make her happy. And then one day she will say, you did this for me Mitka. You gave me this joy. Yes Valerie, this will happen, believe me it will. He said her name over so often in his heart that he felt certain she must hear. But she sat quiet, her eyes half closed, the faint breeze fluttering her long purple veil. Mildred, too, lay back, smiling, soothed by the air and the quick movement to sleepy delight.

"Don't they look lovely," said Mitka to Paddy.

Paddy nodded. "Yes, lovely." He leant across put his hand over Mildred's.

"Are you happy Dredy" he said. I know why he does that, thought Mitka. He is longing for her to look at him a moment. And he was glad for his brother when Mildred pressed his hand & smiled at him. They were in the country flying down the silvered dusty lanes, past fields & fields of hay. The scent of it was in the air like honey. I feel a little drunk, thought Mitka. I wonder is this country really what I see? If so it is the most beautiful –

They drew up at some big iron gates.

"Where are we Paddy."

"It's a place to have tea."

Although he was really so brave and made long speeches to her in his heart and called her by her name, Mitka felt shy of his friend. She seemed to keep him away from her, to join with Mildred in teasing him like a little boy. Quite quite different to the girl of the morning. The afternoon might have been a failure if Mildred had not teased him so much.

"Now's your chance," she said, when tea was over. "Take Valerie away into the garden & lose yourselves. You'll never get such a chance again – she's dying of sentiment."

"Very well," said Valerie. "Come along Mitka. We won't be long. We'll come back for you two here." And he was actually walking with her out of sight of the others down little paths with flowers on either side. They came to a lawn hedged round with holly. A tree covered with yellow flowers grew in one corner. Valerie walked over the grass & sat down under the tree. "Wasn't I clever to take Mildred at her word," she said.

"Wonderfully." Mitka lay down beside her, his face propped in his hands. Flecks of sun & shadow fell on her from the tree & she took up some of the little bell-like flowers that had fallen in the grass & poured them from one hand to the other.

"And now," said Mitka, "you will tell me all about you, won't you. You see, ever since this morning I keep having trembles facing only five days. That is like a clock in me - five days, five days, & then I am gone. Well I must know a lot of you. I can't know enough in five days of a friend, can I?"

"Too much," she said, pouring the flowers through her fingers.

"Please not to laugh," said Mitka seriously.

She bit her lip & glanced at him, sideways. "Well, what do you want me to tell you."

"All," he said eagerly. "As much as possible."

She shook her head. "You'll be sorry."

"No I won't. I can't be. I can only be glad. Oh, please begin - so little time."

Then she was silent & let the flowers fall in her lap & picked them up again & shut them in her hands. "There's nothing to tell you, Mitka," she said.

His heart gave a great thud when she spoke his name. "First time you ever call me by my name is under this tree," he said, and he stared up into the bright branches of this yellow wonder. "Ah, but please please be good to me. Tell me about you."

"What do you want to know?" she said. "You ask me - and I promise to answer." He had to be satisfied with that.

When she had told him, & she told him little enough and all toned down and made fair in the telling, he lay still in the grass & did not look at her. Very slowly he felt his heart beat close to the ground. "And you hate him," he whispered.

"I can't bear him," Valerie shivered.

Mitka put out his hand & stroked her little shoe. "Oh my poor friend, my poor friend," he said. "How terribly brave you are. But surely, surely," he said, "there's some place that you can get away."

She shook her head. "There isn't any. It's not possible. Don't you think if there had been I'd have thought of it by now?"

"To hold you in his power like that. My God!" cried Mitka sitting up & clenching his fists. "What a devil this man must be."

She bent her head. "What makes it so terrible is that he - he -"

"Oh," said Mitka. "Yes, I understand. Oh Valerie - my friend. How am I going to free you? How am I going to make you happy?"

She shook her head & looked at him with her long grey eyes.

"How wonderful you are - how simply marvellous," said Mitka, "and you really are my friend."

"Really." She put a check on his eagerness. "But Mitka you must understand that I have to be careful. We must be secret friends. We mustn't let the world touch us. When you think I am changed & cold you must realize that I have to be like that."

"Once you have explained," he said, "of course I shall never not understand you - and -" he smiled timidly. "Believe me dear friend, we will find out a way."

She brushed the petals off her lap & stood up, looking away from him. "And you don't - despise me," she said.

"I hold you," he said, "like God." They walked back slowly through the shadowy garden. "Is it peculiar in friendship," said Mitka, "for me to tell you how beautiful you are, to voice out loud the way you walk & lift your little head, then smile with your eyes & - all those things?"

IV

On the following evening when Paddy went up to his room to dress for dinner he found his little brother sitting on the side of the bed - in the dark. As he switched on the light Mitka rolled over with his arm across his eyes.

"What's up? What are you doing?" asked Paddy curiously. "Is something the matter, Mitka?"

"No," said a muffled voice. "Only the sudden light, Paddy. It makes me blink." But Paddy was not satisfied. He stooped down and picked up Mitka's

handerchief from the floor, raised his eyebrows as he felt it, and sat down
beside him. It was like old times to come upon Mitka like that - like the days
that Paddy never had time or desire to recall except when he saw his little
brother. What a child he is, thought Paddy - & Mitka, as though he had heard
his words, said, "Yes Paddy, I'm not ashamed before you. I've been crying."
He sat up & caught hold of Paddy's arm. "But not because I am sad,"
he stammered. "No, that's not why. It's because I hate someone so - so fiercely.
I have been crying with rage!"
"I thought you were going to say just the opposite," said Paddy. "I thought,
Mitka, you were crying because you were in love. Sure not?"
"Oh no," said Mitka - his lips quivering - "not a bit - not in the way you
mean. I couldn't be. No, I've been crying in despair, Paddy, in such awful rage.
Ah" - he put up his hands & clutched his head - "terrible, terrible!"
"You won't tell me who it is you hate" & Paddy added to himself: of course
I know.
"No," Mitka shook his head. "I can't do that. Don't ask me. But Paddy - the
sweet and the bitter are such an awful mixture in Life, aren't they? I almost
think it would be better if you couldn't have both at the same time - if you
had all bitter or all sweet. It would be much more bearable - & juster, I think.
Yes really." He looked up at Paddy through his tumbled black hair. "It's so -
impossible," he said, "to be torn by your head & your feet at the same time -
you can't move either way. Tonight," he said, "I don't think God is cruel or
merciful or loving - I think he's really silly, Paddy, & a silly God is a horrible
one to have. I would like to throw up my hands at him and say what an old
fool you are - you imbecile! I suppose you - never - feel like that!"
Paddy shook his head. "Never, Mitka. I'm too hard. I'm too busy thinking
about myself to worry over God. You see, little brother," said Paddy, & he put
his arm round Mitka's shoulders, "you're really in an unfortunate position -
you've never grown a shell. Now to be able to go through Life you've got to
have one, and a thick one too. Everything that touches you makes a mark -
hurts you - or delights you, and as Life isn't all sweet as you say you're bound
to be hurt as well as delighted. Now I'm nearly all shell, Mitka. I couldn't keep
open heart for the world like you do. I want to be powerful - that is, rich
and loved by one woman - and I just fight for those two things on the quiet
& keep myself guarded against everything that can get in the way of them.
So Life's pretty simple for me. But for you," he said, "oh Mitka, you're like
a naked baby on a battlefield."
Mitka rubbed his cheek on Paddy's sleeve. "No," he said, "you're not quite
right. I'll tell you how it is with me. All my life, ever since I can remember,
Paddy, I've had what you call a shell - it's been loneliness. Things have hurt and
delighted me, that's true, but never really badly because I've not been near
them. I've kept quite by myself - lonely, Paddy. Then you see, the life I chose -
to go to sea - I chose because it expressed my lonely feelings better than any
other. Not that I didn't hate and loathe this thing that covered me up - in a
way I did. But in another way, if you can understand me, it was the most
precious thing I could have. You know, although I've known such a lot of

people I've never had any friends because - except for laughing & joking and being on acquaintance terms - I can't understand people, properly. People are too complicated for me & I don't feel at all complicated. I feel - just one thing or another thing as I used to when I was a little boy, that's all." "And now," said Paddy, "you're not lonely any more, is that it?" "In a way - yes, I suppose so." "And you hate the person who's done this to you?"
"Oh my God no," said Mitka quickly. "How could I? No, no, it's not that."
"Oh Mitka," laughed Paddy, "if I sit here any longer with you a long white beard will flow over my chest. You make me feel hundreds of years old. I think I'd better shut you up in a box & take you back to your ship again."

V

And then came Sunday. Mitka remembered the Sundays at Wyndham Square - the untidy idle morning, and then the great dinner at half past one with everybody at the table and then the sleepy hush that fell on the house till tea time. He used to think it a very amusing day. But somehow that Sunday was not today. The dinner was the same, from half past one to half past two - they sat at the long clean table while the German waiter, white & sweating, handed the steaming food. Old Mrs Farmer in a high white cap with a coloured silk butterfly on it pecked at her food just as she used to. The Colonel's shaking hands, the whispering of the South American boys, & Mildred's clear ringing laughter jarred his nerves. What is the matter with me he thought. Why is it all so ugly. And Valerie Brandon sat, proud and mocking by Evershed's side. Mildred would not leave him alone.
"Oh Mitka, you do make me laugh today. I can't keep a serious face when I look at you. What's the matter Paddy, have you been scolding him."
Paddy would not stop her. "Mitka your face is as long as - a double bass. Isn't it, Evershed."
"He is in love," cackled old Mrs Farmer, spilling custard down her black silk bodice. "That's the only reason young people get the dumps."
"Clever mother," mocked Mildred. "Look what a piggy mess you're making of yourself, too."
"You wait," said old Mrs Farmer. It was her everlasting retort. "Just you wait." It was her only defence and she seemed to scent a triumph in it. She munched it over and over in her old mouth - "You wait. Just wait, my lady, that's all."
Is this going on for ever, thought Mitka desperately. But it was over at last, and by and by as on those former amusing Sundays the house grew quiet. What am I going to do now? He went up to Paddy's room but Mildred was there. He peeped into the drawing room - the old people were going to sleep - and on the balcony Evershed and the South American boys were reading out bits from the Sunday papers. There is no place for me, thought Mitka. His heart said, "Where is she, where is Valerie?" Yes, he was miserable, and tired too. He wanted to lean up against things. I'd like to sit on these stairs with my head against the wall, he thought. Then I could be sure of . . .
    He heard her door open and the soft rustle of her silk skirts. She came down the stairs with a pink parasol & a book in her hands.

"What are you doing," she said.

"I'm not quite certain."

"I'm going into the Square to read. Would you like to come." And so they walked out of the house in the hot afternoon sun into the Square. Valerie sat down on a little green bench shaded with her pink parasol. "You haven't got a hat," she said. "Isn't it too hot."

"Oh no, not for me," said Mitka, screwing up his eyes at the sun. "I have a very thick head."

She smiled at him. "You do say funny things."

"Do I" he said anxiously. "You mean silly things."

"No, no, no. I mean funny - and charming - things. I shouldn't like you to talk any other way ... What was the matter with you at dinner today?"

"Ah," began Mitka. "Let me think back. It's such a long way away now, I've forgotten it ... Yes, I remember. I don't know. I felt just miserable."

"But why," she insisted, "why."

"I think perhaps a little piece of your hatred of the house dropped in my heart. And at the same time - there was something else."

"What," said her low kind voice. "Tell me Mitka."

"I'm such a disgusting doubter," he said. "Ever since we walked in that garden I have wanted to ask you again - are you still my friend. You haven't changed? I know you haven't. I hate myself for wanting to hear - & yet when I see you with other people - though I understand why you must be different, I get a sort of fright all the same, & I think: She has forgotten you. It was all a dream! And then I feel I must run to you and ask you & beg you to say it over & over, 'No, not changed - just the same - I am your friend, Mitka.' I won't always be such a fool," said Mitka. "But perhaps it is the newness that makes it so awfully sweet and terrible at the same time. Please don't be offended with me."

"I'm not," she said. "But Mitka -" (what a heavenly name I have, he thought) "- you are content with my friendship, aren't you. I mean if I felt I had made you sad -"

"Oh my God, no. Oh Valerie - if only I could tell you - how all life is changed for ever." She did not seem quite content with his answer. She frowned a little & half shut her eyes as though she were puzzled a little. "But here's another thing," he said, not noticing. "I'm terrified when I think of the letters I want to write to you - you will write to me, often, often."

"Often," she promised, shortly.

"You'll really tell me things."

"Of course I shall."

He moved restlessly. "I go on Tuesday - on Tuesday morning," said Mitka.

"For how long," she asked absently, fingering her rings.

"For - you lied," cried Mitka, catching sight of her drawn brows. "You're tired, Valerie."

"Yes, I believe I am a little. It's the sun." And Mitka had a sudden vision of himself as an immense giant pulling it out of the sky and smashing it because it shone too warmly on Valerie.

That evening was like the first evening. They were all in the drawing room - except Evershed - & Valerie was at the piano again. But Mitka sat alone in a corner and watched, tired & happy. Sometimes as she played she looked across at him. "I am your friend," said her grey eyes - until Evershed came into the drawing room & leant over the piano talking to her in a low voice. Her head was bent. Mitka heard her voice, then saw her look up & smile at Evershed & shrug her shoulders. From his corner Mitka watched the two. All this is nothing, he said to himself. She is your friend. She told you so today. All this does not matter - not at all really. It's nothing to do with you and with her. You are going away on Tuesday & then you need not ever see her with other people. Your thoughts can be quite alone with her. He scolded & comforted his heart, but all to no purpose. His heart began to cry and cry and then to sink in despair in his little shaking body.

## VI

"And so you're going to leave us today," said Mildred. "I don't think you're a very nice boy, Mitka. What were you doing all yesterday. You must have gone out after breakfast - & when did you come in."
"I walked," said Mitka. "I came to a sudden conclusion early in the morning & walked all over London."
"What on earth for?"
"To see it. It isn't anything though. Old webs with no spiders," he said, smiling at her.
"Oh well," said Mildred, "a Mother's blessing. Run along. I must dress. I shan't see you again, shall I?" She had been having breakfast in bed & she had called to Mitka to come & say goodbye.
"No, I suppose not."
"Run along and say goodbye to your little sweetheart," said Mildred.

He had packed his leather bag. He took it downstairs put it in the hall & then went up again to the drawing room. He knew Valerie would be there. She sat on the sofa with her hands in her lap. The blinds were down & the drawing room was very cool & dark. Mitka shut the door & went up to her & stood like a little boy about to say a lesson.
"So you're going," said Valerie.
"Aren't you going to ask me what I did all yesterday" he said in a husky voice.
"Well, I tell you. I made up my mind to say to you: no, please don't write me letters. No, please take back this friendship. I don't want it. I am very sorry."
Valerie opened her eyes at him. "Why," she whispered, watching him keenly, with a sort of delighted surprise waking in her face.
"Because -" he shrugged his shoulders "- I haven't a reason," he said in a low voice. "I haven't a reason at all - except I am not what you thought I was really, and I am a fraud."
"Mitka."
He went over to the piano & leant against it away from her.
"Mitka, if you've changed & you don't want me any longer - if I'm to lose my

friend," she said, "well," she gave a little breathless laugh, "I can't help that, can I - I can't plead for you, can I, Mitka. But I do think that I've got the right to know why - you are - breaking our secret."

He shook his head quickly. "no - I can't tell you. No good asking. The thing to do," he said, speaking slowly, "is for me to say my goodbye and then to go. Goodbye, just like that. Not turn." He turned and looked at her & the words died on his lips. She sat very quiet, her eyes upon him. He could see her little breast rising and falling & he could see her hands half hidden in the black lace shawl. Slowly she seemed to grow and fill the world as he watched her. What did anything else matter. What was anything? Nothing but her remained. "It's no good," he cried sharply. "I can't. I can't tell you," & he stumbled forward & sat beside [her] & put his head in her lap. "I love you, love you, love - "

"Ah," she breathed - in the mirror opposite she smiled at the radiant lovely face that smiled at her, & then she bent over Mitka and laid her hand lightly, lightly on his dark head. "Mitka, are you sure?"

He raised his head and looked up at her, frightened and desperate. His eyes were full of tears and his mouth was set hard. He could not speak - only nod his head; his breath came in shaking sobs.

"Don't," she said tenderly. With infinite gentleness and sweetness she looked at Mitka. "I love you too," whispered Valerie.

"What is that you have said" he stammered. "Say it again. Quickly, quickly." "I love you too."

He seized her hands and kissed them over and over, the backs of her hands, the palms of her hands - each little finger, never taking his eyes off her face. He said in awe & wonder, "You love me," and again, holding her hand against his heart, "You <u>love</u> me!"

She nodded. Smiles flew over her lips. How radiant she was, and yet there was a kind of tired languor in her gestures and her voice. "Oh, for a long time. Didn't you … really know?"

"If God had appeared to me & told me I should not have believed him. How could I believe that this world could hold such a heaven." He gave a queer run-away laugh. "I'm not dreaming, am I? This is I, Mitka, & you are Valerie - and you have said you love me." Suddenly he put his arms around her. She leaned to him and they kissed each other. In that long kiss Mitka gave himself and his brave love and his hopes and all his being into the keeping of Valerie. "Forgive me," he said. "Forgive me."

"Why" she whispered, looking at him in ecstasy - & yet she was calm & he trembled violently.

"I am so unworthy & I am so weak. I can hardly bear my joy. What have I done to be this happy man. Ah!" he cried, "how beautiful you are, my love - how marvellously beautiful - there's a light shining from every little finger in you like the light from a saint. Valerie, Valerie." She lay among the cushions and smiled at him. He bent over her. "And you will be my wife."

Came a tiny pause - long enough for a throb of surprise in Valerie's bosom. Then she said, "Yes, your wife, Mitka."

He made as if to kiss her again then he drew away & clasped his hands together. "No, no!" he said in a strained voice. "Don't let me. Help me, Valerie. Don't let me kiss you too much. If I do I shall go mad and I shall not be able to leave you – and we have to part now. Yes yes we must – if only to come together again, dearest. I must leave you soon."
"So soon as that?" she whispered – and she put her arms round him & drew him to her and pressed his head on her breast. "Forget everything," she whispered, "everything except that we love each other my dearest, my dearest."

He broke away from her arms. "That's just what I can't do," he stammered. "Don't you understand." And he got up & walked quickly up and down the room. "I am lost if I do that. You see this sudden joy, and you, so sweet to me, & my thoughts on fire, and all the future to be settled in just this breath of time – suddenly, you understand. My angel," said Mitka, "my beloved soul, I have to leave you, and we must wait for our caresses and for our happiness until I come back quickly, as quickly as I can, & take you away & we are married. Now," he said, "we have to decide everything, to make our plans." He stopped in front of her & took her hands & began kissing them again. "Already, Valerie, my head is full of plans. I can even see our house already, and our child." She sat quite still with her head bent. "Listen to me, my darling – " and he began to talk and to arrange & plot and settle these marvellous happenings. He was going now to Alexandria to get money. Then he would go to Marseilles. He had friends there. He could get something to do in Marseilles. In the meantime he would borrow enough money for them both & she would come to him there. That was the best. They would start a new life together, far away from everybody, from everything. Now Evershed & his threats did not matter. Nothing & nobody could touch or harm them.

Life unfolded like a sweet flower as he spoke. He smelled its fragrance, he leaned over it and the dazzling miracle of its beauty & colour intoxicated him – he spoke on and on, for years it seemed to the listening Valerie – who never moved or looked up, whose hands lay in his without warmth or pressure. Just once when he knelt by her and said "Ah Valerie, our life together, our children" a little smile crooked her lips & she raised her eyebrows faintly. Otherwise she gave no sign.

## VII

One morning a few weeks later Mildred walked into Valerie's room. The young girl was in bed and asleep. Mildred stood looking down upon her and wondering in a vague way how or why Valerie kept her childishness of appearance. She lay on her back; the sleeves of her nightgown had fallen back leaving her arms bare to the shoulders. Long curls of black hair lay on either side of her cheeks, her eyelashes and brows cast a faint shadow, her lips were parted to her gentle breathing. Yes, she's lovely! thought Mildred. Good Lord how innocent she looks. I expect she's as passionate a little devil as they make them. Mildred drew the curtains from the window but Valerie did not stir.

On the dressing table lay her scarf, long white gloves, a fan, and a big bunch of bruised yellow roses. The room was littered and disordered with her clothes and toilet jars, but Mildred realized this untidiness as something careless and fascinating, a part of Valerie. Yes, if I were a man I'd be in love with this little minx, too. She's so certain of herself and so utterly careless, and yet she keeps her secret. Yes, she's cold and passionate. With her thumb and finger Mildred flicked the envelope she held in her hand, glanced at the writing and postage mark, and made a little grimace. Valerie sighed, flung out her arms, half rolled over and sat up, shaking her head.

"I'm not at all awake yet," she said in a clear unreal voice (children who talk in their sleep speak so).

"Well, its high time you were," said Mildred. "Its after eleven o'clock. There's a letter for you," and she gave it to Valerie.

"You're an angel," said Valerie, just glancing at the letter. "We didn't get in until four. Went to one of those idiotic clubs." She smiled. "Ah, come and sit down a tiny minute by me," she coaxed. Mildred sat down and Valerie put her arms round her.

"So its still going on, is it?" asked Mildred, running her finger up one of Valerie's curls.

"What? You mean these pathetic effusions?" said Valerie.

"Mm. I was in your room the other day when the housemaid was turning it round & she pulled dozens from behind the white paper frill of the fireplace. I knew they were from the same - the poor child uses such funny paper. Do you read them?"

But Valerie did not answer. Instead she said, "Well what am I to do? I can't stop him. I've written and told him its hopeless until I'm tired. Its all very well for you to laugh, but its boring - and so stupid. There's something humiliating in a boy's letters. Gaucherie can be rather delightful when you're with a person - charming eyes, a baby mouth, silky hair can carry it off. But by letter - oh dear <u>no</u>. What are you laughing at."

"You. I am laughing at you troubling to play for me. I know perfectly well you're up to some game with Mitka. I'd love to know what it is. He's a queer little creature. I am sure that if you had told him to stop writing he wouldn't write. He's too proud & too sensitive to do that. Well I don't believe you've told him. But then you're not in love with him, so why keep him on the hop?"

Valerie lay down in bed, threw the letter up in the air and caught it again. "Bother me," she said lightly, "<u>I</u> don't know. But if once I've touched a thing I can't let it go until I've tried to break it or to see if it can break me. Its my one principle - snatched from a weary world - " Then she sat up & tore open the letter. The envelope slipped off the sheet on to the floor. There were pages & pages of fine careful writing. "Like to hear?" she said, making a face at Mildred. But Mildred moved away from the bed.

"No, no. I loathe hearing things being killed - & babies cry worse than pigs. Bon appétit, you little witch." She drifted out of the room.

Dearest of all

Do not be frightened. I am writing to you in my bed. I have caught a fever of some kind on the top of some pleurisy and therefore I am not well. Excuse my stupidity. What a fool I am. I believe it was anxiousness. It is so long since I have had a letter from you & the waiting and thinking from the first to hear has made me a little tired. There have been so many things to do and I am not the man of affairs that Paddy is. But people have been angels. That is because I love you. I have carried you in my heart wherever I went & I do not believe a person has seen me - it is you they have seen in my looks, and it is for you they have been kind. As I told you last week, my father has sent me the money. Everything is ready & waiting for you. I am staying here until you come & we find where you should wish to live. Of course where I am now would not do for you, but for me it is all right, and it saves me money. Besides, everywhere is heaven with you in my heart. In the first days of my illness the room was so full of you I stretched out my arms to it like a child does to a garden. I know there is a good reason why you don't write. I know I must not try you - & you are wise - but still I am so stupid, every time the postman sounds in the street I rush to the stair-case & my heart beats up. Lying here among all other steps I know his now. Even if I lie asleep my heart hears them and wakes me & I run out of bed. Come, my darling. Everything waits for you. Come soon. It will not be hard. I know you are very delicate & fine, but do not be afraid. Such foolishness to write but my head burns. Valerie, Valerie. I kiss your little feet. I implore them to bring you quickly to me. I adore you.

However, I shall burn it, she thought. She got out of bed & dropped this letter too behind the white paper frill in the fireplace. Yes, she was really curious, and the idea of Marseilles was exciting, decidedly. Of course she had never meant to go. Not really, but just for a time. And she saw herself in a white room overlooking a garden of pink waxy flowers that reached down to the sea. Mitka was with her, lying on his back with his eyes closed, very flushed, his ears & lips very pink. Yes, he'd look just like that. He'd be an awfully charming lover - after my commercial bulldog. But you couldn't live up to [it], my child, she said, staring at herself in the glass. Because, you see, my lady, that's what's the matter with you. Her lips smiled gaily, but her eyes said Yes, that is true - you're too clever to be found out, but you'd kill him, you know you would - and oh what complications! But Marseilles. <u>Well</u> - and maybe I can buy white carnations from a dark musky-smelling flower seller who could not keep his eyes off her whiteness. You're a perfect little thing being loving to this boy, she scolded herself, <u>or</u> you're degenerating - choose which one you like the better. I am sure he has [...]

## VIII

Again he heard the sound of those footsteps. Again he rushed to the door, opened it and hung over the iron stair rail. They were coming up the stairs, they were quite near. Again he made that tremendous effort to speak above the throbbing of his heart. "Anything for me?" Oh my God – what had happened? The postman looked up at him, grinned, came up further, dipped into his satchel and Mitka bent and took the letter through the bars.

"V'là M'sieu'," said the postman, passing the letter into the trembling hands as though it were bread he carried.

But Mitka did not answer. He straightened up & holding the stair rail he went slowly, slowly back into his room, shut the door, leant against it, the letter pressed to his heart. There was a piece of mirror on the wall opposite the door. As he raised his eyes he saw himself reflected in it, so transfigured, so mysteriously joyful. Mitka is dead, he thought. Mitka is a saint. For a long time he stood there. And a strange thing happened. He forgot all about the letter that lay on his heart. With wondering eyes he looked at his little room. A funny little room under the roof of a huge building. In one corner stood a bed covered with a red quilt patterned with yellow flowers. In another an iron wash-stand. A table stood in the middle with a chair pushed against it. His luggage was piled against a wall. On a shelf by the bed there were bottles – bottles of all colours. A pencil ray of sun shining on these bottles made them wonderfully beautiful. Over the window hung a battered blind but it did not keep the sun out. The sun shone in rays and big soft spots of gold light on the floor & walls. Tenderly, he smiled at the room and walked to the table & sat down by it. Yes, I lived here, said Mitka. He tapped with the letter on the dusty table. It's rather nice, he said dreamily. The blind lifted and tapped to a little breeze. Through the window there came the sound of long-drawn cries and lazy shouting. AAAI drawled a voice, and then EEEEEE – just the same sound their old gardener made with his tongue when he chased a swarm of bees. AAAI came in lazy shouts – and then the old gardener answered, angry and bustling. He wanted very much to get up from his chair and look out of the window but no, his body would not move. It was no use trying. He sat still. He felt very peaceful, almost as if he were at sea again. Yes, his little room with the spots of sun and beautiful bottles floated in the sea, and those were the voices of sailors. Why do I feel so frail? Yes, I know. It is because I have not been to sleep such a long time – and at the thought he began to breathe slowly but not too profoundly because a deep breath moved a knife that had fallen into the bottom of his lung. But it was good even to breathe like that. How long was it since he had been to sleep? Well, he could not remember. Perhaps he had not been to sleep for years. Now he could move. He got up from the table and lifted his arms above his head, and walking carefully so as not to step upon the quivering spots of lovely light that danced on the floor he reached the bed and lay down, pressing his head into the pillow. Away floated Mitka in the room in the roof. Away he floated. AAAA-iiii came fainter & fainter now and the sun danced on Valerie's letter.

That was how she found him. An African servant with a slop pail had met her at the bottom of the stairs, had struggled in front of her up the five flights, the stinking pail still in her hand. Valerie opened the door & came in – quite quietly. But when she saw Mitka lying on the bed she ran over to him –

terribly frightened for a moment. No – nothing <u>like that</u> had happened. He was only sound asleep, his face covered with beads of sweat, lying on his back, his lips and his ears very pink. Had she dreamed this. But not this disgusting dreadful room, not this vile house, that awful African woman, the smells. So this was where he expected her to come – it was to this place. She looked at the flowers she carried – white carnations bought from a musky-smelling flower seller. She held them to her face. She saw the red & blue bottles, the ugly blobs of sun spilling through the broken blind – and then she saw on the dusty table her unopened letter to him. Her presence of mind never deserted her a moment. Deliberately & making no attempt to hush her steps she walked across to the table, picked up her letter. She even took care to see the petals of her flowers had fallen. I loathe the cheap properties of tragedy, thought Valerie, shutting the door after her.

IX

Evershed was waiting in the room of the hotel, striding up & down, his face dark red, his eyes immense & glazed. When she opened the door he started violently. "Where in God's hell have you been" said Evershed. "You've given me a pretty turn. Here I go out for a jiffy to get some cigarettes & come back to find this – this bloody little note <u>Back in an hour's time</u>. Look here, Valerie, you can't do that sort of thing you know. It's – it's not cricket. It's – it's a damnable trick to play on a man." He was trembling all over & wiping his eyelids & his moustache with a folded handkerchief. "What did you do it for? Why didn't you tell me? Did you want to buy something? What was it?" She looked at him in amazement, a childish smile on her lips. "You poor old boy, I never dreamed you'd feel like that. I merely thought while you were away I'd like to go for a walk after that train. I'd got a headache. And I felt cross. I wanted air & I wanted to walk off my black monkey. Did I really give you a fright." She put up her hands to untie her veil. "You're joking." "Joking!" He gave a great sigh of relief & flopped on to the bed. "I never thought a man could be such a fool about a woman. I nearly howled. I was half mad, Valerie. Everything you could imagine rushed into my brain. Why, I thought you'd done it on purpose. Brought me here and then skeedaddled – no not quite as bad as that, but I – well it's no good going over it again. Was that really all. You weren't chippy with me or anything. I thought you seemed a bit quiet in the train. Thunder!" said Evershed, "that was a nasty scare." "On the contrary," said Valerie. She had taken off her hat. She lifted her hair off her face & went over to him & perched on his knee looking up at him with a strange wistful smile. She put her hands on his hot cheeks. "I believe I'm really falling in love with you," she whispered. "Valerie, my Queen," said Evershed. "I knew you'd come round, little girl."

# Notebook 34

[Notebook 34, qMS–1252][39]

I bought a book by Henry James yesterday and read it, as they say, "until far into the night". It was not very interesting or very good, but I can wade through pages and pages of dull, turgid James for the sake of that sudden sweet shock, that violent throb of delight that he gives me at times. I don't doubt this genius: only there is an extraordinary amount of pan and an amazingly raffiné flash.

One thing I want to annotate. His hero, Bernard Longueville, brilliant, rich, dark, agile etc. though a witty companion is perhaps wittiest and most amused when he is alone, and preserves his best things for himself. All the attributive adjectives apart I am witty, I know, and a good companion – but I feel my case is exactly like his – the amount of minute and delicate joy I get out of watching people and things when I am alone is simply enormous. I really only have "perfect fun" with myself. When I see a little girl running by on her heels like a fowl in the wet and say "My dear there's a Gertie" I laugh and enjoy it as I never would with anybody. Just the same applies to my feeling for what is called "nature". Other people won't stop & look at the things I want to look at or if they do they stop to please me or to humour me or to keep the peace. But I am so made that as true as I'm with anyone I begin to give consideration to their opinions and their desires – & they are not worth half the consideration that mine are.

I don't miss Jack at all now. I don't want to go home. I feel quite content to live here in a furnished room & watch. Its a pure question of weather – though that aside I believe. (A <u>terrific</u> Gertie has just past.) Life with other people

---

[39]Printed on the front cover of this notebook is:

L'EPATANT
Cahier de 50 Pages

Appartenant à        *Katherine Mansfield*
Commencé le         *Toujoursième*
Fini le                    *Jamaisième*
Murry's note: Winter 1915–1916.

becomes a blur: it does with Jack, but its enormously valuable & marvellous when I'm alone - the detail of life - the <u>life</u> of life. Carco feels that too - but nobody else. Perhaps in a negative way, Lesley does. Yes, she does.[40]

[J80-81]

<u>Rough sketch</u>.

This family began very modest with Mamma, extremely fat, with a black moustache and a little round toque covered with poached pansies, and the baby boy, bursting out of an english tweed suit that was intended for a norfolk but denied its county at the second seam. They had barely settled in their places and pinched every separate piece of bread in the basket and chosen the crustiest when two young men in pale blue uniforms with about as much moustache as mother appeared at the doorway of the restaurant and were hailed with every appearance of enthusiam by sonny who waved a serviette about the size of a single bedsheet at them. Mother was embraced; they sat down side by side and were presently joined by an unfortunate overgrown boy whose complexion had enjoyed every possible form of Frühlingserwachen and who looked as though he spent his nights under an eiderdown eating chocolate biscuits with the window shut and reading L'Histoire des Petits Pantalons pas tout a fait fermé.

Five single bedsheets were tucked into five collars. Five pairs of eyes roamed over the menu. Suddenly with a cry of delight up flew Mamma's arms - up flew Sonny's. The 2 young soldiers sprang to their feet, the étudiant came out in no end of a perspiration as a stout florid man appeared & walked towards them. The waitress hovered round the table delighted beyond words at this exhibition of vie de famille. She felt like their own bonne. She felt she had known them for years. Heaven knows what memories she had of taking M. Roue his hot water, of being found by M. Paul, looking for his shirt stud on his bedroom floor on her charming little hands & her still more delicious knees.     [J81-82]

February 13th [1916][41]

I have written practically nothing yet & now again the time is getting short. There is nothing done. I am no nearer my achievement than I was 2 months ago & I keep half doubting my will to perform anything. Each time I make a vow my demon says at almost the very same moment: "Oh yes, we've heard that before!" And then I hear R.B. in the Cafe Royale "Do you still write?" If I went back to England without a book <u>finished</u> I should give myself up. I should know that, whatever I said, I was not really a writer & had no claim to "a table in my room". But if I do go back with a book finished it will be a profession de foi pour toujours. <u>Why</u> do I hesitate so long? Is it just idleness? Lack of will power? Yes, I feel thats what it is & thats why its so immensely

---

[40]The above passage and the following one are written on pages that were not originally part of this notebook. They have been slipped into it subsequently, probably by Murry, and he has dated them 'Paris, May 1915'.

[41]Prior to this passage, which has been numbered page 4 by Murry, two pages have been cut out of this notebook.

important that I should assert myself. I have put a table today in my room, facing a corner, but from where I sit I can see some top shoots of the almond tree & the sea sounds loud. There is a vase of beautiful geraniums on the table. Nothing could be nicer than this spot & its so quiet & so high, like sitting up in a tree. I feel I shall be able to write here, especially towards twilight.

Ah, once fairly alight how I'd blaze and burn! Here is a new fact. When I am not writing I feel my brother calling me & he is not happy. Only when I write or am in a state of writing - a state of 'inspiration' do I feel that he is calm. Last night I dreamed of him and of Father Zossima.[42] Father Zossima said "do not let the new man die." My brother was certainly there. But last evening he called me while I sat down by the fire. At last I obeyed and came upstairs. I stayed in the dark & waited. The room got very light. There were stars outside - very bright twinkly stars that seemed to move as I watched them. The moon shone. I could see the curve of the sea & the curve of the land embracing & above in the sky there was a round sweep of cloud. Perhaps those 3 half circles were "very magic". But then when I leaned out of the window I seemed to see my brother dotted all over the field - now on his back, now on his face, now huddled up, now half pressed into the earth. Wherever I looked there he lay I felt that God showed me to him like that for some express purpose & I knelt down by the bed - but I could not pray. I had done no work - I was not in an active state of grace. So I got up finally & went downstairs again. But I was terribly sad. The night before when I lay in bed I felt suddenly passionate. I wanted Jack to embrace me. But as I turned to speak to him or to kiss him I saw my brother lying fast asleep - and I got cold. That happens nearly always. Perhaps because I went to sleep thinking of him I woke & was he - for quite a long time. I felt my face was his serious, sleepy face. I felt that the lines of my mouth were changed & I blinked like he did on waking.

This year I have to make money & get known. I want to make enough money to be able to give Lesley some. In fact I want to provide for her. That's my idea & to make enough so that Jack and I shall be able to pay our debts & live honourably. I should like to have a book finished & <u>numbers</u> of short stories ready. Ah, even as I write, the smoke from my cigarette seems to mount in a reflective way & I feel nearer that kind of silent crystallized being that used to be almost me.      [J94-96]

14th. I began to think of an unfinished memory which has been with me for years. It is a very good story if only I can tell it right, and is called 'Lena'. It plays in New Zealand and so would go in the book. If only I can get right down to it. Dear brother, as I jot these notes I am speaking to you. To whom did I always write when I kept those huge complaining diaries? Was it to myself? But now as I write these words and talk of getting down to the

---

[42] A visionary and holy man, Father Zossima's position as an elder in a Russian monastery is described in Chapter V ('Elders') of Book I of *The Brothers Karamazov* by Fyodor Dostoevsky.

New Zealand atmosphere I see you opposite to me, I see your thoughtful seeing eyes. Yes it is to you –

We were travelling – sitting opposite to each other & moving very fast. Ah, my darling, how have I kept away from this tremendous joy. Each time I take up my pen <u>you</u> are with me, you are mine. You are my playfellow, my brother, & we shall range all over our country together. It is with you that I see & that is why I see so clearly. That is a great mystery. My brother I have doubted these last few days. I have been in dreadful places. I have felt that I could not <u>come</u> through to you. But now, quite suddenly, the mists are rising and I see and I know you are near me. You are more vividly with me now this moment than if you were alive & I were writing to you from a short distance away. As you speak my name, the name you call me by that I love so – Katie – your lip lifts in a smile. You believe in me, you know I am here. Oh Chummie[43] – put your arms round me. I was going to write – let us shut out everybody, but no – it is not that. Only we shall "look on" at them together.

My brother, you know with all my desire, my will is weak. To do things, even to write, absolutely for myself and by myself is awfully hard for me. God knows why when my desire is so strong. But just as it was always our delight to sit together – you remember? – & talk of the old days, down to the last detail, the last feeling, looking at each other & by our eyes expressing when speech ended how intimately we understood each other – so now, my dear one, we shall do that again. You know how unhappy I have been lately? I almost felt – perhaps "the new man" will not live. Perhaps I am not yet risen … But now I do not doubt. It is the idea (it has always been there but never as it is with me tonight) that I do not write alone. That every word I write & every place I visit I carry you with me. Indeed that might be the motto of my book. There are daisies on the table and a red flower, like a poppy, shines through. Of daisies I will write, of the dark, of the wind – & the sun & the mists, of wharves – ah! of all that you loved & that I too love and feel. Tonight it is made plain. However often I write & rewrite I shall not really falter, dearest – and the book shall be written & ready.     [J96-97]

15. I have broken the silence. It took long. Did I fail you when I sat reading. Oh, bear with me a little. I will be better. I will do <u>all</u> all that we would wish. Love, I will not fail. Tonight it is very wild. Do you hear? It is all wind and sea – you feel that the world is blowing like a feather, springing and rocking in the air like a baloon from Lindsays. I seem to hear a piano sometimes but that's fancy. How loud the wind sounds! If I write into my diary faithfully a little record of how I have kept faith with you – that is what I must do. Now you are back with me – you are stepping forward, one hand in your pocket. My brother, my little boy brother. Your thoughtful eyes! I see you always as you left me. I saw you one moment alone – by yourself, & quite lost, I felt.

---

[43]'Chummie' was a family name for Leslie, KM's brother.

My heart yearned over you then. Oh, it yearns over you tonight & now!
Did you cry? I always felt he never never must be unhappy. Now I will come
quite close to you, take your hand, and we shall tell this story to each other.

16th. I <u>found</u> The Aloe this morning. And when I had reread it I knew that
I was not quite 'right' yesterday. No, dearest, it was not just the spirit.
The Aloe is right. The Aloe is lovely. It simply fascinates me, and I know that it
is what you would wish me to write. And now I know what the last chapter is.
It is your birth – your coming in the autumn, you in Grandmothers arms
under the tree, your solemnity, your wonderful beauty, your hands, your head,
your helplessness – lying on the earth, & above all your tremendous solemnity.
That chapter will end the book. The next book will be yours and mine.
And you must mean the world to Linda & before ever you are born Kezia
must play with you. Her little Bogey. Oh Bogey – I must hurry. All of them
must have this book. It is good, my treasure, my little brother – it is good and
it is what we really meant.      [J97-98]

17th. I am sad tonight. Perhaps it is the old forlorn wind. And the thought of
you <u>spiritually</u> is not enough tonight. I want you by me. I must get deep down
into my book for then I shall be happy. Lose myself, lose myself to find you,
dearest. Oh, I want this book to be written. It <u>must</u> be done. It must be
bound and wrapped and sent to New Zealand. I feel that with all my soul.
It will be.      [J98]

My head is full of only one thing. I can't begin writing or even thinking
because all my thoughts revolve round le seul sujet. It is a real vice avec moi au
présent. I keep thinking round and round it, beating up and down it and still
it stays in my head and wont let me be. I keep figuring it out, making other
plans, feeling sure I still havent got enough <u>wits</u>. How maddening it is!
I despise myself. I must begin to think of other things. The thing is that today
for some maddening reason I simply <u>can't</u> concentrate. Mais c'est joli.
C'est joli comme un [...]. Il y a une cabinet avec[?] de l'eau courante, vous
savez. Je vous dis Madame, c'est une affaire de toute beauté.

> Sunday Morning. Five minutes to eleven.
> F.G.[44]
> Never did cowcumber lie more heavy on a female's buzzum that [sic]
> your last letter to me is as you might say dying and curdling and setting
> up sich an explogion
> > Villa Pauline
> > Bandol
> > (Var)
> > Sunday
> Mr F.G.
> Never did cowcumber lie more heavy on a female's buzzum than your
> curdling effugion which I have read twice and wont again if horses drag

---

[44]Frederick Goodyear. See Volume One, footnote 271.

me. But I keep wondering, and cant for the life of me think, whatever there was in mine to so importantly disturb you. (Henry James is dead. Did you know?) I did not, swayed by a resistless passion[45] say that I loved you. Nevertheless I'm prepared to say it again looking at this pound of onions that hangs in a string kit from a saucepan nail. But, Betsy love, what has that got to do with the Kilner Idea? I recognise the Kilner Idea, I acknowledge it and even understand it, but whats it got to do with me? Nothing. I don't want to rob you of it. . . And why should you write to me as though I'd got into the family way with H.G.W. and driven round to you in a hansom cab to ask you to make a respectable woman of me? Yes, youre bad tempered, suspicious and surly. And if you think I flung my bonnet over you as a possible mill[?], my lad, you're mistook. So shut up about your Five Whores <u>and</u> a Hedgehog and send me no more inventories of those marbil halls wherein of aforetime they did delight to wander.

In fact, now I come to ponder on your last letter I don't believe you want to write to me at all & Im hanged if Ill shoot arrows in the air. But perhaps that is temper on my part; it is certainly pure stomach. Im so hungry, simply empty, and seeing in my minds eye just now a surloin of beef, well browned with plenty of gravy <u>and</u> horseradish sauce and baked potatoes I nearly sobbed. There's nothing here to eat except omelettes and oranges and onions. Its a cold, sunny windy day – the kind of day when you want a tremendous feed for lunch & an armchair in front of the fire to boaconstrict in afterwards. I feel sentimental about England now – English food, <u>decent</u> English <u>waste</u>! How much better than these thrifty french whose flower gardens are nothing but potential salad bowls. There's not a leaf in France that you cant 'faire une infusion avec', not a blade that isn't bon pour le cuisine. By God, I'd like to buy a pound of the best butter, put it on the window sill and watch it melt to spite em. They are a stingy uncomfortable crew for all their lively scrapings. For instance, in their houses – what appalling furniture – and never one comfortable chair. If you want to talk the only possible thing to do is to go to bed. Its a case of either standing on your feet or lying in comfort under a puffed up eiderdown. I quite understand the reason for what is called french moral laxity – you're simply forced into bed – no matter with whom – there's no other place for you ... Supposing a <u>young</u> man comes to see about the electric light & will go on talking and pointing to the ceiling, or a friend drops in to tea and asks you if you believe in Absolute Evil. How can you give your mind to these things when youre sitting on four knobs and a square inch of cane. How much better to lie snug and <u>give yourself up to it</u>.

---

[45]E M Forster in his novel *Howard's End*, published in October 1910, uses the phrase 'resistless power' in Chapter 29.

<u>Later</u>

Now I've eaten one of the omelettes and one of the oranges. The sun has gone in; its beginning to thunder. There's a little bird in a tree outside this window not so much singing as sharpening a note. He's getting a very fine point on it; I expect you would know his name. Write to me again when everything is not <u>too</u> bunkum.

> Goodbye for now.
> With my 'strictly relative' love
> 'K.M.'

[J107-109]

March 4th

Dear Frieda

The new house sounds very nice and I am glad to think we shall be there – all of us together – this Spring. Thank you for your letter, dear, but you really haven't been right in judging us first the kind of traitors that you did. Jack <u>never</u> would hear a word against Lawrence

# *Unbound Papers*

[MS-Papers-4006–04]<sup>46</sup>

## Chapter III

All that day school seemed unreal and silly to Rachael. Round and round, like a musical box with only one tune, went her mind on what had happened the evening before. Her head ached with trying to remember every little detail and every word. She did not want to remember, but somehow, she could not stop trying. She answered questions and made mistakes in her sums and recited "How Horatius Kept the Bridge" like a little girl in a dream. The day crawled by. "That was the first time I've ever stood up to him," she thought. "I wonder if everything will always be different now. We can't even pretend to like each other again." Bottlenose! Bottlenose! She smiled again remembering the word but at the same time she felt frightened. She had not seen her Father that morning. The grandmother told her that he had promised not to mention the subject again. "But I don't believe that," thought Rachael. "I wish it hadn't happened. No, I'm glad it has. I wish that he was dead – Oh, what Heaven that would be for us!" But she could not imagine that sort of person dying. She remembered suddenly the way he sucked in his moustache when he drank and the long hairs he had on his hands, and the noises he made when he had indigestion. No, that sort of person seemed too real to die. She worried the thought of him until she was furious with rage. "How I detest him – detest him!" The class stood up to sing. Rachael shared a book with Tui.

> "Oh forest, green and fair
> Oh pine trees waving high
> How sweet their cool retreat
> How full of rest"

sang the little girls. Rachael looked out through the big bare windows to the wattle trees, their gold tassels nodding in the sunny air, and suddenly the sad

---

<sup>46</sup>Murry published this piece in *The Scrapbook* with 'Rachael' changed to 'Kezia', and 'Mrs Preston' changed to 'Mrs Fairfield'. He titled it 'Kezia and Tui'. Another piece of the story, titled 'Young Country', from Newberry Notebook 2, is reproduced in Volume One, p 261.

tune and the trees moving so gently made her feel quite calm. She looked down at the withered sweet pea that drooped from her blouse. She saw herself sitting on the grandmother's lap and leaning against the grandmother's bodice. That was what she wanted. To sit there and hear grannie's watch ticking against her ear and bury her face in the soft warm place smelling of lavender and put up her hand and feel the five owls sitting on the moon ...[47]

Mrs Preston was in the garden when she came home - stooping over the pansies. She had a little straw basket on her arm, half filled with flowers. Rachael went up to her and leant against her and played with her spectacle case. "Sweetheart, listen," she said. "Its no good saying I'm sorry because I am not. And I'm not ashamed either. Its no good trying to make me." Her face grew hard. "I <u>hate</u> that man and I <u>won't</u> pretend. But because you're more -" she hesitated, groping for the words - "more <u>valuable</u> than he is, I won't behave like that again - not unless I absolutely feel I can't help it, Grannie." She looked up and smiled. "See?"
"I can't make you do what you don't want to, Rachael" said Mrs Preston.
"No" said she. "Nobody can. Can they? Otherwise it wouldn't be any good wanting anything for your own self - would it? Aren't the pansies pretties, Grannie. I'd like to make pets of them."
"I think they're rather like my little scaramouch in the face" said Mrs Preston smiling and pulling Rachael's pink ear.
"Oh, thank Goodness" sighed Rachael. "You're yourself again. We've made it up. Haven't we? I can't bear being serious for a long time together. Oh my Grannie, I've got to be happy with you. When I go thinking of serious things I could poke out my tongue at myself." She took Mrs Preston's hand & stroked it. "You do love me, don't you?"
"Of course, you silly billy."
"We-ll", laughed Rachael, "That's the only real thing, isn't it?"
"There are two bits of cold pudding inside for you and Tui," said Mrs Preston. "Run along & take it to her while I finish the ironing. I only came out while the iron was getting hot."
"You won't be wretched if I leave you alone" asked Rachael. She danced in to the house, found the pudding, and danced over to Beads.
"Mrs Bead. Tui. Where are you," she called stepping over a saucepan, two big cabbages and Tui's hat and coat inside the kitchen door.
"We're upstairs. I'm washing my hair in the bathroom. Come up, darling" cooed Tui. Ray bounded up the stairs. Mrs Bead in a pink flannel dressing gown sat on the edge of the bath; and Tui stood in torn calico drawers, a towel round her shoulders and her head in a basin. "Hallo, Mrs Bead" said Rachael. She buried her head in the Maori woman's neck and put her teeth in a roll of soft fat. Mrs Bead pulled Ray between her knees and had a good look at her. "Well, Tui," she said, "you are a little fibber. Tui told me you'd had a fight with your Father and he'd given you two black eyes."

---

[47]A silver brooch referred to again on p 96 in 'Things happened so simply then'.

"I didn't – I didn't" cried Tui, stamping. "No one is looking after me. Pour a jug of water over my head, Mummy. Oh Ray, don't listen to her."

"Pooh! its nothing new" said Ray. "You're always lying. I'll pour the water over your head." She rolled up her sleeves and deluged Tui who gave little moaning cries. "I'm drowned, drowned, drowned," she said, wringing out her long black hair.

"You have got a lot of it," said Ray.

"Yes." Tui twisted it round her head. "But I shan't be content till it is down to my knees. Don't you think it would be nice to be able to wrap yourself up in your hair?"

"What funny ideas you have," said Ray, considering Tui. "Mrs Bead, don't you think Tui's getting awfully conceited."

"Oh not more than she ought to" said Mrs Bead, stretching herself and yawning. "I believe in girls thinking about their appearance and Tui could do a lot with herself if she liked."

"Well she doesn't think about anything else, do you Tui?"

"No, darling," Tui smiled.

"Well, why should she" remarked Mrs Bead easily. "She's not like you, Ray. She hasn't got any brain for books, but she's real smart in making up complexion mixtures and she keeps her feet as neat as her hands."

"When I grow up" said Tui "I mean to be a terri-fic beauty. Mother's going to take me to Sydney when I'm sixteen – but I mean to be the rage if I die for it. And then I'm going to marry a rich Englishman and have five little boys with beautiful blue eyes."

"Well, you never know," said Mrs Bead. "And if you turn out into a raging beauty, Tui, I'll take you to Sydney, sure. What a pity you couldn't come too Ray."

"We'd make such an uncommon pair," suggested Tui. Rachael shook her head. "No, Grannie and I are going to live by ourselves when I grow up, and I'm going to make money out of flowers and vegetables and bees."

"But don't you want to be rich" cried Ray [ie Tui], "and travel all over the world and have perfect clothes? Oh, dear. If I thought I was going to live all my life with Mummy in this piggy little house I believe I'd die of grief."

"Yes, that's a good thing about you Tui" said Mrs Bead. "Though you're lazy like me you want a lot to be lazy on, and you're quite right, dearie, quite right. I made a great mistake coming to a little town like this, but then I'd got sick of things and I had enough money to keep us and once I got the furniture in here I seemed to lose heart, somehow. You ought to have ambitions, Ray, but I think you'll come on slower than Tui. You do keep skinny, don't you," said Mrs Bead. "Why, Tui's got quite a figure beside you."

"She hasn't got any front at all, Mummy," gurgled Tui. "Have you, cherie? Mummy, go downstairs & make us some cocoa, and I'll get dressed & come down to finish my hair at the fire." Mrs Bead left the two little [girls].

They went into Tui's bedroom. "Look!" said Tui. "Doesn't it surprise you? Mummy and I fixed it yesterday." The shabby untidy little room had changed to suit Tui's romantic mood. White muslin curtains made out of an old skirt of her mother's adorned the bed, and everywhere Rachael looked there were pink sateen bows. Over the looking glass, on the back of the chair, on the gas bracket & the four black iron bed poles.

"Why don't you put a bow on each of the knobs of the chest of drawers" said Ray sarcastically, "and round the washstand jug, too."

"Oh!" Tui's face fell. "Don't you like it, darling. We thought it was lovely. Mummy thought you'd think it fearfully artistic."

"I think it looks awful," said Ray, "and just like you. You're off your head lately, Tui Bead."

"Really and truly you think so" said Tui, making tragic eyes at herself in the looking glass.

"Yes. Besides if I were you I would mend my drawers first," she answered, scorning Tui's eyes.

"I wonder what makes you so hard hard hard. You're never nice to me, now, Ray."

"Yes I am. But you're so dotty. You seem to be getting all different."

"Darling," Tui put her arm round Ray's waist, "in my heart I'm just the same. Feel my hair. Do you think I've washed it successfully. Feel this bit. Is it silky?" Ray gave it a pull.

"Its nearly as soft as you."

"Come along downstairs, you kids" called Mrs Bead. "And Ray you can take a piece of my cocoanut cake to your Grandma. It hasn't ris at all and its a little damp in the middle, but the ingredients are all the best quality."

It was dark when she left the Beads. She went home by the front way through their weedy garden and out of the gate into their own. Hawk Street was quiet. All over the sky there were little stars and the garden with its white flowers looked as though it were steeped in milk. The blinds were pulled down in their house but lamplight shone from the sitting room and she knew her Father was there. But she did not care. "What a lovely thing night is" thought Rachael. "I wish I could stay out here and watch it." She bent her face over the spicy arum lilies and could not have enough of their scent. "I shall remember just this moment," decided the little girl. "I shall always remember what I like and forget what I don't like." How still and quiet it was. She could hear the dew dripping off the leaves. "I wonder" she thought, dreamy and grave, looking up at the stars, "I wonder if there really <u>is</u> a God!"     [s41-48]

[MS-Papers-4006-13][48]

> Last night for the first time since you were dead
> I talked with you my brother in a dream,
> We were at home again walking by a stream
> Fringed with tall berry bushes, white & red –
> Dont touch them they are poisoned, I said
> But your hand hovered & I saw the gleam
> Of strange bright laughter playing round your head.

---

[48]See note 31

Don't you remember, we called them dead man's bread?
I woke & heard the wind moan & the roar
Of the dark tumbling water on the shore
Come back, oh darling dear! my brother stands
Waiting for me & holding out his hands
Full of the shining berries.
By the remembered stream my brother stands
Waiting for me & holding out his hands
Full of the berries that I did not eat.

[MS-Papers-4006-16]

<u>Villa Pauline.</u>

But Ah! before he came
You were only a name
Four little rooms and cupboard
Without a bone
And I was alone!
Now with your windows wide
Everything from outside
Of sun and flower and lovliness
Come in to hide
To play to laugh on the stairs
To catch unawares
Our childish happiness
And to glide
Through the four little rooms on tiptoe
With lifted finger
Pretending we shall not know
When the shutters are shut
That they still linger
Long long after
Lying close in the dark
He says to me hark
Isn't that laughter?

We are <three> robbers & thieves
Your four little rooms and your cupboard
Are full to the brim
That is why
You stand so trim
Under the starry sky
Our sentinel!
And no one believes
We are more than two
You never will tell!
You will play our game!

[MS-Papers-4006-12]

January

### Camomile Tea.

Outside the sky is light with stars
There's a hollow roaring from the sea
And alas for the little almond flowers!
The wind is shaking the almond tree.

How little I thought a year ago
In that horrible cottage upon the Lee
That Bogey & I should be sitting so
And sipping a cup of camomile tea.

Light as feathers the witches fly
The cusp of the moon is plain to see.
By a firefly under a jonquil flower
And a goblin is toasting a bumble bee.

We might be fifty we might be five
So snug so compact so wise are we!
Beside the kitchen table leg
My knee is pressing against Jack's knee.

But our shutters are shut the fire is low
The tap is dripping peacefully
The saucepan shadows on the wall
Are black and round & plain to see.

[MS-Papers-4006-16]

### The Town Between the Hills

The further the little girl leaped and ran
The further she longed to be
The white white field of Jonquil flowers
Danced up as high as her knee
And flashed and sparkled before her eyes
Until she could hardly see
So to the woods went she.

It was quiet in the woods
It was solemn and grave
A sound like a wave
Sighed in the treetops
And then sighed no more
But she was brave
And the sky showed through
A bird egg's blue
And she saw
A tiny path that was running away

Over the hill to who can say ·
She ran too.
But there the path broke
There the path ended
And would not be mended.
A little old man
Sat on the edge
Hugging the hedge
He had a fire
And 2 eggs in a pan
And a paper poke
Of pepper and salt
So she came to a halt
To watch and admire
Cunning and nimble was he!
May I help if I can little old man?
Bravo he said
You can dine with me
I've two red eggs
From 2 white hens
And a loaf from a kind ladie
Some fresh nutmegs
Some cutlet ends
In pink & white paper frills
And - I've - got
A little hot pot
From the town between the Hills.
He nodded his head
And made her a sign
To sit under the spray
Of a trailing vine.
But as the little girl joined her hands
And said the grace she had learnt to say
The little old man gave 2 dreadful squeals
And she just saw the flash of his smoking heels
As he tumbled tumbled
With his two red eggs
From 2 white hens
His loaf from a kind lady
The fresh nutmegs
The cutlet ends
In the pink & white paper frills
And away tumbled
Little hot pot
So much too hot
From the town between the hills.

[MS-Papers-4006-16]

<u>Waves:</u>

I saw a tiny God
Sitting
Under a bright blue Umbrella
That had white tassels
And forked ribs of gold
Below him His little world
Lay open to the sun
The shadow of His Hat
Lay upon a city
When he stretched forth His hand
A lake became a dark tremble
When he kicked up His foot
It became night in the mountain passes.

But thou art small!
There are gods far greater than thee
They rise and fall
The tumbling gods of the sea.
Can thy Breast heave such sighs
Such hollow savage cries
Such windy breath
Such groaning death
And canst thy arm enfold
The old the cold
The changeless dreadful places
Where the herds
Of horned sea monsters
And the screaming birds
Gather together.

From those silent men
That lie in the pen
Of yon pearly prisons
Canst thou hunt thy prey
Like us canst thou stay
Awaiting thine hour
And then rise like a tower
And crash and shatter?
There are neither trees nor bushes
In my country
Said the tiny God
But there are streams
And water falls

And mountain peaks
Covered with lovely weed
There are little shores and safe harbours
Caves for cool, and plains for sun and wind
Lovely is the sound of the rivers
Lovely the flashing brightness
Of the lonely peaks.
I am content.

But thy Kingdom is small
Said the God of the sea.
Thy Kingdom shall fall
We shall not let thee be
Thou art proud
With a loud
Pealing of laughter
He rose and covered
The tiny God's land
With the tip of his hand
With the curl of his fingers
And after - -

The tiny God
Began to cry.

[MS-Papers-4006-16]

<u>Voices of the air!</u>

But then there comes that moment rare
When for no cause that I can find
The little voices of the air
Sound above all the sea and wind

The sea and wind do them obey
And singing singing double notes
On double basses - content to play
A droning chord for the little throats.

The little throats that sing and rise
Up into the light with lovely ease
And a kind of magical sweet surprise
To hear and to know themselves for these.

For these little voices, the bee, the fly
The leaf that taps, the pod that breaks,
The breeze in the grass tops bending by,
The shrill quick sound that the insect makes.
The insect hanging upon a stem

And a thread of water dropping among
The mosses, the big rocks & diadem
All the infinite silent song.
The silent song, so faint, so rare
That the heart must not beat nor the quick blood run
To hear the myriad voices of the air.

# Notebook 13

[Notebook 13, qMS-1254][49]

The Telegraaf of November 11 states that during the night of October 1-2 smugglers attempted to take to Germany 120 cows near the Dutch village of Koolip[?]. Each cow wore a white linen bonnet[?] a pair of sabots, a woollen shirt and an embroidered apron. Forty were seized by the Dutch customs officials who were amazed when they discovered their true prize. The others walked unharmed into Germany.

---

### Egg cards at Munich[50]

The Munchener Neueste Nachrichten states that the Bureau Committee for the food supply has decided that eggs shall be obtained under the following conditions: Cards will be issued for heads of families, single persons, those intending to marry. Each holder must write his name, description and address (not forgetting to state whether Mr, Mrs, Reverend or Title) you know, occupation, copy of birth & marriage certificates, this officer of the supreme menace to sometime pass a short note of not more than ten lines on the subject of [one line illegible] together with the name and address of the shop at which it is proposed (unofficially) to use the vouchers. But cards will only be valid for certain shops (other than those suggested by the intending egg-consumer) holding vouchers approved by the Food Bureau. Each of these will be given a form for his list of customers on which intending customers must inscribe themselves. Each entry is numbered and these numbers must be listed on the egg-card, hen, counterfoil and egg (if laid) of customer. The next procedure is to collect the counterfoils from customers (who retain vouchers)

---

[49]Many pages have been cut out and many are blank in this notebook which appears to have been mainly Murry's since most of the remaining writing is in his hand.

[50]This paragraph and the preceding one are scrawled in a faint pencil, with some words not actually visible, so this reading should be described as 'approximate'. The German newspaper *Müncher Neueste Nachrichten* was published from 1848 until April 1945, but the articles on which these stories are based have not been located.

and forward them to the Egg Distributing Department of the Municipal Food
Bureau which will inform the merchant how many eggs he will receive and
the hen how many eggs and with what regularity she is expected to lay.
People entitled to a medical certificate will be given special and slightly more
complicated advantages.

---

November. It is so strange! I am suddenly back again, coming into my room
and desiring to write. <u>Knock</u> goes Chappers[51] at the door. A man has come to
clean the windows .
. . I might have known it!
And so death claims us. I am sure that just at that final moment a knock will
come & Somebody Else will appear to 'clean the windows'.
Johnnie has given me his fountain pen. The room is full of smoke tonight and
the gas bubbles as though the pipes were full of water. Its very quiet. I have
rather a cold but I feel so absolutely <u>alive</u> after my experience of this
afternoon.     [J119]

Last Words to Youth.

There was a woman on the station platform. A tall scrag of a woman wearing
a little round hat with a brown feather that dropped in a draggled fringe over
her eyes. She was dressed in a brown jacket and a narrow brown skirt and in
her bare hands she clutched a broken down looking leather bag – the outside
pockets bulging with what looked like old torn up envelopes. Round her neck
some indescribable little dead animal bit its own tail, its fur standing up wet
and sticky like the fur of a drowned kitten. Brown button boots showed under
the skirt and an end of white petticoat dabbled with mud. The toss and
tumble, the hurrying threading rush of movement left her high and dry.
She stood as though she were part of the furniture of the station and had been
there for years – an old automatic machine that nobody dreamed of slipping
a coin into, or even troubled to glance at to find out what once it contained –
whether a drop of white rose perfume or a cachet or deux cigarettes à la reine
d'Egypte.
    Even the porters seemed to accept her right to stand there, and all the
people climbing out of the train, the pale women bunched up in furs, the
stout unshaven men buttoned up in overcoats simply did not see her, but met
their friends and lovers and kissed and chattered and squabbled under her very
nose. There is something revolting about her – something humble and
resigned, almost idiotic, thought Marion, and she sat down on her hat box,
waiting for that mysterious porter who had appeared and disappeared to find
a truck to trundle her things into the cloakroom. I wish he would come –
I'm cold, I really am quite dangerously cold. She clutched her muff tight,
tight against her to stop the strange trembling shivers that rippled over her

---

[51]Transcribed by Murry as 'Miss Chapman'.

whole body. But she could not control two little muscles in her cheek bones that moved up & down like tiny pistons. "No, I never sleep in trains," she said to nobody at all, "and my dear, you have no conception of the heat in that carriage - the windows simply ran. There was a strange pale female opposite to me, too, all wrapped up in black shawls which she called her chiffons. In the middle of the night when everybody was asleep she rooted among her baggage, spread a white handkerchief on her lap, produced what I try to believe was the end of a cold rabbit, tearing at the little legs, cracking up the bones and swaying about in the swinging half dark as she munched, like the portrait of a mad baby farmer by that belgian - what is his name? Wirz ... Yes, it was a very sinister, blackish little meal," said Marion, and she smiled, thinking - with half affected dismay - heavens! I seem to be haunted by mad women - that woman last night and now this mad one this morning. A mad woman at night is a sailor's delight, a mad woman in the morning is a sailor's warning - & she looked up to see the draggled bird moving towards her. Yes, she certainly was very ominous indeed - - Heavens! What was she wearing? How absurd how preposterous. Pinned [to] her jacket a knot of faded ribbon set off a large heart-shaped shield inscribed The representative of the society for the Protection of Young Girls - - -[52]    [s89-91]

---

[52]On the facing page is a series of sketches of houses or house-boats and flying creatures of various kinds.

# *Unbound Papers*

[MS-Papers-4006–04]

### The Laurels[53]

Lytton - - - Dr Keit
Carrington - - his grandchild, Muriel Dash
Mansfield - - - Florence Kaziany
Aldous - - - - Balliol Dodd
Maria - - - - - Jane
Murry - - - - - Ivan Tchek

---

(Act I Scene I. Breakfast room. Ivan enters, pours out a cup of coffee, lights a cigarette, stamps on the cigarette, says)

IVAN. And so it goes on. (And walks out, wrapped in gloom. Enter JANE who clears away & resets the table etc., brushes away cigarette ash & goes to the door & calls)

JANE. Miss Muriel.

MURIEL. (in the distance) Just coming. (She comes in with a bird in a cage, takes off cover & hangs the bird in the window, saying) Now you can look out & sing & see the sun (sighs profoundly) shining on the land.

JANE. Mr Tchek has had his breakfast Miss. It's all ready for the master.

MURIEL. Oh, very well Jane. I'll call him. (Looks at Jane) What's the matter Jane? You've been crying.

JANE. (at table) Oh, don't notice me, Miss Muriel. I'm nobody. I'm nothing.

MURIEL. (Shocked) Whatever do you mean Jane? (Jane puts her hand over her eyes and sobs.)

MURIEL. (taking the hand away) Poor Jane & you do look so dreadful. (Brightly) Tell me then[?]

---

[53]Aldous Huxley, in a letter to Julian Huxley from Garsington Manor, December 29 1916: 'An amusing Xmas party here. Murry, Katherine Mansfield, Lytton Strachey, Brett and Carrington, Bertrand Russell and Maria Nys. We performed a superb play invented by Katherine, improvising as we went along. It was a huge success, with Murry as a Dostoevsky character and Lytton as an incredibly wicked old grandfather.' Scrawled in faint pencil at top speed, this is KM's rough outline of Act 1 Scene 1 of this play.

JANE. Oh Miss if you knew what I feel about – It seems funny don't it Miss –
things happen like that. When I saw 'is boots in the passage this morning –
those black button ones with the brown tops – I felt I could bear it no longer.
I felt quite wild Miss, in the kitchen jest now. Oh Mother what 'ave you been
and gone & done. And it's not as though it's my fault Miss. That's what makes
it so hard to bear.

MURIEL. Bewildering – what on earth are you talking about Jane?

JANE. Oh Miss – it's Mr Tchek – the Russian gentleman.

MURIEL. Are you in love with him Jane?

JANE. Oh Miss –

MURIEL. But whatever is there to cry about in that Jane? Oh Jane –
you lucky girl. Just to be in love – isn't that enough? Oh how I envy you,
how I envy you. I've nobody – nobody to be in love with except (she points)
my canary, & there comes a time Jane (taking the cage) when even a canary
isn't half enough. One seems somehow to want more. Oh Jane –

JANE. But you don't understand Miss. If I was like you, with my Pa & me Ma
in a lovely double frame on the dressing table, it'd be alright. But there –
I've got to tell somebody. (Beats her breast) I'm a love child, I am.

MURIEL. (Claps her hands) A love child, Jane? How too divine. What is it?
How pretty it sounds. (dreamily) A love child.

JANE. (leaning towards her curiously) Do you mean to say you <u>don't know</u>,
Miss? It means I haven't got no Father.

MURIEL. But oh, Jane, how perfect. Just like the Virgin Mary.

JANE. (Furious) You ought to be ashamed of yourself, Miss Muriel, that you
ought. Don't you know it's the most horrible thing that can happen to
anybody – not to have a Father. Don't you know, Miss, that's the reason what
young girls like me jump off buses & in front of trains and eat rat poison
& swoller acids & often murder themselves? Just because they 'aven't got a
Father, Miss.

MURIEL. Does it mean . . .

GRANDFATHER. Muriel. (Enters room, rather feebly, kisses Muriel on
forehead & then looks about him, murmuring faintly, gently.) And how is my
little yellow bird this morning – how is my little darling canary?

MURIEL. Very well thank you, Grandfather. Won't you have an egg & some
bread? (Cuts up loaf.)

GRANDFATHER. And what is my little granddaughter going to do today?
Is she going to warm her wings in the pretty garden & sit & read the
newspaper to her grandfather – all about the bad wicked people & the bad
world outside The Laurels?

MURIEL. The world outside The Laurels. (Covers her face with her hands
& bursts into tears.)

GRANDFATHER. Muriel – my child – what is it?

MURIEL. Oh Grandfather I do so want to go out into the world.

GRANDFATHER. What! My little bird to leave the nest & try to fly over the
tall laurels? My little violet to peep from its leaf for prying hands to gather?

My little Muriel to leave her old grandfather to wander quite abandoned on the dusty road? (Puts his hand to his heart & exclaims) Ugh!

MURIEL. Grandfather, Grandfather.

GRANDFATHER. My heart, A chair. (He sits down[?]. Puts Muriel's hand over his heart.) Feel – scarcely at all.

MURIEL. Oh Grandfather, can it be my fault?

GRANDFATHER. (Takes her face in his hands) Happy child! Careless water sprite. One day when little Muriel is older she will understand how she made Grandfather suffer, & the old wounds here closed, open again.

MURIEL. (clasps her hands) And must I never never go, Grandfather?

GRANDFATHER. Never, little mouse. (Muriel drifts towards the door) Where are you going to child?

MURIEL. (solemnly) I am going to look at my father's photograph.

GRANDFATHER. Achk! (Mysteriously) Fatal. Fatal child. But if the bloom must disappear let mine be the tender hands. Come here Muriel. (Muriel kneels beside him, clasps her hands & gazes at him.) The time has come then when my little Muriel must know why it would be useless for her to go out into the world, and why the world will have none of her roses & violets & pretty pretty parsley, but must hide with Grandfather within the Laurels, under the laurels. (standing) The man in the double frame is not your father, Muriel. Draw closer. How the little hands tremble – those shining eyes. (Mysteriously) Mr Tchek is not our first lodger Muriel. Once upon a time another lived in Mr Tchek's room – the first that ever burst. You follow me, Beating Heart?

MURIEL. Yes Grandfather.

GRANDFATHER. And your mother was just the same age as you – just as tender to the old man who was not so old then, Muriel, but only getting on, getting on. Time passed until one fine day Florence & the first lodger went away and after a long time when Grandfather was all alone he found (groans)– how shall I tell her – a basket under the laurel hedge, with a baby and a bottle and a bonnet in it.

MURIEL. (radiant, flings her arms round him) The baby was me Grandfather.

GRANDFATHER. (clasping her to his heart) My treasure is a love child.

MURIEL. (awed) Just like Jane. (leaves his arm) But did Mother never come back Grandfather?

GRANDFATHER. Never. Other grass was green and water flowed. Never came back. (They sway to and fro, clasped in each other's arms. Suddenly the door opens & FLORENCE bursts in in a travelling cape, followed by Jane carrying a bag.)

FLORENCE. (to Jane) Pay my taxi. (rushes forward) Father!

GRANDFATHER. (horrified) Florence!

FLORENCE. No, don't get up my old feeble broken white-headed old Father.

MURIEL. (very embarrassed) Good afternoon Mother. I am your daughter Muriel.

FLORENCE. (as to a child) Well, my little darling. (turns to grandfather) How
old you have become, my poor Father. I should have warned you before I
came. I had no right – I didn't realise how old you were, how feeble, how
almost – (shakes her head at him) It was high time.

GRANDFATHER. (trying to 'carry it off') I have never been better in my life,
Florence.

FLORENCE. ([...]fully) There there. (She unbuttons her cape & Muriel takes it
from her & stands holding the cape in her hands) How hot and stuffy it is in
here. (walks over to the window) Hemmed in by Laurels –

# Notebook 17

[Notebook 17, qMS-1255][54]

Fractures

A bone may be broken by:
a. direct violence
b. indirect violence
c. muscular contraction
d. 'spontaneous' fracture as in the case of disease.
1 A <u>direct</u> fracture is a fracture by a blow, a fall, the wheel of a vehicle or a bullet.
2 An <u>indirect fracture</u> is due to an impact applied at some distance from the spot at which the bone is broken.
2 <u>Transverse fracture</u> i.e. when a bone is snapped directly across its length. This is [a] very infrequent occurrence.
More common is
3 <u>Oblique fracture</u> where the bone is broken on a slant & the edges are jagged. Overlapping of the broken ends of the bone is caused by the contraction of the muscles which pull the lower fragment upwards. These two <u>simple fractures</u> are attended by haemorrhage, swelling & discoloration.
4 A <u>Comminuted Fracture</u> is a more complicated form of <u>simple fracture</u>. It happens when a heavy weight crushes the bone and between the two pieces there are a number of crushed fragments.
<u>Complicated fracture</u> i.e. when a jagged end of bone tears an artery, a vein or a nerve or penetrates an internal organ. If the main <u>artery</u> is torn all pulsation below the seat of injuries will cease. When a large <u>vein</u> is torn the pulsation continues. When a <u>nerve</u> is torn the muscles are paralysed & the skin loses all sensation. (ex:'drop-wrist' in a soldier when the spiral nerve of the arm is torn.)
A <u>compound fracture</u> is compounded of an injury to the skin. (Tetanus.)

---

` [54]Predominantly Murry's notebook, except for the following which is all in KM's hand.

An <u>impacted fracture</u> e.g. When the two ends of the broken bone are driven into each other & can only be separated with great effort. In this case <u>crepitus</u> is absent, the <u>deformity</u> is slight, no <u>gap</u> can be felt and <u>movement</u> is possible.

<u>Note</u>: In all cases of accident there is a sudden fall of temperature. The normal temperature (98.4) may possibly fall to 92. It is therefore urgent that the patient should be immediately covered.

<u>Signs and symptoms of Fracture</u>: (<u>Signs</u> are what you can hear, feel and see. <u>Symptoms</u> are what the patient can tell you.)
1. unnatural position of the foot.
2. one leg longer than the other.
3. mark on clothing.
4. pain.
5. deformity.
6. swelling.
7. discoloration by blood
8. irregularity of outline of the bone.
9. uselessness of limb.
10. crepitus.

The first thing to do in the case of a fractured thigh is to take hold of the injured limb and pull it down to the right length. Then tie the feet firmly together. Put a long splint from under the armpit to beyond the heel and bandage. The great thing is to keep the part above and below the fracture quiet. In the case of a man another small splint is inserted on the inner side of the thigh.

<u>Lecture II</u>
Fractured clavicle. Signs and symptoms are:
(a) the limb is helpless.
(b) on passing the fingers along the collar bone a gap may be felt.

The <u>outer</u> fragment will be found on a lower level than the inner with its end projecting forward. The principles of treatment are to keep the shoulder back and to support the elbow so that the <u>outer</u> fragment may be <u>pulled backwards and raised</u>.

Treatment: Place a large pad under the armpit on the injured side. Pull the shoulder back. Bend the elbow to a right angle. Support the limb while a sling is applied. Lay an unfolded triangular bandage on the front of the chest, the <u>apex</u> over the elbow. Gather up the lower part of the bandage, carry it below the limb over the back & tie off on the sound shoulder, slightly to the front. (This is known as a St. John Sling.) Take a broad fold bandage, place the middle of it over the injured elbow as low as possible, carry the ends one in front and one behind the body & tie off below the hand of the injured side.

A common fracture is that of the upper part of the arm - the <u>Surgical Neck</u>. <u>Treatment</u>. (A tiny pad of cotton wool may be placed under the armpit to avoid friction.) Apply a broad fold bandage round the top of the injured arm, carry it round the body, <u>cross</u> the ends under the <u>sound</u> arm & tie on the top of the sound shoulder. Put the hand in a small arm sling & tie in the hollow over the collar bone bringing the 2 ends forward. The length of this bandage over the hand should be from the first joint of the little finger to 2 inches of the forearm. In a fracture of the upper and the middle of the humerus a small <u>arm</u> sling is applied; for the collar bone a <u>large</u> sling.

Fracture of the arm bone. Take 4 splints, different size, and place

|        |               |
|--------|---------------|
| Size I | in the front  |
| II     | inside the arm |
| III    | outside       |
| IV     | behind.       |

Great care must be taken that these splints do not reach so low as to interfere with the <u>vein</u> in the elbow.

<u>The Brain</u>.
At the back of the skull there is a large bone called the <u>occiput</u>. The brain consists of a large mass called the <u>cerebrum</u> and a smaller mass called the <u>cerebellum</u>. There are two brains. The inside of the brain is pearly white, the outside is of grey matter 1½ thick, covered with <u>convolutions</u>. The white stuff is nerve fibres and the surface consists of nerve cells. If the nerve cells are destroyed one becomes paralysed.

The two brains are held together by bands of nerves. These nerves cross as they knit over the brain. The set which convey information <u>to</u> the brain are known as the <u>sensory</u> nerves, those which transmit information <u>from</u> the brain are called the motor nerves, the effluent & the affluent.

Ethel May:[55]

Ooh la la – I feel as though I had been walking [...] across the ceiling and as though I have been asleep most of the time – soundly profoundly asleep – ooh la la.

But Ethel May & her young man

then I had better phone them in the morning & make quite perfectly sure I've got

8.XII.16
I thought and thought this morning but to not much avail. I can't think why but my wit seems to be nearly deserting me when I want to get down to

---

[55]Murry's note on this page: 'This is quite illegible.' Elsewhere in this notebook, in which Murry composed his verse play *Cinnamon and Angelica*, he wrote 'even though, as I now fear, to others it may be only an obscurity shed over things transparently clear.' Under this KM wrote:

'Even though, as now I fear
It may to others make obscure
Things that aforetime have been clear
Transparent.'

A page of KM's animal and plant drawings is followed by, in her writing, 'cardamon, cinnamon, may, angelica, peppercorn'.

earth. I'm alight – sky high and even in my brain, in my head I can think and act and write – wonders – wonders – but the moment I really try to put them down I fail instantly[?].    [JI19]

> So that Mysterious Mother, faint with sleep
> Had given into her arms her newborn son
> And felt against her bosom the cherished one
> Breathe and stiffen his tiny limbs and weep
> Her arms became as wings folding him over
> Into that lovely pleasance and her heart
> Beat like a tiny bell – he is my lover
> He is my son, we shall never never part
> Never never never never but why
> Did she suddenly bow her head & begin to cry.    [JI18 s59-60]

Tchehov makes me feel that this longing to write stories of such uneven length is quite justified. Geneva is a long story & Hamilton is very short, & this ought to be written to my brother really, and another about the life in New Zealand. Then there is Bavaria: ich liebe dich, ich liebe dich floating out on the air. Then there is Paris! God! When shall I write all these things & how!

Is that all? Can that be all? That is not what I meant at all.

Tchehov is right about women. Yes, he is quite right. These fairies in black and silver, & then tearing down the road, her long brown fur blowing behind her, brushing the leaves with her trailing skirt & crying; of course he was awfully sorry that she did not get satisfaction, just as he would have been awfully sorry if she had not liked strawberries and cream.

Friday – Friday – he could not get the word out of his head – and before him stood the little man with his hair neatly combed, saying "Please take something to eat!" But I cannot believe that at this stage of the proceedings something pretty extraordinary did not happen. I sat with my back to no-one.

Teddie Fisher. Muriel Fisher. This woman I know v. well – vain, eager, beautiful, désenchantée, an 'actress'. I can put a little child's bed into the corner. Which do you like best Daddie – cats or dogs? Well, I think I like dogs best, old chap.
I don't. I'd like to have a kitten about as big as a little teapot.
The character of the man rather beats me.
I want a very quiet man absorbed in his work, who once he realised, really realised that his wife had married him for her own ends, had no more to do with her, but still loved her and simply adored the child. It is all a bit difficult to write but awfully fascinating. And should not be at too great length.

Does this pen write? Oh, I do hope so. For it is really beastly to have a pen that doesn't. And then a clergyman goes up to him & says he's lost the tails off of his sheep. Well, its a comic! You see?    [JI24-125]

The most important wireless message of yesterday consists of an account of an interview with HinterdemBerg sent by Karl von Wegain to the Klokuk Cuspidor.

HinterdemBerg is a man of very few words. Terse and laconic as befits one who is "all soldier" he seldom pronounces the full stops or the commas and his "connectives" are conspicuously absent. He makes it a rule never to speak an entire sentence at a time, but here a bit and there a bit and everywhere a bit must be snapped up and reverently relished by the rare foreign correspondent whom he will deign to see. I, like every other foreign correspondent had been begging an interview ever since he succeeded, but upon one plea or another he declined much to my surprise. At my last request that he would <u>say something</u> he replied that he would <u>see</u> me next time I was in, out or passing but would <u>say</u> nothing whatever. I arrived at dusk accompanied by Captain Sidelights von Sidelights of the famous SideLight Sidelight von Sidelight Sidelight family of the time of Frederick the Great.

The concentrated central combined Brain is located in a 'Dorf', or small town, township, hamlet, or village, which is a small place of 300 inhabitants in the centre of a vast estate unflown over by fliers. The Field Marshal received me in a room in a building. The furniture consisted of a desk, a table, a chair and a picture of the Kaiser (the last named hung suspended from the wall).

# *Unbound Papers*

[MS-Papers-4006-12]

## Butterflies[56]

In the middle of our porridge plates
There was a blue butterfly painted
And each morning we tried who should reach the butterfly
first.
Then the Grandmother said: 'Do not eat the poor butterfly.'
That made us laugh.
Always she said it and always it started us laughing.
It seemed such a sweet little joke.
I was sure that one fine morning
The butterflies would fly out of the plates
Laughing the teeniest laugh in the world
And perch on the Grandmother's cap.

[MS-Papers-4006-16]

## Tragedy.

From the towering, opal globes in the street
The crude, white light streams down
On him, blue-eyed, on her, with hair

Like a beautiful, golden crown.
His cigaret glows in the dusk as he slowly paces
And beside him the woman shivers in silks and laces.

[MS-Papers-4006-14]

## Little Brother's Secret

When my birthday was coming
Little Brother had a secret
He kept it for days and days
And just hummed a little tune when I asked him.

---

[56]Another MS copy of this has the title 'Butterfly Laughter'.

But one night it rained
And I woke up and heard him crying.
Then he told me.
"I planted two lumps of sugar in your garden
Because you love it so frightfully
I thought there would be a whole sugar tree for your birthday
And now it will all be melted."
O, the darling!

[MS-Papers-4006-16]

## The Storm

I ran to the forest for shelter
Breathless, half sobbing
I put my arms round a tree
Pillowed my head against the rough bark
Protect me, I said, I am a lost child
But the tree showered silver drops on my face and hair.
A wind sprang up from the ends of the earth
It lashed the forest together.
A huge green wave burst and thundered over my head
I prayed, implored, Please take care of me.
But the wind pulled at my cloak and the rain beat upon me.
Little rivers tore up the ground and swamped the bushes.
A frenzy possessed the earth: I felt that the earth was drowning
In a bubbling cavern of space. I alone
Smaller than the smallest fly, was alive and terrified.
Then, for what reason I know not, I became triumphant.
Well kill me, I cried, and ran out into the open.
But the storm ceased: the sun spread his wings
And floated serene in the silver pool of the sky
I put my hands over my face: I was blushing
And the trees swung together and delicately laughed.

[MS-Papers-4006-13]

## The Gulf

A gulf of silence separates us from each other
I stand at one side of the gulf - you at the other
I cannot see you or hear you - yet know that you are there.
Often I call you by your childish name
And pretend that the echo to my crying is your voice.
How can we bridge the gulf - never by speech or touch.
Once I thought we might fill it quite up with our tears
Now I want to shatter it with our laughter.

[MS-Papers-4006-12]

## Across the Red Sky

Across the red sky two birds flying
Flying with drooping wings
Silent and solitary their ominous flight.
All day the triumphant sun with yellow banners
Warred and warred with the earth and when she yielded
Stabbed her heart, gathered her blood in a chalice
Spilling it over the evening sky.
When the dark plumaged birds go flying flying
Quiet lies the earth wrapt in her mournful shadow
Her sightless eyes turned to the red sky
And the restlessly seeking birds.

[MS-Papers-4006-15]

## The Man With the Wooden Leg.[57]

There was a man lived quite near us
He had a wooden leg and a goldfinch in a green cage
His name was Farkey Anderson
And he'd been in a war to get his leg.
We were very sad about him
Because he had a beautiful smile
And was such a big man to live in a very little house.
When he walked in the road his leg did not matter so much
But when he walked in his little house
It made an ugly noise.
Little Brother said his goldfinch sang the loudest of all
other birds
So that he should not hear his poor leg
And feel too sorry about it.

[MS-Papers-4006-16]

## When I was a Bird.

I climbed up the karka tree
Into a nest all made of leaves
But soft as feathers.
I made up a song that went on singing all by itself
And hadn't any words but got sad at the end.
There were daisies in the grass under the tree.
I said, just to try them:

---

[57]See note 52 in Volume One.

"I'll bite off your heads and give them to my little children
to eat."
But they didn't believe I was a bird
They stayed quite open.
The sky was like a blue nest with white feathers
And the sun was the mother bird keeping it warm.
That's what my song said: though it hadn't any words.
Little Brother came up the path, wheeling his barrow
I made my dress into wings and kept very quiet
Then when he was quite near I said: "sweet – sweet".
For a moment he looked quite startled
Then he said: "Pooh, you're not a bird; I can see your legs."
But the daisies didn't really matter
And Little Brother didn't really matter –
I felt just like a bird.

[MS-Papers-4006-15]

## Sanary

Her little hot room looked over the bay
Through a stiff palisade of glinting palms
And there she would lie in the heat of the day
Her dark head resting upon her arms
So quiet so still she did not seem
To think to feel or even to dream.

The shimmering blinding web of sea
Hung from the shore and the spider sun
With busy frightening cruelty
Crawled over the sky and spun and spun.
She could see it still when she shut her eyes
And the little boats caught in the web like flies.

Down below at this idle hour
Nobody walked in the dusty street,
A scent of dying mimosa flower
Lay on the air but sweet – too sweet.

[MS-Papers-4006-14]

## Little Brother's Story.

We sat in front of the fire
Grandmother was in the rocking chair doing her knitting
And Little Brother and I were lying down flat.
"Please tell us a story, Grandmother" we said
But she put her head on one side and began counting her
stitches.

"Suppose you tell me one instead."
I made up one about a spotted tiger
That had a knot in his tail
But though I liked that about the knot
I didn't know why it was put there
So I said: "Little Brother's turn."
"I know a perfect story" he cried, waving his hands.
Grandmother laid down her knitting.
"Do tell us, dear."
"Once upon a time there was a bad little girl
And her mummy gave her the slipper – and that's all."
It was not a very special story
But we pretended to be very pleased
And Grandmother gave him jumps on her lap.

[MS-Papers-4006-12]

## The Candle

By my bed, on a little round table
The Grandmother placed a candle.
She gave me three kisses telling me they were three dreams
And tucked me in just where I loved being tucked.
Then she went out of the room and the door was shut.
I lay still waiting for my three dreams to talk
But they were silent.
Suddenly I remembered giving her three kisses back
Perhaps, by mistake, I had given my three little dreams.

I sat up in bed.
The room grew big – O bigger far than a church.
The wardrobe, quite by itself, as big as a house
And the jug on the washstand smiled at me.
It was not a friendly smile.
I looked at the basket chair where my clothes lay folded.
The chair gave a creak as though it were listening for
something.
Perhaps it was coming alive and going to dress in my clothes.

But the awful thing was the window
I could not think what was outside.
No tree to be seen, I was sure,
No nice little plant or friendly pebbly path.
Why did she pull down the blind every night?
It was better to know.

I crunched my teeth and crept out of bed.
I peeked through a slit of the blind

There was nothing at all to be seen
But hundreds of friendly candles all over the sky
In remembrance of frightened children.
I went back to bed.
The three dreams started singing a little song.


[NL]
                    That Woman.
                        by
            Katherine Mansfield.

Sitting astride the low window ledge, smelling the heliotrope - or was it the tea? - half of Kezia was in the garden and half of her in the room.
"Have you put down the Harcourts?"
"Yes, Mrs Phil and Mrs Charlie."
"And the Fields?"
"Mrs <u>and</u> the Misses Field."
"And Rose Conway?"
"Yes, and that Melbourne girl staying with her."
"Old Mrs Grady?"
"Do you think - necessary?"
"My dear, she does so love a good old cackle."
"Oh, but that way she has of dipping everything in her tea! Iced chocolate cake and the ends of her feather boa dipped in tea ..."
"How marvellously that ribbon has lasted, Harrie. Marvellously."
    That was Aunt Beryl's voice. She, Aunt Harrie and Mother sat at the round table with big shallow tea cups in front of them. In the dusky light, in their white, puffed-up muslin blouses with wing sleeves, they were three birds at the edge of a lily pool. Beyond them the shadowy room melted into the shadow; the gold picture frames were braced upon the air; the cut-glass door knob glittered - a song, a white butterfly with wings outspread, clung to the ebony piano.
    Aunt Harrie's plaintive, singing tones: "It's very faded, really, if you look into it. I don't think it can poss–ibly stand another ironing."
"If I were rich" said Aunt Beryl, "with real money to spend - not save ..."
Mother: "What about - what about asking that Gibbs woman?"
"Linda!"
"How can you suggest such a thing!"
"Well, why not? She needn't come. But it must be so horrid not to be asked anywhere!"
"But, good heavens, whose fault is it? Who could ask her?"
"She's nobody but herself to blame."
"She's simply flown in people's faces."
"And it must be so par–ticularly dreadful for Mr Gibbs."
"But Harrie dear, he's dead."
"Of course, Linda. That's just it. He must feel so helpless, looking down."

Kezia heard her mother say: "I never thought of that. Yes, that might be ...
very maddening!"
Aunt Beryl's cool little voice gushed up and overflowed:
"It's really nothing to laugh at, Linda. There are some things one really must
draw the line at laughing at."     [J99-101 S39-41]

# Notebook 24

[Notebook 24, qMS-1257]

Bloc Notes
1917.

In these notes, so help me Lord
I shall be open and above board.

> 141a Church Street
> Chelsea
> London S.W.3.

### Alors, je pars:

It is astonishing how violently a big branch shakes when a silly little bird has
left it. I expect the bird knows it and feels immensely arrogant. The way he
went on, my dear, when I said I was going to leave him. He was quite
desperate. But now the branch is quiet again. Not a bud has fallen, not a twig
has snapped. It stands up in the bright air, steady and firm, and thanks the
Lord that it has got its evenings to itself again. (N.A. 19.IV.17.)

### A Shilling gone bust:

A knock at the door. Two sisters of Nazareth - one, rather pretty and meek,
in the background, attending; the other, very voluble and fluent, her hands in
her sleeves. When she smiled, showing her pale gums and big discoloured
teeth I decided that I had quite got over my sentimental feeling about nuns.
She was collecting for their home for little children. All sorts of little children
were admitted except those suffering from infectious diseases or subject to fits.
I wondered what would happen if one developed fits after admittance and
decided that I should have the most realistic fit the moment the Nazarene
door shut on me. I remember you well from last year, said the nun. But I
wasn't here last year. Ah, people change so quickly, said she. Yes, but perhaps
their faces don't, said I seriously, giving her the shilling I was just going to put
into the gas meter. I wish I had put it into the gas meter five minutes before.

Living Alone:

Even if I should, by some awful chance, find a hair upon my bread and honey
- at any rate it is my own hair. (N.A. 19.4.17)

Beware of the Rain:

Late in the evening after you have cleared away your supper, blown the crumbs
out of the book that you were reading, lighted the lamp and curled up in front
of the fire, that is the moment to beware of the rain. (N.A. 19.4.17)

E.M. Forster:

Putting my weakest books to the wall last night I came across a copy of
Howard's End and had a look into it. But its not good enough. E.M. Forster
never gets any further than warming the teapot. He's a rare fine hand at that.
Feel this teapot. Is it not beautifully warm? Yes, but there ain't going to be no
tea. And I can never be perfectly certain whether Helen was got with child by
Leonard Bast or by his fatal forgotten umbrella. All things considered I think
it must have been the umbrella. (½ N.A. 19.IV.17)

L.Ms Way.
          New Age 19.4.17.
Cephalus.
          " " " " "


Love and Mushrooms:

If only one could tell true love from false love as one can tell mushrooms from
toadstools. With mushrooms it is so simple - you salt them well, put them
aside and have patience. But with love, you have no sooner lighted on
anything that bears even the remotest resemblance to it than you are perfectly
certain it is not only a genuine specimen, but perhaps the only genuine
mushroom ungathered. It takes a dreadful number of toadstools to make you
realise that life is not one long mushroom.

Babies and the dear Old Queen:

Whenever I see babies in arms I am struck again by their resemblance to the
dear old Queen. They have just the same air of false resignation, the same
mournful, regal plumpness. If only her Majesty had deigned to be
photographed in a white woolen bonnet with a little frill of eiderdown round
it there'd be no telling the difference. Especially if she could have been
persuaded to sit on G'ampa G'adstone's knee for the occasion.

Dreams and Rhubarb.

My sticks of rhubarb were wrapped up in a copy of the Star containing Lloyd
George's last, more than eloquent speech. As I snipped up the rhubarb my eye
fell, was fixed and fastened on that sentence wherein he tells us that we have
grasped our niblick and struck out for the open course. Pray Heaven there is
some faithful soul ever present with a basket to catch these tender blossoms as
they fall. Ah, God! It is a dreadful thought that these immortal words should

go down into the dreamless dust uncherished. I loved to think, as I put the rhubarb into the saucepan, that years hence - P.G. many <u>many</u> years hence - when, in the fulness of time, full of ripeness and wisdom, the Almighty sees fit to gather him into His bosom, some gentil stonecutter living his quiet life in the little village that had known great David as a child, would take a piece of fair white marbil and engrave upon it two niblicks crossed, and underneath: <u>In the hour of England's most imminent Peril he grasped his Niblick and struck out for the open course</u>.

But what <u>does</u> rather worry me, I thought, turning the gas down to a pinch as the rhubarb began to boil, is how these mighty words are to be translated so that our Allies may taste the full flavour of them. Those crowds of patient russians, waiting in the snow, perhaps, to have the speech read aloud to them - what dreadful weapon will it present to their imagination? <u>Unless</u> the Daily News suggest to Mr Ransome that he walk down the Nevsky Prospekt with a niblick instead of an umbrella for all the world to see. And the French - what <u>espece de Niblickisme</u> will they make of it? Shall we read in the french papers next week of someone <u>qui manque de niblick</u>. Or that "<u>Au milieu de ces evenements si graves ce qu'il nous faut c'est du courage, de l'espoir et du niblick le plus ferme</u> - -" I wondered, taking off the rhubarb.

A Victorian Idyll.

Yesterday Matilda Mason
In the <u>Parlour</u> by Herself
Broke a <u>Handsome</u> China Basin
<u>Placed</u> upon the Mantelshelf.

You picture Matilda in a little check dress, puce shoulder ties, muslin pantalettes, black sandals, and a pound of rich glossy curls like a pound of the good old fashioned fried sausages, held in place by a velvet band. She tiptoes about the parlour, among the whatnots and anti-macassars and embroidery frames and Mamma's work-box with the ivory fittings and Papa's music stand with the pearl studded flute lying across it ... How did she come to be in the parlour by herself. [J119-122]

58
May 30th. To be alive and to be a 'writer' is enough. Sitting at my table just now I saw one person turning to another smiling, putting out his hand -

---

[58]The following page is in Murry's hand:
'This is a copy of a page of MS, given to Mr Russell of Markwich[?]
Dedication: To John Middleton Murry with my love.

Facing first page of contents in itals. these words:
*...but I tell you, my lord fool, out of this nettle, danger, we pluck this flower, safety ...*
?

Prelude
Je ne parle pas francais
Bliss
The Wind Blows
Psychology

speaking - and suddenly I clenched my fist & brought it down on the table and called out - there is <u>nothing</u> like it.

1 Stay laces. 2 The Coronation. 3 Two 2d ones please. 4 Late at Night.
5 The Black Cap. 6 In Confidence. 7 The Common Round. 8 A Pic-nic.

its good in a way because ones hand gets sure.

The Musicians Daughter - Kissing in the hall. What should he have done - put the books down or kept them in his hand - or - or   She plays the accompaniments, very serious. She stands at the piano striking <u>A</u> with one finger - her head bent a little on one side, and she dresses like a child in frocks that button up the back and slippers with no heels. The old man <u>rumbles</u>.

[J123]

Father is a 'Tolstoi' character. He has just the point of vision of a Tolstoi character. I always felt that Stepan in Anna Karenina reminded me of someone - and his well nourished, fresh body was always curiously familiar to me - of course - it is my Papa's even to the smell of the whiskers.

Things happened so simply then, without preparation and without any shock. They let me go into my mother's room (I remember standing on tiptoe & using both hands to turn the big white china doorhandle) & there lay my mother in bed with her arms along the sheet and there sat my grandmother before the fire with a baby in a flannel across her knees. My mother paid no attention to me at all - perhaps she was asleep for my Grandmother nodded & said in a voice scarcely above a whisper "Come & see your new little sister." I tiptoed to her voice across the room & she parted the flannel and I saw a little round head with a tuft of goldy hair on it and a tiny face with eyes shut - white as snow. "Is it alive" I asked. "Of course" said Grandmother - "look at her holding my finger." And yes a hand scarcely bigger than my doll's in a frilled sleeve was wound round her finger. Do you like her, said the grandmother. Yes. Is she going to play with the dolls house? By & bye said the grandmother - & I felt very pleased. Mrs Heywood had just given us the dolls house. It was a beautiful one with a verandah & balcony & a door that opened and shut and two chimneys. I wanted badly to show it to somebody else.

---

Pictures
The Man Without Temperament (sic)
Mr Reginald Peacock's Day
Sun & Moon
Feuille d'Album
The German Governess (?)
A Dill Pickle
I can't remember any others. Will you give me your opinion of this list. It is does not look very grand - does it? Do you think there is anything else worth adding or should I cut out any? <u>Second Helping</u> I <u>can't</u> get on with here; its so noisy. Its fearfully hard to work. If you would give me till the end of next week it would be done. I promise it × ♡ and S.D.* I shall work as never before or after at the Villa Flora. <u>The aspecks are simply perfect</u>. If I can get The Second Helping finished I think it would be a good title for the book do you?
Tig.'
[*'Cross my heart straight dinkum': a New Zealand slang expression meaning 'I swear'.]

Her name is Gwen, said the grandmother. Kiss her. I bent down & kissed the little goldy tuft – but she took no notice. She lay quite quite still with her eyes shut. Now go & kiss Mother said the grandmother. But Mother did not want to kiss me. Very languid, leaning against the pillows she was eating some sago. The sun shone through the windows & winked on the brass knobs of the big bed.

After that Grandmother came into the nursery with Gwen and sat in front of the nursery fire in the rocking chair with her. Meg & Tadpole were away staying with Aunt Harriet Beauchamp, and they had gone before the new dolls house arrived so that was why I so longed to have somebody to show it to. I had gone all through it myself from the kitchen to the dining room up into the bedrooms into the drawing room with the dolls lamp on the table heaps & heaps of times. <u>When</u> will she play with it? I asked Grandmother. By & bye darling.

It was spring – our garden was full of big white lilies. I used to run out & sniff them & come in again with my nose all yellow. Can't she go out. At last one very fine day she was wrapped in the new shawl & Grandmother carried her into the cherry orchard & walked up and down under the falling cherry flowers. Grandmother wore a grey dress with white pansies on it. The doctor's carriage was waiting at the door & the doctor's little dog Jackie rushed at me & snapped at my bare legs. When we went back to the nursery & the new shawl was taken away little white petals like feathers fell out of the folds – but Gwen did not look at them. She lay in Grandmother's arms, her eyes just open to show a line of blue, her face very white & the one tuft of goldy hair standing up on her head. All day & all night grandmother's arms were full. I had no lap to climb into, no pillow to rest against – they belonged to Gwen. But Gwen did not notice this. She never put up her hand to play with the silver brooch that was a moon with five little owls sitting on it. She never pulled Grandmother's watch out of her bodice & opened the back by herself to see Grandfather's hair. She never buried her head close to smell the lavender water or took up Grandmother's spectacle case & wondered at it being really silver. She just lay still & let herself be rocked.

Down in the kitchen one day old Mrs McElvie came to the door & asked Bridget about the poor little mite. Bridget said "Kept alive on bullocks blood hotted in a saucer over a candle." After that I felt frightened of Gwen. I decided that even when she did play with the dolls house I would not let her go upstairs into the bedrooms – only downstairs & then only when I saw she could look.

Late one evening I sat by the fire on my little carpet hassock & Grandmother rocked, singing the song she used to sing me, but more gently. Suddenly she stopped & I looked up. Gwen opened her eyes & turned her little round head to the fire & looked & looked at it & then – turned her eyes up to the face bending over her. I saw her tiny body stretch out & her hands flew up. Ah! Ah! Ah! called the grandmother. Bridget dressed her [i.e. me] next morning. When I went into the nursery I sniffed. A big vase of the white lilies was standing on the table. Grandmother sat in her chair to one side with Gwen in her lap, & a funny little man with his head in a black bag was standing behind a box of china eggs. 'Now' he said and I saw my grandmother's face change as she bent over little Gwen. Thank you said the man coming out of the bag. The picture was hung over the nursery fire. I thought it looked very nice. The dolls house was in it too – verandah & balcony and all. Gran held me up to kiss my little sister.    [J101-103]

---

I have a lovely idea for a story. Yelski & his wife the children the cinema actor. Plays in Geneva.

---

[59]At half past 2 the servant girl stumped along the narrow passage from the kitchen to the sitting room, thrust her head in at the door & shouted in a loud impudent voice "Alors, je vais Madame. A demain Madame."
Muffi waited until she heard the front door slam, until she heard the servant's steps ring & clatter down the metal stairs, until faint living[?] ripples of silence spread and covered over every corner of the little flat. Then she changed. It was not only the expression of her face that changed – she breathed differently, her walk & her gestures were altered – something mysterious & beautiful – something half joyful & half rapturous seemed to flow from her soul into her very skin, & wind itself upon her eyelids & her parted lips. If she had talked to herself perhaps she would have said now I am free. But she never talked to herself. Instead she lifted up her arms & her bosom in a sigh, & first she went with quick light steps into the hall into the kitchen the bedroom the childrens room the study, to make sure that nobody was there, & then she came back into the sitting room & curled up on the narrow leather sofa before the window, folding herself, her feet tucked under her, her hands idle on her lap.
    The window of the sitting room looked out upon a field covered with long grass & ragged bushes. In one corner sprawled a heap of timber, in another a load of bricks was tumbled. Round 3 sides of the field & separated from it by a wet clay road there reared up three new buildings – white, unsubstantial, puffed with air like immense half baked meringues. A fourth was being built, the fresh walls & palings showed like slabs of cheese. Everything that afternoon was blurred by a thick white mist & somewhere in the field, hidden quite, a man was practising on the cornet. He must have been walking about while he played, for sometimes the notes were loud and harsh and then they sounded full of despair tinged with threatening anger. Sometimes they came from far away, bubbles of melancholy sound floating on the swaying mist. But always he played the same tune over & over.

---

[59]Several more attempts at the story of Muffi are in the Newberry Library. Titled 'Love Lies Bleeding', they may be found on p 113–120.

<u>Ta</u> <u>ta</u> <u>ta</u>
<u>diddle</u> um <u>diddle</u> um
<u>Ta</u> tiddley um tum <u>ta</u>

There was nobody to be seen & there was nothing to be heard except the
noise of the cornet & the knocking of hammers in the building house.
Its Autumn thought Muffi and her lips trembled as though they tasted the mist
& the cold air. Yes, its autumn.

But she was not made sad by it. She merely responded, just as she
opened her eyes very widely if she walked in the dark or held up her face to
taste the sun or the rain. It was not her nature to rebel against anything.
No, she accepted "with cowlike, female stupidity" as Max put it.

You are like all women, he sneered. You love to make men believe you
are rarer beings, more delicately attuned than they. Nothing surprises me,
he minced in a squeaking voice, fluttering his podgy hand, nothing alarms me.
I knew that it was going to rain. I knew that the house would catch on fire,
that we should miss the train, that my children would die. I have my celestial
messengers. When any man old enough to shave himself knows that your
divine calm is simply your cold lack of imagination – women's incapacity to
feel anything <u>at all</u> once they are out of bed.

The children loved their father when he began to talk like this because
the subject excited him & he would walk up & down the room with tiny
steps, holding up his coat tails for a skirt, laughing and jeering at women and
at the ridiculous false importance granted them by fools and at their boundless
unbelievable stupidity. The children used to sit at the table and clap him & beat
the table with their fists & jump up and down. "Ah Papa. Ah, my Papa, my
darling clever little Papa," Rudi would cry. But Susan who was nine years old
& quite a woman realised that her Papa really meant Muffi when he tiptoed
and squeaked and so her chiefest joy was the knowledge that she knew.

Muffi smiled too & when Rudi flung himself on her & squeezing crying
breathlessly "Isn't he wonderful, my Papa", she would reply "Yes he is
wonderful."

I am not really here. je souffre de ce que vous vivez seul. Je voudrais vous avoir
toute. je ne suis jamais sentie vivre qu'avec vous sure de moi, et vous devez
compte sur moi.
m'a jeté dans une tristesse horrible – [60]

There is a scenic railway winding up & up into the air. And at night it is
covered with little lights, red & green and blue. He put his head close & gave
her a necklace of butterfly kisses.
"Shall we go on it – you & I?"
"Yes. Yes."
"And will you scream. The chaps at school say you can't half scream frightfully
– not because you're afraid but – oh well."

---

[60]These lines are squeezed into the top margin of one of the preceding pages about Muffi.

He was floating in a boat down a drowsy[?] river, floating away from Muffi. Muffi! His voice rang over the water like a big bell. Muffi– le petit Muffon! & his lamp[?] fell into the water and ran in a long ripple to where Muffi stood..... Your little feet are wet. He knelt down & took off her shoes. He bent lower & kissed her feet. Oh no, she whispered. Why not. He looked up at her smiling. I want your little feet to fall in love with me so that they will always carry you quickly quickly to me.

Max.

> Et pouvant, il faut bien s'habituer à vivre
> Même seul, même triste, indifferent et las,
> Car, O ma vision troublante, n'est-tu pas
> Un mirage incessant trop difficile à suivre.[61]

He saw the white boat with sails outspread, flying over the swishing waves[?] towards the little island that rose up on the sea like an immense green bouquet in a frill of white foam. He began to sing. Look out said Evie catching him by the arm, there's a bobby. A policeman, a big blue bottle pest stood at the street corner staring up at the gas lamp that leapt & quivered in its little eager[?] glass. I never heard him said the boy. Rubber heels, dearie, said Evie & she yawned, undoing[?] her hairpin, & lifted up her arms to the indifferent sky.

Elena
Brave Love X
The German Governess X

Cinema
The Party
Woman at the Store X
The Fern Tree.

---

[61]This passage has a one-word heading which is illegible.

# *Unbound Papers*

[MS-Papers-4006-05]

A Victorian Idyll.

Yesterday Matilda Mason
In the Parlour by Herself
Broke a Handsome China Basin
Placed upon the Mantelshelf.

You picture Matilda in a little check dress, puce shoulder-ties, muslin
pantalettes, black sandals and a pound of rich glossy curls held in place by
a velvet band. She tiptoes about the parlour, among the what-nots and
antimacassars and embroidery frames, and Mamma's workbox with the ivory
fittings and Papa's music stand with his pearl studded flute lying across it.
How did she come to be in the parlour by herself - rash, foolish child!
Why was she not sitting upon a bead hassock up in the nursery conning
over one of those amiable little tomes for infants from one and a half to three
years . .
(Charles:  Pray, dear Papa! What is the Solar System?
Papa:  Wipe your nose, Charles, and I will tell you.)
Or embroidering God is Love in red thread upon a nightdress case for her dear
Mamma!
She had parted her Papa's 'piccadilly weepers',[62] had been strained to his
flashing bosom before he dashed off to that mysterious place, the City, where
ladies feared to tread; her Mamma, having seen the doctor's gig draw up at
number twelve had put on her second best pair of jet earrings, wrapped herself
in her second best cashmere shawl and taken a flash of eau de cologne

[J122–123]

---

[62]'piccadilly weepers': long, carefully combed-out whiskers.

[MS-Paper-4006-05]

Life is not gay.

but at last she was conscious that a choice had to be made - that before dawn these shadows would appear less real making way for something quite different. There was no hesitation now. She simply knew that she wanted him near her, that he was to her the meaning of love and of others, that without him all the world was a little ball rolling over a dark sky.

Dawn broke, long in coming. She lay in the bed on her back, one arm behind her head, one hand on the counterpane - the window became blue, then suffused with gold light, but when she looked at her watch she was horrified to find that it was only half past five o'clock. Hours had to [be] got through somehow - hours and hours - and you must remember that time was not the sort of thing you could count on at the last to be faithful or to be just. No, it behaved as it liked - it had infinite capacities for lengthening out, for hanging on like a white ribbon of road under your too tired feet. Oh, to have done with it. To run like a little child over the long white places, to be there and in his arms! x x x

She went over to the mirror, took off her cap, shook her hair - and once, adorably seeing his eyes watch her, she glanced over her shoulder & smiled. Carefully she powdered her face, rouged her lips, traced with the tip of her finger her eyebrows. This was our Kezia at work, this being with

[J125-126 S91-92]

[MS-Papers-4006-05]

## TOOTS [63]

Toots: (puts down her tea cup and begins to rock gently) But really, as time goes on I seem to become more and more selfish. I feel I want nothing and nobody except my own home and my own children within hail. Nice for the poor children! The extraordinary thing is that when they were children I never realised they'd grow up and marry and leave the nest. No. I always imagined us as one large family party, living here or travelling about - of course each of them living their own individual lives - but all of them coming down to breakfast in the morning and pulling their pa-man's beard . . Don't you know? . . (She smiles at Bee absently and hands her a plate of biscuits, saying in an absent voice) Have an almond finger, dear, won't you? They're awfully good - so short and nutty! (But before Bee has time to take one she puts the plate

---

[63]'Toots' exists in two drafts. The first, rough draft (labelled by KM 'very rough') is extremely difficult to read but varies in only minor respects from the more legible draft. The latter, where it varies, does so by expanding phrases and paragraphs, and it also extends beyond the limit of the first draft. The first, rough draft has 141A at the top of page 1, indicating that it was written at 141A Church Street in 1917. On 24 April 1917 KM wrote to Ottoline Morrell 'My play, which is called "A Ship in the Harbour" is at its Third Act. I hope it will be good. I know the idea is good. But there is an unthinkable amount of pruning to be done before one can liberate one's people in a play. I hadn't realised it before. It is very hard work.' Although the more legible of the two drafts is untitled, and although this is almost certainly the play she refers to as 'A Ship in the Harbour', it seems safer to call it by the title KM gave it at the top of the rough draft: 'Toots'.

down and gets up and begins to walk slowly about the room) Of course no outsider could know - not even you, Bee dear - how united we were, how happy! What jokes we had, what rare old giggles! How we used to kick each other under the table and make faces when the Pa-man would persist in reading out long lists of figures about frozen meat or wool or something. And how they used to come and sit in my room at night after I had gone to bed and while their Pa-man was massaging his last remaining hairs and <u>would</u> not go - until they were simply chased out with a hairbrush. Long after they were grown up, I mean ... Yes - - I can see them now - - Margot undoing those two lovely rich silky plaits, Irene manicuring her beautiful little nails, Pip smelling all the pots on my dressing table, and Laura <u>mooning</u> over at the window. (She sits down again and blows her nose.) Then came that <u>fatal</u> trip to England when Margot married Duncan Henderson. Of course he is a delightful person and desirable in every way and would have been a charming friend for her to correspond with and keep in touch with - - don't you know? But why - why go to the lengths of marrying him and starting the break up of it all. No, I shall never forget my feelings at having to leave that darling child so many thousands of miles away. Of course I had to keep up for Stanley's sake but I had barely got over it when my precious Irene was snatched from me - before my very eyes - whirled off the very deck of the ship, so to speak, by Jimmy Curwen. (Stretches out her arms) There again - what was there to be said? A delightful person, desirable in every way, rich, handsome, a Southern American - and they are always so perfect to their women . . Before I could look round another child was gone. I fully expected to arrive home here and find that Laura was engaged <u>at least</u> and Pip an old married man ...

<u>Bee</u>: (puts down her cup. Takes a needle out of her bodice and threads it, screwing up her eyes) I took good care that nothing of that sort should happen!

<u>Toots</u>: Oh, I don't suppose it needed such frightfully good care. They are so wrapped up in each other, those two. Pip understands Laura far better than I do and a million times better than her father ever could.

<u>Bee</u>: (dryly) She is difficult, very!

<u>Toots</u>: Oh, I - don't - know - Of course at times I think she is simply intolerable, but then one can't expect all one's children to be alike. Margot and Irene never passed through these phases but I suppose there are hundreds of other brainy brilliant girls just like Laura. She's too clever, really, and far too intense. Intense isn't the word, my dear! She never can take a decent respectable interest in anything; she's always head over ears before one can say fruit knife. When she <u>is</u> good - what I call good - I'm not saying this because I'm her mother, I'm speaking quite impersonally - she's fascinating, irresistible! But then she so very seldom is <u>what I call good</u>.

<u>Bee</u>: I think she has got very handsome lately - don't you?

<u>Toots</u>: Yes, hasn't she! In the evenings, my dear, sometimes I can't take my eyes off her. She looks like some wonderful little foreign princess. And then

perhaps next morning she'll come down in an old black blouse, a bit of black ribbon round her neck, <u>obviously</u> no stays, <u>bags</u> under her eyes, and ask in a hollow voice for coffee without any milk. On those occasions when I go up to her room I always find either Tolstoi under her pillow or that other man, the man with the impossible name - Dosty-something - <u>Dostyosti</u> I always call him. Poor child! How it maddens her!

Bee: I think it is a very good thing for Laura that Margot is coming out here to live. It ought to steady her very much, having Margot here and the interest of Margot's life.

<u>Toots</u>: Yes, I expect you're right. I hadn't really thought what it would mean to anybody except to me. Think of it! I haven't seen the dear child for six months, and she always was - <u>such</u> a mother's baby.

Bee: I shouldn't be surprised if she were feeling more of a mother's baby than ever just now.

<u>Toots</u>: Why? What do you mean by <u>just now</u>?

<u>Bee</u>: Isn't there any talk of a family?

<u>Toots</u>: (energetically) Good Heavens! I hope not! She's never breathed a word to me. I think it's the greatest mistake for young married people to <u>rush</u> into having children. When you're young and with the whole of your life before you surely it's the height of folly to sit down calmly and have baby after baby. Besides it's so easily prevented now-a-days. Certainly if I had my time over again I'd never lead off with a baby. A baby is one of the <u>last cards</u> I should play. Besides there can't be anything of that sort in the wind. If there had been I don't think Duncan would have left her to travel by herself. He'd have waited for her. He never would have come on a month ahead like this.

<u>Bee</u>: Quite frankly - of course it's no affair of mine - I still can't understand why he has rushed on ahead like this and left her to settle up all their affairs. Of course he had his appointment but his appointment could surely have waited a month. It seems to me <u>odd</u>. No doubt I'm old fashioned and behind these independent times.

<u>Toots</u>: No, I agree. I think it <u>is</u> odd, very odd, but I'm <u>afraid</u> - typical. I had a feeling from the first moment that I saw them together that he didn't appreciate the treasure he had got and that he was bound to take advantage of her angelic unselfishness. I only hope I'm wrong. I only hope he is all that she imagines he is. That's why I shall be very glad to have him under my eye for a month and really get to know him without her. I've put him in the Bachelor's Quarters, beside Pip's rooms. He ought to be very snug there all to himself.

(The clock strikes five)

By Jove! it's five already! They ought to be here in half an hour. Stanley is going down to the wharf but he has to go straight back to the office for a board meeting so Pip will drive up with Duncan. I'd better tell the faithful lunatic to put a kettle on. They are sure to be dying for a cup of tea. (She rings and crosses to the window) Heavens! the wind! What a vile day! Just the kind of day one would <u>not</u> choose to arrive anywhere. The garden will be blown to ribbons by tomorrow morning.

(Enter Jennie with her cap on crooked.)

<u>Jennie</u>: Did you ring, Mrs Brandon?

<u>Toots</u>: (vaguely) Er – yes – Jennie – I <u>did</u> take that liberty for once. Would you put on a kettle and have some tea ready for when Mr Henderson arrives. And – Jennie – where is the gardener – I can't see a hint of him in the garden. He's not blown away by any chance is he?

<u>Jennie</u>: Oh, no, Mrs Brandon. He's having a nice 'ot cup of tea in the kitching with me.

<u>Toots</u>: But Jennie he can't <u>still</u> be drinking that nice hot cup of tea; he was at it two hours ago!

<u>Jennie</u>: Oh, Lor no, Mrs Brandon! That was 'is cup with 'is dinner.

<u>Toots</u>: Well, you might just ask him from me <u>not</u> to forget all about the garden, will you? He might just occasionally look at it out of the kitchen window at any rate ... And Jennie – put a can of really hot water covered with a towel in Mr Henderson's room.

(Jennie nods and goes.)

I don't want the poor soul to feel that he has fallen amongst absolute Maoris.

<u>Bee</u>: (very pink, folding up her work) I must say I do disapprove, my dear, of the way you treat your servants. I had Jennie in the most perfect order while you were away. She was like a little machine about the house. And now she answers back – she's got all her wretched Colonial habits again.

<u>Toots</u>: I know – it's my fault. It's my weakness for human beings. If ever I feel that a servant is turning into a machine I always have to give her something to turn her back again – a petticoat that I haven't finished with, or a pair of shoes that I love my own feet in, or a ticket for the theatre. Hark! Do you hear? That's the cab, isn't it?

<u>Bee</u>: (flustered) My dear, I must go.

<u>Toots</u>: No, why should you? Stay and meet Duncan. Of course. I meant you to stay.

(There is the sound of a big door opening, and laughing voices. The door gives a terrific slam. Someone calls excitedly "Toots!")

<u>Toots</u>: (calling) In the morning room! (She runs to the door but it is opened. Duncan and Philip enter in big coats and caps, pulling off their gloves. Their noses are red with the cold wind. Duncan stuffs his gloves and cap into his pocket, comes forward & takes Toots by the elbows. Bends and kisses her. Pip looks on with merry eyes.)

<u>Duncan</u>: My dear little Mater!

<u>Toots</u>: My dear Duncan – welcome to our hearth! How splendid you are looking and how cold – you poor huge creature. Such a day to arrive! (She leads him forward) Bee dear, here he is. Duncan, this is my old friend Miss Wing.

<u>Duncan</u>: (very cordial) How do you do, Miss Wing. I'm delighted!

<u>Pip</u>: (runs forward. He is bursting with laughter and keeps shaking his head as though he had just come out of the sea.) Here, let me give you a hand with your coat – may I? (To Toots) You haven't got an idea of what the weather is like on the wharf, my dear! It's simply too awful, isn't it?

<u>Duncan</u>: It certainly is one of the roughest days I've ever struck.

<u>Pip</u>: (laughing all the while) And if you'd only seen the poor old Pa-man staggering along the railway lines with me, holding on his hat with the crook of his umbrella. I told him to tie his handkerchief over his hat and fasten it in a neat knot under his chin - but he wouldn't hear of it. And when we got to the place where the lighter should have been - the wind simply playing the fiddle with his sciatic nerves - and when the lighter did come & we watched it going up and down - But going <u>up and down</u>, my dear . . . And I thought that in two Ts we'd be going up and down with it I never felt so sorry for anyone in all my life. But of course he stuck to it like a Trojan and all the way out to the ship he pretended he liked it and said he used to go fishing down the Sounds in just that kind of weather.

<u>Toots</u>: Poor old darling. I hope he has a good nip of brandy when he gets back to the office. I've a great mind to phone and tell him to.

<u>Pip</u>: No, of course don't do anything of the kind, silly. He'd be furious with me.

(Duncan and Bee have been talking together. They raise their voices.)

<u>Bee</u>: But what on earth can she have done it for?

<u>Duncan</u>: That's what puzzled me. It really did seem too dangerous a thing to do for the mere fun of it. I thought there must be some Prince Charming on board but I had a good look round and nobody appeared to be signalling. (Turns to Toots) As I was telling Miss Wing, Mater - While we were waiting for the lighter I was looking through my glasses at the shore and I saw a girl walking along a stone embankment by the edge of the sea. A frightfully dangerous place it looked! She was simply blown about in the wind like a little woollen ball. More than once she was blown right over - right on to the rocks. But she got up again each time and came on until she reached a kind of platform or something.

<u>Pip</u>: Yes, where the people fish from.

<u>Duncan</u>: And there she stood, waving at the ship. Just not being blown into the sea!

<u>Toots</u>: (who hasn't heard a word but has been warming Pip's hands in hers - holding one hand against her breast & rubbing it and then holding the other, says in her absent voice) Fan-cy! (waking up) Tell me, how did you leave Margot?

<u>Duncan</u>: Splendid - simply splendid! Of course she sent all kinds of loving messages to you all. I wish, for many reasons, that she could have come with me - but it wasn't possible. For one thing she had so much that she wanted to settle & for another I had a very special piece of writing on hand and I felt a quiet voyage would be just the place to do it in.

<u>Toots</u>: (dryly) Oh, I am sure it was <u>much</u> the wisest plan. I thought it most sensible and <u>modern</u> of you both. Personally I think it's a great mistake at the best of times to travel with one's husband - or any man, for the matter of that.

<u>Pip</u>: Pooh! I like that - what about me! You'd give your eyes if I'd fly off with you.

Toots: Even if I would – that's got nothing to do with it. You're not a man; you're nothing but a child.

Pip: (warmly) And what are you I should like to know. You're nothing but an infant in arms. I could put you in a basket & tuck you under my arm – and only lift the lid and let you sit on my knee when it came out sunny. (Puts his arm round Toots' shoulder & chuckles) We know what Bee is thinking, don't we Toots. (mimics) I may be old fashioned and behind the times but it does seem to me odd that a child should speak so to its parent. (He shades his eyes with his hand and pretends to stagger back a step) Good Heavens! Do I see aright? A <u>new black velvet blouse</u> trimmed with a neat red and white glacé check?? I'm surprised at you Bee! I wouldn't have believed it! Or (goes over to Miss Bee, takes her hand & kissing it says to her ardently and warmly) was it for me? Am I the happy man?

Bee: Let me go this instant, Philip!

(Pip tries to put his arm around her waist)

Toots: Philip, behave yourself, this instant, sir! I don't know what you will be thinking of us Duncan.

Duncan: (cordial to a fault) Ah, Mater, don't apologise. I like it – it makes me feel like one of the family.

Toots: (strangely) That's splendid! (quickly) Wouldn't you boys like some tea? Pip – show Duncan his rooms while the tea is coming. You don't have to go back to the office today, do you?

Pip: No, darling.

Toots: Well, put your slippers on, my son.

Pip: Oui, ma mère. (He puts his hand on Duncan's shoulder) This way, old boy. (At the door) Mother – where is Laura?

Toots: At the Library reading the Chinese Classics.

Pip: Clever Dick! Avanti, signor. Observe with what ease the young Colonial rolls the foreign tongue. (They go out.)

Toots: (at the door) If there is no hot water in Duncan's room – just <u>curse</u> down the kitchen stairs, will you? (She comes back into the room & very deliberately shuts the door.)

Bee: (who has been rearranging herself) Now I really must go, Toots dear.

Toots: (pays no attention) Well, what do you think of him?

Bee: He's far better looking than his photograph made him out to be.

Toots: (reluctantly) Yes, I suppose he <u>is</u> what you'd call goodlooking.

Bee: And his voice is charming – a charming <u>english</u> voice.

Toots: (naively) Isn't it strange that I can't take to him? Somehow he doesn't seem to be in the least one of <u>us</u> – not to belong in the very faintest degree to <u>our tribe</u> if you know what I mean. But I really haven't got any right to say that about him just now – the moment he has arrived and I dare say <u>feels</u> his nose is red and is dying to – – – wash his hands & part his hair. In fact I think it's beastly of me to shut the door on him and begin criticising like that. I take back what I said, Bee. I really am unscrupulous – just as bad as the children.

Bee: (kissing her) My dear Toots, you may always be certain that anything you ever tell me never goes the length of my little finger further.

<u>Toots</u>: Oh, that's not what I care about at all. Goodbye, dear. I'll come with you to the door. And while I remember I'll get you the pot of my new cape gooseberry jam before I forget.

(The stage is empty. It gets dusky. The wind is heard rushing and hooting. Someone wrenches open the french windows and comes through, shutting them after her as though she were being pursued by the furious wind. It is Laura. She wears a big black coat, a scarf round her neck and a white woollen cap pulled over her ears. When she has shut the windows she staggers forward, her hands clasped at the back of her head, panting and laughing silently, and saying in a breathless whisper "How marvellous it was. How marvellous." She crosses her arms over her breast, hugging her shoulders. "And how terrified I was! How absolutely terrified!" She stands quite still for a moment & then blurts out angrily "And the joke was that some arrogant fool actually thought I was waving to him and started waving back!"

It is quite dusky. Only the shapes of things are seen & Laura's white wool cap. The door opens, letting in a bright light from the hall. Duncan enters, hesitates. Laura goes up to him and says in a shy soft voice "Good evening. I am Laura. And you're my new brother-in-law Duncan, aren't you." She puts out her hand and as he clasps hers and is about to speak she says with a strong American accent: "<u>Pleased</u> to meet you, <u>Mr</u> Henderson." And walks out.)

Quick Curtain
End of Act I.

### Act II

[A small ink sketch of a stage set, with the props lettered and listed at the side, thus:]
- A. - door.
- B. - french windows.
- C. - leather sofa.
- D. - piano (upright).
- E. - deep corner couch covered in chinz.
- F. - fireplace and leather seat in front of it.
- G. - revolving bookcase.
- H. - bookshelves above writing table.
- I. - two armchairs covered in same chinz as couch and a low table between them for tea or work.
- J. - writing table.

The Morning Room as before. Mr. Brandon lies on the leather sofa against the back wall to the right of the door. Pip sprawls over the table cutting open & tearing the wrappers from a big packet of new English and American magazines. He wears white flannel trousers, white boots and a white flannel shirt open at the throat, the sleeves rolled up above his elbows. Mrs Brandon walks about the room, now giving herself a glance in the mirror over the mantelpiece, now pulling the blinds half an inch lower, now bending over the back of Pip's chair & looking at the pictures with him. She is dressed in black muslin with a grey ostrich feather scarf dropping from her shoulders.

Mr Brandon's hands are folded over his belly - he has spread his handkerchief over his face and very occasionally he gives a loud beatific-sounding snore. Although the blinds are more than halfway down one realises it is an exquisite hot Sunday afternoon.

Pip: I can't think why it is but I always feel the need of a sweet toothful on Sunday afternoons - do you? Have you got a chocolate button tucked away in the drawer of the sewing machine or do you think there is by any chance an odd, rather <u>gritty</u> jujube at the bottom of your workbag darling?

Toots: No, I know there isn't. There's nothing except a chip of that awful liquorice the Pa-man bought for his cold mixed up with the sealing wax in the pen tray. Any good?

Pip: (shudders & says in a hollow voice) No good! Come here, Toots. Don't you think that girl is awfully pretty?

Toots: Lovely! What a tragedy it is that actresses so often look like Princesses and Princesses so seldom look like actresses. (She bends over him smelling his hair.) How delicious your hair smells, child - like fresh pineapple.

Pip: (leans against her smiling with half shut eyes) Oh, <u>Mother</u> ... Do you ever get a feeling, for no reason at all, just out of the blue - a feeling of such terrific happiness that it's almost unbearable. You feel that it's all bottled up here (puts his hand on his breast) and that if you don't give it to somebody or get rid of it somehow - <u>tear</u> it out of yourself - you'll simply die - of - bliss ... And at the same time, you feel as though you can do anything you want to - <u>anything</u>. Fly, knock down a mountain, or any darned thing. Just the moment you said my hair smelled of pineapples I got one of those <u>waves</u> - you see for no reason - & if I hugged you now I'd break all your little bones. I couldn't help it. I'm a giant... Do you know what I mean?

    (Mr Brandon gives a long snore.)

Pip: (sotto voce, very sentimental, sings)
          Sleep darling sleep the day-light
          Di-i-ies down in the gold-olden west!

Toots: Sh-sh! Don't wake him. He'll make me rush off for a walk & I'm so much happier here.

Pip: Shall I take him out instead of you.

Toots: My dear! The skies would fall.

Pip: Oh well I don't want to particularly. I'm booked to play tennis at the Graces. How awfully quiet the house is. Where's everybody.

Toots: Duncan is writing letters & Laura hasn't come down yet. I can't think what has come over the child. She has simply stayed in bed today. I took her up some fruit after lunch & she said she was getting up then. She didn't look a scrap tired. On the contrary she looked marvellously well. How did she get on last night? Was she a success?

Pip:

———————————

# *Notebook 32*

[Notebook 32, qMS-1256]

as though she expected to hear those hollow bursts[?] roaring like shells  -  -  -

E.M.F.

and that even if we had swung from the roof of one rushing train on to the roof of another rushing train, or allowed ourselves to be chloroformed & snatched away in sinister taxis with the blinds pulled down,[64]

and Miss Mose pluming & preening herself & clucking[?] discreetly her heart tucked[?] well in behind her big smooth bosom - those light glaring eyes - & thin legs and narrow high button boots gave them the look of hens stepping across the wet stable[?] yard, ugly & perplexed that no one appeared to fling the light grain among them & shoo them this way and that  -  -  -

he stared at his watch, & then still holding it in his hand he stared into the air, [...] over [...] as though counting the [...] of the ugly day.

its weird he doesn't see us isn't it said the [...]. My dear, isn't she weird, said the [...]. I believe she is an alien. But she's too weird for words!

Have you often worked for Mr Alexander, asked the Fat girl. Oh, you would like to work for him. What a nice man he is. Oh what a nice man is that Mr Alexander, & she lifted her head as the [...] started to [...] herself on the [...]-like hot coffee cakes of her childhood.

Large heavy limbs & a neck like a turkey.

piece of doormat. Oh, she cried, flinging the tail of that little dead animal yet again round her fat neck.[65]

---

[64]In her review of *The Extra Lady* by Horace W C Newte in *The Athenaeum* of September 24 1920 KM wrote: 'These conjured up a vision of certain theatrical posters of provincial melodrama - girls in the act of being chloroformed and spirited away in malignant-looking cabs by auburn-haired villians in check riding breeches...'

[65]There follows here a long piece which Murry's note says is a translation from Wyspianski (Stanislaw Wyspianski, 1869–1907, Polish dramatist, poet and painter). Since much of it is illegible I have left it alone.

Was it simply her own imagination or could there be any truth in this feeling that waiters – waiters especially and hotel servants – adopted an impertinent, arrogant and slightly amused attitude towards a woman who travelled alone.[66] Was it just her wretched female self-consciousness? No, she really did not think it was. For even when she was feeling at her happiest, at her freest, she would become aware, quite suddenly, of the 'tone' of the waiter or the hotel servant. And it was extraordinary how it wrecked her sense of security, how it made her feel that something malicious was being plotted against her and that everybody and everything – yes, even to inanimate objects like chairs or tables was secretly 'in the know' – waiting for that ominous infallible thing to happen to her, which always did happen, which was bound to happen to every woman on earth who travelled alone! The waiter prodded a keyhole with a bunch of keys, wrenched one round, flung the grey painted door open and stood against it waiting for her to pass in. He held his feather duster upright in his hand like a smoky torch. "Here is a nice little room for Madame," said the waiter insinuatingly. As she entered he brushed past her, opened the groaning window, unhooked the shutters

---

[66]Several of the following manuscripts appear to be pieces of the story Murry subsequently called 'Geneva', written in 1917. They are brought together here for the convenience of the reader.

# *Unbound Papers*

[MS-Papers-4006-04]

Geneva.                                January 1st 1917.

Chapter IV.

letting a cold shadowless light flood into the hideous slip of a room with the
Hotel Rules & the Police Regulations pinned over the washstand & narrow
string furniture that looked as if it were afraid that one fine night the brown
walls would clap together like butter pats & squeeze it.

She crossed to the window and looked out over a court into the back of
another tall building with strangely crooked windows hung with tattered
washing like the windows of a house in a 'comic' picture.

"A very nice little room for Madame" said the waiter & turning to the
bed he slapped it & gave the mattress a punch which really did not seem to be
merely professional. "Very clean you see Madame - very comfortable with
electric light & running water." She could hardly repress a cold shiver of
horror. She said dully "No I do not like this room at all. And besides it has not
got a good table. I must have a good table in my room."

"A <u>table</u> Madame" said the waiter and as he straightened up his long
feather duster seemed to be printed on his blue linen apron in a big
exclamation mark of astonishment. "A table! But Madame desires a bed.
Madame desires a bed as well as a table. N'est ce pas, Madame?" She did not
reply to the fool. Show me a large room, she said. And he took some sliding
gliding steps to the door and she had the fancy that he was about to waltz
down the passage in a frenzy of delighted amusement.

"Mais voila une <u>belle</u> chambre" said the waiter, stopping in front of
another grey painted door and laying across the palm of his hand the bunch
of jingling keys. He cocked his head on one side selecting the right one.
"But its dear, you understand. It costs six francs a day & without breakfast!
You understand, Madame - six francs." And to make his meaning perfectly
clear he held up six keys arranged like a fan. At the moment she would have
paid 60 just to be rid of that grinning ape - just to have the right to shut the
door upon him.

But it really was a very charming room. Big - square with windows on 2 sides. A white wallpaper, pink carpet & curtains, a deep bed covered in a blue wadded quilt, a little pink settee and an armchair with a dab of white crochet lace on its back & a dab on either arm, yellow-waxed furniture and a table covered in a blue cloth. Very nice. Very nice indeed. She put her hands on the table and it was steady as rock.

"Madame is pleased?" asked the waiter. Yes, she told him she would take the room & would he have her luggage sent immediately. When he had gone & the door really <u>was</u> shut she behaved quite wildly for a minute or two, & ran about, flinging up her arms and crying Oh Oh!, as though she had just been rescued from a shipwreck or a burning house. Between the charming net curtains through one window she could see across a square to the railing of what looked like a park full of yellowing trees. The other looked over a street of little cafes half hidden under striped awnings, & enchanting little shops – one was a confectioner's shop with a big white swan in the window filled with silver chocolates, & one was a florist. A woman knelt on the step outside placing flat yellow baskets of flowers. Then there was a tiny hat shop filled with black hats & crepe belts. How funny the people looked as she peered down upon them - so squat & broad. They scuttled from side to side like black crabs – & what absurd noises the drivers made & really this room was almost perfect in this way - absolutely scrupulously clean. <At that moment she caught sight of herself in the glass & stopped. I would not have believed that you would have had such courage, said she. No I wouldn't have believed it.> She would be very happy here; this was exactly

[MS-Papers-4006-11]

.... what she had imagined .... With flowers, with her books arranged and one or two odd pieces of bright silk that she always travelled with, & her lovely embroidered shawl flung over the settee & her writing things out on the table - really - - -

There came a bang at the door followed by a little red-haired boy staggering under the weight of her suitcases. He was very pale, with big splashes of freckles on his nose and under his eyes, and so out of breath that he could not even ask her where she wanted the luggage put, but stood, his head craned forward, his mouth open to suck in the unaccustomed air.
She overpaid him & he went away but with the generous coin she seemed to have given to him all her excitement and her delight. The door shut upon it: it was gone; the sound of it died away.     [S61-65]

[MS-Papers-4006-10]

She stepped down on to the platform & quite suddenly, as though this were part of her programme & she had fully expected & prepared for it to happen, she gave a strange little smile. She felt herself what a frightful mockery of a smile it was and she went up close to Max and stood in front of him.

But before they reached the end of the platform she could bear it no longer. She turned her back on the people & staring up at a huge red & green poster which announced a sale of winter costumes at Breitmans she paused for a moment. She said to herself as she stroked her muff "keep calm!" but it was too late - she had no more power over herself. She couldn't get calm. She was somehow quite out of her own control. She faced Max & lifting her arms she stammered - I must you know, I must have love, have love - I cannot live without love you know its not

At the words that block of ice which had become her bosom melted, melted into warm tears & she felt these tears like great warm ripples flowing over her whole body. Yes, she wept, as it were, from head to foot. She lowered herself over her darling familiar muff & felt that she would dissolve away in tears. It was all over - all over. What was all over. Everything! The battle was lost.    [s65]

she implored & stroked harder with her little shaking hand. Courage my darling. But the soft word was fatal. Down fell her tears - -    [J212]

Outside the station there was a big pebbled square dotted with little iron benches under the lampposts. Over on the far side of the square a big mass of dark shrubs built up high in the air like a wave about to break and sweep all the sticks and stones away. Women with shawls over their heads & baskets in their laps, untidy soldiers, old men leaning on sticks, old women in white muslin caps that gleamed in the light like spiders webs & little children fast asleep, leaning regardless upon the nearest warm shoulder - -

Someone brushed her arm. She turned quickly - Come in - hurry. The train is coming in a minute. The pain was so dreadful that her

[MS-Papers-4006-11]

Thank God! The steps have gone past my door.[67]
In the mirror she saw again that strange watchful creature who had been her companion on the journey, that woman with white cheeks and dark eyes & lips whose secret she shared, but whose air of steady desperation baffled and frightened her and seemed somehow quite out of her control.

[NL]
                 Love - lies - Bleeding

At half past two the servant girl stumped along the narrow passage from the kitchen to the dining room, thrust her head in at the door and shouted in her loud, impudent voice:- "Well, I'm off, Mrs Eichelbaum. I'll be here tomorrow, Mrs Eichelbaum."

Muffi waited until she heard the servant's steps crunch down the gravel path, heard the gate creak and slam, listened until those steps died away quite,

---

[67]KM has drawn a striding stick figure here.

and silence, like a watchful spider began to spin its silent web over the little house ... Everything changed. The white curtains bulged and blew out as though to the first breath of some mysterious breeze, blowing from nowhere; the dark furniture swelled with rich, important life; all the plates on the sideboard, the pictures and ornaments gleamed as if they shone through water; even the lilies, the faded lilies flung all over the green wallpaper, solemnly uncurled again, and she could hear the clock, ticking away, trotting away, galloping away – a rider with a dark plume round his hat riding on a white horse down a lonely road in the moonlight.

Stealthy as a little cat Muffi crept into the kitchen, up the stairs into their bedroom and the children's room down again and into the study to make sure that nobody was there, and then she came back to the dining room and folded herself up on the shabby sofa before the window, her feet tucked under her, her hands shut in her lap.

The window of the dining room looked out on to a paddock covered with long grass and ragged bushes. In one corner lay a heap of timber, in another a load of bricks was tumbled. Round three sides of the paddock there reared up three new houses, white, unsubstantial, puffed up in the air like half baked meringues. A fourth was being built; only the walls and criss cross beams showed. Everything that afternoon was blurred by a thick sea mist, and somewhere, in the paddock, out of sight, a man was playing the cornet. He must have been walking about while he played, for sometimes the notes sounded loud and harsh, full of despair and threatening anger, sometimes they came from far away, bubbles of melancholy sound floating on the swaying mist.

> Ta-ta-ta
> Tiddle-um tiddle-um
> Ta tiddley-um tum-ta!

There was nobody to be seen and nothing to be heard except that cornet and the tap of hammers in the hollow house. "It's autumn!" thought Muffi. Her lips trembled, tasting the mist and the cold air. "Yes, it's autumn!" Not that she felt sad. No, she merely 'responded', just as she held up her face to the sun and wrapped herself together against the rain. It was not Muffi's nature to rebel against anything. Why should she? What good could it do? She accepted life with "cowlike female stupidity" as Max put it. "And you are like all women," he would sneer. "You love to make men believe that you are rare beings, more delicately attuned than they. 'Nothing surprises me'" Max would squeak in a mincing voice, flirting his fat hand, "'nothing alarms me! I knew that it was going to rain, I knew that we were going to miss the train, I knew that my children would catch cold. I have my celestial messengers!' when any man old enough to shave himself knows that your divine calm is simply your lack of imagination, and that no woman ever feels anything – once she is out of bed!"

The children loved their father when he began to talk like that. He would walk up and down the room, holding up his coat tails for a skirt, laughing and jeering at women and at their imbecile unbelievable vanity.

The children used to sit at the table and bang with their fists and clap their hands and jump up and down.

"Ah, Papa! Ah, my Papa! My darling, clever little Papa!" Rudi would cry, but Katerina who was eleven years old and quite a woman realised that Papa really meant Muffi when he tip toed and squeaked, and therein lay her joy.

Muffi smiled too, and when Rudi, quite overcome, would fling himself upon her, squeezing her, crying breathlessly: "Isn't he wonderful, my Papa!" she would answer: "Yes he is wonderful!" What did it matter!

Ta-ta-ta
Tiddle-um tiddle-um
Ta tiddley-um tum ta!

went the cornet. She had never heard him before. She hoped he was not going to be there every afternoon. Perhaps it was only the sea mist that had 'brought him out'. What was he like? He was an old man, wearing a peaked cap and his grey beard was hung with a web of bright drops. She smiled; he stood before her, the cornet under his arm, wiping his face with a coloured handkerchief that smelled of tar ... "Tell me, why do you play the cornet?" No, he was gone again, sitting perhaps behind the heap of timber, far away, and playing more forlornly than ever.

She stirred and sighed and stretched herself.

"What shall I do this afternoon," thought Muffi. Every day she asked herself the same question, and every day it ended in her doing just the same thing - nothing at all. In the winter she lay in front of the fire, staring at the bright dazzle; in summer she sat at the open window and watched the breeze skim through the long gleaming grass (and then those ragged bushes were covered with tiny cream flowers) and in autumn and winter she sat there, too, only then the window was shut, and some days a sea mist covered everything, and other days the wild hooting south wind blew as if it meant to tear everything off the earth, tear everything up by its roots and send it spinning. She did not even think or dream. No, as she sat there, ever so faintly smiling with something mocking in the way her eyelids lay upon her eyes, she looked like a person waiting for a train that she knew would not come, never would by any chance carry her away - didn't even exist.

During the afternoon the baker's boy came and left a loaf on the kitchen window sill. The round basket on his back always reminded her of a snail's shell. "Here comes the snail," she would say. Three times a week an awful butcher, a man so raw and red and willing to oblige that she always felt if he hadn't the pound and a half of steak in his cart he'd be quite willing to cut it off his own person and never notice the difference. And very, very rarely two shabby old nuns wheeling a perambulator knocked at her door and asked her if she had any scraps or bits of things for the orphan children at Lyall Bay.[68] No, she never had, but she liked very much seeing them at her door, smiling

---

[68]Lyall Bay is in Wellington. KM may have been thinking of Island Bay, close by, where Mother Mary Aubert's Home of Compassion opened in 1907. At first called 'The Home for Incurables' it took sick children—both chronic and acute—as well as 'foundlings and illegitimates'. It was for some time dependent on charity.

so gently, their hands tucked in their sleeves. They made her feel so small somehow, so small and young, so like an orphan child herself. One of them always talked and one kept silent.

"You're not married, are you?" asked the talkative nun, on one occasion.

"Oh, yes," said Muffi.

"Glory be!" cried the old nun, and seemed positively to wring her hands in horror.

"You've no children?" she asked, her old mouth falling open.

"Yes, I've a little boy of seven."

"Mother of God!" cried the old nun, and that day they went away, pushing the perambulator very slowly as if it were weighted down with the incredible news. Any time after five o'clock the children came home from school ...

When five o'clock struck. Muffi got up from the sofa and went into the kitchen to put the kettle on. She was bending over the stove when someone tapped at the window. Rudi. Yes, there he was, tapping on the window, smiling and nodding. Ah, the darling! He was home early! She flew to the back door and just had time to open it. She held out her arms and in he tumbled.

"You're early. You darling. You're home so soon – you're so beautifully early," she stammered, kissing and hugging him. How wet and cold his cheeks and fingers were; even his fringe was damp.

"I'm simply sopping from this mist," said Rudi, in his self contained deliberate little way. "Feel my cap, Muffi. Drenched!"

"Drenched!" said she, kneeling down to take off his reefer jacket.

"Oh I'm so out of breath," he cried, stamping and wriggling his way out of the jacket. "I simply flew home."

"Let me jump you on to the table and take off your boots, my precious."

"Oh <u>no</u>." He was quite shocked. "I can take off my own boots, Muffi. I always do."

"Ah no, let me," she pleaded. "Just this once. Just for a treat."

At that he threw back his head and looked at her, his eyes dancing.

"Well, you <u>have</u> got funny ideas of a treat."

"Yes", said she. "I know I have. Awfully funny ideas ... Now the other foot, my son."

When she had finished he sat on the table edge and swung his legs, pouting, frowning, and showing off just a tiny bit. He knew, as he sat there, that he was the most loved little boy in the world, the most admired, the most cherished, and Muffi let him know it. They were alone together so seldom; they couldn't afford to 'pretend', to waste a moment. He seemed to realise that. He said: "Katerina will be home in a minute. I passed her on my way, <u>dawdling</u> along with Lilly Tar. I can't stand Lilly Tar, Muffi. She's always got her arm round someone and she's always whispering."

"Don't bother about her" said Muffi, as much as to say: "if Lilly Tar dares to get in your way I shall see that she is destroyed instantly." Lilly Tar was gone. He looked down at his red little paws. "My fingers are so stiff," he said, "I'll never be able to practise."

"Sit on the hassock here by the fire and give them a good warm."

"It's very nice down here," he decided after a moment. "I love being down low and looking up at things, don't you? At people moving, and the legs of chairs and tables and the shadows on the floor." His voice tailed off, dreamy, absorbed. She let him be. She thought: "He is getting back to himself after that horrible rowdy school."

But a moment later the front door slammed and Katerina came into the kitchen.

"Hullo," said she, very airy. "Why did you tear home so, Rudi. Lilly and I couldn't help screaming at the way you were rushing along."

"I heard you," said Rudi. "I know you meant me to hear, didn't you." At that she opened her big velvety eyes at him, and laughed.

"What a baby you are."

"But you did. Didn't you?" he protested.

"Of course not," jeered Katerina. "We were laughing at something quite different."

"But you said you were laughing at me, Katerina."

"Oh, only in a way," she drawled. Rudi jumped up. "Oh Katerina," he wailed, "why do you tell such awful stories."

Muffi's back was turned, so Katerina made a hideous face at him and sat down at the table.     [s65-73]

II.[69]

"I'm going, children" called Muffi. She stood in the hall, buttoning her gloves. From the dining room came the sound of Rudi's fiddle. <Lisa> Katerina, supposed to be doing her home work in the kitchen, gave no sign. She stood a moment, listening; she must not go in and disturb him. Up he climbed, up the little bright ladder, firmly and quickly, and down he came as though enchanted with what he had seen. He flew up again to look once more and again he ran down laughing. Then up he stole, slowly, sobbing up a little dark ladder, in vain, and down he crept to die. He would go up once again - but no, it was all in vain. He crept back in despair.

"Katerina, I'm going" called Muffi.

"Also gut," came from Katerina.

[at top of page:] Tuesday afternoon in January. Poste Restante

Muffi had a little black astrachan jacket with a collar that stood up to the tips of her ears and the point of her chin. On Saturday afternoon Max did not go to the University. He came into her room while she dressed. He was not still for a moment - popping from the side of the bed to a chair, fingering everything, smelling her hair brushes, talking, begging her to hurry. Can I find anything for you Muffi - your gloves. Do you want your umbrella. Shall I give

---

[69]The following paragraph, though clearly part of this 16 page manuscript, was omitted by Murry from *The Scrapbook* and replaced with another paragraph that I have not been able to locate in manuscript. All of the following pieces of this story were also omitted from *The Scrapbook*.

you your shoes. It was late afternoon, leaves were falling off the trees - large
gold leaves that fell slowly dropping on them as they passed. The air tasted cold
and bitter like wild cherries. In the distance upon the tall mountain tops the
snow was stained with rose. It was very cold. Rudi put his hands in his
pockets, his teeth chattered, his breath blew out in a white fan and Muffi held
her black muff up to her face. But they were both so happy that even this
sharp cold seemed something special, something they had not tasted before
-something to do with the fair.

The bell rumbled. Can I go said Rudi, putting down his spoon
& slipping off his chair. Muffi nodded. "Yes, run." Ah, wailed Lisa, its not fair
its not fair. It was my turn Muffi, wasn't it Papa. Pooh! Max shook his head in
disgust. Don't be such a little fool. Either run to the door in front of Rudi or
hold your tongue. "But Papa," wailed Lisa. Enough! Max reached across the
table & rapped her knuckles with his spoon.

and then we went to a shop where everything played a tune - yes
everything. The man gave me a plate with 2 greengages on it & it began to
play "ach du liebe Augustine". And Muffi sat down on a little chair & it played
Verlassen Verlassen. He jumped up and down with the bollon[?] loaf in his
hands. Papa has gone away said Rudi. He has gone to Dresden today & he has
taken Lisa. Muffi and I are alone. I have married her I am her husband. He has
gone! said Buffon and he turned sharply & leaned on the bridge beside Muffi.
He could not keep out of his voice an immense incredulous joy. He has gone
Madame. She leaned her arms on the stone wall & put her hands on either
side of her face as though she were frightened & could not bear to hear what
he was going to say. The big impatient birds flew closer and closer about their
heads. The little black one seemed to be diving after the long quivering lights
of the lake. Then he said. as though it were at the end of a long conversation -
you know that I love you. I must see you alone. Can I come to you.
She signed 'no' with a little shake of her head. Well, he said, what am I to do.
Help me? At that she turned and looked at him. He saw her strange pallor and
the serious long glance of her eyes. Where do you live, she asked in a faint
voice.

MSS of Love Lies Bleeding.
wants all re-writing. "Its all over the garden wall" at present.
Re-read February 13th 1918[?]

'Love-lies-bleeding.'

At half past two the servant girl stumped along the narrow passage from the
kitchen to the sitting room, thrust her head in at the door and shouted in her
loud, impudent voice:- "Alors, je vais, Madame. A demain, Madame!"
Muffi waited until she heard the front door slam, until she heard the servant's
steps ring and clatter down the stone stairs, listened until those steps died away
quite, and silence, like a watchful spider began to spin its silent web all over

the little flat. And everything changed. The white curtains seemed to bulge and blow out as though to the first breath of some mysterious breeze, blowing from nowhere; the dark furniture swelled with rich, important life; all the plates on the sideboard and the pictures and ornaments gleamed as if they shone through water; the lilies, the faded lilies flung all over the green wall paper uncurled again, and she could hear the clock, ticking away, trotting away, galloping away - a rider with a dark plume round his hat riding on a white horse down a lonely road in the moonlight.

Stealthy as a little cat Muffi crept into the kitchen, their bedroom, the children's room, the study, 'to make sure that nobody was there', and then she came back to the sitting room and folded herself up on the shabby sofa before the window, her feet tucked under her, her hands shut in her lap ...

The window of the sitting room looked out on to a field covered with long grass and ragged bushes. In one corner lay a heap of timber, in another a load of bricks was tumbled. Round three sides of the field there reared up three new buildings, white, unsubstantial, puffed up in the air like immense half baked meringues. The fourth was being built - only the walls and criss-cross beams showed. Everything that afternoon was blurred by a thick mist, and somewhere in the field, out of sight, a man was playing the cornet. He must have been walking about while he played, for sometimes the notes sounded loud and harsh, full of despair and threatening anger; sometimes they came from far away, bubbles of melancholy sound floating on the swaying mist.

Ta–ta-ta
Tiddle–um–iddle um
Ta tiddley–um tum ta!

Nobody to be seen and nothing to be heard except that cornet and the tapping of hammers in the hollow house.

"It's autumn!" thought Muffi. Her lips trembled, tasting the mist and the cold air. "Yes, it's autumn!"

It was evening again. The little flat was sealed for the night. The shutters were shut, the lighted lamp stood in the middle of the round table and in the pool of light Rudi and his father sat working. Max had a brown leather bag on the table stuffed full of essays and as he corrected them with a stump of blue pencil he would mutter 'God' or 'idiot' under his breath, or give a long windy sigh, or read in silence, scratching his head or laying one finger to the side of his nose breathing down one nostril & then down the other in a way he had. Opposite him sat Rudi with a book of french poetry covered in black american cloth open at a poem of Victor Hugo.

Mon père ce heros au sourire si doux.

He bent over it wearily[?] & then he lifted his head, shut his eyes as his lips moved quickly. Then down went his head again.

Suivit d'un grand hussard qu'il amait entre tous and up again. He looked like a little bird drinking at a pool. If he held the book for a long time his fingers stuck to the american cloth & when he pulled them off they left strange little marks that gradually blotted out – he breathed on the cover & wrote R. then he began to learn again.

Pour sa grande bravoure & pour sa haute taille.[70]

On the sofa very languid & pale with dark marks under her eyes lay Katerina. She was not feeling quite well but she was very proud of her illness & she wondered as she smelt her handkerchief sprinkled with eau de cologne, if she would grow a bosom now. Oh she would love to stick out in front like Lilli Thal did & Lilli was only thirteen. Feel me here said Lilli, smiling proudly & laying Katerina's hand on the right place & I'm not filling myself out a bit.

Katerina walked on to the platform in a white silk dress pulled down very tightly in front. A perfect sigh went up from everybody. What a lovely figure! She wore the buttonhole Harold Buffon had given her pinned in the middle. It went up and down as she sang – – – Oh, what bliss!

"I cannot bear it. I cannot bear it!" thought Muffi. She laid down Katerina's pinafore that she was darning & bent over the froth of white in her lap trying to bear this pain in her heart that was unbearable. She saw herself wring her hands & rock to & fro. moving like an old woman & she saw herself fling away this heap of white & start up & rush out of the flat down the stairs into the dark, away away, and she saw herself stagger down the corridor of a train that went so fast & swayed about so that she was banged this side & that, peering in all the carriages until she came to the one where Harold was. Ah! She could not open the heavy door. She beat on the glass – open it quickly quickly. But just as he wrenched it open Rudi rubbed her jacket gently under the table. Papa! he whispered, bubbling with laughter – look! look! Muffi's asleep! She raised her head. She even managed to smile at him and she said – [one line illeg.]

Silence! said Max sternly. Finish your work & he drew a heavy blue line down a whole page.

There is a 3 cornered tear in Katerina's pinafore.

[NL]

with the half opened buds in her bosom through the great? green? bushy? garden went G. seeking her mate.

Widowed! Married or unmarried married or unmarried

Gerhardi
Ottoline
Orton
Moults
Mrs Montgomery
Delamare
Yoi Maraini

---

[70]These lines are from 'Après la Bataille' by Victor Hugo. In the second line KM wrote 'suivit' instead of 'suivi', and 'grand' instead of 'seul'.

[NL]

(To JMM.)              To the Last Moment[71]
by
Katherine Mansfield

## Chapter I.

He was just in time. They were pulling down the blinds in the Post Office when he burst in, pushing his way through the swing doors with a kind of extravagant breast-stroke, and:- "I can still send a telegram, can't I?" he cried to snappy little Miss Smythe who rapped out:- "If it's very important you may. <u>Not</u> otherwise!"
"Oh it is important - frightfully!" said he, giving her such a radiant unexpected beam that it shook two faded old banners into her cheeks. But he did not notice. He wrote in his beautiful flowing hand which even in that blissful moment he couldn't help admiring:- "<u>Got it arrive by morning boat tomorrow cheers</u>" and pushed it under the netting.
"It will go off tonight, won't it!" he asked counting out a whole handful of pennies.
"Yes. I'll send it now," said she, and her dry little pencil hopped over the form. "Is the last word cheese?"
"Oh, no." Again that beam lighting up the dingy little woman; even her Kruger-sovereign brooch seemed to glow with it. "It's cheers - three cheers - you know - Musical cheers - no, that's wrong ..."
He was out again and swinging along the street (about two foot up in the air) swinging along the street that he'd never seen before. Glorious place!
Such happy, splendid people hurrying home, their faces and hands a deep pink colour in the sunset light. Native women, big, dark, and bright like dahlias, lolling on the benches outside the Grand Hotel. The carts and waggons, even the immense two-horse cabs went spanking by as though every horse's head was turned towards home. And then - the shops - fruit shops, a flare of gold - fish shops, a blaze of silver! As for the smell coming off the flower jars that the florist was spraying before he carried them inside for the night - it nearly knocked you over! That hand, too, hovering in the jeweller's window, taking out the little boxes and trays. Just a hand - so mysterious, so beautiful.
To whom could it belong? And then a rolling navvy bumped into him and said:- "Sorry - my lad!" "My lad!" He wanted to fling his arms round the chap for it.
    Although there was everything to be done he couldn't go home yet. He must walk this off a bit, first. He must climb a hill. Well, that wasn't difficult. The whole place was nothing but hills.[72] So he chose the steepest and up and up he went, getting warm, then getting his second wind and simply

---

[71]Murry supplied the title 'The Scholarship' to this piece in *The Scrapbook*. The manuscript is in the Newberry Library but a further two paragraphs of the story, published by Murry in *Journal* without reference to the main part of the story, are in the Turnbull's Notebook 12 and may be found ('He woke, but did not move') on p 140.
[72]The setting is clearly Wellington.

floating on it to the very top – to a white painted rail against which he leaned and looked over.

For the first time, yes, positively for the first time he saw the town below him – the red roofed houses set in plumy, waving gardens, the absurd little city quarter, 'built in american style', the wharves, the tarred wharf sheds and behind these black masses two cranes that looked, somehow, from this distance, like two gigantic pairs of scissors, stuck on end. And then the deep, brimming harbour, shaped like a crater, in a curving brim of hills, just broken in one jagged place to let the big ships through.

For a moment, while he looked, it lay all bathed in brightness – so clear he could have counted the camellias on the trees – and then, without any warning, it was dark, quite dark, and lights began to appear, flowering in the soft hollows like sea anemones. His eyelids smarted. His throat ached; he could have wept. He could have flung out his arms and cried:– "Oh my darling, darling little town!" And all because he was going to leave it in a week's time – because he was off to Europe and God knows – if he'd ever see it again!

But instead of the fling he took a deep breath and in that breath he discovered how hungry he was. He was starving – quite faint with it. Marching down the hill his knees shook like an old woman's. Down and down he went. There was nobody about now because it was supper time. But the lighted houses in their plumy gardens were full of life; they could not hold so much. It broke from them, in voices and laughter, and scattered over the flowers and trees. "Children! Children! Come in at once!" called a woman. And – "Oh, Mother!" answered the children. Ah, how well he understood what they were feeling, poor little beggars. It was no time at all since he and Isobel had answered just like that.

The garden gate was clammy and cold. As he walked up the path a bough of syringa brushed his face wetting his cheeks and lips. And he smiled, with a strange little shiver of delight; he felt that the plant was playing with him… Two oblong pieces of light lay on the grass below the french windows of the dining room. He leapt on to the verandah and looked in. There he saw his brother-in-law, Kenneth, sitting at the table, eating, with a book propped up against a glass jug. "Hullo, old boy," said Henry. "Hullo" said Kenneth, and he stared at Henry in the solemn, absent way that Henry loved. "You're late. Had supper?" "Good God – no!" Henry came in and began wiping the dew and the pollen off his cheeks. "Been crying?" asked Kenneth. "Big boy hit you?" "Yes," said Henry. "Lamb?" Kenneth's glance wandered over the table. Finally he took a water biscuit, broke it in half, put one half in his book for a marker and began to carve. And Henry stood beside him looking at the glorified table. It was an immense relief to have his hand on Kenneth's shoulder. It rested him. But what was there so lovable about that little tuft of hair that always stood up and wouldn't lie down on the top of Kenneth's head. It was such a part of his personality. Whatever he said – there it stood, waving away. Henry gave the shoulder a hard squeeze. "I can imagine Isobel marrying him for that," he thought.

"Stir the mint sauce well," said Kenneth. "All what Maisie calls the 'nice grittay part' is at the bottom." Henry sat down, stirred and stirred and pushed the mint sauce away. He leaned back in his chair and tried not to smile, tried to carry it off, frowned at his plate and then said:- "Oh, I heard this afternoon I've got that Scholarship." He couldn't resist it; he had to look up at Kenneth - who didn't give a sign, but rubbed the side of his nose in a way he had. "Well," he said finally, "I knew you would. It was inevitable." Henry gulped. "Have a drink." Kenneth pushed the glass jug across. "Don't swallow the cherries. The stones disembody, settle in the appendix, fertilise, and send out shoots which have, sooner or later, to be snipped off. When do you sail?"
"A week from tomorrow."
Kenneth was silent. Then he opened his book and ate the book marker. "This is all about whales" he explained, blowing off the crumbs. "It's extraordinarily unpleasant. I shouldn't advise anyone to read it. There's a description of sharks, too, how when they are attacked - in the middle of the fight - they switch round and eat their own entrails - Sickening! ... I suppose you wired Isobel."
"Yes, I'm going over to her by the morning boat. You know I promised, if this came off, that we'd spend our last week together."
"But what about packing - or aren't you going to take anything. Just a change of socks and a rook rifle."[73]
"I'm going to do all that tonight," said Henry. And then he smiled, a blissful, childish smile. "I couldn't <u>sleep</u>, you know," and reached over for the salad.
"Look out for the cowcumber," said Kenneth. "It sticks to the side of the vessel by some curious process of suction, I believe. Well - I'm coming across to the Bay tomorrow afternoon. It's Saturday - you remember - or <u>don't</u> remember. We'll have the weekend together."
"That will be frightfully -" began Henry.
"Only I wish to God," Kenneth went on, "that I wasn't reading this book. I'll never be able to bathe again. The sea is simply teeming with horrors."
He got up and filled his pipe. "Don't worry. I'm going to smoke on the verandah." But Henry couldn't be left alone. Besides he wasn't hungry after all. He chose a big orange and followed after.

They walked into the warm, velvet dark and into another world. Kenneth stood with his hands in his pockets looking over the garden - at all those shapes and shadows built up in the air. As he stared they seemed to move gently, flowing together under a rolling wave. "Those gardens under the sea," he murmured, "must be the very devil!"

Henry sat on the verandah edge, eating his orange and looking at the clematis flowers. Wide open, dazzling, they lay - as if waiting in rapture for the moon. It was strange how frightfully they added to his excitement. He began to quiver all over. He thought, absurdly:- "The top of my head feels just like one of those flowers" - and a hundred miles away Kenneth murmured:- "Well, I'm glad it's you who are going and not me. I've no desire at all to rush into

---

[73]A reference to a Beauchamp family legend about KM's grandfather, Arthur Beauchamp.

this affair that they call Life. No, my job is to hide in a doorway, or squeeze under a porch until it is all over - only issuing forth - if I must issue forth - with Isobel for my Supreme Umbrella or Maisie for my small, coming-on, emergency umbrella - or 'Sunnyshade', as she calls it. That's one reason why I'm in favour of having large numbers of children - that they may be a kind of tent to me in my old age ..."

Henry went off to do his packing. He got into his pyjamas just for the sake of coolness, for of course he wasn't going to bed.

But by one o'clock everything was done and his feet were cold so he just sat up in bed and decided to smoke until it was time to get up. After one cigarette he lay down on his side, curled up, one hand under his cheek, thinking. He felt himself smiling down to his very toes. Yes, every little toe, now that it was warm, had a basking smile on it. And this was so ridiculous that he began to laugh, cuddling down, burying his face in the pillow. And away the little boat floated ...          [s93-100]

[MS-Papers-4006-11]

A stupid, silly poem that she had read years ago, when she was a schoolgirl and marked in the margin with two crosses and written 'how true' underneath somehow or other came back to her as she sat there, crept back into her memory, washed back on reluctant waves of memory, tossed through her brain, now showing a forlorn ghastly face, now half hidden.

"Look in my face, my name is Might Have Been. I am also called Too Late, No More, Farewell —"

You are not too cold? asked Yelski, bending towards her, half smiling, and he put out his hand & stroked her muff. "Strange" he said, "how women love fur!" She was! She was bitterly cold. She shivered, her knees, pressed tight together, her hands clenched inside the little muff, and long strange shivers shook her so violently that she felt that she might break, simply break to pieces -

"Look in my face, my name is Might Have Been." "Yes, give me a cigarette, she said. I will smoke one cigarette and then I must go." He lit a match and made a cup of his hands for her to light it by —

It began to grow quite dark. She saw the lamplighter with his long pole swing by outside the railings and then under the lamps, under the round pools of light, little knots of people. The clang clang of the trams sounded clear and sharp in the dusky air. Bright squares of lovely light showed in the dark houses.

[MS-Papers-4006-07]

Charming! thought Frances, smiling, as she pushed her way through the glass doors into the hairdresser's shop. What she meant by 'charming' was her little hand in a white kid glove with thick black stitching pressed flat on the pane of the swing door a moment . .

Madame, behind the counter, smiled back at her, and 'charming, charming' re-echoed in her smile and in her quick brilliant glance which flew over Frances from top to toe.

"Georges is quite ready" she cried. "If you will sit down one moment I will tell him." And while she spoke her smile widened & deepened until even her black satin dress, her rings, her locket, her jewelled combs seemed to catch a ripple and to flash with it. Even the bottles & jars and high mirrors in the hairdresser's shop gave it back again.     [J127-128 S101-102]

12.1.18.
I shall certainly be able to write in a day or two - if this goes on. I am not quite so wretched tonight!     [J128 S102]

[MS-Papers-4006-07]

February 19th 1918.
I woke up early this morning and when I opened the shutters the full round sun was just risen. I began to repeat that verse of Shakespeare's: "Lo here the gentle lark weary of rest" and bounded back into bed. The bound made me cough. I spat - it tasted strange - it was bright red blood. Since then Ive gone on spitting each time I cough a little more. Oh, yes, of course I am frightened. But for two reasons only. I don't want to be ill, I mean 'seriously' away from Jack. Jack is the 1st thought. 2nd I don't want to find this is real consumption, perhaps its going to gallop - who knows - and I shan't have my work written. Thats what matters. How unbearable it would be to die, leave 'scraps', 'bits', nothing real finished. but I feel the first thing to do is to get back to Jack.
Yes my right lung hurts me badly but it always does more or less.
But Jack & my work they are all I think of (mixed with curious visionary longing for gardens in full flower). L.M. has gone for the doctor. I knew this would happen. Now I'll say why. On my way here, in the train from Paris to Marseilles I sat in a carriage with 2 women. They were both dressed in black. One was big, one little. The little spry one had a sweet smile and bright eyes. She was extremely pale, had been ill - was come to repose herself. The Big One, as the night wore on wrapped herself up in a black shawl, so did her friend. They shaded the lamp & started (trust 'em) talking about illnesses. I sat in the corner feeling damned ill myself. Then the big one, rolling about in the shaking train, said what a fatal place this coast is for anyone who is even threatened with lung trouble. She reeled off the most hideous examples, especially one which froze me finally, of an american belle et forte avec un simple bronchite who came down here to be cured & in three weeks had had a severe haemorrhage and died. "Adieu mon mari, adieu mes beaux enfants..." This recital, in that dark moving train, told by that big woman swathed in black had an effect on me that I couldn't own and never mentioned. I knew the woman was a fool, hysterical, morbid, but I believed her; and her voice has gone on somewhere echoing in me ever since...

Juliette has come in and opened the windows; the sea is so full of 'little laughs' and in the window space some tiny flies are busy with their darting, intricate dance.    [J129-130]

[MS-Papers-4006-12]

### The Butterfly.

What a day to be born!
And what a place!
Cried the flowers.
"Mais, tu as de la chance, ma chere!"
Said the wild geranium
Who was very travelled.
The campions, the bluebells
The daisies and buttercups
The bright little eyebright and the white nettle flower
And a thousand others.
All were there to greet her –
And growing so high – so high
Right up to the sky, thought the butterfly,
On either side of a little lane.
Only, my dear, breathed an old snail
Who was hugging the underside of a dock leaf
Don't attempt to cross over.
Keep to this side.
The other side is just the same as this
Believe me – just the same flowers – just the same greenness.
Stay where you are and have your little flutter in Peace.
That was enough for the butterfly.
What an idea! Never to go out into the open?
Never to venture forth?
To live, creeping up and down this side.
Her wings quivered with scorn.
Really, said she, I am not a snail!
And away she flew.
But just at that moment a dirty looking dog
Its mean tail between its legs
Came loping down the lane.
It just glanced aside at the butterfly – did not bite
Just gave a feeble snap and ran further.
But she was dead.
Little fleck of cerise and black
She lay in the dust.
Everybody was sorry except the Bracken
Which never cares about anything, one way or the other.

[J151-152 S112–113]

[MS-Papers-4006-06]

KMs Notebook[74]

no good

Pulmonary Tuberculosis.[75]
The man in the room next to mine has got the same complaint as I. When
I wake in the night I hear him turning. And then he coughs. And I cough.
And after a silence I cough. And he coughs again. This goes on for a long
time. Until I feel we are like two roosters calling to each other at false dawn.
From far-away hidden farms.      [J139]

Hotels.
I seem to spend half my life arriving at strange hotels. And asking if I may go
to bed immediately. "And would you mind filling my hot water bottle?...
Thank you; that is delicious. No; I shan't require anything more." The strange
door shuts upon the stranger, and then I slip down in the sheets. Waiting for
the shadows to come out of the corners and spin their slow, slow web over the
Ugliest Wallpaper of All.      [J139]

Pic-Nic.
When the two women in white came down to the lonely beach - <u>She</u> threw
away her paintbox - and <u>She</u> threw away her notebook. Down they sat on the
sand. The tide was low. Before them the weedy rocks were like some herd of
shaggy beasts huddled at the pool to drink and staying there in a kind of
stupor.
Then <u>She</u> went off and dabbled her legs in a pool thinking about the colour
of flesh under water. And <u>She</u> crawled into a dark cave and sat there thinking
about her childhood. Then they came back to the beach and flung themselves
down on their bellies, hiding their heads in their arms. They looked like two
swans.      [J140]

Dame Seule.
She is little and grey, with a black velvet band round her hair, false teeth, and
skinny little hands coming out of frills like the frills on cutlets.
As I passed her room one morning I saw her 'worked' brush-and-comb bag
and her Common Prayerbook. Also, when she goes to the 'Ladies', for some
obscure reason she wears a little shawl...
At the dining table, smiling brightly:- "This is the first time I have ever
travelled alone, or stayed by myself in a Strange Hotel. But my husband does
not mind. As it is so Very Quiet. Of course, if it were a Gay Place -" And she
draws in her chin; and the bead chain rises and falls on her vanished bosom.

[J140–141]

---

[74]'KMs Notebook' is not strictly a notebook but a number of separate pages detached from a writing
pad. 'KMs Notebook' on the front page is in her own hand so it is likely that the components of it were
assembled by KM herself. There are two manuscript copies of 'Pic-Nic' and of 'Dame Seule' and of
'Strawberries and a Sailing Ship'.

[75]This piece occurs again in MS-Papers-4006-15 where it is written in verse form and titled 'Malade'.

Grownupedness.

Four o'clock. Is it light now at four o'clock? I jump out of bed and run over to the window. It is half-light, neither black nor blue. The wing of the coast is violet; in the lilac sky there are dark banners and little black boats manned by black shadows put out on the purple water. Oh! how often I have watched this hour when I was a girl! But then - I stayed at the window until I grew cold - until I was icy - thrilled by something - I did not know what! Now I fly back into bed, pulling up the clothes, tucking them into my neck. And suddenly my feet find the hot water bottle. Heavens! it is still beautifully warm.

That really is thrilling.     [J140]

Remembrance.

Always, when I see foxgloves, I think of the Lawrences. Again I pass in front of their cottage and in the window, between the daffodil curtains with the green spots - there are the great, sumptuous blooms.

"And how beautiful they are against whitewash" cry the Lawrences. As is their custom, when they love anything, they make a sort of Festa. With foxgloves everywhere. And then they sit in the middle of them, like blissful prisoners, dining in an encampment of Indian Braves.     [J141]

Strawberries and a Sailing Ship.

We sat on the top of the cliff overlooking the open sea. Our backs turned to the little town. Each of us had a basket of strawberries. We had just bought them from a dark woman with quick eyes - berry-finding eyes.

"They're fresh picked" said she, "from our own garden." The tips of her fingers were stained a bright red. But what strawberries! Each one was the finest - the perfect berry - the strawberry Absolute - the fruit of our childhood! The very air came fanning on Strawberry wings. And down below, in the pools, little children were bathing, with strawberry faces...

Over the blue, swinging water, came a three masted sailing ship - with nine, ten, eleven sails. Wonderfully beautiful! She came riding by as though every sail were taking its fill of the sun and the light.

And "Oh how I'd love to be on board!" said Anne. (The captain was below, but the crew lay about, idle and handsome. "Have some strawberries!" we said, slipping and sliding on the rocking decks, and shaking the baskets. They ate them in a kind of dream...) And the ship sailed on. Leaving us in a kind of dream, too. With the empty baskets...     [J141]

Jour Maigre.

On Wednesday mornings Mrs Honey[76] comes into my room as usual and pulls up the blinds and opens the big french windows. Letting in the dancey light and the swish of the sea and the creak of the boats lying at anchor out in the

---

[76] Mrs Honey was an elderly woman on the domestic staff of the hotel in Looe where KM went in search of health after her legal marriage to Murry in 1918. Mrs Honey's motherly care and solicitude caused KM to become warmly attached to her.

Roads, and the sound of the lawn mower and the smell of cut grass and syringa and the cheeky whistle of that same blackbird. Then she comes back to my bed and stands over me, one hand pressed to her side, her old face puckered up as though she had some news that she didn't know how to break gently. "'Tis a meatless day" says she.     [J139]

[MS-Papers-4006-07]

What happens is that I come in absolutely exhausted, lie down, sit up & sit in a daze of fatigue - a horrible state until 7 o'clock. I can barely walk, can't think, don't dare to go to sleep because if I do I know I'll lie awake through the night & that is my horror. Oh, for a <u>sofa</u> or a very comfortable armchair - this is always the longing at the back of my mind & except for that and a feeling of despair at wasting the time I am simply a blank. The pain continues in my left shoulder and is <u>vile</u>. That adds of course for finally it becomes intolerable & drives me to lie on the bed covered over to support it. But these are, <u>Hard Lines</u>.     [J128–129]

# *Notebook 11*

[Notebook 11, qMS-1258][77]

Katherine Mansfield Murry.

Station is <u>Stresa</u>. Take mountain railway to <u>Guiese</u>. Hotel Bel Alpino.

Aitken, 37 Great Ormond St, Russell Square.
Dr Achkner, 47A Welbeck Street.
Marie Albera, 28 Rue Dabrey, St. Etienne.

Doctor A. Bouchage, 27 Avenue de Verdun Menton.
     Summer:  Port-Blanc, Cotes-du-Nord.
Bartrick-Baker, Vere, Paradise Farm, Cobham, Surrey.
Brett, 28 Thurlow Road, Hampstead N.W.3.
Beauchamp, Miss C., Villa Flora, Menton.
Mrs Beaumont, 41 Upper Church Road, Weston Super Mare.
     Widow Jumper!
Miss A.L. Beauchamp, Marywell, Blackboys, Sussex. 3 Hurlingham
Gardens S.W.

Cannan Mary, Pension Mirasole, Roquebrune.
Colonial Wine Company, 20 Denham Street, London Bridge, S.E.1
     Special hock 45/- dozen
     Muscat - - - - - -
     Ex special hock 69/-
     Ex special claret 69/-
        1908-1909
Cramer, 96 Victoria Street, S.W.1
H.J. Cave & Sons, 81 New Cavendish Street.
Constable telegraphic, Drayola Westrand (10-12 Orange St) London.

Dunn, Coombe Cottage, Kingston Hill, Surrey.
Delamare, 14 Thomsett Road, Averley S.E.

---

[77]A small address book.

Dahlerup, Pension Coupier, Rue des Alpes 3-5, Geneva.
Carl van Direu, Lit Editor, The Nation, 20 Vesy Street, N.Y.
Drey, 80 Church[?] St, Kensington.

Eliot, T.S., 18 Crawford Mansions, Baker Street, London.

Fullerton, Miss E.J., Ladywell, Hampstead Heath.
Foster, Doctor Michael, Villa San Giovanni, San Remo.

Galsworthy John, Grove Lodge, The Grove, Hampstead N.W.3
G.I. Gurdjieff, 74 Rue de Miromessil, Paris.

Hudson, Doctor, Palace Hotel, Montana.

Kotelianski, 5 Acacia Road, St Johns Wood, N.W.8
5038 Bull Kay (tel. add. Bank Zealand, Logocracy, London.)
Kaye-Shuttleworth, Miss J., Villa Luna, San Remo.
Knopf, Alfred A.. 220 West Forty-Second Street, New York. Publisher.

Lowndes Mrs Belloc, 9 Barton Street, Westrim Stn[?], Londres
Lynd Sylvia, 32 Queens Gate, S.W.7
Lynd Mrs Robert, The Stone House, Steyning, Sussex.
Langdale Major Charles, Hotel Farant, Peira Cava sur Nice, A\M
Doctor F.E. Larkins M.D., 75 Harley Street W.1, Padd 5042 & Brampton
Grove, Hendon N.W.4, Finchley 249.
Harry Leggett Esq., c/o Curtis Brown Ltd, 6 Henrietta Street, Covent
Garden W.C.2.

Moult, 3 Milton Park, Highgate 6.
Macdermot G., 34 Half Moon Street, W.1.
Mayne Violet, The New House, Winchester.
Mrs A. Montgomery, Grey Abbey, County Down, Ireland.
Yoi Maraini, 29 Via Benedetto Fortini, Ricorboli, Firenze.
Monendi[?] Hotel and English Pension, San Remo.
Moody, 21 Alfred Terrace, Hampstead.
Maufe, 139 Church St, Chelsea.
Morrell, Lady Ottoline, The Manor House, Garsington.
Morgan Hon Evan, 48 Grosvenor Street, London 1., 2170 Gerr[?]
Moult, 44 Foxley Lane, Purley.
Mitchell Stewart, 152 West Thirteenth Street, New York City. (The Dial)
Millin S.G., Rhodes Avenue, Parktown West, Jo'Burg.
Susan Mills, Ursula Roberts, 19 Woburn Square, W.C.1
Miller, 276 Earls Court Road, S.W.5.
Murry, Richard, 10 Mecklenburgh Square, W.C.1

Ocrum, Edith, 32 Winchester Road N.W.3.
Orage, 59 Chancery Lane.

Perkins 14-19 July, c/o Mrs Morley, Savile Cottage, Aldeburgh Suffolk.
Porter, William A., 11 Welbeck Street W.

Palmer, Clara, Miss, 20 Vicolo S. Nicolo da Tolentino, Roma.
Pinwick, Market Square, Romily. Lady Greenaway.
R.O. Prowse, 47 St Quintin Avenue, S.W.10.

Rebandi Caterina, Ospedaletti, Ligure.
Richards Grant, 8 St. Martins Street W.C.2
Mrs Richmond, 3 Sumner Place, S.W.7.

Sorapure, 47 Wimpole Street W.I., 1556 Padd.
Doctor Sorapure, 58 Montague Square until 11 May. Mayfair 3146.
Sullivan, 16 Oppidans Road, Chalk Farm, N.W.
Small, Gertie Miss, 5 Golden Square, Hampstead N.W.3
Sinclair, May, 1 Blenheim Road, N.W.8.
Sydney Schiff, 18 Cambridge Square, Hyde Park W.2. 6690 Paddington.
The Knole, Crowborough, Sussex. Till the 3rd. Grand Hotel,
Eastbourne. After, Barrow, Oaren Road.

Trinder, Mrs W.H., Northernwood Park, Lyndhurst, Hants.
Mrs F. Temple, The Pond House, Chobham.
Trench Herbert, United Universities Club, Pall Mall, S.W.1

de Villamus, House Agent, San Remo. (Turton).
Vine (Thomas), Villa Flora, San Remo.

Waterlow, Charlotte, 23 St Leonards Terrace, Chelsea S.W.3.
Williams, E, 29 Regent St, Waterloo Place.
Woolf, Hogarth House, Paradise Road, Richmond.
H.G. Wells, Easton Glebe, Dunmow, Essex.
Williams Oslo, 4 Campden Hill Gardens W.
Webster, Roma, Sanatorio Hagana, Milan[?]
Webster Roma, Chez Broom, 68 Via Leccosa, Roma (9) 4.x.1922

Youspenski, 146 Harley Street W.

I think the only thing which is really 'serious' about me, really 'bad'
really incurable, is my temper.     [J212]

25th June
July 14th 18.13.6

# *Notebook 12*

[Notebook 12, qMS-1260]

Paris. March 1918.

Inside and Outside.

25.IV.18.
"Well sit down Mansfield, and reposez-vous" said Ferguson,
"and I'll get on with my dressing."
So he went into his bedroom & shut the door between, and I sat on the end
of the sofa. The sun came full through the two windows, dividing the studio
into four – two quarters of light and two of shadow. But all those things which
the light touched seemed to float in it, to bathe and to sparkle in it as if they
belonged not to land but to water; they even seemed, in some strange way, to
be moving. When you lean over the edge of the rock and see something lovely
and brilliant flashing at the bottom of the sea it is only the clear, trembling
water that dances – but – can you be quite sure? ... No, not quite sure, and that
little Chinese group on the writing table may or may not have shaken itself
awake for just one hundredth of a second out of hundreds of years of sleep.
Very beautiful, oh God is a blue teapot with two white cups attending, a red
apple among oranges addeth fire to flame – in the white bookcases the books
fly up and down in scales of colour, with pink and lilac notes recurring until
nothing remains but them, sounding over and over.
There are a number of frames, some painted and some plain, leaning against
the wall, and the picture of a naked woman with her arms raised, languid, as
though her heavy flowering beauty were almost too great to bear. There are
two sticks and an umbrella in one corner, and in the fireplace – a kettle,
curiously like a bird.
White net curtains hang over the windows. For all the sun it is raining outside.
The gas in the middle of the room has a pale yellow paper shade and as
Ferguson dresses he keeps up a constant whistling.
Reposez-vous.
Oui, je me repose ...     [J131-132]

26.IV.1918.

If I had my way I should stay in the Redcliffe Road until after the war. It suits me. Whatever faults it has it is not at all bourgeois. There is 'something a bit queer' about all the people who live in it; they are all more or less 'touched'. They walk about without their hats on and fetch and carry their food and even their coal. There are nearly four bells to every door – the curtains are all 'odd' and shabby. The charwomen, blown old flies, buzz down each other's basements ... "No 50 'ad a party last night. You never seen anything like the stite of is rooms this morning." "...'Igh time 'e did get married, I say. 'Is fiangse spends the night with 'im already. E says she 'as 'is bed and 'e sleeps on the table. You dont tell me a great stick of a fellow like im sleeps on is table!"

? But do you like this sort of talk? This kind of thing? What about the Poets and – flowers and trees?
Answer: As I cant have the perfect other thing – I do like this. I feel, somehow, free in it. It has no abiding place, and neither have I. And – and – oh well, I do feel so cynical.     [J132–133]

21.v.18.

I positively feel, in my hideous modern way, that I cant get into touch with my mind. I am standing gasping in one of those disgusting telephone boxes and I cant 'get through'. "Sorry. There's no reply" tinkles out the little voice. "Will you ring them again, exchange? A good long ring. There must be somebody there." "I cant get any answer."

Then I suppose there is nobody in the building – nobody at all. Not even an old fool of a watchman. No, its dark and empty & quiet, above all – empty. Note: A queer thing is that I keep seeing it – this empty building – as my father's office. I smell it as that. I see the cage of the clumsy wooden goods lift & the tarred ropes hanging.

22.

The sea here is real sea. It rises and falls with a loud noise, has a long, silky roll on it as though it purred, seems sometimes to climb half up into the sky and you see the sail boats perched upon clouds – like flying cherubs.

Hallo: here come two lovers. She has a pinched in waist, a hat like a saucer turned upside down – he sham panama, hat guard, cane etc., his arm enfolding. Walking between sea and sky. His voice floats up to me: "Of course occasional tinned meat does not matter but a perpetual diet of tinned meat is bound to produce ..." I am sure that the Lord loves them and that they and their seed will prosper & multiply for ever and ever ...

Are you really, only happy when I am not there? Can you conceive of yourself buying crimson roses & smiling at the flower woman if I were within 50 miles of you? Isn't it true that then, even if you are a prisoner, your time is your own, even if you are lonely you are not being 'driven distracted'. Do you remember when you put your handkerchief to your lips & turned away from me. In that instant you were utterly, utterly apart from me – and I have never felt quite the same since. Also – there was the evening when you asked me if

I still believed in the Heron. Isn't it perhaps true that if I were 'flourishing' you would flourish - ever so much more easily and abundantly without the strain and wear of my presence. And we should send each other divine letters and divine 'work' - & you would quite forget that I was 29 and brown-eyed. People would ask - is she fair or dark & you'd say in a kind of daze - oh I think her hair's pale yellow. Well - well - its not quite a perfect scheme. For I should have to hack off <u>my</u> parent stem <u>such</u> a branch - oh such a branch that spreads over you & delights to shade you & to see you in dappled light and to refresh you and carry you a sweet (though quite unrecognised) perfume.

But it is <u>not</u> the same for you. You are always pale, exhausted, in an anguish of <u>set</u> anxiety, as soon as I am near. Now, I feel in your letters, this is going and you are breathing again. How sad it is! Yes, Ive a <u>shrewd</u> suspicion ......
Of course L.M. will keep us one remove from each other; she'll be a 'help' that way. Did you realise that when you were so anxious to keep her. For of course, as you know, I'd have chucked her finally, after the Gwynne[78] night if it hadn't been for your eagerness.     [J133-135 S102-104]

... to meet, on the stopping of the chariot, the august emergence.

... the jewel wrapped up in a piece of old silk and negotiable one day in the market of misery.

... luxuriant complications which make the air too tropical. .

That sense of folded flowers - as though the night had laid its hand upon their hearts & they were folded and at peace like folded flowers.   KM

... plucked her sensations by the way, detached, nervously, the small wild blossoms of her dim forest.

the high luxury of not having to explain..

the ostrich burying its head in the sand does at any rate wish to convey the impression that its head is the most important part of it.   KM (Good)

though she did in a way, simply offer herself to me she was so cold, so rich, so splendid that I simply couldn't see a spoon silver enough to dare help myself with ..   KM

if there were going to be large freedoms she was determined to enjoy them too. She wasn't going to be perched, swaying perilous in the changing jumble like a little monkey dropped from a tree on to an elephant's head, & positively clinging to some large ear.   KM     [J135]

---

[78] Mr Gwynne was the foreman of the factory where LM worked. A later letter of KM to LM (June 8 1918) suggests that LM and Gwynne had discussed KM's health and urged her to enter a sanatorium. LM, as usual, got the blame for this crime.

a cold day – the cuckoo singing and the sea like liquid metal. Everything feels detached, uprooted, flying through the hurtling air or about to fly.
There's almost a sense of having to dodge these unnatural rudderless birds...
To use a homely image – imagine the world an immense drying ground with everything blown off the lines... It is very nervously exhausting.

And the day spent itself. The idle hours blew on it & it shed itself like seed.

She was the same through & through. You could go on cutting slice after slice & you knew you would never light upon a plum or a cherry or even a piece of peel.

Our friends are only a more or less imperfect embodiment of our ideas.

Feature Extraordinary: Shoes that have never squeaked before start up a squeaking.

Later. Mrs Honey explains. She has been crying. Madame spoke to her 'awful crool' about a cracked tumbler. Lied. Bullied. And the poor old creature, who has had 15 rooms to do lately & three flights of stairs to scrub (age 68) 'couldn't help but cry'... I wish Madame would develop a tumour during the night, have it cut out tomorrow and be dead, buried and a' before the Sunday dinner. She is exactly like a large cow in a black silk dress – and she will <u>never never</u> NEVER die.

<u>Later</u>. I went into John's room just now to put a book there, and turned down the pink bed cover to see if he had enough blankets. As I did so I thought of John – as a boy of about 17. I had a sort of <u>prophetic vision</u> of doing just the same thing for my son...in years to come. The moment had no emotional value at all – especially as it was all drowned in the smell of roast mutting. There goes the gong: it sounds like a timid fire alarm. But I wait until the 1st course is done. I wait until the chimpanzees have lapped up their little pool before I start a nut-cracking wiv 'em.

<u>Later</u>. The table was laid for two. I dined opposite a white serviette shaped like a hand with spread fingers. Now I have dressed & am waiting for the motor.
I rubbed some Genêt Fleuri on my collar just now: I look <u>different</u> – as though I were meant to be played on & not just to lie in a corner with the bow in that slot opposite which fastens with two buttons. No. Now the bow is hanging from the peg – <u>at least</u>.      [J135–137]

21.VI.18.
What is the matter with today? It is thin, white, like lace curtains are white, full of ugly noises (e.g. people opening the drawers of a cheap chest and trying to shut them again.) All food seems stodgy and indigestible – no drink is hot enough. One looks hideous, hideous, in the glass – bald as an egg. One feels swollen, and all one's clothes are tight. And everything is dusty, gritty – the cigarette ash crumbles and falls, the marigolds spill their petals over the dressing table. In a house nearby someone is trying to tune a cheap cheap piano.

If I had a 'home' and could pull the curtains together, lock the door, burn something sweet, fast, walk round my own perfect room, soundlessly, watching the lights & the shadows, it would be <u>tolerable</u>, but living as I do in a public house - its très difficile.

A few of its enormities:

1. I decided to faire les ongles de mes pieds avant mon petit dejeuner - and did not - from idleness.
2. The coffee was not hot, the bacon salt and the plate showed that it had been fried in a dirty pan.
3. I could not think of any small talk for Mrs Honey, who seemed silent & distrait - burning with a very feeble wick..
4. John's letter telling of all his immense difficulties - all the impossible things he <u>must</u> do before he could start his holiday left me luke warm. It had somehow a <u>flat</u> taste - and I felt rather I'd read it curiously apart, not united.
5. A vague stomache in my bath.
6. Nothing to read & too rainy to go out.
7. Anne came - & did not ring. I felt she had enough of our friendship for the present ...
8. Very bad lunch. A small tough rissole which was no use to the functions & some rather watery gooseberries. I despise terribly english cooking.
9. Went for a walk & was caught in the wind & rain. Terribly cold and wretched.
10. The tea was not hot. I meant not to eat the bun but I ate it. <u>Oversmoked</u>.

[J138–139]

Now the day was divine - warm soft sunshine lay upon her arms & breast like velvet - tiny clouds, silver ones shone upon the dazzling blue. The garden trees were full of gold light, and a strange brightness came from the houses - from the open windows with their flaring[?] curtains & flower pots ... the white steps & the narrow spiked railings.      [J144]


Knock! Knock

Whenever I have a conversation about Art which is more or less interesting I begin to wish to God I could destroy all that I have written & start again: it all seems like so many 'false starts'. Musically speak[ing] it is not - has not been - in the middle of the note - you know what I mean? When, on a cold morning perhaps, you've been playing & it has sounded alright - until suddenly you <u>realise</u> you are warm - you have only just begun to play. Oh how badly this is expressed!. How confused and even ungrammatical.      [J143–144]

4.45 Friday. Williams 15 Callon Street.

On these summer evenings the sound of the steps along the street is quite different. They knock knock knock along but lightly and easily, as if they belonged to people who were walking home at their ease, after a procession or a picnic or a day at the sea. The sky is pale and clear: the silly piano is overcome and reels out waltzes - old waltzes, spinning, drunk with sentiment - gorged with memory.

This is the hour when the poor underfed dog appears, at a run, nosing the dry gutter. He is so thin that his body is like a cage on four wooden pegs. His lean triangle of a head is down, his long straight tail is out, and up & down up and down he goes, silent and fearfully eager. The street watches him from its creeper covered balconies, from its open windows - but the fat lady on the ground floor who's no better than she should be comes out, down the steps to the gate, with a bone. His tail as he waits for her to give it him bangs against the gate post like a broomhandle, and the street says she's a fool to go feeding strange dogs. Now she'll never be rid of him. (What I'd like to convey is that at this hour, with this half light and the pianos and the open empty sounding houses, he is the spirit of the street, running up & down, poor dog, when he ought to have been done away with years ago.)     [J144-145]

Did M. wear a grey dressing gown with a dark red piping, she asked.
No, he was dressed.
Oh! Then I suppose he was <u>very</u> dressed, he always is. That made her think, suddenly, of another friend of his - a young fattish man who wore spectacles & was extremely serious with a kind of special fatness that she had noticed went with just that kind of seriousness. She saw him standing by a wash table drying his neck, & she saw his braces - tight, & the neckband of his shirt.
His hair was, as usual, too long.
She smiled.
How awful S. must be without a collar.
Without a collar. He looked at her; he almost gaped.
Yes, in a shirt & trousers.
In a shirt & trousers, he exclaimed. I've never seen him in them.
No - but - oh - well -
He positively fixed her at that.
How <u>extraordinarily</u> inconsequential you are!
And all in a minute she was laughing.
Men, she said, men are - - -
And she looked out of the window at the tall poplar with its whispering leaves, with its beautiful top gold in the last sunlight.
On the wall of the kitchen there was a shadow, shaped like a little mask with two gold slits for eyes. It danced up & down.     [J145- 146]

---

Fresh Tea.

I ought to write something brief for the Nation today & earn a bit more money: a little lunch at the Club or something of that kind. Its not difficult, in fact it is too easy for me because if I do err more on one side than t'other - I'm over fluent.

This view from the window is simply superb - the pale sky & the half-bare trees. Its so beautiful it might be the country - <u>russian</u> country as <u>I</u> see it. No, Lawrence & Murry will <u>never</u> hit it off. They are both too proud & M. is too jealous. He is like a hawk over his possessions.

I never connected until today sang froid with cold blood. This is a word which is one of New Zealands queer 'uns like calling the Savoy the Sävoy, or talking of the aeryeighted bread shops.

(I am very greatly surprised that on the first day of the New Regime I.C.B. should be late.) rig-marole rag-a-muffin sang froid sang frêûd      [J150]

21.X.1918. This is simply the most <u>Divine Spot</u>. So remote, so peaceful: full of colour, full of autumn, the sunset is real and the sound of somebody splitting small wood is real, too. If only one could live up here for really a long time and not have to see anybody. It might very well be France - its much more like France than it is like England.

The place - remote - the dresses & scarves old.
The year - fruitful: their talk and laughter gay.      [J149]

<u>Cheery!</u>

And once again the door opened & she passed, as it were, into another world - the world of night - cold, timeless, inscrutable.
Again she saw the beautiful fall of the steps, the dark garden ringed with glittering ivy - on the other side of the road the huge, bare willows - & above them the sky big & bright with stars.
Again there came that silence that was a question - but this time she did not hesitate. She moved forward, very softly & gently, as though fearful of making a ripple in that boundless pool of quiet. She put her arm round her friend. The friend is astonished, murmurs it has been so nice. The other - Goodnight dear <u>friend</u>. A long tender embrace. Yes, that was it - of course that was what was wanting.      [J153]

---

Like a blow on the heart.
I - I have come - for -
She leaned against the door, quite faint.
Yes? said she.
This. Tightly, quickly he caught her up into his arms.      [J153]

25.X.1918.
She <u>has</u> large appetites but they can be satisfied - except when we've really got her - herself somehow or other in the soup tureen. Then she could - oh! she <u>would</u> eat for ever, and Try this little bit Jones?[79] Don't you like it? What's the matter with it? Hasn't it got enough flavour -[80]      [J150 SIII]

---

[79]Jones was one of KM's names for LM.
[80]Some sketches of flowers occur after this passage.

<u>Scenes from The Ladies Club in Wartime</u>.
Ladies to the Centre:
A round hall very dim, lighted from above. A loud reluctant (swing glass) door
that can't bear people trying to burst their way in and loathes people trying to
burst their way out. To one side of the door the porters cave dotted with
pigeon holes, and a desk, a telephone, with usually a big tea-stained china tea
cup crowned with its saucer. In front of it a squeaking revolving chair with
a torn imitation leather seat.     [J152-153]

If the fire burns bright your maän is in a good temper.[81]     [J136]

butter? paper?

April 2nd. I am not doing what I swore I would at Bandol. I must again write
the word
          D I S C I P L I N E
and under that
      W H I C H   D O   Y O U   P R E F E R ?
And from day to day after this keep a strict account of what it is that I fail in.
I have failed very badly these last few days & this evening was a 'comble'.
<u>This</u> to the uninitiated would appear great rubbish. They'd suspect me of G.
knows what. If only they knew the childish truth. But they won't know, blast
their curious eyes. Now, Katherine, here goes for tomorrow. Keep it up, my
girl. Its such a chance now that L.M. is not i spy i.     [J131]

April 3rd. A <u>good</u> day.

He woke, but did not move.[82] Warm and solemn he lay, with wide open
troubled eyes, pouting a little, almost frowning for one long moment. In that
long moment he sprang out of bed, bathed, dressed, reached the wharf,
boarded the ferry boat, crossed the harbour and was waving - waving to Isabel
and Maisie who stood there, waiting for him on the pier. A tall young sailor
standing near him threw a coil of tarred rope and it fell in a long loop over
a landing post. Beautifully done ...
     And all this moment, vision, was so clear and bright and tiny, he might
with his flesh & pout and solemn eyes have been a baby watching a bubble.
I'm there - I'm there. Why do I have to start and do it all so slowly all over
again. But as he thought he moved and the bubble vanished and was forgotten.
He sat up in bed smiling, pulling down his pyjama sleeves.     [J131]

Looe (To be read after IT has happened.)
<u>June</u>.
Paralysis as idea. A pleasant one. Spinal disease. A stroke. Failure of the Hearts
Action. Some "obscure" Horror. Dead before Friday. A cripple - unable to
speak. My face all <u>deformed</u>. But the top and bottom of this sanwick is a

---

[81]One of Mrs Honey's aphorisms.
[82]See note 71.

paralytic stroke – the important middle – heart failure. Well I've cut it for myself and eaten it day after day – day after day. Its an <u>endless</u> loaf. And I'd like to put on quiet record that the physical pain is just not unbearable – only just not.

At four 30 today it did conquer me & I began, like the Tchekov students, to "pace from corner to corner", then up and down, up and down and the pain <u>racked</u> me like a curse and I could hardly breathe. Then I sat down again & tried to take it quietly. But although I've an armchair and a fire & little table all drawn up comfortable I feel too ill to write. I could dictate I think praps – but write, no. Trop Malade.

I have been, in addition, waiting for Anne all this afternoon. I thought, even in this storm, she'd "blow over". "Hillo!" And about 100 Annes with quick deliberate steps have walked up this brick path but got no further. Plus that I have nothing to read. Hurray!!!

One 'salvation' would I think be <u>music</u>. To have a cello again. That I must try . . . . .      [J137-138]

June 20th the twentieth of June 1918
C'est de la misère.
Non, pas ça exactement. Il y a quelque chose – une profonde malaise me suive comme un ombre.
Oh why write bad French. Why write at all. 11500 miles are so many – too many by 11449¾ for me[83]      [J138]

July 5th. Today, this evening, after I have come home (for I must go out & buy some fruit) commence encore une vie nouvelle. Turn over & you'll see how good I become – a different child.

July 5th. I have read – given way to reading two books by Octave Mirbeau – and after them I see dreadfully and finally (1) that the French are a filthy people. (2) that their corruption is so puante – I'll not go near em again. No, the english couldn't stoop to this. They aren't human; they are in the good old english parlance – <u>monkeys</u>. I must start writing again. They decide me. Something must be put up against this.

Ach, Tchekov! Why are you dead! Why can't I talk to you – in a big, darkish room – at late evening – where the light is green from the waving trees outside. I'd like to write a series of <u>Heavens</u>: that would be one.

I must not forget my <u>timidity</u> before closed doors. My debate as to whether I shall ring too loud or not laugh enough.... Its deep deep deep: in fact it is the 'explanation' of the failure of K.M. as a writer up to the present, and Oh! what a good anfang zu einem Geschichte!      [J142]

---

[83]The distance between New Zealand and England. At this point Murry has written out a list of furnishings for each of the rooms in Portland Villas ('The Elephant') and a list of items needing to be bought.

I pose myself yet once more, <u>my</u> Eternal Question: What is it that makes the moment of delivery so difficult for me? If I were to sit down - now - & just to write out, plain, some of the stories - all written, all ready in my mind twould take me days. There are so many of them. I sit & <u>think</u> them out & if I overcome my lassitude & <u>do</u> take pen they ought (they are so word perfect) to write themselves. But its the activity. I havent a place to write in or on, the chair isn't comfortable - yet even as I complain <u>this</u> seems the place & <u>this</u> the chair. And don't I want to write them? Lord! Lord! its my only desire - my one <u>happy issue</u>. And only yesterday I was thinking - even my present state of health is a great gain. It makes things so rich, so important, so longed for ... changes ones focus.

... When one is little and ill and far away in a remote bedroom all that happens <u>beyond</u> is marvellous... Alors, I am always in that remote bedroom. Is that why I seem to see, this time in London - nothing but what is marvellous - marvellous & incredibly beautiful?

C'est très ennuyeux, maintenant, parceque je sais que cette femme arriverait chez moi et je ne

Elle n'est pas arrivée!

The 'tide' is full in the Redcliffe Road. One by one the doors have opened, have slammed shut. Now, in their blind way, the houses are fed. That poor little violin goes on, tearing up note after note - there is a strange dazzling white cloud over the houses and a pool of blue.

All my virtues - all my rich nature - gone, she said - grown over, tangled, forgotten, deserted like a once upon a time garden. She smiled & pulled down her hat & pulled her coat together as though making ready to stumble out into it & be lost too. A dark place, said she, wavering to her feet. And then she smiled again. Perhaps there <u>is</u> just left my - my -[84] about myself. Evening Primrose .... She half shut her eyes, stooping forward, curiously as though the plant sprang up at her feet. I always did hate evening primroses. They <u>sound</u> such darlings, but when you see them they're such weedy - shabby - flower on the grave without a gravestone sort of thing ... I don't mean anything symbolical by that, said she - God forbid! And was gone!     [J142-143]

The Redcliffe Road - Maisie - the student - other lodgers - she risks anything.
The little leaf that blew in - her memory of the park & crocodile. Then there must be her cat called <u>Millie</u>.
That quiet <u>hook on dear girl</u> - & the view[?] so great that she almost sobs. But nothing happens.
Nay though my heart should break I would not bind you. Miss Ruddick who always plays with her music propped against the towel rail & whenever she

---

[84]KM left a blank space but failed to return and supply the missing word. Murry, in *Journal*, supplied 'curiosity'.

pulls out her handkerchief out comes an end of resin gummed on a flannel, as well.[85]     [J144]

> The English Review
> The Continental Times
> Nation
> Hogarth Press

August 2nd 1918.

Her heart had not spoken… When it does – too late – the pain of it. I ought to have felt like this – often often…     [J145]

September 20th(?) My fits of temper are really terrifying. I had one this (Sunday) morning & tore a page up of the book I was reading – and absolutely lost my head. Very significant. When it was over J. came in and stared. What is the matter? What have you done? "Why?" You look <u>all dark</u>. He drew back the curtains and called it an effect of light but when I came into my studio to dress I saw it was not that. I was a deep earthy colour, & was <u>green with pinched eyes</u>. Strangely enough these fits are Lawrence and Frieda over again. I am more like L. than anybody. We are <u>unthinkably</u> alike, in fact.

It is a dark reluctant day. The fire makes a noise like a flag, & there is the familiar sound from below of someone filling buckets. I am very stiff, very unused to writing now and yet, as I sit here, its as though my dear one, my ONLY one came & sat down opposite me and gazed at me across the table. And I think suddenly of the verses which seemed so awfully good in my girlhood

Others leave me – all things leave me
You remain.

L.M. in her turban with her one big eye & one little un – do I love her? Not really. And then, just now I mounted to J's room, and opened the door. He was sitting at the table, working. All was in indescribable disorder & the air was thick with smoke. He held out his hand to me but it was not my place. Oh no – I came away. I came away back into my room – which really has for me a touch of fairy. Is there anything better than my room? Anything outside. The kitten says not, but then its such a hunting ground for the kitten. The sun throws the shape of the window on to the carpet, & in these four little square fields the silly flies wander, ever so spied upon by the little lion under the sommier frill …     [J146-147]

I don't like Jack's family. I could never <u>bear</u> to have them live <u>with</u> us – –
We'll come to blows about them one day. The young brother – so witty that J. choked over his tea, the father who found half a sovereign in his hip pocket, the mother – jam or marma<u>la</u>de and Aunt Doll….
Oh dear, oh dear – <u>where</u> are my people! With whom have I been happiest? With nobody in particular. It has all been mush of a mushness.[86]

---

[85]The page facing this is full of ink sketches of flowers and associated shapes and patterns.
[86]Originally written as 'much of a muchness', then changed.

<u>Later</u>  That kitten took sick, was taken away, lived two weeks in great torture, then for 2 days it lost the will to live & it became just a cotton reel of fur with two great tearful eyes "Why has this happened to me." So the vet. killed it. It had gastric trouble, acute constipation with a distended belly and canker in both ears. The two days before it went away it suffered here. I bought it a ball & it tried to play a little – but no, it couldn't even wash itself. It came up to me, stood on its hind legs, opened its little jaws & <u>tried</u> to mew. No sound came; I never saw anything more pitiful.     [J147]

I hope this pen works. Yes, it does.
The last day in September – <u>immensely</u> cold – a kind of solid cold outside the windows. My fire has played traitor nearly all day & I have been, in the good, old fashioned way, feeling my skin <u>curl</u>. <u>Don't</u> read this. Do you hear that train whistle & now the leaves, the dry leaves & now the fire, fluttering & breaking. ?Why <u>doesn't</u> she bring the lamps? So it is to be a baked meat pudding with a caper or twain and then the rusks cooked in milk with blackberry sauce. Talking of it made us quite friendly after the Fight of the Lamps.     [J147]

24.X.1918. Ida is going to town. I must take some of my dear money out of the Bank & give it her. I am in bed; I feel very sick. Queer altogether – decomposing a bit. Its a pale, silent day. I should like to be walking in a wood, far away.
   <u>Health</u> seems to me now more remote than anything – unattainable. Best to stay in bed & be horrid from there. This sky in waves of blue & cream and grey is like the sky overhanging a dead calm sea, when you hear someone rowing, from far away & then the voices from the boat & the rattle of a chain & the barking of the ship's dog all sound loud.
   There is as usual a smell of onion & chop bones in the house. Perhaps L.M. is just frying something in the pan "for the sake of the nice savoury smell" while she washes up – – –
   What do I want her to buy for me? When it really becomes an urgent matter I want <u>nothing</u> – waste of money – I feel [like] that Mdlle Seguin[87] who wouldn't hang the pictures in her new flat because <u>Life is such a breath, little Dolly</u>.     [J149–150]

[MS-Papers-4006-16]

Verses Writ in a Foreign Bed

Almighty Father of all and Most Celestial Giver
Who hast granted to us thy children a Heart & Lungs & a Liver
If upon me should descend thy beautiful gift of tongues
Incline not thine Omnipotent ear to my remarks on Lungs.     [J129]

---

[87]Mlle Séguin, who taught French at Queen's College for 33 years, including KM's years there, habitually addressed her students as 'little Dolly'.

# Notebook 14

[Notebook 14, qMS-1259][88]

But Lord! Lord! how I do hate the french. With them it is always rutting time.
See them come dancing and sniffing round a woman's skirts.

Mademoiselle complains that she has the pieds glacés. Then why do you wear
such pretty stockings & shoes Mademoiselle, leers Monsieur. Eh - oh la - c'est
la mode.

And the fool grins well content with the idiot answer.

When I am sitting above the rocks near the edge of the sea I always fancy
that I hear above the plash of the water the voice of two people talking
somewhere I know not where. And the talking is always broken by something
which is neither laughter nor sobbing but a low thrilling sound which might
be either and is a part of both.

How immensely easier it is to attack an insect that is running away from
you rather than one that is running towards you. The scuttling tribe. Spiders as
big as half crowns with long gooseberry hairs.

(February 7th) I have been a worm this morning & read poetry when I should
have worked.

Note – A muff like a hard <u>nut</u>.        [J128 S102]

---

[88]Notebook 14, on the front cover of which KM has written 'Mouse', is mostly taken up with a draft
of 'Je ne Parle Pas Francais'.

# *Unbound Papers*

[NL]

The Boy With the Jackdaw[89]
by
Katherine Mansfield.

9
VI
18

## II.

So he sat and smoked his cigarette, looking at the empty fire-place, the frill of paper inside the grate, and the irons, inside too, heaped in a bundle.

"Put a match to them and get a blaze if you can, but that's all the fire you'll get in my house." Very cheering. Very hospitable. But then the cigarette was ¾ parts smoked he thought miserably. That's just about what I feel like. That's a complete picture of myself at this moment. It couldn't be truer.

She sat at the table her hands just touching the long paper of mixed flowers that the landlady had given her to take home. They <u>were</u> mixed. Canterbury bells, sweet william like velvet pincushions, irises, silly flaring poppies, snapdragon & some roses that smell sweetly in water lay half spoiled with greenfly. She was not going to take them home. She had no vases to fit them & besides - she didn't want them. No, she would leave them in the rack of the railway carriage. If only some officious fool wouldn't run after. Excuse me Madame - you've left your flowers. Oh no they were there when we came into the carriage.

In a few hours the ugly room which did not belong to them or to anybody would be emptied of them for ever & tomorrow morning or this evening perhaps the card labelled Apartments would be stuck in the window. After they had gone the landlady & Blackie, her grandson would come in & sneak & pry about looking for pickings. Had they left anything? Nothing but half a bottle of thoroughly bad ink & yes that bowl of dog daisies & sorrel on the mantelpiece. She'd throw away that wild trash. She'd chuck the daisies in to the dustbin & then empty the tea leaves on to them while they were yet

---

[89]The title 'The Boy With the Jackdaw' may not refer to the piece which follows it. Murry called it 'The Quarrel' in *The Scrapbook*.

alive. And she'd say: "She was as nice and pleasant spoken a young woman as you could wish to find, but he was a cool fish-blooded young man, & terrible hard to please sometimes I reckon. Oh <u>yes</u>!" - & then she'd worry about whether she couldn't have charged them a bit more for something they'd never had - & then they'd be forgotten. He flicked the cigarette end on to the hearth & slowly turned towards her but didn't look, saying in a cool unnatural voice Well aren't you coming out. For it had been agreed between them before this last quarrel that when the packing was done they would sit on the beach for ½ an hour and then come back to tea & wait for the cab that was to take them to the station.

That voice! How she hated it! And how it insulted her. How dared he speak to her like that. And the worst of it was it was so put on - so affected. He had a way, after they'd been quarrelling, or even in the middle of a quarrel, of speaking down to her as much as to say - Of course you haven't understood a word of what's happened, but this sort of thing - Shall we have tea, shall we go out - you can understand & you can reply to. She sat up & drew in her chin making her throat longer, very free & soft. She glanced with hot quick eyes & darted the words at him. "I'm certainly not going."

But he saw none of this. Very listless & tired he rolled out of the chair & pulled on his hat. "Oh very well, please yourself!"

But she didn't want to stay in that ugly room looking at those hideous flowers. The landlady would come in too & want to talk & think it funny that she hadn't gone with him. And she hated walking by herself in this strange village and she didn't want him to be down there on the stony beach all alone - a little speck among all the others - lost, unconscious of her, forgetting her. She didn't trust him. He might do something idiotic. He might forget all about the time, he might hire a boat - say he rowed while the tea grew cold & the cab waited & she stood at the window in an anguish of exasperation - dying of it simply! He was at the door. Yes, I will come after all. Was he smiling? Had he known that she would "come round"? He gave no sign at all. Staring at the floor in the same listless, tired way: I'll wait here while you put on your hat. "I've got it on" said she.

And they passed out of the ugly room into the hideous hall. There the landlady caught them: she had the door of the kitchen open on purpose. Out she bounced. "Oh Mrs Tressle I was wondering whether you care to take back a lobster. My cousin the fishmonger has just brought it across to me boiled & all." She was back in the kitchen & out again with the strange red thing on a white dish - offering it to Miriam.

Instead of helping her to get rid of this fool of a woman, instead of even doing his share, he sauntered out of the house & stood at the gate with his hands in his pockets, looking down the road, leaving it, as usual, all to her. This she realized <u>beyond words</u> while she was pleasant & gay & grateful to the landlady. It's awfully kind of you Mrs Trefoyle but my husband - "Don't care for them," said the landlady, smiling her knowing smile, which Miriam pretended not to see. They don't agree with him, she said regretfully making a little murmer of regret at the loathsome red thing in the dish; "I wish they did - it <u>does</u> look a beauty." Oh well, there's likes & there's dislikes said the landlady - & Miriam went out to join him.

It was hot & fine. The air quivered. You would have fancied the whole round world lay open like a flower to the sun, and behind everything, underneath all the little noises there was a stillness, a profound calm, a surrender so blissful that even human beings were moved by it & walked along, easy and confident. The cats lay asleep on the window sills. A row of sea gulls perched on a roof tile. Marble birds.

Nobody saw the queer ugly child dragging between them, clutching a hand of each as they walked side by side down the road. Obstinate, ugly & heavy - their only child, the child of their love. The only thing that held them together & kept them alive to each other.

<u>He</u> knew it - he felt it pulling, but just for the moment he did not care. As always happened after their quarrelling, folded in upon himself, sealed up, he died for the time being, like a sea anemone that has been prodded with a stone. He hadn't even got to the stage where the stone is rejected. No, there it lay ... & he covered it & was still.

She, on the contrary, after the quarrels, always felt so strong so dreadfully full of life. She wanted to snatch the ugly brat up to shake it at him, to cry:- See what you've made me bear! It's yours. It's yours. It's all your fault! I never quarrelled with anybody before I met you. People used to say that I simply radiated happiness & wellbeing. And it was true - it was true. I was made to be happy & to make other people happy, & now you're killing me - killing me. You won't let me be myself even for a single moment. No, all you really want to do - your only real desire in life - is to drag me down, to make me somehow or other as wretched as yourself, to force me to crawl to the office with you every day & endure the torture, & crawl back again.     [s104-109]

[NL]
Love in Autumn.

The leaves are falling on Hampstead Heath, lifting, spinning, flying, tossing, dancing, chasing, but falling falling. It is very cold; the grass looks grey, & the pond is wrinkled & dark. Where the Heath joins the road an old man in a straw hat tries to tidy up the leaves with a broom - tries to sweep them into little heaps. But they won't be tidied. Away they fly - he might as well try to heap up into a neat pile all the years of his life.

A soldier & a girl come walking. He swings along, solid and strong, but she in her high heels trips over the grass like a running bird. Where are they going to so eagerly? It is too cold to sit down on the bench under the tree. Down they sit, & he puts his arm along the back of it & she comes up close. They are so still - they might be having their photographs taken - before he goes back to France. Me and 'er under a tree like - you can see him handing it round.

But the wind blows & big clouds pull over the pale sky, silver clouds, purplish ones - they pass in sober silence over the trees & the grey grass & soldier & the girl. Only the pond sees them. It is going to rain. If they were a little boy & a little girl sitting out there now how their mothers would call – children, children come in at <u>once</u>. You will catch your deaths. Come in <u>immediately</u>. Does he ever think that she was once a little girl in a pink pinafore fastening with a tape? And she ever think of him [in] a tiny sailor suit with a flannel dicky?

Now his arm is right round. But oh dear – her hat. It's not that it's so big either but ... — Won't it come off. No Mr Clever Dick. And she throws it on the grass. There it lies, the last bouquet of the year, round & bright, at their feet.

There is a loud roaring in the trees, & away the leaves fly. She catches one & shuts it up in her fist & he opens the little hand finger by finger & there is the leaf inside. At sight of the little hand outspread with the leaf on it his heart grows big. You've got small hands, says he – & she, seeing his big round fingers close over hers, feels her heart grow tender. Well not so big as yours, says she. Listen – do you hear? That's a bird. That's a bird making that noise. The silver clouds have turned grey. The pond trembles. Down comes the rain.

Do come on its raining. Put on yer 'at. And she pins on the bright bouquet. He stands up, pulling down his jacket, ready to go, & she, leaning against the swaying tree, her feet hidden [in] the grass, the pond behind her, the changing clouds above and [the] tree & the leaves – gently he bends down & fastens her coat together with a long warm kiss.

8.10.18[90]

[MS-Papers-4066]

Katherine [on cover][91]

Watson
Mrs Maufe
Aunt Belle
1.18.9.
Saintsbury

---

Take train midday Friday
Arrive Saturday. Travel Monday.

---

There is as much of the[92]

---

Mother is well. I am preparing for the journey. I doubt it. and am thinking over other places, other plans. But Katherine, don't live apart again or without a servant again. Phone […] and […][93]
– phone Murry.

---

[90]These large numerals are written upside down beside a large X.

[91]This little notebook is a photocopy whose provenance is unknown, as is the whereabouts of the original.

[92]This paragraph, illegible, ends in '... half barking, half <u>uneasy</u>.'

[93]Two lines are illegible here.

the shawl is a good omen
Suggest that Gertler come and travel with us.

Better be imprudent movables than prudent fixtures. Keats to Fanny.

[J127 S101]

But I must admit the russians bore me - they are not couched enough in the
bones of Art.

fish
lettuce
rhubarb
carrots
apples
account book
_____

salad eggs
bread
cakes
rhubarb
turnips
potatoes
onions
_____

salad
onions
rhubarb
artichokes
veg alors
bread
rock cakes

braid paper envelopes wrapping paper Knickers vests
I can't remember who the woman on the back of the book was - Mrs
Hardwick or Mrs Jenkins, & the moral[?] Mrs H. is just like a frenchwoman.
Met Lizzie Flegg today - Chestnut Lodge is all over long long ago & I have an
apartment. It doesn't matter which bus I catch. She reeked of carnations.

Newberry Lodge
Combe Martin
N. Devon.

I never feel so comfortable or at ease as when I am holding a pencil. Note that
& if you have an embarrassing moment see that you meet it armed!

[J127 S101]

[94]

Madame Hunt
1 Great Woodstock St
Off Mary-le-bone High Street.

> hairpins
> needles
> coat buttons
> cushion stuff

The window was broken. Il faut acheter un araignée[?]
<¼ prunes
¼ figs>
Wrote Ottoline[95] and Geoffroi.[96] Posted. The woman with the white fan of wool over her bosom, the toddling baby and the little boys - like the untidy children in Italian painting. I want to say something about a milk tooth or two missing.

---

A woman who is un peu agé and has a youngish man in France shows very plain her jealousy and her desire to keep his attention from wandering. Even if he wants to sleep she takes his eye.     [J127 S101]

January 1st 1918

|  | £. s.d |
|---|---|
| In hand | 13. 0.0 |
| dairy | 18.3 ¼ |
| Jack | 1. 0.0 |
| Laundry | 5.8 ½ |
| passport | 5.0 |
| ticket | 10.7 |
|  | 2.19.7 ¾ |
|  | 8.6 ¾ |
| telegrams | 3.11 |
| taxi | 1.0 |
| porter | 6 |
| papers & cigarettes | 6 |
|  | 13. 0.0 |
|  | 2.19.7 ¾ |
|  | 10. 4.5 ¾ |

---

[94]Some money sums occur here.

[95]Lady Ottoline Morrell (1873–1938), the famous hostess of Garsington, a manor house outside Oxford, to which she contrived to invite all the most interesting people of the contemporary scene. She and KM corresponded warmly but were privately wary of each other.

[96]Dr Geoffroi, Mayor of Carpentras, was married to Régine Geoffroi, an old acquaintance of KM, from Bandol.

[NL]

Keeping Up[97]
by
Katherine Mansfield

Just as she put her suitcase down on the landing and turned the bunch of keys to find the outdoor one she heard steps coming up the stairs. And at the sound, although she herself knew it was absurd, her heart, her stupid heart made, as it were, one great sickening plunge into some deep trembling water... But nonsense, it couldn't be – and they were large, deliberate steps, the steps of a heavy elderly person. Heavy elderly men don't carry them – except once ... at night – in the rain ... in a mackintosh ... an old old man with a lantern who pronounced their name wrong. She picked up the suitcase and began walking down the stairs. And after all it was someone she knew; it was Mr Penridden, stumping up, blowing, out of breath. "Hullo" he said kindly, too kindly, in the voice she was beginning to learn to expect, the voice that men reserved for little children – little children who had fallen down or were being taken to the doctor for the first time. "Now if I'd been a minute later I'd have missed you. I was just coming to ask you if you'd come and have a quiet little dinner with me tonight." He stood before her, stout, ruddy in his tight grey suit, bowler hat, thick shoes. In one hand he grasped a massive umbrella with a thick strap of gold round the handle; in the other he balanced a paper bag.

"Figs" he said, smiling & nodding at her. "I remembered your fondness for them. Fresh figs – and the pick of the season. Just look at them." He crooked the umbrella in the stair rail, undid a pinched corner of the bag & half drew out a plaited basket. "They're just ready to burst" said he. "It's very kind of you very kind indeed" she [said.] The man who bought figs in a basket – that man's an odd man. "But I'm so sorry. I'm just on my way to the station. I've promised to spend the weekend with my sister Carrie at her hospital for officers. You see I can't possibly hear anything until Monday – not possibly – and at any rate they are on the telephone."

His flushed face fell at the mention of it, sympathising. "It's a very good idea" said he. "It'll do you good. Take your mind off & bring the roses back into your little cheeks. I'll come with [you] to the station if you don't mind & these figs will just be the very thing for the train." "Oh no, don't trouble to do that" said she. "It's no trouble at all. It's a pleasure. Wait now while I get you a taxi." And she waited in the dark cold hall while he slipped through the double doors into the sunny glare. There was a wind blowing. It blew his trousers tight against his thick legs, blew his coat back from his round belly. He held up the umbrella & suddenly stepped into the road and roared. A cab drew up & stopped & he came back to her triumphant & radiant.

"I don't know how it is" he cried in his normal reckless voice, "I've the

---

[97]There are two copies of 'Keeping Up': this one is manuscript and the other is a manuscript copy of the first page and a typed copy of the rest of it.

devil's own luck with taxis. Come on now." He put his hand on her arm,
& his voice changed again. "My God!" said he, "your little arm's wasting away.
You mustn't let that happen you know. You must keep your flesh at all costs."
And to the driver, "You'll take us to Waterloo Station." Down he plumped
beside her; the seat bounced. The precious figs he still held – tenderly.
"You wouldn't care to try one – in the car" he said. "No one will see you.
Do now!" She knew how it would please him & yet she just couldn't. "I think
I'd rather keep them for the train" she said, smiling. Her dark eyes begged him
not to urge her.

"Oh, there's plenty for you to eat then" he cried, "see, look – here's a
beauty." Yes, she would have to. Better submit at once. She couldn't bear even
a little scene. He was holding out an envelope to her to keep her dress clean,
& she put it on her lap & drew off her gloves & took the fig while he watched
her, his big eyes popping with delight. "My God. Look at that. It's full of
honey!" he cried, almost awed, as she broke open the fig. "You needn't bother
to skin it. You can eat it all. It's as clean as the back of my hand."

Could she eat it – could she – cold malignant glistening thing. Yes one
can do anything, anything. Anxious, eager, he watched every mouthful.
"That'll do you good" he said. In some strange way he seemed to be eating
the fig with her, tasting as she tasted. "You've got a touch of a relaxed throat
haven't you? I can hear it in your voice. Have another." "Oh no thank you
Mr Penridden" & she wiped her fingers & drew on her gloves again.

They were driving very fast. Suddenly "Look out you bloody fool" from
the driver & the taxi gave a great swerve flinging Mr Penridden against her
like a sack of grain. "What the Hell" said he, heaving himself back. "I didn't
hurt you, did I?" "No not at all." Her suitcase, too, fell across her feet.
"My God! that must have been a narrow shave" said Mr Penridden, & he gave
in his excitement a loud chuckle. "It would have looked very black, really if
we'd been taken to the hospital with one suitcase between us and on our way
to Waterloo on a Saturday afternoon." She tried to smile. "Eh, poor little
woman, you're not in the humour for jokes" said he contritely & he covered
her hand with one of his swollen freckled paws & patted it. "Don't you give
up heart" said he, "it'll come alright – you just keep up. Why a poor woman
came to the office this morning: her husband had been on the staff & she'd just
had the news he'd been blown to pieces – not even a button to pick up & send
to her" said Mr Penridden, feeling in his pocket for change for the taxi.
"What does the Clock say Kitty? Your eyes are sharper than mine." "Five and
fourpence" said she.

(What luck? Any luck? Here is L.M. home from the Post. No luck.)

December 31st[98] 4.45 P.M.
Fly: Oh, the times when she had walked upside down on the ceiling, run up
glittering panes, floated on a lake of light, flashed through a shining beam!

---

[98] 1918.

And God looked upon the fly fallen into the jug of milk and saw that it was good. And the smallest Cherubims & Seraphims of all who delight in misfortune struck their silver harps & shrilled: How is the fly fallen fallen.

[JI53]

Jack came to bed at ten minutes to twelve. Said he: don't go to sleep before the New Year. I lay holding my watch. I think I did go to sleep for a moment. The window was wide open, & it looked out and over a big soft hollow. Far away there were shapes of trees, serpents and fans – with a sprinkle of lights between. Then the hour struck – the bells rang, hooters, sirens, horns, trumpets sounded. The church organ peeled out (reminding me of Hans Andersen) & an Australian called Cooee. (I longed to reply.) I wanted L.M. to hear & to see. I called loudly to her ever so many times but she had 'chosen' to take a bath. Jack was very chagrined because I had thought of her & not only of him. That rather spoiled his New Year. We ought to have clasped [JI54]

[MS-Papers-4006-7]

One was out of draughts. That is too true. The French and the Italians never appear to reckon on living indoors at all. One is either out, eating, or in bed. This may (if I may allow myself to be wicked) account for the proverbial laxity of French morals. Once indoors there is no place where one can conduct a comfortable conversation except in

[MS-Papers-4006-7]

Lame Ducks:
It is seldom that lame ducks are seen together. As a rule, so profoundly unaware do they appear to be of one anothers existence one is almost tempted to believe that a lame duck to a lame duck really is invisible. They may frequent the same cafés for years, attend the same studio parties, feed at the same restaurants, even sit with the same group round a table, but when the others get up to go one lame duck's way is with these – to the right, and the other with those, to the left. [JI89 SI23]

[MS-Papers-4006-8]

May 19th 1919. 6 p.m.
I wish I had some idea of how old this notebook is. The writing is very faint & far away. Now it is May 1919. Six o'clock. I am sitting in my room thinking of Mother. I want to cry. But my thoughts are beautiful & full of gaiety. I think of our house our garden us children – the lawn – the gate, & Mother coming in. Children! Children! I really only ask for time to write it all – time to write my books. Then I don't mind dying. I live to write: the lovely world (God how lovely the external world is!) is there and I bathe in it and am refreshed. But I feel as though I had a DUTY, someone has set me a task which I am bound to finish. Let me finish it: let me finish it without hurrying, leaving all as fair as I can …

My little mother, my star, my courage, my <u>own</u> - I seem to dwell in her now. We live <u>in the same world</u>. Not quite this world, not quite another. I do not care for 'people', and the idea of fame, of being a success - that's nothing - less than nothing. I <u>love</u> my family, as few others, dearly, and I love, in the old - in the ancient way, through & through, my husband. But I want no one more. She is quite solitary. Not a soul knows where she is. She goes slowly, thinking it all over, wondering how she can express it <u>as she wants to</u> - asking for time and for peace.     [J154]

[MS-Papers-4006-7]

Its what you might call indoo weather, said the little man. Oh really - why that, said I, vague. He did not answer. The two polished knobs of his behind shone as he leaned over feeding the black seams of the boat with a brown twist. The day was dull, steaming. There was a blackness out at sea; the heavy waves came tolling. On the sea grasses the large bright dew fell not. The little man's hammer went tap-tap.

L.M. snorted, threw up her head, stamped her foot on the wet sand, scrambled to a boulder, tore at some sea poppies, dug them in her hat, held the hat away, looked, scornful, wrenched them out again.
I looked and felt vague as a wing. "Spades & buckets is round the point with the lobster catch." The hammer tapped. He explained that all the lobsters would be sent away alive in sacks if they were not given a sharp stang with one of these. It was an ordinary grey & red garden trowel. L.M. went off to save their lives, but not joyfully. She walked heavy, her head down, beating the trowel against her side.

We were alone. The watcher appeared. He stood always in profile, his felt hat turned up at the side, a patch on the eye nearest us. His curved pipe fell from his jaws. "Hi Missy," he shouted to me, "why don't you give us a bit of a show out there." The little man remonstrated. The sea was like a mass of half-set jelly - on the horizon it seemed ages fell.
Come on Missy, bawled the watcher. I took off my clothes, stepped to the edge & was drawn in. I tried to catch the stumps of an old wharf but slime filled my nails & I was sucked out. They watched.

Suddenly there came, winnowing landward, an enormous skinny skeleton of a hindoo, standing upright. A tattered pink & white print coat flapped about his stiff outstretched arms; he had a cloth of the same with a fringe of spangles over his head. He stood upright because of the immense sweeping broom of wood growing waist high. Help Help! I called. The noise of the hammer came & I felt the watcher's patched profile. A huge unbreakable wave lifted him, tipped him near. His shadow lay even on the surface of the dusty water - a squat head and two giant arms. It broadened into a smile.     [J175-176]

Its what you might call, said the little old man, indoo weather.
Oh, really, why that, I asked.

The day was dull but steaming. There was a blackness out at sea – like fog, like smoke. In the silence you could hear the dew splash from the sea poppy flower onto the sea poppy leaf.

[NL][99]
It was not at all difficult for the Williamses to leave home. They had no children & their two servants, scotch girls, sisters (such a point, that, if they do happen to get on well together. On the other hand – but in this case they did) were perfectly capable of looking after the house and Busby the Belgian griffon who most fortunately got on with them too. Dear little chap. He was devoted to Annie. And loved going to the post with Harriet which just gave him the little run he needed into the bargain. As for the garden (Mrs W. was a passionate gardener) all was in apple pie order – one could not have chosen a more satisfactory moment to leave it. And perhaps if the truth were known the garden breathed a deep soft sigh of relief at the blissful thought of three weeks freedom from being weeded and turned over and raked out and examined – even from being stared at …

So, the endless preparations over at last, one soft mist-dripping morning, one of those damp typical English mornings when the newspaper arrives damp & smelling like a mushroom, off they went to the Station with their 2 large suitcases, one small, one hat box, one roll of rugs, the Fuller tea basket, and a copy of Punch which they had neither of them had time to look at that week. Both of them sat bolt upright in the taxi, both of them wore new, very practical kid gloves which smelt extraordinarily strong, and both in their own way [were] deeply excited. Gwendolen showed it by her high colour, and by her continually fingering her bag to make sure her keys & ticket were in the inside pocket, and Gerald showed it by a quick distracted glance of his large pale blue eyes and by a slightly increased tempo in his whistling…

(Rough Sketch only)
Charing X[100]
Travelling 1st with 2nd class ticket. Pay 3d.
Buy bun with nail in it. Miss a turn.
Lose your hat out of window. Back to Charing X.
Folkstone. Rough sea. Stay 1 turn at Marine Hotel.
Seasick. Stay at Y.W.C.A. one turn.
Hit sailor with your umbrella. Pay 1d.
Boulogne. Lost ticket. Miss a turn.
        Passport out of order. Back to Charing X.
        No sleeper. Miss a turn.
Paris. Threw bottle out of window. Pay 1d. Miss a turn.
Dijon __ Loop line to Lyon-Geneva.
Frasne: Kissed in tunnel. Miss 2 turns.

---

[99]Murry published 'Mr & Mrs Williams' among the unfinished stories in 'The Dove's Nest' but omitted this final section of it, presumably because it is extremely difficult to read.
[100]This seems to be the invention of a board game with echoes of Snakes and Ladders. Presumably it was devised some time after KM's journey to Sierre in the middle of 1921.

Vallorbe: Carrying gold out of France. Pay 3d.
Lost keys. Lose two turns.
Lausanne __ Loop line to Geneva.
Miss connection. Lose a turn.
Swallow marble in lemonade bottle. Back to Lausanne.
Wearing False Nose. Back to Vallorbe.
Sion. Lose your galoshes. Miss a turn.
Sierre. Asleep. Miss 2 turns.
Give Cigarette Picture for Ticket. Back to Sion.

<u>Chateau Belle Vue</u>
<Read and give to Brett>

Sion to Sierre
Step on Passenger's dog.
Hornet Flys into Carriage.
Cow puts its head in Window = go on to Sierre
Buy puppy [in another hand]
<u>Mad</u>man enters carriage.

# Notebook 42

[Notebook 42,[101] qMS-1261]

Saturday. Peaceful and gay. The whole house takes the air.

×     Athenaeum[102] is asleep & then awake on the studio sofa. He has a silver spoonful of my cream at lunch time, then hides under the sofa frill & plays the Game of the Darting Paw. I gather the dried leaves from the plant in the big white bowl; they are powdered with silver. There is nobody in the house and yet whose is this faint whispering? On the stairs there are tiny spots of gold – tiny footprints ....     [J156]

×     The red geraniums have bought the garden over my head and taken possession. They are 'settled in', every leaf & flower unpacked & in its place & never do they mean to move again! Well – <u>that</u> I could bear. But why because I've let them in should they turn me out? They won't even let me lie in the grass without their shouting:"<u>Im</u>-pudence."

[J157]

√     J. digs the garden as though he were exhuming a hated body or making a hole for a loved one.     [J166]

√     The ardent creature spent more than half her time in church praying to be delivered from temptation. But God grew impatient at last & caused the door to be shut against her. "For Heaven's sake," said he "give the temptation a chance!"     [J166]

Cook to see me.

√     As I opened the door I saw her sitting in the middle of the room, hunched, still... She got up, obedient, like aprisoner when you enter a cell. And her eyes said, like a prisoner's eyes say:"Knowing the life I've had I'm the last to be surprised at finding myself here."     [J162]

---

[101]Murry's note on Notebook 42: 'It is difficult to say when this fair copy of notes was made. I think from the cribbage scores on the cover in 1921 - though many of them are <u>much</u> earlier (1919 chiefly).' KM's ticks and crosses in the margin beside some of these paragraphs are, presumably, her indication of their passing or failing inclusion in some projected publication.
[102]Athenaeum, or Athy—a cat.

Its raining but the air is soft, smoky, warm. Big drops patter on the languid leaves, the tobacco flowers lean over. Now there is a rustle in the ivy. Wingley[103] has appeared from the garden next door; he bounds from the wall. And delicately, lifting his paws, pointing his ears, very afraid that a big wave will overtake him, he wades over the lake of green grass.

[j166]

B.[104] loves the louse for its own sake. He has pedigree lice & keeps them in tiny boxes. They feed from his arm. And he spends his life dissecting them & finding their <u>glands</u> and so on.

As he stood at the door he said, quietly: "Nothing is incurable. It is all a question of time. What seems so useless today may just be that link which will make all plain tomorrow." We had been discussing hydatids, the egyptian parasite that begins its new cycle of being in a water snail & the effects of hydrophobia. He smiled gently. There was nothing to be alarmed or shocked or surprised at. It was all a question of knowing these things as they should be known and not otherwise. But he said none of this & went off to his next case     [j168-169]

✓     At breakfast time a mosquito and a wasp came to the edge of the honey dish to drink. The mosquito was a lovely little high stepping gazelle, but the wasp was a fierce roaring tiger. Drink, my darlings.     [j169]

✗     When the coffee is cold L.M. says:  These things have to happen sometimes. And she looks mysterious & important, as if as a matter of fact she had known all along that this was a cold coffee day.     [j169]

✓     What I felt was, he said that I wasn't in the whole of myself at all. I'd got locked in, somehow, in some little...top room in my mind, and strangers had got in - people I'd never seen before were making free of the rest of it. There was a dreadful feeling of confusion, chiefly that, and ...vague noises - like things being moved, changed about, in my head. I lit a candle & sat up & in the mirror I saw a dark, brooding, strangely lengthened face.

"The feeling roused by the cause is more important than the cause itself." That is the kind of thing I like to say to myself as I get into the train. And then, as one settles into the corner "For example" or "Take, for instance..." Its a good game for <u>one</u>.     [j169]

She fastens on a white veil and hardly knows herself. Is it becoming or is it not becoming? Ah, who is there to say. There is a lace butterfly on her left cheek and a spray of flowers on her right. Two dark bold eyes stare through the mesh - surely not hers. Her lips tremble; faint, she sinks on her bed. And now she doesn't want to go. Must she? She is being driven out of the flat by those bold eyes. Out you go. Ah, how cruel! (Second Violin)

---

[103] Wingley, or Wing—a cat, brother to Athenaeum.
[104] Bateson, William, FRS (1861–1926), naturalist and geneticist. Prolific writer on Mendelian principles of heredity. See p 172.

But her hand is large & cold with big knuckles and short square nails. It is not a little velvet hand that sighs, that yields - faints dead away and has to be revived again only to faint once more. (S.V.)

What do I want? she thought. What do I really want more than anything in the world? If I had a wishing ring or Ali Baba's lamp - no, it wasn't Ali Baba, it was - oh, what did it matter! Just supposing someone came ... "I am here to grant your dearest wish." And she saw, vaguely, a fluffy little creature with a silver paper star on a wand - a school fairy ... What should I say? It was cold in the kitchen, cold & dim. The tap dripped slowly, as tho' the water were half frozen ...

Miss Todd and Miss Hopper were second violins. Miss Bray was a viola.

√ Midday strikes on various bells - some velvety soft, some languid, some regretful, and one impatient - a youthful bell ringing high and quick above the rest. He thought joyfully: That's the bell for me!" ...

[J169-170]

√ Cinderella:
Oh, my sisters - my beautiful Peacock-proud sisters - have pity on me as I sit with my little broom beside the cold ashes while you dance at the Prince's party. But why - is the Fairy Godmother, the coach, the plumes and glass slipper just - faery - and all the rest of the story deeply, deeply true? Fate I suppose - Fate. It had to be. These things happen so. La reponse: Poor old girl - of course one is awfully sorry for her, but she does become a bore, doesn't she. There's no getting away from it.

√ When they got into bed together her feet rushed to greet his like little puppies that had been separated all day from their brothers. And first they chased one another and played and nudged gently. But then they settled down, curled up, twined together under the edredon (like puppies on a warm hearth rug) and went to sleep.

√ Dark Bogey is a little inclined to jump into the milk jug to rescue the fly.

√ Fairy like the fire rose in two branched flames like the golden antlers of some enchanted stag.     [J170-171]

× So he sat there, burning the letters & each time he cast a fresh packet in the flame his shadow, immense, huge, leapt out of the wall opposite him. It looked, sitting so stiff and straight, like some horrible old god toasting his knees at the flames of the sacrifice.     [J175]

√ Two Climates. I'd always rather be in a place that is too hot rather than one that's too cold. But I'd always rather be with people who loved me too little rather than with people who loved me too much.

√ "She has made her bed" said Belle. "She must lie on it." I reflected thankfully that in this case that would be no hardship. On the contrary indeed, I hoped it was what they were both longing to do ...

√ North Africa. The whole valley is smothered in little white lilies. You never saw such a sight! They make me feel so wretchedly homesick. They smell just like dear old Selfridges.[105]　　[J174]

√ "Don't you think it would be marvellous," she said, "to have just one person in one's life to whom one could tell everything?" She bent forward, put down her cup, but stayed bent forward touching the spoon against the saucer. She looked up. "Or is it just childish of me - just absurd to want such a thing? ... All the same," she leaned back, smiling, "childish or not, how wonderful it would be - how wonderful! to feel, from this person, this one person I really don't need to hide anything.
It would be such heavenly happiness!" she cried, suddenly, "it would make Life so ..." She got up, went to the window, looked out vaguely & turned round again. She laughed. "Its a queer thing" she said, "I've always believed in the possibility, and yet - in reality ... Take R. and me, for instance." And here she flung back in a chair & leaned back, still she was laughing but her body leaned to the chair as though exhausted. "I tell him everything. You know we're - rather different from most people. What I mean is - don't laugh! - we love each other simply tremendously - we're everything to each other! In fact, he's the one person on earth for me - and yet" & she shut her eyes & bit her lip as though she wanted to stop laughing herself: "try, try try as I can, there's always just one secret - just one - that never can be told, that mocks me." And then for a moment she lay still ...　　[J175]

√ I saw S[106] as a little fair man with a walrus moustache, a bowler much too small for him and an ancient frock coat that he keeps buttoning & unbuttoning. D.B.[107] saw him as a grave gentleman with long black whiskers. Anyhow, there he was, at the end of a dark tunnel, either coming towards us or walking away... That started us on a fascinating subject. There are the people in D.B.'s life I've never seen (very few) and the immense number in mine that he has only heard of. What did they look like to us? And then, before we meet anyone, while they are still far too far off to be seen we begin to build an image ... how true is it? Its queer how well one gets to know this stranger; how often you've watched him before the other comes to take his place ... I can even imagine someone keeping their "first impression" in spite of the other.

[J177]

√ For a long time she said she did not want to change anything in him, and she meant it. Yet she hated things in him & wished they were otherwise. Then she said she did not want to change anything in him and she meant it. And the

---

[105]Selfridges—a London department store. In 1915 KM wrote a letter to her brother on notepaper with the printed heading SELFRIDGE & CO. LTD./ OXFORD STREET/ LONDON-W. THE LOUNGE, READING AND WRITING ROOMS. Clearly 'dear old Selfridges' was, for her, something like a London club. 'North Africa' at the beginning of this paragraph is unexplained.

[106]George Santayana (1863–1952), philosopher, literary critic and essayist. Author of *The Life of Reason*, 1905–6.

[107]Dark Bogey, an occasional nickname for Jack.

dark things that she had hated she now regarded with indifference. Then she said she had not wanted to change anything in him. But now she loved him so that even the dark things she loved, too. She wished them there; she was not indifferent. Still they were dark and strange but she loved them. And it was for this they had been waiting. They changed. They shed their darkness – the curse was lifted and they shone forth as Royal Princes once more, as creatures of light.     [J230]

✓ She sat on the end of the box ottoman buttoning her boots. Her short fine springy hair stood out round her head. She wore a little linen camisole and a pair of short frilled knickers. "Curse these buttons" she said, tugging at them. And then suddenly she sat up & dug the handle of the button hook into the box ottoman. "Oh dear" she said. "I do wish I hadn't married. I wish I'd been an explorer." And then she said dreamily "The Rivers of China, for instance." "But what do you know about the rivers of china, darling" I said. For Mother knew no geography whatever; she knew less than a child of ten. "Nothing" she agreed. "But I can _feel_ the kind of hat I should wear." She was silent a moment. Then she said "If Father hadn't died I should have travelled and then ten to one I shouldn't have married." And she looked at me dreamily – looked through me, rather.     [J234]

Souvent j'ai dit a mon mari: "Nous en prenons un?" Et il me dit Ah, non, non, ma pauvre femme. Notre petit moment pour jouer est passé. Je ne peux rien faire que rester dans ma chaise en faisant les grimaces, et ça fait trembler plus que ça fait rire un petit enfant.     [J174]

At The Bay.

At last the milk white harbour catches the glitter and the gulls floating on the trembling water gleam like the shadows within a pearl.

The house dog comes out of his kennel dragging the heavy chain and kalop kalops at the water standing cold in the iron pan. The house cat emerges from nowhere & bounds on to the kitchen window sill waiting for her spill of warm morning milk.     [J231]

✓ Children children!
Oh no. Not yet. Oh, it can't be time. Go away. I won't. Oh, why must I. Children! children!
They are being called by the cold servant girls. But they simply can't get up. They simply must have one more little sleep – the best sleep of all – the warm, soft, darling little rabbit of a sleep ... Just let me hug it one minute more before it bounds away.

Soft little girls rolled up in rounds, just their bunch of curls showing over the sheet top; little long pale boys stretching out their slender feet; other little boys lying on their bellies pressing their heads into the pillow; tiny little fellows with fresh cut hair sprouting from a tuft, little girls on their backs, their fists clenched, the bedclothes anyhow, one foot dangling; girls with pigtails or rings of white paper snails instead of hair ... And now there is the sound of plunging water, & all those youthful, warm bodies, the tender exposed boy children, and the firm compact little girls, lie down in the bath tubs and ruffle their shoulders scattering the bright drops as birds love to do with their wings ...

Squeech! Squeech! Tchee. Quee! Little boys with plastered hair, clean collars & brand new boots squeak from the nursery to the lobby to the cupboard under the stairs where the school kits are hung. Furious young voices cry: "Who's <u>stolen</u> my ink eraser that was in the well of my pencil box." They hiss through their teeth at the stolid servant girls carrying the porridge pots: "You've been at this! Thief! Spy!!"    [J231-232]

Have you noticed how very <u>smug</u> those mountains look that are covered with snow all the year round. They seem to expect one to be so full of admiring awe. It never seems to enter their silly tops to wonder whether it isn't rather dull to be so for ever & ever above suspicion.    [J234]

✓   Such a cultivated mind doesn't really attract me. I admire it. I appreciate all "les soins et les peines" that have gone to produce it, but it leaves me cold. After all, the adventure is over. There is now nothing to do but to trim & to lop and to keep back - all faintly depressing labours. No, no the mind I love must still have wild places - a tangled orchard where dark damsons drop in the heavy grass, an overgrown little wood, the chance of a snake or two (real snakes), a pool that nobody's fathomed the depth of, and paths threaded with those little flowers planted by the wind.
It must also have <u>real</u> hiding places, not artificial ones - not gazebos and mazes. And I have never yet met the cultivated mind that has not had its shrubbery. I loathe & detest shrubberies.    [J234-235]

When I read Doctor Johnson I feel like a little girl sitting at the same table. My eyes grow round. I don't only listen; I take him in <u>immensely</u>.
                                  [J174-175]
Let me remember when I write about that fiddle how it runs up lightly and swings down sorrowful; how it <u>searches</u>.    [J235]

✗   "You merely find yourself in the old position of trying to change me. And I refuse to change. I won't change. If I don't feel these things I don't feel them and there's an end of it."
For a moment he stood there, cold, frigid, grasping the doorhandle, staring not at her but over her head. He looked like a stranger who had opened her door by accident, and felt it necessary, for some reason or other to explain the accident before he closed it again and went out of her life for ever.    [J227]

✓   I have just partaken of that saddest of things - a cup of <u>weak</u> tea. Oh, why must it be weak! How more than pathetic it is to hear someone say as she puts it down before you: "I am afraid it is rather weak." One feels such a brute to take advantage of it until it is a little stronger. I grasp the cup; it seems to quiver, to breathe – "Coward!" I confess, I can never hear a person at a tea party say (in that timid whisper, you know, as though they were shamefully conscious) "<u>Very</u> weak for me, please" without wanting to burst into tears. Not that I like desperately strong tea. No, let it be of a moderate strength – tea that rings the bell. Very strong tea does seem to give you your penny back – in the teapot from the taste of it.      [J233]

Now and again Fred talked in his sleep. But even then you could say he was quiet… She would wake up and hear him say suddenly: "it wants a couple of screws" or "try the other blade", but never more than that.      [J233-234]

In the white lace, the spreading veil and the pearls she looked like a gull. But a quick hungry gull with an absolutely insatiable appetite for bread. "Come feed me! Feed me!" said that quick glare. It was as though all her vitality, her cries, her movements, her wheelings depended upon the person on the bridge who carried the loaf.      [J230]

But the champagne was no good at all. She turned the glass in her fingers. But there was something positively malicious in the way the little bubbles hurled themselves to the rim, danced, broke … They seemed to be jeering at her.

No, no, said Miss P. That really isn't fair. I love serious books. Why I don't know when I've enjoyed a book as much as – as – dear me! How silly! Its on the tip of my tongue. Darwin's – one moment – its coming – Darwin's Decline & Fall. No, no. That wasn't the one. That's not right now. Tchuh! Tchuh! You know how it is. I can see it quite plainly and yet … I've got it! Darwin's Descent of Man!.. Was that the one, though? Do you know <u>now</u> I'm not certain? I feel it was and yet somehow its unfamiliar. This is most extraordinary. And yet I enjoyed it so much. There was a ship. Ah! <u>That's</u> brought it back. Of course. Of course! <u>That</u> was the one. Darwin's Voyage of the Bugle!

"La mère de Lao-Tse a conçu son fils rien qu'en regardant filer une étoile."      [J235]

# Notebook 16

[Notebook 16, qMS–1263]

May 21st 1919[108]
She was sure I would be cold & as usual tried to make of my departure une petite affaire serieuse: I always try to thieve out, steal out. I should like to let myself down from a window, or just withdraw like a ray of light. "Are you sure you won't have your cape ... etc etc etc?" Her attitude made me quite sure. I went out. At the corner the flying, gay, eager wind ran at me. It was too much to bear. I went on for a yard or two, shivering - then I came home. I slipped the yale key into the lock, like a thief, shut the door <u>dead</u> quiet. Up came old L.M., up the stairs. "So it <u>was</u> too cold after all!"

I couldn't answer or even look at her. I had to turn my back & pull off my gloves. Said she: "I have a blouse pattern here I want to show you." At that I crept upstairs, came into my room & shut the door. It was a miracle she did not follow ... What is there in all this to make me HATE her so? What do you see? She has known me try & get in and out without anyone knowing it dozens of times - that is true. I have even <u>torn</u> my heart out & told her how it hurts my last little defences to be questioned - how it makes me feel just for the moment an independent being to be allowed to go & come unquestioned. But that is just Katie's 'funniness'. She doesn't mean it, of course ...

We hardly spoke at lunch. When it was over she asked again if she might show me the pattern. I felt so ill, it seemed to me that even a hen could see at a side glance of its little leaded eye how ill I felt. I don't remember what I said. But in she came & put before me - something. Really I hardly know what it was. "Let the little dressmaker help you ..." I read. But there was nothing to say. She murmured "purple chiffon front neck sleeves" I don't know. Finally I asked her to take it away. "What <u>is</u> it, Katie? Am I interrupting your work?" "Yes, we'll call it that."     [J155-156]

He is so inclined to cast himself into the milk jug after the fly.

---

[108]Written inside the front cover.

Saturday: This joy of being alone. What is it? I feel so gay and at peace –
the whole house takes the air. Lunch is ready. I have a baked egg, apricots
& cream, cheese straws & black coffee. How delicious! A baby meal.
Mother shares it with me. Athenaeum is asleep & then awake on the studio
sofa. He has a silver spoon of cream – then hides under the sofa frill & puts out
a paw for my finger. I gather the dried leaves from the plant in the big white
bowl & because I <u>must</u> play with something I take an orange up to my room
& throw it & catch it as I walk up & down ...          [J156]

The red geraniums have bought the garden over my head. They are there,
established, back in the old home, every leaf and flower unpacked and in its
place – and quite determined that no power on earth will ever move them
again. Well, <u>that</u> I don't mind. But why should they make me feel a stranger?
Why should they ask me every time I go near: "And what are <u>you</u> doing in a
London garden?" They burn with arrogance & pride. And I am the little
colonial walking in the London garden patch – allowed to look, perhaps, but
not to linger. If I lie on the grass they positively shout at me. Look at her lying
on <u>our</u> grass, pretending she lives here, pretending this is her garden & that tall
back of the house with the windows open & the coloured curtains lifting is
her house. She is a stranger – an alien. She is nothing but a little girl sitting on
the Tinakori hills & dreaming: I went to London and married an englishman
& we lived in a tall grave house with red geraniums & white daisies in the
garden at the back. <u>Im</u>-pudence!     [J156-157]

* * * *

Sometimes I glance up at the clock. Then I know I am expecting Chummie.
The bell peals. I run out on to the landing. I hear his hat & stick thrown on
to the hall table. He runs up the stairs, three at a time. "Hullo darling!"
But I can't move, I can't move. He puts his arm round me, holding me tightly
& we kiss – a long, firm family kiss. And the kiss means: We are of the same
blood; we have absolute confidence in each other; we are proud of each other;
we love; all is well; nothing can ever come between us. We come into my
room. He goes over to the glass. "By Jove, I am hot." Yes, he is very hot.
A deep childish colour shows in his cheeks, his eyes are brilliant, his lips burn,
he strokes the hair back from his forehead with the palm of his hand. I pull
the curtains together & the room is shadowy. He flings himself down on
the sommier & lights a cigarette, and watches the smoke rising so slowly.
"Is that better?" I ask. "Perfect, darling – simply perfect. The light reminds me
of – – –" And then the dream is over & I begin working again.     [J157-158]

* * * *

The two brothers were on one side of the room – I on the other. Arthur[109] sat
on the floor inclined towards Jack. Jack lay on the stickleback, very idly.

---

[109]Arthur Murry was JMM's younger brother. KM, who did not like the name Arthur, began to call
him Richard, which became the name by which he was generally known for the rest of his long life.

"If you could have your wish where would you be?" First he thought a café in some foreign town - in Spain - Grenoble perhaps, sitting listening to music & watching the people. We are just passing through ... There is a lake or a river near ... But then NO. A Farmhouse in Sussex, some good old furniture, knocking about in my garden, rolling the lawn perhaps - yes, rolling the lawn. An infant, two good servants. And then when it grew dark - to go in, have some milk, then I to go to my study & you to yours - work for about an hour & a half & then trundle off to bed. I would like to earn my living but <u>not</u> by writing. I feel that my talent as a writer isn't a great one - I'll have to be careful of it. Yes, that's what I'd like - no new places, no new things - I don't <u>want</u> them. Would you like that? I felt his brother was with him. The brother inclined towards him, understanding & sharing that life - the homestead on the Downs, the English country, the sober quiet. "Would you like that?"

No, I don't want that. No, I don't want England. England is of no use to me. What do I mean by that? I mean there never has been, there never will be any rapprochement between us - <u>never</u>. There is the inexplicable fact that I love my typical english husband for all the strangeness between us. I <u>do</u> lament that he is not warm, ardent, eager, full of quick response, careless, spendthrift of himself, vividly alive, <u>high spirited</u>. But it makes no difference to my love. But the lack of these qualities in his country I HATE - these & others - the lack of its <u>appeal</u> - that is what I chiefly hate. I would not care if I never saw the english country again. Even in its flowering I feel deeply antagonistic to it, & I will never change.

Arthur, I believe, through his sensitive love for Jack, felt this. They were of one nation, I of another, as we sat talking - I felt Arthur offered himself to his brother - in my stead.     [J158-159]

\* \* \* \*

Jack digs the garden as though he were exhuming a hated body or making a hole for a loved one.

30th.
First comes Ida. I give her orders. Ask her to supervise the maid until Monday. Be gentle with her, help her to make the bed & just tell her how everything must be. Then in detail I sketch out the maid's programme. "Send Ralph,[110] please." Ralph arrives. I arrange the food. <u>Then</u> settle all that must be done - coercing Ralph, putting her mind in order if I can, making her see the bright side of things, sending her away (I hope) feeling important & happy. I go upstairs to see Maud - to say 'good morning', to hope 'she will be happy'. "Just take things gently; I'll quite understand you can't get into our ways at once. Ask Miss Baker and the cook for what you want. But if you wish to see me don't hesitate to come in. I was so glad you were early." She was very reassured. Her eyes shone (she's only a little girl), she said it was like the

---

[110]Mrs Ralph was apparently the cook.

country. As she walked up from the tram the birds sang 'something beautiful'.
This instead of the long drag up the hill was very cheering. I left her happy.
I know I did. Downstairs just to say good day to Mrs Moody & to say there
were some flowers for her to take home. The good creature was on her knees
polishing & saying it was such a fine day. Bless her 60 years. We had a little
joke or two & I came away. Ida again - just for a moment to say: As you have
a machine don't hem dusters by hand as I see you are doing. Keep your
energies for something <u>important</u>. Then I sit down to work & there comes a
steady, pleasant vibration from the ship. All goes well for the moment. If only
I could always control these four women like this. I must learn to.     [J159-160]

<u>Work</u>. Shall I be able to express, one day, my love of work - my desire to be a
better writer, my longing to take greater pains. And the passion I feel. It takes
the place of religion - it <u>is</u> my religion - of people - I create my people - of
'life' - it <u>is</u> Life. The temptation is to kneel before it, to adore, to prostrate
myself, to stay too long in a state of ecstasy before the <u>idea</u> of it. I must be
more busy about my master's business.

Oh God - the sky is filled with the sun, and the sun is like music - the
sky is full of music. Music comes streaming down these great beams. The wind
touches the harp-like trees, shakes little jets of music - little shakes, little trills
from the flowers. The shape of every flower is like a sound. My hands open
like five petals. Praise him! Praise him! No, I am overcome; I am dazed; it is
too much to bear.

A little fly has dropped by mistake into the huge sweet strong cup of a
magnolia. Isaiah (or was it Elisha) was caught up into Heaven in a chariot of
fire <u>once</u>. But when the weather is divine & I am free to work such a journey
is positively nothing.     [J161]

The cook is evil. After lunch I trembled so that I had to lie down on the
sommier, thinking about her. I meant, when she came up to see me, to say <u>so
much</u> that she'd have to go. I waited, playing with the wild kitten. When she
came I said it all and more & <u>she</u> said how sorry she was & agreed
& apologised and quite understood. She stayed at the door, plucking at a
d'oyley. "Well I'll see it doesn't happen in future. I <u>quite</u> see what you mean."
So the serpent still slept between us. Oh! why won't she turn & speak her
mind. This pretence of being fond of me! I believe she thinks she is. There is
something in what Ida says: she is not consciously evil. She is a FOOL, of
course. I have to do all the managing and all the explaining. I have to cook
everything before she cooks it. I believe she thinks she is a treasure ... no,
wants to think it. At bottom she knows her corruptness. There are moments
when it comes to the surface, comes out, like a stain, in her face, & then her
eyes are like the eyes of a woman prisoner - a creature looking up as you enter
her cell and saying: if you'd known what a hard life I've had you wouldn't be
surprised to see me here _ _ _     [J161-162]

Its raining, but the air is soft, smoky, warm.

'Mr Despondency's daughter, Muchafraid, went through the water singing.'[111]

[J166]

The day the housemaid had to leave because her husband didn't want her to work no more and to consolidate his authority had punched her so hard in the neck that she had a great red swelling under her ear, the cook became a kind of infallible being – an angel of mercy. Nothing was too much for her – stairs were rays of light up which she floated. She wore her cap differently – it gave her the air of a hospital nurse – her voice changed. She suggested puddings as though they were compresses, whiting because they were "so delicate & harmless". Trust me! Lean on me! There is nothing I cannot do! was her attitude. Every time she left me she left me for her mysterious reasons – to lay out the body again & again, to change the stiffened hand, to pull the paper frill over the ominous spot appearing.      [J160-161]

She said: "I don't feel in the least afraid. I feel like a little rock that the rising tide is going to cover. You won't be able to see me  – –  big waves  – –  but they'll go down again & I shall be there – winking bright."
(Oh what sentimental toshery.)      [J166-167]

R's first husband was a pawnbroker. He learned his trade from her uncle with whom she lived & was more like her big brother than anything else from the age of 13. After he had married her they prospered. He made a perfect pet of her, they used to say. His sisters put it that he made a perfect fool of himself over her. When their children were 15 – 9 he urged his employers to take a man into their firm – a great friend of his, and persuaded them – really went security for this man. When Ralph saw the man she went over cold. She said Mark me you've not done right. No good will come of this. But he laughed it off. Time passed – the man proved a villain. When they came to take stock they found all the stock was false; he'd sold everything. This preyed on her husband's mind, went on preying, kept him up at night, made a changed man of him, he went mad as you might say, over figures, worrying. One evening, sitting in his chair – well it was very late – he <u>died</u> of a clot of blood on the brain.

She was left. Her big boy was old enough to go out but the little one was still not more than a baby: he was so nervous & delicate. The doctors had never let him go to school.

One day her brother-in-law came to see her & advised her to sell up her home, and get some work. All that keeps you back, he said, is little Bert. Now I'd advise you to place a certain sum with your solicitors for him and put him out – in the country. He said he'd take him. I did as he advised. But funny! [I] never heard a word from the child after he'd gone. I used to ask why he didn't write & they said when he can write a decent letter you shall have it – not before. That went on for a twelvemonth & I found after he'd been

---

[111]From *Pilgrim's Progress* by John Bunyan.

writing all the time, grieving to be took away & they'd never sent his letters. Then, quite sudden, his uncle wrote & said he must be taken away. He'd done the most awful things - things I couldn't find you a name for - he'd turned <u>vicious</u>, he was a little criminal! What his uncle said was I'd spoiled the child & he was going to make a man of him - & he'd beaten him and half starved him & when he was frightened at night & screamed he turned him out into the new forest and made him sleep under the branches.

My big boy went down to see him. Mother, he says, you wouldn't know little Bert. He can't speak. He won't come near anybody. He starts off if you touch him; he's like a little beast. And oh dear! the things he'd done. Well, you hear of children doing those things before they're put into orphanages but when I heard that & thought it was the same little baby his father used to carry into Regents Park bathed & dressed of a sudden[112] morning, well, I felt my religion was going from me.

I had a terrible time trying to get him into an orphanage. I begged for three months before they'd take him. Then he was sent to Bisley. But after I'd been to see him there - in his funny clothes and all - I could see is misery. I was in a nice place at the time, cook to a butcher in a large way in Kensington, but that poor child's eyes - they used to follow me - and a sort of shivering that came over him when people went near.

Well, I had a friend kept a boarding house in Kensington. I used to visit her and a friend of hers, a big well set up fellow, quite the gentleman, an engineer who worked in a garage, came there very often. She used to joke, say he wanted to walk me out. I laughed it off until one day she was very serious. She said you're a very silly woman. He earns good money; he'd give you a home & you could have your little boy. Well, he was to speak to me next day & I made up my mind to listen. Well, he did & he couldn't have put it nicer. I can't give you a house to start with, he said, but you shall have three good rooms & the kid and I'm earning good money and shall be more.

A week after he come to me, "I can't give you any money this week," he says. "There's things to pay from when I was single. But I daresay you've got a bit put by." And I was a fool, you know, I didn't think it funny. Oh yes, I said, I'll manage. Well so it went on for three weeks. We'd arranged not to have little Bert for a month because he said he wanted me to himself and he was so fond of him - a big fellow, he used to cling to me like a child & call me mother - - After three weeks was up I hadn't a penny. I'd been taking my jewellery & best clothes to put away to pay for him until he was straight but one night I said - where's my money. He just up and gave me such a smack in the face I thought my head would burst. And that began it. Every time I asked him for money he beat me. As I said, I was very religious at the time, used to wear a crucifix under my clothes & couldn't go to bed without kneeling by the side & saying my prayers - no, not even the first week of my marriage.

Well I went to see a clergyman & told him everything and he said

---

[112] ie 'Sunday', perhaps.

My child, he said, I am very sorry for you, but with God's help, he said, its your duty to make him a better man. You say your first husband was so good. Well, perhaps God has kept this trial for you until now. I went home – and that very night he tore my crucifix off & hit me on the head when I knelt down. He said he wouldn't have me say my prayers; it made him wild. I had a little dog at the time I was very fond of, & he used to pick it up & shout I'll teach it to say its prayers & beat it before my eyes – until – well, such was the man he was.

Then one night he came in the worse for drink & wet the bed. I couldn't stand it. I began to cry. He gave me a hit on the ear & I fell down striking my head on the fender. When I come to he was gone. I ran out into the street just as I was. I ran as fast as I could, not knowing where I was going – just dazed – my nerves were gone. And a lady found me & took me to her home & I was there three weeks. And after that I never went back. I never even told my people – I found work – and not till months after I went to see my sister. "Good gracious" she says, "we all thought you was murdered." And I never seen him since ...

Those were dreadful times. I was so ill I could scarcely hardly work & of course I couldn't get my little boy out. He had to grow up in it. And so I had to start all over again. I had nothing of his, nothing of mine. I lost it all, except my marriage lines. Somehow I remembered them just as I was running out that night & put them in my body – sort of an instinct, as you might say.

[J162-165]

10.XI.1919. I have discovered that I cannot burn the candle at one end & write a book with the other – – –    [J167]

Often I reproach myself for my 'private' life – which after all, were I to die, <u>would</u> astonish even those nearest to me. Then, (as yesterday) I realise how little Jack shares with me. Last week I had no idea what was going in the paper, no copy of the paper and J. hadn't the smallest curiosity as to whether I had seen or had not seen it. He never even asked. It might have been a report for the Home Office. I found from Milne[113] that he still goes to Somerset House. I found from him today that he is paid £250 a year for it.

Knowing my agony if anyone is <u>late</u> – having shared it with me a dozen times, saying he knows the difficulties of our domestic arrangements, he was 25 minutes late yesterday, and when he realised how he had hurt me he sulked because he could not do as he liked – was always driven, <u>ALL</u> his pleasure spoilt, even at St Albans, by worrying about my 'complex' about the time. He went to St. Albans yesterday & stayed until four & never told me a thing of the journey – had nothing to tell.

Today he is with his brother. We met for lunch & he discovered for me

---

[113]H J M Milne, a friend of Murry's who worked in the British Museum. He lived with Murry at 2 Portland Villas when KM left London for Menton in September 1920.

afterwards (when I asked) a number of new books which he has brought into the house & never shown me - just put away. He knows I can seldom go out, he knows I can <u>never</u> get to a bookshop, he knows how I <u>love</u> books - love dipping into them, love just a moment's chat about them, but all the same, he has never thought to share these finds with me - never for a moment.

 All this hurts me horribly, but I like to face it and see all round it. He ought not to have married. There never was a creature less fitted by nature for life with <u>a woman</u>.

 And the strange truth is I don't WANT him to change. I want to see him and then adjust my ways & go on alone & WORK.

 Life without <u>work</u> - I would commit suicide therefore work is more important than life.  [J165-166]

Bateson and his love of the louse for its own sake. Pedigree lice. £100 a year from the Royal Institute; a large family - desperately poor, but he never notices. The lives he saved in the Balkan War with shaving & Thymol. Cases reduced from 7000 to 700. No reward, not even an O.B.E. He dissects them, finds their <u>glands</u> and so on. Keeps them in tiny boxes; they feed on his arm - the louse & the bed bug.

 Hydatids - the australian who got them - handfuls of immature grapes. They attack the liver. In the human body they reproduce <u>in</u>definitely. When they are passed and a sheep is attacked by them they develop <u>hooks</u> & become long worms.

 The Egyptian disease - a parasite which attacks the veins & arteries & causes fluxion - constant bleeding. It is another egg drunk in water. After it has been in man the only thing it can affect is a water snail - it goes through an entirely new cycle of <u>being</u> until it can attack man again.

 Dysentery - another parasite.

<u>Hydrophobia</u>.
The virus from the dog is taken and a rabbit is infected. That rabbit is used to infect another rabbit, the 2nd a third & so on till you get a rabbit who is practically <u>pure</u> virus.

 The spinal chords are then taken from these rabbits, & dried by a vacuum. The result is pounded up fine into an emulsion - 1st rabbit 2nd rabbit 3rd etc. and the patient is injected progressively till at last he receives a dose which, if he had not been so prepared to resist it would kill him outright. The disease develops very slowly; the treatment is very expensive. Symptoms are a profuse shiny bubbly saliva and gasping & groaning as in gas poisoning. No barking - no going on all fours.

 In lockjaw the jaw does not lock.

Pasteur was a very dreamer of dreamers.
Human beings are a <u>side line</u>.
Science.

All this I talked over with Sorapure[114] June 21st. His point of view about medicine seems to me just completely right. I'd willingly let him take off my head, look inside & pop it on again if he thought it might assist future generations. Quite the right man to have at ones dying bedside - hed get me at any rate so interested in the process - gradual loss of sensitiveness, coldness at the joints etc. I'd lie there thinking: this is very valuable to know - I must make a note of this. As he stood at the door talking - nothing is incurable, its all a question of time, what seems so useless today may just be that link that will make all plain to a future generation ... I had a sense - of the larger breath - of the mysterious lives within lives, and the egyptian parasite beginning its new cycle of being in a water snail affected me like a great work of Art. No, that's not what I mean: it made me feel how perfect the world is, with its worms & hooks and ova. How incredibly perfect. There is the sky & the sea & the shape of a lily & there is all this other as well. The balance how perfect. (Salut, Tchekov.) I would not have one without the other.

The clocks are striking ten. Here in my room the sky looks lilac, in the bathroom it is like the skin of a peach. Girls are laughing - Jack & Sullivan[115] are down in Somerset - happy, I feel - if they are warm enough - enjoying each other.

I have consumption. There is still a great deal of moisture (& pain) in my BAD lung. But I do not care - I do not want anything I could not have. Peace, solitude, time to write my books, beautiful external life to watch & ponder - no more. O, I'd like a child as well - a baby boy - mais je demande trop.

[J167-168]

July 20th Beware!

August 1st Beware!!

It is pleasant to plant cuttings of futurity if only one in ten takes root. [J179]

Psychologie Féminine
It is said that the turtle dove never drinks clear water but always muddies it first with its foot so that it may the better suit its pensive mind. [J215]

Then there is Teague [?] and his worms.[116]

---

[114]Dr Victor Edgar Sorapure (1874–1933) was the physician whom KM came to trust more than any of the many others she consulted, and who influenced her thinking about her illness during the last five years of her life. As a Professor of Clinical Medicine at Fordham University in New York, and then, after the outbreak of war, as a diagnostician and tireless general medical practitioner in London, he was highly esteemed by colleagues and patients alike. He died of tuberculosis before his 60th birthday.

[115]J W N Sullivan was Assistant Editor of the *Athenaeum*, of which Murry was Editor, and was a friend of both KM and Murry.

[116]Here follow some pages of Murry's notes on and quotes from Chaucer's *Troilus and Criseyde*. KM has turned the book over and started again from the back.

arnica - a paint for a sprain
mix ammonia
aconite for fever
ephicaquahna[117] for colds

Tuesday night. May 21st.[1919] Temperature 101.2.
Severe pain in lung. Had a prolonged coughing attack & brought up blood.
Slept very little on account of cough; expectoration streaked with blood.

Wednesday morning. Temp 100.2. Cough troublesome. Signs of blood persist
until noonday. Severe pain in the lung & feel very cold and nauseated.
Shivered all the afternoon but temperature 101. Lung still very painful at each
breath.     [J155]

B.L. of J.[118] page 350.

The insolence of wealth is a wretched thing but the conceit of parts has some
foundation ...

M:  A temporary poem always entertains us.
J:  So does the account of the criminals hanged yesterday entertain us.

Criticism: Nobody has the right to put another under such a difficulty that he
must either hurt the person by telling the truth or hurt himself by telling what
is not true ... Therefore the man who is asked by an author what he thinks of
his work is put to the torture, and is not obliged to speak the truth; so that
what he says is not considered as his opinion; yet he has said it and cannot
retract his opinion.

352: All censure of a man's self is oblique praise. It is in order to show how
much he can spare. It has all the invidiousness of self-praise, and all the
reproach of falsehood.[119]
B: Sometimes it may process from a man's strong consciousness of his faults
being observed. He knows that others would throw him down & therefore he
had better lie down softly of his own accord ...
... It is thus that mutual cowardice keeps us in peace. Were one half of
mankind brave & one half cowards, the brave would be always beating the
cowards. Were all brave they would lead a very uneasy life; all would be
continually fighting; but being all cowards we get on together very well ...

S: So, sir, wine is a key which opens a box & this box may be either full or
empty?
J: Nay, sir, conversation is the key; wine is a pick-lock which forces open the
box & injures it. A man should cultivate his mind so as to have that confidence
& readiness without wine, which wine gives.     [J148-149 S110-111]

---

[117]Murry has written, underneath this word, his version of it: ipecachuana.
[118]Boswell's *Life of Johnson.*
[119]This passage, '352 ... falsehood.' is marked by a heavy line in the margin.

baum analgysèphe
Bergeré Paris
Parke Davis
10 teaspoonsful.                                    mulled ale.

Old Court House.[120] <u>callous</u>. pariah p'riah. philoprogenitive.
The Arrow of Gold

59 the childlike stamping
75 the old old story

I wouldn't judge you. What am I before the knowledge you were born to?
You are as old as the world. She accepted this with a smile. gd. the vulgar old
tricks – upsetting boxes and so on.

Then what will I do for one? [KM][121]
buy another [J]
I will sell you my watch for 2 quid [KM]
perfect! [J]
but a male [KM]
All right. [JM]

Here reigned Lydia and <u>herself</u> worked at a lattice with the rest.[122]
its disintegration as rag and its apotheosis as paper –
<u>apotheosis</u>.
It is extremely pleasant work because there is really such a deal of wholesome
life in it.
Of the two stories that run side by side in Mr Philpott's new novel we prefer
that which deals with the process by which handmade paper is made. The
scene is a small village on the river Dart.

of the two stories that run side by side in Mr Philpott's new novel we confess
we prefer that which describes the process by which handmade paper is made
– – This little village[123]

---

[120]These are notes on *The Arrow of Gold* by Joseph Conrad, which KM reviewed in the *Athenaeum*
on 8 August 1919.
    [121]Murry's note: 'This is a conversation, carried on when KM's cough was very troublesome, with
me.' The attributions in square brackets are supplied by Murry.
    [122]Murry's note: 'These are notes on Eden Philpott's novel *Storm in a Teacup*, KM's review of which
appeared on August 29, 1919.'
    [123]Between the pages of this notebook is a printed version of 'Truthful Poem By An Ex-Serviceman.
Written by an UNEMPLOYED Ex-Soldier.'

# Notebook 46

[Notebook 46, qMS-1262][124]

[1] Criticism: Not good enough. Uneven, shallow, forced. Very thin, pocket muslin handkerchief vocabulary! K.M.

[2] This is jerky & the second review is thoroughly bad. It never gets there! The C. & C. is <u>smart</u> somehow. 'after the model'.

April 18th 1919.

[3] Too vague. Too much in the air. <u>Un</u>-telling. Rebecca West beat me to a frazzle on the same subject. <u>She</u> got in my school 98 marks. <u>I</u> got 44.    [s117]

[4] I did not say what I set out to say. It is not close knit enough. No, it won't do.

[5] Top verses far too facile. I like the lower ones.

---

[124]This hard-backed ledger book was originally used by someone (not KM or Murry) as a record of books, with author, publisher, description, price and publication date. KM appropriated it and at one end pasted in copies of some of her published book reviews, with her own comments on each review, and at the other end she wrote the first part of a story which takes place in a cabin on board ship, and which appears here following these comments. Her comments refer to the following reviews:

1. *Hope Trueblood* by Patience Worth (Skeffington 6s 9d net)
   *The House of Courage* by Mrs Victor Rickard (Duckworth 7s net)
   *The Tunnel* by Dorothy Richardson (Duckworth 7s net) (April 4th 1919)
2. *Christopher and Colombus* by the author of "Elizabeth and her German Garden" (Macmillan 7s 6d net)
   *What Not* by Rose Macauley (Constable 6s net) (April 11th)
3. *Old Junk* by H M Tomlinson (Melrose 6s net) (April 18th 1919)
[KM has also pasted in here Tomlinson's letter to her about her review: 'Dear Mrs Murry, On reading your appreciation of me for a second time I was the more puzzled by my amazing good luck. I told J.M.M., & it is quite true; your review of my book was more to me than the Legion of Honour. And how finely the decoration was bestowed! When a reviewer who writes like that can give so noticeable a tribute to another writer, the honour is more than doubled. It has a rarer and different quality altogether. My astonishing good fortune! Yours sincerely, H.M. Tomlinson.']
4. *My War Experiences in Two Continents* by S Macnaughton (Murray 10s 6d net) (April 25th)
5. Two poems by 'Elizabeth Stanley': 'Covering Wings' and 'Firelight'.

[6] You seem to have a mania for 'such' a detestable word & the weakest of links in a chain & 'so'. You'd better stop playing that particular tune now, nous avons assez entendu sonner.      [s119-120]

[7] Nothing like good enough. Too big an avenue; practically <u>no</u> house at the end of it – at any rate no solid house & no firm hold. <u>Very very bad.</u>

[8] Shows traces of hurry, & at the end, is pompous!

[9] I think this is too short. It wants expanding & developing. Also the last sentence is inadmissable. It is not complete – not a <u>whole specimen.</u>

[10] Not bad. Touch of my gran'pa in it.

[11] Fish:
The day had been endless without him – endless – endless.

Chapter I[125]

It was neither dark nor light in the cabin. The ring of the porthole shone very bright and cold like the eye of some huge dead bird. In that eye you saw an immense stretch of grey waving water, a vague sky above, and between, a few huge live birds flying so aimless and uncertain they didn't look like birds at all, but like bits of wave, torn off, or just shadows ...

Shadows, too, birds of shadow, flew across the cabin ceiling - across its whiteness, iron girders, splashes of rust, big nails coated with paint, paint blisters. There was a strange gleam on the walls. A tiny day seemed to be breaking all on its own in the mirror above the washstand and another tide rose and fell in the thick bottle.

It was cold. The damp air smelled of paint and rubber and sea water. The only thing of life in the silent cabin was the little doll-like curtain hanging at the porthole. In the quiet it lifted - lifted - fluttered - then blew out straight and stiff, tugging at the rings. And then gently, gently it fell again. Again it folded, drooped, only to begin puff puffing out once more, filling, swelling, stretching out stiff with only a quiver, dancing a secret dance as it were while those birds of silence chased over the ceiling. The minute day deepened very slowly in the mirror, and in the thick bottle rose & ebbed the heavy tide.

"... But my dear child its no earthly use simply to say that you've lost it. That won't help you. How can it? You must stir yourself, rouse yourself, begin looking for it. It must be somewhere. Things don't simply disappear, vanish into thin air. You know that as well as I do. Pull yourself together. Concentrate. Now when did you last have it? When did you first realise it

---

6. Not a review but a satirical piece, 'Perambulations', about publishers, signed Katherine Mansfield. (May 2nd)
7. *The Gay-Dombeys* by Sir Harry Johnston (Chatto & Windus 7s net) (May 2nd)
8. *The Moon and Sixpence* by W S Maugham (Heinemann 7s net) (May 9th)
9. *Loose Ends* by Arnold Lunn (Hutchinson 6s 9d net) (May 16th)
10. *Pink Roses* by Gilbert Cannan (Fisher Unwin 7s 6d net) (May 23rd)
11. The final comment does not refer to a review but occurs in isolation in the middle of the book.
    [125] Murry supplied the title 'Strange Visitor' to this piece in *Scrapbook*.

was gone. When did you feel that terrific shock, that – Good Heavens – where on earth – don't you know? You must remember that. And Oh! don't mind me laughing, darling, but you look so tragic. I can't help saying it is so exactly like you. So just the sort of thing that would be bound to happen to you of all people. One might almost say that you've been working up to it, don't you know, all your life.

Lost Stolen or Strayed. We shall have to advertise. Three shillings a line for the first two lines and something enormous a word afterwards. You don't think I'm cruel, do you, pet? Everything has its funny side, hasn't it? And if one can bring one's sense of humour to bear upon a thing – what can be better? Don't you agree? Of course I'm a philosopher. I don't believe there's a single thing that we aren't really better without, but I can't expect you to agree with that. Cheer up! We've only one life after all. That's cheap I know – but you could not say a truer thing – not even if you were willing to spend millions on it. And here's what I would do. If I were you I should put it all out of my mind – make a fresh start, behave as though it was not. Ah, I know that sounds hard to you now, girlie (you don't mind me calling you girlie & just patting your hand as I do. I enjoy it – and the tremor you can get on girlie – marvellous) but Time heals all. Not with his scythe dear, no – with his eggtimer – my facetious way of saying his hour glass. Ha! Ha! Ha! You hate me I know. Well I'm just going. But one day if you are honest with yourself you will remember and you will say Yes, she was right and I was wrong – she was wise and I was foolish."

The odious little creature who had been sitting on the edge of the lower berth drew on a pair of dirty white kid gloves, tucked her tail under her arm, gave a loud high cackle and vanished.

The figure on the bunk gave no sign. She lay on her back, her arms stretched down by her sides, her feet just touching the wooden rim at the end of the berth, the sheet up to her chin. Very pale, frowning, she stared at the spot where little monkey had been sitting, shut her eyes, opened them, looked again – nobody was there.

And the night was over. It was too late to expect anybody else. She shut her eyes again – a great loud pulse beat in her body or was it in the ship? In the ship. She had no body – she just had hands feet and a head, nothing else at all. Of course they were joined together by something, but not more than the stars in the Southern Cross were joined together. How otherwise could she feel so light – so light.     [s73-76]

# *Notebook 26*

[Notebook 26, qMS-1264]

17.XII.19.[126]                    The Walking Stick.[127]

When I had gone to bed I realised what it was that had caused me to 'give
way'. It was the effort of being up with a heart that wouldn't work. Not my
lungs at all. My despair simply disappeared - yes, <u>simply</u>. The weather was
lovely, every morning the sun came in & drew those squares of golden light on
the wall. I looked round my bed on to a sky like silk. The day opened slowly
slowly like a flower & it held the sun long long before it slowly, slowly folded.
Then my homesickness went. I not only didn't want to be in England, I began
to love Italy - and the thought of it - the sun - even when it was too hot
always the sun - and a kind of <u>wholeness</u> which was good to bask in.

     After a few days J's letters in response to <u>my</u> depressed letters began to
arrive. There were a series of them. As I grew depressed <u>he</u> grew depressed but
not <u>for</u> me. He began to write (1) about the suffering I caused him: <u>his</u>
suffering, <u>his</u> nerves, <u>he</u> wasn't made of whipcord or steel, the fruit was bitter
for <u>him</u>. (2) a constant cry about money. He had none: he saw no chance of
getting any, 'heavy debts', 'as you know I am a bankrupt', 'I know it sounds
callous', 'I can't face it'. These letters, especially the letters about money bit
like a knife through something that had grown up between us. They changed
the situation for me, at least, for ever. We had been for 2 years drifting into a
relationship different to anything I'd ever known - we'd been <u>children</u> to each
other, openly confessed children, telling each other everything, each
<u>depending</u> equally upon the other. Before that I'd been the man and he had
been the woman & he had been called upon to make no real efforts.
He'd never really 'supported' me. When we first met, in fact, it was I who kept
him and afterwards we'd always acted (more or less) like men friends. Then this

---

[126]At the top of this page Murry wrote 'Casetta - the day after my arrival - Dec. 16 1919.' Then he
wrote, 'The 17th must be a mistake, and I'm pretty sure she would not have written this the day after my
arrival. J.M.M.' In his published version of this passage he has changed the date to the 15th. There is some
authority for him to do this in that KM has twice inserted the date in the following pages, and both times it
is 15.XII.1919.
     [127]Murry's note: 'Title of a story - quite irrelevant.'

illness – getting worse & worse & turning me into a woman and asking him to put himself away & to <u>bear</u> things for me. He stood it marvellously. It helped very much because it was a 'romantic' disease (his love of a 'romantic appearance' is <u>immensely</u> real) and also being 'children' together gave us a practically unlimited chance to play at life – not to live. It was child love.

Yes, I think the most marvellous, the most radiant love that this earth knows: terribly rare. We've had it. But we were not <u>pure</u>. If we had been he'd have faced coming away with me. And that he would not do. He'd not have said he was too tired to earn enough to keep us here. He always refused to face what it meant – living alone together for 2 years on not much money. He <u>said</u> – & ¾ of him believed – I couldn't stand the strain of it with you ill. But it was a lie & a confession that all was not well with us. And I always knew it. Nevertheless I played up & truly even in October I <u>clung</u> to him still – still the child – seeing as our salvation a house in the country in England <u>not later than next May</u> & then never to be apart again … The letters – ended all of it. <u>Was</u> it the letters? I must not forget something else.

All these 2 years I've been obsessed by the fear of death. This grew & grew & grew <u>gigantic</u> & this it was that made me cling so, I think. Ten days ago – it went – I care no more. It leaves me perfectly cold. Well it was that <u>&</u> the letters perhaps. Gone is my childish love, gone my desire to live in England. I don't particularly want to live with him. I'd like to if it could be managed, but <u>no sacrifices please</u>. As to leaning, as to being a "little lovely darling" its not conceivable. I want to <u>work</u> – travel – get a good maid in place of L.M. – & that's all. Quite all? Yes, all. I am become Mother. I don't care a <u>rap</u> for 'people'. I shall always love Jack & be his wife, but I couldn't get back to that anguish – joy – sweet madness of the other years. Such love has gone for me. And Life either stays or goes.

I must put down here a dream.[128] The first night I was in bed here – i.e. after my first day in bed I went to sleep. And suddenly I felt my whole body <u>breaking up</u> – it broke up with a violent shock – an earthquake, & it broke like glass. A long terrible shiver, you understand, & the spinal cord & the bones and every bit & particle quaking. It sounded in my ears – a low confused din, and there was a sense of flashing greenish brilliance, like broken glass. When I woke I thought there had been a violent earthquake. But all was still. It slowly dawned upon me – the conviction that in that dream I died. I shall go on living now – it may be for months, or for weeks or days or hours. Time is not. In that dream I died. The <u>spirit</u> that is the enemy of death & quakes so & is so tenacious was shaken out of me. I <u>am</u> (15.XII.1919) a dead woman & <u>I don't care</u>. It might comfort others to know that one gives up caring but they'd not believe any more than I did until it happened. And oh – how strong was its hold upon me – how I <u>adored</u> Life & <u>dreaded</u> Death. I'd like to write my books & spend some happy time with Jack (not very much faith in that)

---

[128] The words 'Imp/ort/ant!/for/the/conf/essi/ons' were written vertically in the left hand margin of this paragraph. Beside them Murry wrote, 'I could not decipher this.'

and see Lawrence in a sunny place & pick violets - all kinds of flowers. Oh, I'd like to do heaps of things really, but I don't mind if I do not do them.

That quiet simplicity, that deep simple love <u>is</u> not. It only existed until we put it to the test. Then, when I cried out, Jack beat me - because it hurt him to hear me - I stopped his play, I made the house all wrong ... How clear it all is. Immediately I, as a tragic figure, outfaced or threatened to outface him (yes, that's exactly the truth) the truth was revealed. He was the one who really wanted <u>all</u> the tragedy. It must have been a fearful blow to spare at all ... I am glad it is over. I wouldn't call it back. Honesty - (why?) - is the only thing one seems to prize beyond life, love, death, everything. It alone remaineth. Oh those that come after me - will you believe it? At the end <u>truth</u> is the one thing <u>worth</u> <u>having</u> - its more thrilling than love, more joyful, & more passionate. It simply can<u>not</u> fail. All else fails. I, at any rate, give the remainder of my life to it & it alone. (15.XII.1919) I'd like to write a <u>long long</u> story on this & call it "Last Words to Life." One <u>ought</u> to write it, and another on the subject of HATE.      [J183-185]

It often happens to me now that when I lie down for sleep at night instead of getting drowsy I feel wakeful and lying here in bed I begin to <u>live</u> over little scenes from real life or imaginary scenes. Its not too much to say they are almost hallucinations: they are marvellously vivid. I lie on my right side & put my left hand up to my forehead as though I were praying. This seems to <u>induce</u> the state. Then for instance its 10.30 p.m. on a big liner in mid ocean ...
People are beginning to leave the Ladies Cabin. Father puts his head in & asks if one of you would care for a walk before you turn in. Its glorious up on deck. That begins it. I am <u>there</u>. Details - father rubbing his gloves, the cold air, the <u>night</u> air rather he brings to the door, the pattern of everything, the feel of the brass stair rail & the rubber stairs. Then the deck. The pause while the cigar is lighted, the look of all in the moonlight, the <u>steadying</u> hum of the ship, the 1st officer on the deck, so far aloft the bells, the steward going into the smoking room with a tray, stepping over the high brass-bound step. All these things are far realer, more in detail, <u>richer</u> than Life. And I believe I could go on until .... there's <u>no end</u> to it. I can do this about anything. Only there are no personalities. Neither am I there personally. People are only part of the silence, <u>not</u> of the pattern - vastly different to that - part of the <u>scheme</u>. I could always do this to a certain extent - but its only since I was really ill that this shall we call it "consolation prize" has been given me. My God, its a marvellous thing!

I can call up certain persons - Doctor Sorapure for instance. And then I remember how I used to say to J & A[129] "he was looking very beautiful today." I did not know what I was saying. But when I so summon him & see him 'in relation' he <u>is</u> marvellously beautiful. There again he comes to every

---

[129]Jack and Arthur

tiny detail to the shape of his thumbs, to looking over his glasses, his lips as he writes & particularly in all connected with putting the needle into a syringe - I relive all this at will.

But my life with Jack I'm not inclined to. It doesn't enter my head. Where that life was there's just a blank. The future - the present life with him is not. It has got to be lived. There's nothing in it. Something has stopped - a wall has been raised and its too recent for me to wish to go there even. Wait till it looks a little less new .... is the feeling. I'm not in the least curious either - & not in the least inclined to lament.

If one wasn't so afraid - why should I be - these aren't going to be read by Bloomsbury et Cie - I'd say we had a child - a love child & its dead. We may have other children but this child can't be made to live again. J. says forget that letter. How can I? It killed the child - killed it really & truly for ever as far as I am concerned. Oh, I don't doubt that if I live there will be other children but there won't be that child.     [J186-187 S125-127]

Any children? he asked, taking out his stethoscope as I struggled with my nightgown. No, no children. But what would he have said if I'd told him that until a few days ago I had had a little child, aged five & ¾ - of - - indeterminate sex. Some days it was a boy. For two years now it had very often been a little girl ...[130]     [J187]

    The Wrong House.

Miss Lavinia Bean sat at the diningroom window finishing another pink vest for the mission. She was crocheting up the sides and after that there was the long tie of chain stitch to make and then it was done. The day was chill

    She liked to lie in the bath & very gently swish the water over her white jellified old body. As she lay there, her arms at her sides, her legs straight out, she thought this is how I shall look, this is how they will arrange me in my coffin. And it seemed [to] her as she gazed down at herself terribly true that people were made to fit coffins - made in the shape of coffins. Just then she saw her wet shining toes as they were pressed against the end of the bath. They looked so gay, so unconscious of their fate. They seemed really to be smiling all in a row - the little toe so small. "Oh!" She gave the sponge a tragic squeeze.
                                              [J187 S127]

Alone with W. She took his [.....] boyish look & like the little girl with her [...] loaf in the Hans Andersen story she flung it on the mud & used it as a stepping stone.

She will go out and buy the vegetables and take our heavenly father's hat & stick when he goes to visit his father ...

---

[130]Following this is the story 'This Flower', another version of which, titled 'Late Spring' is in the Newberry Library and may be found on p 246.

Sitting up in bed she put a pink fascinator over her head and shoulders, drew the spectacles out of the case & looked through the album –

After tea it was her habit to play patience until the evening paper came.[131]

Surely I do know more than other people. I have suffered more, endured more. I know how they long to be happy and how precious is an atmosphere that is loving, a <u>climate</u> that is not frightening. Why do I not try to bear this in mind and try to cultivate my garden? Now I descend to a strange place among strangers. Can I not make myself felt as a real personal force. (Why should you) Ah, but I <u>should</u>. I have had experience unknown to them. I should by now have learnt Campbell's obiter dictum – how true it might be. It <u>must</u> be.

[J188]

A Lost Love. By Ashword Owen. John Murray 3/6 net. The tone is too low. This is a very interesting monograph. Browning, Swinburne & Tennyson [...] to this little book. Published London 1854. Show Georgy London[?] Lord Erskine. His winning ways. Constance Everett & the nightcaps. All good.

> My Neighbours. By Caradoc Evans. 6/- Melrose.
> Short [...] Welsh[?] Life.
> Mrs Warrens Profession. By Sir Harry Johnson. 7/6 net.
> Chatto & Windus.
> Honoria Frazer. Michael[?] Rossiter
> Villa Beau Séjour. Too garrulous.

---

[131] This is an unpublished sentence at the end of 'A Strange Mistake', published as 'The Wrong House'. Facing the last page of this story is a page of pencilled flower drawings with '<u>Jack</u>!' written in the middle.

# *Notebook 22*

[Notebook 22, qMS-1265]

Miss Smith c/o Constable & Co.
grey silk stockings
Mrs Beaumont 7 Oriel Terrace Lower Church Road Western[132] S. Mare.
Mrs P's sister 4 Lanks Terr.[?] Leads in Sloane[?] Street.

Love Birds at 47B
Male and female.
male green underbody, wings mole tipped with yellow, broad at base, gradually growing smaller until the head feathers as close as can be, yellow faces, a touch of pale blue on the chops and the top of the beak. On the male exquisite black spots, points of jet under the beak. Tail of male bird blue. Female yellow with overbody of pale green in delicate pencil lines. The bird is yellow but a green yellow. Male bird burrows in its back, finds        [J330]

| 7/6. | Friday. | 193.17.0 |
|---|---|---|
| | | 30. 0.0 |
| | | 20.13.9 |
| | | £244.10.9 |

        Dinner Blunden.

Hotel d'Angleterre
        Beau Rivage
        Bellevue
        de la Paix
Quai du Mont Blanc

How's Hotel, 37 Queens Gate Gdns, South Ken. 3268 Ives.

---

[132]ie 'Weston'

Rising above all pain and all infirmity – rising above <u>everything</u> – the child trying on gloves banging

Robinson Crusoe
Pilgrims Progress
Coleridge Biographia Literaria
  "     Lectures on Shakespeare
One or Two Jane Austen
Shakespeare and the O.B.E.V.[133]
The Sea and the Jungle
Chaucers Canterbury Tales
Spenser's Faerie Queen.     [J214-215]

sachets (2)
pocket mirror
comb
poudre milde
sponge bag
toothbrush case & soap
sotol tablets[134]
Kolynos
Floss silk
Powder
<u>veils</u>
<u>shoes</u>

<u>Name</u>  Katherine Middleton Murry[135]
<u>Address</u>  c/o Bank of New Zealand, 1 Queen Victoria St, London E.C.4.
<u>Motor Car No.</u>  0194
<u>Bicycle No.</u>  Stores 109750
<u>Height</u>  5 <u>feet</u> 4½ <u>inches</u>
<u>Size of Gloves</u>  6
<u>Size of Boots</u>  4
<u>In case of serious accident or other urgent need please notify</u>
John Middleton Murry, Athenaeum, 10 Adelphi Terrace W.C., London.

29 MONDAY[136]

Catherine brought maid. Jack returned exhausted from San Remo. Bathed his head. In the afternoon played demon. Jack was furious at my lack of sympathy.

---

[133]Oxford Book of English Verse.
[134]Sotol tablets—a brand of antiseptic mouthwash tablets; Kolynos—a proprietary brand of toothpaste.
[135]The underlined headings here constitute a printed form on an introductory page of this commercial diary. The personal information not underlined was written in by KM.
[136]December 1919.

He was dying Egypt dying. But he could laugh heartily at the Smallwood family. 'That's first chop.'

### 30 TUESDAY

Calm day. In garden. Read early poems in Oxford Book. Discussed our future library. In the evening read Dostoievsky. In the morning discussed the importance of 'external life'. Played our famous Stone game (Cape Sixpence and Cornwall). But something is wrong.

### 31 WEDNESDAY

Long talk over house. Marie Foster said I could walk. Sea sounded like an island sea. Happy. Lovely fire in my bedroom. Succès éclatant avec demon[137] before dinner. Listened to Wingley's fiddle. The wooden bed.  [J190]

### 1920. 1 JAN. THURSDAY

Jack prepares to go. Drying figs on the stove, & white socks drying from the mantelpiece. A dish of oranges & rain-wet leaves, a pack of cards on the table. It rains but it is warm. The jonquil is in bud. We linger at the door. L.M. sings.

### 2 FRIDAY A.M.[138]

Jack left for London. The house very empty and quiet. I was ill all day – exhausted. In the afternoon fell asleep over my work & missed the post. My heart wont lie down. No post. Cashed cheque for 1,089 lire: Y. During the night the cat picture became terrifying.

### 3 SATURDAY

A load of wood. Sent review. Letters from Marie and Clara. Cold day. Miss K.S.[139] called – deadly dull. Her yawn and recovery. Storm of wind and rain. I had nightmare about Jack. He and I 'separated'. M.K.S. talked about tulips but she makes all sound so <u>fussy</u>, the threads of her soul all ravelled.

### 4 SUNDAY

Cold, wet, windy, terrible weather. Fought it all day. Horribly depressed. Dickinson[140] came to tea but it was no good. Worked. Two wires from J. According to promise. I cannot write. The jonquils are out, weak and pale. Black clouds pull over. Immediately the sun goes in I am overcome – again – the black fit takes over. I <u>hate</u> the <u>sea</u>. There is nought to do but WORK, but

---

[137]Demon Patience: a card game for one person.

[138]Aunt Martha: menstrual period.

[139]Miss Kaye-Shuttleworth. KM wrote about her on 23 November 1919 in a letter to Murry: 'I lay down again. The bell rang. A LADY, Miss Lionel Kaye-Shuttleworth, Villa Giovanni, San Remo, to call – a friend of Dent's aunt in Nice. Elderly, typical, good family, dowdy gentlewoman with exquisite greenish ermine scarf, diamond ear rings & white suede gloves. The combination suggested <u>arum lilies</u> to me somehow. I liked her very much. She knows a great deal about Italy, she was <u>gay</u>, <u>sociable</u>, full of life and <u>pleasant talk</u>, and she was a 'perfect lady'.' KM seems not to have known that this visitor was the daughter of Janet, Lady Kay-Shuttleworth, sister-in-law to John Addington Symonds, a writer who was of much interest to KM in her youth.

[140]Dickinson: an English acquaintance and occasional visitor in Ospedaletti.

how can I work when this awful weakness makes even the pen like a walking stick.

5 MONDAY

Henry IV. Nuit blanche. Decided at 3 a.m. that Dickin was a homicidal maniac. <u>Certain</u> of this. Started my story 'Late Spring.' A cold bitter day. Worked at Tchekhov all day and then at my story until 11 p.m. Anna came. We talked about her to her face in English. No letters. Post Office strike. Anna's bow & velvet blouse.

6 TUESDAY E.A.M.[141] <u>Black day</u>. Winter's Tale. Dark - no sky to be seen, a livid sea; a noise of boiling in the air. Dreamed the cats died of <u>anti-pneumonia</u>. Heart attack 8 a.m. Awful day. No relief for a moment. Couldn't work. At night changed the position of my bed but it was no good: I did not sleep. At five o'clock I thought I was at sea tossing - for ever. <u>N.B.</u>

7 WEDNESDAY

On the verandah. I don't want a God to praise or to entreat but to <u>share</u> my vision with. This afternoon looking at the primula after the rain. I want no-one to 'dance & wave their arms' I only want to <u>feel</u> they see too. But Jack won't. Sitting out there in the sun - where is my <u>mate</u>. <u>He</u> wants neither external life <u>nor</u> depression?!!!

8 THURSDAY

BLACK. Wrote to Jinnie.[142] A day spent in Hell. Unable to do anything. Took brandy - determined not to weep - wept. Sense of isolation frightful. I shall die if I don't escape. Nauseated, faint cold with misery. Oh I <u>must</u> survive it somehow.

9 FRIDAY

BLACK. Another of them. In the afternoon Foster[143] came and agreed that I must leave here. I somehow or other wrote a column. Broke my watch glass. In the evening L.M. and I were more nearly friendly than we have been for years. I couldn't rest or sleep. The roaring of the sea was insufferable. Posted to Jinnie.

10 SATURDAY

Father's marriage: news from Marie.[144] Spent the evening writing another column. Help me God! and then L.M. came in to say I was ½ an hour slow. Just did it in time. Had talk with L.M. our friendship is returning - in the old

---

[141] Probably 'Exit Aunt Martha'.

[142] Jinnie Fullerton, companion and colleague of KM's cousin, Connie Beauchamp. The two women lived in Menton and took KM under their wing when she 'escaped' from Ospedaletti to Menton.

[143] A local doctor.

[144] 'Marie' was the grown-up family name (as opposed to the childhood family name, 'Chaddie') of KM's older sister Charlotte Beauchamp, at this time a widow, Mrs Perkins.

fashion. Thought out The Exile.[145] Appalling night of misery deciding that
J. had no more need of our love.

11 SUNDAY N.B.
Worked from 9.30 a.m. to a quarter after midnight only stopping to eat.
Finished the story. Lay awake then till 5.30 too excited to sleep. In the sea
drowned souls sang all night. I thought of everything in my life and it all came
back so vividly – all is connected with this feeling that J. and I are no longer as
we were. I love him but he rejects my <u>living</u> love.[146] This is anguish. These are
the worst days of my whole life.

12 MONDAY
Last day I heard from Jack. Posted the story and a telegram. Very tired. The sea
howled and boomed and roared away. When will this cup pass from me?
Oh misery! I cannot sleep. I lie <u>retracing</u> my steps – going over all the old life
before .... The baby of Garnet's love.

13 TUESDAY
Bad day. A curious smoky effect over the coast. I crawled crept about the
garden in the afternoon. I feel terribly weak and all the time on the verge of
breaking down. Tried to work could not work. At six o'clock went back to
bed. Had a dreadful nightmare. Wrote Jack and Marie.

14 WEDNESDAY
Foster came. Says my lung is remarkably better but must rest absolutely for
2 months & not attempt to walk at all. I have got a 'bigger chance'. Bell rang
at night. My life pains me. <u>Cannot</u> get a move on. Dreamed about Banks.[147]
She gave me her baby to look after. Heard from Jinnie.

15 THURSDAY
Sat in my room watching the day change to evening; the fire like a golden
stag. <u>Thinking of the past</u> always dreaming it over. The cotton plant has turned
yellow. Tonight the sea is <u>douce</u>. P.O. strike. No, no letters.

16 FRIDAY
Wrote & sent reviews. Stayed in bed worked. Had a bath. The day was very
lovely. I had to work hard. In the evening began my new story A Strange
Mistake. P.O. strike for letters <u>and</u> telegrams. At night I could not sleep.
My life in London seems immeasurably far and all like a dream. L.M. talked
of herself as a child.

---

[145]Afterwards called 'The Man Without a Temperament'.
    [146]Murry's note: 'This word cannot be love. J.M.M.' But in *Journal* he has transcribed it as 'love',
which indeed it is.
    [147]Georges Banks, a woman artist, and her friend the sculptor Henri Gaudier-Brzeska, both
contributors to *Rhythm*, together physically attacked Murry in his office in 1913 because they thought,
wrongly, that he had cheated them.

17 SATURDAY

Postal strike no letters no wires. Tearing up and sorting the old letters.
The <u>feeling</u> that comes – the anguish – the words that fly out into one's breast
my <u>darling</u> my <u>wife</u>. Oh what anguish! Oh will it ever be the same! Lay awake
at night listening to the voices. Two men seemed to sing – a tenor and a
baritone. Then the drowned began. Love's Labours Lost.

18 SUNDAY

No letters strike still on. A fine day. But what is that to me. I am an <u>invalid</u>.
I spend my life in bed. Read Shakespeare in the morning. I feel I cannot bear
this silence today. I am <u>haunted</u> by thoughts of Jack perpetually. Dickinson's
flowers & dog. And then little Flock and dark- eyed Catherina!! All the flowers
& the two dogs. They seem to be running in and out among the daisies and
jonquils. Flock puts his paws on the bed "Oh that monkey" the sky & sea
behind him, and the chill, smoky air.

19 MONDAY

Alls Well that Ends Well. Comedy of Errors. No letters or papers. Vince[148] came
& Mrs V and Mr T. and Miss Sheila[?] in white. The trouble I've had with you
Mrs Murry & the expense it's put to me - more fuss than if you had died
there. The women against the flowers were so lovely - even Miss S. I had a
dreadful crying fit about 'noise & cleanliness'. It was horrible.

20 TUESDAY

Twelfth Night. Washed my hair. L.M. out nearly all day. Here alone on a
perfect day. I wandered in the garden & the flowers blew in the wind.
There was a ship white & solid on the water. Overcoat disappeared. The fire in
my room and the double light. All was exquisitely beautiful. 'Goodbye.' It now
believes we are going and it is safe.

21 WEDNESDAY[149]

Measure for Measure. A day like a dream. Vince's hair, stick, jacket, teeth, tie -
all to be remembered - to use a <u>volgarism</u> I'm fed up. The journey, the
flowers, & these women here. Jinnie's black satin neckcloth & pearl pin.
This exquisite cleanliness turns me into a cat. Dreamed of Jeanne, Marie and
Violet.

22 THURSDAY

Saw the doctor - a fool. Thinking of the Casetta left to itself - the little winds
blowing, the shutters shut, the cotton plant turning yellow. Heard from J. wire
& letter. Spent a day recovering. My heart tires me. The meals downstairs are a
fearful strain. But the people newly risen[?].

---

[148]Thomas Vince, the English agent for the Casetta Deerholm, the house KM was renting in
Ospedaletti.
[149]This was the day of KM's escape to Menton.

23 FRIDAY

Saw two of the doctors - an ass, and an ass. Spend the day at my windows.
It was very lovely & fair. But I was trying to work all day and could not get
down to it. In the night had appalling nightmare.

24 SATURDAY

Cousin Connie brought the tiny dog to see me - a ravishing animal. The same
despairing desire to work and could not work. I suppose I started reviewing T.
nine or ten times. Felt very tired as a result of this.

25 SUNDAY

A year has passed away ... and that's all.[150] Missed J. Connie & Jinnie came.
She is a really wonderful creature. Her gaze, her hands, her quietness.
Both have this quiet, restful air. L.M. came très embarrassée - I don't know
why. I grudge L.M. money - it's very dreadful. The meals here are a horror.
I seem to be sitting hours & hours there & the people are ugly. Nevertheless
thank God I <u>am</u> here, in sound of the train, in reach of the post.
Italian letters came today.

26 MONDAY

Posted Kay[151] two cheques. Felt ill with fatigue and cold & my lungs hurt.
It is because I am not working. All is a bit of a nightmare for that reason.
My temper is so bad! I feel I am horrid and can't stop it. It's a bad feeling.

27 TUESDAY

The woman who does the massage is not really any good. My life is queer
here. I like my big airy room but to <u>work</u> is so hard. At the back of my mind
I am so wretched. But all the while I am thinking over my philosophy -
the defeat of the personal. Received advice from Kay that my account is
HH.F.E.[152]

28 WEDNESDAY

I shall not remember what happened on this day. It is a blank. At the end of
my life I may want it, may long to have it. There was a new moon - that I
remember, but who came or what I did, all is lost. It's just a day missed, a day
crossing the line.[153]

29 THURSDAY

I have received an abominably selfish letter from Jack - telling me about
Sussex. It has hurt me so much. I wrote back, but won't post it. I feel it must
be a mistake. 'Drunken with the magnificence' 'pure sheer spring'.

---

[150]This sentence, squeezed in above the entry for the 25th, is in ink, and the 25 is underlined in ink,
whereas the rest of the diary is in pencil. It is obviously a comment made on 25 January 1921.

[151]Alexander Kay, Manager of the London Branch of the Bank of New Zealand.

[152]According to Murry HH.F.E. is a coded form of £88.6.5.

[153]KM had had experience of crossing the equatorial date-line while sailing from the Northern to the
Southern Hemisphere, and so 'losing a day'.

30 FRIDAY

No letter from him today – other letters came. I tried all day to work and feel dog tired. Perhaps it's the massage. Jinnie came to see me & brought me a present from her little dog.

31 SATURDAY

Changed my room for this other – I prefer it. It is more snug & there is only one bed. I sent the reviews off today & a letter to Jack. W.G.[154] sent a little[?]. Wrote to several people. Father.        [J191-196]

1 FEB. SUNDAY

No F. No G.[155]

A.M. My room is horrible. Very noisy. A constant clatter & a feeling as though one were <u>doorless</u>. French people don't care a hang how much noise they make. I hate them for it. Stayed in bed. Felt very ill but didn't mind because of the reason. The food was really appalling. Nothing to eat. At night <u>old Casetta</u> feelings. Like madness. Voices and words & half visions. No F  No M.

2 MONDAY

F only.

C & J came & the Times notice of my book.[156] Sent to the bank. J. brought me more flowers. <u>Saw the lovely palm</u>. Work will win if only I can stick to it. It will win after all & through all.

3 TUESDAY

F only no gouter. No letter from John today. Went for a little walk in the garden & saw all the pale violets. The beauty of palm trees. To fall in love with a tree. Heard the ladies in the Harem talking. Japonica is a lovely flower, but people never grow enough of it.

4 WEDNESDAY

Paid bill. Gouter F. & M. A letter card obscure and later a telegram & another card obscure. Horrible day. I lay all day & <u>half</u> slept in this new way, hearing voices, drifting off. Heard from Ottoline. The attendance here is really abominable. Wrote to Jack about the G. Pension.[157] No good.

5 THURSDAY

M. No F. Sent wire. Letter re Constable. Replied. Went for a drive. All way gay. The house & the girl. Couldn't work – slept again – dreadful pain in joints.

---

[154]Murry suggests this might be *The Westminster Gazette.*

[155]Murry's note: 'No F = no Friction. No G = no Goûter.' At the end of this entry KM wrote 'No M' after which Murry has put a question mark. Presumably friction and massage were not the same thing—the former being a matter of rubbing down with towels. Goûter was a snack between meals: morning or afternoon tea.

[156]*Bliss.*

[157]*In A German Pension* was KM's first book, published in 1911. In her letter to Murry, referred to here, she wrote 'I cannot have the German Pension republished under any circumstances. It is far too <u>immature</u> & I don't even acknowledge it today. I mean I don't 'hold' by it. I can't go foisting that kind of stuff on the public – <u>its not good enough</u>.'

Jack talks of insurance & ideas far from reality. Fearfully <u>noisy</u> house! Saw an orange tree, an exquisite shape against the sky. When the fruit is ripe the leaves are pale yellow.

### 6 FRIDAY

Received Lawrence's[158] last letter & reply from J. Determined to review 2 books today and to get on with Second Helping. Saw the <u>fool</u> of a doctor today, diddle-dum dum de! <u>Cod</u> is the only word! Badin-ag-e! Flat-ter-ie! Gallan-ter-ie! Frogs!!! Vous pouvez vous promenez. <u>Liar</u>. The palm tree. Did not finish review but no matter, it goes.

### 7 SATURDAY

Exit A.M. 2.55 laundry. Wrote & sent reviews. House in a perfect uproar. Dreadfully nervous. Dressmaker came & her little apprentice who gave me the flowers. Had a bath – but all was in a tearing hurry & clatter. Had a strange dream. "She is one with the moonlight." Georges Sand – ma soeur.

### 8 SUNDAY

To Villa Flora. In the garden with the unhappy woman lying on the hard bench. Seeing them all at tea in their beauty. The spanish brocade cloth, the piece of heliotrope. Jinnie's plan that I shall go and live there. Came back & wrote it all to Jack in delight. Then a nuit blanche, dreadful nightmare. I think I should like to join the Roman Catholic Church. I must have something!

### 9 MONDAY

Hell. Letter from Jack. It was too much. I wept all the morning. In the afternoon sitting in the sun – alas alas! The sun is so warm – like summer. All's over then. My dream was right.     [J197-199]

### 11 WEDNESDAY

Mrs Dunn[159] came in the afternoon & squeezed up on the chair or crouched on the floor.

### 12 THURSDAY

A lie is the unjust denial of the truth. She stood here. Yes, <u>64</u> dear, sat & raised her hands. Can I help her? I want to. Here is a woman whom I would <u>love</u> to make just a little happy – a great woman.

### 13 FRIDAY

Dressmaker 11 a.m.

### 4 APRIL SUNDAY

Easter eggs in the folded napkins. A Happy Easter. I am given the Mass for the day to read. We drink to absent friends, but carelessly – not knowing whether to bow or no.

---

[158] The novelist D H Lawrence (1885–1930) with whom KM had a deep and difficult relationship.
[159] Mrs Bunnie Dunn, an American friend of KM's cousin Connie Beauchamp, living in Menton.

9 FRIDAY

Schiffs[160] are coming to tea. Cold and windy. Out of the window the writhing palms - the dust - the woman with a black veil. Mrs D. knowing nothing of England "I'm an Imperialist." Jinnie in bed "I like to be fair." Connie lies on the couch and reads. I feel I must live alone alone alone - with <u>artists</u> only to come to the door. Every artist cuts off his ear & nails it on the outside of the door for the others to shout into.

11 SUNDAY

I never can remember what happens. It is so without outline. 'Yesterday' pales into the general shade. But all the same one looks back & there are wonders. There is always Miss Helen stretching her hands out to the great defiant bouquet, crying with a kind of groan Oh - the <u>darlings</u>. She flushed. That remains for ever. And then one must never forget the dog which gets all the love of children. Going nice ta-tas with Missie, my ducksie pet!

12 MONDAY

Went to the fish museum at Monaco. Must remember the bubbles as the man plunged the rod into the tanks. The young girl. How naice! Young girls make me feel <u>40</u>. Well one certainly doesn't want to look 21. The woman with her three little children at Monte ...      [J204]

13 FRIDAY

Send passports to Genoa.

12 JULY MONDAY

4 p.m. injection at Harley Street.      [J206]

why ink in an actresses hand? Most unlikely.[161]
pass quite unregarded.
your book isn't re-al poetry.
There was no need for you to trouble ...
We know you so well by reputation ...
Young precisians  older hands
Once again so pleased about Boston
Agreeing on the subject of Miss Bison.
Niagara in a barrel.  Too sudden.
Once a month - too definite.
The letter.  He had read it <u>much</u> later  -  -  -
It fascinated him to read it over  -  -  -
A flush forced[?] high on her cheek
<u>Glenshwa[?] blushed</u>
I should hate to die ugly.
He would go in and asking for a cup of tea
He had an impulse to put his hand on the gate.  But would he have?  Why not?

---

[160]Sydney and Violet Schiff were living at Roquebrune, near Menton. He was the novelist Stephen Hudson.

[161] Murry's note: 'I don't understand the references here. ?Notes on a novel she was reviewing.'

1 choux fleur
un morceau de veau
4 eggs
1 kilo de pommes de terres.

After the talk with Dunning[162] there <u>is</u> a change.
He woke and still with his eyes closed he turned & kissed her shoulder.
That's a good beginning?
I believe that D. has the secret of my recovery and of J's awakening. All that he spoke of yesterday ... the terms were strange, but what he <u>said</u> was what she had known for a long time. He made the Casetta story plainer: I saw how it could be made to 'fit'.

But this short sketch by[163] Boulestin must be extremely simple and yet decisive ... It must not be in even the slightest degree 'thin'. If I can include the glittering sheep, the pond, the[164]      [J211 S143-144]

At the Queens Hotel. The last Thursday. I am very tired.

One must write a story about a doctor's waiting room. The glass doors with the sun from outside shining through, the autumn trees pale and fine, the cyclamen - like wax. Now a cart shakes by.

Think of the strange places that illness carries me into, the strange people one passes from hand to hand, the succession of black coated gentlemen, the men to whom she'd whispered 99, 44, 1-2-3, the servants she'd smiled at. The last waiting room, all before had been so cheerful.
Then you don't think my case is hopeless?
The disease is of long standing but certainly <u>not</u> hopeless.
This one, however, leaned back & said You really want to know?
Yes of course. Oh you can be quite frank with me.
Then I <u>DO</u>!
The carriage came & drove her away, her head buried in her collar.      [J242-243]

<A fortnight before send passports to Genoa with letter from S. and 11/- postal order. On their return four days before go to Vintimille with photographs for the French visa probably 10 francs to pay. Proceed to San Remo with permis de sejour for the police visa. Take 12 o'clock train from here to Vintimille. Lesley to Vintimille for tickets in early March. Ask at Banca di Sconti[?] if she can buy french money.>

---

[162] Miller Dunning, an English mystic interested in yoga, lived in Ditchling, Sussex, where Murry joined him (living next door) when KM entered the Institute at Fontainebleau in 1922.
[163] ie 'for'.
[164] Murry's note: 'The sketch which Katherine then had in mind for M. Boulestin's <u>Keepsake</u> apparently developed into *At The Bay*. It was not published in *The Keepsake*, to which she sent *The Black Cap* instead.'

Hotel Belle Vue William Eliot of Auckland & Syd. Phillips.

'Tis a morning to tempt Jove from his ningle
'magnificoes'[?]
The inaudible and noiseless force of Time.
The word which haunts me is <u>egocentric</u>.         [J212 S145]

Travelling.
Toilet paper & hand towels. Zotos.[165] Soap.
Cold chicken, wine <u>like</u> marsala, coffee.

In.   201.4.6
In.   170.10.6
P.i. today       22.14.0
                 8. 0.0

| Date | | Received | Paid |
|---|---|---|---|
| Jan 1st | Cheque from H.K. | 2. 2. 0 | |
| Jan 2nd | Drew for Housekeeping | 22. 0. 0 | |
| Jan 4th | Cheque from Kot | 1. 10. 0 | 25 |
| | allowance | 25. 0. 0 | |
| Jan 23rd | Cheque from A. | 11. 10. 0 | |
| | Cheque for books | 1. 0. 0 | |
| | | 41. 2. 0 | 47. 0. 0 |

inquire re A. cheque which is entered as 10.11.6 by the Bank & entered by me
as 11. 0. 0.

| | In hand | 100. 16. 5. | |
|---|---|---|---|
| | allowance paid in | 25. 0. 0 | |
| | Jack paid in | 10. 0. 0 | |
| | 3rd Living[?] exes | 25. 0. 0 | |
| 20th | Ida gave me | 20. 0. 0 | 10. 0. 0 |
| Jack | paid in | 10. 0. 0 | |
| 2nd | Athenaeum cheque | 11. 2. 0 | |
| | Koteliansky | 1. 7. 6 | |
| 25th | | | 10. 0. 0 |
| | | 178. 5.11 | 45. 0. 0 |
| | | 45. 0. 0 | |
| | | 133. 5.11 | |
| | In hand | 133. 5.11 | |
| 1st | allowance paid in | 25. 0. 0 | 25. 0. 0 |
| 2nd | Self | 10. 0. 0 | 20. 0. 0 |
| | Jack | 11. 9. 6 | 10. 0. 0 |

---

[165]Zotos contained chlorbutol which was used as a mild sedative and local analgesic, as well as for
motion sickness.

|        |            |           |           |
|--------|------------|-----------|-----------|
|        | Athenaeum  | ————————— |           |
| 24th   | Self       | 179. 11. 6 | 55. 0. 0 |
|        |            | 55. 0. 0  |           |
|        |            | —————     |           |
|        |            | 124. 11. 6 |          |
|        |            | 79        |           |
|        |            | 95        |           |
|        | eau        | 72        |           |
|        | Marie      | 3. 50.    |           |
|        |            | 5. 01     |           |
|        |            | —————     |           |
|        |            | 95        |           |
| April  |            |           |           |
|        | In hand    | 124. 11. 6 | 25. 0. 0 |
| 1st    | a. paid in | 25. 0. 0  | 10. 0. 0 |
|        | Kot. cheque| 1. 4. 9   | 15. 0. 0 |
|        | drew out   | 5. 0. 0   |          |
| 12th   | Constable  | 40. 0. 0  | 5. 0. 0  |
|        | Ath.       | 3. 0. 6   | 5. 0. 0  |
|        | G & S      | 2. 5. 0   | 4. 10. 0 |
|        |            | —————     | ————     |
|        |            | 196. 2. 1 | 68. 10. 0 |
|        |            | 68. 10. 0 |          |
|        |            | —————     |          |
|        |            | 127. 12. 1 |          |

| Paid in | In hand    |
|---------|------------|
| 25. 0.0 |            |
| 8.0     | 150. 19. 2 |
| 2. 5.0  | 5. 0. 0    |
| 3. 0.6  | 11. 10. 0  |
| 7. 7.0  |            |

Must buy a decent account book.

Oh Bogey I can't help laughing at the hymns & prayers at your lecture! Did YOU sing? I feel you were (I'd truly swear to it) specially mentioned in a prayer. Did you kneel down? And all those rubber tikis showed on your shoes. Oh <u>dear</u> me. Did you have a hymn book of your own or ½ the parson's? Signes cabalistiques. I often used to [think] what a horror they would have given Crusoe.[166]    [J251 S176-177]

The little heads were like pink fondants in a gilt lined chocolate box.[167] Its something I know. I <u>must</u> have heard it. Her head was wound with old purple grapes.

———————

[166]Murry's note: 'I had given Katherine an account of a lecture at which, to my surprise and embarrassment, prayers were offered and hymns sung. The rubber <u>tikis</u> refer to the bold designs on the rubber soles of my shoes.'

[167]Murry's heading in *Journal* for the following notes is 'At Mary Rose' ie at a performance of James Barrie's play *Mary Rose*.

The introductory music raking the hard soil of ones heart & preparing it for fairy seed. The voices of the singers were like celestial <u>gargling</u>.
Scene I. Housekeeper in the worst tradition. The Australian soldier - <u>rattles</u> on the stairs. His whole manner- & the loud voices. They should have been all vague & remote. The light should have been dim. (He's very complicated Barrie but charming oh so charming!) Modern - quite modern. The same author married 16, married twice. Boy about 8 V G handsome - awfully sweet beautiful woman. Robert Loraine - splendid - terrible Fantasy - delightful.
I like New York better its more noisy London so quiet I like plenty of Life.

[J212-213]

Act I Scene I. The clergyman is a little fantastic - the other man overacts.
<u>We'll be good won't we.</u>
Fantastic.
The scene on the island is <u>terrific</u>. It is a terrible idea.
And as soon as it was over the tea the maid of the mountains - quick quick quick - & the heads The old heads & the young heads. 'How he ever thought of it is beyond me.'

£50 for something worth about 2d. I bought things for £1000 - about 2d for 10d.

But they don't progress do they. They don't go out into the world. Is that good for a country. Oh a lovely life I should love my husband to be a farmer!

But the natives are nice aren't they when they are young.
First it was the linnet & then the sea.      [J213 S145-146]

Trench no. 30. The day of the attack. I got the orders by phone & scrambled off with them to my officer - putting a 2 franc piece down my collar, inside my shirt for luck. We all set [off] together. I knew it was all up with me. So did another. Our number was up. The feeling of <u>waste</u>. My hand on the hilt of a revolver. You can always turn it on yourself. Some people <u>are</u> really. The man who keeps improving his charwoman is 30 francs to the good. It's always the nearest man who's killed. I chose a safer position.
If I could get back the little grave should have what he wanted ... But I shan't get back. They suggest a slight wound - but not for me.      [J213-214 S146]

Act I. Scene II. King Richard III.
Vouchsafe to wear this ring.
To take is not to give.

I don't want you to be other than yourself.
But if I am myself I won't do what you ask me to do... I feel it's forcing me. It's not <u>me</u>; it's not my <u>geste</u>. They looked at each other & for some reason they smiled - actually <u>smiled</u>.
I really & truly don't <u>know</u> what I want to do. Life isn't so simple as all that, you know ...
And the music went on, gay, soothing, reassuring. All will be well, said the music. Life is so easy - - so easy - why suffer ...

He shivered faintly & held up a paw – but he seemed to smile …
But if you knew. I am looking out of a <u>dark dark net</u>. It is only accident that it's I sitting beside him. This is the music where the elephants come in & drink out of bottles. The clown comes in & takes the bottles away & drinks himself.

[J227]

Smith Allabon House, Highway Cres. [?]

J. Lewin Payne, 18 Portland Place.

# *Unbound Papers*

[MS Papers 4006-7]

A Dream. November 1st.[168]

Walking up a dark hill with high iron fences at the sides of the road and immense trees over. I was looking for a midwife, Mrs Nightingale. A little girl, barefoot, with a handkerchief over her head pattered up and put her chill hand in mine; she would lead me. A light showed from a general shop. Inside a beautiful, fair, angry young woman directed me up the hill & to the right. "You should have believed <u>me</u>" said the child and dug her nails into my palm.

There reared up a huge wall with a blank notice plastered on it. That was the house. In a low room sitting by a table a dirty yellow and black rug over her knees an old hag sat. She had a grey handkerchief on her head. Beside her on the table there was a jar of onions and a fork. I explained. She was to come to Mother. Mother was very delicate: her eldest daughter was 31 and she had heart disease: so please come up at once! "Has she any adhesions?" muttered the old hag & she speared an onion, ate it & rubbed her nose. "Oh yes", I put my hand on my breast, "many many plural[sic] adhesions." "Ah that's bad that's very bad" said the crone, bunching up the rug so that through the fringe I saw her square slippers. "But I can't come. I've a case at four o'clock." At that moment a healthy, bonny young woman came in with a bundle. She sat down by the midwife & explained "Jinnie has had hers already." She unwound the bundle too quickly - a new born baby with round eyes fell forward on her lap. I felt the pleasure of the little girl beside me - a kind of quiver. The young woman blushed and lowered her voice. "I got her to ..." and here she paused to find a very <u>medical private</u> word to describe washing: "to <u>navigate</u> with a bottle of English water," she said "but it isn't all away yet."

Mrs Nightingale told me to go to her friend, Madame Léger, who lived on the terrace with a pink light before her house. I went. The terrace of houses [was] white & grey blue in the moonlight with dark pines down the

---

[168] 1919 is Murry's suggested date.

road. I saw the exquisite pink light, but just then a clanking sound behind me
& there was the little girl, bursting with breathlessness, hugging in her arms
a huge black bag. "Mrs Nightingale says you forgot this."

　　So I was the midwife. I walked on thinking: I'll go and have a look at the
poor little soul but it won't be for a long time yet.　　　[j180-181]

[MS-Papers-4006-11]

The courier was so late. She rang and asked the eternal déja passé & heard the
eternal 'pas encore Madame.' At last Armand appeared with a letter from him
& the papers. The letter. She read - she read to "don't give me up entirely".
When she read those words it happened <u>again</u> - again there seemed to be
a dreadful loud shaking & trembling, her heart leaped, she sank down in the
bed. She began to weep and could not stop. What was he made of - to talk of
them giving each other up. The cruel - the ghastly ice-cold cruelty. Never say
again you have imagination - never say you have the capacity to love and that
you know pity. You have said things to me that have wounded me for ever.
I must go on but I'm wounded for ever by you.

　　The first bell rang. She got up. She began to dress, crying & cold.
The second bell. She sat down & steeled herself - her throat ached, ached.
She powdered herself thickly & went downstairs. In the ascenseur: Armand
cherchez-moi une voiture pour deux heures juste. And then 1 hour and a
quarter in the brilliant glaring noisy salle, sipping wine to stop crying & seeing
all the animals crack up the food. The waitress kept jerking her chair offering
food. It was no good. She left & went upstairs but that was fatal. Have I
a home? A little cat? Am I any man's <u>wife</u>? Is it all over? He never tells me
a thing - never a thing - just all those entirely self-absorbed letters and now
just these notes. What will come next? He <u>asks</u> if I believe he loves me & says
"don't give me up" but as though <u>perfectly prepared</u> for it. She wrote out the
telegram. He is killing me, killing me. He wants to be free - that's all.

　　She dressed & went downstairs into the horrible hall because there with
the monde drinking coffee & cigarettes she dare not cry. A little brougham
drove up with an old dragging man. She got in. A la poste. Oh these little
broughams, what I have gone through in them - the blue buttoned interior
the blue cords & ivory tassels, all, all. She leaned back & lifted her veil & dried
her tears. But it was no use. The post office was full. She had to wait in a
queue for the telegrams among horrible men who shouted over her shoulder -
horrible men. And now - where? A dose of sal volatile at the chemist. While
he made it up she walked quickly up & down the shop twisting her hands.
There was a box of Kolynos. It said Jack. Jack in her room, talking about the
foam, saying he'd leave his. Four francs seventy-five.

　　She bought and drank the mixture, & now - where. She got into the cab,
the old man hung at the door. She couldn't speak. Suddenly down the road on
the opposite, looking very grave, came Jinnie. She crossed over & taking her
hand said "Deo gratias." And then was silent a moment. Then she said
suddenly "Come along & see Rendall now. Let's fix it now this moment."

They waited in a very quiet room <u>rich</u> with books and old dark coloured prints & dark highly polished furniture. Jinnie went out for a preliminary talk & then came back for her and they entered the doctor's room. He was short, dry, with a clipped beard & fine shrewd eyes. A fire burned, there were books everywhere - German books too, reminding her of Croft Hill.[169] Jinnie stayed while the long familiar careful examination went on again. The doctor took infinite pains. When he had done she dressed & Jinnie said "Doctor its the desire of my life to cure this - little friend of mine. You must let me have her - you must let me do it." And after a pause which the other thought final he said "I think it would be ideal for her to be with you. She ought not to have to suffer noise and the constant sight of repellent people. She is highly sensitive & her disease - of such long standing - has increased it a thousandfold." He was quiet, grave, gentle. Oh, if they could have known or seen my heart that had been stabbed & stabbed. But she managed to smile & thank the doctor & then Jinnie put her back into the brougham & it was arranged she would leave in a week.

All that afternoon she had been seeing wallflowers. Let me never have a sprig of wallflowers if ever I have a garden. Oh anguish of Life! Oh bitter bitter life! He just threw her away - well "don't give me up entirely." That reminded her of wallflowers & Shakespeare. Yes how in a Winters Tale Perdita refused gillyflowers in her garden. "They call them nature's bastards." She came back into her room & lay down. it was like Bavaria again - but worse worse - & now she could not take a drug - or anything. She must just <u>bear it and go on</u>.     [J199-201]

[MS-Papers-4006-8]

I should like this to be accepted as my confession.

<u>Suffering</u>.
There is no limit to human suffering. When one thinks: "now I have touched the bottom of the sea, now I can go no deeper" - one goes deeper. And so it is for ever. I thought last year in Italy any shadow more would be Death, but this year has been so much more terrible that I think with affection of the Casetta! Suffering is boundless - it is eternity. One pang is eternal torment. Physical suffering is - child's play. To have one's breast crushed by a great stone - one could laugh!

I do not want to die without leaving a record of my belief that suffering can be overcome. For I do believe it. What must one do? There is no question of what Jack calls passing beyond it: this is false. One must <u>submit</u>. Do not resist. Take it. Be overwhelmed. Accept it fully - make it <u>part of Life</u>. Everything in Life that we really accept undergoes a change. So suffering must become Love. This is the mystery. This is what I must do. I must pass from personal love which has failed me to greater love. I must give to the whole of

---

[169]Murry's note: 'Dr Croft Hill had been our doctor in London, much admired by us both.'

Life what I gave to him. This present agony will pass - if it doesn't kill. It won't last. Now I am like a man who has had his heart torn out - but - bear it - bear it. As in the physical world so in the spiritual world - pain does not last for ever. It is only so terribly acute now. It is as though a ghastly accident had happened. If I can cease reliving all the shock and horror of it, cease going over it, I will get stronger. Here, for a strange reason, there rises the figure of Doctor Sorapure. He was a good man. He helped me not only to bear pain but he suggested that perhaps bodily ill health is necessary, is a repairing process - and he was always telling me to consider how man plays but a part in the history of the world. My simple kindly doctor was pure of heart as Tchekhov is pure of heart. But for these ills one is one's own doctor. If 'suffering' is not a repairing process I will make it so. I will learn the lesson it teaches. These are not idle words. These are not the consolations of the sick.

Life is a mystery. The fearful pain of these letters - of the knowledge that Jack wishes me dead - and of his killing me - will fade. I must turn to <u>work</u>. I must put my agony into something - change it - 'sorrow shall be changed into Joy.'

It is to lose oneself more utterly - to love more deeply - to feel oneself part of Life - not separate. Oh Life! accept me - make me worthy - teach me -

I write that. I look up. The leaves move in the garden, the sky is pale, I catch myself weeping. It is hard - it is hard to make a good death! And the horrible vulgar letters of this woman about "John's fou rire" and so on, and his <u>cruel</u> insulting letter about "no <u>physical attraction</u>" (!!) "I think she is in love with me" and so on - were they necessary? He now claims his right not to suffer on my account any more. Oh God! How <u>base</u> in its selfishness.

But <u>no no</u>. I must not blame him any more and I must not go back. Thus was it. Let it be. To live - to live - that is all - and to leave Life on this earth as Tchekhov left Life and Tolstoi.

After a dreadful operation I remember that when I thought of the pain of having stitches out I used to cry. Every time I felt it again & winced & it was unbearable. That is what one must control. Queer! The two people left are Tchekhov - dead - and unheeding indifferent Doctor Sorapure. They are the two good men I have known.

Katherine Mansfield
19.XII.1920.     [J228-229]

[MS-Papers-4006-8]

Mon pauv' mari rolled over and said "Tu as peur. Que tu est bete. Ce sont des rats. Dors encore." I thought after she'd told me these words kept rippling & rippling through my mind. Something had disturbed the long silent forgotten surface. How many of his words were remembered. Did anybody ever quote the living words he'd spoken? Tu as peur - que tu est bête. Words spoken at night in the dark - strangely intimate, reassuring. He turned over & lifted himself in his grave as Marie spoke. Mournful, mournful - - -

What about a cauliflower, I said. A cauliflower with white sauce. But they are so dear Madame, wailed Marie, so dear - one little cauliflower for

2.50. Its robbery - its - Suddenly through the kitchen window I saw the moon. It was so marvellously beautiful that I walked out of the kitchen door through the garden & leaned over the gate before I knew what I was doing. The cold bars of the gate stopped me. The moon was full, transparent, glittering. It hung over the sighing sea. I looked at it for a long time. Then I turned round & the little house faced me - a little white house quivering with light, a house like a candle shining behind a feather of mimosa tree. I had utterly forgotten these things when I was ordering the dinner. I went back to the kitchen. Let us have the cauliflower at any price, I said firmly. And Marie muttered, bending over a pot (<u>could</u> she have understood), en effet, les times are dangerous!   [J219-220]

Does nobody want that piece of bread & butter says L.M. You really think from her tone that she was saving the poor little darling from the river or worse, willing to adopt it as her own child & bring it up so that it never should know that it was once unwanted. She cannot bear to see solitary or little pieces of bread & butter or a lonely little cake or even a lump of sugar that someone has cruelly, heartlessly left in his saucer. And when you offer her the big cake she says resignedly - Oh well my dear I'll just try a slice - as though she knows how sensitive & easily hurt the poor old chap's feelings are, if it's passed by. After all it can't hurt her.

   L.M. is also exceedingly fond of bananas. But she eats them so slowly, so terribly slowly. And they know it somehow: they realise what is in store for them when she reaches out her hand. I have seen bananas turn absolutely livid with terror on her plate - or pale as ashes.   [J220]

[MS-Papers-4006-11]

… particularly large olive or standing whistling for a taxi like a forlorn rooster piping before break of day - - or that, although you did talk so amazingly about Stendhal your hat was too small. Enfin, you are ridiculous in some way and I am hurt I am hurt." I have not said a bit what I mean to say - it's so difficult to explain - I've only hinted - - <u>Do</u> you ever feel like that about the world? Of course this sensitiveness has its reverse side, but that, for some extraordinary reason has never anything to do with present people but is nearly always connected with "things". Today, for instance, in my search for a lovely coloured rug, very bright and silky to touch, with perhaps a pattern of wild fruit trees growing on the borders of a lake and gay coloured beasts standing on the brink - - for not more than fifteen shillings at the outside - I found myself in a carpet shop.   [s27–28]

[MS-Papers-4006-8]

When autograph albums were the fashion - sumptuous volumes bound in soft leather, the pages so delicately tinted that each tender sentiment had its own sunset sky to faint, to die upon - the popularity of that most sly, ambiguous, difficult piece of advice: "To thine own self be true" was the despair of collectors. How dull it was, how boring, to have the same thing written six times over. And then, even if it was Shakespeare that didn't prevent it – oh, l'age d'innocence! – from being dreadfully obvious! Of course it followed as the night the day that if one was true to oneself . . . True to oneself! Which self? Which of my many – well, really, thats what it looks like coming to – hundreds of selves. For what with complexes and suppressions, and reactions and vibrations and reflections – there are moments when I feel I am nothing but the small clerk of some hotel without a proprietor who has all his work cut out to enter the names and hand the keys to the wilful guests.

Nevertheless, there are signs that we are intent as never before on trying to puzzle out, to live by, our own particular self. Der mensch muss frei sein – free, disentangled, single. Is it not possible that the rage for confession, autobiography, especially for memories of earliest childhood is explained by our persistent yet mysterious belief in a self which is continuous and permanent, which, untouched by all we acquire and all we shed, pushes a green spear through the leaves and through the mould, thrusts a sealed bud through years of darkness until, one day, the light discovers it and shakes the flower free and – we are alive – we are flowering for our moment upon the earth. This is the moment which, after all, we live for, the moment of direct feeling when we are most ourselves and least personal.   [J205 S136-137]

# Notebook 38

[Notebook 38, qMS-1266]

Second Helping
by
Katherine Mansfield[170]


There is No Answer[171]
by
Katherine Mansfield


Certainly it was cold, very cold. When she opened her lips & drew in a breath she could taste the cold air on her tongue, like a piece of ice. But though she shivered so and held her muff tightly pressed against her to stop the strange uneasy trembling in her stomach she was glad of the cold. It made her feel, in those first strange moments, less strange and less alone; it allowed her to pretend in those first really rather terrifying moments that she was a tiny part of the life of the town, that she could, as it were, join in the game without all the other children stopping to stare and to point at the entirely new little girl. True, there had been two seconds when she was a forlorn little creature, conspicuous and self-conscious, stuffing her luggage ticket into her glove and wondering where to go next, but then, from nowhere, she was pelted with that incredible snowball of cold air, and she started walking away from the station, quickly, quickly ...

In all probability those simple people passing, so stout and red, those large, cheerful bundles with a friendly eye for her, imagined that she was some young wife and mother who had arrived home unexpectedly because she could not bear to be away another moment. And while she walked down the station hill, quickly, quickly she smiled. She saw herself mounting a flight of shallow, waxed stairs, pulling an oldfashioned red velvet bell cord, putting her

---

[170] This title and author are written on the front cover.

[171] This 17 page piece did not belong originally with this notebook. It has been inserted inside the front cover of it and is probably not contemporary with the rest of the notebook. It may even be one of the 'Geneva' fragments from 1917.

finger to her lips when the ancient family servant (her old nurse, of course) would have cried the house about her, and rustling into the breakfast room where her husband sat drinking coffee and her little son stood in front of him with his hands behind his back, reciting something in french. But now her husband grew long ears and immense boney knuckles, and now she was Anna, kneeling on the floor and raising her veil the better to embrace and clasp her darling Serozha.

Which was all very well, but what a time and place to choose for this nonsensical dreaming! She had better find a café where she could have breakfast and devour the hotel list with her coffee. By now she was right 'in the town' and walking down a narrow street full of half open shops.
She bought a newspaper from an old hag squatting beside a kiosk, her skirt turned back over her knees, munching a mash of bread and soup, and was just going into a discreet 'suitable-looking' café when she saw a lovely flower stall. The flower seller knelt on the pavement surrounded by a litter of flat yellow baskets. She took out and shook, and held up to the critical light bunch after bunch of round, bright flowers. Jonquils and anemones, roses and marigolds, plumes of mimosa, lilies-of-the-valley in a bed of wool, stocks, a strange pink like the eyes of white rabbits, and purple and white violets that one longed not only to smell but to press against ones lips and almost to eat. Oh! how she loved flowers! What a passion she had for them and how much they meant to her. Yes, they meant almost everything.

And while she watched the woman arrange her wares in tin cups and glasses and round china jars she was strangely conscious of the early morning life of this foreign town. She heard it, she felt it flowing about her as though she and the flowers stood together on an island in the middle of a quick flowing river - but the flowers were more real. And the crowning joy and wonder [was] that she was perfectly free to look at them, to 'take them in' for just as long as she liked ... For the first time she drank a long heady draught of this new wine, freedom. There was no-one at her elbow to say: "But my dear, this is not the moment to rave about flowers", no-one to tell her that hotel bedrooms were more important than marigolds, not a soul who simply by standing there could make her realise that she was in all probability in an abnormal, hysterical state through not having slept all night. So, she drank the cup to the sweet dregs and bought an armful of mixed beauties and carried them into the café with her.

They were heaped on the table beside her and their scent mingled with the delicious smell of the coffee, and the cigarette she smoked was too sweet, too exciting to bear. She almost felt that the flowers, in some fairy fashion, changed into wreaths and garlands and lay on her lifting bosom and pressed on her brow until she bent her head, gazing with half shut eyes at the white ring of the cup & the white ring of the saucer, the round, white shape of the pot and jug & the four crossed pieces of sugar on a white dish on the bluey white marble table, at the cigarettes, spilled out of a yellow wrapper and her little hands, folded together so mysteriously, as though they held a butterfly.

"Daisy! Daisy! giv me your onze heures, do!"
sang someone. She looked up. A young man in a light tweed cap stood against the counter, playing with a black kitten. Except for the flat-footed old waiter who shuffled among the tables at the far end like a forlorn aged crab, she and the young man were quite alone in the café. The kitten was very tiny; it could not even walk yet. It knew all about what to do with the front half of itself but its two little back legs were the trouble. They wanted to jump along, or to bound along in a kind of minute absurd galop. How very confusing it was! But the young man leaning over the counter and singing 'Daisy, Daisy' hadn't a grain of pity in him. He threw the kitten over, rolled it into a ball, tickled it, held it up by its front paws and made it dance, let it almost escape and then pounced on it again and made it bite its own tail.

"Give me your onze heures do!"
he sang, in his swaggering, over-emphasised fashion. She decided he knew perfectly well that someone was watching and listening ... But how wonderfully "at home" he looks, she thought. How lazily, how lightly he leans and stretches, as though it were impossible for anything to upset his easy balance, and as though if he chose, he could play with life just like he played with the kitten, tumble it over, tickle it, stand it on its hind legs and make it dance for him.

Quite suddenly the young man threw the kitten away, caught up his glass of dark purplish coffee, and facing her he began to sip and stare. Cool, cool beyond measure, he took his time, narrowed his eyes, crossed his feet and had a good, good look at her. Well - why not? She took another cigarette, tapped it on the table and lighted it, but for all her manner a malignant little voice in her brain warned her: "Keep calm!" She felt his eyes travel over her big bunch of flowers, over her muff and gloves and handbag, until they rested finally upon her, where she sat with her purple veil thrown back and her travelling cape with the fur collar dropping off her shoulders. Her heart beat up hot and hard; she pressed her knees together like a frightened girl and the malignant little voice mocked: "If you were perfectly certain that he was admiring you you would not mind at all. <u>On the contrary</u>."

Then just as suddenly as he had turned he wheeled round again and stood with his back towards her. Again he began to sing:

"Daisy, Daisy, giv me your onze heures do."
Was it just her fancy or did she really detect in his shoulders and in his twanging voice real, laughing contempt. Wasn't he singing again just to show her that he had looked and seen quite enough, 'thank you'. But what did he matter - an insolent underbred boy! What on earth had she to do with him! She tapped with her spoon for the waiter, paid, gathered up her flowers, her muff, her bag, and keeping her eyes fixed on the café door as though she was not perfectly certain whether it was the door or not, she walked out into the street.

It had positively grown colder while she was in that café. The sun was hidden for a moment behind a wing of cloud and the clatter and rattle of the

morning traffic pouring over the cobbles sounded so loud and harsh that it
bruised her nerves. How tired she was – very tired! She must find a room and
escape from this street immediately. It was ridiculous to walk about like this
after a racking night in the train. She longed to take off her tired clothes, and
to lie in a hot bath smelling of carnation crystals. At the thought of gliding
between incredibly smooth gleaming sheets she gave a nervous shiver of
delight.

"But what has happened to your blissful happiness of half an hour ago?"
mocked the tiny voice. No, no, she wouldn't listen! ... If only she could get
rid of this absurd bunch of flowers. They made her look ridiculous, feel
ridiculous, feel like a gushing schoolgirl returned from a school picnic.
What would the hotel people think when she arrived without any luggage but
'simply' carrying flowers. "Very touching! Dear me – really!" she stormed;
"you might have waited!" If only she could find some place to throw them
away! "Do not throw us away!" pleaded the flowers. No, she couldn't be so
cruel. But how she hated them! And she hid them under her cape, like a lady
in a melodrama trying to hide a baby, she thought, as she pushed through the
swing doors of an hotel.

II

Late afternoon. She woke, she opened her eyes but did not move – did not
move a finger. She lay so still that she tricked her body into believing that she
was still asleep. All warm and relaxed it lay, breathing deeply and beating with
slow, soft pulses.     [s76–83]

Imp.
Oh to be a <u>writer</u> a real writer given up to it and to it alone! Oh I failed today
I turned back, looked over my shoulder and immediately it happened I felt as
tho' I too were struck down. The day turned cold & dark on the instant.
It seemed to belong to summer twilight in London – to the clang of the gates
as they close the garden – to the deep light painting the high houses to the
smell of leaves & dust, to the lamp light, to that stirring of the senses to the
languor of twilight – the breath of it on one's cheek – to all those things which
(I feel today) are gone from me for ever ... I feel today that I shall die soon –
& suddenly but not of my lungs.     [J203]

Colour. Pink. 5 petalled flower with seed purse darker colour, thick reddish
stem, small leaf like a bramble leaf. The seed purse is highly glazed, it is – in 3,
one long wing & 2 little ones. Attached to it is the 5 petalled flower.
It always falls in delicate clusters.[172]

marqueterie – which they make here. The design style [......] – made into
paper cutters boxes servers, brushes – style for the writing tables – the large
pieces. All is the design for the writing table – all the pieces are mounted on

---

[172]Pencil drawings of flowers illustrate this page.

bois d'ochré – the cutting of it is done in erable naturelle. [.....] in rose wood
– the wood which is [...] in white is on cypre or orange wood – for the
mosaique one takes one long piece of wood, adds the design of both sides to
the middle designs, cuts all out in long fine strips, puts the solid piece
underneath one on top and then makes each small piece coloured. The effect
is of small tiny designs in red and white & green. The father is 68 and at 8
years they learn – it goes from father to son. The travail is italian and it comes
from Sorrento, it is handed from father to son. They are du pays. One gets the
pattern from one hole to another by a very fine saw – perfectly [.....] a design
of leaves roofs, birds and a [...] It is pressed into a small movable frame – and
two pieces of white [...] or lemon wood are then entered into the dark wood
– and then it is varnished added to the well polished. The boxes are made by
the women.
The whole family works and it is all made by hand.

The Persones Tale
he is a jabere and a gabbere      [J212 S145]

And yet one has these 'glimpses' before which all that one ever has written
(what has one written) all (yes, all) that one ever has read, pales ... The waves,
as I drove home this afternoon – and the high foam, how it was suspended in
the air before it fell ... What is it that happens in that moment of suspension?
It is timeless. In that moment (what <u>do</u> I mean) the whole life of the soul is
contained. One is flung up – out of life – one is 'held' – and then, down,
bright, broken, glittering on to the rocks, tossed back – part of the ebb and
flow. I don't want to be sentimental. But while one hangs, suspended in the air
– held – while I watched the spray I was conscious <u>for life</u> of the white sky
with a web of torn grey over it, of the slipping, sliding, slithering sea, of the
dark woods blotted against the cape, of the flowers on the tree I was passing –
and more – of a huge cavern where my selves (who were like ancient seaweed
gatherers) mumbled, indifferent and intimate ... and this other self apart in the
carriage grasping the cold knob of her umbrella thinking of a ship, of ropes
stiffened with white paint & the wet flapping oilskins of sailors ... Shall one
ever be at peace with oneself, ever quiet and uninterrupted – without pain –
with the one whom one loves under the same roof? Is it too much to ask?

[J202-203]

There are moments when Dickens is possessed by this power of writing – he is
carried away – that is bliss. It certainly is <u>not</u> shared by writers today.
For instance the death of Merdle[173] – dawn fluttering[174] upon the edge of night.
One realises exactly the mood of the writer and how he wrote as it were for
himself. It was not his will he <u>was</u> the fluttering dawn and he was Physician
going to Bar. And again when the [...]      [J203]

---

[173]A reference to Chapter xxv of Charles Dickens' *Little Dorrit, Book II*. In *Journal* Murry transcribed
'Merdle' as 'Cheedle', thus throwing generations of Dickens enthusiasts into confusion.
　[174]Both this word and the repeat of it two sentences later look like 'falling' or 'flitting' but are
probably a telescoped 'fluttering', since the phrase in *Little Dorrit* to which KM refers is 'and the wings of day
were fluttering the night when Physician knocked at the door.'

maugre
#### Second Helping.

At mid-day the Walking Club streamed through the ancient beautiful gates and clattered over the cobblestone of the inn courtyard. They disturbed a great ring of blue and white pigeons pecking among the stones; away they flew with a soft clapping.     [J212 S144]

> Catherine Magnaldi Joseph Vigliecca
> Andre Botton
> Laure Blanchard.

"Something to do with lilacs" - an old air of France.

> Le temps des lilas et le temps des roses
> Ne reviendra plus ce printemps-ci     [J212 S145]
> Le temps des lilas et le temps des roses
> Est passé - the temps des oeillets aussi.

> Le vent a changé les cieux sont moroses
> Et nous n'irons pas couper et cueillir
> Les lilas en fleurs et les belles roses
> Le printemps est triste et ne put fleurir.

> Oh, joyeux et doux printemps de l'année
> Qui vint, l'an passé, nous ensoleiller
> Notre fleur d'amour est si bien fanée
> Las! que ton baiser ne peut l'eveiller.

> Et toi, que fais-tu? Pas de fleurs ecloses
> Point de gai soleil ni d'ombrages frais;
> Le temps des lilas et le temps des roses
> Avec notre amour est mort à jamais.

29.ii.1920. Life's a queer thing. I read this today and in my mind I heard it sung in a very pure voice to a piano and it seemed to me to be part of the great pain of youthful love.     [J201–202]

Twelfth Night. Viola.
If one should be a prey how much the better
To fall before the lion than the wolf!

Some are born - - some achieve - - and some have - - thrust upon them.

# Newberry Notebook 4

[Newberry Notebook 4]

K.M.M.
I.V.I920[175]

But this morning she'd been awakened by the great slam of the front door. Bang! The flat shook. What is it! She jerked up in bed, clutching the eiderdown, her heart beat. Then she heard voices in the passage, the clatter of crockery. Marie knocked – entrez, she cried faintly, and as the door opened, with a sharp tearing rip out flew the blind and the curtain, stiffening, flapping, jerking. The tassel of the blind knocked knocked against the window. Ah, voila, said Marie, setting down the tea & running to the window. She cried in a high sharp voice as though she were trying to make herself heard in a storm at sea 'C'est le vent, Madame, c'est un vent insupportable.'

Up flew the blind. The window pane jerked upward – a whirling grayish light filled the room. Monica caught a glimpse of a huge pale sky with a cloud like a torn sheet dragging across, before she hid her eyes with her sleeve. Marie the curtains. Quick draw the curtains. Monica fell back into the bed. No, no tea – impossible. My valena[?] tablets in the little gold box on the dressing table – & then go. She almost broke down on the last word. She shut her eyes & she felt big tears ready to fall. But if Madame would take one in a little cup of tea instead of water, coaxed Marie. At last she understood. Monica was past speech. She heard Marie pour out the tea.

Ring ting a ting ping. Ring ting a ting ping. It was the telephone. At that she grew quite calm. There are always these moments in life when the limits of suffering are reached and we become heroes and heroines. Monica sat up in bed & sipped her tea. Go and see who it is Marie. It is M. said M. He wishes to know if Madame will lunch with him at 1.30 at Princes today. Yes, it was M. himself. Yes, he has asked that the message be given to Madame. Instead of replying she put the tea cup down & asked Marie in a small wondering voice

---

[175.]The following is an earlier draft of 'Revelations'.

what time it was. It was half past nine. She lay still & half closed her eyes.
Tell Monsieur I cannot come – and as Marie waited – that's all, said she gently.
But as the door shut that strange bedfellow who had slipped in invisible with
Marie's message, suddenly gripped her close close, violent, half strangling her –
while she gave way.

How dared he. How dared Ralph do such a thing when he knew how
agonizing her nerves were in the morning. Hadn't she explained, implored
& even – though lightly of course – one couldn't say such a thing directly –
given him to understand that was the unforgiveable thing! Did he think it was
just a fad of hers, a little feminine folly to be laughed at & tossed aside.
And only last night he had said: You know I know you much better than you
know me, though of course you won't believe it, and I know myself better
than you know me. You see you do have a way of flying off at awfully brilliant
tangents and men, dull, stodgy, half alive men go plodding on, collecting
impression after impression, testing them, verifying them. Yes laugh – do laugh.
I love the way your lip lifts and your eyes light. And he leaned across the table
as if intoxicated. I adore you – you're more beautiful than all the [. . . .] of the
world. I don't care who sees that I love you. Let them look. My darling I'd like
to be on a mountain top with you & all the searchlights of the earth might
play upon us!

'Heavens.' Monica almost clutched her head. How incredible men were!
Was it possible she really loved him? How could she love a person who talked
like that. What had she been doing all these months – ever since that dinner
party when he had seen her home & asked her if he might come & see her
afterwards. I want to come & see again your slow Arabian smile. Oh what
nonsense – what utter nonsense! And she remembered how at the time a
strange deep thrill unlike anything she ever had felt before had made her
almost faint . . . But now –

   Coal coal coal
     and
   Old iron old iron old iron

sounded from below – it was all over. Understand her? He had understood
nothing. That ringing her up on a windy morning was immensely immensely
significant. And it was the end. Anger, her strange bedfellow, slipped away.
She felt empty and cold. When Marie came in later to take her to her bath she
said: M. replied he would be in the vestibule at half past one if Madame
changed her mind. And Monica said – No, carnation, not verbena.
Two handfuls Marie.

A wild white morning, a tearing rocking wind. As she waited for the
maid to thread a ribbon she looked through the window at the hurrying
people below. In the flats opposite a little grey nurse with a red nose flopped
a perambulator down the steps and a woman like a pillow tapped the grime of
the window & waved her hair pins to the baby. Monica almost found herself
nodding her head, too. Idiot. She turned away.

She sat down to the mirror. She was pale. The maid combed back her dark hair - combed it all back & her face was like a mask. There was a shadow under her eyes - her lips were dark red - her cheeks[?] very pink. As she stared at herself in the bluish shadowy glass she suddenly felt - oh, the strangest most tremendous excitement filling her slowly, slowly - & she wanted to fling out her arms to laugh, to scatter everything, to cry I'm free, I'm free - I'm free as the wind! And now all this vibrating, trembling, exciting, flying world was hers - it was her Kingdom. No, no, she belonged to nobody but Life.

That will do, Marie, she stammered. My hat. My coat. My bag. And then get me a taxi. Where was she going? Oh, anywhere. She could not stand this silent flat, noiseless Marie, this ghostly quiet interior. She must be out. She must be driving quickly - anywhere anywhere.

The taxi is there, Madame.

As the big outer door of the flats pressed open the wild wind caught her, floated her across the pavement. Where to? Oh, where. She got in & smiling radiantly at the cross sleepy man she said - To - and then gave him the name of her hairdressers. What would she have done without her hairdresser. Whenever Monica had nowhere else to go to or nothing to do, she drove there. She might just as well have her hair waved & by the time it was done she would have thought out a plan. The first leaves of autumn came flying past the windows. One fell on to her lap. I love autumn, I love autumn she said, lying back in the cab.

The sleepy driver drove at a tremendous pace, threading in and out of the traffic and she let herself be tossed from side to side. She wished he would go faster and faster! Oh to be free of Princes at 1.30, of being the kitten in the swansdown basket, of being an Arabian and a grave delighted child and a strange wild little creature and ... Never again she cried aloud, clenching her small hand. But the taxi stopped. The driver was standing holding the door open for her.

The hairdressers shop was warm & glittering. It smelt of soap and burnt paper and wallflower brilliantine, and there was Madame behind the counter, round, white, fat, her head like a powder puff rolling on a black satin pincushion. Monica always had the feeling that they loved her in this shop & understood her - the real her - far better than many of her friends did. She did not know why. She was herself here. She & Madame had often talked - quite strangely together & Georges who did her hair - young, dark, slender Georges she was really fond of.

But today - how curious! Madame hardly greeted her. Her face was whiter than ever, but rims of bright red showed round her blue bead eyes, & even the rings on her tiny fingers did not flash. They were cold, dead, like chips of glass. When she turned her back to Monica & called over the wall telephone - Georges, there was a note in her voice that had never been there before. But Monica would not believe it - no - she refused to. It was just imagination & she sniffed greedily the warm scented air, & passed behind the curtain into the small cubicle.

Her hat & jacket were off & hanging on a peg & still Georges did not come. This was the first time he had ever not been there to hold the chair for her, to take her hat, to hang up her bag, dangling it in his fingers as though it were something he'd never seen before - something faery. And how quiet the shop was. There was nobody else there, no sound from Madame. Only the wind blew, the old house seemed to shake, the wind hooted, the portraits of Ladies of the Pompadour period looked down & smiled, cunning & sly. Monica wished she hadn't come. Oh, what a mistake to have come. Fatal! Fatal! If Georges did not come the next moment she would go away. She took off the white kimono. She didn't want to look at herself any more. When she opened a pot of cream on the glass shelf her fingers trembled. There was a tugging feeling at her heart as though her happiness her marvellous happiness were trying to get free.

Oh, I'll go. I'll not stay. She took down her hat. But just at that moment there was a murmur from outside & steps sounded, & looking in the mirror she saw Georges bowing in the doorway. How strangely he smiled. It was the mirror of course. She turned round - quickly his lips curled back in a sort of grin & - wasn't he unshaved? He looked almost green in the face. Very sorry to have kept you waiting he said, sliding, gliding forward.

Oh no, she wasn't going to stay. I'm afraid she said. But he had lighted the gas & laid the tongs across, & was handing her the kimono. It's a wind he said. Monica submitted. She smelt his fresh young fingers pinning the jacket under her chin. Yes there <u>is</u> a wind, said she, sinking back into the chair. And silence fell.

Georges took out the pins in his expert way - her hair tumbled back but he didn't hold it as he usually did, as tho to feel how fine & soft & heavy it was. He didn't say it was in a lovely condition - he let it fall, and taking a brush out of a drawer he coughed faintly & said: Yes it's a pretty strong one. I should say it was. She had no reply to make. The brush fell on her hair - but oh how mournful - how mournful. It fell quick & light, it fell like leaves, & then it fell more heavy, tugging tugging like the tugging at her heart. That's enough, said she shaking herself free.

Did I do it too much, said Georges & he crouched over the tongs. I'm sorry. There came the smell of burnt paper - the smell she loved - & he swung swung swung the hot tongs round in his hand. 'I shouldn't be surprised if it rained' and he was just taking up the first piece of her hair when she stopped him.

She looked at him. She saw herself looking at him in the white kimono like a nun looks. 'Is there something the matter. Has something happened.' But Georges gave a queer half shrug & grimace. Oh no Madame. Just a little occurrence - & he took up her piece of hair again. Just the front - only the front. Just a wave or two here & there. Oh dear she said.

Oh, she wasn't deceived. That was it. Something had happened! The silence - really, the silence seemed to come drifting through the air like flakes of snow. It was cold in the little cubicle, all cold & glittering. The nickel taps the jets the sprays looked somehow almost malignant. The wind rattled the window frame – a piece of iron banged, & the young man went on changing the tongs crouching over her. Oh, how terrifying Life is – how dreadful. It is the loneliness which is so appalling. We whirl along like leaves, & nobody knows, nobody cares where we fall, in what dark river we float away. The tugging feeling seemed to rise into her throat. It ached ached. She wanted to cry.

'That will do' she whispered. Give me the pins. And as he stood beside her with the pins in his hand, bending forward, so submissive, so silent, she nearly dropped her arms & sobbed. She couldn't bear it. Like a wooden man, the gay young Georges still slided, glided, handed her her hat & veil, & her coat, taking the note & bringing back the change. She stuffed it away. Where was she going to now.

Georges took a brush. 'There is a little powder on your coat,' he murmured. He brushed it away. And then suddenly he raised himself, & looking at Monica he gave a strange wave with the brush & said: The truth is Madame, since you are an old customer – my little daughter died this morning. A first child – & then his white face crumpled like paper and he turned his back on her & began brushing the kimono. The tears ran down Monica's cheeks. How old? she whispered. Two and a half came from Georges. She ran out of the shop into the taxi. The driver, looking furious, swung off his seat & slammed the door again. Where to?

'Princes!' she sobbed. And all the way there she saw nothing but a tiny tiny wax doll with a feather of hair, lying meek, its little hands & feet crossed. And then just before they came to Princes she saw a flower shop full of white flowers. Oh what a thought what a perfect thought. Lilies-of-the-valley and white pansies & double white violets sent to the hairdresser's shop. From an unknown friend. From one who understands. For a little girl. She tapped against the window, but the driver did not hear, and, anyway, they were at Princes already.

### The Baby
by
Katherine Mansfield

Call for him once a week!
with worn black button boots, like squashed fruits. "No" he said, lowering his withered legs from the sofa & rubbing his knee joints, "I'll wait a bit yet before I'm called for." She was pinning on her hat in the mirror above the mantelpiece, but when he said that she turned round & stared, a long pin in her hand. "I'm sure I don't know what you mean" she said loftily.

### Hansbury Mansions
He sucked in his cheeks & rubbed away, blinking. Even as he thought this he collapsed, he fell sideways on the pillows, and suddenly ... in a voice that he'd never heard before, a high queer rasping voice that got louder, angrier, shriller every moment, he began to cry ...

you know we've got you, she hissed. And he nodded his quick nod in queer approval.     [J204-205 S137-138]

This pen simply must not get crossed.

thereby the way we should eke it out would be by sharing it with those who need it less.

176
The Pen Corner, Kingsway.

J. Middleton Murry
J. Middleton Murry
Miss Katherine Mansfield
There is no doubt that this is an excellent pen and I congratulate you on your choice.
Hour £1 Waterman's Font
9 carat. So enormous
A Penny.[177]
A Writers Cramp.
Katherine Mansfield
Lady Ottoline Morrell
John Middleton Murry
Ca marche seule
Have I made a mistake.  Yes!
178

>   Darling Bogey,
>           Yes, there is more to be said for Sorley than I admitted to you, but until I began to talk about him to my enemy I wasn't anti-Sorley as you thought. Really, really not. That's the curse: you're not

>   Dear Darling,
>           Forgive me, too.

Letters to L.H.B.
How beautiful little children are.  Yes, I shall kneel before them and

[J206 S138]

>   two jumpers
>   crepe de chine skirt
>   white stockings
>   grey stockings
>   blue dress
>   pink camisole
>   black knickers
>   pink nightgown

---

[176] Some drawings of boxes occur here.

[177] The above signatures and comments are in Murry's hand.

[178] Further signatures in Murry's hand occur here.

jacket
handkerchiefs

I.VII.1920.                                    2 Portland
My dear Sydney,
<The idea that we might possibly get that house in your village for August is
very exciting. Jack is awfully keen. I shall be much beholden to you if you do
find time to inquire>

Tuesday lunch Schiffs
Sydney to dinner Tuesday
Virginia Wed. afternoon
Blundens dine Friday
Monday. Boulestin

# Notebook 25

[Notebook 25, qMS-1267]

<u>By Moonlight</u> [179]

I hate this book so awfully!!

August 1920.

"And if a man will consider life in its whole circuit, and see how
superabundantly it is furnished with what is extraordinary and beautiful and
great, he shall soon know for what we were born."

9.VII.20. I should like to have a secret code to put on 'record' what I feel today.
If I forget it may my right hand forget its cunning ... the lifted curtain ... the
hand at the fire with the ring & stretched fingers ... no, its snowing ... the
telegram to say he's not ... just the words arrive 8.31. But if I say more
I'll give myself away. B.O.C. <u>412</u>.

I wrote this because there is a real danger of forgetting <u>that kind</u> of intensity,
& it won't do. [180]
No, there is <u>no</u> danger of forgetting. 8.XII.1920.

I must ask Doctor Sorapure what is the immediate treatment for and what are
the symptoms of fractured base.      [J206–207]

12.VII.20. More beautiful by far than a morning in Spring or Summer.
The mist - the trees standing in it - not a leaf moves - not a breath stirs.
There is a faint smell of burning. The sun comes slowly, slowly the room
grows lighter. Suddenly, on the carpet there is a square of pale red light.
The bird in the garden goes 'snip - snip - snip' - a little <u>wheezy</u> like the sound
of a knife grinder. The nasturtiums blaze in the garden; their leaves are pale.
On the lawn, his paws tucked under him, sits the black and white cat.
    As he sits, dumb, staring, there comes that weak light - autumn.

---

[179] Written on the front cover.
[180] This sentence is written in the margin beside the paragraph above.

I cough and cough and at each breath a dragging boiling bubbling sound is heard. I feel that my whole chest is boiling. I sip water, spit, sip, spit. I feel I must break my heart. And I can't expand my chest - it's as though the chest had collapsed. Life is - getting a new breath. Nothing else counts. And Murry is silent, hangs his head, hides his face with his fingers <u>as though</u> it were unendurable. "This is what she is doing to me! Every fresh sound makes <u>my</u> nerves wince." I know he can't help these feelings. But oh God! how wrong they are. If he could only, for a minute, serve me, help me, give <u>himself</u> up! I can so imagine an account by him of a "<u>calamity</u>"... I could do nothing all day. MY hands trembled. I had a sensation of UTTER cold. At times I felt the strain would be unbearable, at others a <u>merciful numbness</u> and so on. What a fate to be so self imprisoned!! What a ghastly fate. At such times I feel I never could get well with him. It's like having a cannon ball tied to one's feet when one is trying not to drown. It is just like that.          [J207 S139]

Brett[181] in her letters to Murry is unbalanced. This morning when she wrote how she wanted to rush into the cornfield - <u>horrified</u> me. And then he must <u>smack</u> her hand and she threatens to cry over him until he's all wet. Poor wretch! She's 37, hysterical, unbalanced, with a ghastly family tradition - and he had 'awakened' her. Her face is entirely changed: the mouth hangs open, the eyes are very wide, there is something silly and meaning in her smile which makes me cold. And then the bitten nails - the dirty neck - the film on the teeth! Whatever he may feel about it now the truth is she flattered him and got him! She listened and didn't criticise & sat at his feet and worshipped and asked for the prophet's help and he told her the old old tragedy. If Murry hadn't met me which would have won? His vanity & self absorption would have delivered him into the arms of countless INFERIOR females (it's always the 5th rate who play this 'game'.) At the same time his honesty and his faith in Art might have saved him. It would have been a rare toss up. Look what happened last winter, par example, while I was away. X "thought him very distinguished", Y "said she was frightened of him" - and so forth. He was puffed up tremengous - and wouldn't hear one single word contrary to his opinions. I'll never forget it. He was <u>furious</u> at a sign of criticism. I wonder if the whole thing will be repeated this winter. I suppose so ....[182]

Bought and Paid for. A bouquet - all her expenses - sometimes only vegetables to bring away. Fortune teller & crystal gazer.          [J207 S139]

Can't you help me? Can't you? But even while she asked him she smiled as if it didn't matter so much whether he could or couldn't.
My nature ... my nerves ... the question is whether I shall change or not.
Per-sonally ... you see him? And he has a friend, a confidant, an old

---

[181] The Hon Dorothy Brett (1883–1937), daughter of Viscount Esher, was a painter whom KM met at Garsington. They became close friends although Brett's deafness was a difficulty, and eventually KM became troubled by the familiarity between Brett and Murry.

[182] Murry's note under this passage: 'Not used because of B, & J.M.M. a little.'

schoolfellow, small, shabby, with a wooden leg whom he has rediscovered.
He's married. The friend enters the new menage. Little by little he gets to
know the wife. No <u>tragedy</u>. He feels like a one-legged sparrow. Talking
together in the house before she comes in. "Is that you Beaty? Can we have
some tea?"

Let the sparrow - let the sparrow. Suffer the sparrow to ...

<u>Charades</u>. Roger of course commits suicide cuts his throat with a paper
knife & gurgles his life away. Listen to me. I have been married to you for
15 years ...

<u>The Dud</u>. This is in Society. We know it all. Then Wyndham is his friend & in
his trouble appeals to him - <u>in vain</u>. One mustn't forget his writing table, so
exquisite, and his graceful style of reply. To write a letter was a little act of
ritual ... His rooms are off Baker Street - Upper Gloucester Place, in fact.

[J207-208 s139]

The daughter of the watch smith. Her piano playing. Her weak heart, queer
face, queer voice, <u>awful</u> clothes. The violets in their garden. Her little mother
& father - the scene at the baths - the coldness, the blueness of the children,
her size in the red twill bathing dress trimmed with white braid. The steps
down to the water - the rope across.

Edie has a brother Siegfried. 17. You never know whether he has begun to
shave or not. He and Edie walk arm in arm ... Her Sunday hat is <u>trimmed</u>
<u>beyond words</u>.

Oh that tree at the corner of May Street. I forgot it until this moment. It was
dark and hung over the street like a great shadow. The father was fair
& youthful to look at. He was a clockmaker.     [J214]

|            |             |            |
|------------|-------------|------------|
| Lindsey .. | Swaith ..   | Charlie    |
| Sinclair .. | Page ..    | Edie Bengel|
| Duncan ..  | Harcourt .. |            |

19.VII. Murry let fall this morning the fact that he <u>had</u> considered taking
rooms with Brett at Thurlow Road this Winter. Good. Was their relationship
friendship? Oh, no! He kissed her and held her arm and they were certainly
conscious of a dash of something far more dangerous than <u>l'amitié pure</u>.
And then he considered taking rooms with her ... He said "Doesn't Gertler[183]
live there too?" But Gertler never had the very beginnings of such a
relationship with Brett as Murry knows.

I suppose one always thinks the latest shock is the worst shock. This is
quite unlike any other I've ever suffered. The lack of sensitiveness as far as I am
concerned - the <u>selfishness</u> of this staggers me. This is what I must remember
when I am away. Murry thinks no more of me than of anybody else. I mean

---

[183]Mark Gertler (1892–1939), a painter and member of the Bloomsbury group of artists and writers of
which the Murrys were on the fringe.

I am the same: the degree of his feeling is different but it's the same feeling.
I must remember he's one of my friends - no more. Who could count on such
a man! To plan all this at such a time and then on my return the <u>first words</u>
I must be nice to Brett. How disgustingly indecent. I am simply <u>disgusted</u> to
my very soul!

I've read this over today (8.XII.1920). And now I wouldn't mind a straw if he
went & lived at Thurlow Road. Why on earth not? I don't love him less but
I do love him differently. I don't aspire to a <u>personal</u> life; I shall never know it.
I must remind him to do so at Christmas.

And again I read this over (9.VI.1921) and it seemed to me very stupid and
strange that we should have hidden from each other. By stupid I mean of
course stupid in me to write such stuff.
And again (24.VII.1921). Neither stupid nor strange. We both failed.

[J208-209 S140-114]

By Moonlight.
(From The House in The Sun.)

Aren't we alike said Laurie.
Yes but you've got much better eyebrows, said Laura. I'm still rather sparse
& when I was a baby, ong dit I hadn't got any at all - not a brow to bless
myself with, said Laura. Mother was terrified. She used to pat them on with
a feather dipped in train oil - olive oil, I mean. Oh whoever told you such a
story! cried Laurie to that laughing face in the glass. I don't know dear, said
Laura. One of the servants - Lizzie I believe it was. Do you remember old
Lizzie? Well, said Laura quickly, she came after Jane & she was followed by
Rose Spiers. But why I remember her so particularly is that it was in her time
that that policeman came to the front door & rang the bell.
My God! said Laurie. He plumped down on Laura's bed. I never shall forget
that. The sheer horror of it! I thought everything was over for us, didn't you.
Oh absolutely. And the worst of it was Meg was practising. She'd just begun
learning the piano, you remember. She was playing Rousseau's Dream.
I thought that would make him even more furious. Stop that piano barked
Laura - like a furious policeman.
        Did you always feel that there was something awfully mysterious about
the dining room.
Always.
When one went into it in the afternoon for a dish for Cook it was so dark
& so dead quiet & then the sideboard. You remember the strange winey
& [...] smell & how funny one's face looked reflected in the sideboard glass,
with little fern fronds round one's head. And did you awfully feel that the
selzogene[184] was like a very proud but also awfully indignant bird.
That <u>hiss</u> when you pulled the handle - Furious!
I know - I used to almost jump away like a cat. And the dumb waiter. A real
man - enchanted one awfully of course - a real man. I was so sorry for him

---

[184]Soda water dispenser.

weren't you? because even if he'd been a man he was dumb – just bowing his head when you gave him orders, & <u>wheeling</u> silently away.

It always happens to me near midi and demi to simply expire of hunger.

Do you know she said dreamily, I think that new hair tonic is going to be a most marvellous success. Don't worry dear. The entire top of your head is covered with a trim of golden down, a trim of baby rabbit fur.
But you've made that discovery about every hair tonic I've bought for the last fifteen years, said Father. The trouble is it never seems to get past the baby rabbit fur stage.
No, said Father gloomily passing his hand over his head, I think I'm doomed. I may be able to preserve about ½ a dozen hairs each side just to soften the picture – but <u>can't hope for more</u>.
Don't let's ever die she said in a low confiding whisper. Oh we won't said Laurie reassuringly. We couldn't – not you & I. Either the end of the world will come in our time or – something will be found out that stops people dying – some marvellous discovery, you know.
     And gazing upon the boundless velvety sky it seemed to her the white moon & the joyful glittering stars were trying to attract their attention, were trying to say: it's quite alright. Don't be afraid. We know the secret – we know it already!
     Dinner was over. There came a whiff of Fathers cigar from the hall & then the door of the smoking room shut, clicked. Mother went rustling to & fro to and fro – to the dining room door speaking to Zaidee who was clearing away giving Hans who helped Zaidee his orders for tomorrow – to the music room speaking to the girls – – Francie darling run upstairs & get me my cream feather boa will you? My cream one – out of the tall wardrobe. Come here child. How beautifully you've done your hair.
Really dearest? I just threw it up – I was in such a hurry. How mysterious it is that if one really tries to get that effect – –
Yes – isn't it.
There came a long soft chain of sound from the music room as though Meg had flung a bright loop & snared the dreaming piano.
We're going to try over Francie's new song, she said. This Life is Weary.
This Life is Weary, cried Mother. Oh dear – is it another tragic one. I can't understand why all these modern songs are so depressing. It seems so unnecessary – why can't one for a change – –
Oh but its fascinating said Meg. And softly she played over This Life is Weary. You cant say you like Cupid at the Ferry better than that.
I do said Mother. I like songs about primroses & cheerful normal birds and – spring & so on.
But Francie came floating down the stairs with a feather boa. It wasn't in the wardrobe you little story said she, winding her mother up in it. It was among your hats. And then you always pretend to be so tidy & so amazed at us.
If you don't speak to me with more respect, said Mother, I shall go straight & tell your Father. Thank you, darling child.

Francies little wooden heels tapped over the parquet floor to the music room. Shut the door while we're practising will you please Mother? The door shut & the piano seemed to have been waiting until it was alone with them - it burst out so passionately This Life is Weary!

Silence from the hall. Mother was still - her head bent turning her rings. What was she thinking of? She looked up. The double doors on to the porch were open & the light in the glass lantern flickered faintly. Dreamily she went over to the hall stand & picked something up. Why she murmured aloud - is there always one <u>odd</u> glove. Where does it come from? Then she went in to the smoking room.

Down the passage through the green baize door that led to the kitchen regions sailed Zaidee with her trays of trembling glass & winking silver and moon white plates & Hans followed with the finger bowls, with the fruit dishes & the plates piled with curls of tangerine peel & spiky shavings of pineapple-outside. The last tray was carried - the heavy baize door swung to with a 'whoof'. There came a faint ghostly chatter from the kitchen - very far away it sounded.

Where was Laurie? He'd gone straight off to his dark room after dinner. She wouldnt disturb him. But all the same Laura slid off the landing window sill parted the embroidered velvet curtains that hid her so beautifully & coming on to the stairs leaned her arms along the bannisters. What was she to do.

This Life is Weary
A tear a sigh
A dream a waiting

sang Francie & suddenly from that faraway kitchen there sounded a shrill little peal of laughter.

How much bigger the house felt at night, thought Laura. All the lighted rooms & the passages that were dark & the cupboards & the front & back stairs. As to the cupboard under the stairs - Lauras eyes widened at the thought of it. She saw herself suddenly exploring it with a candle end - there was the old croquet set there were the goloshes, the shelf of old lamps & the buffalo horns tied up with ribbons. It was like exploring a cave.

Big - big & empty. No not empty exactly but very strange. For though the lights were up everywhere (the Sheridans were dreadfully extravagant about lights & fires) through the open windows the darkness came flowing in from outside. It was the darkness that so gently breathed in the curtains, gathered in pools under the tables & hid in the folds even of the coats down there in the hall. And the stairs! Stairs at night were utterly different to what they were by day & people went up & down them quite differently. They were much more important somehow. They might have led to anywhere. But just as Laura thought that, she had an idea that someone on the top landing was looking down at her. Someone had suddenly appeared from nowhere & with a brilliant round white face - was staring. Oh how awful! And it was shameful, too, to think such things at her age. She even decided the face was a chinaman's before she had the courage to look up. What nonsense. It was the moon shining through the top landing window. And now there

were moonbeam fingers on the bannisters. Laura walked up the stairs slowly –
but for some reason she tried not to make a sound, & looking down at her
little satin shoes she pretended they were two little birds tiptoeing up a branch.

By Moonlight[185]
To: W.J.D.[186]

Dinner was over. There was a whiff of Father's cigar from the hall and then the
door of the smoking room shut, clicked. Mother went rustling to and fro, to
and fro - to the dining room door, speaking to Zaidee who was clearing away,
giving Hans, who was helping Zaidee, his orders for tomorrow, to the music
room, speaking to the girls.
"Francie, darling, run upstairs & get me my cream feather boa will you?
My cream one. On the top of the tall wardrobe. Come here, child, how
beautifully you have done your hair!"
"Really dearest? It was simply thrown up. I was in such a hurry."
"How mysterious it is that if one really <u>tries</u> to get that effect …"
"Yes, isn't it!"
There came a soft chain of sound from the music room as though Meg had
flung a bright loop & snared the dreaming piano.
"We're going to try over Francie's new song" said she. "<u>This Life is Weary</u>."
"This Life is Weary" cried Mother. "Oh dear, is it another tragic one? I can't
understand why all these modern songs are so depressing. It seems so
unnecessary. Why can't one for a change …"
"Oh, but it's fascinating!" said Meg. "Listen." And softly she played "This Life
is We-ary." "You can't say you like <u>Cupid at the Ferry</u> better than that?"
"I do" said Mother. "I like songs about primroses and cheerful normal birds
and - spring and so on."
But Francie came floating down the stairs with the feather boa. "It wasn't
on the tall wardrobe, you little story" said she, winding her Mother up in it.
"It was among your hats. And then you always pretend to be so tidy and so
unlike us."
"If you don't speak to me with more respect said Mother, "I shall go straight
off and tell your Father. Thank you, darling child."
Francie's little wooden heels tapped over the parquet floor of the music room.
"Shut the door while we're practising, will you please, Mother?" The door
shut and the piano seemed to have been waiting until it was alone with them,
it burst out so passionately "This Life is Weary."
Silence from the hall. Mother was still, her head bent, turning her rings.
What was she thinking of? She looked up. The double doors on to the porch
were open and the light in the glass lantern flickered faintly. Dreamily she
went over to the hall stand and picked something up. "Why", she murmured
aloud, "is there always one odd glove. Where does it come from?" Then she
went into the smoking room.

---

[185]This fair copy of the preceding piece incorporates some new material.
[186]The poet Walter de la Mare (1873–1950), one of KM's most valued friends.

Down the passage, through the green baize door that led to the kitchen regions sailed Zaidee with her trays of trembling glass and winking silver and moon white plates. And Hans followed with the finger bowls, with the fruit dishes, and the plates piled with curls of tangerine peel and shavings of pineapple-outside.[187] The last tray was carried; the heavy baize door swung to with a 'whoof'. There came a faint, ghostly chatter from the kitchen. Very far away it sounded.

Where was Laurie? He'd gone straight off to his dark-room after dinner. She wouldn't disturb him - no! But all the same Laura slid off the landing window-sill, parted the embroidered velvet curtains that hid her so beautifully and coming on to the stairs leaned her arms along the bannisters. What was she to do?

"This Life is We-ary!
A Tear - a Sigh
A Love that Chang-es!"

sang Francie. And suddenly from that far away kitchen there sounded a shrill little peal of laughter ...

How much bigger the house felt at night, thought Laura. All the lighted rooms and the passages that were dark and the cupboards and the front and back stairs. As to the cupboard under the stairs - Laura's eyes widened at the very thought of it ... She saw herself, suddenly, exploring it with a candle end. There was the old croquet set, last year's goloshes, the shelf of dead lamps, and the buffalo horns tied up with ribbons. It was like exploring a cave.

Big - big and empty. No, not empty, exactly, but awfully strange. For though the lights were up everywhere through the open windows the darkness came flowing in from outside. It was the darkness that so gently breathed in the curtains, gathered in pools under the tables, and hid in the folds even of the coats down there in the hall. And the stairs! Stairs at night were utterly different to what they were by day, and people went up and down them quite differently. They were much more important, somehow; they might have led to anywhere.

But just as Laura thought that, she had an idea that some one on the top landing was looking down at her. Someone had suddenly appeared from nowhere and with a brilliant round white face was staring! Oh, how awful! And it was shameful, too, to have such ideas at her age. She even decided the face was a chinaman's before she had time to look up. What nonsense! It was the moon shining through the top landing window. And now there were moonbeam fingers on the bannisters. Laura walked up the stairs slowly but for some reason she tried not to make a sound and looking down at her satin shoes she pretended they were little birds tiptoeing up a dark branch. "But now we're at the top of the tree" she told them. And she stood with her head bent and her arms by her sides, waiting for someone ... "It's only because people don't know she's there that they don't come" thought Laura. "She is wearing a white tulle dress with a black velvet sash - very nice!

---

[187]Murry underlined 'outside' and wrote 'I altered this to rind'.

Charming! I say, Laurie, introduce me to your sister!" And someone came forward stroking his white kid gloves.

Laura was so delighted she gave a little jump for joy and forgetting all about her resolve she ran across the landing, down the passage, past the american bathroom & knocked on the dark-room door.

This isn't bad, but at the same time it's not good. It's too easy … I wish I could go back to N.Z. for a year. But I can't possibly just now. I don't see why not in two years' time, though.      [s180-184]

I am stuck beyond words - and again it seems to me that what I am doing has <u>no form</u>! I ought to finish my book of <u>stories first</u> and then when it's gone really get down to my novel <u>Karori</u>.

Why I should be so passionately determined to disguise this I don't quite know. But here I lie pretending, as Heaven knows how often I have before, to write. Supposing I were to give up the pretence & really did try? Supposing I only wrote ½ a page in a day - it would be ½ a page to the good, and I would at least be training my mind to get into the habit of regular performance. As it is every day sees me further off my goal, <u>and</u> once I had this book finished I'm free to start the real one. <u>And</u> it's a question of money. But my idea, even of the short story, has changed rather, lately.

That was lucky! Jack opened the door softly & I was here apparently really truly engaged … And - no, enough of this. It has served its purpose. It has put me on the right lines.      [j262]

A moment later and there was nothing left of Netta Skeritt but a dent in the pillow and one long - much too long - blue black hairpin gleaming on the pale carpet.      [j266 s196]

On her way back to the garden Susannah sat down on the hall chair for a minute to take a pebble out of her shoe. And she heard her mother say: No, I can't possibly do that. I can't possibly turn that dear good Mr Taylor out of the house simply to make room for this Skeritt girl. Susannah

It was a little difficult to explain the facts of the case to the Reverend Mr Taylor, and Mrs Downing hated having to do so. It seemed so unreasonable to ask him to turn out of the spare room for an unknown girl for the night when he was their regular guest, as it were, for the whole Synod and so appreciative - poor lonely up-country man - of the spare room double bed. But there was nothing else to be done. In that extraordinary way men have Harry Downing had rung up from the office to tell her that a Netta Skeritt had called on him that morning. She was passing through Wellington on her way to Nelson and though neither of the Downings had ever seen her before, simply because her father and Harry Downing had known each other in the old days, Harry had immediately asked her to stay the night with them.

And you really won't mind Susannah's bed for the night, Mr Taylor? said Mrs Downing anxiously, pouring him out a second cup of tea.

Not at all Mrs Downing. I shall be as happy as a king, said good cheerful
Mr Taylor.

At that moment Susannah herself came in from the garden. She leaned her
elbows upon the round walnut table, crossed her legs, & cupped her burning
cheeks in her hands. But Susannah's eyes opened very wide. Her lips parted.
She stared first at her Mother & then at Mr Taylor's black coat, gleaming collar
& big yellow hands.

Is Mr Taylor going to sleep in my bed, Mother? said she, astounded.

Yes dear but only for tonight, said her mother, absently folding a piece of
bread & butter. Mr Taylor smiled his broad smile. She imagined him lying in
her bed, his head tilted back, snoring like he snored on Sunday afternoons.
How awful.

With me, she asked, horrified.

Mother flushed faintly & Mr Taylor gave a loud snort that might have been
laughter.

Don't be such a silly little girl, Susannah. Of course not. You are going to sleep
in the spare room with Miss Skeritt.

This was more mysterious still. Oh dear! Why were grownups like this.

She had only run in for a piece of bread & butter. She wanted to get back to
the garden & here they were sitting in this dark room - it looked very dark
& the white cups shone on the walnut table like lilies on a lake after the bright
outside.    [J264-266 S194-196]

Mrs M.[188] knows Ernestine well. She was there while her servant was away
for holiday. Excellent! Clean, reliable, and very kindly. But not what you'd call
a good cook. However most willing & anxious.

About coal & wood. 150 francs - and she suggests 30 francs for the 30 lbs of
jam! But that I said I'd pay her when I had found from L.M. just how much
jam was there - she was not sure.

Masses of wood there.

In November there is 6 foot of snow!!

Elizabeth is FEARFULLY keen on your work. She reads it all. Never has
known anyone develop so. It seems to her each week somehow freer.

She says: Do you think he likes me? I am a dog-like nature & can't live if
people don't whistle to me & give me a strictly spiritual little pat occasionally.

Mrs D. her talk is so bad, Katherine. She has such a big big remnant basket
& I don't like remnants.

Ida. What a joy it must be to get rid of a perfect friend. That's what is so very
difficult.    [J253]

September is different to all other months. It is more magical. I feel the strange
chemical change in the earth which produces mushrooms is the cause, too, of

---

[188] Murry's note: 'The following is a fragment of K.M.'s conversation when, on reaching Montana,
she dared not talk for fear of bringing on an attack of coughing, but wrote what she had to say in her
notebook. The first part refers to the taking of the Chalet des Sapins.' The Chalet was owned by
Mrs Maxwell who leased it to the Murrys for seven months from June 1921.

this extra 'life' in the air - a resilience, a sparkle. For days the weather has been the same. One wakes to see the trees outside bathed in green-gold light. It's fresh - not cold. It's clear. The sky is a light pure blue. During the morning the sun gets hot. There is a haze over the mountains. Occasionally a squirrel appears, runs up the mast of a pine tree, seizes a cone & sits in the crook of a branch, holding it like a banana. Now and again a little bird, hanging upside down, pecks at seed. There is a constant sound of bells from the valley - it keeps on all day from early to late.

Midday - with long shadows. Hot and still. And yet there's always that taste of a berry rather than scent of a flower in the air. But what can one say of the afternoons? Of the evening. The rose, the gold on the mountains - the quick mounting shadows. But it's soon cold. Beautifully cold, however.     [J260–261]

It's nothing short of loathsome to be in my state. Two weeks ago I could write anything. I went at my work each day and at the end of each day so much was written. Whereas <u>now</u> I can't say a word![189]     [J262 S185]

Darling Veen,[190]
It's like this. It's no good her being here any more - it's too hot & the food has gone off. Also I must tackle my affair seriously, you know. So I am going to Montana. Stephani[191] says that he would far rather I went to him for a month at least so that he could keep my heart under his <u>eye</u> or <u>ear</u>. Good. I agree. But there's my Bogey. Will he go to a pension 5 minutes away for a month & visit me? As soon as I find out how the place suits me we can get a little chalet. I send you a p.c. of your pension. Stephani's place is not a real live - or dead - Sanatorium. He of course thinks you would like to be with me there. Why not? It is quite usual. But I sang <u>No</u> to that & I'm sure you agree. You'd hate it. So would I.     [J250 S179]

Tedious Brief Adventure of K.M.

A doctor who came from Jamaica
Said: This time I'll mend her or break her
I'll plug her with serum
And if she can't bear 'em
I'll call in the next undertaker.

His <u>locum tenens</u> Doctor Byam
Said: Right O, old fellow, let's try 'em
For I'm an adept O

---

[189] At this point KM turned the book over and started at the other end.
[190] 'Veen' is a nickname KM occasionally used for Murry. Its origin is not known.
[191] Dr Stephani, a famous chest specialist in Sierre.

At pumping in strepto
Since I was a surgeon in Siam.

The patient. who hailed from New Zealing
Said: "Pray don't consider my feeling
Provided you're certain
'Twill not go on hurtin'
I'll lie here and smile at the ceiling."

Those two very bloodthirsty men
Injected five million, then ten
But found that the strepto
Had suddenly crept to
Her feet - and the worst happened then!

Any day you may happen to meet
Her alone in the Hampstead High Street
In a box on four wheels
With a whistle that squeals
And her hands do the job of her feet.      [J178-179]

Marie.[192] She is little and grey with periwinkle - I feel inclined to write peritwinkle - blue eyes and swift sweeping gestures. Annette said she is "une personne très superieure - la veuve d'un cocher", and "qu'elle a son appartement à Nice ... Mais que voulez-vous, la vie est si chère, on a forcée." But Marie does not look like any of these imposing, substantial things. She is far too gay, too laughing, too light to have ever been more than a feather in the coachman's hat. As to an appartement I suspect it was a chair at a window which overlooked a market.

Throttling strangling by the throat a helpless exhausted little black silk bag. But one says not a word & to the best of one's belief gives no sign. I went out into the gentle rain & saw the rainbow. It deepens, it shone down into the sea & then it faded: it was gone. The small gentle rain fell on the other side of the world. Frail - Frail - I felt Life was no more than this.      [J219]

Look here my love & my dear,
I'm not really up to chalets yet. This is what would be BEST of all.
Do you agree? We go to Montana. I go to Stephani's for a month at least
- you have a room at this <u>pension du lac</u>. Stephani then can keep his eye
& his ear on my heart & I can lie absolutely low for that month. Then in
the meantime, we have looked around & we take a chalet.
[Does] that seem possible to you?      [J250-251 S179-180]

---

[192]The maid at the Villa Isola Bella, Menton.

and she flung back her head, sucked in her underlip and half shut her eyes, just as she had seen Grace Palotta[193] do at the Theatre Royal, the week before. "And you call yourself" she mocked in a low quivering voice, "you dare to call yourself a married man."

But Potts was far too crushed to act his part properly. Besides at that moment there was a sound of wheels & the yellow-painted butcher's cart rattled round the bend of the road & drew up sharp close by. Then the hearty, common young butcher leapt off the seat, unhooked the back of the cart & let it down with a bang & began in a reckless, careless, horribly indifferent manner to sharpen his long knives.

> avant c'etait un jardin de Paris
> il y a rien a faire que de mourir Madame.
> They fatten, Madame, they fatten - - -

She is the kind of woman who if she did eat raisins she would fatten.

---

[193]Grace Palotta (d 1959), actress, whose hey-day was in London in the 1890s, but who also toured extensively in the US, Australia, India, and the Far East.

# *Notebook 9*

[Notebook 9, qMS-1268]

July 21st Conrad review.[194] bad[?] ditto. <u>The lift boy & the bread tray</u>.
Sweetness of home Life.

<u>Isola Bella. How shall I buy it?</u>

Lying facing the window I woke early. The blind was half pulled down. A deep
pink light flew in the sky and the shapes of the trees, ancient barns, towers,
walls, were all black. The pools & rivers were quicksilver. Nearing Avignon the
orchard in the first rays of sunlight shone with gold fruit – apples flashed like
stars.

   L.M.'s legs dangled. She dropped down, slowly waving her big grey legs,
as though something pulled her, dragged her – the tangle of rich blue weeds
on the red carpet. Avig –avig – avignon she said. One of the loveliest names in
the world done to death, said I. A name that spans the ancient town like a
delicate bridge. She was very impressed. But then, George Moore <u>would</u>
impress her!   [J215]

Woman & woman. What I feel is she is never for one fraction of a second
unconscious. If I sigh I know that her head lifts – I know that those grave large
eyes solemnly fix on me. Why did she sigh. If I turn she suggests a cushion or
another rug. If I turn again then it is my back. Might she try to rub it for me?
There is no escape. All night a faint rustle, the smallest cough and her soft
voice asks did you speak. Can I do anything. If I do absolutely nothing then
she discovers my fatigue under my eyes. There is something profound
& terrible in this eternal desire to establish contact.   [J215-216]

Stove brushes.

Mysterious is man and woman. She sat on the flat seat in the corridor & he
stood above her while the dark fat man beat them up a couple of beds.

---

[194]KM's long appreciative review of Joseph Conrad's *The Rescue* had appeared in the *Athenaeum*
of 2 July 1920.

She looked sulky, stubborn and bored. But it was plain to see she suited him. Bang on the door when you're ready old girl, and the door slammed. He sat on the flap seat, smoothed his thin smooth hair, folded his bony hands, a neat foot dangled from a thin ankle. The light shone on his glasses. Seeing him thus one could not imagine a man who looked less like a woman's man. But I admired him immensely. I was proud of them as "made in England."    [J216]

It grew hot – everywhere the light quivered green-gold. The white soft road unrolled with plane trees casting a trembling shade. There were fields of pumpkins & gourds – outside the house the tomatoes were spread in the sun. Blue flowers & red flowers & tufts of deep purple flared on the roadside edges. A young boy carrying a branch stumbled across a yellow field followed by a brown high-stepping little goat. We bought figs for breakfast, immense thin-skinned ones. They broke in one's fingers & they tasted of wine and honey. Why is the northern fig such a chaste fair-haired virgin – such a soprano. The melting contraltos sing through the ages.

The great difference. England so rich – with the green bowers of the hops & gay women & children with their arms lifted pausing to watch the train. A flock of yellow hens led by a red rooster streamed across the edge of the field. But France – an old man in a white blouse was cutting a field of small clover with an oldfashioned half-wooden scythe. The tops of the flowers were burnt. The stooks (are they stooks) were like small heaps of half burned tobacco. The pale […] sun[?] swam on a grey lake like some lone sere-breasted bird.    [J216-217]

A Dance at the  – – –
Is Life going to be all like this? thought Laura. And she lay down in bed & put her arms round the pillow and the pillow whispered "Yes – this is what Life is going to be like – only always more & more splendid, more and more marvellous!"
But supposing said Laura, speaking very fast with the greatest possible earnestness, supposing you were terrifically successful & were married to the person you adored & you had every single thing you wanted and – and your first child was just born (that's supposed to be a marvellous moment, isn't it?) would you be really happier than you are now?
They stared hard at each other a moment.
Then no, said Laurie. I simply couldn't be.
At his words Laura gave a beaming smile, a great sigh, & squeezed her brother's arm. Oh what a relief! she said. Neither could I – not possibly!
Laura, Laurie. What are you doing up there. Come down at once. The Ns have arrived.

Laura stooped down & kissed her grandmother. You're by far the most beautiful girl in the room, my little precious, she whispered. As Grandma passed on, the Major and Laura suddenly turned round to catch her eye.

She raised her eyebrows in a very curious astounded way, & sucked in her cheek. The old woman actually blushed.     [J209–210 S141-142]

potage - oeufs sur le plat fromage. Veal haricots. meat vegetables entremets fromage fruits.

|  | Isola Bella |  |  |
|---|---|---|---|
| soap[195] | 4.60 | carried forward | 50.80 |
| soda | 85 | vanilla | 2.25 |
| torelion[?] | 1.30 | Saint Galmier | 15. |
| powder | 1.50 | ink | 1.20 |
| T paper | 2.25 | telegram | 5. |
| sanitas | 2.50 | oil | 1.20 |
| condy | 4.50 | eggs | 2.80 |
| cottonwool | 1.25 | essens[?] | 5 |
| lettuce | 25 | Annette | 18.05 |
| tomatoes | 80 | voiture | 10. |
| onions | 60 |  | ——— |
| potatoes | 70 |  | 112.40 |
| garlic | 50 |  |  |
| rice | 2.50 |  |  |
| flour | 90 |  |  |
| oatmeal | 1.50 |  |  |
| oil | 14. |  |  |
| vinegar | 2.60 |  |  |
| mustard | 2.40 |  |  |
| nutmeg | 20 |  |  |
| chocolate | 1.30 |  |  |
| rennet | 3.50 |  |  |
|  | ——— |  |  |
|  | 50.80 |  |  |

Four little boys. One minute, three larking. When the three ran on to the lines & tried to dash themselves to death the little one obviously suffered torture & did his best to drag them back again. I realised this would have been just the same if it had been deep water.

An old man, an old woman, a tiny boy in a cape. When the old woman disappeared, the ancient took the little boy with such tender care. He had a little pipe in his beard - it looked as though his beard were curling ... Poplars springing in green water - red willows. The luxury of trees!

[J217 S147]

A man poked his head in at the door & said tea was served. "Tea! Dear me!" she fussed at once. "Would you care to go ... Shall we do you think. On the other hand I have some tea here. I'm afraid it will not be very good. Tea that is

---

[195] In this list sanitas was a household disinfectant and oxidiser. Condy—either crystals or liquid—was a disinfectant. Saint Galmier was a mineral water.

not fresh and then there is that [...] water – what it is I do not know but – Shall we care to try it?" "Might as well." "In that case dear perhaps you would not mind lifting down my suitcase. I am sorry to say the tea is in there. Such a bother. These racks are so very high. I think they are decidedly higher than English racks. Mind! Do take care! Oh!"

He: Ugh!

Finally she spread out a piece of paper, put on it a little cup & an odd saucer, the top of the thermos flask, a medicine bottle of milk, and some sugar in a lozenge tin. I am very much afraid said she. Would you like me to try it first? He looked over the top of his paper and said drily Pour it out. She poured it out and gave him the cup and saucer of course, while she filled the most uncomfortable little drinking cup in the world for herself, and sipped & anxiously watched. Is it so very ...

Might be worse!

Fidgeting in her handbag, first she pulled out a powder puff, then a nice substantial handkerchief, then a paper parcel that held a very large wedge of cake, of the kind known as Dundee. This she cut with a penknife while he watched with some emotion.

This is the last of our precious Dundee, said she shaking her head over it & cutting it so tenderly that her gesture almost seemed an act of cannibalism. That's one thing I have learned, said he, and that is never to come abroad without one of Buszard's[196] Dundees. Oh how she agreed.

And each taking a large wedge they bit into it and ate solemnly with round astonished eyes like little children in a confectionery shop who are allowed to eat sitting up to the counter.

More tea dear?

No thanks.

Sure?

A glance. (I sympathise with his glance for reply.)

I think I will just have a cup, said she gaily, so relieved to have a sip after all. Another dive into her bag and chocolate was produced. Chocolate. I had never realised before that chocolate is offered playfully. It is not a solemn food. It's as though one thought it rather absurd, but then who knows?

Perhaps.

What, said he & peered over the paper. No, no – dismissing the chocolate. She had thought as much.

And having torn up little shreds of paper & wiped the cup the saucer & the knife clean she packed all tight again. But a final rummage in her bag produced an oval shaped paper, which, unwrapped, was an egg! This sight seemed to fill her with amazement. But she must have known the egg was there. She did not look as though she had. Brighteyed, her head on one side, she stared, and I fancied I heard an interrogatory clucking ...

[J217-218 s148-150]

---

[196]Buszard's was a high-class tea-shop in London whose famous cakes could be purchased whole as well as eaten in the shop.

– – – For a story little boys [......] and a yard paved with hard little stones[?].
Heirloom[?] homes. Why are the town doors all guarded with bars and tines
of iron. Hideous shapes. Villas oleanders & birches & pretty with lead pencil
spires. Beau Sejour – with dim lights, Belle Bague, Pension des Amis.
Bague. The lake very cold with little diving steps pegged out into the water.
Lecons de piano & behind a pair of trousers hanging out to dry.
Why do people always put on such airs when they are saying goodbye.
They smile – [.....]
They seem so exquisitely glad to be staying. Are they? Or it is envy?

This is John's Fountain pen and I don't think much of it. It's all on one side!

[J148 S109]

Wallington, Grange Road, Lewes.

She has <u>lids</u> on all the chamberpots.

| | | | |
|---|---|---|---|
| taxis | 5.50 | vests | 44. |
| " | 6.50 | oranges | 1.20 |
| milk | 55 | apples | 1.50 |
| hat | 9. | milk | 55 |
| tip | 1. | cakes | 1. |
| block | 3.75 | supper | 50 |
| telegrams | 3.25 | | |
| " | 4.50 | | 48.75 |
| [...] | 4.75 | [...] | 1.75 |
| milk | 55 | oxo | 1.25 |
| oranges | 70 | fares | 60 |
| metro | 60 | DN | 30 |
| milk | 55 | ink | 2. |
| butter | 1.45 | stamps | 5. |
| | | milk | 1.90 |
| | 36.85 | cakes 1. | |
| | | mail | 30 |
| | | trams | 1.95 |
| | | milk | 90 |
| | | papers | 60 |
| | | cakes | 1. |
| | | trams | 1.20 |
| | | wire | 5.60 |
| | | letter | 1.50 |
| | | cakes | 1. |
| | | milk | 90 |
| | | butter | 55 |
| | | taxi | 15. |

48.75
28.50
_____
77.25

Swiss: changed 50 francs for 115 fr.

| | |
|---|---|
| tickets | 15. |
| water | 1. |
| porters | 2.50 |
| voiture | 5. |
| ticket | 2.60 |
| porter | 2. |
| ticket | 15. |
| | 44.10 |

| French | | supper | 1. |
|---|---|---|---|
| Taxi | 8.50 | envelopes | 1.50 |
| porter | 3. | fares | 1.30 |
| stamps | 5. | milk | 55 |
| wire | 4.35 | cakes | 1. |
| fares | 1.30 | milk | 55 |
| fruit | 1.50 | cream | 1.10 |
| flowers | 5.50 | doctors | 100. |
| paper | 30 | taxis | 11. |
| oil | 1. | taxis | 12. |
| milk | 55 | taxis | 7. |
| cakes | 1. | | |
| Ida | 4. | | 146.95 |
| eggs | 1.60 | | 48. |
| butter | 1.30 | | |
| salt | 30 | | 194.95 |
| meat | 1.80 | | |
| orange | 30 | | |
| medicine | 6.40 | | |
| | 48.0 | | |

# *Unbound Papers*

[MS-Papers-4006–8]

14:XII:1920.     <u>Singing</u>          Madame <u>Lavena</u>

kissed & kissed the dark, sweet smelling hand with the silver ring.
Pa-pa! Pa-pa!

the baby became covered with inkspots & served her as a little reminder for
days & days of the things she had forgotten to say and the things she might
have said so differently!     [J226 S163]

(here he used to sit & sometimes on the path below there sat a small white
& yellow cat with a tiny flattened face. It sat very still & its little peaked
shadow lay beside it ... This little cat never ran straight. It wound its way along
the path, skirting the tufts of grass, crept now by the fence, now to the side
of a rubbish heap & its little paws seemed to touch the ground as lightly as
possible as though it were afraid of being followed - <u>traced</u>.)

I shan't say it like that. It's only a note. But Ah my darling how often
I have watched your small silent progress. I shall not forget you, my little cat,
as you ran along your beat on this whirling earth.     [J235–236]

When Jean-Paul was undressed his breast was like a small cage of bent
bamboos. And she hated to see it. "Cover yourself!" & he shot his small arms
into his woollen shirt.     [J236]

[MS-Papers-4006–8]

... I kissed her. Her flesh felt cold, pale, soft. I thought of nuns who have
prayed all night in cold churches ... All her warmth and colour and passion
she had offered up in prayer in cold, ancient churches ... She was chill, severe,
pale; the light flickered in her raised eyes like the light of candles - her skirt
was worn shiny over her peaked knees: she smelt faintly of incense.
"No, Father. Yes, Father. Do you think so, Father?" (But still haven't said what
I want to say.)     [J220–221]

The Doll:
Well, look, muttered Miss Sparrow - I've nothing to be ashamed of. Look
as much as you like - I defy you. It's what I've wanted all my life. She cried
brokenly - and now I've got it. I defy you. I defy the world! And she drew
herself up in front of the window, proudly, proudly, her eyes flashed, her lips
gleamed, pressing the doll to her flat bosom. She was the Unmarried Mother.
18.X.1920.
Of course I <u>can't</u> write that: I'm surprised to have made such a crude note.
That's the raw idea as they say. What I ought to do, though is to write it,
<u>somehow</u>, immediately, even if it's not good enough to print. My chief fault,
my overwhelming fault is in <u>not writing</u> it out. Well, now that I know it
(and the disease is of very long standing) why don't I begin at least to follow
a definite treatment? It is my experience that once an 'evil' is recognised <u>any</u>
delay in attempting to eradicate it is fatally weakening. And I who love order,
with my mania for the 'clean sweep', for every single thing being 'ship-shape'
... I to know there's such an ugly spot in my mind! Weeds flourish in neglect.
I must keep my garden open to the light and in order. I must at all costs plant
these bulbs and not leave them (oh shameful!) to rot on the garden paths!
Today (October 18th.20) is Monday. I have raised my right hand & sworn.
Am I ever happy except when overcoming difficulties? Never. Am I ever free
from the sense of guilt, even? Never. After I had finished that slight sketch
The Young Girl wasn't there a moment which surpasses all other moments?
Oh, yes. Then - why do you hesitate? How can you! I take my oath - not one
day shall pass without I write something - original.    [J221]

# Notebook 35

[Notebook 35, qMS-1269]

<u>Notes: Personal</u>[197]

Isola Bella.

December 27th. [1920] When I stuck the small drawing to the side of the mirror frame I realised that the seal – the mark – the cachet rouge – had been set on the room. It had then become the room of those two – and not her room any more. It is not that the room was dead before, but how it has gained in life! Whence has come the tiny bouquet of tangerine fruits, the paste pot on the writing table, the fowl's feather stuck in Ribni's[198] hair, the horn spectacles on the chinese embroidery. The 'order' in which I live is not changed, but enriched – in some strange way it is enlarged.

This is <u>en effet</u> just the effect of Jack's mind upon mine. Mysterious fitness of our relationship! And all those things which he does impose on my mind please me so deeply that they seem to be <u>natural</u> to me. It is all part of this feeling that he and I, different beyond the dream of difference, are yet an <u>organic whole</u>. We are, as I said yesterday, the two sides of the medal – separate, distinct, and yet making one. I do not feel that I need another to fulfil my being and yet having Jack I possess something that without him I would lack. In fact we are – apart from everything else – each other's <u>critic</u> in that he 'sees' me – I see myself reflected as more than I appear and yet not more than I AM and so, I believe, it is with him. So to be together is apart from all else <u>an act of faith in ourselves</u>.

... I went out into the garden just now. It is starry and mild. The leaves of the palm are like down-drooping feathers; the grass looks soft, unreal, like moss. The sea sounded, and a little bell was ringing, and one fancied – was it real, was it imaginary – one heard a body of sound, one heard all the preparations for night from within the houses. Someone brings in wood from the dark,

---

[197] Written on the cover.
[198] Murry's note: 'Ribni was Katherine's Japanese doll, so named after Captain Ribnikov, the Japanese spy who is the hero of Kuprin's story of that title.'

lamp-stained yard, the evening meal is prepared, the charcoal is broken, the dishes are clattered, there is a soft movement on the stairs & in the passages & doorways. In dusky rooms where the shutters are closed the women, grave & quiet, turn down the beds and see that there is water in the water jugs. Little children are cheeping.

Does it always happen that while you look at one star you feel the other stars are dancing, flickering, changing places - almost playing a game on purpose to bewilder you. It is strange that there are times when I feel the stars are not at all <u>solemn</u>: they are secretly gay - I feel this tonight. I sat on the cane chair and leaned against the wall. I thought of Jack contained in the little house against which I leaned - within reach - within call. I remembered there was a time when this thought was a distraction. Oh it might have been a sweet distraction - but there it was! It took away from my power to work ... I, as it were, made him my short story. But that time belongs to the Past ... One has passed <u>beyond it</u>.

... I thought also of the Princess B.[199] It's a bit bewildering - her unlikeness to the faces 'we' recognise or would recognise. She has a quick rapacious look - in fact she made me think of a <u>gull</u> with an absolutely insatiable appetite for bread, and all her vitality, her cries, her movements, her wheelings depend upon the person on the bridge who carries the loaf. This would of course be <u>hidden</u>. But this is what she is when she is really <u>she</u> and not 'enchanted.'     [J232-233]

... But the champagne was no good at all. It might have been writing water. I had to drink it because it was there, but there was something positively malicious in the way the little bubbles hurled themselves to the rim, danced, broke - they seemed to be jeering at me.     [J227-228 S162]

... Does one ever know? One never knows. She realised how foolish it would be to ask the question: "What are you thinking of?" And yet if she did not ask the question she would never be sure he was not thinking of ... Even if she asked it how could she be certain he did not make up the answer.     [J236]

Peace of mind. What is peace of mind? Did I ever have it. It seems 'yes' and yet perhaps that is only deception. But at Bandol for instance or even Hampstead - Ah - who knows? Peace of mind. The other will not give up his secret. What <u>is</u> it? He evades the answer. "I swear on my honour", "look here I'm absolutely in the dark". She cannot believe and yet she has to believe - she <u>does</u> not believe. The letters <u>disappear</u>. All the other letters are left on the table but not those. Why? I am to forget everything - to behave as though everything has not been. But I <u>can't</u>. Because I don't know what has been. I only know he denies a wrong (not an obvious wrong) which was committed. It must have been committed. People don't write like that pour rien - de

---

[199]Princess Elizabeth Bibesco, daughter of Herbert and Margot Asquith and wife of Antoine Bibesco, a Roumanian diplomat. Murry had a brief flirtation with her in 1920 which KM did not take calmly.

l'amitié pure. So whenever I look at him and whenever I am with him there is that <u>secret</u> and I can't give him all I long to give him nor can I <u>rest</u> in him because of it. I have no abiding place. Peace of mind. Yes, I had it when I was first here. Yes, I had it fully when I wrote Miss Brill.

No, I've been poisoned by these 'letters'. How <u>can</u> he know someone so 'strange' to me? To us? Not only know her but cherish her?

[J229-230 S161-162]

Accounts with Jack (temporary)[200]

---

[200]Written on the back cover.

# *Unbound Papers*

[MS-Papers–4000–36]

Dream I.

I was living at home again in the room with the fire escape. It was night:
Father & Mother in bed. Vile people came into my room. They were drunk.
Beatrice Hastings led them. "You dont take me in old dear" said she.
"You've played the Lady once too often, Miss - coming it over me." And she
shouted, screamed <u>Femme marqué</u> and banged the table. I rushed away. I was
going away next morning so I decided to spend the night in the dark streets
and went to a theatre in Piccadilly Circus. The play a costume play of the
Restoration had just begun. The theatre was small and packed. Suddenly the
people began to speak too slowly, to mumble: they looked at each other
stupidly. One by one they <u>drifted</u> off the stage & very slowly a black iron
curtain was lowered. The people in the audience <u>looked</u> at one another.
Very slowly, silently, they got up and moved towards the doors - stole away.

An enormous crowd filled the Circus: it was black with people.
They were not speaking - a low murmur came from it - that was all.
They were still. A whitefaced man looked over his shoulder & <u>trying to smile</u>
he said: "The Heavens are changed already; there are six moons!"

Then I realised that <u>our</u> earth had come to an end. I looked up. The sky
was ashy-green; six livid quarters swam in it. A very fine soft ash began to fall.
The crowd parted. A cart drawn by two small black horses appeared. Inside
there were salvation army women doling tracts out of huge marked boxes.
They gave me one. "Are you Corrupted?" It got very dark and quiet and the
ash fell faster. Nobody moved.

What is milk a <u>metre</u> now? L.M.[201]

Dream II.

In a café. Gertler met me. "Katherine you must come to my table. Ive got
Oscar Wilde there. Hes the most marvellous man I ever met. Hes splendid!"

---

[201]Written on the back of the above page.

Gertler was flushed. When he spoke of Wilde he began to cry - tears hung on his lashes but he smiled.

Oscar Wilde was very shabby. He wore a green overcoat. He kept tossing & tossing back his long greasy hair with the whitest hand. When he met me he said "Oh <u>Katherine</u>!" - very affected. But I did find him a fascinating talker. So much so I asked him to come to my home. He said would 12.30 tonight do? When I arrived home it seemed madness to have asked him.
Father & Mother were in bed. What if Father came down & found that chap Wilde in one of the chintz armchairs? Too late now. I waited by the door. He came with Lady Ottoline. I saw he was disgustingly pleased to have brought her. Dear <u>Lady</u> Ottoline & Ottoline in a red hat on her rust hair '<u>hounyhming</u>'[202] along. He said "Katherine's hand - the same gentle hand!" as he took mine. But again when we sat down - I couldn't help it. He <u>was</u> attractive - as a curiosity. He was fatuous & brilliant!

"You know Katherine when I was <u>in that dreadful place</u> I was haunted by the memory of a <u>cake</u>. It used to float in the air before me - a little delicate thing <u>stuffed</u> with cream and with the cream there was something <u>scarlet</u>. It was made of <u>pastry</u> and I used to call it my little Arabian Nights cake. But I couldn't remember the name. Oh. Katherine it was <u>torture</u>. It used to <u>hang</u> in the air and <u>smile</u> at me, and every time I resolved that next time they let some one come and see me I would ask them to tell me what it was but every time, Katherine, I was <u>ashamed</u>. Even now ..."

I said "mille feuilles à la creme?"

At that he turned round in the armchair and began to sob, and Ottoline who carried a parasol opened it and put it over him ...

[NL]

### Sorrowing Love

And again the flowers are come
And the light shakes
And no tiny voice is dumb
And a bird breaks
On the humble bush and the proud restless tree.
Come with me!

Look, this little flower is pink
And this one white.
Here's a pearl cup for your drink,
Here's for your delight

A yellow one, sweet with honey,
Here's fairy money
Silver bright

---

[202] Whinnying: In Jonathan Swift's *Gulliver's Travels* the houyhnhnms were intelligent horse-like creatures.

Scattered over the grass
As we pass.

Here's moss. How the smell of it lingers
On my cold fingers.
You shall have no moss. Here's a frail
Hyacinth, deathly pale.
Not for you, Not for you.
And the place where they grew
You must promise me not to discover,
My sorrowful lover!
Shall we never be happy again?
Never again play?
In vain - in vain!
Come away!
                    Elizabeth Stanley.[203]


"You love me - still?"[204]
                    by
          Katherine Mansfield.

As Gertie the parlour maid pressed through the green baize door that led from the kitchen regions she nearly dropped the tray of dinner silver she was carrying. For there, beyond the stairs, in the very middle of the big dim hall stood Miss Cassandra - Mrs Brook - wearing a little black hat with a thick black veil, a long black cape, and clasping her hands as if she was praying. Oh, she did give Gertie a turn, coming on her so sudden, all in black, too, and standing there so strange. But immediately she saw Gertie, Miss Cassandra came to life, darted forward and said in her sweet husky voice - the servants loved Miss Cassandra's - Mrs Brook's - voice - "Oh good evening Gertie. Where is Mother?"
"Good evening Miss - Ma'am. In her room. She must have just about finished dressing." "Is Father with her?" asked Cassandra, putting her hand on the banister. "No Miss. It's Wednesday. One of his late nights, you know." "Oh yes, I forgot." Then Cassandra said quickly "Where are the others?" "Miss Jinnie's in the drawing room & Mr Jack's in his dark room." "Thank you Gertie, then I'll run up."
        And run she did - skimmed rather, like a bird. She knocked at the big cream panelled door and turned the glass handle. "Mother it's me. Can I come in?" "Cassandra!" cried her mother. "Do darling, of course. What a surprise. What a strange hour." Mrs Sheridan sat at the dressing table clasping her pearls. As she spoke she settled them & drew down her daughter's little dark head & kissed her. The black veil only came to Cassandra's nose. Her mother noticed that her lips were hot & through the thick mesh her eyes looked dark

---

[203]Elizabeth Stanley, the maiden name of KM's paternal grandmother, was a pseudonym she adopted during this period for her occasional poems published in the *Athenaeum*.
[204]'Cassandra' in *Scrapbook*.

- enormous. But that meant nothing with Cassandra. The child had been to a concert, or she'd been reading or stargazing simply or tracking down a crying kitten. Anything threw Cassandra into a fever. "Do you know how late it is, my child" she said tenderly. "It's just on dinner time. And I thought Richard only got back today." "Yes he did" said Cassandra. "This afternoon." She gave a little gasp. "Then why didn't you - " Her mother broke off. "But before we begin talking darling, you'll stay to dinner of course. I'll just let Cook know. She'll be so furious if I don't." And she moved towards the bell beside the fireplace before Cassandra stopped her. "No, mother, don't. I'm not stopping to dinner. I don't want any dinner." Suddenly she threw back the cape & with that gesture she seemed to reveal all her excitement and agitation. "I've only come to speak to you - to tell you something. Because I must, I simply <u>must</u>" - & here Cassandra clasped her hands as she had in the hall below - "confide in somebody." "My precious child don't be so tragic" said her mother, "you're frightening me now - you're not going to have a baby, are you? Because I'm no good at that kind of thing. What is it? And don't begin crying if you can help it. It's so exhausting!"

She was too late. Cassandra had begun. Pressing her little handkerchief to her eyes she sobbed "I can't talk in this room - I'm afraid we'll be interrupted. Come into my old room, Mother." And away she sped, across the wide hall and down the passage into her bedroom-that-was, next to the nursery. The door of the cold, dim little room was shut behind them. Cassandra almost sprang upon her mother. "Mother!" she cried, "I've been betrayed - I've been wickedly cruelly deceived - Richard's been false to me - but so false" cried Cassandra, walking away from Mrs Sheridan & shaking her little fist at the ceiling. "But <u>so</u> false, so utterly, abominably false!" "Child - what are you saying" cried Mrs Sheridan. She really was taken aback by this. "It can't be true. Richard - of all people. How? When? With whom? Instead of replying Cassandra ran back to her mother & half shutting her eyes, smiling like an actress she declaimed in low passionate tones: "Dearest you love me - <u>still</u>? Ah, my dear one," pleaded Cassandra, flinging out her hand to her astonished mother - "end each of our daily letters with 'Yes I love you still' as well as 'Bless you' and don't forget - " & here Cassandra raised her hand - "do listen to this bit mother," she implored - as if her mother was not listening - "that though I bask, I gloat in the fact that I so perfectly understand your silence - I have a jigsaw of longing to hear you speak ..."

After this extraordinary oration Cassandra smiled again & simply stared at her mother. Mrs Sheridan really thought the child had become unbalanced - - - "But what does it <u>mean</u>" she said. "Did you hear this? Did someone say it to him?" "No," said Cassandra. She gave a little wave and almost laughed. "I found it - and it's a <u>mild</u> specimen, my dear - in his collarbag!"[205]

[s157-161]

---

[205]It is probably significant that KM wrote this piece during the same period in which she was expressing anxiety about Elizabeth Bibesco's love letters to Murry. The possibility that she employs here actual quotations from them is an interesting one.

[NL]

Late Spring[206]

"... But I tell you, my lord fool, out of this nettle danger, we pluck this flower, safety."

The doctor - for Roy, of course, unable to resist the smallest dramatic opportunity, had obtained a rather shady Bloomsbury address from the man in whom he always confided everything, who, although he'd never met her knew "all about them" - did not show the least surprise when she said in her untroubled soft voice "Do you mind not mentioning anything of this to Mr King." He was, on these occasions, inclined to be jocular - to swagger a bit - to make it an affair of - he and she across the table with the secret between them, to clinking glasses, tossing it down, to "alright, little lady, don't you worry. You leave it to me, my dear. I'll tell him you've swallowed the kitten and want a bit of sea air to drown it in." But the whole surroundings in which he found himself and particularly the owner of the untroubled soft voice had thrown him clean off his beat. Why the Hell had they knocked him up. Standing in the middle of the exquisite fragrant room he was so nervous he broke into a sweat and it was only while he mopped his forehead and moustaches that he discovered he'd still got his stethoscope slung round his neck.
"If you'd tell him I'm a little run down and that my heart wants a rest. For I have been complaining about my heart." He hadn't time to reply when there was a soft knock at the door. "Come in" [he] cried, and Roy - he really did look pale - smiling his half-smile, came in and asked the doctor what he had to say.
"Well!" said the doctor, stowing away the stethoscope with hands that positively shook, "all I think Mrs - hm - Madam wants is a bit of a change. She's a bit run down. Her heart wants a bit of a rest."
    In the street a barrel organ struck up something gay, laughing, mocking, with little trills, shakes, jumbles of notes. It finished him. [It] made him feel like a sick cat. "That's about it" he said, taking up his bag which lay on a white enamelled table and looked somehow like a broken old brown canvas shoe. She saw over her shoulder Roy's smile deepen, his eyes took fire. He gave a little "ah" of relief and happiness. And just for one second he allowed himself to gaze at her, without caring a jot whether the doctor saw or not, drinking her in as she stood tying the pale ribbons of her camisole, stooping for her little purple cloth jacket. That purple cloth against the pale tea-rose of her arms and bosom! He jerked back to the doctor.
"She shall go away. She shall go away to the sea at once" said he. "And about her food?" He saw her in the long mirror, buttoning her jacket and laughing at him - oh so charmingly - in the way that delighted him.
    "That's all very well" he protested, laughing back at her and at the unfortunate doctor who tried a grin and couldn't manage it. "But if I didn't

---

[206]Another version of the published story 'This Flower'.

manage her food, doctor, she'd never eat anything at all except caviare
sandwiches and - and - white grapes. About wine - ought she to have wine?"
"Wine'll do her no harm" said the doctor.
"Champagne?"
The doctor cocked his eye at Roy. Was this a joke. But Roy appeared to be
hanging upon the answer.
"Oh yes champagne" he stammered, and then with an immense effort "She
can have a brandy & soda with her lunch every day if she fancies it" he
brought out.
Roy loved that. It tickled him immensely.
"Do you fancy a brandy and soda with your lunch, Marina?" he asked her
solemnly, blinking and sucking in his cheeks to keep from laughing out.
The blarsted barrel organ burst into "All night <u>Long</u> you Call me" and the
doctor snatched his hat. Roy went with him to settle his fee. She heard the
front door close and then rapid steps down the passage. He was back, in her
room - she was in his arms - crushed up small while he kissed her quickly,
quickly - warm quick kisses - until she was half stifled and cried for mercy.
But still he kept his arms round her and she leant against his shoulder as
though quite exhausted. He was laughing too, and she felt as though his
laughter were running in her veins.

   "How beautiful you are, you little beauty. Look up at me, my darling,
my delight." And she looked up at the face bent over her - at the tanned skin
with a reddish light on the cheek bones, the short clipped auburn moustaches,
the eyes like blue fire and the rust coloured hair as smooth as paint. He pleased
her - oh but immeasurably - and he knew it.[207]
"What is it" he whispered, bending down to her. "What is it, my treasure."
But "nothing" said she, shaking her head. Then "You smell very nice. Not of
cigars ..."
"Of nuts?" he laughed. That was peculiarly his kind of joke.
But she did not mind it. She let him pull her down gently into the deep chair
between the windows.

[MS-Papers-4006–15]

### The Ring

But a tiny ring of gold
Just a link
Wear it, and your heart is sold
... Strange to think!

Till it glitters on your hand
You are free
Shall I cast it on the sand
In the sea?

---

[207]In the margin beside this paragraph KM has written 'Too much description'.

Which was Judas' greatest sin
Kiss or gold?
Love must end where sales begin
I am told.

We will have no ring, no kiss
To deceive.
When you hear the serpent hiss
Think of Eve.

—————————————

[MS-Papers-4006-16]

Sunset.

A beam of light was shaken out of the sky
On to the brimming tide, and there it lay
Palely tossing like a creature condemned to die
Who has loved the bright day.

"Ah, who are these that wing through the shadowy air"
She cries, in agony. "Are they coming for me?"
The big waves croon to her: "Hush now. There-now-there!
There is nothing to see."

But her white arms lift to cover her shining head
And she presses close to the waves to make herself small ...
On their listless knees the beam of light lies dead
And the birds of shadow fall.

Elizabeth Stanley.      [J159 S120]

[MS-Papers-4006-13]

Et Après.

When her last breath was taken
And the old miser death had shaken
The last, last glim from her eyes
He retired.
And to the world's surprise
Wrote these inspired, passion-fired
Poems of Sacrifice!
The world said:
"If she had not been dead
(And burièd)
He'd never have written these.
She was hard to please
They're better apart.
Now the stone

Has rolled away from his heart
Now he's come into his own
Alone."

                    Elizabeth Stanley.     [J182]

[MS-Papers-4006-13]

                    He wrote

Darling Heart if you would make me
Happy, you have found the way.
Write me letters. How they shake me
Thrill me all the common day

With our love. I hear your laughter
Little laughs! I see your look
"They Lived Happy Ever After"
As you close the fairy book.

Work's been nothing but a pleasure
Every silly little word
Dancing to some elfin measure
Piped by a small chuckling bird.

All this eve – as though I've tasted
Wine too rare for human food
I have dreamed away and wasted
Just because the news was good.

Where's the pain of counting money
When my little queen is there
In the parlour eating honey
Beautiful beyond compare!

How I love you! You are better.
Does it matter – being apart?
Oh, the love that's in this letter
Feel it, beating like a heart.

Beating out – 'I do adore you'
Now and to Eternity
See me as I stand before you
Happy as you'd have me be.

Don't be sad and don't be lonely
Drive away those awful fears
When they come remember only
How I've suffered these two years.

Darling heart, if you must sorrow
Think: "My pain must be his pain"
Think: "He will be sad tomorrow"
And then - make me smile again.

Elizabeth Stanley.       [j181-182]

[MS-Papers-4006-16]

## Winter Bird

My bird, my darling,
Calling through the cold of afternoon -
Those round, bright notes,
Each one so perfect
Shaken from the other and yet
Hanging together in flashing clusters!
'The small soft flowers and the ripe fruits
All are gathered.
It is the season now of nuts and berries
And round, bright, flashing drops
In the frozen grass.'       [j197 s130]

[NL]

## A Little Girl's Prayer.

Grant me the moment, the lovely moment
That I may lean forth to see
The Other buds, the Other blooms
The Other leaves on the tree.

That I may take into my bosom
The breeze that is like his brother
But stiller, lighter, whose faint laughter
Echoes the joy of the Other.

Above on the blue and white cloud-spaces
There are small clouds at play.
I watch their remote, mysterious play-time
In the Other far-away.

Grant I may hear the small birds singing
The song that the Silence knows ...
(The Light and the Shadow whisper together
The lovely moment grows

Ripples into the air like water
Away and away without sound
And the little girl gets up from her praying
On the cold ground.)

Elizabeth Stanley.

# *Notebook 36*

[Notebook 36, qMS-1272]

Le travail – même mauvais – vaut mieux que la rêverie.

1. Baby
2. Thief
3. Snow [208]

But I can't see why you should mind so much, she said for the hundredth time. I can't see what it is you object to. It isn't as though people would notice you even. Goodness me! I'm always meeting them since – since – she broke off. And it seems such a waste, too. There it is standing in the hall, doing nothing. It seems so ungrateful after it's been lent to you not to give it a trial, at least. Why don't you say something?

She was pinning on her hat in front of the mirror in the sitting room. Her outdoor jacket & gloves lay across a chair. And when he still didn't answer she made a little weary hopeless face at the mirror which meant: "Oh dear, we're in one of our moods again!" If it's me you're thinking of by any chance, she said quickly, snatching at the jacket –

Here is M. [209] with the supper. And I shall have to endure her jawing until it is over. But that is not important. What <u>is</u> is that I have not written anything today worth a sou. I have passed the day in a kind of idleness. Why? Does it take so long to begin again? Is it my old weakness of will?     [J238-239]

Oh, I must not yield! I must, this evening, after my supper, get something done. It's not so terribly hard after all. And how shall I live my <u>good life</u> if I am content to pass even one day in idleness. It won't do. <u>Control</u> – of all kinds. How easy it is to lack control in little things. And once one does lack it the small bad habits – tiny perhaps – spring up like weeds & choke one's will. That is what I find.

---

[208]These are written on the front cover.
[209]Marie, the maid.

My temper is bad; my personal habits are not above reproach. I am ungracious, mentally untidy. I let things pass that I don't understand (unpardonable) and I excuse myself - invent pretexts for not working. Yet is my desire to be idle greater than my desire to work. Is my love of <u>reverie</u> greater than my love of action. Treacherous habit! Habit above all others evil & of long standing. I must give it up <u>at once</u> or lose my self-respect... It is only by making myself worthy of Jack that I shall be worthy of what I mean our relationship to be. He that faileth in little things shall not succeed in great things. Even my handwriting. From this moment <u>it</u> too must change. After supper I must start my journal & keep it day by day - a record of my progress towards spiritual health... But can I be honest? If I lie it's no use.

[J240]

... Once they're found out - once the taint's discovered, you might as well try and get rid of a touch of the tar brush. ...[210] "No," he thought, staring at a drowned leaf that bobbed against the edge of the cup, "it's no good. It won't work. Charlie must go."

... And now, thinking over Charlie's cleanliness and cheerfulness and good temper, it seemed to him that it had all been acting. An astonishing example in so young a boy of criminal cleverness. What else could it have been? Look how, even after he had been forgiven and the whole thing wiped out, after he'd been allowed to get off 'Scott free'    [S230-231]

---

After a succession of idle, careless, or clumsy, or unwilling little boys had passed through the office, after horrid little boys that the typists couldn't bear to come near them: "Stand further off, please", or clumsy young idiots who tripped on the Boss's doormat every time they came to him with a message, the appearance of Charlie Parker on the scene was more than a relief - it was hailed with positive pleasure by everybody. His mother was good old ma Parker, the office cleaner, whose husband, a chimney sweep, had died in a chimney! Really - the poor seem to go out of their way to find extraordinary places to die in! Charlie was the eldest of goodness knows how many little Ps - so many, in fact, that the clergyman's wife who was tired of delivering parcels of flannelette at the tiny house with the black brush over the gate, said that she didn't believe Mr Parker's death had made the slightest difference to Mrs Parker. I don't believe anything will stop her. I am sure there has been a new one since I was there last. I believe it has simply become pure habit and she will go on and on - eating into the maternity Bag, said the clergyman's wife crossly. "I confess my dear, I find you slightly difficult to follow" said her husband.

Well, if they were all like Charlie it wasn't greatly to be wondered at. What trouble could he have given his mother? He was one of those children who must have been a comfort ever since he found his legs. At fourteen he was a firm, upstanding little chap - on the slender side perhaps, but quite

---

[210]'The Office Boy' in *Scrapbook*.

a little man, with bright blue eyes, shining brown hair, good teeth that showed when he smiled – he was always smiling – and a fair baby skin that turned crimson when the typists teased him. But that wasn't all. He was so neat, so careful of his appearance, so – brushed & combed. There was never a speck on his blue serge suit. When you looked at his tie you wanted to smile, you could see how solemnly that knot had been drawn just so. Beams came from his hair and his boots, and his childish hands were a deep pink colour as though he'd just finished drying them.

From his first day at the office Charlie found his place as though he had been dreaming all his life what he would do when he was an office boy. He changed the blotting paper on the desks, kept the ink pots clean and filled, saw that there were fresh nibs, carried wire baskets of letters from the typists room to the Boss, to the Acting Manager, to Mr Tonks of the Wholesale Order Department, went to the post office, bought immense quantities of different kinds of stamps, asked the various callers who it was they wished to see, answered the store room phone. And at four o'clock when Miss Wickens, the head typist, had boiled the kettle on the electric heater she was so proud of, he took in the Boss's tea. A knock at the door. "Come in." Enter Charlie, with the tea tray, very serious and yet trying not to smile. He walks so straight that his knees rub together and if as much as a saucer clatters he draws in his breath and frowns... "Ah Charlie!" The Boss leans back. "That my tea." "Yes Sir." And very carefully the tray is lowered & a pink hand reaches out & ventures to move back a paper or two. Then Charlie stands upright like a soldier on parade, & glaring at the sugar as if he dared it to take wings & fly he says: "Have you everything you want, Sir?" "Yes I think so Charlie" says the Boss, easy and genial. Charlie turns to go.
"Oh one moment Charlie." And the little boy turns round & looks full at the Boss, & the Boss looks back into those candid innocent eyes. "You might – you might tell Miss Wickens to come in to me in half an hour."
"Very good, Sir" says Charlie. And he is gone. But the Boss pours out his tea & the tea tastes wonderfully good. There is something especially crisp about the biscuits too & there's no doubt afternoon tea is refreshing – he's noticed it particularly lately.

It was extraordinary the difference one little boy made in the office. 'E couldn't be made more fuss of if 'e was a little dog, said the storeman. It's like aving a pet in the ouse, that's what it is. And he was right. To have someone who was always eager & merry & ready to play – someone to whom you could say silly things if you wanted to – someone who, if you did say a kind word, as good as jumped into the air for joy. But why wasn't he spoilt. That was what the typists couldn't understand. When everybody went out of their way to be nice, to be kind to him – when even the Boss made a favourite of him why didn't he become an odious little horror? Mystery ... However ...

One October afternoon, blustery, chill, with a drizzle of saltish rain

[s227-230]

This story won't do. It is a silly story.      [s231]

I took them last just after you & Dent went. Do you think I dare take another dose. I feel as tho'I am suffocating.[211]     [J242]

I suppose doctor, my patients are fond of saying, for patients flatter their doctors you know, just as much as doctors flatter their patients - the reason why you always look so very stern in your car & never glance to the right or left is that you know so many people. I mean if once you began to recognise anybody it would be - a - a kind of royal procession from door to door. Too dreadfully boring!

I more than smile - I fling back my head, wrinkle my eyes & give my famous silent little laugh. Then I spring to my feet lightly, almost youthfully, incline towards the patient, take that confiding little hand in mine & say as I press it reassuringly "But it needs the most dreadful discipline you know - sometimes - goodbye!" And I am gone before the patient has done thinking "Then he did see me that day - after all that, I was right."

But the patient is wrong, of course. Not that it is a matter of any importance. But what really happens is - I emerge from the hotel, chateau, villa - whatever it is. The grey car is drawn up to the pavement edge & the figure of Giovanni leaps to attention on the instant. I cross rapidly, pause one moment, my foot on the step, & not looking at Giovanni but looking over his shoulder, give him the next address, & then leap in, light an Egyptian cigarette, thrust my hands into my pockets so as to be ready, at the very first movement, at the very first gliding motion of the car, to relax, to lean back, to give myself up, to let myself be carried, without a thought or a feeling or an emotion . . .

But that star - that green star that shines so brightly!     [J243-244 S175-176]

It fell so softly so gently it seemed to him that even tenderly it fell. It floated through the air as if it were sorry about something and wanted to reassure him, to comfort him. Forget! Forget! All is blotted out, all is hidden - long ago, said the snow. Nothing can ever bring it back - nothing can ever torture you again. There is no trace left. All is as if it never had been. Your footsteps & hers are long since covered over. If you were to look for her you never would find her. If she were to come seeking you it would be in vain. You have your wish, your wish! whispered the snow. You are safe, hidden, at peace. Free.

At that moment, upon that word a clock struck one loud single stroke. It was so loud, so mournful, so like a despairing groan that the feathery snowflakes seemed to shiver, to hesitate an instant, to fall again faster than ever as though something had frightened them - - -     [J241-242 S173-174]

---

[211]Murry's note: 'A question evidently addressed to me at a moment when Katherine dared not speak for fear of bringing on a fit of coughing.'

Aah! Baah! Aaah! Baah! like thousands of tired sheep in the shearing pens at evening time.

and the gum leaves, like tufts of cock's feathers ruffled in the faint breeze.

[J242]

The café was all but deserted. Over in the corner there sat a poor little creature with 2 loops of velvet in her hat that gave her the look of a rabbit. She was writing a letter. First she wrote a little, & then she looked up & the two bows of ribbon seemed to pout, to listen. Then she hunched down again & scribbled another sheet. Again she looked up. The grey waiter had his eye on her ...

 Over in the corner there sat a stout man with a swollen shabby black leather bag at his feet. He was yawning over a timetable but occasionally he stopped & gave the black bag a little dig, a kick, as if to warn it that it was no good falling too fast asleep - they'd have to be off soon.  [J242 S174]

I kissed her. Her cheek felt cold white, and somehow moist. It was like kissing a church candle. I looked into her eyes, they were pale, flickering with dim far off lights. She smelled faintly of incense. Her skirt was rubbed and bulged at the knees. But how could you say that about the Blessed Virgin! said she. It must have hurt Our Lady so terribly. And I saw the B.V. throwing away her copy of Je ne Parle pas francais & saying "Really this K.M. is all that her friends say [of] her to me."  [J202]

By night and at early morning I love to listen to my darling roosters crowing to one another from lonely yards. Each one has a different note. I have never heard two roosters crow alike. But the hens who seem from their cackle to be laying eggs all day long sound as like one another as - as - - In fact there is no possible distinguishing between them. L.M. says they are not <u>all</u> laying eggs. Some of them are frightened, surprised, excited - or just - playful. But this seems to me to make the affair even <u>more</u> - - - humiliating.  [J202]

<u>Burton's Anatomy of Melancholy</u>

# Notebook 6

[Notebook 6, qMS-1280]

<u>Shakespeare</u> [212]

Anthony [sic] and Cleo: Act I. Scene I.

> 'The triple pillars of the world ...
> The wide arch of the ranged empire ...

> 'Tonight we'll wander through the streets and note
> The qualities of people.' (That is so <u>true</u> a pleasure of lovers.)
> Sc. II. 'A Roman thought hath struck him ...'

> A:Ah then we bring forth weeds
> When our quick minds lie still ...

<u>Enobarbus</u> constantly amazes me. i.e. his first speeches with A. about Cleo's celerity in dying.
> 'Your old smock brings forth a new petticoat.'

Scene III like Scene II. 1. Saw you not my lord? 2. Where is he? The <u>married</u> woman. There's jealousy! And then her fury that he's not more upset at Fulvia's death! Now I know how you'll behave when I die.

These are beautiful lines of Anthony's
> 'Our separation so abides and flies
> That thou, residing here, goes yet with me,
> And I, hence fleeing, here remain with thee.'

> Scene IV  'Like to a vagabond flag upon the stream
> Goes to and back, lackeying the varying tide
> To rot itself with motion.'

Marvellous words! I can apply them. There is a short story. And then it seems that weed gets caught up and one night it is gone out to sea and lost.

---

[212] On front cover.

But comes a day, a like tide, a like occasion and it reappears more sickeningly rotten still! Shall we? Will he? Are there any letters? No letters? The post? Does he miss me? No. Then sweep it all out to sea. Clear the water for ever! Let me write this one day.

> ... thy cheek
> so much as lanked not.
> The economy of utterance.

> Scene V.  Now I feed myself
> With most delicious poison.
> An arm-gaunt steed? Oh yes, of course.

> Act II. Sc. I. <u>Salt</u> Cleopatra ...
> Scene II  Every time
> Serves for the matter that is then born in it.

> Caesar:  You praise yourself
> By laying defects of judgement to me but
> You patched up your excuses.

> Enobarb:  That truth should be silent I had almost forgot.

- - - The short scene between Anthony and the soothsayer is very remarkable. It explains the tone of Caesar's remarks to Anthony ...
And Anthony's concluding speech shows his uneasiness at the truth of it.
He'll go to Egypt. He'll go where his weakness is praised for strength. There's a hankering after E. between the lines.

Scene V. "<u>tawny</u> finned fishes" "their <u>slimy</u> jaws" and the adjectives seem part of the nouns when Shakespeare uses them. They grace them so beautifully, attend and adorn so modestly and yet with such skill. It so often happens with lesser writers that we are more conscious of the servants than we are of the masters, and quite forget that their office is to serve, to enlarge, to amplify the powers of the master.

> "Ram thou thy fruitful tidings in my ears
> That long time have been barren."

Good lines! And another example of the choice of the place of words.
I suppose it was instinctive. But fruitful seems to be just where it ought to be to be resolved (musically speaking) by the word 'barren'. One reads fruitful expecting barren almost from the 'sound' sense ...

> Cleo:  Thou shouldst come like a fury crowned with snakes,
> Not like a formal man.

> 'But yet' is as a jailer to bring forth
> Some monstrous malefactor.

There's matter indeed! Does not that give the pause that always follows those hateful words. 'But yet' and one waits - and both look towards the slowly opening door. What is coming out? And sometimes there's a sigh of relief after. Well, it was nothing so very awful. The gaol mouse, so to speak, comes mousing through & cleans his face with his paw.

"I am pale, Charmian": Reminds me of Mary Shelley. "Byron had never seen anyone as pale as I." Something of John too. I can't remember what. Was he as pale as she? He must have been for he felt the blood creeping back into his cheeks. I don't know whether Bogey <u>wrote</u> creeping or whether that's caricature. It makes me smile. It's <u>so</u> like him.

> "Since I myself
> Have given myself the cause."

What does that mean exactly? That she sent Anthony away? Or let Anthony go?

Cleo: In praising Anthony I have dispraised Caesar?

– – –

I am paid for't now.

A creature like Cleopatra always expects to be paid for things.    [J276-279]

# *Notebook 7*

[Notebook 7, qMS-1270]

1. The Pessimist.
2. The New Year.[213]

When she reached home the New Year was there already, pale, mysterious, gentle and so timid. It hung in the folds of the curtains, in the shadows of the stairs, it waited for her on the landing. She undressed quickly making as little noise as possible & quickly she plaited her hair. But as she parted the sheets it seemed to her that another hand – the hand of the New Year – drew them down too and after she was in bed that gentle hand helped to cover her.

[J236 s164]

The last day of the old year was dull and cold. All day the light was weak and pale and smoky like the light of a lamp when the oil is all but finished & the wick begins to burn. Everything looked shabby – even the trees, even the sky with its big grey patches. The church bells seemed never to stop ringing, the trams groaned, dragged past as if they expected every journey to be their last and when there was no other sound a little dog, tied up somewhere, began to yelp like young dogs yelp when they are frightened ...      [J236 s164]

What was there about that little house at the corner which made you feel sure a widow lived there. In the tiny sloping garden there grew candytuft, mignonette, pansies, star of Bethlehem. A narrow asphalt path led to the door. But there was something about the windows – something quenched, expressionless. They had nothing to hide, nothing to reveal. And there was something about the door that made you know when you rang the door would not be answered at once. There would be an interval of strange dead quiet & then there would come a faint rustling ...

Sophie Bean sat at the dining room window in her black dress, hemming pillow slips. She was pale but in the dusky room a whiteness came from the pillow slips with the whiteness of snow & made her paler. Her hands moved

---

[213]On front cover.

slowly – sewing depressed her – but it had to be done. Nevertheless she very often put it down and looked out of the window at the drooping trees, the heavy trams dragging along & the people who passed by, stooping & hurrying as though there was a secret reason why they should not be seen ... All that day –    [J239 s164-165]

The Dud

Today passing the kitchen the door was open. Charles sat up to the table darning socks. And there sat beside the ball of wool a large black cat with a red bow round its neck. When he took up the scissors the cat squeezed up its eyes as if to say that's quite right & when he put the scissors down it just put out its paw as if to straighten them but then it drew its paw back, deciding it wasn't worth it.    [J239 s165-166]

Sunday Janvier 2d. This afternoon is dreary it is growing dark, but I am waiting for somebody. Somebody will come in & not go again. He will stay to supper, sleep here & be here when I wake in the morning ...    [J237 s168]

I thought, a few minutes ago that I could have written a whole novel about a <u>Liar</u>. A man who was devoted to his wife but who <u>lied</u>. But I couldn't. I couldn't write a whole novel about <u>anything</u>. I suppose I shall write stories about it. But at this moment I can't get through to anything. There's something like a great wall of sand between me and the whole of my 'world'. I feel as though I am <u>dirty</u> or <u>disgusted</u> or both ... Everything I think of seems false.    [J228 s162]

The Pessimist.[214]

After luncheon the weather was so enchanting (enchanting was the word that weekend: it had been brought from town by Moyra Moore & everybody was using [it]) the day was so perfectly enchanting that they wandered into the garden and coffee was served on the lawn under the – yes actually – wasn't it too wonderful! – spreading chestnut tree!

The three pekes & the baby pekums who had just had their dinners of underdone steak mixed with a morsel of heart & the merest dash of liver (their favourite combination) started a kind of intricate game of chase in and out of people's ankles which was slightly bewildering. But nobody really minded except the Cabinet Minister who was terrified of dog bites; he shook his finger at the little loves & said – Not so fast my young friends, in a would-be playful tone which didn't deceive a soul. It certainly didn't deceive the pekes ...

Standing at the table pouring out the coffee in a yellow muslin dress with a green silk hat, green stockings & black satin shoes, the hostess felt wonderfully like somebody in the Russian ballet. She lifted the pots with

---

[214]In *Scrapbook* Murry has placed this story in 1917, although the earlier pieces in this notebook he has placed in 1921. His transcription differs from this manuscript in so many places that one supposes he must have used a different, presumably later and now vanished, draft of the story.

strange little angular gestures & when she had filled a thimble-like cup she held it up high in the air & cried Coffee! Coffee! as though she were summoning her little negro page ...

Moyra Moore, kneeling on the grass before a tulip - she always knelt before the flowers she admired - (could one do less) - murmured: It's quite as good as a Matisse you know - I mean the line is quite as strange! Real flowers [are] often so dreadfully cosy looking. And the young gentleman of the moment who was trying dreadfully hard to live up to this & couldn't, heard himself say, but couldn't stop himself: Roses are very nice, aren't they!

On the garden bench under the round billowing tree sat a little lady with a fan & such a large comb in her hair that every time you looked at her it gave you [a] fresh small shock. Was it as big as that last time. Beside her sat a fair woman with that trembling perfect smile that hovers on the lips of young mothers; as a matter of fact she had just published a first novel - it was just out, as she told everybody, staring into the distance as if she seemed to see it being wheeled away in a white perambulator. And at the end of the bench a very dark young man stretched his legs & made rings of smoke. His play Freud Among the Ruins had been accepted by the Stage Society though they had given him no definite date as yet - but in time.

Hovering under the tree & looking up through the branches there was a very young poet. The hostess did wish he would sit down - one couldn't really look as vague as that. And besides it would give the Cabinet Minister such a wrong impression.
Coffee, Spenser, your coffee is <u>here</u>, she cried gayly.

The woman.

What was there about that publishing couple in cane chairs on the other side of the table. He was tall, lean, with a long clean-shaven face that looked dreamy. And she was one of those women - one of those women who still exist in spite of everything. Then they are rare, but were they ever anything but rare? Where do they come from & what happens to them? Have they ever been girls? Do they ever become old ladies. One cannot <u>imagine</u> them except between thirty & forty. They are exquisite, elusive, flawless-looking, with slow movements & perfect hands, perfect hair. When they travel their luggage is a paper of parma violets or a few long-stemmed yellow roses - & in the background hovers the ideal maid with the russian leather dressing case & the fur coat tied with oyster brocade. Their jewel is pearls - pearl earrings, a string of pearls, pearls on their fingers. And the curious thing is that whatever they say - & they seldom say anything very remarkable - I always sleep in my pearls or I am afraid I know very little about modern music or I always think it's so clever to be able to write - one feels charmed, gratified, and even a little carried away. Why?

Dearest, said Moyra Moore, moving over to the hostess & stroking her cheek with a poor pale tulip, do tell me about the spreading chestnut tree - was it before my time or after? Oh you wicked child, said the hostess, looking regretfully at the tulip. But the poet piped: It was a poem by Longfellow!

At that the dark young man sat up suddenly & stopped making rings. Goldsmith, please! he said shortly - as though Goldsmith was a friend of his & that really was a bit too steep. The young poet looked as if he was going to cry. Oh come now, said the Cabinet Minister pleasantly - & the hostess sighed with relief that they had begun to talk about something simple enough for him to join in. Surely it was Longfellow. It was certainly Longfellow in my young days. And because he was a Cabinet Minister they all smiled kindly as though he had said something quite amusing!
All but the dark young man - who looked terrible!

"Under the spreading chestnut tree
The village smithy stands."

said the lady with the fan. I've always wanted to ask & I've never dared to - was he the same smith as that dreadful harmonious one that one used to have to practise on a cold piano in the early morning.
Varats by Handel, murmured the lady novelist.
The dark young man spoke again. Haydn, please, said he loudly[?]. At that the Cabinet Minister looked quite distressed. What a bother it was, thought the hostess, they were really worrying him.
I am afraid, he said, still quite pleasantly, you're not quite right in your facts. I fancy - in fact I feel quite certain on this point - the name was Handel.

But this time the young man refused to be subdued. I thought Samuel Butler had proved that Handel didn't exist. Samuel Butler! cried the Cabinet Minister - but he was obviously staggered. Then how on earth - how on earth does he account for the Messiah? The Messiah! cried Moyra Moore & she waved the tulip like a wandering angel.

But this was too much for the hostess. She ran to the rescue of the Cabinet Minister. You must come - you must come & see my asparagus, she pleaded. It's so wonderful this year. The Cabinet Minister was delighted & away they wandered. Then the little lady with the fan tinkled with laughter. Do - do look at his trousers, she cried. They are just like crackers - chinese crackers after a funeral. If only the ends were cut into fringes!
The couple in the cane chairs stirred, too.
Do you care - he murmured.
I should like to, murmured she & they too wandered away across the brilliant green lawn. I wonder what they are saying about me, said the tall man gloomily. The pearl lady opened her grey sunshade & smiled faintly.
It's quite hot, said she. At her words he put his hand to his head with a look of alarm. Hot! My God, so it is! Do you mind waiting here for a moment while I get my hat? And he said something about the heat being fatal as he strode away. She bent towards a huge creamy magnolia flower & smelled it with that distrait expression with which women smell a cake of soap or a sachet while waiting at the chemist's shop. Back he came really adorned with a wide silver grey hat.

I'm afraid I don't quite know, said the hostess vaguely. He used to ride with my brothers - years ago. I remember he once had an extraordinary

accident – well hardly an accident. But they were all dismounting & his foot got jammed in the stirrup. He'd no idea it was caught & he fell off – exactly like the White Knight, & there he lay with one foot in the air ...
But how too odd for words! said the lady with the fan.
And he doesn't look at all the type those things happen to, mused the pearl lady.
Did you notice at lunch he upset his wine? said an animated young thing who seemed to belong to nobody & to thirst to be adopted – by somebody, anybody.
No! Did he. How too tiresome! wailed the hostess. My lovely cloth!
Yes & he said, cried the young thing, revelling in her success, I dreamed last night I was going to do this – – –
If poetry is an overwhelming emotion – –

At that moment there came a sharp pit–pat on the crown of his hat. Good Lord, he said. A drop of rain. How extraordinary. But when he took off his hat to see, he laughed bitterly. That's done it, he said – that's finished it completely. And a tiny bird that had been perched on the tree just above their heads flew away & its wings sounded like breathless laughing. But the weather was still enchanting!     [s83-89]

# *Notebook* *44*

[Notebook 44, qMS-1281]

Shakespeare[215]

The First Lord in Alls Well that Ends Well is worth attending to. One would
have thought that his speeches & those of the Second Lord would have been
interchangeable; but he is a very definite, quick-cut character. Take, for
example, the talk between the two in Act IV Scene III. S.L. asks him to let
what he is going to tell dwell darkly with him.
F.L. 'When you have spoken it, 'tis dead, and I am the grave of it.' And then his
comment: 'How mightily sometimes we make us comforts of our losses.'
And this is most excellent: 'The web of our life is of a mingled yarn, good
and ill together; our virtues would be proud if our faults whipped them not;
and our faults would despair if they were not cherished by our virtues.'
I like the temper of that extremely – and does it not reveal the man?
Disillusioned and yet – amused – worldly – and yet he has feeling. But I see
him as quick, full of Life, and marvellously at his ease with his company, his
surroundings, his own condition, and the whole small, solid earth. He is like
a man on shipboard who is inclined to straddle just to show (but not to
show off) how well his sea-legs serve him …

    The Clown – 'a Shrewd Knave and an unhappy' comes to tell the
Countess of the arrival of Bertram and his soldiers. 'Faith, there's a dozen of
'em, with delicate fine hats and most courteous feathers, that bow and nod the
head at every man.'
In that phrase there is all the charm of soldiers on prancing, jingling, dancing
horses. It is a veritable little pageant. With what an air the haughty (and
intolerable) Bertram wears his two-pile velvet patch, with what disdain his
hand in the white laced French glove tightens upon the tight rein of his silver
charger. Wonderfully sunny, with a little breeze. And the Clown, of course,
sees the humour of this conceit …

---

[215]On front cover.

Parolles is a loveable creature, a brave little cock sparrow of a ruffian.
... 'I am now sir, muddied in Fortune's mood, and smell somewhat strong of
her strong displeasure.'

I must say Helena is a terrifying female. Her virtue, her persistence, and
disguised as a pilgrim – so typical!, her pegging away after the odious Bertram
and then telling the whole story to that <u>good</u> widowwoman! and that tame
fish Diana. As to lying in Diana's bed and enjoying the embraces meant for
Diana – well, I know nothing more sickening. It would take a respectable
woman to do such a thing. The worst of it is I can so well imagine Vera[216] for
instance acting in precisely that way, & giving Diana a present afterwards.
<u>What</u> a cup of tea the widow and D. must have enjoyed while it was taking
place, or did D. at the last moment want to cry off the bargain. But to forgive
such a woman! Yet Bertram would. There's an espece de mothersboyisme in
him which makes him stupid enough for anything.

The old King is a queer old card – he seems to have a mania for
bestowing husbands. As if the one fiasco were not enough Diana has no sooner
explained herself than he begins:

> 'If thou be'st yet a fresh uncropped flower
> Choose thou thy husband, and I'll pay thy dower.'

I think Shakespeare must have seen the humour of that. It just – at the very last
moment in the play, puts breath into the old fool.

Coleridge on Hamlet. 'He plays that subtle trick of pretending to act only
when he is very near being what he acts.'
... So do we all begin by acting & the nearer we are to what we would be, the
more perfect our <u>disguise</u>. Finally there comes the moment when <u>we are no
longer acting</u>; it may even catch us by surprise. We may look in amazement at
our no longer borrowed plumage. The two have merged; that which we put
on has joined that which was; acting has become action. The soul has accepted
this livery for its own after a time of trying on and approving.

To act ... to see ourselves in the part – to make a larger gesture than
would be ours in life, to declaim, to pronounce, to even exaggerate, to
persuade ourselves(?) or others(?) To put ourselves in heart? To do more than is
necessary in order that we may accomplish ce qu'il faut.
And then Hamlet is lonely. The solitary person always acts.
But I could write a thousand pages about Hamlets.

Mad Scene. If one looks at it with a cold eye is really very poor.
It depends entirely for its effect upon wispy Ophelia. The cardboard King
& Queen are of course only lookers on. They don't care a ½d. I think the
Queen is privately rather surprised at a verse or two of her songs ... And who
can believe that a solitary violet withered when that silly fussy old pomposity
died. And who can believe that Ophelia really loved him, & wasn't thankful to
think how peaceful breakfast would be without his preaching. The Queen's

---

[216]KM's eldest sister, Vera Mackintosh Bell.

speech after O's death is exasperating to one's sense of poetic truth. If no-one saw it happen - if she wasn't found until she was drowned how does the Queen know how it happened? Dear Shakespeare has been to the Royal Academy ... for his picture.[217]

Tempest. To say that Juliet & Miranda might very well be one seems to me to show a lamentable want of perception. Innocent, early-morning-of-the-world Miranda, that fair island still half dreaming in a golden haze, lapped about with little joyful hurrying waves of love ... And small, frail Juliet, leaning upon the dark - a flower that is turned to the moon & closes, reluctant at chill dawn. It is not even her Spring. It is her time for dreaming: too soon for love. There is a Spring that comes before the real Spring & so there is a love - a false Love. It is incarnate in Juliet.

Romeo & Juliet. When the old nurse cackles of leaning against the dove-house wall it's just as though a beam of sunlight struck through the centuries & discovered her sitting there in the warmth with the tiny staggerer - one positively feels the warmth of the sunny wall ...

Malvolio "or ... play with some rich jewel." There speaks the envious servant heart that covets his master's possessions. I see him stroking the cloth with a sigh as he puts away his master's coat - holding up to the light or to his fingers the jewel before he snaps it into its ivory case. I see the servant copying the master's expression as he looks in the master's mirror.
And that "having risen from a day bed where I have left Olivia sleeping." Oh, doesn't that reveal the thoughts of all those strange creatures who attend upon the lives of others!      [J273-276]

Vaihinger.
Die Philosophie des Als Ob: How comes it about that with consciously false ideas we yet reach conclusions that are in harmony with Nature & appeal to us as Truth? It is by means of and not in spite of these logically defective conceptions that they obtain logically valuable results. The fiction of Force. When two processes tend to follow each other to call the property of the first to be followed by the other its "force" and to measure that force by the magnitude of the result (Force of character). In reality we only have succession and co-existence & the 'force' is something we imagine.

Dogma: absolute and unquestionable truth.
Hypothesis: possible truth (Darwin's doctrine of descent).
Fiction: is impossible but enables us to reach what is relatively truth.
The myths of Plato have passed through these three stages & passed back again i.e. they are now regarded as fiction.

---

[217]In her Urewera notebook in Volume One of this edition KM referred to the famous painting of the drowned Ophelia by Millais in the Tate Gallery. This painting was from time to time exhibited in the Royal Academy.

? Why must thinking and existing be ever on two different planes? Why will not the attempt of Hegel to transform subjective processes into objective world-processes not work out?

"It is the special art & object of thinking to attain existence by quite other methods than that of existence itself." That is to say. reality cannot become the ideal, the dream, and it is not the business of the artist to grind an axe, to try and impose his vision of Life upon the existing world. <u>Art</u> is not an attempt to reconcile existence with his vision: it is an attempt to create his own world <u>in</u> this world. That which suggests the subject to the artist is the <u>unlikeness</u> of it to what we accept as reality. We single out, we bring into the light, we put up higher.　　[J272-273 S200-201]

# Notebook 15

[Notebook 15, qMS-1273]

5.v. Genève, Salle d'attente. The snow lay like silver light on the tops of the mountains. In the chill, greenish light the wide motionless rivers looked as though they were solid, and the pale furrowed earth with white fruit trees like coral branches looked as it were water.
Later. The station clock.      [J247-248]

June 8th 1921. For the first time since the war I talked German to a German. Wollen Sie fragen ob man warten kann?
And so on. It was simply extraordinary. Why?      [J251]

Lenz   Grillon not too high. Villa.
Lens   near Sierre.

7.30. A.M. Hotel Beau Site.

My precious Bogey,

I keep walking & walking round this letter, treading on my toes & with my tail in the air; I dont know where to settle. There's so much to say & the day is so fine – Well here goes, darling.
      The journey to Geneva took no time. My watchet seemed to be racing the train. We arrived some time after one & I went & sat in a green velvet chair while L.M. saw to things. I suppose we had a long wait there; it did not seem long. Ever since early morning those mountains that I remembered from last time had been there – huge, glittering, with snow like silver light on their tops. It was absolutely windless, and though the air was cold, it was cold like Spring. In fact (perhaps you realise Im putting a terrific curb on myself) it was delicious. Only to breathe was enough. Then we got into an omnibus train & it waddled slowly round the lake, stopping at every tiny station. Germans were in the carriage; in fact I was embedded in Germans, huge ones, Vater und die Mama und Hänsl. Every time we saw a lilac bush they all cried schön. This was very old world. There was also a notice in

the carriage to say that the company had thoughtfully provided a cabinet. This they read aloud (1) Vater - then die Mama & then little Hänsl. We arrived at Clarens just as the station clock (which was a cuckoo clock: that seems to me awfully touching doesn't it to you?) struck seven & a motor car, like a coffee mill, flew round & round the fields to Baugy. Oh dear, you realise Im just telling you facts. The embroidery Ill have to leave for now. The hotel is simply admirable so far. Too clean. Spick is not the word nor is span. Even the sprays of white lilac in my salon were fresh from the laundry. I have two rooms and a huge balcony, and so many mountains that I havent even begun to climb them yet. They are superb. The views from the windows, Betsy love, over fields, little mushroom-like chalets, lake, trees, & then mountains are overwhelming. So is the green velvet & flesh pink satin suite in the salon, with copper jugs for ornaments & a picture on the wall called Jugendidyle. More of all this later.

I am posing here as a lady with a weak heart & lungs of spanish leather! It seems to 'go down' for the present. Well, I had dinner in my room - consommé, fish, cream sauce, roast turkey new potatoes braised laitue & 2 little tiny babas smothered in cream. I had to send the turkey & trimmings away. Even then ...

Saint Galmier is superseded by Montreux[218] which the label says is saturated with carbonic acid gas. But my physiology book said this was deadly poison & we only breathed it out - never unless we were desperate took it in. However according to Doctors Ritter, Spingel and Knechtli its marvellous for gravel and makes the urine sparkil like champagne. These are the minor mysteries.

Sierre.   The room with seven doors.   Each door is different & the 7th is a very tiny little door.   It opens into a cupboard painted white with an arched top, sky blue, sprinkled with stars.

> The furniture stern & dark.   [J248-250]

---

[218]Murry's note: 'Saint Galmier and Montreux are both mineral waters.'

# *Notebook 21*

[Notebook 21, qMS-1271]

Household:  6:iii:1921[219]

| | | |
|---|---|---:|
| 7th | Notebooks | 3.20 |
| 8th | house | 28.20 |
| 9th | " | 30.25 |
| Wed. | " | 1.50 |
| Jeudi. | " | 22.65 |
| Ven. | " | 18.05 |
| S.S. | " | 42.10 |
| Dim. | | 3.40 |
| | Laundry | 21.20 |
| | | 170.55 |

| | | |
|---|---|---:|
| March 26th: | Saturday | 42.15 |
| | Sunday | 26. |
| | Monday | 52.40 |
| | Tuesday | 5.40 |
| | Wednesday | 30.65 |
| | Friday | 34.90 |
| | | 191.50 |

---

[219]On front cover.

It is remarkable how much there is of the ordinary man in J. For instance, finding no towels in his room tonight his indignation, sense of injury, desire so to shut his door that it would bring the house down – his fury, in fact in having to look for the blarsted things – all was just precisely what one would have expected of his Father. ... It makes one think again of the separation of the ARTIST and the MAN.

It's like his <u>Why is lunch late</u>? As tho' I had but to wave my hand and the banquet descended. But doesn't that prove how happy he would have been with a real WIFE!

"Tis thus:
Who tells me true, though in his tale lay death
I hear him as he flattered."

Act I. Scene II

"If I were to follow all your instructions and advice I don't think I should have any pleasures in Life at all." [J147-148 S109]

# Notebook 43

[Notebook 43, qMS-1274]

Katherine Mansfield. 1921[220]

Ah, that was she! That was his wife, bending out of the dark porch, half hidden by the over-hanging passion vine that drooped sorrowful, mournful even, as though it understood. Small warm arms were round his neck, a face little & pale lifted to his and a voice breathed: goodbye my treasure! My treasure! Goodbye my treasure. Which of them had spoken – whose voice was it he heard?[221]

> Many thanks for your stuffy letter. As for the candlestick dear – if you remember I gave it to you on your last birthday. No wonder it reminded you of me. I have kept it in its paper & intend to return it to you with a pretty little note on your next. Or shall I first send it to you as an early Christmas present & do you return it as a late one or a New Year's gift? Easter we shall leave out. It would be a trifle excessive at easter. I wonder which one of us will be in possession of it at the last. If it is on my side I shall leave it to you in my will, all proper, and I think it would be nice of you, Camilla, to desire that it should be buried with you. Besides, one's mind faints at the idea of a candlestick whirling through space and time for ever. Fliegende candlestick, in fact!

I have been suffering from wind round the heart. Such a tiresome complaint but not dangerous. Really, for anything to be so painful I think I would prefer a spice of danger added. The first act was brought on by a fit of laughing.

[J260]

Flaubert Notes.[222]

---

[220]On front cover.
[221]Murry's note: '"Old Mr Neave" - conclusion.'
[222]On back cover.

# Newberry Notebook 5

[Newberry Notebook 5]

xi.viii.1921[223]

I don't know how I may write this next story.[224] It's so difficult. But I suppose I shall. The trouble is I am so infernally cold!

Oh!
Oh!!
Oh!!!
je meurs de quelque chose

"I have been writing a story about an old man"
She looked vague.
"But I don't think I like old men, do you" said she. "They <u>exude</u> so."[225]
This horrified me. It seemed so infernally petty and more than that ... it was the saying of a vulgar little mind.

Later:  I think it was shyness.      [J259]

<u>Widoed</u>
by
Katherine Mansfield

Jimmy! His boots! How can a person be dead when their boots look like that. When Geraldine Cullen lost her husband it all happened so quickly, so unexpectedly, and she was called upon for such a display of courage and

---

[226]But just enough to keep one keen on one's appearance and so on. Otherwise one is apt to get grumpy ... But I was only thinking the other night in bed love is really absolute torment for anybody. One is never at peace, one is

---

[223]This date precedes 'Marriage à la Mode' which, as a published story, is not transcribed here.
[224]'The Voyage'.
[225]A remark, 'Elizabeth' later ruefully admitted, made by her.
[226]The following three paragraphs are part of an early draft of 'Hat With a Feather', some other parts of which occur in Newberry Notebook 7 and may be found on p 278. Murry brought them together in *Scrapbook* under his title 'Harden Your Heart'.

always thinking about the other person, worrying over them or being worried over – which is just as bad. Whereas now I have time for myself. I haven't the constant feeling of a man in the background. Not that one doesn't like a man in the background now & again, said Claire, laughing & pulling at her fur. But not seriously. Just a little affair to keep one keen on one's appearance, otherwise one is apt to get grumpy or eccentric.

But I can see my dear, said Claire, & she put her arms round Margaret & gave her a quick strained hug, you're not out of the wood yet. You're still in danger. Oh yes. She stepped away from Margaret & pulled on white suede gloves with quick little twitchy tugs, looking down at her hands. When she looked up her eyes were narrowed & cold, though her lips smiled. You've got to harden your heart my dear, said Claire. That's the whole secret. Harden your heart! Keep it <u>hard</u>!

Margaret said something, it might have been anything, went with Claire to the door. The day was over – the air blew cold and under the light sound of Claire's footsteps running over the gravel path to the road she heard the long slow pull of the cold sea.      [s188-189]

> exhausted
> angry
> quick

<u>The panting of the saw</u>      [j261 s190]

… constitutes a serious menace to health …

29.viii.1921.

"If I could only sweep all my garden up the hill to your doors."
her perfect little gesture as she said this.      [j260]

"Two women – and both Beauchamps!"[227]

A sudden idea of the relationship between 'lovers'. We are neither male nor female. We are a compound of both. I choose the male who will develop & expand the male in me; he chooses me to expand the female in him. Being made 'whole'. Yes, but that's a process. By love serve ye one another … And why I choose <u>one</u> man for this rather than many is for safety. We bind ourselves within a ring, and that ring is as it were a wall against the outside world. It is our refuge, our shelter. Here the tricks of Life will not be played. Here is <u>safety</u> for us to <u>grow</u>.

<u>Why I talk like a child.</u>      [j259]

(3) A smell of thyme startled the silence as the scream of a hawk.
(7) the hot sheet between her teeth, as she lay there damp & shivering.
It is impossible to 'take in' all these views and changes of light.

---

[227] Apparently this was a remark of Murry's, referring to his wife and her father's cousin 'Elizabeth'.

The innocent girl who barely knew the word 'obscene' could not think in this fashion: Was it merely as a potentiality that he obsessed her thoughts?[228]

[J261 s190]

<Little children run in and out of my world, never knowing the danger; and sick persons feel it slowly building up about them, trying to thrust its way into the place of the other. That is why they have such a horror of being alone ... anything to 'break' the silence; and lonely people, rather than face it, walk the streets, gape at shows, drink.>[229]     [s190]

> Dear Ida
>
>        Thank you for your letter. I would have written a card before but I have been - am - ill, & todays the first day I've taken a pen even so far. I've had an attack of what Doctor H. calls acute enteritis. I think it was poisoning. Very high fever & sickness & dysentery and so on. <u>Horrible</u>. I decided yesterday to go to the Palace but today makes me feel I'll try & see it out here. Jack is awfully kind in the menial offices of nurse & I have not been able to take any food except warm milk so E. can't work her worst on me. She seems poor creature to be much more stupid than ever! Burns everything! Leaves us without eggs & went off for her afternoon yesterday without a word. We didn't even know she was gone.
>
> [J259]
>
> In fact you are awfully in request. My very soul revolted though at your letter about your pension again. How can you have such a <u>passion</u> for people to hold up their hands & tell you over & over & over that they need you!! Or are you simply insincere when you take on a job? You don't ever mean to make anything your job - you're just a kind of vaccuum. I don't know. It's difficult. It's maddening. I suppose it gives you a trumpery sense of power. But no-one wants a slave, you know. There's your mistake. One only wants to feel sure of another. That's all. A pity you can't resist the female in you. I like people to be 'gay' & to be happy but I can't bear <u>flirts</u> ...

20.  The Biblical quote. Is it right?
27.  remembering something nice to compare you to
29.  big as a postage stamp
61.  why count the handkerchiefs
72.  Birds don't fit[?]
86.  I think you're a v. unhappy man
94.  Let's get married
96.  grey veil
101.  Does it hurt?
123.  passion of love for HIM?[230]

---

[228]Murry's note: 'Apparently quotations from a novel Katherine was reading with distaste.'

[229]At the end of the manuscript of 'A Married Man's Story' is this brief crossed out passage which Murry picked up and published in *Scrapbook* as 'Silence'.

[230]Murry's note: 'I fancy these are notes on *The Things We Are.*' His novel of that title was published by Constable in 1922.

An Outing        30.viii.1921

<So devoted to children.
The first year their mother had a flat in London for the season Betty and Susannah met more people who were not relations in a fortnight than they had seen in the whole of their lives. Not that they were very old. Betty wore stockings in the winter, bathed herself and used a small knife to cut up her own meat, but Susannah was still small enough to sit on knees, to believe everything people said and to drink out of her christening mug.>        [J261 s189]

<<u>Widowed</u>. The small buds at her breast. "Married or unmarried". The fires in the squares – the sweeper – the barrow. Lying in bed and still not able to feel anything but excitement.>

Emily Plack.        [J261 s190]

> The Garden–Party.
> At the Bay.    Prelude
> The Daughters of the Late Col.    Je ne parle.
> The Stranger
> Miss Brill.    Miss Moss
> The Young Girl.    Feuille
> The Ladies Maid.    The Wind blows
> Life of Ma Parker
> Sixpence
> Mr and Mrs Dove
> An Ideal Family
> Her First Ball
> Marriage à la mode
> The Singing Lesson
> The Voyage
> Bank Holiday.
>
> Widowed
> Barrington
> The Golden Birds
> Second Violin.

<u>100 Bedford Park</u>

# Newberry Notebook 6

[Newberry Notebook 6]

13.xi.1921

It is time I started a new journal. Come, my unseen, my unknown, let us talk together. Yes, for the last two weeks I have written scarcely anything. I have been idle; I have <u>failed</u>. Why? Many reasons. There has been a kind of confusion in my consciousness. It has seemed as though there was no time to write. The mornings, if they are sunny, are taken up with sun-treatment; the post eats away the afternoon. And at night I am tired. But it all goes deeper. Yes, you are right. I haven't felt able to yield to the kind of contemplation that is necessary. I have not felt pure in heart, not humble, not good. There's been a stirring up of sediment. I look at the mountains and I see nothing but mountains. Be frank! I read rubbish. I give way about writing letters. I mean I refuse to meet my obligations, and this of course weakens me in every way. Then I have broken my promise to review the books for the Nation. Another <u>bad spot</u>. Out of hand? Yes, that describes it - dissipated, vague, not <u>positive</u>, and above all, above everything, not working as I should be working - wasting time.

Wasting time. The old cry - the first and last cry. Why do ye tarry! Ah, why indeed? My deepest desire is to be a writer, to have a "body of work" done, and there the work is, there the stories wait for me, <u>grow tired</u>, wilt, fade, because I will not come. When first they knock how fresh and eager they are. And I hear & I <u>acknowledge</u> them & still I go on sitting at the window playing with the ball of wool. What is to be done.

I must make another effort, at once. I must begin all over again. I must try and write simply, fully, freely, from my heart. <u>Quietly</u>, caring nothing for success or failure, but just going on.

I must keep this book so that I have a record of what I do each week. (Here a word. As I re-read At the Bay in proof it seemed to me flat, dull, and not a success at all. I was very much ashamed of it. I am.) But now to resolve! And especially to keep in touch with Life. With the sky and this moon, these stars, these cold candid peaks.     [J270-271]

Katherine Mansfield Murry
Katherine Mansfield Murry[231]

---

[231] Both signatures in Murry's hand.

# *Newberry Notebook 7*

[Newberry Notebook 7]

> For the moment only:  Hotel Beau-Site
> > Baugy-sur-Clarens
> > La Suisse.

Bele Beatrice[232]
> I can't tell you how glad I am to hear you are dancing again
– albeit 'delicately' as you say.

> Lo! how sweetly the Graces do it foot
> To the instrument!
> They dauncen deftly and singen sooth
> In their merriement.

That means you are really better. Don't get ill again. Isn't it awful –
being ill. I lie all day on my old balcony lapping up eggs and cream
& butter with no-one but a pet goldfinch to bear me tompanëë. I must
say the goldfinch is a great lamb. He's jet tame & this morning, after it
had rained he came for his Huntley & Palmer crumb with a little
twinkling raindrop on his head. I never saw anyone look more silly and
nice. Switzerland is full of birds but they are mostly stodgy little german
trots flown out of Appenrodt's[233] catalogue. (Which reminds me of Bertha
<u>K</u>, ma chère.) But all Switzerland is on the side of the stodges.     [J248]

July. I finished Mr and Mrs Dove yesterday. I am not altogether pleased with
it. It's a little bit made up. It's not inevitable. I mean to imply that those two
may not be happy together – that that is the kind of reason for which a young
girl marries. But have I done so? I don't think so. Besides it's not <u>strong</u>
enough. I want to be nearer, far, far nearer than that. I want to use all my force
even when I am tracing a fine line. And I have a sneaking notion that I have, at
the end, used the doves <u>unwarrantably</u>. Tu sais ce que je veux dire. I used them
to round off something, didn't I? Is that quite my game? No, it's not. It's not
quite the kind of truth I'm after. Now for Susannah. All must be <u>deeply felt</u>.

---

[232]Beatrice Campbell, Lady Glenavy.
[233]Appenrodts (Criterion Restaurants Ltd) was a chain of foreign provision merchants in London.

But what is one to do with this wretched cat and mouse act? There's my difficulty! I must try and write this afternoon, instead. There is no reason why I shouldn't! No reason except the after-effects of pain on a weakened organism.

23rd. Finished <u>An Ideal Family</u> yesterday. It seems to me better than the 'Doves' but still it's not good enough. I worked at it hard enough, God knows & yet I feel I didn't get the deepest truth out of the idea, even once. What <u>is</u> this feeling? I feel again that this kind of knowledge is too easy for me; it's even a kind of trickery. I know so much more. This looks & smells like a story but I wouldn't buy it. I don't want to possess it - to live with it. <u>NO</u>. Once I have written 2 more I shall tackle something different - a long story - <u>At the Bay</u> with more difficult <u>relationships</u>. That's the whole problem.     [J256-257]

Out of the pocket of the mackintosh she took an ample bag which she opened & peered into & shook. Her eyebrows were raised, her lips pressed together.

And a very long shining blue-black hairpin gleaming on the faded red carpet.

She shuddered. And now when she looked at his photograph even the white flower in his button-hole looked as though it was made of a curl of mutton fat.

And she saw Mr. Bailey in a blue apron standing at the back of one of those horrible shops. He had one hand on his hip, the other grasped the handle of a long knife that was stuck into a huge chopping block. At the back of him there hung a fringe of small rabbits, their feet tied together, a dark clot of blood trembling from their noses.     [J257]

10.iv[?].1921.     A Sweet Old Lady
Montana.

    <Darling,[234]

        Do treat me just for once as a weekly paper that pays you let's say £950 a year for one article a week - a 'personal' article - intimate - only about yourself. For 3 days no-one has been near my bed with a letter. Your postcard in the train came this evening - but that's all.>

The <u>Tig Courier</u>, Sir is a weekly paper that pays you £950 a year for an article, personal as possible, the more intimate the better. For three days the editor has been waiting for your copy. Tonight she got a p.c. written in a train; but that was all. Will you tell her (a) your reasons for withholding it (as subtle as you like) or (b) when she may expect it.
Address:
    Tig
        Stillin
            Bedfordshire.     [J248]

---

[234]The following two notes to Murry were written on blank verso pages of the MS of 'An Ideal Family'.

Switzerland. May 1921.

One thing I am determined upon. And that is <u>to leave no sign</u>.

There was a time – it is not so long ago – when I should have written <u>all</u> that has happened since I left France. But now I deliberately choose to tell no living soul. I keep silence as Mother kept silence. And though there are moments when the old habit 'tempts' me – I may even get so far as to write a page – they are only moments & each day they are easier to conquer.

<u>Chalet des Sapins</u>. Just as now I say scarcely a word about my treacherous heart. If it is going to stop it is going to stop & there's an end of it. But I have been in this little house for nearly 2 days & it has not once quietened down. What dread to live in. But what's the use of saying aught? No, my soul, be quiet …

July 10th. And now, just as I felt a little better and less worried about my HEAD and my heart, the gland has become inflamed & all the surrounding tissue too. It looks as tho' an abcess were forming. So here is another <u>scare</u>. And with it I've one of my queer attacks when I feel nauseated all the time & can't bear light or noise or heat or cold. Shall I get through this, too? It is not easy to still find the courage to cope with these onslaughts …

July 13th. Went to the Palace & had the gland punctured. It is very unlikely that they will save the skin. I am sure, from the feeling, that they won't & that this affair is only beginning. I shall be back at the Palace before the week is out. In the meantime I am exhausted & can't write a <u>stroke</u>.

Well I must confess I have had an idle day – god knows why. All was to be written but I just didn't write it. I thought I would but I felt tired after tea and rested instead. Is it good or bad in me to behave so? I have a sense of guilt but at the same time I know that to rest is the very best thing I can do. And for some reason there is a kind of booming in my head – which is horrid.
But marks of earthly degradation still pursue me. I am not crystal clear – above all else, I do still lack application. It's not right. There is so much to do and I do so little. Life would be almost perfect here if only when I was <u>pretending</u> to work I always was working. But that is surely not too hard? Look at the stories that wait and wait just at the threshold. Why don't I let them in? And their place would be taken by others who are lurking just beyond out there – waiting for the chance.

Next day. Yet take this morning, for instance. I don't want to write anything. It's grey; it's heavy and dull. And short stories seem unreal & not worth doing. I don't want to write; I want to <u>Live</u>. What does one mean by that? It's not too easy to say. But there you are!

Queer this habit of mine of being garrulous. And I don't mean that any eye but mine should read this. This is – <u>really private</u>. But I must say nothing affords me the same relief. What happens as a rule is, if I go on long enough I <u>break through</u>. It's rather like tossing very large flat stones into the stream.

The question is, though, how long this will prove efficacious. Up till now,
I own, it never has failed me ...

One's sense of the importance of small events is very juste here. They are not
important at all ...!? Strange! I suddenly found myself outside the library in
Worishofen. Spring - lilac - rain - books in black bindings.

    And yet I love this quiet clouded day. A bell sounds from afar. The birds
sing one after another, as if they called across the tree tops. I love this settled
stillness, and this feeling that, at any moment, down may come the rain.
Where the sky is not grey it is silvery white, stroked with little clouds.
The only <u>dis</u>agreeable feature of the day is the flies. They are really maddening
and there is nothing to be done for them: I feel that about hardly anything.

[J254–255]

Mon seul désir ici c'est dire <u>Besfe</u>[?] Feel apposed[?] to the distance.
The barmaid. She wore an immense amount of fuzzy hair piled up on top of
her head, & several very large rings which from their bright flashing look you
were certain were engagement rings.

Above all cooking smells I hate that of mutton chops. It is somehow such an
ill-bred smell. It reminds me of commercial travellers & second class N.Z.

I'll stand in front of the house & knock & when the door is opened run in,
past the maid, & call for whoever is there.

Should you say wasted? No - not really. Something is gathered. This quiet time
brings one nearer.    [J256]

Hat With a Feather [235]
by
Katherine Mansfield

Claire replied most enthusiastically. My dear how extraordinary that we should
be unbeknown within reach of each other all this time! I shall love to come to
tea on Sunday. It's ages since Ive had a real talk with a fellow-creature. I am
lunching with a Mrs Beaver at the Royal and shall come on from there by
tram. My carriage days are over! Lucky you to have managed to snare a small
villa. As soon as I can get the present people out I am moving into a minute
one myself. I loathe hotels & as to pensions!..

Until Sunday alors, Lovingly
Claire.

P.S. Hannah C. told me your news. Ought I to be sorry? I am - because you
must have suffered. Otherwise I can't help being wickedly glad that another
of them has been found out!

Isobel read the letter over twice. It was curious how important letters became
when you lived by yourself. They seemed to be somehow much more than

---

[235]This was published in *Scrapbook* under Murry's title 'Harden Your Heart'.

written words on a page. They breathed, they spoke, they brought the person before you, and - was it fancy - Isobel heard a new sharp note in Claire's gay childlike voice, and a something careless. Not careless exactly, reckless was more the word - that was quite new. And yet, after all, perhaps it was just her imagination. One dashed down a little note like that in some hotel writing-room, with people asking for a loan of your blotting paper or whether there was such a thing as an uncrossed nib in your pen tray. But what can it be?     [s187-188]

1) The Daughters of the Colonel
2) The Stranger
3) The Young Girl
4) The Lady's Maid
5) Miss Brill
6) Ma Parker
7) Sixpence
8) The Music Lesson
9) Mr & Mrs Dove
10) An Ideal Family

# *Notebook 28*

[Notebook 28, qMS-1275][236]

## The New Baby.

It is late night, very dark, very still. Not a star to be seen. And now it has come on to rain. What happiness it is to listen to rain at night; joyful relief, ease, a lapping round and hushing and brooding tenderness, all are mingled together in the sound of the fast-falling rain. God, looking down upon the rainy earth, sees how faint are these lights burning in little windows - how easily put out.

Suddenly quick hard steps mount the stone staircase. Someone is hurrying. There is a knock at my door and at the same moment a red beaming face is thrust in and Ernestine announces 'He is born!' Born! 'He is born!' Oh, Ernestine, don't turn away. Don't be afraid. Let me weep too.

You ought to keep this my girl, just as a <u>warning</u> to show what an arch-wallower you <u>can</u> be![237]     [J266]

It is a curious fact that once a writer has attained to a certain eminence we English cease to bother ourselves about him. There he is, recognized, accepted, labelled.     [J241 S175]

## <u>Keith and Isobel</u>[238]

Among the passengers by the afternoon boat was Keith Kember. He had his bicycle on board.

<u>Reste toi ici - tu es mort</u>.

children are marvellous!

and all the while the little girl sat in the railway train & nursed her baby.

---

[236] This notebook begins with a draft of the first part of 'Second Violin'.
[237] This sentence is written in the top margin of the above passage.
[238] This is followed by a draft of 'All Serene'.

"Do you think that marriage would be of any use to me?" His friend considered gravely. He frowned, knocked his pipe against his heel & thrust out his underlip. "It depends" said he, "very much on the woman." "Oh but of course" said Archie, eagerly.

"Granted the right woman" said Wyndham largely, "I can imagine it might immensely benefit you."

The problem is 2 friends and a woman enters. One marries.[239]

[J253-254 S184-185]

Lucien's mother was a dressmaker. They lived in the village with the big church down in the valley. It was a very big church, it was enormous; it had two towers like horns. On misty days when you climbed the hill and looked down and you heard the great bell jangle it reminded you of a large pale cow. Lucien was nine years old. He was not like other boys. For one thing he had no father; and for another he did not go to school, but stayed at home all day with his mother. He was delicate. When he was very small his head had gone so soft, so soft, like a jelly, that his mother had had to clap two boards to it to prevent it from shaking. It was quite hard now but the shape was a little bit queer and his hair was fine like down rather than real hair. But he was a good child, gentle, quiet, giving no trouble, and handy with his needle as a girl of twelve. The customers did not mind him. The big, blousy peasant women who came to his mother's room to try on, unhooked their bodices and stood in their stays scratching their red arms and shouting at his mother without so much as a glance at him. And he could be trusted to go to shop. (With what a sigh his mother rummaged in the folds of her petticoat, brought out her shabby purse with a clasp and counted and thumbed the coins before she dropped them into his little claw.) He could be trusted to leave at the right houses large bulky newspaper parcels held together with long rusty pins. In these excursions Lucien talked to nobody & seldom stopped to look. He trotted along like a little cat out-of-doors, keeping close to the fences, darting into the shop and out again, and only revealing himself fully when he had to stand tiptoe on the top step of a house and reach up to the high knocker. This moment was terrifying to him.     [J303-304 S197-198]

---

[239]Murry's note: 'This is, I think, the first "idea" of the unfinished story <u>Honesty</u> of which fragments have been published in <u>The Doves' Nest</u>.' This attribution, though probably right, might have been less convincing if Murry had not changed 'Wyndham' to 'Rupert' in his version.

# Notebook 30

[Notebook 30, qMS-1276]

Katherine Mansfield

'Lives like Logs of Driftwood'. Etc.

Begun September 27th 1921.[240]

These pages from my journal. Don't let them distress you.
The story has a happy ending - really & truly.

14.x.1922.
I have been thinking this morning until it seems I may get things straightened
out if I try to write ... where I am. Ever since I came to Paris I have been as
ill as ever. In fact yesterday I thought I was dying. It is not imagination.
My heart is so exhausted and so tied up that I can only walk to the taxi and
back. I get up at midi and go to bed at 5.30. I try to 'work' by fits and starts,
but the time has gone by. I cannot work. Ever since April I have done
practically nothing. But why? Because, although Manoukhin's[241] treatment
improved my blood & made me look well and did have a good effect on the
lungs it made my heart not one scrap better, and I only won that improvement
by living the life of a corpse in the Victoria Palace Hotel.

My spirit is nearly dead. My spring of life is so starved that it's just not
dry. Nearly all my improved health is pretence - acting. What does it amount
to? Can I walk? Only creep. Can I do anything with my hands or my body?
Nothing at all. I am an absolutely hopeless invalid. What is my life? It is the
existence of a parasite. And five years have passed now, and I am in straighter
bonds than ever.

Ah, I feel a little calmer already to be writing. Thank God for writing.
I am so terrified of what I am going to do. All the voices out of the 'Past' say -

---

[240]On front cover.
[241]Dr Manoukhin, a Russian medical man practising in Paris, claimed to be able to cure tuberculosis
by a series of treatments which irradiated the spleen. In desperation and at great expense KM underwent
these treatments which not only did her no good but probably hastened her death.

"don't do it". Bogey says 'Manoukhin is a scientist. He does his part. It's up to you to do yours.' But that is no good at all. I can no more cure my psyche than my body. Less it seems to me. Isn't Bogey himself, perfectly fresh and well, utterly depressed by boils on his neck? Think of five years imprisonment. Someone has got to help me to get out. If that is an expression of weakness – it is. But it's only lack of imagination that calls it so. And who is going to help me? Remember Switzerland. "I am helpless." Of course he is. One prisoner cannot help another. Do I believe in medicine alone? No. Never. In science alone? No. Never. It seems to me childish and ridiculous to suppose one can be cured like a cow <u>if one is not a cow</u>. And here, all these years I have been looking for someone who agreed with me. I have heard of Gurdjieff [242] who seems not only to agree but to know infinitely more about it. Why hesitate?

Fear. Fear of what. Doesn't it come down to fear of losing Bogey? I believe it does. But good heavens! Face things. What have you of him now! What is your relationship. He talks to you - sometimes - and then goes off. He thinks of you tenderly. He dreams of a life with you <u>some day</u> when the miracle has happened. You are important to him as a dream. Not as a living reality. For you are not one. What do you share? Almost nothing. Yet there is a deep sweet tender flooding of feeling in my heart which is love for him and longing for him. But what is the good of it as things stand? Life together, with me ill, is simply torture with happy moments. But it's not life. I have tried through my illness (with one or two disastrous exceptions) to prevent him facing wholly what was happening. I ought to have tried to get him to face them. But I couldn't. The result is he doesn't know me. He only knows Wig-who-is-going-to-be-better-some-day. No. You do know that Bogey and you are only a kind of dream of what might be. And that might be never never can be true unless you are well. And you won't get well by 'imagining' or 'waiting' or trying to bring off that miracle yourself.

Therefore if the Grand Lhama of Thibet promised to help you - how can you hesitate! Risk! Risk anything! Care no more for the opinions of others, for those voices. Do the hardest thing on earth for you. Act for yourself. Face the truth.

True, Tchekhov didn't. Yes, but Tchekhov died. And let us be honest. How much do we know of Tchekhov from his letters. Was that all? Of course not. Don't you suppose he had a whole longing life of which there is hardly a word? Then read the final letters. He has given up hope. If you de-sentimentalize those final letters they are terrible. There is no more Tchekhov. Illness has swallowed him.

But perhaps to people who are not ill all this is nonsense. They have never travelled this road. How can they see where I am? All the more reason to go boldly forward alone. Life is not simple. In spite of all we say about the

---

[242]George Gurdjieff, an Armenian mystical philosopher, founded The Institute For the Harmonious Development of Man at Fontainebleau, in France. KM, believing that Gurdjieff possessed the kind of wisdom that could guide her initially to a spiritual cure, joined the Institute in October 1922 and died there three months later.

mystery of Life when we get down to it we want to treat it as though it were a child's tale ...

Now, Katherine, what do you mean by health? And what do you want it for? Answer: By health I mean the power to live a full, adult, living breathing life in close contact [with] what I love - the earth and the wonders thereof, the sea, the sun. All that we mean when we speak of the external world. I want to enter into it, to be part of it, to live in it, to learn from it, to lose all that is superficial and acquired in me and to become a conscious, direct human being. I want, by understanding myself, to understand others. I want to be all that I am capable of becoming so that I may be - (and here I have stopped and waited and waited and it's no good - there's only one phrase that will do) a child of the sun. About helping others, about carrying a light and so on it seems false to say a single word. Let it be at that. A child of the sun.

Then I want to work. At what? I want so to live that I work with my hands and my feeling and my brain. I want a garden, a small house, grass, animals, books, pictures, music. And out of this - the expression of this - I want to be writing. (Though I may write about cabmen. That's no matter.)

But warm, eager living life - to be rooted in life - to learn, to desire to know, to feel, to think, to act. That is what I want. And nothing less. That is what I must try for.

I wrote this for myself. I shall now risk sending it to Bogey.[243] He may do with it what he likes. He must see how much I love him. And when I say 'I fear' - don't let it disturb you, dearest heart. We all fear when we are in waiting rooms. Yet we must pass beyond them and if the other can keep calm it is all the help we can give each other.

Suppose if this worries you, you show it to Dunning? I trust Dunning in spite of my thinking he did not really solve your problem. Let him see that, too. He will understand.

And this all sounds very strenuous and serious. But now that I have wrestled with it it's no longer so. I feel happy - deep down. May you be happy, too.

I'm going to Fontainebleau on Monday & I'll be back here Tuesday night or Wednesday morning. All is well.

Doctor Young the London man who has joined Gurdjieff came to see me today & told me about the life there. It sounds wonderfully good & simple and what one needs.      [J331-334]

My first conversation with Orage[244] took place on August 30th 1922. On that occasion I began by telling him how dissatisfied I was with the idea that Life must be a lesser thing than we were capable of 'imagining' it to be. I had the feeling that the same thing happened to nearly everybody whom I knew and

---

[243] Murry's note says she changed her mind about sending it to him. He found it among her papers.

[244] A R Orage, Editor of the *New Age*, became important to KM in 1910, encouraging her and publishing her work over the next two or three years. He came back into her life at the end as a disciple of Gurdjieff. KM had discussions with Orage about Gurdjieff and his Institute before both of them joined it at about the same time.

whom I did not know. No sooner was their youth, with the little force and impetus characteristic of youth, over, than they stopped growing. At the very moment when one felt that now was the time to gather oneself together, to use one's whole strength, to take control, to be an adult in fact, they seemed content to swop the darling wish of their hearts for innumerable little wishes. Or the image that suggested itself to me was that of a river flowing away in countless little trickles over a dark swamp.

They deceived themselves of course. They called this trickling away greater tolerance, wider interests, a sense of proportion so that work did not rule out the possibility of 'life'. Or they called it an escape from all this mind probing and self consciousness - a simpler and therefore a better way of life. But sooner or later, in literature at any rate, there sounded an undertone of deep regret. There was an uneasiness, a sense of frustration. One heard, or one thought one heard, the cry that began to echo in one's own being. "I have missed it. I have given up. This is not what I want. If this is all then Life is not worth living."

But I <u>know</u> it is not all. How does one know that? Let me take the case of K.M. She has led, ever since she can remember, a very typically false life. Yet, through it all, there have been moments, instants, gleams, when she has felt the possibility of something quite other.     [J329-330]

Important

When we can begin to take our failures non-seriously, it means we are ceasing to be afraid of them. It is of immense importance to learn to <u>laugh at ourselves</u>. What Shestov calls "a touch of easy familiarity and derision" has its value.

What will happen to Anatole France and his charming smile? Doesn't it disguise a lack of feeling - like M's weariness ... Life should be like a steady, visible light.

What remains of all those years together? It is difficult to say. If they were so important how could they have come to nothing. Who <u>gave up</u> and <u>why</u>?

Haven't I been saying, all along, that the fault lies in trying to cure the body and pay no heed whatever to the sick psyche. Gurdjieff claims to do just what I have always dreamed might be done.

The sound of a street pipe hundreds & hundreds of years old.     [J331]

Our Hilda.

On a fine spring morning, one of those delicious spotless mornings when one feels that celestial housemaids have been joyfully busy all through the night, Mrs Quill locked the back door, the pantry window, and the front door and set off for the railway station.

"Good-bay, wee house!" said she, as she shut the gate, and she felt the house heard and loved her. It was not quite empty. In her bedroom, in his cradle Chi-chi lay sleeping his morning sleep. But the blind was down and he was so beautifully trained. She counted on him not waking up until they were back.

At that hour, all the little houses in Tyrell Street basked in the radiant light; all the canaries in their little houses hanging from the verandah poles, sang their shrillest. It was difficult to understand how the infants in perambulators who shared the verandahs with the canaries slept through the din. But they apparently did; no sound came from them. Up and down spanked the important-looking light yellow butcher's cart, and in and out of the back gates went the baker's boy with his basket clamped to his back, like a big shell. It had rained in the night. There were still puddles – broken stars – on the road. But the pavement was beautifully dry. What a pleasure it was to walk on the nice clean pavement!     [J323 S218]

% Mme Dubois, Val Richer, Lisieux (Calvados).

# Notebook 31

[Notebook 31, qMS-1278]

Oct. 16th. Another radiant day. J. is typing my last story The Garden Party, which I finished on my birthday. It took me nearly a month to 'recover' from At the Bay. I made at least three false starts. But I could not get away from the sound of the sea and Beryl fanning her hair at the window. These things would not <u>die down</u>. But now I am not at all sure about that story. It seems to me it's a little 'wispy' – not what it might have been. The G. P. is better. But that is not <u>good enough</u>, either.

The last few days, what one notices more than anything is the blue. Blue sky, blue mountains, all is a heavenly blueness! And clouds of all kinds - wings, soft white clouds, almost hard little golden islands, great mock-mountains. The gold deepens on the slopes. In fact, in sober fact, it is perfection.

But the late evening is the time of times. Then with that unearthly beauty before one it is not hard to realise how far one has to go. To write something that will be worthy of that rising moon, that pale light. To be 'simple' enough as one would be simple before God ...     [J267]

Nov. 21st. Since then I have only written The Doll house. A bad spell has been on me. I have begun 2 stories but then I told them and they felt betrayed. It is absolutely fatal to give way to this temptation ... Today I began to write, seriously, 'The Weak Heart', a story which fascinates me <u>deeply</u>. What I feel it needs so peculiarly is a very subtle variation of 'tense' from the present to the past & back again. And softness, lightness, and the feeling that all is in bud, with a play of humour over the character of Ronnie, and the feeling of the Thorndon Baths, the wet, moist, oozy ... no, I know how it must be done.

May I be found worthy to do it! Lord make me crystal clear for Thy light to shine through.     [J271]

The woman from upstairs has just been down to put her milk can out. She was furious when she found me in the hall. She simply - rounded on me - there's no other word for it. Told me I ought to be ashamed of myself for waiting up for him, that it served me right if he came in later and later, that she'd be ashamed at my age, not to know better. Little spitfire. I'm still

trembling! And what right has she to say anything at all. She has none.
She can't understand. She's a hard little thing. The very way she shut the door
on the milk can just now showed she had no feeling for anyone else.

It's a long time now since he started going out every evening. I can't stop
him – I've tried everything but it is useless – out he goes. And the horrible
thing is I don't know where it is he goes to – who is he with? It's all such a
mystery, that's what makes it so hard to bear. Where have you been. I've asked
him and asked him that. But never a word, never a sign. I sometimes think he
likes to torture me.

But then I've got nobody else. I suppose that sounds strange. But I can
say as truly as a girl in love: He is all the world to me.      [J251-252 S185-186]

The deep grudge that L.M. has for me really is fascinating. She keeps it under
for a long time at a stretch but oh – how it is there! Tonight, for instance, in
the salon we hated each other – really hated in a queer way. I felt I wanted her
out of my sight; she felt that she must insult me before she went. It was very
queer. It was peculiarly horrible. When she said I hope you are satisfied I had
a real shrinking from her – something I never feel at other times. What is it?
I don't understand, either, why her carelessness or recklessness should be so
repellent to me. When she tosses her head and says in a strange voice, at ease,
"Oh a lot I care" I want to be rid of the very sight.      [J269-270 S191]

These last days I have been awfully rebellious. Longing for something. I feel
uprooted. I want things that Jack can so easily do without, that aren't natural
to him. I long for them. But then, stronger than all these desires is the other
which is to <u>make good</u> before I do anything else. The sooner the books are
written, the sooner I shall be well, the sooner my wishes will be in sight of
fulfilment. That is sober truth, of course. As a pure matter of fact I consider
this enforced confinement here as God-given. But on the other hand, I must
make the most of it quickly. It is not unlimited any more than anything else is.
Oh, why – oh why isn't anything unlimited. Why am I haunted every single
day of my life by the nearness of death and its inevitability! I am really diseased
on that point! And I can't speak of it. If I tell J. it makes him unhappy. If I
don't tell him it leaves me to fight it. I am tired of the battle. No one knows
how tired.

Tonight when the evening star shone through the side window and the
pale mountains were so lovely I sat there thinking of death, of all there was to
do – of Life which is so lovely – and of the fact that my body is a prison.
But this state of mind is <u>evil</u>. It is by acknowledging that I, being what I am,
had to suffer <u>this</u> in order to do the work I am here to perform – it is only by
acknowledging it, by being thankful that work was not taken away from me,
that I shall recover. I am weak where I must be strong. 24.XI.1921.

And today, Saturday, less than ever. But no matter. I have progressed – a little.
I have realised <u>what</u> it is to be done – the strange barrier to be crossed from
thinking it and writing it ... Daphne.[245]      [J271-272]

---

[245]A draft of 'Daphne' follows here.

Have you seen my cosmias dear? Have you noticed my cosmias today? Really, even though they are mine I must say I've never seen so fine a show. Everybody remarks on them. People stop to stare. I think it's so marvellous of the children not to pick them now that they show over the fence. Those mauve ones. Did you ever see anything so delicate! Such an uncommon colour, too. And when I think all that beauty came out of one little 3d packet from the D.I.C!²⁴⁶

Frail as butterflies the petals of the cosmias fluttered like wings in the gently breathing air. They were moon white, mauve, pale pink, and lemon yellow. And peering through the delicate green you could still see in the garden bed, the little soiled seed packet stuck in a cleft stick. Kezia remembered the day when she had watched Aunt Fan tear off a corner, shake the seed, like minute canary seed, then pat the fine earth over. And afterwards they had stood together, just as they were standing now, gazing at nothing but seeing – just what they looked at this very minute. What was the difference really? It was too hard to understand.

She said "They are most lovely, Aunt Fan."
"Look at that bee Kezia. Look at that great velvety fellow."
They watched him. When he clung to a cosmia the flower leaned over, swung, quivered – it seemed to be teasing him. And when he flew away the petals moved as though they were laughing.
"But I really must go, Aunt Fan."
"One moment darling. I'll just get my kitchen scissors & snip off a dead head or two while you're here." She was there and back again on the instant, & before Kezia realised what was happening, quickly, lavishly, Aunt Fan had begun cutting her finest largest flowers.
"Oh Aunt Fan what are you doing!" Kezia was horrified. "Stop! I don't want them. Why will you always give everything away. We've millions & billions of flowers at home. The vases were only done yesterday. Oh Aunt <u>Fan</u>."
"Only these, Kezia. Only this little selection for your own vase in your room." She thrust them into Kezia's hand & squeezed the reluctant fingers.
"They flower all the better for being cut. You know that's true."
Yes that was comforting. Kezia smiled at an exquisite half-open bud, the petals springing from the centre like the feathers of a tiny shuttlecock.
"Well – goodbye, Aunt Fan." She turned. Aunt Fan took her in her arms, held her close, looked, just an instant, intently & gravely at her before she gave her a quick light kiss.

Aunt Fan. <u>No</u>.    [J311-313]

----

Paris. May 3rd 1922

I must begin writing for Clement Shorter²⁴⁷ today. 12 'spasms' of 2000 words each. I thought of the Burnells but no, I don't think so ... Much better the

----

²⁴⁶The DIC - a department store in Wellington.
²⁴⁷Clement Shorter, editor of the *Sphere*, commissioned a good deal of work from KM and so eased her financial burdens at this time.

Sheridans - the three girls and the brother and the Father and Mother and so on, ending with a long description of Meg's wedding to Keith Fenwick. Well, there's the first flown out of the nest. The sisters Bead who come to stay. The white sheet on the floor when the wedding dress is tried on ... Yes, I've got the details all right. But the point is - where shall I begin? One certainly wants to dash.

Meg was playing. I don't think I ought to begin with that. It seems to me the mother's coming home ought to be the first chapter. The other can come later. And in that playing chapter what I want to stress chiefly is: which is the real life - that or this - late afternoon, these thoughts, the garden, the beauty, how all things pass ... and how the end seems to come so soon ...

And then again there is the darling bird. I've always loved birds. Where is the little chap?

What is it that stirs one so? What is this seeking - so joyful, ah, so gentle. And there seems to be a moment when all is to be discovered. Yes, that is the feeling. The queer thing is I only remember how much I have forgotten when I hear that piano. The garden of the Casino, the blue pansies. But oh, how <u>am</u> I going to write this story!     [J313-314]

Dear Ida,

Just a line to say - Jack and I both have so much work to do this summer that we have decided when we leave here (end of this month) to go to the Hotel d'Angleterre, Randogne. Does that make you open your eyes! But in the summer June and July that place was so lovely & I know it. It would only take a day to settle and a look at the mountains before one could work. All other arrangements are too difficult - Germany & so on. We have not, literally, the time to discover a new place and take our bearings. Then we shall be near Elizabeth, too. The winter we are going to spend in Bandol at the Beau Rivage. I am going to get a maid now at once. I can't do without one. I simply have not the time to attend to everything and I can't bear as you know 'untidiness'. I shall advertise in the Daily Mail. Jack may be going to lecture in England this autumn too, so I should like to have a really trustworthy person to post letters and so on and be with me. By the way it may interest you Jack is really <u>very</u> successful now. His reputation is at least double what it was. He has a new job with The Times for which [he] is being enormously successful. Don't speak of our plans, by chance - will you?

There is a really superb professional pianist here. He plays nearly all day & one writes <u>to</u> his music. Au revoir. K.M.[248]     [J316]

---

[248] At the end of this notebook is an ink-drawn temperature chart with the morning and evening temperatures recorded, though without dates, for 2½ days. All of them were above 'normal'.

# Notebook 41

[Notebook 41, qMS-1277]

Finished and sent to put into my book.[249]
B
This is a moderately successful story - and that's all. It's somehow, in the episode at the lane, scamped.        [J266]

16.XI.1921. To go to Sierre if it goes on like this ... or to - or to -
        Ka        [J271]

It happened that Alexander and his friend missed the Sunday morning train that all the company travelled by. The only other for them to catch so as to be at their destination in time for the rehearsal on Monday morning was one that left London at midnight. The devil of a time! And the devil of a train, too. It stopped at every station. Must have been carrying the London milk into the country said Alexander bitterly, and his friend, who thought there was no one like him said "That's good, that is. Extremely good. You would get a laugh for that in the Halls I should say." They spent the evening with their landlady in her kitchen. She was fond of Alexander: she thought him quite the gentleman.[250]        [J264 S194]

And then finally there is his first leave.[251] She does not go to the station to meet him - Daddy goes alone. As a matter of fact she is frightened to go. The shock may upset her & spoil their joy. So she tries to bear it at home.
    Late afternoon. The lights on. Gorgeous fires everywhere - in his bedroom too, of course. She goes to see it too often - but each time there is something to be done - the curtains to be drawn, or she makes sure he has enough blankets. For some reason there is no place for the girls in this

---

[249]Above this is the first part of 'The Garden Party'.
[250]Murry has written 'Second Violin' above this piece. For a discussion of problems with this title see note 254.
[251]The draft of 'Six Years After', at this point, includes this passage which is not part of the published story.

memory; they might be unborn. She is alone in that warm, breathing lighted house except for the servants. Each time she comes into the hall she hears that distant twitter from the kitchen - or the race of steps down the area. They are on the lookout. And at this point she always remembers his favourite dinner - roast chicken, asparagus, meringues, champagne. And then - oh God help me to bear this moment - there's the taxi. It's turned into the square. Is it slowing. No.

There it is'm.

No, Nellie, I don't think so.

Yes, yes. It is. Courage. Be brave. It's stopping. Is that father's glove at the window. Then the door is open - she is on the step. Father's voice rings out. Here he is - and all at one & the same moment the taxi stops & bursts open, a young muffled figure bounds up the steps. Mummy.

My precious precious son! And here it's no use - here she must break down - just a moment, just one - pressing her head against the cold buttons of his British Warm while he holds her & his Father is behind him patting his shoulder & his laugh rings out.

Well you've got him. Are you satisfied?

The door is shut. He is peeling off his own world[?] - his gloves & scarf & coat & tossing them on to the chest in the hall. The old familiar quick shot back of his head while he looks at her laughing, then he describes how he spotted Daddy immediately & Father absolutely refused to recognise him.

oh, my <u>hatred</u>!<sup>252</sup>

<u>Don't reply to this</u>.

Dear <u>Friend</u>

I like your criticism. It is right you should have hated those things in me. For I was careless and false. I was not <u>true</u> in those days. But I have been trying for a long time now to "squeeze the slave out of my soul" ... I just want to let you know.

Oh, Koteliansky, I am in the middle of a nice story.<sup>253</sup> I wish you would like it. I am writing it in this exercise book & just broke off for a minute to talk to you.

Thank you for the address. I cannot go to Paris before the Spring, so I think it would be better if I did not write until then. I feel this light treatment is the right one. Not that I am ill at present. I am not in the least an invalid, in any way.

Its a sunny, windy day - beautiful. There is a soft roaring in the trees and little birds fly up into the air just for the fun of being tossed about.

Goodbye. I press your hand. But do you dislike the idea we should write to each other from time to time?

Katherine.     [J266]

---

<sup>252</sup>This fragment was written at the bottom of one of the pages of 'Six Years After'.
<sup>253</sup>Murry's note: 'The Garden Party'

Its queer how even when the <u>need</u> is removed she waits in a fury of impatience for the post.

I wonder why it should be so difficult to be humble. I do not think I am a good writer; I realise my faults better than anyone else could realise them. I know exactly where I fail. And yet, when I have finished a story & before I have begun another I catch myself <u>preening</u> my feathers. It is disheartening. There seems to be some bad old pride in my heart; a root of it that puts out a thick shoot on the slightest provocation ... This interferes very much with work. One can't be calm, clear, good as one must be while it goes on. I look at the mountains, I try to pray, & I think of something <u>clever</u>. It's a kind of excitement within one which shouldn't be there. Calm yourself. Clear yourself. And anything that I write in this mood will be no good; it will be full of <u>sediment</u>. If I were well I would go off by myself somewhere & sit under a tree. One must learn, one must practise to <u>forget</u> oneself. I can't tell the truth about Aunt Anne unless I am free to enter into her life without selfconsciousness. Oh God! I am divided still. I am bad. I fail in my personal life. I lapse into impatience, temper, vanity & so I fail as thy priest. Perhaps poetry will help.

I have just thoroughly cleaned & attended to my fountain pen. If after this it leaks then it is <u>no</u> gentleman!     [J269]

And the friend opposite gazed at him thinking what an attractive mysterious fellow he was. And the train sped on.

flashy and mean –

It was spouting with rain yet there was that feeling of spring in the air which makes everything bearable.

The big sprays of flowers. What on earth

He shot out his legs, flung up his arms, stretched, then sat up with a jerk & felt in his pocket for the yellow paper of cigarettes. As he felt for them a weak strange little smile played on his lips. His friend opposite was watching it. He knew it. Suddenly he raised his head; he looked his friend full in the eyes. That was a queer thing to happen, he said softly & meaningly. What? asked the friend, curious. Alexander kept him waiting for the answer. Practised liar that he was, the[254]     [J263-264 S193-194]

> N.Z.  <u>Honesty</u>. The Doctor & his wife, Arnold Cullen, Lydia & Archie.
> L.    <u>One Kiss</u>. Arnold Alexander & his friend in the train. <u>Wet lilac</u>.

---

[254]Immediately following this piece is one of KM's lists of her stories in which 'One Kiss' seems to refer to this piece. However, in the next list, 'One Kiss' has disappeared and 'Second Violin' seems to be the same story. Among the unfinished stories in *The Dove's Nest* Murry has published a longer piece about Alexander and his friend as part of a story, called 'Second Violin' which begins with Miss Bray on her way to orchestra practice with her violin. It is probable that 'Second Violin' (about Miss Bray) and 'One Kiss' (about Alexander and his friend) are two quite distinct but, alas, unfinished stories.

N.Z.  <u>Six Years After</u>. The wife & husband in the steamer. The cold
        buttons.[255]
N.Z.  <u>Aunt Anne</u>. Her life with the Tannhauser Overture.
L.     <u>Lives Like Logs of Driftwood</u>.
N.Z.  <u>A Weak Heart</u>. Edie & Ronnie.
L.     <u>Widowed</u>. Geraldine and Jimmie.
N.Z.  <u>Our Maude</u>. "What a girl you are!"
        <u>The Washerwoman's Children</u>.      [J263 S192]

I wish that <u>my</u> silence was only a 2 minute one!
... fallen out of the nest, without wings or feathers to help them bear the cold.

[J270]

27.X.1921.
Stories for my new book.
N.Z. <u>Honesty</u>:  The Doctor, Arnold Cullen & his wife Lydia, and <u>Archie</u> the
friend.
L. <u>Second Violin</u>:  Alexander and his friend in the train. Spring - spouting
rain.
N.Z. <u>Six Years After</u>:  A wife & husband on board a steamer. They see
someone who reminds them.
L. <u>Lives Like Logs of Driftwood</u>:  This wants to be a long, very well written
story. The men are important, especially the lesser man. It wants a great deal of
working ... newspaper office.
N.Z. <u>A Weak Heart:</u>  Ronnie on his bike in the evening, with his hands in his
pockets <u>doing marvels</u> by that dark tree at the corner of May Street.
L. <u>Widowed</u>:  Geraldine & Jimmie, a house overlooking Sloane Street
& Square. Wearing those buds at her breast. "Married or not married ..."
From Autumn to Spring.
N.Z. <u>Our Maude</u>:  Husband & wife play duets and a <u>one</u> a <u>two</u> a <u>three</u> a one
a <u>two three one</u>! His white waistcoats. Wifeling & Ma hub!
N.Z. <u>At Karori</u>:  The little lamp. I seen it. And then they were silent. Finito
<u>30</u>.X.21.     [J267-268]

Mr Kelvie was the scandal of the neighbourhood.[256] He drove a fish cart, when
he was out of prison or out of the hospital. For he was such a hopeless
drunkard that the wonder is he could sit in the cart at all - he never did for
long. Horses have scent[?] of the Devil's plan - if he [...] one he was pitched
out at the other - & there he lay angry & swearing until the police came
round to remove him.
    Happily there were only 2 little Kelvies. Lil, a stout plain child with big
freckles and a high forehead and her little sister whom her mother & everyone
called 'our Else'. Our Else was so small that people said there was something

---

[255] It is worth noting that 'the cold buttons' occur only once in this story—in the piece (on p 295)
which did not find its way into the published version.
[256] A draft of 'The Dolls House' occurs here. This section of it was deleted from the final version.

wrong with her; she was nearly a dwarf. A little wishbone of a child with cropped hair, enormous eyes in a pale solemn little face. No-one had ever seen her smile, she could scarcely be made to speak. The teachers gave her up after two days & she had a [...] little bench by herself and looked on during lessons. Out of school she did not seem to exist except as a part of Lil. It seemed to be her one idea that if she let go of Lil she let go of Life altogether. And so in the playground, or down the road, going to and from school Lil marched in front & our Else tagged behind holding on to her sisters dress with one hand like a claw. When she wanted anything or when she was out of breath she gave Lil a tug or twitch, & Lil stopped dead & turned round. She never failed to understand.

<He is dead. The doctor is there and Major Hunter is still there. Her sister has been telephoned for and Jimmie's brother, Arnold. Both are on their way. He is dead. His riding boots stand side by side, his cold[?] clothes are put away. But his watch still ticks on the dressing table. The glass has cracked, but it seemed to be going quite normally otherwise. The watch has escaped.>[257]

---

[257]This crossed out paragraph of 'Widowed' was part of its first draft.

# Unbound Papers

[MS-Papers-4006-8]

Behind the hotel - à deux pas de l'hotel, as the prospectus said - there was an immense stretch of gently rising turf dotted with clumps of pine and fir trees. Beyond was the forest, threaded with green paths and hoarse, quick tumbling little streams. Dark blue mountains streaked with white rose above the forest and higher still there was another range, bright silver floating across the still, transparent sky.

What could be more pleasant, after the long terribly cold winter, than to sit outside on a fine Spring afternoon and to talk, slowly, softly, at one's ease. Nothing has happened, and yet there seems so much to say. In the winter one can go for weeks without saying a word more than is necessary. But now, in the warmth and light there is such a longing to talk that it is hard to wait for one's turn ... It was hot in the sun. Auntie Marie had a newspaper over her head, Auntie Rose a handkerchief, but little Anna's father, whose hair was thick like fur, refused to cover himself. They sat the three of them in a row on canvas chairs outside the back door [of] the hotel & little Anna danced now before them now behind them now from side to side like a gnat.

Little Anna and her father had come up from the valley by the funicular to spend the day with the Aunties who owned this immense, airy hotel with its wide windows & wider balconies and glassed-in verandah lounge.
What! All this was owned by these two insignificant little grey haired creatures in their black shift dresses. They themselves seemed to realise how dreadfully inappropriate it was and hurriedly explained in almost a horrified whisper that it had been left to them. And as they could never sell it or let it they tried to make a living out of it. But very very few people came. It was too quiet for young people - there was no dancing or golf, nothing on earth to do but to stare at the view. And, thank Heaven, they hadn't come to that yet! And it was too quiet for old people. There was no chemist, no doctor within call. As for the view, when one did stare at it one felt inclined to whimper, the mountains looked so cruelly unsympathetic.

I seem to have lost all power of writing. I can think, in a vague way, and it all seems more or less real and worth doing. But I can't get any further. I can't write it down. Sometimes I think my brain is going. But no! I know the real reason. It's because I am still suffering from a kind of nervous prostration caused by my life in Paris. For instance, those interviews with the dentist. If anyone else – anyone with imagination had realised what I suffered they would have known I was really at the end of my strength. And then the strain of keeping going; of brushing my clothes, making the constant renewed effort, talking to Brett, coughing … Bogey was perfectly marvellous. But watching him do everything was really nearly as tiring as doing it oneself. And then, on other journeys, look at the care I had taken of me – everything was spared. There was nothing to do but to keep still. This time I felt at the mercy of everything. Tchekhov, by the way, felt this disenchantment exactly. And who could not feel it who lives with a pessimist. To keep another going is a million times more tiring than to keep oneself going. And then there is always the feeling that all falls on <u>stony ground</u>. Nothing is nourished, watched, cherished. He hears. It gives him a vague sense of life, and then it passes away from him as though it never had been and he      [J321-322 S239-242]

[MS-Papers-4006-10]

<Then after lunch when I came out of the Kiwi Café I knew for the first time why men want to send women flowers and all that – what not. I'd always thought it was [what] you see in the pictures. It was useless of course. She – the other – was ½ way to Napier²⁵⁸ by then. But if I could have been at some station & waited for her train & handed her roses – only roses – big long-stemmed ones, a whole mass of them – 5 bob's worth – But it hurt to think about it. I didn't go on thinking about it.>²⁵⁹

[MS-Papers-4006-9]

The Lily.

As old Mr Rendall sat at the window with the rug over his knees, with his spectacles, folded handkerchief, medicine and newspaper on a little table beside him; as he sat there, looking out, he saw a large, strange cat bound on to the fence and jump right into the very middle of his lawn. Old Mr R. hated cats. The sight of this one, so bold, so carefree, roving over the grass, sniffing, chewing at a blade of something as though the whole place belonged to it, sent a quiver of rage through him. He shifted his feet in the felt slippers, his hands lifted, trembled, and grasped the knobs of his chair.

"Tss!" he said, glaring spitefully at the cat. But it was a small feeble sound; of course the cat did not hear. What was to be done? His yellowish old eyes glanced round the parlour for something to throw. But even supposing there had been something, a shell off the mantelpiece or a glass paperweight

---

²⁵⁸It is impossible to tell whether this word is Napier or Naples. Napier is a city on the east coast of the North Island of New Zealand, some 200 miles north of Wellington.

²⁵⁹A crossed out section of 'A Bad Idea' at the end of the 4th paragraph which in the published version ends '… asked me if I had a headache.'

from the centre table, surely old Mr R. knew he could no more throw it at the cat than the cat could throw it back at him.

Ah, the hateful beast! It was a large tabby with a thin tail and a round flat face like a penny bun. Now, folding its paws it squatted down exactly opposite the parlour window and it was impossible not to believe that its bold gaze was directed expressly at him. It knew how he hated it. Much it cared. It had come into his world without asking; it would stay there as long as it chose and go again when the fancy seized it.

A cold snatch of wind raked the grass, blew in the fur of the tabby, rattled the laburnum and sent the kitchen smoke spinning downwards over the stony little garden. High up in the air there sounded a loud hooting and shrieking as the wind raced by. And it seemed to old Mr Rendall that the wind was against him, too, was in league with the cat and made that shrill sound on purpose to defy him.     [J306-307 S216-217]

Bowing deeply as though bitterly ashamed the little girl crept out after her grandmother.

When they were gone old Mr Rendall lay down on the horsehair sofa. He felt better altogether – easier and lighter now he had torn the lily from its stem. Hm! the wan blood tingled in his veins. He threw his handkerchief over his face, thinking with almost a chuckle there was life in the old dog yet!

Well, said Janet, sighing – she always sighed at moments of leave taking – if we are to catch that tram we must be going. And lifting her chin she began to retie her bonnet strings.
Get down Susannah.
Susannah slid over the slippery chair. She was glad to go. I'll look in again when I'm passing, said Janet. Shake hands Susannah & say goodbye. No, not that hand child, the other.     [J307]

[MS-Papers-4006-9]

By great good fortune the tram was empty. The sisters had it all to themselves. Feeling grand, down they sat in one of the small wooden pens. The conductor blew his whistle, the driver banged his bell, the fat small horses started forward and away they swung. Merrily danced the pink bobbles on the fringes of the cotton blinds and gaily the sunlight raced under the arched roof.
"But what on earth am I to do with this" cried Gertrude, gazing with exaggerated scorn and horror at the bouquet that old Mr Phipps had cut and bound together so lovingly. Agnes screwed up her eyes and smiled at the unearthly white and gold arum lily and the dove blue columbines.
"I don't know" said she. "You can't possibly cart it about with you. It's like a barmaid's wedding bouquet." And she laughed and put her hand to her glorious coil of thick hair. Gertrude tossed it on to the floor & kicked it under the seat. Just in time, as it happened.     [J309 S199]

And smiling faintly he looked into his wife's faintly smiling face. Wherever the house happened to be he added, softly.     [J313]

[MS-Papers-4006-8]

One great advantage in having your clothes made by Miss Phillips was that you
had to go through the garden to get to the house. Perhaps it was the only
advantage for Miss Phillips was a strange, temperamental dressmaker with ever
a surprise up her - no, indeed - in your own sleeve for you. Sleeves were her
weakness, her terror. I fancy she looked upon them as devils, to be wrestled
with but never overcome. Now a 'body', once she had tried it on first in
newspaper, then in unbleached calico and finally in the lining she would make
a very pretty fit to the figure. She liked to linger over her bodies, to stroke
them, to revolve round them, hissing as was her wont, faintly. But the moment
she dreaded came at last.
"Have you cut out the sleeves, Miss Phillips."
"Yes, Miss, I 'ave. One moment Miss. If you please." And with a look half
peevish, half desperate, the strange funnel shaped thing was held up for your
arm to be thrust into.
"The armhole is <u>very</u> tight, Miss Phillips."
"They're wearing them very small this seasing, Miss."
"But I can't get my hand near my head."
"Near your read, Miss" echoed Miss Phillips, as though it was the first time
she had ever heard of this gymnastic feat being attempted. Finally she repinned
it & raised it on the shoulder.
"But now it's much too short, Miss Phillips. I wanted a lo-ong sleeve.
I wanted a point over the hand. Points over the hand always seemed to me -
still seem to me - excessively romantic."
"Oh Miss !"
    The big scissors that went 'sneep sneep' like a bird on a cold morning cut
out a brown paper cuff & Miss Phillips fixed it on with fingers that trembled;
while I frowned at the top of her head & even made faces at her in my rage.
Her hair was so strange. It was grey, all in little tufts. It reminded you of a
sheepskin hearthrug. And there were always threads, minute triangles of stuff,
pieces of fluff sticking to it. It didn't want brushing, I thought, so much as
sweeping and a shaking out of windows. In person Miss Phillips was extremely
thin and squeezed in so tightly that every breath creaked, and at moments of
emotion she sounded like a ship at sea. She invariably wore the same black
alpaca apron, frilled, and on her left breast - oh how cruel, how sinister it
looked to me - a tight little red plush heart pierced all over with needles &
pins and a malignant looking safety pin or two to stab deeper - "If you please
Miss while I unpin you." Her small hard hands flew up, perched, gripped like
claws. She had a thin nose with just one dab of red at the tip as though some
wicked child with a paint brush had caught her sleeping.
    "Thank you Miss Phillips. And you'll let me have it on Saturday?"
"Satterday for certing, Miss" hissed Miss Phillips through a bristling mouthful.
    While I dressed in front of the long mirror that had spots on the side like
frosted finger prints I loved to discover again that funny little room. In the
corner by the fireplace stood the 'middle' covered in red sateen. Its solidity

ended at the hips in wire rings that reminded one of a doves egg beater. But what a model it was. What shoulders, what a bosom, what curves, and no horrible arms to be clothed in sleeves, no head to be reached up to. It was Miss Phillips god. It was also, I decided, a perfect lady. Thus and thus only do perfect ladies appear in the extreme privacy of their apartments. But above all - it was godlike. I saw Miss Phillips, alone, abstracted, laying her stuffs upon that imperturbable altar. Perhaps her failures were to be excused. They were all part of a frenzy for sacrifice ...        [J299-300 S231-233]

[MS Papers 4006/9][260]

A very small railway train came along with a wooden whistle. First it stopped, blew the whistle & then moved slowly forward with a wonderfully expressive motion of the right arm. People mattered not at all. It went through them, past them - skirted them. Then down it fell, full length. But two gentlemen picked it up, patted its behind and in a minute it whistled (rather longer than usual) and started off again ...

A little bird-like mother with a baby in her arm, and tugging at one hand a minute little girl in a coat made out of a pleated skirt & a pink bow - it looked like pink flannel - on her bobbed hair. A very rich child in a white beaver hat passed & fell quite in love with the pink flannel bow. When its nurse was not looking it hung back & walked beside its little poor sister, looking at her wonderingly & very carefully <u>keeping step</u>.

A little person in a pink hat passed very carefully dragging a minute doll's pram. It was <u>so</u> minute she had to drag it on a thread of cotton. Naturally once she stopped looking & her hand gave a jerk down fell the pram & for about 2 minutes she pulled it along on its side. Then she discovered the accident, rushed back, set it up & looked round very angrily in all directions, <u>certain</u> some enemy had knocked it over on purpose. Her little dark direct gaze was quite frightening. Did she see someone?

And then suddenly the wind lifts and all the leaves fly forward so gladly - so eagerly as if they are thankful it is not their turn yet to        [J334-335]

[MS-Papers-4006-9]

## Poor Auntie B!

On Sunday mornings as early as half past ten, and in spite of the fact that the kitchen arrangements in the Tindalls' large luxurious flat were cut off by baize doors and a passage, there was a whiff, a discreet whiff but an unmistakable one, of the very finest roast surloin. Priscilla and Betty who were too young to recognise the smell as roast beef - unless the roast beef was actually there before them - called it the Sunday smell. They had a dim idea - at least Betty had - that it came from Heaven and that little children who did not go to church with [a] bright 6d in their gloves were not allowed to smell it.

---

[260] Murry's heading for this piece is 'October. The Luxembourg Gardens'.

Bring them straight back across the park Mam'selle, please. said Mrs T. who liked to go into the day nursery and survey Priscilla & Biddy when they had been through the maids and Mamselle's

[MS-Papers-4006-9]

There are certain human beings on this earth who do not care a safety-pin whether their loved one is beautiful or pretty or youthful or rich. One thing only they ask of her and that [is] that she should smile.

"Smile! Smile now!" their eyes, their fingers, their toes and even their tiny jackets say. In fact, the tassel of little Jean's cap, which was much too big for him and hung over one eye with a drunken effect, said it loudest of all. Every time his mother swooped forward to put it straight it was all she could do not to lift him out of the pram and press him - squeeze him to her shoulder while she rubbed her cheek against his white cheek & told him what she thought of him.

Jean's cheeks were white because he lived in a basement. He was, however, according to his mother, a perfectly healthy child, and good, lovely. He had merry, almost cunning little eyes. "Smile!" said Jean's eyebrows, which were just beginning to show.

On a perfect spring afternoon he and his mother set off for the Jardins Publiques together. It was his first spring. A year ago he had been of course much too young - six months only! - to be in the open air for any length of time. Even now his mother wheeled him out in the teeth of his grandmother's awful prophecies and the neighbours' solemn warnings. The open air is so weakening for a baby and the sun, as everyone knows, is very very dangerous. One catches fever from sitting in the sun, colds in the head, weeping eyes. Jean's gran, before daring to face its rays, plugged her ears with wool, wrapped herself round in an extra black shawl, gave a final twist which hid her mouth and her pale beak-like nose, & pulled black woollen mitts over her cotton ones. Thus attired, with a moan of horror she scuttled away to the bread shop and having scuttled back she drank something blue out of a bottle as an extra precaution ...

But there was a wicked recklessness about his mother. First she had made up her mind to buy a pram and then she had bought one second hand. Then she had set her heart on taking Jean to the Jardins Publiques, and here they were!

It is lovely in the public gardens; it is full spring. The lilac is in flower & the [...] the new grass quivers in the light, & the trees, their delicate leaves gold in the sun, stand with branches outspread as if in blessing ...

Up the path go Jean and his mother. She is extremely proud of him and then proud of herself for having managed to bring him there. The wheel of the pram squeaks & this delights her, too, for she thinks everybody will notice it and look at Jean. But nobody does. Mothers, nurses, babies, lovers, students go by in a stream. A little boy tugs his grandfather's hand. Run, he says - run. And they stagger off together. It is hard to say which will fall down first.

But all this is absolutely mysterious to little Jean. First he looks one side, then he looks the other. Then he stares at his mother who nods & says cuckoo! But how does cuckoo explain anything. For a moment he wonders if he ought to cry. But there seems to be nothing to cry about, so he jumps up and down instead & tries to burst out of some of the tight hot little coats & shawls that are half smothering him. The heat in the pram is terrible. He is sitting on a blanket, a broad strap cuts across his legs, and on either side, at his feet & there behind his head, there are large newspaper parcels which contain his mother's mending.

Are you hungry? Are you hungry? Hungry? Hungry? asks his mother as she wheels the pram over to a bench & sits down. Jean is never hungry. But he takes the biscuit that she shows to him, nibbles it, & stares at the grass on the other side of the low railing.    [J301-303 S224-227]

The kitchen hearth rug with a tail on it very big and sniffing at the trees.
The pram was not new. It had belonged to
life saving apparatus.
Do you want to go home, want to go home, want to go home? said she.
Why she asked him so many times nobody will ever know.    [S189]

There are certain human beings on this earth who do not care a safety-pin whether their loved one is beautiful or pretty or youthful or rich. One thing only they ask of her and that is that she should smile. Nothing else matters. Paul Verdun was one of them. Smile! he commanded. Smile now! And he searched his mother's face as though it were the heavens & her smile the sun.

And for the last time she folded up her newspaper parcels, packed them round little Paul, lifted him, set him down again, put his cap straight, & strapped him in. But as she drew the strap tight he realised what all this preparation meant. Shall we go home - go home, home! repeated his mother.

It was horrible at home in the dark basement kitchen. His grandmother padded about in felt slippers. She wore a black handkerchief on her head & her hands were covered with little black mitts. And she was always shaking something that smelt disgusting in a saucepan over the fire. He hated his grandmother. He would have hated her more had he known how she scolded his mother for being sure that he should be taken into the open air every day. What could be more dangerous than the sun? It gave you fever, it gave you colds in the head. His grandmother declared the open air was weakening.

[MS-Papers-4006-9]

Why should Sunday be so different to every other day? Why should the air, the sky, the clouds be different. Why should the dew take so much longer to dry on the bluish grass and how do the birds know it's Sunday? One can understand it in the town where all the shops are shut and the trams don't run until church time, but in the country - that stillness, that brightness, that sense of joyful ease ... where does it come from.

"Ting-a-tan! Ting-a-tan! Ting-a-tan-tan-tan" rang very faint from the little tin church over the hill. It sounded rather charming from a distance. The Skeritts never dreamed of going any nearer. She washed her hair on Sunday mornings if the weather was fine; if it was wet she cleaned her white kid gloves. And he lay in a long chair on the verandah & read something or other. There had been a time when she had always come to dry her hair in the sun on the verandah. She stood in her white kimono against the big blue plumbago, looking solemn & fanning that flag of hair until he put down his book & drawled lazily "I say what a lot. How jolly it looks." There had been a time when she had always pinned the helpless exhausted-looking gloves to the verandah poles to air while he murmured "They look like absurd little mice." But that was over. Nothing had been said but both of them understood why.

[s238-239]

[MS-Papers-4006-10]

I do not think I have the right to criticise any of this. Please ignore the pencil marks & the comments. I am <u>sure</u> I should have left your work as it is.
It is <u>you</u>.

K.M.

[MS-Papers-4006-9]

It was the late afternoon when Mrs Sheridan after having paid Heaven knows how many calls turned towards home.

"Thank Heaven that's all over!" she sighed as she clicked the last gate to, and stuffed her little chinese card-case into her handbag.

But it was not all over. Although she hadn't the faintest desire to remember her afternoon, her mind, evidently, was determined she should not forget it. And so she walked along seeing herself knocking at doors, crossing dim halls into large pale drawing rooms, she heard herself saying no, she would not have any tea, thank you. Yes, they were all splendidly well. No, they had not seen it yet. The children were going tonight. Yes, fancy, he had arrived. Young & good-looking too! Quite an asset! Oh dear no! She was determined not to allow any of her girls to marry. It was quite unnecessary nowadays, and such a risk! And so on and so on. What nonsense calling is! What a waste of time! I have never met a single woman yet who even pretended to like it. Why keep it up then? Why not decide once and for all. Mock orange. And Mrs Sheridan woke out of her dream to find herself standing under a beautiful mock orange bush that grew against the white palings of old Mr Phipps garden. The little sponge-like fruit - flowers? which were they? - shone burning-bright in the late afternoon sun. They are like little worlds, she thought, peering up through the large crumpled leaves & she put out her hand & touched one gently. The feel of things is so strange, so different: one never seems to know a thing until one has felt it - at least that is true of flowers. Roses for instance - who can smell a rose without kissing it. And pansies - little darlings they are! People don't pay half enough attention to pansies.

Now her glove was all brushed with yellow. But it didn't matter. She was glad, even. "I wish you grew in my garden" she said regretfully to the mock orange bush, and she went on, thinking I wonder why I love flowers so much. None of the children inherit it from me - Laura, perhaps. But even then it's not the same - she's too young to feel as I do. I love flowers more than people - except my own family of course. But take this afternoon for instance. The only thing that really remains is that mock orange.

But this is not expanded enough or rich enough. I think still a description of the house and the place should come first and then the light should fall on the figure of Mrs S. on her way home. Really I can allow myself to write a great deal - to describe it all - the baths, the avenue, the people in the gardens, the chinaman under the tree in May Street. But in that case she won't be conscious of these things. That's bad. They must be seen and felt by her as she wanders home. That sense of flowing in and out of houses - going and returning like the tide. To go and not to return - how terrible! The father in his dressing room, the familiar talk. His using her hair brushes, his passion for things that wear well. The children sitting round the table, the light outside, the silver. Her feeling as she sees them all gathered together, her longing for them always to be there. (Yes, I'm getting nearer all this. I now remember S.W. and see that it must be written with love - real love. All the same the difficulty is to get it all within focus, to introduce that young doctor & bring him continually nearer and nearer until finally he is part of the Sheridan family, until finally he has taken away Meg ... That is by no means easy ...)

Now her white glove was all brushed with yellow. But it did not matter. She was glad, even. Why don't you grow in my garden, she said regretfully to the mock orange bush. And she went on, thinking I wonder why I love flowers so much. I love them more than people - except my own family of course. But take this afternoon, for instance. The only thing that really remains is that mock orange. I mean, when I was standing under that bush it was the only moment when I felt in touch with something. These things are very difficult to explain. But the fact remains I never feel the need of anybody - apart from Claude & the children. If the rest of the world was swept away tomorrow

Return again! Come. It was an agony to Mr Sheridan to be late, or to know that others were late. It had always been so. Talking with his wife in the garden - the stillness, the lightness, the steps on the gravel, the dark trees, the flowers, the night scented stocks - what happiness it was to walk with him here. What he said did not really matter so very much. But she felt she had him to herself in a way that no other occasion granted her. She felt his ease and although he never looked at what she pointed out to him it did not matter. His 'very nice, dear' was enough. He was always planning, always staring towards the future 'I should like, later on'. But she - she did not in the least, the present was all she loved and dwelt in.

I have been thinking over this story this morning. I suppose I know as much about it now as I shall know. So it seems. And if just the miracle happened I

could walk into it and make it mine. Even to write that brings it all nearer. It's very strange, but the mere act of <u>writing anything</u> is a help.
It seems to speed one on one's way. But my feet are so
cold.    [J323-6 s219-23]

[MS-Papers-4006-9]

<Late Afternoon.
The Theatre.

It was the late afternoon and Mrs Sheridan, after having paid Heaven knows how many calls, was on her way home. Who invented calling? What a ridiculous waste of a fine afternoon it is! But she could not get out of it, more especially now the children were grown up. People were so absurdly touchy. For her part she would be only too thankful if there was never another card on the salver. Cards again are most absurd. Why did she have to leave 2 of Henry's, and one of her own? And as she walked along The Terrace she was like a person waking out of a succession of faint-dreams - each dream the same and yet not the same. A door, a dim hall, a chintz drawing room, with silver[?] tables & tall vases of roses. "No thanks I won't have any tea", "Yes, isn't it exquisite weather", "No, the children are going tonight - they say it's very good", "Yes, I hear he has arrived? Young and goodlooking too? Oh, please don't suggest anything so frightful - I shall never let any of my children marry.>

[MS-Papers-4006-9]

              Late Afternoon.

It was the late afternoon when Mrs Sheridan, after having paid Heaven knows how many calls, turned towards home. "Thank goodness that's over" she thought, "Thank goodness!' She hated calling. But then she had never met a woman who didn't. Who invented it? And why if they all agreed it was a waste of time did they keep it up? Slowly she walked along Clive Terrace, slowly that succession of faint dreams faded.

Really & truly? You're not making a martyr of yourself? My dear! How <u>can</u> you!

[NL]
              A Family Dance
                   by
           Katherine Mansfield

The excitement began first thing that morning by their father suddenly deciding that, after all, they could have champagne. What! Impossible! Mother was joking! A fierce discussion had raged on this subject ever since the invitations were sent out, Father pooh-poohing and refusing to listen, and Mother, as usual, siding with him when she was with him ("Of course,

darling: I quite agree") and siding with them when she was with them
("Most unreasonable. I more than see the point."). So that by [this] time they
had definitely given up all hope of champagne, and had focussed all their
attention on the hock cup instead. And now, for no reason whatever, with
nobody saying a word to him - so like Father! - he had given in.

"It was just after Zaidee had brought in our morning tea. He was lying
on his back, you know, staring at the ceiling, and suddenly he said: 'I don't
want the children to think I am a wet blanket about this dance affair. If it's
going to make all that difference to them; if it's a question of the thing going
with a swing or not going with a swing, then I'm inclined to let them have
champagne. I'll call in and order it on my way to the Bank.'"

"My dear! What did you say!"

"What could I say? I was overcome. I said: That's very generous of you,
Daddy dear, and I placed the entire plate of cut bread and butter on his chest.
As a kind of sacrifice to the darling. I felt he deserved it and he does so love
those thin shaves of bread and butter."

"Can't you see the plate" cried Laurie, "gently rising and falling on his
pyjama jacket."

They began to laugh, but it really was most thrilling. Champagne did
make all the difference - didn't it? Just the feeling it was there gave such a
different ... Oh, absolutely!      [J326-327 S223-224]

[MS-Papers-4006-9]

September 30th 1922.
Do you know what individuality is?
No.
Consciousness of will. Conscious that you have a will and can act.
–  –  –  –  –  –
Yes it is. It's a glorious saying.      [J330]

[MS-Papers-4006-8]

21.ii.1922
           Confidences.

"You know, my dear," said Kitty, standing in the middle of the drawing room
and stripping off her white gloves, "your house is too lovely for words. But too
lovely!" She had just arrived, a little out of breath as usual, but so charmingly
breathless, her eyes wide, her lips half open, and the parma violets agitated in
the front of her gown.
"I don't know what it is," she went on gaily, "but one always has the feeling it's
so alive." And she turned quickly towards her friend. "You know what I mean.
Don't you feel it too?"

But Eva, who was lighting a cigarette, made no reply for a moment.
She took a puff, breathed deeply, and then fixing her eyes on the lighted tip of
the cigarette, she said, rather queerly, "Yes, I certainly used to feel that."

Used to? Why used to? Now that Kitty looked at her closely she fancied Eva was pale. Her expression changed (she was a marvellously sympathetic little thing) and lifting her hands to her violets she sank into a chair and said softly "This weather's awfully trying - don't you agree?"

Eva sat down too. But still she did not look at her friend. With her finger tip she flattened the tobacco in her cigarette and in the same unnatural voice she murmured "Yes, I suppose it is. I've not been out. I haven't noticed."

This seemed to Kitty so strange that quickly she leaned forward and laid her hand on her friend's silken knee. "You're not ill, darling, are you" she asked tenderly. But Eva as quickly drew back. "Oh please please don't touch me" she pleaded, waving Kitty away, "don't be too nice to me." And now there was no doubt about it. There were tears in her eyes, her lids were trembling. "I shall make a fool of myself if you do. I ... I ought not to have seen anybody this afternoon ...    [J307-308]

[MS-Papers-4006-8]

Carriages are not allowed to drive up to the doors of the clinique because of the noise. They stop at the iron gates. Then comes a little walk - on the level it is true, but still quite a walk, before the yellow glass porch is reached. But there is a compensation, if only the patients would realise it. On either side of the gravel are flowerbeds full of purple and pink stocks, wallflowers, forget me nots and creamy freezias with their spears of tender green like the green of young bamboos. The front of the clinique is hung with heliotrope, banksia roses and pink ivy geranium. And there is such a coming & going of brown bees and white butterflies, the air smells so sweet, there is such a sense of delicate trembling life that however ill anyone might be it was impossible surely not to be cheered and distracted.

"Look. Look how lovely," said the plain girl, pointing them out to her companion. But the young man in a black double breasted jacket put his hand to his ribs & breathed[?] a-huh a-huh - as if he were playing trains.

"How pretty they are - how very pretty!" said the sentimental old mother, wagging her head at them and glancing at her daughter. But the pale daughter stared back at her spitefully, very spitefully, & flung the end of her shawl over her shoulder.

Now a bath chair is pushed along carrying an old man. In his stiff, much too big overcoat with his hat squeezed down to his ears he looks marvellously like a Guy Fawkes. The nurse stops the chair & says 'flowers' as one says flowers to a baby. But there is no response at all; she smiles & wheels it on again ...

(Stupefaction) total. I feel unable to do anything. It is a proof of the horribly soporific nature of the codeine mixture.    [J244-245 S177-178]

# Notebook 20

[Notebook 20, qMS-1282]²⁶¹

<u>ai écrit à</u>

Richard
Anne
Brett
Ottoline
Sydney
Manoukhine
Kot
Drey
Vere
Sadleir
. . . . . . . . . .
Cousin Lou
E.B.
Marie
Jeanne
Roma
Sydney
Elizabeth

1.  To escape from the prison of the flesh – of matter. To make the body an instrument, a servant.

2.  To act and not to dream. <u>To write it down</u> at all times and at all costs.

What is the universal mind?

OM. "<u>Kratu smara Kritam smara Kratu smara Kritam smar</u>."

From the Isha Upanishad.²⁶²      [J291-292 S205]

---

²⁶¹ This is a diary for 1922 with a Heron Bookplate and with 'Katherine from Boge' written in Murry's hand.
²⁶² Murry's note: 'Quoted from *Cosmic Anatomy* (p106) where the author says: "The accepted translation is 'Om (my) mind, remember (thy) acts, remember (O) mind, remember (thy) act remember.'"' *Cosmic Anatomy or the Structure of the Ego* by 'MB Oxon' was written by Dr Wallace, a Theosophist. Murry described it as 'a book of occult doctrines' and reacted strongly against it, while KM found that it contained much food for thought.

SUNDAY, JANUARY 1

I dreamed I sailed to Egypt with Grandma, a very white boat.

<u>Cable</u>

Cold, still. The gale last night has blown nearly all the snow off the trees, only big, frozen looking lumps remain. In the wood where the snow is thick bars of sunlight lay like pale fire.

I have left undone those things which I ought to have done and I have done those things which I ought not to have done e.g. violent impatience with L.M.

Wrote The Doves Nest this afternoon. I was in no mood to write; it seemed impossible, yet when I had finished three pages they were 'alright'. This is a proof (never to be too often proved) that once one has thought out a story nothing remains but the <u>labour</u>. Wing Lee disappeared for the day. Read W.J.D.'s[263] poems. I feel very near to him in mind. I want to remember how the light fades from a room – and one fades with it, is <u>expunged</u>, sitting still, knees together, hands in pockets …

MONDAY, JANUARY 2

Letters from Marie & J.[264]

Little round birds in the fir tree at the side window, scouring the tree for food. I crumbled a piece of bread but though the crumbs fell in the branches only two found them. There was a strange remoteness in the air, the scene, the winter cheeping. In the evening for the first time for – – I felt rested. I sat up in bed and discovered I was singing within. Even the sound of the wind is different. It is joyful, not ominous, and black dark looks in at the window and is only black dark. In the afternoon it came on to pour with rain, long glancing rain falling aslant.

I have not done the work I should have done. I shirk the lunch party. This is very bad. In fact I am disgusted with myself. There must be a change from now on. What I chiefly admire in Jane Austen is that what she promises she performs i.e. if Sir T. is to arrive we have his arrival at length and it's excellent and excels our expectations. This is rare; it is also my very weakest point. Easy to see why …

TUESDAY, JANUARY 3

I dreamed I was at the Strand Palace, W.L.G.[265] having married Marie Dahlerup[266] – big blonde – in quantities of white satin … There was a great deal more snow this morning; it was very soft, 'like wool'. The coconut was bought and sawn in half and hung from J's balcony. The milk came tinkling out of the nut in brightest drops – not white milk. This was a profound surprise. The flesh of the nut is very lovely – so pure white. But it was that dewy, sweet liquid which made the marvel. Whence came it? It took one to the island.

---

[263]Walter de la Mare.
[264]KM's sisters, Marie (i.e. Chaddie) and Jeanne.
[265]W L George, the novelist, through whom KM first met Murry in 1911.
[266]Marie Dahlerup, an old acquaintance of KM and her sisters, probably from their schooldays.

I read The Tempest. The papers came. I over-read them. Tell the truth.
I did no work. In fact I was more idle and hateful than ever. Full of sin. Why?
"Oh self oh self wake from thy common sleep." And the worst of it is I feel so
much better in health. It is strange! The Tempest seems to me astonishing this
time. When one reads the same play again it never is the same play.

WEDNESDAY, JANUARY 4
Dreamed of Michael Sadleir.[267] An important dream, its tone was important.
That gallery over the sea and my "isn't it beautiful" and his weary "no doubt".
His definition of the two kinds of women.
A.M. which served as one excuse not to do any creative work. But I was not
so wicked today. I have read a good deal of Cosmic Anatomy - understood it
far better. Yes, such a book does fascinate me. Why does Jack hate it so?
To get even a glimpse of the relation of things, to follow that relation & find it
remains true through the ages enlarges my little mind as nothing else does.
Its only a greater view of psychology. It helps me with my writing for instance
to know that hot + bun may mean Taurus, Pradhana, substance. No, that's not
really what absorbs me, its that reactions to certain causes & effects always have
been the same. It wasn't for nothing Constantia[268] chose the moon & water -
for instance! Read Shakespeare. The snow is thicker, it clings to the branches
like white newborn puppies.

THURSDAY, JANUARY 5
A long typical boat dream. I was, as usual, going to N.Z. But for the first time
my stepmother was <u>very</u> friendly - so nice. I loved her. A tragic dream as
regards Ida. She disappeared & it was too late to find her or tell her to come
back <u>at last</u>.
    Read Cosmic Anatomy. I managed to work a little. Broke through.
This is a great relief. Jack & I put out food for the birds. When I went to the
window all the food was gone, but there was the tiny print of their feet on the
sill. J. brought up the ½ coconut, and sprinkled crumbs as well. Very soon,
terrified, however one came, then another, then a third balanced on the
coconut. They are precious little atoms. It still snows. I think I <u>hate</u> snow,
downright hate it. There is something stupefying in it - a kind of 'you must be
worse before you're better' and down it spins. I love, I long for the fertile
earth. How I have longed for the S. of France this year! So do I now.
Soundly rated Ida about food & clothing. She has a food 'complex'. J. & I read
Mansfield Park with great enjoyment. I wonder if J. is as content as he
appears? It seems too good to be true.

FRIDAY, JANUARY 6
First Quarter of the Moon. Jour de Fête. The Tree is dismantled. I had a v. bad
night & did not fall deeply asleep enough to dream. In the morning all white
all dim and cold and snow still falling. While waiting in my room I watched

---

[267]Michael Sadleir, born Michael Sadler, changed the spelling of his name to avoid confusion with his
father. An undergraduate friend of Murry at Oxford, he became a director of Constable, KM's publisher.
    [268]Murry's note: 'One of the sisters in "The Daughters of the Late Colonel".'

the terrific efforts of a little bird to peck through the ice and get at the sweet food of the nut. He succeeded but why must he so strive? My heart is always bad today. It is the cold. It feels congested and I am uneasy, or rather my body is. Vile feeling. I cough. Read Shakespeare, read C.A., read the Oxford Dictionary. Wrote. But nothing like enough.

In the afternoon Woodyfield[269] came to tea. I suspect he is timid, fearful and deeply kind. Deep within that vast substance lurks the seed. That is not sentimental. He wished me sun as he left. I felt his wish had power and was a blessing. One cant be mistaken in such things. He is in his stockings - pea green and red!

J. came up after skiing, excessively handsome - a glorious object no less. I never saw a more splendid figure. I am wearing my ring on my middle finger as a reminder not to be so base. We shall see. No letters. Picture of Anna Wong.[270] It asked for a story.

SATURDAY, JANUARY 7

It ceased snowing and a deep, almost gentian blue sky showed. The snow lay heaped on the trees, big blobs of snow, like whipped cream. It was very cold but I suppose beautiful. I cannot see this snow as anything but hateful. So it is. A letter came from Violet & one from Brett. Answered Brett. My birds have made a number of little attacks on the coconut but it is still frozen. I read Cosmic Anatomy, Shakespeare & the Bible. Jonah. Very nice about the gourd & also on his journey paying the fare thereof. I wrote at my story but did not finish the lunch party as I ought to have done. How very bad this is! Had a long talk with Ida, and suddenly saw her again as a figure in a story. She resolves into so many. I could write books about her alone!

I dreamed a long dream. Chummie[271] was young again, so was Jeanne - Mother was alive. We were going through many strange rooms - up in lifts, alighting in lounges. It was all vaguely foreign.

SUNDAY, JANUARY 8

All night dreamed of visiting houses, bare rooms, no 39, going up & down in lifts etc.

Heavily, more heavily than ever falls the snow. It is hypnotising. One looks, wonders vaguely how much has fallen & how much will fall and - looks again. Bandaged Jack's fingers. The Mercury came with A.T.B.[272] I am v. unsatisfied.

In the afternoon J. and I played cribbage, with nuts for counters. I recalled the fact that I used to play so often with such intense - heavens with what feelings! - in the drawing room at Carlton Hill while Tommy[273] played

---

[269] Woodifield was a patient in a large clinic called The Palace in Montana where KM also was a patient for a day or two before finding the Chalet des Sapins, and which she then attended once or twice to have her tubercular gland drained.

[270] Anna May Wong was a well-known Chinese film actress who appeared in Hollywood movies.

[271] KM's brother Leslie Beauchamp who died in 1915 in the war, aged 21.

[272] 'At The Bay'

[273] Tommy was Arnold Trowell who, with his family, was living in Carlton Hill in London in 1908 when KM, having left New Zealand finally, arrived in London in pursuit of Life.

the piano. But it meant absolutely <u>nothing</u>. J. giving me a bad nut & me
paying him back the bad nut again was all that really mattered. After tea we
knitted and talked and then read. We were idle - snow-bound. One feels there
is nothing to be done while this goes on. Had a letter from The Sketch asking
for work. I must obey. J. & I talked Paris yesterday and he quite understood.
This is a proof that one must be <u>calm & explain</u> and be TRUE. Remember
that!

MONDAY, JANUARY 9
Snow. The vegetable fence was all but gone. Hudson came & said there was
between 6 & 7 feet of snow. He was very cheerful and friendly. Off his guard.
Speaking of Miss S. he declared "Well the fact is she is not normal.
And anyone who is not normal I call <u>mad</u>. She is unconventional, that is to
say, and people like that are no good to anyone except themselves." When he
said "mad" a look came into his eyes - a flash of <u>power</u> and he swung the
stethoscope, then picked up my fan and rattled it open.
    Read and knitted and played cards. A long letter from Sydney [Schiff].
I want to believe all he says about my story. He <u>does</u> see what I meant.
He does not see it as a set of trivial happenings just thrown together. This is
enough to be deeply grateful for - more than others will see. But I have this
continual longing to write something with all my power - all my force in it.

TUESDAY, JANUARY 10
Dreamed I was back in New Zealand.
Got up today. It was fine. The sun shone and melted the last traces of snow
from the trees. All the morning big drops fell from the trees, from the roof.
The drops were not like raindrops, but bigger, softer, more <u>exquisite</u>.
They made one realise how one loves the fertile earth and hates this
snowbound cold substitute.
    Two men worked outside in the snowy road trying to raise the telegraph
pole. Before they began they had lunch out of a paper sitting astride the pole.
It is very beautiful to see people sharing food. Cutting bread & passing the
loaf, especially cutting bread in that age old way - with a clasp knife.
Afterwards one got up in a tree & sat among the branches working from there
while the other lifted. The one in the tree turned into a kind of bird as all
people do in trees - chuckled, laughed out, peered from among the branches,
careless. At-tend! Ar-ret! Al-lez.

WEDNESDAY, JANUARY 11
In bed again.
Heard from Pinker[274] the Dial has taken the Dolls House. Wrote & finished
<u>A Cup of Tea</u>. It took about 4-5 hours. In the afternoon Elizabeth came.
She looked fascinating in her black suit; something between a Bishop and a
Fly. She spoke of my "pretty little story" in The Mercury. All the while she was
here I was conscious of a falsity. We said things we meant; we were sincere but

---

[274]In 1920 KM had asked J B Pinker, D H Lawrence's literary agent, if he would act for her too. He
was instrumental in placing a good many of her stories and she remained grateful to him.

at the back there was nothing but falsity. It was very horrible. I do not want ever to see her or to hear from her again. When she said she would not come often I wanted to cry <u>Finito</u>. No, she is not my friend. There is no feeling to be compared with the joy of having written and finished a story. I did not go to sleep but nothing mattered. There it was <u>new</u> and complete. Dreamed last night of a voyage to America.

THURSDAY, JANUARY 12
A short note from Johnny,[275] a card from 'Meg'.[276] A vile cold day. The parcel came from Elizabeth. But when one compares it with Anne's exquisite coat ... Jack and I 'typed'. I hate dictating but the story still seems to me to be good. Is it?

All the whole time at the back of my mind slumbers, not now sleeps, the idea of Paris and I begin to plan what I will do <u>when</u> – Can it be true? What shall I do to express my thanks? I want to adopt a Russian baby, call him Anton & bring him up as mine with Kot for a godfather and Mme Tchekhov for a godmother. Such is my dream.

I don't feel <u>so</u> sinful this day I think because I have written something and the tide is still high – the ancient landmarks are covered. Ah, but to write better. Let me write better, more deeply, more <u>largely</u>. Baleful icicles hang in a fringe outside our window panes.

FRIDAY, JANUARY 13
Full Moon.
Heard from Mimi.[277] Her letter was almost frightening. It brought back the inexplicable Past. It flashed into my mind too, that she must have a large number of letters of mine which don't bear thinking about. In some way I fear her. I feared her at Chancery Lane.[278] There was a peculiar recklessness in her manner and in her tones which made me feel she would recognise no barriers at all. At the same time of course, one is <u>fascinated</u>.

Wrote to Koteliansky. Began a new story but it went too slowly. M. typed for me. I am again held up by letters to write. Letters are the real <u>curse</u> of my existence. I hate to write them. I have to. If I don't there they are like great guilty gates barring my way. Hudson came and suggested my heart condition was caused by the failure to expand the diaphragm. Then why in that case not learn to expand it?

SATURDAY, JANUARY 14
Posted my story to Pinker. Heard from China[279] and from Michael Sadleir. I got up today & felt better. It was intensely cold. Elizabeth came in the

---

[275]Johnny: probably J W N Sullivan.
[276]'Meg' was the name KM gave to her sister Vera when she was writing about the family in the 'Sheridan' pieces which culminated in 'The Garden Party'.
[277]Mimi was Vere Bartrick-Baker, a close friend of KM at Queen's College. She eventually married J W N Sullivan, Murry's friend and colleague.
[278]Chancery Lane, London, was a one-room flat where the Murrys lived and worked to produce *Rhythm* in the winter of 1912-13.
[279]China remains unidentified.

afternoon. She and I were alone. She wore a little blue hood fastened under the chin with a diamond clasp. She looked like a very ancient drawing. She suggested that if I did become cured I might no longer write ...

Dreamed last night I was in a ship with the most superb, unearthly, in the heavenly sense, seas breaking. Deep, almost violet blue waves with high foaming crests & this white foam bore down on the blue in long curls. It was a marvellous sight. The dream was about C.[280] He had married a girl without permission and Father & Mother were in despair. I 'realised' it was to be what had happened if he had not died. Wingley made a dash at the bird window today.

SUNDAY, JANUARY 15
Dreamed I was shopping, buying underclothes in Cooks and then in Warnocks.[281] But the dream ended horribly. Wrote to China, Anne, Sydney. Another chill, bloodless day. I got up but all was difficult. In the afternoon J. went to the Chalet & came back in the evening with a letter for me from Elizabeth, so generous, so sweet a letter that I am ashamed of what I said or thought the other day.

I have worked today but in discomfort - not half enough. I could have written a whole story. Saw for the first time an exquisite little crested bird. Its call is a trill, a shake, marvellously delightful. It was very shy, though, and never had the courage to stop and eat. Saw people in sleighs & on luges. Snow is very blue. The icicles at dawn this morning were the colour of opals – blue, lit with fire. E. lent us Will Shakespeare. Really awful stuff. I had better keep this for a sign.[282]

MONDAY, JANUARY 16
A wonderfully pleasant dream about Paris. All went so well. The doctor and his friends all had the same atmosphere. It was good, kind, quietly happy. I don't know when I have had a dream more delightful. But the day has not been delightful. On the contrary. It snowed heavily, it was bitter cold & my congestion worse than ever. I have been in pain & discomfort all day. My functions won't work normally either. My lung creaks. I have done no work. After tea I simply went to sleep out of sheer inertia. I am in a slough of despond today and like everybody in such an ugly place I am ugly, I feel ugly. It is the triumph of matter over spirit. This must not be. Tomorrow at all costs (here I swear) I shall write a story. This is my first resolution pour un date fixé in this journal. I dare not break it.
H.M.T.'s[283] letter to M. came yesterday. It was a beautiful letter - not to be forgotten. But why am I so bad?

TUESDAY, JANUARY 17
Tchekhov made a mistake in thinking that if he had had more time he would have written more fully, described the rain & the midwife & doctor having

---

[280]Chummie.
[281]Cooks and Warnocks were both, as Murry noted, shops in Wellington.
[282]A small square is drawn at the end of this sentence.
[283]H M Tomlinson, who had written gratefully to KM about her review of his book (see note 124).

tea. The truth is one can get only <u>so much</u> into a story; there is always a sacrifice. One has to leave out what one knows & longs to use. Why? I haven't any idea but there it is. It's always a kind of race, to get in as much as one can before it <u>disappears</u>.

But time is not really in it. Yet wait. I do not understand even now. I am pursued by time myself. The only occasion when I ever felt at leisure was while writing The Daughters of the Late Col. And then at the end I was so terribly unhappy that I wrote as fast as possible for fear of dying before the story was sent. I should like to prove this, to work at <u>real leisure</u>. Only thus can it be done.

WEDNESDAY, JANUARY 18
Hudson is a man to remember. At tea that day. Mrs M. before the huge silver kettle and pots and large plates. The <u>ornate</u> cake. One must remember that cake. "It seems such a pity to cut it", and the way the old hand, so calmly, grasped the knife. Hudson leaning back, slapping two pieces of bread and butter together. "More tea, Tim." "No thanks. Yes. Half a cup." Pouring from the kettle to the teapot, the fat finger on the knob. "And how is he?" "Bleeding like a pig!" "Oh dear," gathering her scarf into her lap, "I'm sorry to hear that"

H. always collects something - always will. China, silver, "any old thing that comes along". He's musical & collects fiddles. His feeling for his children is so <u>tender</u> that it's pain. He can't understand it. One must remember too his extraordinary insecurity. The world rocks under him and it's only when he has that stethoscope that he can lay down the law. <u>Then</u> lay it down he does. "What I say is - she's <u>mad</u>. She's not normal, and a person who isn't normal I call <u>mad</u> - <u>barmy</u>." And you hear pride in his voice, you hear the unspoken "I am a plain man you know" ...

I imagine there is a vein of tremendous cynicism in him too. He feels sometimes that all is ashes. He likes to go to church, to take part, to sing when others sing, to kneel, to intone the responses. This puts his heart at rest. But when it is over and he is at home & there is a smell of beef there comes this restlessness. When he was little I imagine he pulled the wings off flies. And I still see suicide as his end - a kind of melancholia, & nobody wants me & damned if I won't.

FRIDAY, JANUARY 20
Last Quarter of the Moon. Wrote to W.J.D. Why it should be such an effort to write to the people one loves I cannot imagine. It's none at all to write to those who don't really count. But for weeks I have thought of DelaMare, wanted to - longed to write to him, but something held back my pen. What? Once started, really started, all goes easily. I told him in this letter how much I thought of him. I suppose it is the effect of isolation that I can truly say I think of W.J.D., Tchekhov, Koteliansky, HMT and Orage every day. They are part of my life.

I have got more or less used to pain at last. I wonder sometimes if this is worse or better than that has been. But I don't expect to be without. But I have a suspicion like a certainty that the real cause of my illness is not my lungs at all. But something else & if this were found and cured all the rest would heal.

SATURDAY, JANUARY 21
Grandma's birthday.
Where is that photograph of my dear Love leaning against her husband's shoulder, with her hair parted so meekly and her eyes raised. I love it. I long to have it. For one thing Mother gave it to me at a time when she loved me. But for another – so much more important – it is <u>she</u>, my own grandma, young and lovely. That arm, that baby sleeve with the velvet ribbon – I must see them again. And one day I must write about Grandma at length, especially of her beauty in her bath – when she was about sixty. Wiping herself with the towel. I remember now how lovely she seemed to me. And her fine linen, her throat, her scent. I have never <u>really</u> described her yet. Patience! The time will come.

SUNDAY, JANUARY 22
My feeling about Ernestine[284] is shameful. But there it is. Her tread, her look,the way her nose is screwed round, her intense stupidity, her wrists, revolt me. This is <u>bad</u>. For she feels it, or I am sure she does. When we speak together she blushes in a way that doesn't seem to me natural: I feel that her self-respect is shamed by my thoughts.

<u>Lumbago</u>. It is a very queer thing. So sudden, so painful. I must remember it when I write about an old man. The start to get up, the pause,, the slow look of fury – and how lying at night one seems to get <u>locked</u>. To move is an agony. Finally one discovers a movement which is possible. But that helpless feeling about with the legs first.

MONDAY, JANUARY 23
Paris?
To remember the sound of wind – the peculiar wildness one can feel while the wind blows. Then the warm soft wind of spring searching in the heart.
The wind I call The Ancient of Days which blows here at night. The wind that shakes the garden at night when one runs out into it. Dust. Turning one's back on a high tearing wind. Walking along the Esplanade[285] when the wind carries the sea over. The wind of summer – so playful that rocked and swung in the trees here. And wind moving through grass so that the grass quivers.
This moves me with an emotion I don't even understand. I always see a field, a young horse, and there's a very fair Danish girl telling me something about her stepfather. The girl's name is Elsa Bagge.

TUESDAY, JANUARY 24
Wrote and finished Taking theVeil. It took me about 3 hours to write finally. But I had been thinking over the décor and so on for weeks – nay – months,

---

[284]the maid.
[285]In Wellington.

I believe. I can't say how thankful I am to have been born in N.Z., to know Wellington as I do and to have it to range about in. Writing about the convent seemed so natural. I suppose I have not been in the grounds more than twice. But it is one of the places that remain as vivid as ever. I must not forget the name of <u>Miss Sparrow</u>[286] nor the name <u>Palmer</u>.

### WEDNESDAY. JANUARY 25
Received cheque from Mercury for 25.0.0. Wrote Pinker & sent 2.10.0. Played cribbage with Bogey. I delight in seeing him win. When we play he sometimes makes faces at me – the same kind of faces that Chummie used to make. I think I am never so fond of him as when he does this.
We were talking of the personality of the cat today & saying that we ought to write it down. It is true he has become as real as if he could talk. I feel he does talk and that when he is silent it is only a case of making his nettle[?] shirt and he will begin. Perhaps the most engaging glimpse of him is playing his fiddle with wool for strings or sitting up to the piano & playing Nelly Bly. But his love Isbel, his whole complete little life side by side with ours, ought to be told. I shall never tell it though.

### THURSDAY, JANUARY 26
Wrote Bank Manager, Brett and Anne. Heard from Hotel. Pinker writes to say The Nation has taken The Doll House. A letter from Vera and Jeanne. I felt these 2 letters had nothing whatever to do with me. I would not care if I never saw Vera again. There is something in her assumed cheerfulness which I can't bear. I'd never get on with her. And J. – is it fancy – just a touch of carelessness. I feel they are so absolutely insincere. What on earth would I do at Woodhay?[287] It doesn't bear thinking about. I am much nearer Brett for instance.
  I am sure that meditation is one cure for the sickness of my mind i.e. its lack of control. I have a terribly sensitive mind which receives every impression and that is the reason why I am so carried away and <u>borne</u> under.

### FRIDAY, JANUARY 27
New Moon.
Posted to Pinker the story. Got the tickets from Cooks. Heard from Pinker. Wrote to Massingham.[288] Long letter from Ottoline. Elizabeth came wearing her woolly lamb. A strange fate overtakes me with her. We seem to be always talking of physical subjects. They bore and disgust me for I feel it is waste of time and yet we always revert to them. She lay back on the pillows talking. She had an absent air. She was saying how fine women were – – – and it was on the tip of my tongue to be indiscreet. But I was not. Thank Heaven! I have been in pain, in bad pain all day. I ache all over. I can barely stand. It seems

---

[286]See 'The Doll', p 238.
[287]'Woodhay' was a house near Southampton which Harold Beauchamp had provided for his daughters Chaddie (widowed) and Jeanne (not yet married). The style of life in Woodhay was the style KM had suffered much to escape from in Wellington.
[288]H W Massingham, editor of the *Nation* and a friend of Murry.

impossible that I am going away on Monday. "Every umbrella hides a warm bud of life."

SATURDAY, JANUARY 28

These preparations for flight are almost incredible. The only way to keep calm is to play crib. J. and I sit opposite each other. I feel we are awfully united. And we play and laugh and it seems to keep us together. While the game lasts we are there. A queer feeling ...

The N.A. came. I have a deep suspicion of Bechhofer. He is horrid and I feel he is going to attack me. It's a prophetic feeling.[289] There was an article of psychoanalysis so absurd, ugly and ridiculous that it's difficult to understand how any editor could let it pass.[290] J. read me his review of Orage. It seemed to me brilliant. He has improved out of all knowledge. I don't think he has any idea how he has found himself lately. All sounds so easy, so to flow off his pen, and that hard dogmatic style has quite gone. He is a real <u>critic</u>.      [s204–205]

SUNDAY, JANUARY 29

Hudson came. He says my R lung is practically all right. Can one believe such words. The other is a great deal better. <u>He</u> thinks my heart will give me far less trouble at a lower level. Can this be true? He was so hopeful today that TB seemed no longer a scourge. It seemed that one recovered more often than not! Is this fantastic. Tidied all my papers. Tore up and ruthlessly destroyed much. This is always a great satisfaction. Whenever I prepare for a journey I prepare as though for Death. Should I never return all is in order. This is what Life has taught me. In the evening I wrote to Orage about his book. It has taken me a week to write the letter. J. and I seemed to have played cribbage off and on all day. I feel there is such love between us. Tender love. <u>Let it not change</u>!

---

[289]'The N.A.' was transcribed by Murry as *The Nation and Athenaeum*, but was, in fact, *The New Age*. C E Bechhofer-Roberts (1894–1949) wrote for the latter but not for the former. He was Murry's secretary at the War Office, and was later, like KM, a follower of Gurdjieff.

The issue of *The New Age* KM is referring to here is that of 26 January 1922, although her receipt of it in Switzerland on the 28th must mean that it was posted a day or two prior to publication date. Bechhofer was writing a column called 'Readers and Writers', and KM's suspicion of him probably began a few weeks earlier, as a result of his first column, in the issue of 5 January, where he stated that 'Literature in England has become stagnant.' He said there was a younger generation, and he named some of them, including 'Miss Katherine Mansfield', 'from some of whom one may expect very good work, but little inspiration either for themselves or others in most cases. I will try to deal with the possible exceptions another time.' (He did not do so during the period of his contribution of this column.) On 26 January he expatiated on the preponderance of 'literary crimes', and mentioned, in particular, plagiarism. He suggested that he was at risk of becoming the sponsor of a literary equivalent of 'The Police Gazette' in writing about literary crimes. In view of KM's earlier appropriation of one of Tchekov's stories which she turned into her own 'The Child Who Was Tired', it is unsurprising that she was apprehensive of Bechhofer.

[290]The 'article of psychoanalysis' was 'Social Analysis' by J A M Alcock, and was a discussion of *Psycho-Analysis and Sociology*, a book by Aurel Kolnai which offered a psychoanalytic interpretation of Capitalism and Communism, employing such concepts as subsidiary anal-eroticism and the significance of constipation as a masculine protest. When one imagines KM trying to make sense of 'Where one man owns a Rolls-Royce and ninety-nine men drive a tinker's cart, there is going to be an affect of inferiority with compensatory revolt. Where the affect is overpowering and the intellect stunted, as happens with the libido-inhibition of the wage-slave (I include the so-called professional man), this revolt is going to be crude, will be in fact as Kolnai says, a plain incest-wish.', her response seems temperate.

MONDAY, JANUARY 30

There was a tremendous fall of snow on Sunday night. Monday was the first
real perfect day of the winter. It seemed that the happiness of Bogey and of
me reached its zenith that day. We could not have been happier; that was the
feeling. Sitting one moment on the balcony of the bedroom for instance, or
driving in the sleigh through the masses of heaped up snow. He looked so
beautiful too, hatless, strolling about, his hand in his pocket. He weighed
himself. 10 stone. There was a harmonium in the waiting room. Then I came
away after a quick but not hurried kiss ...

I had letters from Pinker, Richard, Galsworthy. Pinker told me the
Westminster has taken The Garden Party. It was very beautiful on the way to
Sierre, but I kept wondering if I was seeing it all for the last time. The thorn
bushes, the leafless trees. "I miss the buns."

TUESDAY, JANUARY 31

Travelling is terrible. All is so sordid and the train shatters one. Tunnels are hell.
I am frightened of travelling. We arrived in Paris late, but it was very beautiful
– all emerging from water. In the night I looked out and saw the men with
lanterns. The hotel all sordid again, fruit pies, waste paper, boots, grime, ill
temper. In the evening I saw Manoukhine. But on the way there, nay, even
before, I realised my heart was not in it. I feel divided in myself and angry and
without virtue. Then L.M. and I had one of our famous quarrels & I went to
the wrong house. Don't forget, as I rang the bell the scampering & laughter
inside. M. had a lame girl there as interpreter. He said through her he could
cure me completely. But I did not believe it. It all seemed suddenly
unimportant and ugly. But the flat was nice – the red curtains, marble clock
& picture of ladies with powdered hair.

WEDNESDAY, FEBRUARY 1

At 5.30 I went to the clinique & saw the other man Donat.[291] I asked him to
explain the treatment and so on. He did so. But first. As I approached the door
it opened & the hall, very light, showed, with the maid smiling, wearing a
little shawl, holding back the door. Through the hall a man slipped quickly
carrying what I thought was a cross of green leaves. Suddenly the arms of the
little cross waved feebly and I saw it was a small child strapped to a wooden
tray. While I waited voices came from another room. Very loud voices – M's
over and above them. Da. Da, and then an interrogatory Da?[292] I have the
feeling that M. is a really good man. I have also a sneaking feeling – I used that
word sneaking advisedly - that he is a kind of unscrupulous imposter.
Another proof of my divided nature. All is disunited. Half boos half cheers.

THURSDAY, FEBRUARY 2

Yes, that is it. To do anything, to be anything, one must gather oneself together
and one's faith make stronger. Nothing of any worth can come from a
disunited being. It's only by accident that I write anything worth a rusk and

---

[291]Dr Donat was Dr Manoukhin's assistant.
[292]Da is Russian for Yes.

then it's only skimming the top – no more. But remember The Daughters was written at Menton in November when I was not as bad as usual. I was trying with all my soul to be good. Here I try and fail & the fact of my consciousness makes each separate failure very important – each a <u>sin</u>. If, combined with M's treatment I treated myself, worked out of this slough of despond, lived an honourable life, and above all made straight my relations with L.M. I am a <u>sham</u>. I am also an egoist of the deepest dye – such a one that it was very difficult to confess to it in case this book should be found. Even my being well is a kind of occasion for <u>vanity</u>. There is nothing worse for the soul than egoism. Therefore ...

FRIDAY, FEBRUARY 3
I went [at] 3 for a treatment. A curious impression remains. M's beautiful gesture coming in to the room was perfect. But D. shouted so, pushed his face into mine, asked me <u>indecent</u> questions. Ah, that's one horror of being ill. One must submit to having one's secrets held up to the light and regarded with a cold stare. D. is a proper frenchman. 'Etes-vous constipé?' Shall I ever forget that & his face pushed into mine & the band of his tie showing over his white coat. M. sits apart, smoking, and his head, which is a curious shape – one is conscious of it all the time as of an instrument – hangs forward. But he is deeply different. He desires to reassure. "Pas de cavernes." Had palpitations from the moment of getting on to the table until 5 o'clock. But when I felt them coming on while the rays were working I felt simply horribly callous. I thought well if this kills me – let it. Voila! That shows how <u>bad</u> I am.

SATURDAY, FEBRUARY 4
Massingham accepts the idea of a regular story. Heard from Koteliansky about 'people'. It was rather a horrible day. I was ill, and at night I had one of my terrible fits of temper over a pencil. Is it possible one can be so unruly!

Heard from M.[Murry] saying he prefers to remain in Montana. All his letters now are the same. There breathes in them the relief from strain. It is remarkable. He does not believe a word about Manoukhine & talks of coming to 'fetch' me in May. Well, if I am any better there will never be any more <u>fetching</u>. Of that I'm determined. The letter kept me awake until very late, and my sciatica! Put it on record in case it ever goes, what a pain it is. Remember to give it to someone in a story one day. Ida is a very tragic figure. Remember her eyes – the pupils dark-black, and her whiteness. Even her hair seems to grow pale. She folded the quilt & held it in her arms as though it was a baby.

SUNDAY, FEBRUARY 5
First quarter of the moon. Wrote at my story, read Shakespeare. Read Goethe, thought, prayed. The day was cold and fine but I felt ill and could do nothing but lie still all day. This going to Paris has been so much more important than it seemed. Now I begin to see it as the result, the ending to all that reading. I mean that even Cosmic Anatomy is involved. Something has been built – a raft, frail and not very seaworthy, but it will serve. Before, I was cast into the

water when I was 'alone'. I mean during my illness, and now something supports me. But much is to be done. Much discipline and meditation is needed. Above all it is important to get work done. Heard from Pinker that Cassells had taken a <u>Cup of Tea</u>. Wrote giving my change of address to various people. Thought about French women and their impudent confidence in the power of sex.

MONDAY, FEBRUARY 6
Letters from Brett and M. Brett's letter was the most beautiful I have ever received. It gave me a strange shock to find M. never even asked how things were going. A boyish letter like so many I have had but absolutely impersonal. It might have been written to anyone. True, he was anxious for the post. But ... that was because he is alone. Do I make M. up? Is he thankful to sink into himself again? I feel relief in every line - there's no strain, nothing that binds him. Then let it continue so. But I will not take a house anywhere. I too will be free (I write exactly as I feel). I do not want to see M. again just now. I shall beg him not to come here. He is at present just like a fish that has escaped from the hook. A bad day - I felt ill in [an] obscure way - horrible pains and so on and weakness. I could do nothing. The weakness was not only physical. I <u>must heal my Self</u> before I will be well.

Yes, that is the important thing. No attention is needed here. This must be done alone and at once. It is at the root of my not getting better. My mind is not <u>controlled</u>. I idle, I give way, I sink into despair. And tho' I have 'given up' the idea of true marriage now (By the way what an example is this of the nonsense of time. One week ago we never were nearer. A few days ago we were fast - and now I feel I have been away from M. for months. It's true I cannot bear to think about the things I love in him ... little things. But if one gives them up they will fade.) I am not complete as I must be.

WEDNESDAY, FEBRUARY 8
Heard from Gerhardi,[293] Sara Millin,[294] Pinker. Sketch has taken T.T.Veil and wants more. A day passed in the usual violent agitation such as Jack only can fling me into. Now he will come. There is no stopping him. But it's put down to my wanting him. He is absolutely entangled in himself as usual. First my novel wouldn't then it would. Never was such a (coin a word) <u>shell</u>fish! I hate this in him. It's low to put it all down to me, too. And when he chooses to find tears - he'll find them. There wasn't a suspicion of a tear. In fact this whole horrible devastating affair which nearly kills me - revolts me, too. His very frankness is a falsity! In fact it seems falser than his sincerity. I've often noticed that. Went to that flat with the "girls and Uncle". The view outside, the stockings like snakes in the bath. Con showing off the bedroom - voila la CHAMBRE.

THURSDAY, FEBRUARY 9
Walk to Coxs. Drew 2000 francs. Gave them a cheque on B.N.Z. for £25. Wrote Barclay's manager asking them to transfer my £100 deposit to Coxs

---

[293]William Gerhardi, a young novelist whom KM helped and encouraged.
[294]Sarah Millin, one of whose novels KM had reviewed.

here. Sent cheques from Pinker 12.2.11 and J. 3.3.0 to Barclays. Heard from
Naomi R-S,[295] Jack, Richard, press, Pinker, Swin[?].

Have got a bad chill. Find[?] I have in the Bank at this moment £103
odd. Ida has been noble about this looking for flats for she is worn out and she
absolutely does not complain once. Just goes and does it all. I have fever and
feel as though I've got a very bad attack of chill coming on. Nothing makes
me ill like this business with Jack. It just <u>destroys</u> me.

Wrote Cox, N.R. Smith, Pinker, Barclays, Richard. it was a miserable
day. In the night I thought for hours of the evils of uprooting. Every time one
leaves anywhere something precious which ought not to be killed <u>is</u> left to die.

FRIDAY, FEBRUARY 10
5 o'clock at the clinique. I did not go to the clinique because of my chill.
Spent the day in bed reading the papers. The feeling that someone was coming
towards me was too strong for me to work. It was like sitting on a bench at the
end of a long avenue in a park and seeing someone far in the distance coming
your way. She tries to read, the book is in her hand, but it's all nonsense and
might as well be upside down. She reads the advertisements as though they
were part of the articles.

I must not forget the long talk Ida & I had the other evening about <u>hate</u>.
What is hate? Who has even described it? Why do I feel it for her? She says:
It is because I am nothing, I have suppressed all my desires to such an extent
that now I have none. I don't think. I don't feel. I reply: If you were
cherished, loved for a week you would recover. And that is true, and I would
like to do it. It seems I ought to do it. But I don't. The marvel is that she
understands. No one else on earth would understand. All that week she had
her little corner. I may come into my little corner tonight, she asks timidly.
And I reply - so cold, so cynical - if you want to. But what would I do if she
didn't
come! ..

Jack arrived early in the morning with a letter for me - <u>never to be
forgotten</u>. In half an hour it seemed he had been here a long time. I still regret
his leaving there for <u>his</u> sake. I know it is right for our sake. We went together
to the clinique. Bare leafless trees, a wonderful glow in the sky - the windows
flashed fire. Manoukhine drew the picture of my heart. I wish he had not.
I am haunted by the hideous picture, by the thought of my heart, like a heavy
drop in my breast. But he is good.

SUNDAY, FEBRUARY 12
Full moon.
We put the chessmen on the board & began to play. It was an unsettled day -
Ida in and out with no home, no place, whirled like leaf along this dark
passage and then out into the raw street. Jack read the Tchekhov aloud. I had
read one of the stories myself & it seemed to me nothing. But read aloud it
was a masterpiece. How was that? I want to remember the evening before.

---

[295]Naomi Royde-Smith (d 1964), literary editor of the *Westminster Gazette* from 1912–1922, was also
a novelist, playwright and biographer.

I was asleep. He came in – thrust his head in at the door & <u>as</u> I woke I did not know him. I saw a face which reminded me of his mother and Richard. But I felt a kind of immediate dread confusion. I knew I ought to know it and that it belonged to him, yet he was as it were not present. I think this is what people who are going out of their minds must feel about the faces that bend over them and old old people about their children, and that accounts for the foolish offended look in their faces sometimes. They feel it's not right they should not know.

MONDAY, FEBRUARY 13
A.M. Felt ill all day. Plenty of violent congestion in my body & head. I feel more ill now than ever, so it seems. Jack went out and bought teapot and so on, also a game of chess & we started playing. But the pain in my back and so on make my prison almost unendurable. I manage to get up, to dress, to make a show [of] getting to the restaurant & back without being discovered. But that is literally all. The rest is rather like being a beetle shut in a book, so shackled that one can do nothing but lie down – and even to lie down becomes a kind of agony. The worst of it is I have again lost hope. I don't & can't believe this will change. I have got off the raft again and am swept here and there by the sea.

TUESDAY, FEBRUARY 14
Brett sent me a nice wire and [...] a little grubby book. Another hellish day. But Jack found some pastilles which help my throat & it seemed to me they had a calming effect on my heart. I had one of my perfect dreams – was at sea, sailing with my parasol open to get a 'freshet' of wind. Heavenly blue sea, blue sky, blue land, parasol pink, boat pale pink. If I could only get over my discouragement. But who is going to help with that! Now that Ida is away I have more to do, all my clothes and so on to put away & pull out, as well as a bowl or two to wash. The effort uses what remains of my strength. By 5 o'clock I am finished & must go to bed again. It is a very dull day. The canaries sing. I have been reading Bunin's stories. He's not a sympathetic soul but it is good to read him ... he carries one away. Heard from Cox.

FRIDAY, FEBRUARY 17
Went to the clinique. I felt that all was wrong there. Manoukhine was distrait and a little angry. Donat as usual sailed over everything. But that means nothing. It seemed to me there had been some trouble or some trouble was brewing. The servant there is a very beautiful plump woman with a ravishing smile. Her eyes are grey. She curls her hair in a small fringe and she wears a little grey shawl, an apron and a pair of rather high boots. Stepping lightly with one small plump hand holding the shawl she opens the door.

[J279-299 S205-206]

SATURDAY, FEBRUARY 18
Last quarter.

MONDAY, FEBRUARY 20
Finished 'The Fly'.

SUNDAY, FEBRUARY 26
New Moon.

MONDAY, MAY 1
Oh what will this beloved month bring!

SUNDAY, SEPTEMBER 3
Selsfield.

MONDAY, SEPTEMBER 4
Tea with Papa.

TUESDAY, SEPTEMBER 5
O.[296] Dinner with Mrs Richmond.

WEDNESDAY, SEPTEMBER 6
Webster. 12 o'clock.[297]

THURSDAY, SEPTEMBER 7
Tea with Papa & the children.

FRIDAY, SEPTEMBER 8
Lunch with Edward Garnett.[298]

SATURDAY, SEPTEMBER 9
The Search for the Cardigan.
Gave Minnie notice.

SUNDAY, SEPTEMBER 10
Orage 7.30 here.

TUESDAY, SEPTEMBER 12
Children to tea.

THURSDAY, SEPTEMBER 14
Lunch with Papa.
Saw Marion Ruddick
Lecture at 28 Warwick Gardens.

FRIDAY, SEPTEMBER 15
Webster at 12
Saw doctor Sorapure.
Wrote Roma Webster.

SATURDAY, SEPTEMBER 16
Orage 8.30.
Kot at 2.

---

[296]Murry's identified this in *Journal* as Orage.

[297]Murry's note: 'Probably the first treatment.' Dr Webster continued KM's radiation treatments until the end of September.

[298]Edward Garnett, literary critic and dramatist, husband of Constance Garnett who translated the works of Chekhov and Dostoievsky.

SUNDAY, SEPTEMBER 17
Lunch with Sydney & Violet. <u>Odious</u>.[299]
Children to tea.

MONDAY, SEPTEMBER 18
Kot at 2.

TUESDAY, SEPTEMBER 19
Flower show with Mrs Richmond.
Lunch 1.30 Belgravia Restaurant, Grosvenor Gardens.
Vivian Locke Ellis & Sullivan to dinner. Dull.
Cough very troublesome.
Saw Webster.

WEDNESDAY, SEPTEMBER 20
Lunch with Beresford[300] at 1 p.m.
Richard to tea
Sullivan to dinner.

THURSDAY, SEPTEMBER 21
Charlotte to tea.
146 Harley Street 8 p.m.
Kot in afternoon.

FRIDAY, SEPTEMBER 22
Lilian.
Lunch with Anne.
Richard to tea.

SATURDAY, SEPTEMBER 23
Kot 3 p.m.

SUNDAY, SEPTEMBER 24
Charlotte to tea.      [J328–329]

TUESDAY, SEPTEMBER 3
Cashed a cheque for 100 francs
Arrived Paris. Took rooms in Select Hotel, Place de la Sorbonne, for 10 francs
per day per person. What feeling? Very little. The room is like the room where
one could work - or so it feels. I have been a perfect torment to Ida who is
pale with dark eyes. I suspect my reactions so much that I hardly dare say what
I think of the room and so on. Do I know? Not really. Not more than she.
I have thought of M. today. We are no longer together. Am I in the right way,
though? No. Not yet. Only looking on - telling others. I am not in body and
soul. I feel a bit of a sham ... And so I am. One of the K.M. is so sorry. But of
course she is. She has to die. <u>Don't</u> feed her.      [J330–331]

SATURDAY, OCTOBER 14
Orage goes to Paris.      [J33]

---

[299]Murry's note: 'This I <u>think</u> was the lunch at which Wyndham Lewis was offensive.'
[300]J D Beresford (b 1873), novelist and literary critic.

SUNDAY, OCTOBER 15
Nietsche's Birthday.
Sat in the Luxembourg Gardens. Cold, wretchedly unhappy. Horrid people
at lunch, everything horrid from angfang bis zum ende.   [J335]

TUESDAY, OCTOBER 17
Laublatter. The Four Fountains. The Red Tobacco Plant.
English dog. The funeral procession. Actions & Reactions.
The silky husk, like the inside of the paw of a cat.
'Darling'. Ida! Ida! waving the tambourines. Fire is sunlight & returns to the
sun again in unending cycle. One shakes the tambourine with the base of the
hand. He looks exactly like a desert chief. I kept thinking of Doughty's
Arabia ...
To be wildly enthusiastic, or deadly serious – both are wrong. Both pass.
One must keep ever present a sense of humour. It depends entirely on yourself
how much you see or hear or understand. But the sense of humour I have
found true of every single occasion of my life. Now perhaps you understand
what to be indifferent means. It's to learn not to mind, and not to show you
mind.

WEDNESDAY, OCTOBER 18
In the autumn garden leaves falling. Like footfalls, like gentle whispering.
They fly, spin, twirl, shake.   [J335–336]

>Addresses of Teeth Snatchers à Paris.
>Dr Holly Smith, 22 Place Vendôme
>Dr W.S. Davenport, 6 Avenue de l'Opera
>Dr Wilson, Bd Hausmann (?)
>Dr Hipwell, 91 Avenue de Champs Elysées.

>Hotel Paradis
>Diano Marino, Italian Riviera. A place to remember **IF**

List of people to whom I must send copies:
>H.G., Koteliansky, Galsworthy, Ed. Street, Mrs B. Lowndes, Sydney,
>(Tom), Orage. <Elizabeth, W.J.D., H.M.T., Clement Shorter.>

>Galsworthy, Grove Lodge, The Grove, Hampstead N.W.3.
>Roma, Piessa Broom[?], 68 Via Seccosa, Roma (9).
>Charles Gallup, Overlook, Coxsackie on Hudson, New York.

>The Major & the Lady
>The Mother
>The Fly
>An unhappy Man
>Lucian
>Down The Sounds
>A Visit (The Lily)
>Sisters
>The New Baby
>Confidences

The Dreamers
Aunt Fan
Honesty
Best Girl

{ A Cup of Tea
{ Taking the Veil
{ The Dolls House     [J301]

| January 1st | Credit | £ | S | D |
|---|---|---|---|---|
|  | In hand | 115 | 12 | 3 |
| 1st | B.N.Z. | 25 | 0 | 0 |
| 28th | Mercury | 25 | 0 | 0 |
|  |  | 165 | 12 | 3 |
|  |  | 77 | 10 |  |
|  |  | 88 | 2 | 3 |
| February | Pinker | 12 | 2 | 11 |
|  | Jack as per agree. | 3 | 3 | 0 |
|  |  | 15 | 5 | 11 |
|  |  | 88 | 2 | 3 |
|  |  | 103 | 8 | 2 |
|  |  | 35 | 12 | 6 |
|  |  | 67 | 1 | 8 |

| January 1st | Debit | £ | S | D |
|---|---|---|---|---|
| 1st | Ida | 8 | 0 | 0 |
| 15th | Self | 17 | 0 | 0 |
| 25th | Pinker | 2 | 10 | 0 |
| 26th | Self | 50 | 0 | 0 |
|  |  | 77 | 10 | 0 |
| February | Jeanne | 1 | 0 | 0 |
|  | A.J. |  | 10 | 6 |
|  | Doctor Hudson | 32 | 0 | 0 |
|  | Ida | 2 | 2 | 0 |
|  |  | 35 | 12 | 6 |

| March | Credit | £ | S | D |
|---|---|---|---|---|
| 3rd | JMM | 12 | 10 | 0 |
|  | " (in account) | 5 | 15 | 0 |
|  | In hand | 67 | 15 | 8 |
| 175.16.2 | Pinker (for Constable) | 89 | 15 | 6 |
|  | Pinker | 27 | 8 | 2 |
|  | Jack | 2 | 5 | 0 |

| July | In hand | 227 | 0 | 0 |
|---|---|---|---|---|
| | JMM | 10 | 0 | 0 |
| | Pinker | 41 | 10 | 0 |
| August | I.B. | 100 | 0 | 0 |
| | Pinker | 12 | 12 | 8 |
| | Debit | | | |
| July | Self | 37 | 0 | 0 |

## Cox's Account

| Credit | | **Frcs** | |
|---|---|---|---|
| August 8th | In hand | 4682 | 75 |
| Octobre | Cheque JMM (approx) | 812 | |

| Debit | | | |
|---|---|---|---|
| Oct 3rd | self | 100 | |
| " 5th | S.H. | 621 | |

| Credit | | frcs | |
|---|---|---|---|
| Feb? | Sent from Menton – Paris | 5000 | |
| Feb 13th | Remainder of M. account | 2757 | 15 |
| " " | Transferred £100 from deposit | 4985 | |
| " 8th | Bank of N.Z. £25 | 1247 | 75 |
| March | " " " £25 | 1223 | 75 |
| ?April | " " " | 1165 | |
| May | Pinker 42.9.5 | 2120 | |
| ? June | allowance | 1165 | |
| July | " | 1354 | 25 |
| | | 17,139 | 80 |

| Debit | | | |
|---|---|---|---|
| Feb | Self | 500 | |
| | Self | 2000 | |
| | Self | 2500 | |
| March 11 | Self | 2500 | |
| Avrilo | | 2500 | |
| May | | 3000 | |
| May | Wire | 500 | |
| May | Self | 1000 | |
| " | Goddard[?] | 250 | |
| " | X ray | 50 | |
| June | Dressmaker | 212 | |
| Dressmaker | | 400 | |
| | | 17412 | |

Denn jeder sieht und stellt die Sachen anders, eben nach seiner Weise.[301]

[J291 S205]

---

[301]The translation of this sentence is: For everyone sees and presents things differently, in his own way.

# Notebook 5

[Notebook 5, qMS-1283]

I find the rapture at being alone hard to understand. Certainly when I am
sitting out of sight under a tree I feel I would be content to <u>never return</u>.
As to 'fear', it is gone. It is replaced by a kind of callousness. What will be will
be. But this is not a very useful statement for I've never put it to the test.
Should I be as happy with anyone by my side? No. I'd begin to talk, & it's far
nicer not to talk. Or if it were Jack he'd open a little blue book by Diderot,
Jacques le Fataliste, & begin to read it & that would make me wretched.
Why the devil want to read stuffy sniffy Diderot when there is this other book
before one's eyes ... I do not want to be a book <u>worm</u>. A worm burrows
everlastingly. If its book is taken away from it the little blind head is raised,
it wags, hovers, terribly uneasy, in a void until it begins to burrow again.

    Loneliness: 'Oh Loneliness of my sad heart is Queen.' It isn't in the least
that. My heart is not sad except when I am among people & then I am far too
distracted to think about Queens. (Oh dear. Here is a walking tragedy –
Madame with a whole tray of food!) when I begged for a bastick, only a
bastick! She came, wandered afield while I sat and then sat beside me, covering
her white stockings with her big limp bouquet. And she talked of the <u>womb</u>,
worms in eggs & the horrors of Stepheni. The irate husband.

I[302] have watched this big heavy woman, moving so sullen, plodding in and out
with her pails and brushes, coming to the door at midday and evening to look
for her husband and child. She looks neither sad nor happy; she looks resigned
and stupified. Sometimes when she stops and stares round her she is like a cow
that is being driven along a road, & sometimes when leaning out of the
window she watches her quick husband, so jaunty, cutting up logs of wood,
I think she hates him. The sight of her suffocates him.

    But today, it being the first fine day since the lodgers have come, they
went off for a walk & left the nurse girl in charge of the baby. A 'cradle' made
of two straw baskets on trestles was brought out into the sun and the baby
<u>heaped</u> up in it. Then the nurse girl disappeared.

---

[302]Murry's note: 'The following description is of a family who lived in a small chalet within view of
Katherine's window at Randogne.'

Round the side of the house came my woman. She stopped. She looked round quickly. No one was in sight. She leaned over the cradle & held out her finger to the baby. Then it seemed she was simply overcome with the loveliness and the wonder of this little thing. She tiptoed round the cradle, bent over, shook her head, shook her finger, pulled up a tiny sleeve, looked at a dimpled elbow. Her little girl in a white hat (in honour of the lodgers) danced up. I imagine my woman asked her how she would like a little brother. And the little girl was fascinated as small creatures are by smaller. 'Kiss his hand' said my woman. She watched her daughter, very serious, kiss the tiny hand, and she could hardly bear that anyone should touch the infant but herself. She snatched her daughter away ...

When finally she dragged herself away she was trembling. She went up the steps into the house, stood in the middle of the kitchen, & it seemed that the child within realised her love & moved. A faint timid smile was on her lips. She believed & she did not believe.

Gyp their dog is the most servile creature imaginable. He is a fat brown & white spaniel with a fat round end of tail which wags for everybody at every moment. His passion is for the baby. If anyone throws him sticks he dashes off & brings them back to lay at the foot of the cradle. When his mistress carries the baby he dances round them so madly in such a frenzy of delight that one doesn't believe in him. He feels himself one of the family – a family dog.

The master is a very stupid conceited fellow with a large thin nose, a tuft of hair, and long thin legs. He walks slowly, holding himself perfectly rigid. He keeps his hands in his pockets always. Yesterday he wore all day a pair of pale blue woolen slippers with tassels, and it was obvious he admired himself in these slippers tremendously. Today he is walking about in his shirt sleeves, wearing a sky blue shirt. He wears black velvet trousers and a short coat. I am sure he thinks he is perfectly dressed for the country. Ah, if he only had a gun to carry over his shoulder! When he came home he walked stiff, rigid, like a post, hands in pockets up to the front door & stood there. Did not knock, gave no sign. In less than a minute the door opened to him. His wife felt he was there.

(What a passion one feels for the sun here.)

The friend is a dashing young man in a grey suit with a cap always worn very much on one side. This cap he does not like to take off. He is the kind of man who sits on the edge of tables or leans against the counter of bars with his thumbs in his waistcoat. He feels a dog. He is sure all the girls are wild about him & it's true each time he looks at one she is ready to titter. For all his carelessness he's close with money. When he & his 'friend' go up to the village for stores he lounges in the shop, smells things, suggests things, but turns his back & whistles when it comes to adding up the bill. He thinks the friend's wife is in love with him.

(When the dog is tied up it cries pitifully, sobs. The sound, so unrestrained, pleases them.)

The wife is small, untidy, with large gold rings in her hair. She wears white canvas shoes & a jacket trimmed with artificial fur. She is the woman

who is spending a day at the seaside. She looks dissatisfied - unhappy. I am sure
she is a terrible muddler.
(The dog is really very hysterical.)

They have a little servant maid of about 16 with a loose plait of dark
steely hair & silver-rimmed spectacles. She walks in a terribly meek but
self-satisfied way, pushing out her stomach. She is meekness <u>itself</u>. How she
bows her head & walks after her master! It is terrible to see. She wishes to be
invisible - to pass unseen. Do not look at me & she effaces herself. (This must
be written very directly.) She it is who holds the baby. When the others are
gone she rather lords it over the baby, turns up his clothes and exclaims with
quite an air.

The baby is at that age when it droops over a shoulder. It is still a
boneless baby, blowing bubbles, in a little blue muslin frock. When it cries it
cries as though it were being squeezed. Its feet, in white boots, are like 2 little
cakes of dough.
(The dog's enthusiasm is enough to make you want to kick it. When they
come out, cold, damp, depressed, there he is leaping, asking when the fun's
going to begin. It is sickening.)     [J317-320]

Queer bit of psychology. I had to disappear behind the bushes today in a
hollow. That act made me feel nearer to normal health than I have felt for
years. Nobody there. Nobody wondered if I was all right, i.e. there was
nothing to distinguish me at that moment from an ordinary human being.

Each little movement of this bird is made so ostentatiously as if it were
trying to show itself as much as possible. Why?

But to continue with this <u>alone</u>-ness. To follow it up a little. Could
I ... ? It seems to me to depend entirely on health in my case. If I were well
& could spend the evenings sitting up writing till about 11. (Do look up
through the trees to the far away heavenly blue.) Now it's getting late
afternoon and all sounds are softer, deeper - the sough of the wind in the
branches is more <u>thoughtful</u>.

This - this is as great happiness as I shall ever know. It is greater happiness
than I had ever thought possible. But why is it incompatible with - only
because of your weakness. There is nothing to prevent you living like this.
In fact don't you yet know that the more active & apart you make your own
life the more content the other is. What he finds intolerable is the lack of
privacy. <u>But so do you</u>. It makes him feel as though he were living under a
vacuum cap. So it does you. You hang on thinking to please him while he
burns for you to be gone. How badly how stupidly you manage your life.
Don't you realise that both of you have had enough contact to last you for
years. That the only way for each of you to be renewed and refreshed is for
you to go apart. Not necessarily to <u>tear</u> apart but to go apart as wisely as
possible. You are the most stupid woman I have ever met. You never will see

that it all rests with you. If you do not take the initiative nothing will be done. The reason why you find it so hard to write is because you are learning nothing. I mean of the things that count – like the sight of this tree with its purple cones against the blue. How am I to put it that there is gum on the cones – gemmed? no beaded? no they are like crystals. Must I? I am afraid so ...     [J320-321]

Ida is going to find it.

a pump at 2 in the morning?

an arrival

What are you going to do?[303]

    Jack
    Brett
    Kot
    Violet S.
    Richard
    Marie
    Jeanne
    Orage
    Gurdjieff

        Lunches and Dinners & Teas etc.[304]

| Octr 3rd | Lunch | 14.0 |
| | dinner | 12.15 |
| | lemon | 40 |
| | | 26.55 |
| 4th | Lunch | 12.80 |
| | supper | 14.70 |
| | | 27.50 |
| 5th | Lunch | 12.75 |
| | dinner | 10.40 |
| | Fruit | 1. 5 |
| | | 24.20 |

---

[303]After this passage comes a page of Russian/English vocabulary: parts of the body, colours, family members—followed by several pages of miscellaneous Russian/English vocabulary. I have omitted the Russian-language vocabulary lists because of the difficulty of reading KM's hand in a language with which I have no familiarity.

[304]Paris 1922 was written above this in Murry's hand.

| | | | |
|---|---|---|---|
| <u>6th</u> | Lunch | 13.75 | |
| | supper | 11.80 | |
| | | 25.25 | |
| <u>7th</u> | lunch | 11.60 | |
| | supper | 15.50 | |
| | | 27.10 | |
| <u>8th</u> | lunch | 15.0 | |
| | supper | 11.50 | |
| | | 26.50 | |

# Notebook 3

[Notebook 3, qMS-1284][305]

This is a damning little note book, quite in the old style. How I am committed!

Today is Tuesday. Since leaving M.[306] I have written about a page. The rest of the time I seem to have slept! This of course started all the Old Fears, that I could never write again, that I was getting sleeping sickness and so on. But this morning I nearly kicked off & this evening I feel perhaps a time of convalescence was absolutely necessary. The mind was choked with the wrack of all those dreadful tides. I wrote to Kot today. It seems to bring things nearer. It's only now I am beginning to see again & to recognise again the beauty of the world. Take the swallows today - their flitter flutter, their delicate forked tails, their transparent wings that are like the fins of fishes. The little dark head & the breast golden in the light. Then the beauty of the garden, and the beauty of raked paths ... Then, the silence.

I should like to write the Canary story tomorrow. So many ideas come and go. If there is time I shall write them all, if this uninterrupted time continues.

The story about this hotel would be wonderful if I could do it ...

If there is a book to be read, no matter how bad that book is - I will read it. Was it always so with me? I don't remember. Looking back, I imagine I was always writing. Twaddle it was, too. But better far write twaddle or anything, anything, than nothing at all.

Rebecca is a mixture of W.L. George, Disraeli, and Mrs Henry Dudeney.

I wage eternally a war of small deceits. Tear this book up! Tear it up, now. But now I am pretending to be taking notes on a book I have already read & despise ... What dreadful awful rot!     [J327]

---

[305]Murry's note at the beginning of this notebook: 'After a great deal of puzzling I finally decided that these entries belong to July 1922.'

[306]'M', according to Murry, means 'Hotel d'Angleterre, Montana'.

# Unbound Papers

[NL]

'Room 135'

Well! - who could have believed it - who could have imagined it! What a marvellous what a miraculous thing to [have] happened! I'm trembling; I feel quite ... But I mustn't get too excited; one must keep one's sense of proportion. Be calm!

I can't, I can't! Not just for the moment. If you could feel my heart! It's not beating very fast, not racing, as they say, but it's simply quivering - an extraordinary sensation - and if I am quite sincere I feel such a longing to kneel down. Not to pray. I scarcely know what for. To say Forgive me! To say my darling. But I should cry if I said it. My darling! My darling! Do you know I've never known anyone well enough to call them that. It is a beautiful word, isn't it. And one puts out one's hand when one says it & just touches the other ... No, no. It's fatal to think such things. One mustn't let oneself go.

Here I am back in my room. I should like to go over to the window and open it wide. But I daren't yet. Supposing he were looking out of his and he saw; it might seem marked. One can't be too careful. I will stay where I am for the present until my - my excitement dies down a little. No. 134 That is the number of my room. I only realised at that moment that I am still holding my big flat door-key. What is his number? Oh, I have wondered that so often. Shall I ever know. Why should I? And yet after what has just happened

If a flash-light photograph had been taken at that moment, or if a fire had broken out & we had been unable to move and only our charred bodies found it would have been the most natural thing in the world for people to suppose we were - together. We must have looked exactly like the other couples. Even his reading the newspaper & not speaking to me seemed to make it more natural.

This tenderness this longing. This feeling of waiting for something. What is it. Come! Come! And then one goes out and there are new leaves on the trees, the light shakes in the grass and everywhere there is a gentle stirring. I have never been very good at imagining things. Some people have so much imagination. They make up long stories about the future.     [J315-316 S212-213]

[MS-Papers-4006-16]

## The Wounded Bird

In the wide bed
Under the green embroidered quilt
With flowers and leaves always in soft motion
She is like a wounded bird resting on a pool.

The hunter threw his dart
And hit her breast.
Hit her, but did not kill.
Oh, my wings, lift me – lift me
I am not dreadfully hurt!
Down she dropped and was still.

Kind people come to the edge of the pool with baskets
"Of course what the poor bird wants is plenty of food!"
Their bags and pockets are crammed almost to bursting
With dinner scrapings and scraps from the servants' lunch.
Oh! how pleased they are to be really <u>giving</u>!
"In the past, you know you know, you were always so fly-away
So seldom came to the window-sill, so rarely
Shared the delicious crumb thrown into the yard.
Here is a delicate fragment and here a tit-bit
As good as new. And here's a morsel of relish
And cake and bread and bread and bread and bread."

At night, in the wide bed
With the leaves and flowers
Gently weaving in the darkness
She is like a wounded bird at rest on a pool.
Timidly, timidly, she lifts her head from her wing.
In the sky there are two stars
Floating, shining –
Oh, waters – do not cover me!
I would look long & long at those beautiful stars!
Oh my wings – lift me – lift me
I am not so dreadfully hurt ...

Katherine Mansfield.

---

[MS-Papers-4006-10]

Darling one,
Please send Wig[307] an immediate note + say what she ought to receive
for an english money order for 9.18.6 – <u>which</u> is my 10.0.0 minus
"the charges" just arrived. Here are a few fruits of my calculations –
but only a few.[308]

---

[307]'Wig', a variation of 'Tig', short for 'Tiger': a nickname for KM used by Murry and by KM herself.
[308]Three quarters of this page is taken up with bits of arithmetic.

Luncheon.

eggs. scrambled, poached, fried, omelette, baked, dutch eggs, curried eggs, on
mashed potatoes, boiled, sauce tomate. Welsh rarebit, chestnut curry, stuffed
tomatoes, potatoes in jackets, sardines on toast, potted meat. jam, cheese,
biscuits, chocolate. Fresh fruit.

Dinner.

Hors d'oeuvres, radishes, tomatoes, anchois, hareng, sardines, mayonnaise,
salade suisse, cold vegetable. chicken, rabbits, pâte. potatoes fried, sauté, boiled
with butter, whisked, mixed with egg. rice with saffron, meat liquor,
watercress. coffee cream, orange salade of slices, baba cakes, crème caramel,
baked apples.

| nightdresses | underclothes |
|---|---|
| blue | 2 heavy combin. |
| pink | 2 medium |
| mauve | 2 light |
| small flower | 2 vests |
| large flower | 2 silk vests |
| 18th century | 2 chemises & knickers |
| | 1 crepe de chine top & knickers |
| | 1 white silk        "             " |
| | 1 white lawn       "             " |
| | stockings about 1 dozen. |

| Coats & skirts | dresses |
|---|---|
| Black flannel | 2 black dresses |
| mole face cloth | 1 blue evening |
| beige jersey cloth | 1 purple silk |
| black cloth | 1 russian linen |
| | 2 silk jumpers |
| | 1 crepe de chine skirt |
| | 1 panne velvet skirt |
| | 1 jaegar wooly |
| | little coats various |
| | 1 crepe de chine jumper |

1 overcoat  1 cape  1 scarf  1 silk shawl  1 fur

1 brown hat  1 grey hat  1 black fruit  1 shiny black
1 small chiffon  4 pairs gloves  6 lace handkerchiefs
4 large coloured silk handkerchiefs about  1 dozen ordinary handkerchiefs

2 pairs mules ⊥ black suede shoes ⊥ grey cloth
⊥ pair slippers ⊥ black walking shoes.

---

1 blue silk kimono 1 dressing gown with fur.

---

veils, ribbons, boxes, powder, scent, amethyst brooch 2 rings

---

I was late because my fire did not burn.
weather
this morning was a heavy frost
The grass was white
The sky was blue as in summer
Winter - spring - autumn.
The trees still have apples. Apple.
I fed the goats
I eat - she eats
Bring me
long
I go for a walk
What is the time. Time
month - week
Days of the week
day - night - morning
midday - midnight
year - one year - century.

| neck | waist | blue clear | woman |
|------|-------|------------|-------|
| shoulders | legs | red dark | man |
| hand | back | yellow | child |
| fingers | rib | green | girl |
| nails | ribs | pink | boy |
| chest | skin | grey | children |
| stomach | | colours | people |
| | | costumes | old young |
| | | | good boy |
| | | | mother |
| bed | | | father |
| wash table | | | brother |
| table | | | sister |
| chair | head | | son |
| carpet | arms | | daughter |
| divan | legs | | |
| armchair | eyes | | |

| Floor | nose |
|---|---|
| walls | mouth |
| ceiling | hair |
| door | ears |
| window | body |
| fireplace. | forehead |
| | cheeks |
| | chin |
| | = under |
| | lips |
| | teeth |
| | eyelashes |
| | eyebrows?[309] |

---

[309]After this is a list of Russian words for bed, to wash, wash table, table, carpet, divan, chair, floor, walls, ceiling, door, window, fireplace.

# *Newberry Notebook 3*

I am cold[310]
bring paper to light a fire
paper
cinders
wood
matches
flame
smoke
strong
strength
Light a fire
No more fire
because there is no more fire
white paper
black paper
what is the time
it is late
it is still early
good!

I would like to speak Russian with you.        [J336 S243]

breakfast

This is their brother's house
Where is the booking office?
Here is your telegram
The lady's luggage is there

---

[310] Murry's note: 'The following list of words and phrases, for which she sought the Russian equivalent, is eloquent of the discomforts which Katherine deliberately endured at the Gurdjieff Institute at Fontainebleau.'

Where is his friend's hotel?
This is the number of their house
Here is his doctor's address
Our street is there
There is a glass of wine
I am glad; you are right, he is not ready
She is busy; they are not right, they are glad.
I was, she was, we were.
he was not, you were not, they were not.
was he? was not she? we were not. were you not?
was he not?

[NL]

At The Bay.

At the Bay
The Daughters of the Late.
Mr and Mrs Dove
The Young Girl
Life of Ma Parker
Marriage à la Mode
The Voyage
Miss Brill
Her First Ball
The Singing Lesson
The Stranger
Bank Holiday
Sixpence
An Ideal Family
The Ladies Maid.

| Thursday | In hand | 15.75 |
|---|---|---|
| | metro | 30 |
| | lunch | 1.85 |
| | papers | 45 |
| | cigarettes | 65 |
| | stamps | 50 |
| | books | 3.20 |
| | supper | 65 |
| | | 7.60 |
| Friday | candles | 1.20 |
| | papers | 30 |
| | tea | 20 |
| | lunch | 1.95 |
| | stamps | 35 |
| | milk | 15 |
| | | 4.15 |

|           |       |      |
|-----------|-------|------|
| oranges   |       | 40   |
| eggs      |       | 50   |
| butter    |       | 20   |
| stamp     |       | 25   |

| coffee     | 50   |
|------------|------|
| stamp      | 25   |
| cigarettes | 65   |
| matches    | 10   |
| bread      | 20   |
| paper      | 15   |
|            | ———  |
|            | 1.85 |
| milk       | 15   |
|            | ———  |
|            | 2.0  |
| eggs       | 30   |
| butter     | 60   |
|            | ———  |
|            | 2.90 |
| paper      | 30   |
| coffee     | 50   |
| dejeuner   | 1.75 |
| stamp      | 25   |
| milk       | 15   |
|            | ———  |
|            | 2.95 |

Montana 23.vii.1921. "Hat With a Feather."

### The New Baby.

At half past ten the yacht steamed into the Sound, slowed down. "Hullo!" said someone, "we've stopped!" For a moment, and it seemed like a long moment, everybody was silent. The crying of little waves sounded from the distant beach; the soft moist breath of the night wind came flowing over the dark sea. And looking up at the sky one fancied that even the bright-burning moon had stopped too and was waiting to see what was going to happen ...

Then "Come on, girls" cried the genial old mayor. And Gertrude Pratt began to bang out The Honeysuckle and the Bee on the squat, tinny little piano. As they had sung the same song every night for the last three weeks the noise was considerable, but very pleasant. It was a strange relief after the long day to lie on deck and to put one's whole heart into

> "I love you dearly dearly and I
> <u>Want</u> you to love me!"

You couldn't say these things and yet you felt them. At least – the ladies did. Not for anybody in particular but for everybody. It really seemed that ever since they came on board they had been haunted by love: there was no escaping from it. It was all very well to pretend to be interested in other things, to look through the glasses, to ask the Captain intelligent questions as you stood on the bridge

The New Baby.

At half-past ten the yacht steamed into the Sound, slowed down … "Hullo" said someone, "we've stopped." For a moment, and it seemed like a long moment, everybody was silent. They heard the crying of little waves from the distant beach, the soft moist breath of the large wind came flowing gently over the dark sea. And, looking up at the sky one fancied that even those merrily-burning stars were telling one another that the yacht had anchored for the night.

Then "Come on girls" cried the genial old mayor. And Gertrude Pratt began to bang out The Honeysuckle and the Bee on the squat tinny piano. As the whole party had sung the same song every night for the past three weeks the noise was considerable, but very pleasant. It was an extraordinary relief after the long dazzling day to lie on deck and to put all one's heart into

> "I love you dearly dearly and I
> <u>Want</u> you to love me."

You couldn't say these things. And yet you felt them. At least – the ladies did. Not for anybody in particular but for everybody, for the lamp, even, hanging from the deck awning, for Tanner the steward's hand as it stroked the guitar. Love! Love! There was no escaping it. It was all very well to pretend to be interested in other things, to look through the glasses, to ask the Captain intelligent questions as you stood on the bridge, to admire Mrs Strutt's marvellous embroidery.

There were exquisite small shells to be found on these beaches, small greeny-blue kinds, coral spirals, and tiny yellow ones like grains of maize.

| 26 | The New Baby |
| ii | by |
| 1922 | Katherine Mansfield. |

At half past ten the yacht steamed into the Sound, slowed down. "Hullo" said someone, "we've stopped." For a moment, and it seemed like a long moment, everybody was silent. They heard the crying of little waves on the distant beach, they felt the moist soft breath of the large wind breathing so gently from the boundless sea. And looking up at the sky one fancied that even those merrily-burning stars accepted the fact that they were anchored for the night.

Then "Come on girls, lets have another" cried the genial old mayor. And Gertrude Pratt began to bang out 'The Honeysuckle and The Bee' on the squat, tinny little piano. As the whole party had sung the same song every night for the last three weeks the noise was considerable, but very pleasant. It was an extraordinary relief after the long dazzling day to lie out on deck and sing at the top of one's voice

> "I love you dearly dearly and I
> Want you to love me!"

You couldn't say these things. And yet you felt them. Not for anybody in particular, for everybody, for the lamp even, hanging from the deck awning, for Tanner the steward's hand as he stroked the guitar.

and they came away thinking "What a life!" All very well to land there for an hour or two on a glorious morning but imagine being stuck there month in – year in year out. With nothing to look at but the sea with for one's greatest excitement getting fresh ferns for the fireplace! "Christ what a life!" thought the men pacing up & down the deck waiting for the lunch bell, and "My dear, just imagine it" thought the ladies powdering their noses in the flat cabin mirrors. And lunch in the bright saloon with the portholes open & the stewards flying to & fro in their linen jackets always seemed particularly good, particularly delicious, afterwards.

the sun flowing through the saloon porthole ...

They asked them questions, had a good look at everything, ate the fruit or whatever they were offered and took photographs. If there was a swing – and there was usually an old fashioned one hanging from a branch in the orchard, the girls got the men to push them. Out they flew, their gossamer veils streaming, while the mayor sat on the verandah talking to their host and the older ladies had a quiet chat somewhere within doors.

Father!
We – my wife that is – but it would not do. He began to smile and it seemed he could not smile ... simple ... childish ... yes – "as a matter of fact our first kid turned up this morning at half past three. A fine boy."

The mayor stopped & dug his sun umbrella into the sand. He didn't quite grasp it for the moment. You mean – was born? said he.
That's it said the other nodding. Great Scott! said the mayor & he turned back & called his wife. Mother they've got a new baby!

The flowers in the garden <u>look like it</u>. So do the little wet shells on the beach. So does the house. All seems to breathe freshness, peace. I especially see those shells – so naive looking ...

Take them he said gently & bending down he ruffled the leaves & began to gather the fruit. Stop! Stop! she said shocked. You're cutting them all. You'll have none on the bush. "Why not?" he said simply. "You're welcome."

[J309-311 S206-209]

The Boy Who Couldn't Stand Girls.

The train stopped. When a train stops in the open country between two stations it is impossible not to put one's head out of the window and see what's up. But when it stops and shunts and clanks about & whistles and you know for a fact that two extra engines are being added to it surely no human being worth anything (except a silly woman) would go on sitting in his corner as though nothing had happened. But that is what Smith did.
But it is an intensely difficult story to write! It is difficult to get going ...

The New Baby

As the little steamer rounded the point and came into the next bay they
noticed the flag was flying from Putnam's Pier. That meant there were
passengers to bring off. The Captain swore. They were half an hour late already
and he couldn't bear not to be up to time. But Putnam's flag, cherry red
against the green bush on this brilliant morning, jigged gaily, to show it didn't
care a flick for the Captain's feelings. There were three people and an old
sheepdog waiting. One was a little old woman, nearing seventy perhaps, very
spry, with a piece of lilac in her bonnet & pale lilac strings. She carried a
bundle wrapped in a long shawl white as a waterfall. Beside her stood the
young parents. He was tall, broad, awkward in a stiff black suit with banana
yellow shoes & a light blue tie & she looked soft & formless in a woollen coat;
her hat was like a child's with its wreath of daisies, and she carried a bag like a
child's school-kit, stuffed very full & covered with a cloth. As the steamer drew
near the old sheepdog ran forward & made a sound that was like the beginning
of a bark but he turned it off into an old dog's cough as though he'd decided
that little steamer wasn't worth barking about.

The coil of rope was thrown, was looped, the one-plank gangway was
spanned across and over it tripped the old woman, running & bridling like a
girl of eighteen. Thank you Captain said she, giving the Captain a bird-like
impudent little nod. That's all right Mrs Putnam said old Captain Reid who
had known her for the last 40 years. After her came the sheepdog, then the
young woman looking lost, & she was followed by the young man who
seemed terribly ashamed about something. He kept his head bent, he walked
stiff as wood in his creaking shoes as the long brown hand twisted away twisted
away at his fair moustache.

Unruffled sea. the gulls moved like the lights within a pearl[311]

Old Captain Reid winked broadly at the passengers. He stuffed his little hands
in his short jacket, drew a breath in as if he was going to sing. "Morning
Mr Putnam" he roared. And the young man straightened himself with an
immense effort & shot a terrified glance at the Captain. "Morning Cap'n" he
mumbled. Captain Reid considered him, shaking his head. "It's all right my
lad" he said "we've all been through it. Jim here", & he jerked his head at the
man at the wheel, "had twins last time. Hadn't you Jim." "That's righ' Cap'n,"
said Jim, grinning broadly at the passengers.

The little steamer quivered, throbbed, started on her way again, but the
young man, in an agony, not greeting anyone, creaked off to the bows.
The two women (they were the only women on board) sat themselves down
on a green bench against the white deck rail. As soon as they had sat down:
"Here Mother let me take him," said the young woman anxiously, quickly.
She tossed the kit away. But Gran didn't want to give him up. "Now don't you
go tiring yourself," said she. "He's as nice as can be where he is." Torture!

---

[311]Written at the top of the following page.

The young woman gave a gasp like a sob. "Give him to me!" she said & she actually twitched at her mother-in-law's sleeve. The old woman knew perfectly well what she was feeling. Little channels for laughter showed in her cheeks. "My goodness gracious me" she pretended to scold. "There's impatience for you." But even while she spoke she swung the baby gently gently into its mother's arms. "There now!" said Gran, & she sat up sharp & gave the bow of her bonnet strings a tweak as though she was glad to have her hands free after all.

It was an exquisite day. It was one of those days so clear, so still, so silent you almost feel the earth itself has stopped in astonishment at its own beauty.

[J304-306 S233-236]

**Katherine Mansfield** (1888–1923) was born in Wellington, New Zealand, as Kathleen Mansfield Beauchamp. After she moved to England in 1908, she never returned to her native country. Among her publications are *In a German Pension, Prelude, Bliss and Other Stories, The Garden Party and Other Stories, Poems, The Dove's Nest and Other Stories,* and *Something Childish and Other Stories.* After her death from tuberculosis, her husband, John Middleton Murry (1889–1957), edited selections from her notebooks and published many of her works and letters.

**Margaret Scott** transcribed "The Unpublished Manuscript of Katherine Mansfield" for six installments in the *Turnbull Library Record* in 1970–74, and she has coedited five volumes of *The Collected Letters of Katherine Mansfield.* She is the author of *Recollecting Mansfield.*